14.99

Contemporary British Society

Third Edition
Completely Revised and Updated

Nicholas Abercrombie
Alan Warde

with

Rosemary Deem, Sue Penna, Keith Soothill,
John Urry, Andrew Sayer, Sylvia Walby

POLITY PRESS

First edition published 1988
Reprinted 1988, 1989 (twice), 1990, 1991, 1992

Second edition published 1994
Reprinted 1995 (twice), 1996, 1998

This edition first published in 2000 by Polity Press
in association with Blackwell Publishers Ltd

Editorial office:
Polity Press
65 Bridge Street
Cambridge CB2 1UR, UK

Marketing and production:
Blackwell Publishers Ltd
108 Cowley Road
Oxford OX4 1JF, UK

Published in the USA by
Blackwell Publishers Inc.
Commerce Place
350 Main Street
Malden, MA 02148, USA

A catalogue record for this book is available from the British Library.

Library of Congress Cataloging-in-Publication Data

Abercrombie, Nicholas.
    Contemporary British society / Nicholas Abercombie, Alan Warde;
  with Rosemary Deem . . . [et al.]. — 3rd ed.
        p.   cm.
    Includes bibliographical references and index.
    ISBN 0-7456-2296-8
    ISBN 0-7456-2297-6 (pbk.)
    1. Great Britain—Social conditions—1945–. I. Warde, Alan. II. Deem, Rosemary.
  III. Title.
    HN385.5 .A24 2000
    306′.0941—dc21   99-42479
                                                              CIP

Typeset in 10 on 12 pt Sabon
by Ace Filmsetting Ltd, Frome, Somerset
Printed in Great Britain by T.J. International, Padstow, Cornwall

This book is printed on acid-free paper.

Contents

Detailed Chapter Contents

Acknowledgements

The authors wish to acknowledge the help of Pennie Drinkall, Judith Henderson, Dale Southerton and Karen Westall in the preparation of the manuscript. As always, Polity Press has been extremely efficient, helpful and tolerant and particular thanks are due to Sophie Ahmad, Hilary Frost, Thelma Gilbert, Fiona Sewell, Serena Temperley and Pamela Thomas.

The publishers wish to thank the following for permission to use copyright material:

Ashgate Publishing Ltd for **Tables 4.3–5** from N. Millward et al. *Workplace Industrial Relations in Transition*, Dartmouth (1992) pp. 94, 224, 238; **Table 13.3** from A. Heath et al. in R. Jowell et al., eds, *Labour's Last Chance?: the 1992 election and beyond*, Dartmouth (1994) Table 15.4; and **Table 10.2–5** from F. McGlone et al., in R. Jowell et al., *British Social Attitudes*, Dartmouth (1996) pp. 56, 57, 59, 61;

David Austin for **Plate 15.2**, cartoon from *The Guardian*, 10.10.91;

Blackwell Publishers Ltd for **Box 4.1** from C. P. Hales, 'What do Managers Do?: A critical review of the evidence', *Journal of Management Studies, 23:1 (1986) p. 104; Table 6.16*, **Fig. 6.2**, from J. Scott, *Who Rules Britain?*, Polity (1991) pp. 83, 66; **Fig. 3.8** from J. Scott, 'The British Upper Class' in D. Coates et al., eds, *A Socialist Anatomy of Britain*, Polity (1985) p. 45; and **Fig. 9.3** from J. Gershuny, 'Change in the doemstic division of labour in the UK 1975–1987: dependent labour versus adaptive partnership' in N. Abercrombie and A. Warde, *Social Change in Contemporary Britain*, Polity (1992) p. 78;

Butterworth Heinemann for **Table 15.5** from K. Melia et al., 'Introduction' to *Classic Tests in Health Care* (1988) Table 1; and **Tables 13.1, 13.4–5, 13.7** from A. Heath et al., *Understanding Political Change* (1991) pp. 13, 209, 220, 108;

Cambridge University Press for **Table 13.2** from I. Crewe et al., *The British Electorate 1963–1987: A Compendium of Data from the British Election Studies* (1991) p. 19;

Campaign for Press & Broadcasting Freedom for **Fig. 12.1** from data researched by Jo Treharne (1994) Fig. 4.3;

Christian Research for **Fig. 10.3** from P. Brierley, *'Christian' England* (1991) p. 203; and **Fig. 10.1, 10.3, Tables 10.6–7** from P. Brierley and H. Wraight, *UK Christian Handbook* (1998/97) p. 284, 203, 240, 282–3;

Edward Elgar Publishing Ltd for **Fig. 3.7** from R. Clarke, 'Trends in concentration 1980–9 in UK manufacturing' in M. Casson and J. Creedy, eds, *Industrial Concentration and Economic Inequality* (1993) p. 125;

European Communities Office for Official Publications for **Table 4.8** from *The Employment Situation in the EU* (1997);

The Guardian for **Table 6.17** using data from *The Guardian*, 22.7.98, p. 24;

The Controller of Her Majesty's Stationery Office for **Figs. 3.9, 4.2, 7.1, 8.1–2, 9.1–2, 9.4–5. 14.1–2, 15.1–3, 15.5–6, 16.2–7, 16.9–10, Tables 3.2, 3.4, 3.10, 4.1, 4.6, 4.9–10, 5.1, 6.5, 6.12–14, 7.1, 7.3, 7.5, 7.6–12, 8.1, 8.7–8, 8.14, 9.1, 9.3–4, 9.6, 9.8, 9.10, 11.1–2, 11.5–8, 12.1, 12.3–4, 13.9, 14.1–4, 15.1–4, 15.6, 15.11–12, 16.1–4, 16.10, Plate 15.3** and **Box 7.1**. Crown copyright ©;

McGraw-Hill Ryerson Ltd for **Fig. 16.1** from J. Hagan, *The Disreputable Pleasures* (1984) p. 111;

Macmillan Ltd for **Fig. 13.5, Table 13.6** from D. Butler and D. Kavanagh, *The British General Election of 1997* (1998) pp. 255, 246; **Table 6.11** from R. Price and G. S. Bain, 'The Labour Force' in A. H. Halsey, ed., *British Social Trends Since 1900*, (1988) p. 164; **Table 3.3** from J. Gershuny, *After Industrial Society* (1978); and **Box 6.1** from R. Crompton and G. Jones, *White Collar Proletariat* (1984) p. 62;

Gareth Morgan for **Fig. 4.1** from G. Morgan, *Images of Organization*, Sage Publications, Inc (1986) p. 21;

Open University Press for **Box 11.2** from P. Willis, *Common Culture* (1990) pp. 85–7;

Organisation for Economic Co-operation and Development for **Table 4.9** for data from *Economic Surveys* (1998) p. 184;

Oxford University Press for **Figs. 5.2–4, 5.7** from J. Goldthorpe et al., *Social Mobility and Class Structure in Modern Britain*, 2nd ed. (1987) pp. 45, 49, 39–41; **Tables 5.5–7** from G. Marshall et al., *Against the Odds: Social class and social justice in industrial societies*, Clarendon (1997) p. 42, 83, **Tables 5.4–5**; **Fig. 4.5** from D. Gallie and Catherine Marsh, 'The Experience of Unemployment' in D. Gallie et al., eds, *Social Change and the Experience of Unemployment* (1994) p. 3; **Table 4.2** from D. Gallie et al., *Restructuring Employment Relationship* (1998), p. 52; **Table 9.7** from J. Pilcher, *Age and Generation in Modern Britain* (1995) p. 62; **Box 14.3** from A. M. Halsey et al., *Origins and Destinations: Family class and education in modern Britain*, Clarendon (1980); and **Table 4.7** from C. Hakim, *Social Change and Innovation in the Labour Market* (1988) p. 227;

Policy Journals for **Tables 15.8–10** from A. Harrison, 'British Social Attitudes Surveys' in *Health Xare UK 1991* (1992) and *Health Care 1997* (1998);

Policy Studies Institute for **Tables 8.2–6, 8.9–11** from T. Modood, 'Culture and Odentity', pp. 292, 293, 331, 109, 110, 121, 91, 92, **Table 8.15** from S. Virdee, 'Racial Harrassment', p. 266, **Table 8.13** from R. Berthoud, 'Income and Standards of Living',

p. 160, and J. Lakey, 'Neighbourhoods and Housing', p. 199, in T. Modood, R. Berthoud et al., *Ethnic Minorities in Britain: Diversity and disadvantage* (1997);

Punch Ltd for **Plate 16.1**, cartoon 'A Briton in time of peace' (1856);

Rivers Oram Press Ltd for **Table 9.5** from P. Hewitt, *About Time: The revolution in work and family life* (1993), p. 61;

Joseph Rowntree Foundation for **Fig. 5.1–5 from J. Hills**, *Inquiry into Income and Wealth*, Vol. 2 (1995) pp. 13, 24, 23, 96, 9;

Sage Publications for **Figs. 3.3, 3.6** from P. Dicken, *Global Shift*, 3rd ed. Paul Chapman Publishing (1988) pp. 190, 296; **Table 12.2** from P. Barwise and A. Ehrenberg, *Television and its Audience* (1988) p. 26; and **Box 11.1** from K. Roberts, 'Great Britain: socio-economic polarization and the implications for lesure' in A. Olszewska and K. Roberts, eds, *Leisure and Life-Style* (1989) pp. 52–4;

Scarlet Press for **Table 7.13** from P. Snyder, *The European Women's Almanac* (1992) p. 370;

The Sociological Review for **Tables 11.3–4** from J. Gershuny and S. Jones, 'The changing work/lesure balance in Britain: 1961–84' in J. Horne et al., eds, *Sport, Leisure and Social Relations*, Sociological Review Monograph 33 (1987) pp. 38–9, 42;

Taylor and Francis for **Tables 10.1, 6.7**, from P. Saunders, *A Nation of Home Owners*, Routledge (1990) p. 287, 285; **Tables 6.1–2, 6.8–9**, from G. Marshall et al., *Social Class in Modern Britain*, Routledge (1988) pp. 148, 208, 217, 146; **Table 13.8** from N. Pleace etal., 'Homelessness in contemporary Britain' from N. Pleace et al., eds, *Homelessness and Social Policy*, Routledge (1997) p. 15; **Table 3.1** from L. Hannah, *The Rise of the Corporate Economy*, Methuen (1983) p. 144; and **Table 6.15** from A. Heath and M. Savage, 'Political alignments with the middle classes, 1972–89' in T. Butler and M. Savage, eds, *Social Change and the Middle Classes*, UCL Press (1995) p. 281;

University of Durham, Dept. of Geography for **Fig. 3.5** from H. Benyon et al., *The Growth and Internationalisation of Teeside AE's Chemical Industry*, Durham Working Paper 3, Middlesbrough Locality Study (1986) p. 72;

Veronica Wallis for **Fig. 10.2** from R. Wallis, *The Elementary Forms of the New Religious Life*, Routledge and Kegan Paul (1984) p. 6;

World Health Organization for **Fig. 15.4** from G. Dahlgren and M. Whitehead, *Policies and Strategies to Promote Equity in Health* (1992) p. 6.

Every effort has been made to trace the copyright holders but if any have been inadvertently overlooked the publishers will be pleased to make the necessary arrangement at the first opportunity.

How to Use this Book

We have tried to write an approachable and accessible textbook on contemporary British society that looks at the society, rather than debates within sociology, and reviews relatively recent work rather than sociological classics. The following points may help you to get the best out of this book.

1 | Many readers will be familiar with the second edition of this book. The third edition is very substantially revised to bring it up to date. In addition, to reflect changes in the subject we have added some new chapters – on associations, leisure, and the mass media. There are other changes designed to help the reader. There is a glossary, each chapter is introduced by an overview and there are references throughout the text to readings from the new companion volume, *Readings in Contemporary British Society*.

2 | The book is divided into *chapters*, which are further subdivided into *sections*. We have assumed that many people will read only one section of the book at a time. Each section is therefore designed to stand on its own as a review of a particular topic, although in many chapters there is also an argument that connects sections.

3 | In general we have avoided cluttering up the text with academic references. Where we do refer to a book or article we use the author-date system; that is, the reference appears as the name of the author or authors, followed by a date. You can find the full details by looking in the bibliography at the back of the book under the author and date.

4 | At the beginning of each chapter you will find a very brief outline of the contents of each section of the chapter.

5 | In every chapter after chapter 1, at the end of each section, you will find a summary of the topic. You will also come across references in the text to other parts of the book which are especially relevant. In addition, there are references throughout

the text to extracts from books and articles on British society to be found in the companion volume to this book, entitled *Readings in Contemporary British Society*.

6 | At the end of each chapter, there is a brief list of books (further reading) that explore in more detail the issues raised in the chapter, and also a brief section which refers you to relevant discussion in other parts of the book.

7 | There are illustrations of various kinds throughout the book. Courses in sociology now often include exercises in interpreting social statistics presented in various ways. We suggest that you use our tables, diagrams and graphs to find out information that is not discussed in the text; a close reading of a table can often tell you more, or suggest more interesting problems, than pages and pages of text. All tables and figures are for the UK unless stated otherwise.

8 | We have found that people often have only a very hazy idea of the geography of the British Isles. To help all our readers we have included maps of Britain and London, with all the places mentioned in the book marked on them.

9 | You may find some of the terms that we use unfamiliar. At the back of the book there is a glossary which provides definitions of technical terms used in the book.

10 | Lastly, enjoy reading our book!

Map 1 Britain, showing places mentioned in the text

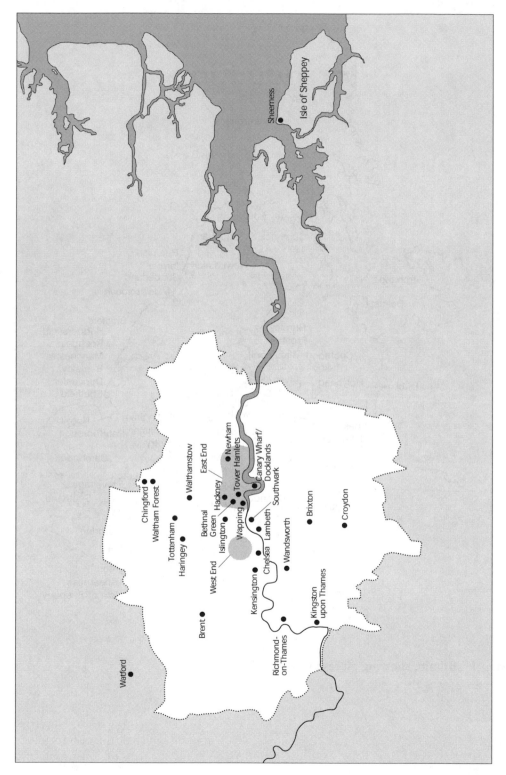

Map 2   London, showing places mentioned in the text

1 Introduction

1.1 Approaching sociology

This book is both an introduction to sociology and an outline of the structure of contemporary British society.

Sociology is the outcome of sustained systematic investigation of social institutions and social relations. Sociology formed as a discipline at the end of the nineteenth century. During the twentieth century it developed most in continental Europe and the United States, its presence in Britain being very limited until the 1960s. Since then it has become a subject for research and teaching in most universities and increasingly also in schools. Expansion encouraged diversity, both of approach and in terms of topics to be explored. Confrontation and collaboration with other disciplines – economics, anthropology, geography, cultural studies – further extended intellectual horizons. Nevertheless there remains a set of core concerns and basic orientations which distinguish sociology. It insists that individual behaviour can be understood only in terms of constraints and opportunities furnished by specifically social arrangements. Social institutions prescribe appropriate modes of conduct, partly in the form of legal or moral pronouncements, partly through formal and informal incentives and sanctions. Institutions solidify over time, but are continually open to challenge and hence change more or less rapidly. Sociology seeks to account systematically and reliably for the changing institutional order and its effects on the behaviour of individuals and groups.

There are many ways in which sociology may be introduced. One way is via the grand questions of how societies in general cohere or change, questions classically addressed by social theorists such as Marx, Durkheim, Weber and Parsons. A second way is by examining and defining concepts that belong to the sociological vocabulary – concepts like *identity, status, network, authority, community* – which are related to one another and have more specialized and restricted meanings than they do in ordinary language, and through which it becomes easier to talk about and understand social processes. Or one could show what sociologists do, the methods they use to investigate the social world and the problems that arise in interpreting the data they collect. Yet another way is to present some of the findings about social practices and social relations in particular societies. This is the approach we adopt.

We follow Runciman (1983) in claiming that sociology consists of four distinct and separable activities: reportage, explanation, description and evaluation. Sociologists, first, *report* on what happened, on events, processes or situations. Second, they try to *explain* why those events or processes happened, what were the reasons or causes for their occurrence. Third, sociologists attempt to *describe* what it was like for people who experienced these events or processes: how did it feel? How did the participants understand and interpret what was going on? Finally, sociologists may *evaluate* events or processes, declaring them to be good or bad, desirable or not. In practice these four activities tend to become intertwined, but in principle they are separate and different. Thus a reader is able, say, to accept explanations for gender inequalities offered in this book without sharing the evaluations; or facts reported may be seen as accurate without the reader necessarily agreeing with the descriptions of, say, what it is like to be a woman in contemporary Britain. As Runciman (1983, p. 38) puts it:

> It takes little familiarity with the writings of sociologists, anthropologists and historians to be aware how often and how intricately the four are intertwined. In any full-length account of a complex event, process or state of affairs, the writer's purpose is likely to encompass reportage, explanation, description and evaluation alike. He is likely, that is, to want not only to persuade the reader that the events, processes or states of affairs which he has chosen to report came about as he reports them and for the reasons or causes which he has put forward, but at the same time to convey to the reader his idea of what it was like for the participants and to bring the reader round to his view of them as good or bad. But however intricately the four are connected in his account, it will always be possible in principle for the reader to disentangle them.

Sociologists, of course, disagree among themselves and all the elements of sociological inquiry are open to controversy. One sociologist can dispute the accuracy of another's report or offer a different explanation. But this is a feature of all kinds of knowledge: debate and argument, trying out competing explanations, and confronting one report with another are, it is often said, the basis for the development of knowledge. In recent times, textbooks of sociology have tended to introduce sociology in terms of apparently mutually exclusive theoretical traditions – functionalist, structuralist, interactionist, Marxist, for example. There are, of course, theoretical disagreements among sociologists, and theories affect explanations, descriptions and evaluations. But the significance of such theoretical disputes for understanding change in contemporary Britain is easily exaggerated. *In practice*, sociologists tend to use techniques, concepts, explanations and interpretations which draw on many, if not all, theoretical traditions. Concepts are taken from a number of competing theoretical positions, referring to action, meaning, structure and function, when discussing social relations and today's societies. Sometimes from reading textbooks one gets the impression that understanding and analysing the social world is complicated because sociologists make it so, unnecessarily, by adopting obscure and mutually exclusive theoretical positions. Rather, to our way of thinking, the difficulties of sociological analysis arise *because the social world is extremely complex*. We have, therefore, set about giving a concrete sociological analysis of one society, Great Britain, respecting its complexity rather than focusing on sociologists' perceptions of societies. We have tried to write a book about British society, not about sociologists.

1.2   Modern societies

Modern industrial societies are probably the most complex of those known in human history. This is partly reflected in their density: relatively large populations are maintained in a comparatively limited space. What is now Britain supported a population of around 3 million in 1600, 6 million in 1800, but 59 million in 1996. This expansion of population was made possible by two developments: an increasing division of labour and urban growth. The division of labour, through which more specialized work tasks were divided between different firms and individuals, increased the efficiency with which those things necessary to support the growing population could be produced (food, clothes, tools, houses, etc.). The expansion of cities provided a physical environment which helped the organization of the division of labour in production and a new social environment for the larger population. Perhaps the major cause of the complexity of contemporary British society is, however, the speed of social change: Britain (like all modern societies) is a *dynamic* society. This dynamism originated from and is sustained by capitalist social relations.

Britain is fundamentally a capitalist society. By this we mean that:

1   there is private ownership of the means of production (property, plant, machinery, etc.);
2   economic activity is geared to making profits;
3   profits go to the owners of the means of production;
4   workers generally do not own productive property but work for wages;
5   the processes of production and sale of goods and services are organized into markets; transactions are commodified.

To define capitalism in such a way does not, of course, mean that it has remained unaltered since its origins in the seventeenth and eighteenth centuries. Quite the contrary: as we show in this book, there have been drastic changes in capitalism. The pattern of ownership of the means of production, changes in the distribution of income and wealth, the increasing complexity and fragmentation of the class structure, and the growth of the welfare state are but a few of the changes that have radically altered capitalist society. Indeed, capitalism by its very nature is an economic system that produces changes and diversity, and this is one of its main features. It produces a self-propelling, ever-accelerating sort of society.

Max Weber, among many others, noted how early capitalists of the seventeenth and eighteenth centuries used what he considered a peculiar logic – devoting their lives to accumulating wealth, or capital, but without spending it. He described this as the development of a Protestant ethic which forbade the use of wealth and encouraged 'asceticism'. At the same time, the Protestant ethic promoted hard work and made worldly success a positive religious virtue. Manufacturers, farmers and merchants of the Protestant faith thus sought business success, which was then, as now, measured by profit-making, but had no way of spending their increasing wealth other than reinvesting in their businesses. This process of profit-making and reinvestment, when seen in the light of competition between private enterprises, led to constant innovation. Firms cannot stand still. They must reinvest and reorganize their operations continually, otherwise their competitors will put them out of business.

The most simple example of this process is that of the introduction of new machinery. If firm A buys machines which make it possible to produce goods more cheaply than firm B, then B will be unable to sell its products and will go out of business, unless it responds. To purchase the same, or better, machinery is one response, but there are others – getting workers to work harder, making new products, or buying out firm A, for instance. The point, however, is that this innovation and change is self-perpetuating, inevitably built into an economic system where individuals and firms are free to produce any goods they choose, how they choose, constrained only by profitable competition. This 'logic' can be seen quite clearly in contemporary economic life: machinery becomes obsolete very quickly; there are frequent mergers, takeovers and closures; new firms are continually being set up; and new generations of products appear increasingly rapidly.

Rapid economic change is closely linked to cultural change. Partly because of continual economic development, British people are used to change. Though not always welcoming it, many people positively seek change. This may occur at the personal and individual level: moving to another town, joining a new religious movement, buying new types of goods, taking a different job. It also occurs collectively, in the political sphere and in the neighbourhood: radical political parties and new social movements are associations of people who collectively set about changing the social world. Britain is an 'active' society: people act as if they can alter the circumstances under which they live, to improve their own conditions and those of others.

This constant change and innovation generates a distinctive kind of social experience which some contemporary sociologists refer to as 'the experience of modernity'. Rapid change leads to uncertainty about the future, feelings of insecurity and anxiety, a sense of lost bearings in negotiating everyday life. Yet, at the same time, it brings a restlessness with permanence, a seeking after new experiences in pursuit of self-development, and selfish concern with personal well-being. The modern experience generates particular personality types. It also threatens social instability as norms and behaviour change, old values and practices are discarded, new kinds of fads and fashions emerge, and traditional institutions become obsolete or are transformed. The experience of modernity is, thus, contradictory. On the one hand, it is exciting, bringing new and diverse experiences and fresh horizons. On the other hand, it removes all certainties, leaving people groping around in a social world without any established norms or guidelines.

Arguably, the modern experience has been amplified and reformed in the last two decades. Many sociologists perceive an emergent postmodern condition. Postmodern culture is one in which the foundations of knowledge are subject to radical doubt, ways of life become less uniform, social interactions less predictable, commitments less permanent and self identities less fixed. The postmodern experience leads people to be more experimental and less dogmatic, to adopt a playful attitude towards identities, images and meanings, to appreciate social and cultural variety, and perhaps to be increasingly tolerant of differences between groups. Such changes are mostly considered a radical extension of implicit features of modern culture. However, these attributes undermine aspirations to plan and control social arrangements. The collapse of the communist regimes of Eastern Europe at the end of the 1980s signalled the end of the main alternative to the capitalist form of organization of industrialized societies. With their demise went also confidence in the capacity to plan social institutions and regulate social change. Social engineering, by means of centralized policy and legislation, was a secondary feature of modernity and one of the traditional fields for the application of sociological knowledge. The extent to which the more fluid and fragmentary characteristics of postmodern culture prevail is highly controversial, but, regardless, the paradoxical kernel of modern experience remains.

Some of the possibilities for new experience and social experimentation associated with capitalist modernity are to be welcomed, others not; the paradox is that we tend to get both the beneficial and the detrimental consequences at the same time. For example, family relationships are changing: new laws and new attitudes to divorce permit women, especially, to escape miserable marriages, but that often leaves them in situations of social and economic insecurity, with heavy responsibilities for their children. The growth of youth subcultures is equally typical of modernity. Unconventional styles of dress, language, music and entertainment alter frequently as young people pursue distinctive, and new, group identities. Such styles are tied up with a capitalist commercialism which, in seeking to persuade people to buy more, encourages changes of fashion.

In an important sense the experience of modernity is an urban phenomenon, an experience that is strongest in the largest of cities. In the city, social relations are relatively impersonal, impermanent, varied and unpredictable. Of course, not all social relations are like that. There are urban communities that are tightly knit and long established, where everyone knows everybody else and where there are collectively enforced rules of behaviour. A sense of community survives within a more general culture of modernity, and this shows the complexity of modern social experience. Complexity involves a multiplicity of experiences, and an enormous diversity.

Diversity can also generate inequality and thus, possibly, conflict. Key themes of sociological inquiry concern inequalities between classes, sexes, ethnic groups, status groups and age groups. Such differences need not produce conflict but they often do, particularly when difference is interpreted as inequality. The pursuit of equality, along with the pursuit of liberty, has been a fundamental base of actions to promote social change in Britain throughout the capitalist era. Social groups seeing themselves as unequally treated have organized together to improve their position. The struggle over the franchise (who should be able to vote), won first by middle-class men, then by working-class men, then by women, is a well-known example of the pursuit of one aspect of political equality – the right of equal citizenship.

Inequalities are perpetual sources of conflict in capitalist societies, though in most cases conflict is institutionalized, that is to say there are channels or institutions which resolve conflicts peacefully, by negotiation, without recourse to the use of force or violence. Thus, parliamentary democratic procedure, bargaining procedures in industrial relations and regulation of competition between firms are all ways of institutionalizing conflict. Of course, these are not always effective: internal war in Northern Ireland, riots in the inner city and protests against roadbuilding are all contemporary instances of conflict escaping from institutional regulation. But the point is that diversity generates conflict, fuelling experiences of instability, encouraging people to act to re-establish stability, which in turn produces further change.

Diversity, complexity and change are, then, features of contemporary British society. Any individual will know of, or share, only a very small proportion of the variety of experiences that make up the social mosaic of the modern society. That, indeed, is one of the fascinations of reading good sociological reportage and description: it allows some access to the range and pattern of the experiences of social groups other than those to which the reader belongs. Sociology, however, also seeks to connect together context and experience, to show how certain social mechanisms or structures constrain and shape experiences. For all the diversity and complexity of everyday life, there are patterns to social action and interaction. The social world is *structured*. Just as the mosaics of the floors of Roman houses are made up of hundreds of pieces which, nevertheless, make a complete design, the patterning of social relations cannot be seen by looking at the individual elements. The mosaic has to be examined in terms of the *relative* positions of its different pieces, how they stand in relation to one another.

One of the outstanding features of societies is the way in which component parts are highly interrelated, or *interdependent*. Thus, for instance, the social organization of work affects the way education is organized, changes the role of the family in bringing up children and results in the unequal distribution of income and wealth. It is this, the interdependence of social institutions, which makes sociological explanation so difficult and complicated. If one part of the mosaic changes then the whole pattern is altered, making it difficult to pin-point a single cause of any particular event, process or change.

The concepts that we have discussed above are ones which we will use in our analysis of change in British society. We stress that Britain is a diverse, changing and complex society. At the root of that diversity is a capitalist economic system and a modern culture. These are fundamental bases of social change, generating sometimes order and harmony, at other times disorder and conflict. They are the structures behind everyday life with all its variety, ambiguity and contradiction.

1.3 Contemporary Britain

Some of the implications of the preceding remarks are briefly illustrated in the following thumb-nail sketch of key structures and changes of contemporary British society, which we discuss in greater detail in the chapters that follow.

Our understanding of contemporary Britain begins by recognizing that we cannot consider the country in isolation from other societies. Very rapidly, a global society is developing in which nation-states are inextricably bound together by international flows of money and communication, an increasing internationalization of ownership of companies, global travel, mass media which easily cross national frontiers, and environmental risks such as global warming which will affect everywhere. This process of globalization contributes to an increased speed of events. It also makes societies like Britain increasingly vulnerable to changes happening elsewhere over which they have no control. The collapse of east Asian economies in 1998, for example, had marked effects on countries around the world. At the same time, globalization presents opportunities – for travel, for the enjoyment of goods from other countries, for contact with other cultures.

Globalization also provides the context for the process of industrial change which the country has experienced since the mid-1970s. The British economy has declined by comparison with those of other advanced nations in the world system. Many British firms have lost out in competition with foreign equivalents, though it has to be recognized that, increasingly, the most important firms are multinational corporations anyway. In response to a harsh external environment many firms have undergone restructuring, with changes in ownership as a result of takeovers, and changes in their internal organization. This restructuring has serious effects upon employees, partly as new machinery is introduced making workers redundant, and partly as jobs are redesigned so as to save money by making each worker more productive. In fact, British workers increased their productivity very considerably during the 1980s, but this did not improve the relative competitiveness of British industry. The British state, in the 1980s and 1990s, was either unwilling or unable to improve the situation, preferring to allow the cold winds of capitalist competition to reshape the economy rather than intervening directly.

Industrial change inevitably affects class relations and the class structure, because occupation is a fundamental basis of class position. The shape of the occupational structure has been changing in recent years, the numbers of manual workers declining, and the numbers of professional and semi-professional jobs increasing. A debate rages about the effects of this on class relations. In the twentieth century, the working class, through the organizations of the labour movement (primarily trade unions and the Labour Party), has exerted much political pressure for social reform. The main supporters of the labour movement were, however, manual workers, who were the majority of the working population and whose social situation was visibly distinct from that of the upper and upper-middle class. The changing size and composition of British social classes have reduced the strength of the working class as a force for change.

Women have played a critically important part in the redefinition of the social division of labour since the late 1960s. For instance, there are more married women in paid work today than there have been at any time in the twentieth century. However, the jobs women have tend to be relatively poorly paid and carry little authority. The segregation of men's work from women's work, which is the way that gender differentials are maintained, is increasingly a source of frustration and annoyance to women, who have organized to improve their position. This is to be expected since, apart from education, where opportunities for girls and women have improved markedly in recent years both at school and in higher education, the inequalities between men and women have not been correspondingly reduced. Much of this inequality has its roots in cultural stereotypes of women as in, for example, the unequal distribution of housework, in images of femininity which describe women as helpless and passive, and in male violence against women.

In a similar way, we can see that the labour market intersects with cultural stereotypes to create a further social division which is a source of social conflict – that between ethnic groups. Many members of ethnic groups, particularly those of Caribbean and Asian descent, even if many of them have been born in Britain, suffer social and material deprivation when compared with white people. The very presence in Britain of many different ethnic groups is one mark of the diversity of culture and experience among different sections of the population. Family forms and religious experience distinguish ethnic groups, and some of the most vital of contemporary cultural products – food, music, oriental religions – are the result of the presence of people with different cultural traditions. These differences are, however, frequently turned into bases for much-resented inequalities. There can be no doubt that black people tend to get poorer jobs than whites. What is more, they tend to suffer the consequences of white racism, the hostile or deprecatory attitudes and behaviours which are directed at them merely on the basis of their skin colour.

The next aspect of the contemporary social structure that we deal with is more directly concerned with the cultural experience of modern society. The family is one institution which exemplifies the degree of variety and complexity that characterizes social experience in Britain, and one which illustrates the insecurity and instability of social relations in the contemporary world. One of the most striking features of the contemporary British family is the variety of forms it assumes. Besides distinctive household patterns of ethnic minorities, which are often adapted from their particular religious and cultural traditions or the need to provide accommodation for newly arrived immigrant kinsfolk, there is a remarkable diversity of household forms among other sections of the population too. There is a dominant image of what a 'normal' family is in contemporary Britain – a small, nuclear family of parents and dependent children. In reality, this is not normal at all, and only a small proportion of households is like this. Various social changes, including the facts that people live longer than they used to, that many more people are getting divorced, and that people expect more from marriage than before, have meant a rise in the numbers of single-person households, of one-parent families and of families formed by remarriage and step-parenting. The increasing diversity of household forms in Britain is partly produced by changing attitudes to family and marriage. Not only is the divorce rate high, but more couples are living together without getting married and are deciding to have children together, and increasing numbers of people are opting to live by themselves.

Since the 1950s, British families have had greater opportunity for leisure as hours of work have, in general, fallen and family incomes have risen. A whole range of industries has grown up to service this demand. Some are oriented to home-based leisure, particularly the expansion of the range of offerings in the mass media, especially television. At the same time, there has been expansion in commercial provision outside the home – in tourism, for example. These developments have persuaded some sociologists that Britain is becoming a consumer society in which people's identities are being formed by shopping, television and holidays rather than by work and family. This is undoubtedly an exaggeration and neglects the importance that people attach to involvements with the network of associations outside the immediate family and work – friends, more remote family, voluntary and religious organizations and the local community.

Many of the contradictions of contemporary British society, and some of the points of tension between the organization of economic life and the culture of modernity, are reflected within the education system. Educational institutions both express and create social divisions. Current emphasis upon making education relevant for work – training for economic life – typifies these contradictions. On the one hand, educating people for future work roles always entails selection and differentiation: some people are made into successes, others into failures. Schools create inequalities between individuals by preparing their pupils differently by class, gender and ethnic group. On the other hand, schools are expected to transmit a common culture – to educate young people for citizenship and to be full members of a national community. To what extent schools actually do either of these things very effectively is open to debate. However, the complicated role that educational institutions play gives some indication of the complex interdependencies between institutions in British society: they are intended to fit in with the entire industrial and occupational complex, with the family, and with the dominant political institutions. What schools do is relevant to, and interdependent with, all other major institutions in contemporary Britain.

Diversity and change in modern society and domination and resistance are the very stuff of politics. In parliamentary democracies people have the power, even if it is rather restricted, to change things. The most obvious way is through voting, but the means by which people seek to change their situations have also become more diverse. British society is characterized by a multiplicity of social movements and pressure groups. Women, ethnic groups and environmentalists are but three voices represented in new social movements which express specific grievances and wishes.

It has to be recognized, however, that the capacity to change society, either by voting or by involvement in pressure groups, is limited. The powers of the state have very greatly increased since the beginning of the twentieth century, especially since the Second World War. This is partly because the state has come to intervene more extensively in citizens' lives, and partly a result of the vast resources the state can deploy. It also has the ultimate capacity for authoritative and direct control. The growth in numbers of the police in Britain, and of their powers, is a significant example. The character of the police force is changing: it is becoming more professional and technologically sophisticated. Some of these changes have been brought about in response to the fear of a rising rate of crime. Others are introduced because of the civil disturbances which, as we indicated earlier, have to be seen as elements of a rapidly changing society showing symptoms of strain.

Contemporary British society, as we have argued, is increasingly diverse and complex and is, furthermore, changing very quickly. Underlying this complexity are some basic structuring elements, two of the most important of which are capitalist social relations and a culture of modernity. The rest of this book looks at these issues in much greater depth. Its principal message is that social groups have very different social experiences. Our sociological description and explanation seek to portray the extent of this diversity, and to respect the complexity of social life. At the same time, we try to account for its distinctive features in terms of underlying social-structural mechanisms which produce experiences in the social world. What any individual experiences, and what any social group shares, are significantly constrained by the way in which the society as a whole is structured. There is both diversity and structure.

Further reading

There are many sources outlining other approaches to the introduction of sociology which are complementary to ours. The best recent general introduction to the sociological way of thinking is Bauman (1990). Giddens (1997) is a textbook that seeks to offer a comprehensive introduction to all aspects of sociology, including to theoretical approaches, methods and the analysis of social institutions. Hughes et al. (1995) deals with classical sociological theory. Dictionaries of sociology, like Abercrombie et al. (2000), define and describe the development of specifically sociological concepts.

2 Globalization

2.1   Introduction

It is widely believed that we are currently living through some extraordinary times, times involving exceptional changes to the fabric of our social life. In particular, it is often now argued that these changes result from the globalization of economic, social and political relationships. In this chapter we consider such a thesis of globalization (some of the more economic aspects of globalization will also be analysed in chapter 3).

   In popular writing, three global trends have been particularly noted. First, it is often said that contemporary economies have become global. Huge flows of money move between foreign exchange markets in different countries (much greater than the amounts necessary for world trade); companies pursuing a global strategy have developed with an annual turnover greater than that of whole national economies (such as Microsoft, Nike, Virgin, Sony, McDonalds); and a wide array of products from many different countries is readily available worldwide (such as tropical fruit, Brazilian TV, Japanese Walkmans, South African wine and so on). Local factories and offices can be opened and closed seemingly at will, while individual states which can both promote and constrain global processes are often unable to determine their own national economic policies. Some writers have argued that there are no longer *national* economies, such as the British economy.

Second, one particular set of global companies has been especially noted, namely those huge corporations that control the world's mass media. These media seem to be producing homogeneous programmes based upon a very large international market. The power of such global media reduces the impact of local programmes and of local

Plate 2.1 | The blue earth
Source: Geosphere Project / Science Photo Library

identities. It seems that we are living in a world of media sameness, defined by football World Cups, American talk shows, Australian soap operas, British period dramas, adverts for Coca-Cola and so on. The globe is itself very popular as a global image. The earth or globe is used in the advertising of products (airlines, for example) and for recruiting people to join groups protesting about the environment (see plate 2.1 for a famous picture of the earth as seen from space).

Third, new technologies are dramatically reducing the apparent distances between places and peoples (see M. Waters 1995). These include mass jet transportation, fax machines, high-speed trains, mobile phones, fibre-optic cabling, satellite communications, cable television, the networked computer and the internet. These technologies are redrawing the very categories of time and space, compressing distance through reducing the time taken to move people, or images or information, and increasing some sense of global interdependence. These are technologies of time-space compression.

We will examine each of these global aspects below. It should also be noted that, if there is some development of global social relationships, then this has implications for the discipline of sociology, which has been based upon the idea that we study the characteristics of each separate 'society'. However, globalization may well produce a new social science focused upon the study of these global relationships and not upon examining separate societies. Any particular society, such as Britain, will only be analysable in terms of its connections with other societies and especially through its location within a set of global relationships. The existing social sciences, including sociology, could gradually disappear and be replaced by the study of this broader global social order.

So far we have used the word 'globalization' without much clarification. It is a somewhat confusing word, since it refers both to certain global processes and to certain global outcomes. These two senses are set out below:

1   Globalization 1 (process): processes operating on an emergent global level which over time are compressing the distances between peoples and places within different societies, and which increase the sense that we live in a single world.
2   Globalization 2 (outcome): an end-state in which the whole earth is criss-crossed by global processes and in which individual places, groups of people and individual societies have lost their significance and power – there is a single global economy and society.

In this book we use 'globalization' in the first sense, globalization 1. We do not consider that there is a single global society as implied in globalization 2. Many of the processes we discuss in this chapter are incomplete. We shall see that there are incipient global processes but there is so far nothing that approaches a single global economy and society.

In the next section we outline some interconnections between Britain and the rest of the world. We consider to what degree the contemporary world is subject to global processes. In section 2.3 we consider the complex balance of the benefits and the costs of globalization. In section 2.4 we consider one particular set of costs, namely various 'global risks' which impact upon, and have helped to generate, contemporary environmentalism.

2.2 British society and globalization

It has become increasingly difficult to talk about 'Britain' as a separate society that can be analysed on its own. Various global processes appear to be making societies less obviously autonomous from each other.

We will examine this through the conceptual distinction between scapes and flows. We will consider how people, ideas and images especially flow along various scapes organized through and across different societies. One example of this involves the movements of television images that flow along the scapes that connect together three kinds of places. There are those sites where TV programmes are made (such as Hollywood, London, Liverpool, Melbourne): the places where transmission masts, satellites, cables under pavements are located: and the places where television sets, decoders and satellite dishes are located within houses, clubs and pubs.

Scapes comprise the networks connecting together machines, technologies, organizations and documents. Together they produce sets of nodes that are connected together in complex and often lengthy forms. The following are the main global scapes:

- the systems of transportation of people by air, sea, rail, motorways and other roads;
- the transportation of objects via postal and other systems;
- the wire, co-axial and fibre-optic cables that carry telephone messages, television pictures and computer information and images;
- the microwave channels used by cellular phones;
- the satellites used for transmitting radio and television signals.

Once such scapes have been established, then individuals and especially large companies will try to become connected to them, to become nodes within a particular scape or network. Examples of this in Britain include the ways in which different towns try to get connected to the motorway network or to have flights organized to major 'hub' airports. People will also endeavour to get their local schools plugged into the worldwide internet. Towns try to attract the laying of cables for receiving television programmes from BSkyB and other providers.

Various flows occur along these scapes once they are established. These flows consist of:

- *people* travelling along transportation scapes for work and for holidays;
- *objects* being sent and received by companies and individuals, which move along postal and other freight systems;
- *information and images* flowing along telephone and television cables and between satellites;
- *messages* travelling along microwave channels from one mobile phone to another.

In short, there is extensive *information* flowing along these scapes, including financial, leisure, economic, scientific, news data and images.

Such scapes and flows create new social inequalities. These can be called inequalities of access. Some groups in Britain are well 'plugged in' to these scapes (such as those schools with good internet access) while others are excluded. What has become significant is the relative, as opposed to the absolute, location of a particular social group or town or city in relationship to these scapes. These telecommunication and transportation structures reshape the very nature of time and space. Scapes pass by some areas while connecting others along information-rich and transportation-rich 'tunnels', such as that between London and Birmingham. These tunnels in effect compress the distances of time and space between places.

The rapid increase in the scale and velocity of such scapes and flows represents a striking change in the organization of British (and other) societies. These scapes and flows are relatively independent of each individual nation-state, although they are shaped by various kinds of legal and other forms of government regulation, such as the attempts to censor what appears on the internet.

Scapes connect together specific towns and cities. In the case of money, one of the most significant of such flows, the main connections throughout the world are those between the three world-cities of London, Tokyo and New York. These are the main financial nodes in the world-system. They contain the most influential stock exchanges, the largest concentrations of banks and investment houses, the most significant exchanges for buying and selling foreign currencies (such as dollars, marks, yen and sterling) and the greatest concentrations of specialist financial advisers such as accountants and lawyers. In relation to money, the connections between London, Tokyo and New York are more important than the ones between London and the rest of Britain. As a result of interdependence across the globe, national governments find it very hard to control these scapes and flows of money. It is not so much that money makes the world go round as that the world is money going round faster and faster.

More generally, national territories are less subject to effective governance by national states as these scapes and flows criss-cross national borders. Besides the huge flows of money, there are flows of refugees, asylum seekers, information about almost every subject on the internet, television images and so on. States cannot act effectively in many traditional domains without international collaboration (so as to regulate against internet pornography, for example). Governments have had to increase their integration with each other in order to offset the destabilizing effects of these forms of global interconnectedness. This can be seen particularly in the development of the European Union, which plays a significant role in social regulation (see chapter 13). More generally, states are involved in both promoting and constraining global processes.

Many of these scapes have become partially organized at the global level itself. Some organizations involved in globalizing them include the United Nations, the World Bank and the International Monetary Fund, Bill Gates's Microsoft software company, broadcasting stations such as CNN or the BBC, Rupert Murdoch's News Corporation, the World Intellectual Property Organization, the International Air Transport Association, the Olympic movement, which organizes the global Olympic Games, and the World Health Organization.

Globalization and national identity

It would be misleading to argue that globalization means that a sense of national identity has disappeared. On the contrary, nationalism is the other side of the coin of globalization; as global flows increase, so too does an awareness of differences between nations and national identities. Becoming aware of other cultures sharpens the consciousness of the domestic culture.

It is useful to distinguish hot from cool nationalism. The former is manifested in those outbursts of passionate nationalism that have characterized the modern world for some time in such diverse places as Iran, Serbia or Argentina. Cool nationalism refers to the sense of national identity that forms an unexamined, often unconscious, background to everyday life. Billig (1995, p. 93) argues that this 'banal nationalism' is very important, precisely because it is not obvious:

> The thesis of banal nationalism suggests that nationhood is near the surface of contemporary life. If this is correct, then routinely familiar habits of language will be continually acting as reminders of nationhood. In this way the world of nations will be reproduced as 'the' world, the natural environment of today. As has been argued, nationalism is not confined to the florid language of blood myths. Banal nationalism operates with prosaic routine words which take nations for granted and which, in so doing, inhabit them.

Banal nationalism is manifested in a number of different ways – in the flying of flags, the defence of national currencies, and civic rituals such as coronations, the opening of Parliament or national days. It even creeps into the very language used every day to describe ourselves. Billig illustrates this by means of a study of British newspapers on one day in June 1993. On that day the newspapers all carried stories about the bombing of Baghdad (it was the start of the Gulf War) and it is not surprising that these were couched in nationalistic language. However, Billig identifies other ways in which a banal nationalism was represented. For example, there was persistent use of the word 'our', as in a *Sun* editorial which complained that the European Community had taken 'our money'. The assumption made here, and made routinely throughout, is that the newspaper is addressing a nation with a strong sense of collective identity which can be contrasted with others. The *Daily Telegraph*, similarly, headlined an article 'Why our taxes need never rise again'. Again, the idea of the nation is invoked by a large number of stories which mention 'British' or 'Britain'. For example, the *Sun* began a story 'Britain got a triple dose of good news yesterday' while the *Mirror* announced 'A new eating fad is about to hit Britain'. The sports pages, of course, promote an even sharper sense of nationhood. On this day in June, for example, the newspapers were celebrating the survival of a British tennis player into the second round of the Wimbledon tennis tournament. Again, 'our' and 'we' were common. In the European athletics championship the British men's relay team came second, provoking the *Sun*'s headline 'That's relay great lads'. The reports of a variety of other sporting events were similarly focused on the success or failure of British competitors.

Just as nations exist in tension with an emerging globalization, so also is there an ambiguous relationship between parts of nations as a whole. Indeed an 'identity politics' at the regional level seems to be more pronounced as globalization develops. This process is expressed in a number of ways which mirror the markers of nationhood itself

– language, religion, political movements, even tourism.

Although regional identities are stronger in other parts of Europe, they are clearly seen in Britain, where Scotland, Wales and Northern Ireland all press for a measure of autonomy. This is probably most powerful in Scotland, which has long had a claim to be a nation in its own right despite not being differentiated from the rest of the United Kingdom by language or religion. As McCrone (1992, p. 21) points out, Scotland 'ceded political sovereignty to Westminster while retaining considerable civil autonomy'; Scotland exists, in other words, very much as a separate society accompanied by a certain degree of local control of the economy. This identity is reinforced by an image of what Scotland is, a 'landscape in the mind', as McCrone puts it. To some extent, this set of images is manufactured as part of the heritage industry. McCrone, Morris and Kiely (1995), for example, point out how Glasgow has been promoted as a city of culture, how the highlands have become romanticized for the tourist trade, and how Scotland's independent history is celebrated in castles and in the sites of ancient battles.

The sense of a separate Scottish identity is expressed in Scottish nationalism. For example, in an opinion poll carried out in 1991, 40 per cent of Scots considered themselves to be Scottish, not British, 29 per cent more Scottish than British, and a further 21 per cent equally Scottish and British. Recently this sense of a distinct national identity has been turned into greater political independence as the Westminster Parliament has devolved significant powers to a Scottish Parliament.

Summary

1 Globalization takes a variety of forms.
2 The most useful way of thinking about globalization is in terms of scapes and flows.
3 Such scapes and flows create major new social inequalities; states are often unable to ameliorate the impact of such flows.

2.3   Globalization and social life

There are three very different kinds of academic response to the thesis of globalization: global scepticism, global enthusiasm and global pessimism. We begin this section by summarizing these three positions.

Global sceptics argue that the thesis of globalization is overstated. Hirst and Thompson (1996) set out the sceptical thesis. They argue, on the basis of considerable statistical information about the economy, that the present international economy is not so distinct as many argue and that in some ways it is less open than in the period 1870–1914. They also argue that most large companies are based within a given society (such as Ford being American, Sony being Japanese, Vickers being British) and that there are relatively few truly international companies. Most investment, they say, occurs between the rich countries, especially between the triad of Europe, Japan and North America, and it is not equally spread across the globe. Governments are able to intervene and make a difference to the conditions of life of their citizens. We should not be pessimistic about the possibilities of state intervention. Overall, Hirst and Thompson say that while the economy has become internationalized it has not been globalized.

Against this thesis three critical comments can be made. First, Hirst and Thompson concentrate upon the economic aspects of globalization and ignore global processes in the areas of culture and the environment. They do not consider the globalization thesis in its entirety. Second, they do not sufficiently consider how some of the phenomena they discuss may be in the process of further development in a global direction. Indeed, they implausibly suggest that the globalization of money markets may only be a temporary phenomenon that will go into reverse. Finally, much of what they call internationalization is what we have called globalization 1 – they take globalization 2 as *the* form of the globalization thesis.

Global enthusiasts see global processes as producing a new world order, a kind of cosmopolitan borderlessness in which wars and other conflicts will gradually disappear. This new global epoch is seen as offering huge new opportunities, especially in overcoming the limitations and restrictions that national governments have exercised on the freedom of both corporations and individuals. Global processes are celebrated because of the new freedoms and opportunities that they make available.

Global pessimists see globalization not as a borderless utopia but as a new dystopia. The global world is seen as a new kind of medieval world. The old medieval world was characterized by a lack of clear societies; there were empires with centres and peripheries and there were powerful city-states. The new medieval global world likewise consists of strong empires, such as Microsoft and Coca-Cola, which are often more powerful than societies. At the same time, there is the growth of competing city-states, such as London, New York, Sydney and Tokyo. Also there is a weakness of each society that is unable to reform itself so as to improve the social conditions of the population.

In the following, we do not simply adopt one of these positions. We show that globalization is by no means complete, and that so far it has created some very dangerous risks while simultaneously facilitating new opportunities and desires. It produces new kinds of social relationship, linking different people and their social activities within very varied kinds of town and city. Global scapes and flows create novel risks and uncertainties in people's lives, as well as providing new opportunities and desires.

Some of the risks entailed by globalization include:

- the spread of AIDS and other diseases throughout the world since the mid-1980s or so;
- the growth of environmental risks moving across national borders, such as those which followed the explosion at Chernobyl nuclear plant in 1985 in what was then the USSR;
- the loss of national sovereignty as these various global scapes and flows have increasingly bypassed national governments;

- being exiled from one's country of origin, or finding that one is an asylum seeker with very limited rights of residence in the country that one arrives in;
- the homogenization of the culture of different places and the loss of local distinctiveness. This has sometimes been described as the 'Coca-Colonization' or 'McDonaldization' of contemporary social life (see box 2.1).

Box 2.1   McDonaldization

George Ritzer (1998) shows how a network of technologies, skills, texts and branding ensure that, in every country where companies like McDonald's operate, more or less the same product is delivered in more or less the same way. He calls this process 'McDonaldization'. Many other 'global' enterprises, such as British Airways, Virgin, American Express, Coca-Cola, Disney and Sony, are organized on the basis of a similar global network.

These global products are produced in predictable, calculable, routinized and standardized environments, even where there is franchising and not single ownership. These global companies have produced enormously effective networks across the globe. Thus an African McDonald's Big Mac will be every bit as 'good' as one sold in a British McDonald's (incidentally the first McDonald's only sprung up in Britain in 1974; McDonald's started in the USA in 1955).

Such networks depend upon allocating a very large proportion of resources to branding, advertising, quality control, staff training and the internalization of the corporate image in each country where that company operates. These aspects of the brand cross societies in standardized patterns, so sustaining the global brand image.

The development of McDonaldization is very influential. It has generated new ways of organizing companies on a global scale with a minimum of central organization. The development of American Express or Disney Parks is an example of similarly organized companies operating at a global level. Furthermore, McDonaldization generates new kinds of low-skilled, standardized jobs which are particularly directed at young people. These are sometimes described as McJobs. There is also the development of new products such as Big Macs or the entirely simulated Chicken McNuggets. These alter people's eating habits, even in countries like China or Russia where McDonald's is especially popular with young people. McDonaldization also encourages the eating of standardized fast food bought from takeaway restaurants. It popularizes what is often called 'grazing' rather than sitting down for a prolonged family meal.

At the same time, the development of global connections allows people new opportunities and new activities to develop. These new opportunities include:

- relatively cheap travel, so that many people in Britain can go on overseas holidays at least every few years;
- the ability to buy consumer goods and lifestyles from across the world (such as

Mexican food, Indian rugs, African jewellery, South American coffee, Scandinavian furniture and so on);

● the opportunity to communicate with people in many countries through the use of the internet;

● the ability to form new social groups, which are often opposed to, or provide alternatives to, aspects of globalization;

● the possibility of participating in global cultural events, such as the World Cup;

● listening to 'world music' and participating in other new global cultural experiences;

● reinforcing and marketing certain kinds of local identity which can have a global appeal, such as the development of Irish drinks, Irish bars, Riverdance and Irish culture generally.

Overall, then, we have seen that global processes create both new risks and new opportunities. In box 2.2 these contradictory effects are illustrated through a discussion of the £625 m bid made by BSkyB in September 1998 to buy the football club Manchester United.

Box 2.2   Football as the global game

The World Cup has, of course, become a huge business, with complex links between national football associations, FIFA, national media interests such as the BBC, Channel 5 or ITV, and global television companies. In Britain the most visible global company is BSkyB, which has bought the rights to many domestic and international football games.

In September 1998, BSkyB made what many saw as an outrageous and, in the end, unsuccessful bid for the largest and financially most successful British soccer club, Manchester United. The bid valued the club at over £600 m, while only ten years earlier no buyer for the club could be found when it was priced at £20 m.

What is significant about Manchester United is that it is a global club. There are thought to be 100 m supporters across the globe, of whom a staggering 98 per cent have never been to a match at Old Trafford. There are over 200 supporters' groups in at least 24 countries, including Australia, India, Malaysia, Malta, Germany and Ireland. It is thought that in the Scandinavian countries there are more United fans than there are fans supporting any of the local teams. There are said to be 17,000 unofficial web sites on the internet devoted to Manchester United. No other sporting club in the world sells so many replica shirts. Over 100,000 copies of the official magazine are sold across 30 countries.

Even within Britain there are reckoned to be over 4 m supporters, the vast majority of whom can never expect to see a game at Old Trafford. Even many local fans have great difficulty in getting seats in the 55,000-seater stadium (about to be increased to 67,000). Most fans cannot see the club play.

Thus BSkyB and Manchester United presume that there is a massive unfulfilled demand to see their games on television, both in Britain and, more importantly, across the globe. The potential income, especially from pay-for-view digital television, is colossal. Fans across the globe could, for example, watch every home game, since BSkyB possesses the rights to transmit in every continent. For example, it is part of the same media group as Star Television, which now transmits TV programmes across most of Asia.

So the bid for Manchester United is a bid for a global football club which will permit the 100 m supporters worldwide to see their team play. There will be a real benefit from globalization for those supporters living away from Manchester, especially overseas.

But at the same time many local supporters of the club are strongly opposed to the bid from BSkyB, since they consider that the club's traditions, based on and around Old Trafford and Manchester, will be lost, even including the colour of their shirts. Local supporters say that the club will have to fit in with the requirements and schedules of the global media giant BSkyB. The local traditions of the club will be destroyed by becoming part of Rupert Murdoch's global company, News Corporation.

The takeover bid for Manchester United thus brings out the complex disputes that globalization generates, between various new benefits and new risks.

In conclusion to this section, we consider the formulation of the sociologist Michael Mann:

> Today, we live in a global society. It is not a unitary society, nor is it an ideological community or a state, but it is a single power network. Shock waves reverberate around it, casting down empires, transporting massive quantities of people, materials and messages, and finally, threatening the ecosystem and atmosphere of the planet. (Mann 1993, p. 11)

There are a number of points to note about this. He argues that there is not a unified global society but exceptional levels of global interdependence; unpredictable shock waves spill out from one part to the system as a whole; there are not just societies but massively powerful empires roaming the globe; and there are mass flows of peoples, objects and human wastes, some of which are beneficial, some very dangerous. In the next section we examine these dangerous flows of human wastes – of global environmental risks.

Summary

1   There is a variety of different views as to the overall impact and significance of globalization, ranging from scepticism through enthusiasm to pessimism.
2   McDonaldization produces powerful effects on the nature of economic and social life within Britain.
3   The consequences of globalization are diverse and contradictory – some social groups benefit, others lose out. Most people both lose and gain from its consequences.

2.4   Global environmental risks

We begin here with one of the best-known definitions of globalization. Giddens defines it 'as the intensification of world-wide social relations which link distant localities in such a way that local happenings are shaped by events occurring many miles away and vice versa' (1990, p. 64). One clear way in which this can be seen is in the environment, where what happens in one place critically affects what happens in other places and indeed what may well happen in the very distant future. Tree felling in the Amazon rainforest today will affect future climate patterns throughout the world for many years to come.

The best-known sociological approach to the study of these environmental risks is Ulrich Beck's thesis of the risk society (see box 2.3).

Box 2.3   Risk society

Beck (1992) distinguishes between industrial societies and risk societies. In the former, political conflicts are defined by the distribution of 'goods' within each national society. People conflict over their rights to education, health care, pensions, unemployment benefits and so on. These are goods normally provided by the government in each society, and political debate is organized around access to them.

In the risk society, by contrast, political conflicts are defined by the distribution not of goods but of 'bads'. Such bads comprise the flows of hazards, waste products and environmental risks. Such a risk society is partly global since these hazards flow everywhere. No person and no country remains safe from their consequences. The risk society affects everyone, rich and poor, young and old, although those living in very poor countries tend to be worse affected by the distribution of bads.

Beck distinguishes between those 'natural' catastrophes that happened in pre-modern societies, such as floods and hurricanes, and the 'created' hazards that occur in the contemporary risk society. The latter are systematically caused by human innovations, especially by science, governments and companies, which have come to treat the parts of the whole globe as a laboratory. Examples of such risks manufactured in one place and then having untold consequences elsewhere include the chemical pollution of rivers, BSE (mad cow disease), nuclear radiation, ozone depletion, acid rain and global warming. Each of these manufactured risks flows across the borders of each society.

These risks have a number of features. First, their effects are not limited to specific places or specific times. Indeed, there are future generations who will suffer from the explosion at the Chernobyl nuclear power plant in 1985 (see plate 2.2). These risks affect the whole globe including its biosphere. Sheep farmers in Cumbria and Wales are still affected by the fallout from Chernobyl.

Second, these are risks that cannot be compensated for, since the effects are global. It is not possible to insure against them. Further, these are mostly risks that cannot be sensed. We are unable to see, hear, smell or touch nuclear radiation. These are risks of extraordinary danger and yet they are mostly invisible. Beck describes this as the 'disempowerment of the senses' (see Macnaghten and Urry 1998).

Finally, we become particularly dependent upon experts to inform us as to the consequences of these risks, and yet at the same time such experts are often mistrusted because they have helped to generate them. A risk society is particularly based upon conflicts between experts and those who possess lay knowledge. In such conflicts, global expert systems often become seen as part of the problem rather than the solution to environmental risks.

So far we have seen how industrial societies have shifted into a risk society. In current debates it is then said that there are processes of *global* environmental change involved here. However, that people see these risks as global and part of a common crisis of the environment is not something that simply follows from the development of these global risks.

What happened in Britain and elsewhere is that many different kinds of risk and damage came to be interpreted as 'environmental'. Developments in the 1970s and 1980s, such as nuclear power, the building of motorways, the loss of greenfield land, threats to areas of special scientific interest, and a reduced biodiversity, had all come to be regarded as part of the 'environment' and not as separate and unconnected phenomena.

The concepts that now make up the environmental agenda involved a process of active construction by environmental groups during the 1970s and 1980s, in response to concerns about the more general character of contemporary society. New forms of

Plate 2.2 | The explosion at Chernobyl generates invisible global risks, 1985

environmental protest were related to widespread anxiety about a technocratic economy and politics, as with the specific nature of the health-threatening properties of the physical environment. Such developments had, moreover, to be viewed as novel and disruptive and not as naturally part of our experience of modern life.

Furthermore, the environmental movement came to use the global media, often very effectively. Greenpeace, for example, is expert at packaging environmental action in simple, black-and-white, media-sensitive fashion. Greenpeace activism has come to symbolize heroic action pitted against corporate greed, self-interest and the behaviour of states. Some environmental groups have developed very effective employment of media images, including those which indicated the effects of acid rain on lakes, forests, various industries, birds and so on. The media are now an integral part of the cultural process by which environmental meanings are created, circulated and consumed. Andrew Ross summarizes:

> In recent years we have become accustomed to seeing images of a dying planet, variously exhibited in grisly poses of ecological depletion and circulated by all sectors of genocidal atrocities. The clichés of the standard environmental movement are well known to us all: on the one hand, belching smokestacks, seabirds mired in petrochemical sludge, fish floating belly-up, traffic jams in Los Angeles and Mexico City, and clearcut forests; on the other hand, the redeeming repertoire of pastoral imagery, pristine, green, and unspoiled by human habitation, crowned by the ultimate global spectacle, the fragile, vulnerable ball of spaceship earth. (Ross 1994, p. 171)

Also, viewing the environment as threatened by global changes resulted from the emergence of various institutions that operate at the level of 'one earth'. These include Greenpeace, Friends of the Earth, Bandaid, the Brundtland Report on the environment, large media conglomerates, the Rio Earth Summit in 1992, and so on. These organizations have generated some sense of the fact that there are citizens of the globe who share some common problems, and may be willing to engage in actions on behalf of humanity as a whole (such as recycling their waste, making fewer car journeys or not using CFC-based sprays).

Finally, we can again note the double-edged quality of globalization. On the one hand, such processes appear to produce a heightened sense of 'insecurity', because of the relentless media reporting of environmental catastrophes around the globe and the sense that global forces, especially working through money markets, are determining futures in ways largely unrelated to people's wants and aspirations. Yet on the other hand, they lead to a sense of global connectedness, largely due to new information technologies and the almost instantaneous media reporting from around the globe, and a heightened knowledge of different cultures, experiences and forms of life.

Summary

1   There seems to be a shift from an industrial to a risk society.
2   There are complex processes involved by which such risks are interpreted as global.

3   The role of the global media is important in generating some sense of global interdependence.

Related topics

Sections 3.2 and 3.3 discuss some of the economic aspects of globalization in more detail. Chapter 12 deals with the global organization of mass media. Section 13.2 considers further political consequences of globalization, including the development of the European Union as a new kind of organized multinational state, and the regional devolution of power within the UK. Aspects of British nationalisms are considered in section 8.5. The significance of holidays overseas is analysed in section 11.4.

Further reading

Useful general books on globalization are M. Waters (1995) and Albrow (1996). For in-depth studies of the limits of globalization see A. Scott (1997). On global risks see Macnaghten and Urry (1998).

Cross-references to *Readings in Contemporary British Society*

Bennett on the relationship between global and local music making; **Roseneil** on the interaction between a local political protest and the global political context; **Bechhofer et al.** on national identity; **Dicken** on the global economy.

3 Economic Organization

3.1   Introduction

The development of the capacity to produce the vast range of goods and services now expected of advanced economies has had an inestimable impact on most aspects of social life. Economic production occurs under specific social relations, with or for others, in particular kinds of organization. Organizations which secure the necessary level of co-ordination of economic activities are diverse, complex and remarkably effective. Increasingly, firms, networks and markets, many extended on a global scale, shape a daily existence which becomes ever more dependent on their inputs. Economic activities, in both the formal or cash economy and the informal domestic economy, can be socially organized in a wide variety of ways. While peasant economies have very limited division of labour, so that households produce much of what they consume, in modern economies such as Britain most people do a highly specialized job, for which they receive wages or salaries, with which in turn they buy the things they require. In capitalist societies production is driven primarily by the pursuit of profit by those who own the means to produce goods and services which can be sold. Privately owned, industrial and commercial organizations undertake an increasing proportion of the productive activity which is the basis for the mass consumption which currently characterizes the UK. Much of the dynamism of British society arises from changing patterns of corporate organization, and the successive and alternative strategies for economic development which organizations adopt. Understanding the forces involved underpins appreciation of the consequences of economic organization for the distribution of social power.

In this chapter we will examine from a sociological perspective the causes and consequences of economic restructuring and the changing nature and distribution of employment, the patterns of ownership and control (who owns what), the major forms of economic organization, and the changing industrial structure.

3.2   Economic restructuring

Capitalism is an extraordinarily dynamic economic system whose turbulence affects virtually the whole of society. The basic unit of organization, the capitalist firm, depends for its survival on being profitable. If it becomes relatively unprofitable, owners and others investing in it are likely to switch their money to more lucrative activities, and the firm may become bankrupt. To make profits in the face of competition, firms cannot stand still: they must change continually. Where this change takes a qualitative form, such as changing the product or the way it is made and delivered, it is called restructuring. As a result of countless, uncoordinated changes of this kind, the economy as a whole is continually being restructured, though the process tends to be more intense and traumatic in times of economic crisis than during booms.

We can illuminate the dynamics of capitalist firms by reference to 'the circuit of capital', which operates within each firm (see figure 3.1).

At the top of the circuit, money capital (M) is advanced by the firm to buy the commodities (C) required for carrying out production – the means of production (MP), consisting of machines, buildings, raw materials and energy, and the workforce or labour power (LP). There then follows the production process (P), in which MP and LP are set to work, indicated by the dashed line. At the end of this process the result are commodities (C′), which are worth more than those used in their production (C). They are then sold to realize their value (M′), the difference between this and the initial outlay (M) being the profit (m). This profit can then be reinvested in the firm, invested in other firms, or spent by the owners on their own consumption. Other competing firms are doing the same, trying to undercut or outsell rivals.

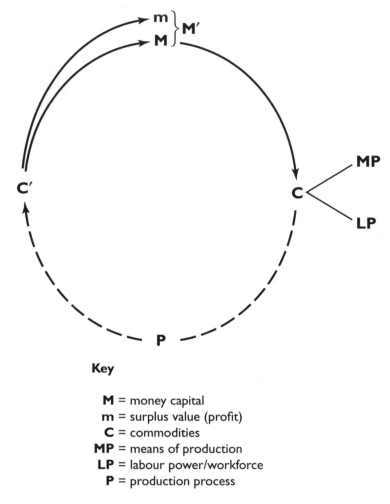

Key

M = money capital
m = surplus value (profit)
C = commodities
MP = means of production
LP = labour power/workforce
P = production process

Figure 3.1 | The circuit of capital

In response to the threat to their profits posed by competition, firms have four main types of restructuring options open to them. They can:

1 find cheaper inputs – whether raw materials, energy, machines and buildings (MP), or cheaper labour (LP). This may involve either moving to places where these inputs are currently located – perhaps in different countries – or alternatively importing them, as in the case of migrant workers;
2 seek out new markets. This again may involve moving overseas;
3 introduce new, more attractive products;
4 find faster, more efficient, ways of producing and delivering their products – speeding up the circuit, in other words – either by simply getting workers to speed up,

or by reorganizing the work process, or by automating tasks by introducing new technology.

This last option in particular illuminates the dynamic character of capitalism. Every activity involves the outlay of money, and the more quickly the firm can make and deliver the product or service and get the payment back from the buyer, the more quickly it can reinvest it and make more profit. It is not just the amount of profit that is important but the rate per month or year. Firms only have their workforces available for a certain number of hours per week, so within that time it is essential for them to maximize their output if they are to remain competitive. This is where the idea that 'time is money' comes from. It is the pursuit of time economies that increases the pace of work and life, and makes studies of time and motion necessary. Frequently, multinational firms compare the output per hour of employees working on comparable tasks in different countries in order to press the slowest into speeding up. Employees dealing directly with the public are taught scripted conversations which enable them to conduct their business in the minimum time while keeping the customer happy. Even workers in non-profit-making activities such as doctors' surgeries get pressured into working faster in order to keep costs down.

Restructuring produces 'creative destruction', as the economist Joseph Schumpeter (1943) put it – not only adding new products and processes but destroying or abandoning old ones. Those who were employed in the old activities are likely to find themselves unemployed unless they can develop new skills and find new jobs. As the rate of restructuring and associated technical change speeds up, fewer people can expect to retain the same kind of job for life and more may periodically have to reinvent themselves and move into new fields.

Some of the social effects of restructuring are illustrated in figure 3.2. This diagram does not exhaust all the effects, but it indicates how restructuring affects not only the division of labour but further aspects of everyday life such as changes in status and education and politics. There are, of course, also other influences on the phenomena listed on the right of the diagram.

The international division of labour

The search for new markets and inputs encourages firms to become bigger and to operate in many countries, becoming multinational firms. The division of labour under capitalism has therefore become increasingly international. This has happened in several stages.

At first, separate specialist producers in different countries engaged in international trade, often as a result of colonialism and imperialism; for example, British metal manufacturers imported raw materials from many Commonwealth countries, and British machine producers exported their products back to them. Large international flows of migrants in search of work and economic improvement have also developed since the beginnings of capitalism. As the twentieth century progressed, increasing numbers of firms began to operate on an international basis, not merely buying from and selling to other countries but producing within them. Employment in Britain is now increasingly affected by decisions taken by companies that are headquartered elsewhere and

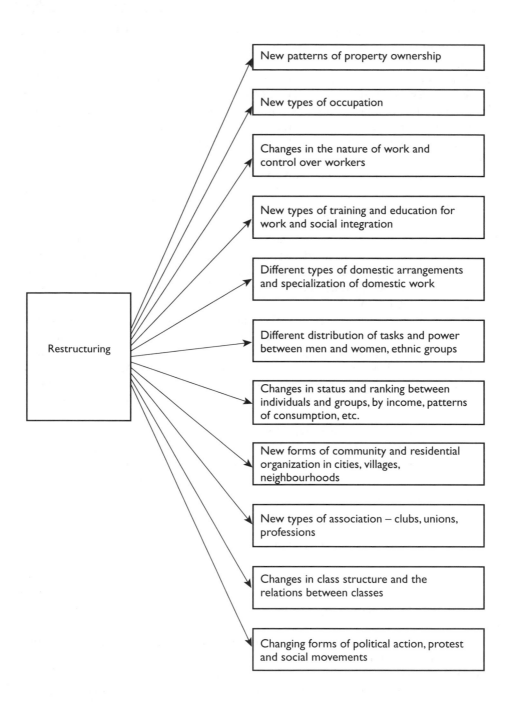

Figure 3.2 | Some social effects of restructuring

calculate the comparative advantages of producing and selling goods in different locations throughout the world.

Multinational companies

Multinational companies (MNCs) now dominate the capitalist world economy. Some of these corporations have enormous turnovers – much greater than the national income of many countries. They are both 'multi-plant' and 'multi-product' organizations. At first they tended to reproduce free-standing production and sales activities in each major country, so that, for example, the plant needed to produce and sell each product was self-contained. More recently they have tended to rationalize these into international production systems, wherein different parts of final products are made in different countries. Thus, if you look at a personal computer, different parts may have been made, and different stages of production may have been carried out, in different countries. The more technical, skill-intensive tasks such as the design of microprocessors often takes place in rich countries like Germany or the US, and the low-skill activities like assembly in low-wage countries like Mexico, Ireland or Taiwan.

Although MNCs may be extremely large, most face severe competition. Indeed it is this competition which drives them to the far corners of the world. Once one US MNC finds a new market, say in Europe, or a cheap source of labour, say in east Asia, its competitors are likely to have to do the same to keep up.

Operation on an international scale creates many strategic advantages. In the first place MNCs are able to benefit from the varied social and economic conditions in different countries. Firms selling to individual consumers will generally benefit from being located in rich countries with affluent consumers. Many companies sell mainly to other companies and to get their custom they need to form close relationships with them, through face-to-face contact. This is why so many European and Japanese information technology firms want to locate in Silicon Valley in California, where many key, leading-edge industrial customers are based. On the cost side, MNCs can take advantage of differential wage rates. As figure 3.3 indicates, the differences are considerable. Operations which are labour-intensive and low-skilled (i.e. wages rather than machines or raw materials are the major cost to the enterprise) tend to be undertaken in developing countries where wages are very low. Those which require scarce skilled labour, whether technical or managerial, are likely to be restricted to rich countries where those kinds of worker tend to live. MNCs' headquarters and their research and development and sales units tend to remain in or near financial centres and major markets in the advanced countries. Though less spectacular, something similar happens in Britain, where the 'higher-order functions' of research, finance and corporate planning in the big corporations are concentrated in the south-east of England, with lower-level managerial and routine activities being located more widely, both in the south-east and elsewhere.

The exploitation of cheap labour may be the most striking feature of the international division of labour but it is not the most important in determining its shape. The fact that the international division of labour is dominated by rich countries and multinationals from the North investing in other developed countries shows that getting access to affluent markets is the dominant consideration. Labour costs are often not the main factor in competition. If they were, the first world would be fast losing its

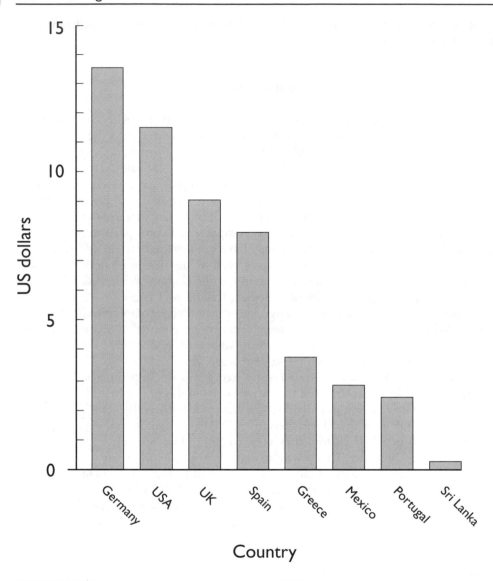

Figure 3.3 | Hourly earnings in selected countries, 1995
Source: Dicken 1998, p. 190

dominance to the third world. It is not. Globalization turns out to be mainly a first world phenomenon.

While MNCs are highly responsive to differences between national economies, they also shape them. As Hymer explained, albeit with some degree of exaggeration:

> the transnational corporation tends to create a world in its own image by creating a division of labour between countries that corresponds to the division of labour between various levels of the corporate hierarchy. It will tend to centralize high-level decision-making

occupations in a few key cities (surrounded by regional sub-capitals) in the advanced countries, thereby confining the rest of the world to lower levels of activity and income. (Hymer 1972, p. 59)

Figure 3.4 represents Hymer's claim. Columns show the social profile or composition of each type of area according to the functions it performs within the divisions of labour internal to multinationals. Gradually the social composition of the areas in which each function is performed will come to conform to that required by MNCs; for example, top management jobs are concentrated in major centres, leaving those areas – the hinterlands – at the bottom of the hierarchy tending to have 'headless' social structures. Note, however, that the absolute volume of middle-level activities in world cities B exceeds that in regional capitals C, just as the absolute amount of routine execution work in world cities D exceeds that in regional centres E, which in turn exceeds that in hinterlands F.

Much has been made of the power of MNCs relative to national governments. Certainly MNCs have more options than national companies. They may be able to evade pollution-control laws by relocating hazardous activities to countries with no environmental legislation, usually in the third world. They can evade unions and restrictive employment legislation by locating where these are absent or banned. They can also reduce tax liability by shifting financial assets to take maximum advantage of differences in national policies; thus, for example, US MNCs can locate their dollar reserves outside the US where US policy can have no effect. Moreover, in order to bring money and employment to their countries, governments often compete to attract MNCs by

	World cities: e.g. London, New York, Tokyo	Regional capitals: e.g. Toronto, Madrid, Kuala Lumpur, Manchester	Hinterlands: e.g. third world free trade zones, south Wales, Durham
Top-level decision-making	A		
Middle-level decision-making	B	C	
Routine execution	D	E	F

Figure 3.4 | The international division of labour according to Hymer

offering incentives such as tax concessions, rent-free premises, grants towards site development, etc. Ironically, this often means giving advantages to foreign firms and increasing competitive pressures on domestic companies. Thus, the influx of Japanese auto and electronics firms into Britain has hastened their victory over their British competitors, and the former have subsequently been lauded for swelling British exports. As a consequence of this internationalization, the meaning of 'British industry' becomes more complex; it could be taken to mean not only British-owned firms, but British branches of foreign firms, and perhaps British-owned MNCs' operations abroad.

MNCs are undoubtedly powerful and can influence politics, particularly where they have few competitors in their industries, as in the case of Rupert Murdoch's media empire. But they are still dependent on national governments. Few MNCs have lost their original national identity altogether, and many rely heavily on their home governments and sometimes host governments for contracts and favours. Furthermore they have to be careful to avoid countries which are politically unstable in case their international production systems are disrupted. Finally, they are still vulnerable to competition and takeover; thus the computer giant IBM, which once dominated the computer industry but was slow in responding to developments in information technology, has now lost much of its share of the market to other computer firms and to software firms, particularly Microsoft. Box 3.1 summarizes MNCs' impact.

Box 3.1   The impact of multinationals

Like Hymer, we could sum up the impact of multinationals by quoting Karl Marx and Friedrich Engels, the nineteenth-century social theorists and revolutionaries, in the *Communist Manifesto* and replacing their word 'bourgeoisie' with 'MNC':

> The MNC cannot exist without constantly revolutionizing the instruments of production, and thereby the relations of production, and with them the whole relations of society . . . The need of a constantly expanding market for its products chases the MNC over the whole surface of the globe. It must nestle everywhere, settle everywhere, establish connexions everywhere . . . The MNC has through its exploitation of the world market given a cosmopolitan character to production and consumption in every country. To the great chagrin of Reactionists, it has drawn from under the feet of industry the national ground on which it stood. All old-established national industries have been destroyed or are daily being destroyed . . . In place of the old wants, satisfied by the productions of the country, we find new wants, requiring for their satisfaction the products of distant lands and climes. (Original quotation Marx and Engels 1872, p. 38)

Global competition

MNCs are leading agents in the process of uneven geographical development. Global competition is especially fierce in manufacturing, for goods can be transported and stored in a way which is either impossible or difficult for services (although financial, scientific and tourist services are internationally highly competitive). British manufacturing firms have often failed to compete with foreign MNCs, especially when the latter have set up operations in Britain.

Imperial Chemical Industries (ICI) was created by the merger of four British compan-ies in 1926. It always operated abroad to some degree, though in its early days primar-ily in the countries of the British empire – thus the title 'Imperial'. By the 1980s it was a massive corporation with truly global operations, having factories in more than 40 coun-tries and offices in more than 60 (I. M. Clarke 1982). Its factories produce a vast range of products which include organic chemicals, fibres, general chemicals, industrial explo-sives, oils, paints, pharmaceuticals and plastics. In response to the world recessions since the 1970s the company rationalized its production, often by closing down British operations. Figure 3.5 shows both how the number of workers in ICI has fallen since 1971 and also how the proportion working in Britain has declined. Whereas, in 1971, 72 per cent of ICI employees were in Britain, by 1981 they were a mere 51 per cent. To take just one example of the way this happens, ICI in 1981 opened a plant in Wilhelmshaven in Germany, manufacturing exactly the same product (chlorine) as it was already producing in Cheshire and Teesside. This was done primarily because elec-tricity, which accounted for 80 per cent of the cost of producing chlorine, was cheaper by half in Germany (I. M. Clarke 1982). What is economically rational for ICI is omi-nous for the employment prospects of the population of northern England.

Chemicals is an industrial sector dominated by large companies. Other sectors con-

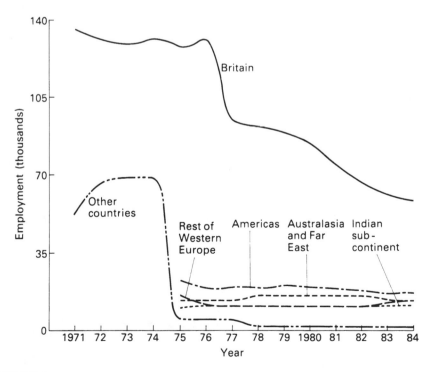

Figure 3.5 Employment in ICI worldwide, 1971–84
Source: Beynon, Hudson and Sadler 1986, p. 72

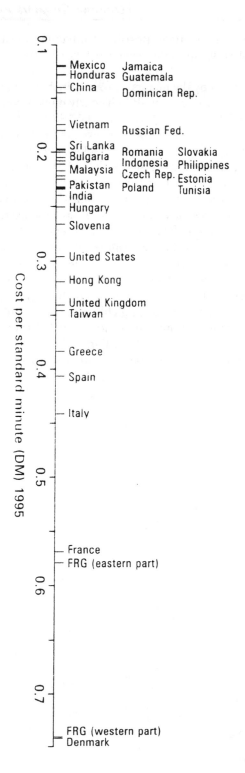

Figure 3.6 | Labour costs per standard minute in the clothing industry, 1995
Source: Dicken 1998, p. 296

sist of enormous numbers of separate firms, but they too are much affected by internationalization. Phizacklea's (1990) study of the fashion clothes industry is instructive. Clothing used to be mostly made in Britain. Since the early 1970s, a considerable amount of all clothing sold in Britain has been manufactured overseas. 180,000 jobs were lost in the UK clothing industry between 1970 and 1993 (Dicken 1998). The primary reason for this is that wage rates are considerably lower in south-east Asia and assembling clothes is a labour-intensive process. Figure 3.6 indicates the relative cost per hour of labour in the clothing industry in different countries. Products for which there is stable demand, like underwear and men's shirts, are likely to be made by young women workers in less developed countries. Fashion goods, by definition, are characterized by the very rapid turnover of styles, which require fast response to new demands and short production runs. In the women's fashionwear section of the market, much of current manufacture still takes place in Britain.

For expensive fashion clothing, advanced technologies, especially computer-assisted design and manufacture (CAD/CAM), are profitable for some British firms, as they more obviously are also in Germany and Italy. Phizacklea points out that in terms of money value a significant proportion of British imports comes from Italy and Germany, whose competitiveness depends on design and quality rather than cheap labour. Less expensive items are also sourced in Britain, but these are usually produced by a vast number of small operators, typically in the inner cities and the East End of London, who are engaged as subcontractors to cut cloth and assemble articles for the retail chains. The position of small entrepreneurs is highly unfavourable for there is severe competition, partly because it requires very little capital to set up such a business. Consequently, working conditions in some businesses resemble the sweat-shops of the nineteenth century, with workers very poorly paid, casually employed and rarely unionized. Ethnic minority workers figure prominently in these workplaces, and also as homeworkers, earning very low wages and lacking job security, especially in the latter case, where rates may be below £1 per hour. Using skills learned in the home, and excluded from more attractive labour markets by racist and patriarchal mechanisms, ethnic minority women produce many of the fashion clothes available in the high-street stores. Their low wages permit small British businesses to survive without introducing expensive and advanced machinery.

The effects of restructuring

The social consequences of economic restructuring on an international scale have been momentous. As in previous periods, the methods of the most successful producers tend to be emulated by competitors. Thus, the global success of Japanese corporations has led to their widespread imitation in Britain since the mid-1980s, as is evident in attempts to introduce Japanese-style working practices in some industries. While advanced industrial countries have always faced competition from low-wage producers in developing countries, this has become more acute as a result of the rise of MNCs taking advantage of this opportunity to cut costs. However, the primary destination of foreign investment by MNCs has been rich countries, indicating the importance of access to affluent and advanced markets. The MNCs grew in size partly by taking over small companies, thereby extending their influence in new markets across the globe. Meanwhile, government, management, regulation and planning became difficult as world markets and foreign companies increasingly determined economic outcomes. Intense reorganization accompanied the new international division of labour.

Summary

1   Modern economies are dominated by companies operating on a multinational basis.
2   Multinationals are courted by governments for their economic power yet governments have limited control over their behaviour.

3.3   Ownership and control

It is a familiar argument that, since the beginning of the twentieth century, the whole structure of the ownership and control of British industry has changed. A series of factors contribute to this: firms have grown larger by merger and takeover; increasingly, businesses are owned not by single entrepreneurs or capitalists and their families but by many shareholders; and large financial institutions have gradually assumed ownership of significant sectors of British industry. In 1932, Berle and Means argued that ownership was becoming increasingly dispersed, while the control formerly associated with it was becoming ever more concentrated in the hands of a few corporate managements. Whether this is true has been hotly debated. Do professional managers take control or do groups of shareholders dictate decisions? There are in fact a number of different issues raised by these questions and we start by considering the way in which the ownership of firms has become more concentrated.

Concentration and control

British industry might appear to be composed of a mass of competing, independent firms. But how far is this true? As consumers we are often faced with a welter of brand names. In the supermarket, for instance, a large number of manufacturers are represented, offering a wide range of different types of product. On the other hand, firms often merge or are taken over, to form ever larger businesses. Often large corporations battle to gain control of another firm which may be in quite a different area of business.

    Are firms typically independent or are they linked with others? Do the many competing brands, for example, conceal the fact that a few firms manufacture them all? The general answer to these questions is yes, since until recently there has been a concentration of ownership in British industry since the beginning of the twentieth century.

Concentration and the corporate economy

Until 1980 there was a trend for fewer and larger firms to take a larger proportion of sales in each industry:

It is a commonplace that in the course of the twentieth century British industry has witnessed a transformation from a disaggregated structure of predominantly small, competing firms, to a concentrated structure dominated by large, and often monopolistic, corporations. The 100 corporations which now occupy the dominant positions account for something approaching one half of total manufacturing output, whilst at the turn of the century the largest 100 accounted for barely 15 per cent of output. (Hannah 1976, p. 1)

The British economy is dominated by large corporations. Indeed it has become a corporate economy. The rise of the corporate economy can be investigated in a number of ways. An initial approach is to look at the concentration ratio, which usually refers to the proportion of sales in any particular industry accounted for by the five largest firms in that industry.

The increase in concentration in the post-war boom can be seen for a range of industries in table 3.1. It shows that in several industry groups, roughly three-quarters of sales are taken by the five largest firms, and in tobacco the proportion is 100 per cent. Even in the industry with the lowest concentration ratio – non-electrical engineering – the five largest firms account for one-quarter of the sales. The increases in concentration are also clear in that period.

TABLE 3.1 | **Concentration in industry groups: shares of the largest five firms, 1957 and 1969 (percentages)**

Industry	1957 firms	1969 firms
Tobacco	96.5	100.0
Clothing and footwear	63.8	78.4
Shipbuilding	62.1	74.2
Chemicals	71.0	73.7
Vehicles	50.4	71.0
Drink	32.7	69.5
Electrical engineering	47.2	68.0
Textiles	44.2	65.1
Paper and publishing	47.5	63.2
Metal manufacture[a]	45.7	59.5
Food	41.3	52.7
Building materials	53.1	51.1
Non-electrical engineering	29.8	25.3

[a] Excluding the nationalized British Steel Corporation and its constituents
Source: Adapted from Hannah 1983, p. 144

Evidence of the degree of concentration in non-manufacturing industries is less easy to come by. It is high in food retailing, for example, where the big five increasingly dominate the industry, but low in the hotel industry, where the three largest hotel groups, for instance, control only 8 per cent of the total number of beds available.

However, since 1980 concentration has reduced. As figure 3.7 shows, the dominance of the largest five firms in each industry has lessened since then. The share of the largest manufacturing firms in each sector fell by over 3.5 per cent, from nearly 46 per cent to 43 per cent, following a rise of 1.5 per cent in the 1970s.

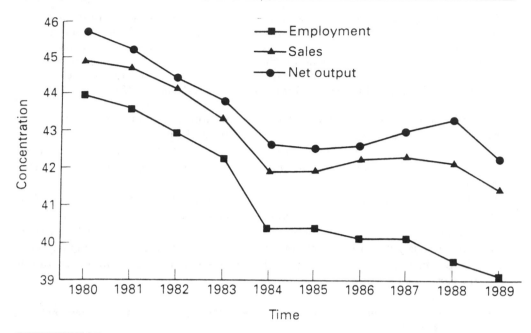

Figure 3.7   Trends in concentration in manufacturing: top five firms' shares, 1980–9
Source: R. Clarke 1993, p. 125

The reasons for this reduction are probably a growth in the number of small firms, partly as a result of a trend in the 1980s for large companies to hive off functions to other firms (downsizing), plus the increasing penetration of the British market by foreign firms. Nevertheless, the British economy remains dominated by large firms. It should also be noted that the data refer to market *shares*; large firms are likely to have increased their output in absolute terms even if their relative shares have declined.

However, the way in which a few firms dominate particular industries or markets is not necessarily the most sociologically interesting aspect of concentration. We also need to look at the economy as a whole and the way in which relatively few firms dominate it. This is particularly important as businesses have grown larger by absorbing other firms that operate in quite different areas of industry. The result is the increased importance of conglomerates with diversified interests in a very wide range of products.

The growth of conglomerate enterprises

The most important single cause of concentration in the British economy is merger, or the acquisition of one firm by another. During the 1960s and 1970s most of the disappearances of firms quoted on the stock exchange were due to mergers with other firms. In addition to restructuring in various ways, as discussed above, firms may strengthen their position by merging with competitors or others in order to get a larger share of the market and more resources. Related to this is a point we made earlier about the diversification of large firms. Firms grow bigger often by the acquisition of other firms not trading in their sector of the economy, and not necessarily based in their home country.

Interlocking directorships

Concentration means that industry and commerce are no longer made up of a multiplicity of firms with little connection with each other, but are dominated by a few hundred firms. The evidence presented so far rather understates the links between firms. This partly arises from the fact that firms may own only relatively small parts of other firms, less than required to give total control. These smaller overlaps in ownership do not count as a merger, yet they clearly represent a considerable degree of co-operation and interdependence between firms. Equally significant is the phenomenon of interlocking directorships. The ease of communication between firms is very much enhanced by the fairly common practice of having directors of one large company sitting on the boards of other similarly powerful firms.

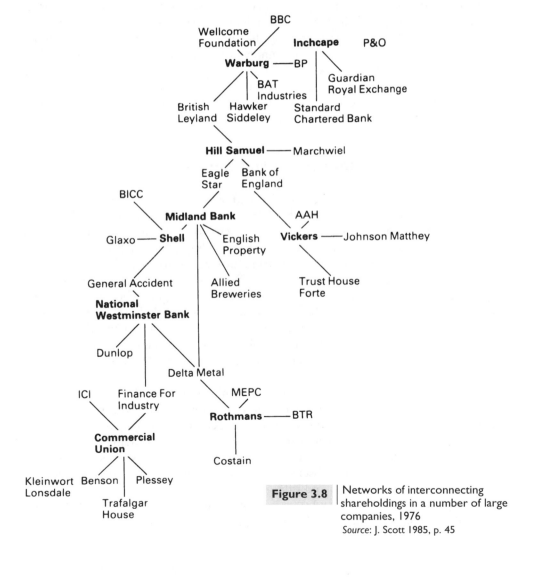

Figure 3.8 | Networks of interconnecting shareholdings in a number of large companies, 1976
Source: J. Scott 1985, p. 45

Figure 3.8 shows part of the network of interlocking directorships of large companies in 1976. In the survey from which the illustration is taken, 11 people had a total of 57 directorships in the top 250 companies, and many others in subsidiaries of these companies and in smaller companies. The directorships of 9 people linked together 39 very large companies. This is clearly only a section of a large network but one which is, nevertheless, held together nationally, at least in the larger firms, by a remarkably small number of people. J. Scott (1985) argues that at the heart of this network are those companies which dominate the capital market and are able to provide finance for investment. The banks, particularly, are organized into cliques and clusters which occupy a central position. But this centrality should not be seen as bank control over the non-financial sector as a whole; rather it simply reflects the banks' importance as providers of capital. Besides providing capital, the network of interlocking directorships also makes for more efficient flow of information between firms. Thus not only has there been a major concentration of capital in the last half century, but the running of the economic system is facilitated by the personal contacts between directors. Interlocking directorships are, however, not the only vehicle by which personal relationships unify British industry. Family and kinship relations continue to be important (see section 6.5 on the upper class). At the same time an increasing number of ownership links and interlocking directorships has developed between firms from different countries. Consequently, '[i]nstead of being linked into a cohesive national economy, the various elements in the advanced economies are tied into an extensive, but decentralized, global network of intercorporate relations' (A. Scott 1997, p. 19).

Ownership and control

Berle and Means (1932) thought that the dispersal of share ownership would lead to the disappearance of the traditional capitalist forms of ownership in all but smaller enterprises, leaving them increasingly under management control. The discussion here applies mostly to large companies with multiple shareholdings. In small firms there may be no separation of ownership and control, while in large firms each shareholder owns only a relatively small proportion of the shares. With ownership diversified in this way, it *appears* that real control passes to the professional managers who, working in the company full-time, have a much better idea of the company's business than do the shareholders. The latter are likely to have a purely speculative, opportunistic interest in the companies in which they hold shares, while managers' dependence on their company for employment arguably makes them more committed to its success, rather than that of any other firm.

J. Scott (1990) points out that the terms 'ownership' and 'control' are rather misleading, and he proposes replacing them with the terms 'ownership', 'control' and 'rule'. Ownership simply refers to the right to receive an income. Control is the capacity possessed by a particular group of owners to determine policy and strategy by a number of means, including having representatives on the board of directors. Rule describes actual involvement in decision-making. Essentially, then, the question is: what is the relationship between ownership, control and rule?

The first point to decide here is who actually owns shares in British companies. Figure 3.9 presents some data on this issue. In 1990 the proportion of shares held by individual

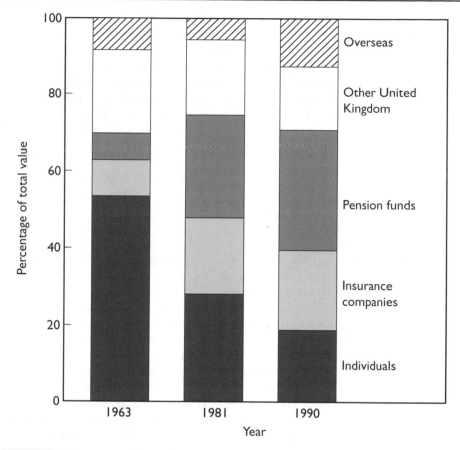

Figure 3.9 | Who owns Britain's shares?
Source: Social Trends 1992, p. 103. Crown copyright

persons amounted to 20 per cent while pension funds held 31 per cent and insurance companies about 20 per cent. The balance between these two kinds of shareholder has been shifting. In 1963, personal shareholders held 54 per cent of all shares while these financial institutions held only about 13 per cent.

There has, therefore, been a move away from the personal ownership of shares towards ownership by large financial institutions. This is a depersonalization of ownership, in that individual people no longer own companies. This does not mean that wealth in the form of company shares is more evenly spread among the population. What has happened is only that the minority of wealthy families no longer hold their wealth in a single company but spread it more widely by buying shares in a number of companies (see chapter 5). The shift in share ownership has given great power to the largest financial institutions. For example, the 10 largest institutions are responsible for investing about one-quarter of the total value of the stock market.

Financial institutions have an increasing role in the ownership and control of large British firms, particularly where they are able to form alliances with each other. How then are the financial institutions – banks, pension funds, unit trusts and insurance companies – themselves owned and controlled? The short answer to this question is that the process of depersonalization of ownership applies to financial companies as well as to other branches of the economy. Despite these links British capital is less organized than that of many developed economies like Germany and Japan, where companies form networks in which they are committed to one another's success in the long run. It is not only that shareholding has dispersed ownership but that shareholders are not likely to be committed to the firms in which they hold shares, since it is in their interest to sell them and buy another firm's as soon as the latter offer a better return. Consequently companies have to pay shareholders large dividends to encourage them to stay. The shareholders may have little influence on companies through lobbying, but they have the power of exit – the ability to take their money somewhere else. Thus there is in Britain a daily market in company ownership and shareholding.

Just how much the power of large firms has been enhanced by these links is controversial. Their existence does not necessarily mean that there is less competition among firms in Britain than hitherto. The reduction in the number of firms in a sector may be accompanied by more aggressive competition among those that remain. This is especially so where formerly isolated regional markets have been penetrated by outside firms, killing off large numbers of firms that previously faced little real competition. Conglomerates require their component firms to be as profitable as possible and to do that each must be competitive. They continue to compete not only for sales in the market for their products but for continued investment, and the latter in particular depends on their profitability. Similarly, directors involved in several firms have an interest in each one of them being profitable. Trying to protect them from competition is likely to fail in the long run as other firms will out-compete them. If a firm belonging to a conglomerate underperforms, it is likely to be cut or sold. The fact that large firms or parts of them still run into difficulties and have to be closed down shows that competition persists. Nor does the concentration of capital necessarily mean that modern economies like Britain's are now more controllable. Indeed the recurrence of economic crises indicates that they continue to be as intractable as ever. Directors and managers today may be controlling vastly more resources than hitherto, but they cannot actually make their customers buy their firms' products. Nor can they control important conditions like the value of currencies or the rate of inflation. They have some influence within markets but much of the control they exercise is in trying to gain advantages by predicting market changes rather than by making them happen. Interlocking directorships and conglomerates indicate a concentration of what power or control there is into the hands of a small number of people and institutions. Their power relative to that of other people is considerable, but their power *vis-à-vis* the economy should not be overestimated.

'Popular capitalism' and the growth of shareownership: a case study

The Thatcher and Major governments of 1979–97 privatized a succession of nationalized industries and public services, from British Telecom to British Rail. These privatizations were advertised so as to encourage people who had not had shares before to buy them, thereby, it was hoped, encouraging the rise of a popular capitalism. More specifically, Conservative politicians argued that wider share ownership would help develop a culture of enterprise, giving more people a stake in the system and countering what they feared was a tendency of both the working class and the middle class to become detached from the core values of capitalism.

In 1979, the first year of the Thatcher government, there were 2.5 million shareowners in Britain. That number rose to about 11 million by 1992. In the General Household Survey of 1988, 21 per cent of adults were found to be shareholders. These were predominantly men (55 per cent), they were disproportionately concentrated in the 45–64 age group, and their average gross income was twice that of non-shareholders. The social composition of new shareholders as a result of the privatizations was less middle class than that of established shareholders. Consequently, to some extent the government could be said to have succeeded in broadening the social base of shareownership. While there was a strong response to the share issues of the newly privatized companies, most of them subsequently lost around half of their shareholders over the first few years of their existence in the private sector, with about a quarter going in the first few months after the sale. The shares were bought up mainly by financial institutions, so that the result of the privatizations has been to increase their domination of share ownership (A. Scott 1997). Although the number of shareholders began to fall, implying a concentration of ownership, it has not returned to its previous level, and therefore in quantitative terms the privatizations have made a more permanent impact. However, there are qualitative differences between the old and the new shareholders. Unlike the established shareowners, who tended to hold shares in a range of companies, many of the new shareholders either just bought shares in a single privatized company and no others, or bought and sold just in successive privatization share issues.

A study conducted by Saunders and Harris (1994) attempted to assess the impact of these privatizations in more depth. Saunders and Harris sought to establish just how far shareownership had spread, and to what extent the behaviour and attitudes of new shareowners indicated a movement towards an enterprise culture. The research focused on the case of water privatization and was based on interviews with households (1,444 in the first instance) drawn from a sample weighted towards the higher occupational classes so as to include a significant number of people who were likely to buy shares in water companies. The sample was split into two areas corresponding to the North West and Southern water regions. The households were interviewed first in autumn 1989, approximately three months before the privatization, and again in spring 1991, roughly 15 months after the privatization. This made it possible to trace changes in the interviewees' views and experience before and after the privatization.

The privatization of water supply was probably the most difficult and contentious of all the privatizations of nationalized industries, with over three-quarters of the British public opposing the sale. Nevertheless, when the water companies were finally privatized in December 1989, 2.7 million people applied for water shares and the sale was oversubscribed 5.7 times. At the close of the first day's trading, when 30 per cent of water shares had changed hands, the 100 p part-paid shares were trading at between 131 p and 157 p, showing an average profit for those who sold the issue of 44 per cent.

The researchers looked into the new shareowners' motives for buying shares. A fifth said they intended selling to make a quick profit ('the gamblers'), a quarter intended them to be a form of long-term saving and did not seem to distinguish shareowning from other forms of saving, and another fifth expected them to provide a good dividend

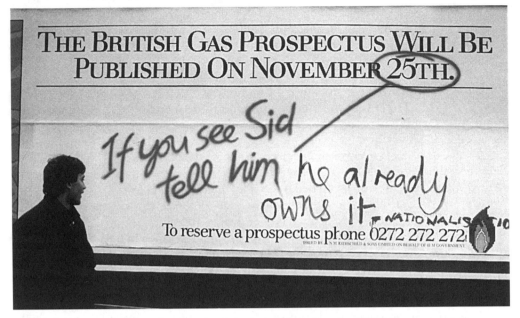

Plate 3.1 | Advertisement for the sale of shares in British Gas: the 'Tell Sid' campaign, with graffiti, 1986
Source: Format/Joanne O'Brien

and rise in value, while the remainder had diverse motives. Many of the new share-holders who had intended to sell their shares immediately to make a high profit did not do so, though dividends were relatively high anyway. Only the third of these groups was judged by Saunders and Harris to have 'appropriate' enterprising behaviour for share-holders.

How these motives relate to enterprise culture is unclear. Some advocates of popular capitalism argued that new shareholders would feel more 'involved' in the companies in which they had invested. Others countered that shareholding involved no commitment whatsoever and was a speculative venture in which the only concern was financial gain. However, Saunders and Harris found little evidence to support either view. While the new shareholders took no interest in the companies, most took little interest in possible short-term financial gains either, for over half of the respondents could not give a rea-sonably accurate current market price for their shares. Indeed, some seemed to have little understanding of the nature of shareholding or how to buy further shares. Saunders and Harris also estimated that only 1 in 240 shareholders would attend the AGM of the water company in which they had invested.

Whether the motives and behaviour of the new shareholders represented enterprising behaviour and fostered a greater understanding of and sympathy for capitalist enter-prise is unclear. This is partly because of the ambiguity of the concept of 'enterprise' itself and the relationship of shareholding to capitalist activity. If enterprise involves self-reliance and risk-taking, buying the shares required a limited amount of initiative, it was made very easy by the government, and the starting prices were set so low that there was no risk of loss. As regards enterprise as a quality needed for running a business, shareholding is far removed from this, since once the shares have been bought it is largely a matter of passively waiting for dividends or a suitable time to sell or make further purchases. Saunders and Harris are doubtful whether the privatizations have succeeded in encouraging a culture of enterprise. While the number of shareholders increased significantly with the privatizations, few became 'active investors', acquiring a range of shares, and buying and selling as prices and dividends changed. This suggests that the impact on attitudes and ways of life has been quite limited. Further, while one might expect new shareowners' political attitudes to shift to the right, the survey suggested their attitudes had become more egalitarian between 1989 and 1991. As the authors conclude (Saunders and Harris 1994, p. 161): 'British culture does not seem to place a high value on individual effort, self-reliance and entrepreneurship' and 'Sociologically, the great privatization crusade has turned out to be much ado about nothing.' While the broadening of the social base of shareownership and the windfall gains made may have been significant in relation to the government's political support, any changes in popular attitudes to capitalism appear to have taken a different form to that desired by the government.

Summary

1   The British economy is dominated by a few hundred large companies whose dominance is becoming more pronounced as firms merge with one another.
2   Companies are also linked by networks of interlocking directorships.
3   There has been a depersonalization of ownership of British companies, with the financial institutions taking a larger proportion of the shares of large companies.
4   The bulk of British companies are still effectively controlled by owners, though often through constellations of agents each of which has a minority holding in any one firm.
5   Although the leading companies have become more powerful, they still have to compete. Control is limited by the essential unpredictability of the competitive market context on which firms depend.
6   The broadening of shareownership prompted by privatizations had a limited effect, both quantitatively and qualitatively, in terms of attitudes or behaviour of the new shareowners.

3.4   Forms of economic organizations

The vast range of specialized activities comprising the formal economy is socially organized in various ways. Formal organizations – particularly firms but also other institutions like hospitals and universities – control particular bundles of activities which are usually strongly related to one another. Within such units bureaucratic organization is perhaps the dominant means by which activities are co-ordinated. In capitalist societies, co-ordination between organizations involved in disparate activities is achieved primarily through markets. The state also plays an important role in economic activities, not only in the public sector but also in the private sector through regulations and taxation. Finally, some activities take place within households and the community and are organized outside the formal economy.

Bureaucratic organization

The founding father of the sociology of organizations, Max Weber, analysed the most widely recognized and most commonly maligned form of organizational structure, bureaucracy. The key features of Weber's ideal type of bureaucracy are listed in box 3.2.

Box 3.2   Key features of bureaucratic organization

The key features of bureaucratic organization are:

1   a specialized division of tasks, undertaken by officials, each with his or her own duties;
2   a hierarchy of authority – 'a clearly established system of super- and sub-ordination in which there is a supervision of the lower offices by the higher ones' (Weber 1968, p. 957) – and a clearly demarcated system of command and responsibilities;
3   a formal set of rules governing operations and activities which co-ordinates behaviour in a predictable, uniform and impersonal fashion;
4   a body of officials who are permanent, full-time workers, appointed by superiors, trained in a specialized task, paid a salary according to rank in the hierarchy, and to whom a career is open on the basis of ability and seniority.

In practice, despite the fact that 'bureaucracy' has become a pejorative term in everyday language, almost all complex organizations exhibit some of the features in the box, though few approach the 'pure' type. Most important in considering contemporary economic organizations are two features, hierarchy and formal rules:

1   In the ideal type of bureaucracy, authority can be represented as a pyramid. Higher offices have authority over lower offices: subordinate officials are responsible to the official immediately above in the hierarchy. The result, in principle, is a single line of authority (see figure 3.10). This provides an integrated vertical chain of command, but prohibits horizontal communication between officials of the same rank.
2   The tasks and the decisions made in the course of operations are governed by formal rules in the sense that officials have limited discretion in dealing with cases. Their activities are closely prescribed, which encourages predictability and impartiality.

Such a bureaucratic organization thus has a highly centralized structure of authority and a highly regulated set of activities.

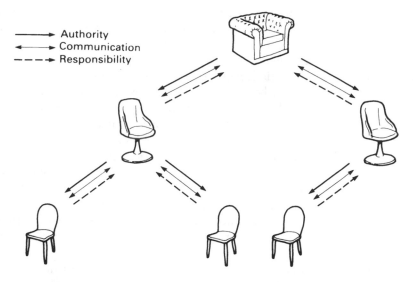

Figure 3.10 | Authority, communication and responsibility in a bureaucracy

Weber thought bureaucracy was a more technically efficient mode of organization than any other previously developed. Its virtues, relative to earlier modes, included 'precision, speed, unambiguity, knowledge, continuity, discretion, unity, strict subordination, reduction of friction and of material personal costs' (Weber 1968, p. 973). When you fill in a form, say to apply to a university, the information requested is precise and unambiguous (e.g. what grades you got in what subject, which courses at which particular universities you want to apply for). Those who process these forms can do so very quickly since there is little room for ambiguity. Where there are any uncertainties, for example concerning applicants with qualifications from other countries, they can normally be referred to a bureaucrat with the appropriate specialist knowledge. If you compare this bureaucratized system with an alternative in which each applicant just wrote a personal letter to whomever they saw fit including whatever information they thought appropriate, the selection process would be extremely inefficient and lacking in consistency and impartiality.

In popular thinking, these virtues of bureaucracy are often overshadowed by its potential disadvantages for clients, officials and organizational efficiency alike. For example, clients of the welfare state frequently complain of impersonality, inflexibility, buck-passing and excessive rule-following. Very long chains of command separate control and authority from responsibility. This causes problems because those in authority have little concrete knowledge of what those at the bottom of the hierarchy, who may be front-line workers dealing with the public, have to do. Restrictions on horizontal communication can limit opportunities for problem-solving between related departments. Studies of the behaviour of officials in such organizations tend to show either a creeping timidity in decision-making by officials closely bound by both formal rules and responsibility to higher authority or a tendency to subvert the organizational structure by developing informal and unauthorized practices.

These difficulties prompt many organizations to develop less bureaucratic systems so that they are more flexible and less hierarchical. In such organizations, rules are less formal, authority and responsibility are less direct, jobs and tasks are less tightly defined, and communication is more varied and not restricted to hierarchical channels. Such organizational structures demand more initiative and personal responsibility from officials. Outcomes are less predictable but may be more inventive and problem oriented.

In practice, workers often either do not know all the rules or do not follow them. They also tend to resist a purely impersonal form of relationship to other workers. From the point of view of efficiency and effectiveness of the organization, much depends on how individuals get on with their immediate co-workers, superiors and subordinates. Organizational behaviour is often characterized by gift relationships, in which favours are given by individuals or departments on the tacit understanding that they will be reciprocated at some future date. Thus, 'getting things done' may depend not on following the rules but on a combination of initiative and being on good terms with others who can help. Ironically, breaking the rules may sometimes help rather than hinder effectiveness.

Bureaucratization also tends to vary with size, not least because of the difficulty of maintaining personal relationships and co-ordination among large numbers of people. In very large institutions and firms, some departments or divisions may be designated as semi-autonomous in order to reduce the separation between control and responsibility if this is felt to benefit performance. In small firms, more personal control through face-to-face contacts is feasible, though this can take oppressive as well as benign forms.

Technology also sets limits to alternative organizational structures. Machines tend to be much less flexible than people, though faster and more accurate at repetitive tasks, where they can generate economies of scale, as in mass production. This involves extreme specialization of tasks and division of labour and so organizations involved in mass production tend to be bureaucratically organized. In this sense, technology and size are related. However, even here, there are problems of rigidities, especially in coping with problems such as breakdowns or absenteeism, and even mass production firms have increasingly sought ways of making both machines and people more flexible. Thus the workforces of this kind of firm are no longer differentiated into large numbers of categories, each with its own specialized job description, but are allocated to a general category and expected to move between jobs as and when required.

The complexity of the environment, particularly with respect to information, also affects structure. The more numerous and complex the sources of information and the more specialized the knowledge needed to interpret information, the more likely is decentralization. This happens because those with the specialized knowledge can gain some degree of independence from their superiors. As section 4.4 shows, this is one basis of the power of professions.

Those at the top of hierarchies tend to want more centralization, especially during crises, yet if they are dependent on the arcane, specialized knowledge of those they direct, then they may not be able to exercise much control over them. Whether those with specialized operational knowledge use their power for their own benefit – to do things as they want at their own pace – or for the good of the organization (or whether the two can be reconciled) is crucial. Since the early 1980s there have been new experiments in dealing with such problems. They are sometime called 'tight–loose' forms of control because they often combine increased delegation and opportunity for discretion with tightened control. An example is making groups or departments responsible for their own budgets, but giving them tighter budgets than hitherto. Another is allowing more discretion over how groups meet their objectives, coupled with tighter inspection or auditing of performance, and gearing subsequent remuneration accordingly, as in performance-related pay.

Virtually all organizations have some bureaucratic procedures, because of the advantages noted above relating to specialization and standardization. Bureaucratic structures and procedures tend to be most effective for organizations which operate in stable environments and with unchanging objectives. In more changeable conditions, less rigid forms tend to be adopted.

In conclusion, note that factors such as size, technology and environment do not determine organizational structure – they merely tend to influence decisions regarding the latter. One of the powers of people exercising strategic control is that of making choices about organizational form, and those choices are one element in the processes of competition between firms and of conflict between managers and their staff.

Markets

No sociology of a market economy like that of Britain is complete without an acknowledgement of the role of markets themselves as a form of economic organization. Whereas bureaucratic control co-ordinates related activities within organizations, for example the processing of insurance claims in an insurance company, markets co-ordinate different activities produced mainly by separately owned firms. Thus an insurance company gets its stationery and computer equipment by buying them from other producers in separate organizations, through the market. Markets are an essential feature of capitalist societies, and they have continued to expand into new areas. Thus, in many countries, especially Britain, activities which used to be run by the state are now governed by markets or market-like forces.

Again, we can start from an ideal type. Markets are generally defined either as routine exchanges of commodities for money or the setting and institutional preconditions for such exchanges, as in the case of the stock exchange. Commodities are goods produced for sale, as opposed to immediate use or barter. They have not only use-value, as in the nutritious character of food or the entertaining character of a video, but also exchange-value, a value expressed in money that is relative to that of any other commodity, whatever its use-value. Although a restaurant meal and a car have utterly different use-values, their exchange-values can be measured and compared in the same terms, through money.

In addition to markets where individuals buy goods and services there are labour markets and financial markets. Most market exchanges take place between firms. Buying and selling are critical for their survival, and certain employees may specialize in these activities, sometimes dealing with just a single major customer or supplier.

Markets presuppose private property. For it to be possible to sell something, someone must own it, so it is theirs to sell. When the good is sold, property rights over it are transferred to the buyer, and by paying for the good, the buyer fully discharges his or her obligations to the seller. The social relation between buyer and seller need not go beyond this functional and impersonal level. As Weber wrote:

> The market community . . . is the most impersonal relationship of practical life into which humans can enter with one another . . . its participants do not look toward the persons of each other but only toward the commodity; there are no obligations of brotherliness or reverence, and none of those spontaneous human relations that are sustained by personal unions. (Weber 1968, p. 636)

In a strictly market relationship, all the buyer and seller have to do is honour their contract: the buyer must pay the sum agreed and the seller must provide the goods or services agreed. Once they have done that, the market relationship is over and it does not have to be renewed unless both parties decide it is in their self-interest to make another exchange. If the buyer wants to take her or his money elsewhere next time, then she or he is free to do so. Marx used the phrase 'the icy waters of egotistical calculation' to refer to the way markets encourage us to put the calculation of our self-interest before sentiment or loyalty.

One of the most striking and remarkable features of many markets is their anonymity, especially as market relationships stretch around the world. Even if we know the seller we are unlikely to know the producers of the commodities they sell. As markets have developed we have become increasingly reliant on goods made by people about whom we know little or nothing. The extraordinary geographical expansion of markets is perhaps the most basic element of globalization.

Closely related to the impersonality and anonymity of markets is their 'neutrality' or indifference to who happens to be the buyer or seller. It is not generally in the interest of buyers and sellers to discriminate against one another according to personal characteristics such as gender or race, for the main consideration is to get the best deal. For example, it is in the interest of a salesperson to take your money from you regardless of who you are, though sometimes other influences such as sexism and racism override this. If sellers do take an interest in those to whom they are selling, for example by conducting market research on them, this is a means for increasing sales, not a consequence of any personal interest in their customers.

The fact that market relations between particular buyers and sellers do not have to be renewed, but can be changed when either sees fit to do so, means that markets generate insecurity; to be free to choose is also to be free to lose. Wherever people rely on producing for markets or being employed in firms, in principle, and often in practice, their livelihoods become insecure. Proponents of markets argue that this insecurity is a spur to effort and efficiency, because too much security leads to complacency. As we shall see, the degree of insecurity varies considerably according to the kind of job. Where, as in Britain, markets are being extended and employment is being made more 'flexible', then it becomes easier for firms to hire and fire. Since the 1970s men's employment careers have become markedly less stable. Women's involvement in paid work has increased, but they too have become more vulnerable to unemployment. However, professional and managerial employees are still significantly less vulnerable to unemployment than manual workers (Gallie et al. 1998).

Markets are one way in which divisions of labour can be co-ordinated. In addition to allowing the transfer of commodities between producers and users, they regulate how much is produced and consumed. They thereby influence how the division of labour develops, and how many people work in each sector, firm and specialized occupation. This happens through the price mechanism. Profits will rise or fall in each line of activity according to the costs of producing the commodities and the level of demand for them. As businesses and investors seek out the the highest return on their money, investment will switch towards the most profitable activities and out of the least profitable. As a consequence, new jobs may be created in some activities while jobs are lost in others. Such changes happen continually. The forces which drive them result from myriad decisions made by producers, sellers and buyers, each of them pursuing his or her own self-interest and either ignorant of or unconcerned about others' interests. No one plans these changes at the level of a whole society. Unlike bureaucracies, markets are not hierarchically governed but both reflect and influence the decisions of independent buyers and sellers.

Since the late 1970s in Britain, there has been a shift away from bureaucratic, state organizations towards favouring markets and private firms as a way of socially organizing the economy. Advocates of this shift – mainly on the political right – argue that markets are more efficient and more responsive to consumers than is state provision. Arguably, the presence of several competing sellers, each dependent on finding buyers, who can always take their money elsewhere, forces them to become efficient, whereas those who know they have no competition, so that users have nowhere else to go, can afford to be complacent and inefficient. Whether this is true is hotly debated.

For good or ill, market relationships have become more important in Britain, partly as a product of the privatizations that we discussed earlier. Thus now, instead of getting our gas or electricity from a nationalized producer, we are bombarded with advertising material from competing energy producers seeking our custom. Even in health and education, there are movements towards market-like provision, encouraging us to think of ourselves as individual consumers seeking the best buy, rather than citizens voting for the best general state-provided system. Where previously health and social services were run on bureaucratic lines, they operate now on a mixture of bureaucratic regulation and market (or 'quasi-market') co-ordination, in which 'providers' of services have to bid for the custom of 'purchasers', like general practitioner (GP) fundholders. This affects not only the security of employment in these services but the day-to-day experience of work, as cost considerations come to play an increasing role in decisions. Where previously health and social service workers had only to consider what kind of service to deliver, they now also have to consider how much it costs. Where previously headteachers were primarily concerned with organizing teaching, they now have to look after their own budgets too. They thus gained a degree of autonomy from their local authority bureaucracies but face tighter restrictions on spending.

Although these are often thought of as economic matters, they have major implications for social relations and social organization. The extension of markets into new areas tends to increase insecurity, make us more money-minded and less reliant on national systems of provision, position us as consumers rather than citizens, and arguably (!) make us more self-reliant.

Market – or market-like – forces introduce forms of restructuring and impacts on workers in public services similar to those found in the private sector. In the National Health Service (NHS), increasing pressure on costs resulted from the need of hospital trusts to compete for money from purchasers, particularly GP fundholders. As labour costs account for about 75 per cent of budgets, labour is particularly vulnerable in the resulting restructuring. In a study of four hospitals Lloyd and Seifert (1995) found that nursing costs had been reduced by separating skilled from unskilled work, reducing the proportion of the former to the minimum. State Registered Nurses (SRNs) and State Enrolled Nurses (SENs) were relieved of more routine work, which was devolved to auxiliaries. Redundancies across a wide range of occupational groups, including professionals, were made in some of the hospitals. There were also attempts to cut absenteeism, make fuller use of temporary staff, and reduce demarcation between different jobs so as to achieve greater numerical and functional flexibility (see below, section 4.2). Another way of cutting costs and increasing flexibility has been through contracting out services like laundry. Other surveys have reported greater levels of stress, demoralization and higher workloads among nursing and ancillary workers. While these changes are very similar to the kinds of restructuring found in private industry, the dangers of cost-cutting leading to a reduction in the quality of service are particularly high in public service work such as health care.

So far we have relied upon an ideal type of market, but as with the ideal of bureaucracy, in practice real markets often diverge significantly from the model.

First, many markets are not as impersonal as the ideal type suggests. Certainly, you do not have to know the petrol station attendant to refuel your car, but for many transactions the buyers and sellers need to interact more extensively to carry out their business. This is generally because market transactions require trust. We need to trust the persons, products and institutions that we are dealing with, which is why firms try to cultivate a trustworthy brand and image. For a firm like Marks and Spencer, for example, its value is not just a matter of what it owns but also its reputation.

The greater the element of risk in the transaction, the greater the need for the buyer and seller to trust each other. For a simple product like petrol, it is not a problem, and buyer and seller may be complete strangers. But for something complex and expensive like major car repairs or buying a house, each party needs reassurance that the other is both honest and competent. We can develop trust by various means: by establishing a good reputation, providing guarantees, getting legal protection, or forming a close, long-term relationship with the other party. Thus, long-term relationships develop between firms selling complex products and services to each other. If firm A needs a specialist computer system and firm B could supply it, the two firms may need to spend considerable time negotiating over what kind of system A needs and B can offer, and arranging for servicing and updating it. In the process they collaborate and build trust. As in many social situations, there are likely to be norms regarding the class, gender and race of the participants in the process. The individuals involved must behave in the manner expected for the situation, following the established dress code, having the right social skills, exchanging pleasantries and hospitality, whether wining and dining or playing golf. Nevertheless, in the final analysis, however sociable such relationships may become, the reasons for developing them are likely to be ones of self-interest in the pursuit of profit. They are ways of doing business.

Such relationships are far removed from the minimal, anonymous and impersonal relations of the ideal type of markets. In practice then, market exchanges tend to be in varying degrees and ways socially embedded, that is embedded in networks of social relations. These are generally routinized – sellers sell and buyers buy routinely, acquiring practical, though often taken-for-granted, knowledge about each other, the product and the setting. Often, success depends on who you know in the market as well as what you know.

Plate 3.2 shows a familiar scene, reflecting the growing importance of financial mar-

Plate 3.2	Traders at the Stock Exchange, 1988
	Source: Network/John Sturrock

kets for the economic health of the country. Note the uniformity of the traders – all male, white, youngish, similar in their demeanour and dress – even where they do not wear blazers to identify their role, there is normally an informal uniform. They also share similar lifestyles in terms of socializing and consumption. These are not merely incidental features. If the traders are to gain the necessary information to carry out their job, they must be able to interact with others, and to do this they must be accepted by them. In turn, to achieve this, they must conform to such norms.

There is always a tension in such situations between the pulls of loyalty and trust resulting from long periods of collaboration and the attractions of breaking the relationship and switching to another buyer or supplier as soon as a more financially attractive option turns up. While the latter may bring short-term advantages, the sacrifice of the long-term understanding and trust may be costly. The conflict between loyalty and economic self-interest is also clear in employment, where employees on fixed-term contracts may find that their commitment and loyalty count for nothing when they need to renew their contracts.

Consider another example: labour markets. In seeking a job, you are putting yourself and your skills up for sale. From the point of view of the prospective employer, especially one seeking to employ someone for a long period, this is a risky proposition. How do they know you will be a good employee? They can ask for your curriculum vitae and references, but how much trust can be placed in these? They will draw upon all their social knowledge to assess you, trying to make inferences from the slightest hints of dress and manner, and you, presumably, will try to meet their expectations.

We rely on markets to an unprecedented degree. The fact that they allow us to choose from whom we buy and to whom we sell, according to our self-interest, makes them a strong individualizing force in society. But that does not mean we become isolated or independent individuals. On the contrary, we become dependent on an ever larger number of other individuals, most of them through anonymous market relations, and it is this anonymity which gives us the illusion of independence. A key element of globalization is the extension of markets linking people to others in distant countries: the British consumer to the Chinese sports goods manufacturer, the Argentinian meat producer or the US credit card company.

State provision

The state is a major actor in organizing economic activities. Through public services and nationalized industries, states are heavily involved in economic production, though most of the latter and some of the former have been privatized in Britain. They also play an indispensable role in regulating the formal economy, collecting tax revenues and enforcing economic policies. A large number of people are employed to provide education, health and social services, in organizations which are predominantly bureaucracies. Since the Second World War, state services have been responsible for the growth of professional and administrative jobs. Such services are ultimately paid for by taxation.

Access to state services is a matter of rights, established through political channels and exercised by virtue of being an eligible citizen. All citizens have a right to state health care at no (or minimal) cost. These entitlements are gradually changing. Conservative governments since 1979 and more recently the Labour government have been concerned to reduce the cost of state-provided services, in order to cut public expenditure. They have had little success in achieving the latter, largely because of the cost of expenditure on benefits for the unemployed, and the effect of an ageing population on demand for health services and pensions. Nevertheless there has been a reduction in state employment and a curtailment in public services, especially those freely available. Thus while all citizens with appropriate qualifications used to be entitled to free higher education, this has ended with the introduction of tuition fees. Demand for private services, such as private health care, is likely to increase from those who can afford them. Such changes have the effect of positioning people as private consumers rather than citizens. Those who cannot afford to pay for services privately will suffer.

Communal and domestic provisioning

A significant amount of economic activity occurs outside the formal economy, in the community and households, often without the use of money or employment. Individuals and households may exchange services, such as baby-sitting, by making use of social networks and without any money payments. Local Economic Trading Schemes (LETS) organize such exchanges more formally, although they remain a very limited phenomenon.

A larger volume of services is provided by individuals for their own or for their family's use. Such domestic services range from house repairs, through child care, to cooking and cleaning. The most striking feature of this, sociologically, is that most of this work continues to be done by women (see sections 7.3 and 9.5). Women have moved much more quickly into the traditionally mainly male sphere of employment than men have moved into the traditionally female sphere of domestic work. The result is a double shift for women workers – doing both paid and unpaid work – which helps to perpetuate gender inequalities in paid work, and produces major differences in the lifestyles of men and women. Most of these domestic services could be obtained by other means – by employing domestic servants, for instance – but are mainly done by people for themselves.

One of the interesting questions about communal and domestic provisioning is whether it provides an alternative to dependence on employment for getting a living. According to research by Pahl (1984), there is little evidence of much working for money informally within communities among the unemployed. However, in terms of domestic provision, he found that an enormous amount of work was being done. Perhaps surprisingly, it was not the unemployed who did a lot of domestic self-provisioning, despite the time they had available. Rather, the more people in a household who were in formal paid employment, the more work they did at home – car repairs, home cooking, DIY, etc. The reason for this division between unemployed and employed households was that the latter, but not the former, could afford to buy the materials and equipment required for self-provisioning. They were therefore able to enhance their standard of living beyond the level that employment alone could. Unemployed households are likely to subside into a state of deprivation and are unable to do much to improve their deteriorating domestic environment. Domestication and home ownership are highly unattractive without the resources which are still only obtainable at a satisfactory level through regular employment (Pahl and Wallace 1985).

Summary

1 Economic activities are socially organized in several ways. Amongst the most important are bureaucratic organization, markets, the state and domestic provisioning.
2 Although popularly seen in negative terms, elements of bureaucratic organization are likely to be found in most large organizations operating in a relatively stable environment.
3 Markets link together firms and consumers in a way which allows them to pursue their own self-interest. An increasing range of commodities and activities is provided through markets, offering not only increased scope for choice but insecurity too.
4 The social relations of market exchange can vary from transient, anonymous and impersonal to enduring and strongly socially embedded.
5 The state both engages in economic activities and regulates them in the wider society. While these activities are politically regulated they are influenced by market forces too.
6 A significant amount of work goes on in the form of self-provisioning in households, though mainly in employed households.

3.5 Services and the changing industrial structure

The industrial revolution is always associated with the rise of manufacturing industry, but it has also involved service industries, such as retailing, tourism, and banking and insurance. As in many advanced economies, employment in manufacturing has fallen while employment in services has risen steadily, prompting many to talk of deindustrialization. This is misleading for three reasons. First, although employment in manufacturing has fallen, its output has risen, since output per employee has risen more rapidly than employment has fallen. Second, services like tourism and transport can also claim to be industries, and employment in many of these has grown. Moreover, as we shall see shortly, the definition of 'services' is far from clear and so it is debatable whether their expansion amounts to deindustrialization or continued industrialization.

The particular mixture of different sectors – primary (agriculture), secondary (manufacturing) and tertiary (services) – and the relative size of each of these within a country is sometimes referred to as its 'industrial structure' (see table 3.2). Figure 3.11 shows that it has changed markedly, but why has this happened? One reason has been the replacement of manufacturing labour by machines. Routine, volume production of goods such as cars and TVs is especially susceptible to mechanization and automation. Another is that much of British manufacturing has been only weakly competitive for decades. This has affected

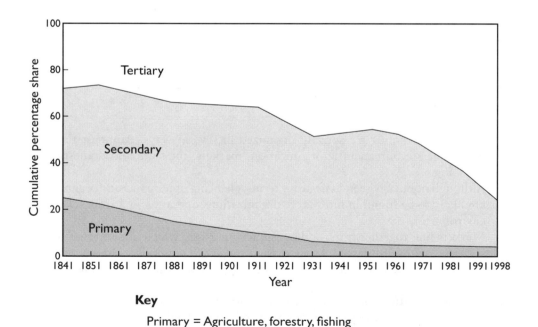

Key

Primary = Agriculture, forestry, fishing
Secondary = Manufacturing, mining, construction, utilities
Tertiary = Services

Figure 3.11 | Britain's changing industrial structure: sectoral shares of employment
Source: Adapted from Allen 1988, updated from *Labour Market Trends* various years

both labour-intensive industries like textiles, where low wages in less developed countries reduce costs, and capital-intensive industries like motor manufacturing, where other advanced economies display higher rates of capital investment. Meanwhile, in many services there is often less scope for automation – and hence less displacement of labour.

TABLE 3.2 | **Employment by industry, March 1998**

Industry	No. employed
Agriculture, hunting, forestry and fishing	289,000
Total primary industry	289,000 (2%)
Mining and quarrying, supply of electricity, gas and water	221,000
Food products, beverages and tobacco	454,000
Clothing, textiles, leather and leather products	371,000
Wood and wood products	89,000
Paper, pulp, printing, publishing and recording media	470,000
Chemicals, chemical products and synthetic fibres	242,000
Rubber and plastic products	226,000
Non-metallic mineral products, metal and metal products	719,000
Machinery and equipment not elsewhere counted	400,000
Electrical and optical equipment	514,000
Transport equipment	400,000
Coke, nuclear fuel and other manufacturing	228,000
Construction	994,000
Total production and construction industries	5,107,000 (23%)
Wholesale and retail trade and repairs	4,033,000
Hotels and restaurants	1,334,000
Transport and storage	854,000
Post and telecommunications	512,000
Financial intermediation	1,059,000
Real estate	284,000
Renting, research, computer and other business activities	2,697,000
Public admin. and defence, compulsory social security	1,348,000
Education	1,870,000
Health and social work	2,585,000
Other community, social and personal activities	1,025,000
Total service industries	17,602,000 (75%)
Total all industries and services	23,219,000

Source: Labour Market Trends 1998a

Services are often defined in contrast to manufactured goods, which are generally tangible and capable of being stored. Services are intangible – 'anything that can't be dropped on your foot' – and they have to be 'consumed' at the same time as they are produced. Some accounts highlight the significance of information, as in teaching or counselling, and face-to-face relations with customers, clients or students. However, much information is embodied in material form such as books and floppy disks and can be communicated without face-to-face interaction. A glance at the list of service industries in table 3.2 reveals many activities which do not necessarily involve intangibles or people-work (see below) with customers: catering involves manufacturing meals, cleaning produces material transformations, and transport involves the movement of materials. Many other jobs combine elements of both manufacture and service; restaurants provide both manufactured material goods – meals – and personal service and ambience. The officially defined services or tertiary industries, then, tend to be residual categories, covering activities which do not fall clearly under primary (extractive) or secondary (manufacturing) headings.

Matters become more complex when we look at service work, like training, design or consultancy. Many people who do these kinds of work are employed in manufacturing (and even primary-sector) firms and are therefore not classified as service-sector employees, though they would be if they worked in specialist training, design or consultancy firms. Part of the increase in service-sector employment has resulted from manufacturing firms hiving off or contracting out their service functions to specialist service firms. Also, manufacturing and services are not necessarily independent sectors; manufacturers need producer services like advertising, legal and financial advice, while most services, whether for producers or consumers, make use of manufactured goods. Therefore much of the service sector represents not so much a departure from manufacturing industry as a support and extension to it.

Social consequences: a post-industrial society?

Notwithstanding the enormous variety of activities included in the service industry category, many do indeed provide intangible services, and involve face-to-face contact with the public – so-called people-work. These present a radically different kind of experience of work from that in manufacturing. Compare the difference between being, on the one hand, a building society cashier, travel agent or nurse and, on the other, an engineer, assembly worker or garment worker. Arguably the meaning of 'industrial society' changes when only a minority of the working population have first-hand experience of the latter kinds of work and a majority are involved in people-work.

Daniel Bell (1973) and other exponents of the post-industrial society thesis argued in the 1970s that these changes in the industrial structure would generally improve the quality of life and work in the Western world. It was anticipated that unpleasant, dirty and routine jobs in factories would be eliminated. Instead, a greater proportion of workers would be dealing with people, doing more rewarding work, in better surroundings, providing assorted services to clients. The post-industrial society thesis assumed that full employment would be maintained as new, more desirable jobs in services multiplied.

However, the realities of economic change in Britain have turned out rather differently. Some of the jobs in the new industries, like cleaning or working in a fast-food outlet, are no more attractive, and less well remunerated, than traditional manual factory jobs. Furthermore, despite the increase of jobs in some service sectors, they have not compensated for the decline of manufacturing employment; consequently full employment has not been known in Britain since the early 1970s.

| TABLE 3.3 | Buying goods rather than services: shifts in household expenditure on transport, 1953–91 (percentage of total household expenditure) |

Years	Purchase and maintenance of vehicles	Fares
1953–4	3.5	3.5
1958	5.1	2.9
1963	8.6	2.6
1968	10.5	2.1
1973	11.2	1.9
1978	11.0	1.8
1985	13.0	2.1
1991	13.5	1.9

Source: Gershuny 1978; *Family Expenditure Survey,* various years

Gershuny (1978), an opponent of Bell's thesis, argued that the contraction of some final consumer services is especially significant. He maintained that the reason why cinemas, laundries and passenger transport have declined is that many people now have personal access to machines which allow them to service themselves – TVs, videos, washing machines and cars. Hence a 'self-service' economy was emerging. A clear instance of this is the proportion of average income spent on transport goods (cars, bikes, etc.) as opposed to transport services (trains and buses) since the late 1950s. As table 3.3 shows, people are spending more of their incomes on goods. The economic impact of this is to boost the car industry, but to reduce employment in public transport. Since the manufacture of cars is less labour-intensive than public transport, jobs have been lost overall. The preference for self-servicing is partly due to cost – labour-intensive services are expensive – but it is also a matter of personal convenience and new lifestyles based on aspirations to own mass consumption goods. As usual there are counter-tendencies too; rising spending on restaurants and takeaway food indicates a decline in self-servicing in producing meals. Table 3.4 shows that some of the more intangible objects of household expenditure – recreation, entertainment and education – have grown rapidly since 1971.

There has been considerable debate about how widespread are the tendencies outlined by Gershuny. If he were correct, Bell's (1973) post-industrial society thesis would have to be dismissed in so far as prospects for employment in existing service industries would be poor. But in any case, Bell's thesis is undermined by his remarkable ignorance of the continuing operation of capitalist mechanisms. Whatever the differences in the experiences of work in manufacturing and services, with the exception of public services like local government, education and health, most manufacturing and service jobs have a crucial feature in common – they are located in capitalist firms. This means that both sectors are subject to competition, pressures to cut costs and speed up, and thus risks of redundancy and closure. For example, one of the main activities in which jobs have been lost through automation in the 1990s is banking, where information technology has radically reduced the need for cashiers and face-to-face contact with customers. Further, as we saw in our discussion of markets, even public services are becoming more

TABLE 3.4 | Household expenditure, 1971–96

Area of expenditure	Indices at constant prices[a] (1971=100)					
	1971	1981	1986	1991	1996	1996[b]
Transport and communication	100	132	171	194	219	81.5
Housing[c]	100	119	136	147	155	74.7
Food	100	104	109	115	124	52.0
Recreation, entertainment and education	100	153	191	240	300	49.7
Household goods and services	100	115	143	166	197	29.9
Alcohol	100	127	134	132	132	28.0
Clothing and footwear	100	129	178	193	246	27.4
Fuel, light and power	100	110	120	126	131	16.1
Tobacco	100	89	74	71	59	11.8
Other goods and services	100	121	163	218	238	92.9
Less expenditure by foreign tourists, etc.	100	152	198	181	257	−14.3
Household expenditure abroad	100	193	229	287	379	14.4
All household expenditure	100	121	144	165	183	464.1

[a] At constant 1990 prices
[b] £ billion (current prices)
[c] Includes domestic rates, but excludes community charge and council tax

susceptible to similar pressures, through cost squeezes and the introduction of quasi-markets. So even if we were to insist on calling Britain 'deindustrialized' or 'post-industrial', we would have to acknowledge that it is no less capitalist than hitherto.

Summary

1   A growth in employment in service industry has partially compensated for severe job loss in British manufacturing since the mid-1960s.
2   There is considerable debate over the implications of the increased proportion of workers in the service sector, not least because of the ambiguities of the meaning of 'services', but they are associated with a growing number of jobs involving people-work.
3   Service industry shares with manufacturing industry the same capitalist economic rules or logic.

Related topics

Relationships between firms and their workforces are dealt with in sections 4.2, 4.3 and 4.4. Information on property ownership, wealth and power appears in section 6.5 on the upper class. Aspects of the globalization of economic activity are reviewed in section 2.3, with the political implications being reviewed in section 13.2 and the political pre-conditions in section 13.4. Material on public service providers can be found in sections 14.2 and 15.6. More information on various economic organizations can be found throughout the book, but especially in chapter 12 on media organizations.

Further reading

For global movements in employment and work see Dicken (1998) and Held et al. (1999). Saunders and Harris (1994) deals with the privatization issue while Gallie et al. (1998) explores changes in the employment relationship. Grint (1998) is a textbook on the area.

Cross-references to *Readings in Contemporary British Society*

McNair on the changing political economy of the British press; **Hesmondhalgh** on the British dance music industry; **Dicken** on the global economy; **Gallie et al.** on changes in organizations; **McDowell** on aspects of financial services in the City of London; **Gewirtz et al.** on the privatization of economic organizations and the introduction of market processes within the school system.

4 Employment

4.1 Introduction

In a capitalist economy, workers are paid wages or salaries to bring them to workplaces to produce commodities – goods and services for sale. Thus there are labour markets, institutional arrangements which facilitate the striking of contracts between employers and employees. The employment relation is one of the most basic elements of modern social structure. As table 4.1 shows, the vast majority of adults are economically active, either as employers, self-employed or as employees. Many of the most important institutions in British society – the education system, the family, the law and politics – are tailored to meet the requirements of work. The social significance of work is evident in the fact that we commonly define an individual's identity in terms of what work she or he does. The quality and subjective experience of work vary enormously, having a major influence on the individual's quality of life. How long you live, whom you marry or live with, how much money you have, where you live and how children fare are all affected by work.

TABLE 4.1 | **Population of working age:[a] by gender and employment status, 1986 and 1997 (millions)**

	1986			1997		
	Males	*Females*	*All*	*Males*	*Females*	*All*
Economically active						
In employment						
Full-time employees	11.3	5.3	16.6	11.0	6.0	17.0
Part-time employees	0.3	3.9	4.2	0.9	4.5	5.4
Self-employed	2.0	0.6	2.7	2.4	0.8	3.1
Others in employment[b]	0.3	0.1	0.4	0.2	0.2	0.3
All in employment	13.9	10.0	23.9	14.5	11.4	25.9
Unemployed[c]	1.8	1.2	3.1	1.3	0.7	2.0
All economically active	15.8	11.2	26.9	15.7	12.1	27.9
Economically inactive	2.2	5.3	7.5	2.9	4.9	7.8
Population of working age	18.0	16.4	34.4	18.7	17.0	35.7

[a] At spring each year, males aged 16–64, females aged 16–59
[b] Those on government employment and training schemes and from 1992 unpaid family workers
[c] Based on the International Labour Organization
Source: Social Trends 1998, p. 75

We have seen in chapter 3 how the occupational structure has changed over time and how it is currently. Table 4.1 shows that the number of people economically active rose by 1 million between 1986 and 1997, to 27.9 million. This was entirely the effect of more women joining the labour market. Of those in employment in 1997, 12 per cent were self-employed. The comparable figure in 1981 was 8 per cent of all people in work. Other data sources show that just over two-thirds of the self-employed are without employees (*Labour Market Trends* 1998b, p. 515). Thus, in 1997, 88 per cent of workers were employees, selling their labour power for wages. There are, however, distinctions within the category of employees. A substantial proportion of people are in managerial, supervisory or professional roles, thus exercising some authority or control at work. While most such people are far from being powerful, they are above the bottom rank in hierarchies of authority at work. In total, according to the 1991 Census, about 66 per cent of all workers were without any degree of authority, though this does not necessarily mean that they were without some autonomy at work. There are significant differences between men and women with respect to employment status.

The nature of the tasks, the social relations of the workplace, and the associated financial rewards are the key features of employment. The diversity of jobs and experience of work is enormous and this differentiation of work is a major influence on social inequalities, divisions and conflicts.

Many of the inequalities deriving from work are well known to everybody. In 1998, average annual incomes for workers in full-time employment ranged from £8,112 for kitchen porters to £54,343 for treasurers and company financial managers (*New Earnings Survey* 1998). Again, some jobs have more prestige than others. Prestige is usually related to income and to the nature of the work done. Pay differences reflect not only differences in skill, but differences in the status of the work and in the degree of power and control vested in the job, and the scarcity of job vacancies relative to job applicants. For example, financial managers' high pay and kitchen porters' low pay can be explained in terms of these factors. Some jobs offer more freedom than others. Some work is creative, much more is very routine. Perhaps more important, some jobs give authority to their occupants: managerial and supervisory positions carry with them some degree of power. In all these respects, the division of labour produces social inequality.

Although employers have most power to determine job content and wage level, employees can, primarily through collective organization and negotiation, exert some influence over the conditions under which they labour. Hence, conflict arises as individuals and social groups attempt to alter the organization of work to their own benefit. Firms, their owners and managers, try to organize work to pursue the goals of profit, growth, efficiency and control in the face of competition from other firms. This generates conflict with workers. In non-profit organizations too, there are invariably constraints on resources and hence pressures to economize. Indeed, since the late 1970s, public-sector workers have come under increasing pressure not only to cut costs but to compete for funding. The balance of power between workers and management and between different kinds of workers is continually shifting. Sometimes the conflicts become generalized. Class struggles are those based on shared interests of many groups of workers against many managements, and – often overlooked – vice versa. Gender struggles are those based upon a recognition of generalized, antagonistic interests between women and men. This second kind of struggle appears both in employment and in other spheres of work.

Work can be paid or unpaid – making a meal at home for someone is work no less than making meals for a wage in a café. Employment is just one kind of work, though it is often the only kind that is generally recognized, so that many people, particularly housewives, who do large amounts of unpaid work are sometimes not considered to be working. (One wonders if this would be true if most of the unpaid work was done by men.) This is certainly work, but not employment. The distinction is very important. Employment is the kind of work classified as an occupation and paid for in wages or salaries. It is employment which produces the inequalities of power and income which are part of the sphere of industrial relations. Domestic work is also unequally distributed and income from employment is generally unequally shared within the household. The inequalities between men and women in the household economy interact in complex ways with gender inequalities in employment (see sections 7.3 and 9.5).

This chapter first considers aspects of the employment relations and the work that are a necessary part of economic production. It considers the role of management in general and its influence on the way in which work tasks are specified and co-ordinated. This is analysed in terms of managerial strategies for control and their effects on the experience of work, and the autonomy and skill of workers. The chapter then examines the means by which workers organize to make their conditions of work more advantageous. Trade unions and professional associations, the most effective institutions for collective control of working life on the part of labour, are described and compared. Finally, the situation of people of working age who are unable to obtain any position in the labour market is described, documenting the personal and social disadvantages of unemployment.

4.2　Management and the labour process

Firms, indeed any institution with a division of labour, require management, just as an orchestra requires a conductor. In small firms, management may be nothing other than the directives of the owner: the owner will personally supervise the implementation of his or her own strategic decisions. As economic organizations grew larger from the end of the nineteenth century, managerial jobs became more common. In the large economic organizations of contemporary Britain, whether private enterprise or public agencies, management involves a complex network of independent roles and activities, hierarchically structured and itself requiring co-ordination.

Particularly in the formal economy, work is organized in terms of specific procedures, cycles and stages, involving specific divisions of labour. This organization is called a labour process. It comprises the material organization of technology and inputs and outputs, the particular way in which jobs are done, and the social relations among workers involved in the process. In this section we shall first outline the nature of management, then proceed to look at labour processes – how they vary and how they are managed.

'Management' is a rather loose concept. At its broadest, it refers to all people in positions of authority over others within a firm – from the managing director at the top to the supervisor on the shop floor. It is therefore essential to distinguish between different types of managerial position: executives, who exercise strategic control, should be distinguished from middle managers with operational control, and also from supervisory workers. Though these categories are blurred at the edges they reflect important differences in power, prestige and function. In this section we are primarily interested in middle management – managers who are neither in a position of strategic control nor directly supervising workers on the shop floor. They are employees of the firm, but they exercise authority and discretion at plant or office level.

The purposes of management

Management has a number of purposes or functions which include liaison, filtering and transmitting information, allocating resources, directing subordinates, and planning and handling disruptions of work. Managers generally combine some specialist, technical activities and some general, administrative work, the proportion varying considerably from one manager to another. For example, an accounts manager may well work more or less alone on the specialized activity of accountancy, while some other managers, so-called line managers, are largely concerned with directing and monitoring the performance of other workers. It should be remembered that many managers are not concerned with supervising work but are involved in the external relations of the firm, particularly with suppliers and major customers, where they are in effect managing key markets. The principal purpose of modern middle management is to plan, co-ordinate and control operations in the everyday running of the firm.

Management practices

As in many social processes, the fit is poor between the formal aims of roles like management and the behaviour of the people who fill those roles. Studies of what managers actually do when at work suggest that, with the exception of some specialist functions, the job of manager is a very fluid and indefinite one. Hales (1986) summarizes the

---

Box 4.1 Key features of managerial work

Hales (1986, p. 104) gives the following as key features of managerial work:

1 It combines a specialist/professional element and a general 'managerial' element.
2 The substantive elements involve, essentially, liaison, people management and responsibility for a work process, beneath which are subsumed more detailed work elements.
3 The character of work elements varies by duration, time span, recurrence, unexpectedness and source.
4 Much time is spent in day-to-day trouble shooting and *ad hoc* problems of organization and regulation.
5 Much managerial activity consists of asking or persuading others to do things, involving the manager in face-to-face verbal communication of limited duration.
6 Patterns of communication vary in terms of *what* the communication is about and with *whom* the communication is made.
7 Little time is spent on any one particular activity and, in particular, on the conscious, systematic formulation of plans. Planning and decision-making tend to take place in the course of other activity.
8 Managers spend a lot of time accounting for and explaining what they do, in informal relationships and in 'politicking'.
9 Managerial activities are riven by contradictions, cross-pressures and conflicts. Much managerial work involves coping with and reconciling social and technical conflict.
10 There is considerable choice in terms of *what* is done and *how*: part of managerial work is setting the boundaries of negotiating that work itself.

literature on managerial behaviour, isolating ten widely agreed attributes of managerial work (see box 4.1). The daily activities of management seem fragmentary and unpredictable: 'little time is spent on any one particular activity.' It seems that for many managers, work entails little decision-taking. This is particularly the case at lower levels where the degree of discretion is very limited.

The labour process

For many people, the factory symbolizes a debased work environment. A woman employee cooking meals in a large community-centre site with several canteen and snack-bar outlets said of the kitchens she worked in:

> It's just like a factory making radios. It is a factory. When we prepare the food, we don't think that someone is going to sit down and enjoy it. As long as it looks right we are not making any effort to improve the quality. There is no variety . . . Everything by the book, always the same way. (Gabriel 1988, p. 58)

Boredom, lack of variety and the absence of opportunity to make decisions about how to set about work tasks are typical complaints.

But not everyone finds work as unpleasant as this. Another woman working in a small snack-bar on the same site said: 'I like working on this small bar better than anywhere else; you get to know the students who come here, we have a laugh and a chat. The bosses leave us alone; it's a first rate job' (Gabriel 1988, p. 70). Some workers in unskilled jobs even appreciate not having to think about what they are doing. Yet many workers derive intrinsic satisfaction from their work.

The experience of work varies considerably, not only between blue-collar and white-collar, between skilled and unskilled, manual and non-manual, but between working with things and working with people. Those who deal directly with people, such as shop assistants, travel couriers, teachers and doctors face a very different task from those whose work is primarily concerned with things – be it accounts, manufacturing goods, driving a lorry or cleaning floors. The former group have to pay attention to the way they present themselves, and to encourage trust – the quality of the relationship with the customer, supervisee or client is part of what their work is about.

Workers' reactions to their jobs are understandably mixed. The deprivations resulting from not having a job – poverty, social isolation and low social status (see section 4.5) – are sufficient to persuade people that any work is better than none. In this sense, people want to work. Further, with the rise in women's employment, it has become central to the identity of a larger proportion of the population. Most people will say that they are satisfied with their job, partly because the realistic alternatives are not much better. Previous experience, qualifications and the local availability of other employment all severely limit any individual's choice of work. On the other hand, employees usually feel that their talents and skills are poorly utilized in work which they perceive as dull and monotonous. As one study of unskilled work in Peterborough observed, 95 per cent of the workers used more skill driving a car to work than they exercised on their job (Blackburn and Mann 1979). Variation in the experience of work is considerable. Most people accept, instrumentally, the financial necessity of having a paid job.

But they also expect to derive other benefits – self-satisfaction, self-actualization, performance of a duty and companionship among them – from their employment.

Adults typically spend a lot of time working, so that the actual quality of the experience of work deeply affects both personal and social relationships. Sociologists have, therefore, examined closely the precise content of jobs and the kind of relationships established between employers, supervisors and employees. These are elements of the so-called labour process.

In order to chart the consequences of work experience, it is necessary to compare the qualities of jobs. Since there are thousands of jobs, each distinctive, we need to reduce differences to a few, important dimensions. For sociological purposes, jobs may be grouped in terms of:

1   the range of tasks involved;
2   the range and character of relations to others involved;
3   the degree of discretion given to the worker to decide how to accomplish those tasks;
4   the mode of control used by managers and supervisors to try to ensure that those tasks are completed satisfactorily.

In these respects, an unskilled manual worker in a factory and a schoolteacher are in very different types of labour process. The former worker is likely to be involved in a strictly limited range of tasks, repeated in a tightly prescribed manner, often paced by the machinery and closely overseen by a supervisor. The schoolteacher, by contrast, undertakes a wider range of tasks; the way of working is left to the teacher's initiative, that is, how teachers teach varies from one person to the next; they have to respond continually to pupils, using social skills, making educational and sometimes moral judgements in interacting with them – for example, regarding the treatment of disruptive pupils. Consequently, no two lessons may be identical. Despite the heavy responsibilities they bear, teachers are also given considerable trust and are subject only to distant and intermittent supervision from the headteacher. What accounts for these huge contrasts in labour process?

Skill levels

One of the main kinds of variation in the nature of jobs, and one which strongly affects work satisfaction, is the degree of autonomy and control that workers have over their work. This in turn is closely related to the type and degree of skill involved in the job. Some may have scarcely any control at all – they may merely have to respond in fixed ways to machines, and be under close surveillance. At the other extreme, some workers may have considerable freedom to use their discretion in how they do their work, and even in what they do.

Much depends on the nature of the work. Repetitive work such as that found in mass production tends to be organized on the basis of a high degree of division of labour, in which tasks are simplified so as to make their execution simpler and to facilitate automation. A large volume of research in the 1970s and 1980s was inspired by Braverman (1974), who examined the history of work in the USA. He argued that fragmentation and specialization of work had reduced the skill required for most jobs, and that this process of deskilling was a deliberate policy pursued in order to increase management's control over the labour process by concentrating knowledge in their hands, so that profits could be maximized. Specifically, control was achieved by the widespread introduction of the techniques of scientific management of the kind advocated by F. W. Taylor, the American work study expert of the early twentieth century. Taylorism, as it came to be known, sought to break work tasks down into their smallest possible units, to control the fashion and the speed in and with which each operation was completed, and to co-ordinate these operations as efficiently as possible. Braverman argued that deskilling would continue to be the dominant tendency in capitalism.

Empirical studies to test the deskilling thesis have produced mixed results (Penn, Rose and Rubery 1994; Gallie et al. 1998). Deskilling and Taylorism are especially suitable for mass production, particularly under conditions where, as in much of the USA in the early twentieth century, there is high labour turnover and hence little point in training workers beyond a minimal level. However, it should be noted that only a small minority of workers are employed in mass production industries. Furthermore, not all mass production businesses follow the Taylorist strategy completely. Large Japanese firms involved in mass production, such as Toyota, have lower labour turnover and expect workers to be skilled in many tasks, and to take responsibility for some decisions, such as dealing with minor technical breakdowns. At the same time, surveillance and control are strong, and so their workers tend to use the limited discretion they have in the firm's interest rather than their own.

To some extent, businesses have learned the limitations of Taylorism. Workers who have been taught only one job can hardly be expected to solve problems that occur in their work area, especially those that arise between different jobs, and they are not allowed to try even if they feel so disposed. It is also difficult to centralize the concrete, practical knowledge of the shop or office floor into the hands of managers who are distant from it. Consequently, although Taylorism was intended to increase control over the work process, it may create new control problems. One of the lessons of Japanese industrial success is that if workers can be suitably motivated and trained, they can handle many operational problems better than managers. Moreover, putting speed of work before quality of work can also be very wasteful, and untrained workers are unlikely to achieve high quality. Taylorism is just one among many means towards the end of improving or defending profitability, and in many cases not a particularly effective one.

For any given job whose end product remains the same, it is quite probable that in the long run there will be a tendency to simplify and deskill the job, or eliminate it through automation, so that the number of workers employed falls even though output may remain high or increase. But under capitalism, new products and new jobs are continually being developed, sometimes in new sectors. These are likely to contain a mixture of skill levels – low in fast food, high in information technology. The skill level depends heavily on the kind of work involved. Some, like teaching or management, cannot be deskilled, and there are many others which it would not be sensible to try to deskill. To assess whether deskilling is dominant one would have to look at all these cases.

Resolving questions about skill changes and differences partly depends on obtaining an acceptable measure of skill. This is difficult, however. All occupational groups would like to be called skilled, since that is grounds for demanding high wages and is a source of social status. The very label 'skill' is a valuable resource which does not necessarily reflect the technical difficulty of a given job. It is significant that few occupations filled predominantly by women are called 'skilled'. For example, some of the intricate and dextrous work done by women, in electronics assembly or in the clothing industry, clearly requires special aptitudes and a lengthy learning process, but it is not considered as skilled and is poorly paid, indicating sexist influences on skill categorization. This suggests that trade union organization is at least as important as knowledge or aptitude in establishing work as skilled. If this is the case, then evaluation of Braverman's thesis is extremely difficult. It is for this reason that earlier we described jobs not in terms of the skill required, but in terms of tasks, discretion and control.

Bearing in mind these problems, there seems to be little evidence that Braverman was right for most employees in Britain. Research conducted by sociologists under the Social Change and Economic Life programme in Britain (Penn, Rose and Rubery 1994) and the Employment in Britain survey (Gallie et al. 1998) shows that a majority of the respondents (63 per cent in the latter study) who had held jobs five years earlier said they had experienced some skill gains in that time, although the extent of the upskilling was generally modest. A large minority reported no change and a small minority claimed significant deskilling. New technology was a factor in this, with the proportion of workers working with automated or computerized technology rising from 39 per cent in 1986 to 56 per cent in 1992.

TABLE 4.2 | **Main type of work by sex (percentages)**

	Male	Female	All
Caring	4	21	14
Dealing with clients/customers	16	28	22
Organizing people	12	8	10
Producing with machines	9	5	7
Maintenance (machines/vehicles)	8	–	4
Assembly-line workers	3	2	3
Analysing/monitoring information	19	12	15
Driving	7	1	4
Other or no main activity	21	21	21
Number	1,803	1,667	3,469

Source: Gallie et al. 1998, p. 52

Technical skills are not the only kind of skill. As we have seen there are also social skills, and these are becoming more important as the proportion of workers involved in people-work increases. In the Employment in Britain survey, 46 per cent of employees were engaged predominantly in some form of people-work, such as caring for others, dealing with clients, and organizing others. There is a major gender difference here, with 57 per cent of women employees involved in such work but only 32 per cent of men (see table 4.2). By contrast, despite the enduring image of assembly-line work in the popular imagination of work, only 6 per cent of employees were found to be involved in it for even a part of their worktime. Significantly, it was this kind of work in which deskilling was most common (Gallie et al. 1998). As one would expect, people-work is

The best nurses have the essential qualifications before they go to school.

Providing you have what it takes to start with, you could qualify as a State Enrolled Nurse in two years or, if you have O'levels as well, as a State Registered Nurse in three.

Send us the coupon and we'll send you more information. Post to the Chief Nursing Officer, Dept of Health and Social Security **(G/QT2)**, PO Box 702, London SW20 8SZ.

Name & Address

Nursing.
Make a career out of caring

Plate 4.1 | Job advert appealing to the social skills of potential recruits
Source: Advertising Archives

most common in the welfare services, leisure services and retailing (mostly gaining in employment) and least common in industries such as metal and chemicals (mostly losing employment).

Some of these trends can be illustrated by reference to banking, a sector studied by Halford, Savage and Witz (1997) in their work on gender and careers in organizations.

Banking is a sector which has increasingly emphasized people-work in the last thirty years, even though many jobs have been eliminated or deskilled by information techno-logy. Prior to the 1970s, high-street banks enjoyed rising demand as increasing numbers of people opened bank accounts, and little change was needed to attract their custom. Banks were then relatively inward-looking, remote and conservative institutions, whose managers were custodians of their traditional values. As most adults came to have bank accounts, the rise in demand for banking services slowed, competition intensified and banks had to try harder to get new custom. This coincided with the rise of information technology, which reduced the number of clerical workers and cashiers needed. For example, automatic cash-dispensing machines made it unnecessary for customers to interact with bank employees for many transactions. The range of discretion allowed to branch managers in decision-making was reduced by increased bureaucratic regulation, for example regarding lending limits. Simultaneously, banks took on new kinds of work or 'product', such as mortgages, which required the acquisition of new skills. Also at the same time, they had to become more sales-oriented to attract business. This was re-flected in an increasing tendency to employ young women as cashiers who would give their banks a more attractive image, and a shift towards more customer-friendly branch managers.

This case illustrates a number of things. First, especially where people-work is in-volved, restructuring can mean a change in the type of the worker – sometimes women replacing men, or younger replacing older women, but sometimes the same workers having to change their work identity. Second, organizations both respond to and make use of the gender characteristics of their employees, including their appearance and sexuality. Third, any organization typically involves a range of diverse activities, which vary in their susceptibility to deskilling, so a simple pattern of skill change cannot be expected. Fourth, at any time, organizations are typically undergoing change on several fronts at once; hence changes to their labour processes tend to have multiple causes.

Organizations, technology and the quality of work

The nature of work is partly dependent upon the organization of the enterprise provid-ing employment. Generally, large firms are more complex, rules and procedures are formally specified, and the element of administrative authority is more prominent. Thus there is a tendency for work to be more specialized and authority relations more imper-sonal than in small firms. Work may then be more fragmented, with less discretion left to the worker. However, the effect of size should not be exaggerated, for, as we saw in section 3.4, there are differences between large firms, some more bureaucratic, others more flexible, depending upon the economic environment in which they operate.

The type of technology (equipment and machinery) used by an enterprise is obviously one important cause of the quality of work experience. A teacher's work might be much altered by the introduction of information technology. In higher education, the Open University offers an instructive example. The use of television means that proportion-ately little lecturers' time is spent personally teaching students. The same lecture can be broadcast to thousands of students simultaneously or transcribed and sent out to them in booklets or on the internet.

It is important to realize that when technology is designed there is invariably a significant degree of choice as to its form, particularly regarding the interface with workers. Whether it demands physical strength or dexterity or specialized know-how to operate, and even whether it is clean or dirty, noisy or quiet, depends to a large extent on how it is designed and how it is incorporated into the workplace, with its social relations and routines. Designers and managers tend to have certain assumptions and strategies concerning technology and the kinds of workers who will work with it. Technology is not merely a technical matter.

It can be designed to facilitate control over workers or in a way that enhances their autonomy. Which strategy is uppermost is likely to be influenced by the kind of firm – whether it relies upon workers' creativity, as in, say, a firm designing computer games, or on driving down costs in producing a standard service, as in a telephone sales company where workers' calls are monitored.

The interplay between technology and power can be seen in the transformation of newspaper production by information technology (Cockburn 1983). The old method of linotype production involved workers called compositors – invariably men – sitting at typesetting machines which had large keyboards (not organized in the usual QWERTY layout used for typewriters and word processors) with about 90 characters. Punching a key would release a tiny mould of the required letter. Streams of these letters were set into blocks and molten metal was poured into the moulds to form lines of text, which, when cooled, could be assembled into columns and, later, whole page blocks ready for use in printing. The work was skilled but dirty, noisy and pressured and had a masculine character about it. Production of newspapers has of course to be done in an extremely short time and to an immovable deadline. Since getting the newspapers out depended on these linotype operators they and their trade union had a great deal of power, and were relatively highly paid.

Fundamental changes in technology are often accompanied by a change in the workforce, but in the case of the London newspaper compositors, such was the strength of their union, that the employers were obliged to retain and retrain workers who wanted to stay. However, the changeover in technology was still used as an opportunity for changing the social relations within the workplace, in particular for attacking the power of the compositors. The new technology was very different, allowing typesetting of both articles and whole pages at a computer with a QWERTY layout, and bypassing most of the old compositing jobs. Control over the keyboards was a crucial issue in the conflicts, which included an 11-month-long battle between the print unions and Times Newspapers in 1978–9. Those who underwent retraining found it both difficult and frustrating to have to become beginners again. The net effect was deskilling. For example, where previously they had been responsible for maintaining their machines they were now using a technology which either did not need maintaining or required electronic expertise they did not have. Interestingly, it would have been technically possible to retain the old keyboard layout in the new technology, but that would have had less effect in reducing the power of the old compositors than a QWERTY layout, which enabled the use of relatively cheap female typists. Cockburn argues that the creation of a more 'feminine' technology and atmosphere was used deliberately to weaken the compositors' power.

Managerial strategies and control at work

Managerial strategies are ways of getting employees to spend their working hours in a fashion that advances the economic goals of the management. Given that much work is unpleasant, management has a problem of motivating workers to complete their allotted tasks quickly and effectively. Care and effort on the part of workers are not guaranteed merely by their presence at work. A major source of industrial conflict is the so-called effort bargain, the negotiable definition of what constitutes a 'fair day's work'. Management has two, intertwined, resources at its command – payment and authority.

Management's control is based ultimately on the threat to stop paying ineffective workers; that is, if the worker's effort falls beneath a certain acceptable minimum, he or she can be sacked. There are, however, more subtle ways in which payment can be used to generate effort. Payment by piece-rates, for example, whereby a worker gets a certain amount for each article completed, means that wages are directly related to work effort. The productivity deal is the equivalent system in workplaces where, since no individual completes any particular product, collective incentives are provided to encourage high output. Performance-related pay is a similar way of obtaining output and quality targets. Finally, the possibility of promotion onto higher pay scales is an incentive to workers to work hard and effectively.

The other main managerial resource is authority, which is exercised in association with payment. By and large, workers accept that management has some right to instruct them what to do. The presence of managers and supervisors watching over workers is thus regarded as legitimate. At the same time, though, in practice that authority is frequently resented and challenged or ignored by workers. The concept of managerial strategy refers to the various ways of exercising authority at work, of making managerial control effective in the face of resistance, and of encouraging workers to be co-operative, efficient and adaptable. A considerable number of strategies have been identified. Here we will consider four pure (or ideal) types of strategy – those based on direct control, technical control, bureaucratic control and responsible autonomy. We will then consider methods of culture management.

Direct control

The employer or manager in small establishments, and the supervisor in larger enterprises, may watch over the worker, threatening to stop part of the worker's payment, or dismiss the worker, if he or she is not working sufficiently quickly or accurately. This is a method of direct control, sometimes called 'simple control' because it is the most basic way to ensure effort. Not surprisingly, such a method tends to cause considerable resentment on the part of the workers. This strategy is probably less used than it once was, though it still characterizes small firms and firms where workers are poorly organized. It is less effective in large establishments, partly because workers organize collectively to resist the authority of supervisors, and partly because supervisors and lower-level managers are not necessarily as enthusiastic about disciplining workers as an owner might be. Many occupational groups succeed in regulating their own work effort by taming supervisors.

Technical control

Here the rate of work is determined directly by the technology. Management chooses the machinery, the speed at which it operates and the range of tasks to be done by each worker, so that the latter has no discretion over how to go about his or her work. Technical control is associated with scientific management and Taylorism. The Taylorist strategy of breaking the labour process down into the smallest possible operations and designing them so each can be completed in the fastest way possible is aided by time-and-motion studies. The classic setting for this strategy is the assembly line, where each individual's tasks are few, discretion is absent, and the speed of work is determined by the line itself. The attraction for management of technical control is great. Partly, it defuses interpersonal conflict between supervisor and worker because the process is technical and impersonal. Partly, it makes output fast and predictable. But technical control also generates worker resistance. Since such methods are generally only applicable in large enterprises, lots of workers, equally bored, are likely to be gathered together. Such workers are relatively easy to organize in unions and are likely to refuse to co-operate willingly with management. The kinds of resistance offered in such situations vary from 'soldiering', that is working slowly when the work study expert comes to assess the rate for individual tasks, to active sabotage. Managerial control is often strongly contested in such situations.

Bureaucratic control

This is the staple form of control in the civil service, though it is now common in advanced sectors of industry, especially among large corporations. Basically, as we saw in section 3.4, the worker's approach to the job is governed by formal rules and policed by a minutely differentiated hierarchy of authority. From one angle this hinders solidarity among workers: resentment is dispersed as each rank complains about its immediate superiors and co-workers rather than about the organization as a whole. Furthermore, because it is hierarchical, a bureaucracy offers promotion prospects. Promotion is used as a reward for obedience and loyalty, thus suppressing resistance. This strategy is used to control workers in many institutions through the operation of internal labour markets. Companies recruit new workers from outside at only a very few levels and always promote workers from inside the company. Thus a worker's future depends upon a satisfactory performance within that company, which may make her or him reluctant to oppose management. Work in a modern bank is a good example of bureaucratic control. The cashier does a fairly wide range of tasks – dealing with customers, checking records, exchanging money – but has little discretion in the design of work and, being at the bottom of the hierarchy, has no authority. Wherever cashiers are confronted with tasks falling outside their specified sphere of responsibility they have to pass them on to their superiors.

Responsible autonomy

Under this mode of control, the worker is given a much greater degree of discretion and is less subject to supervisory authority. The classic cases are craft workers – skilled engineers, technicians, software designers – or professionals such as teachers. These workers are typically left to design and organize their own working time, largely because they have more knowledge than management about the work itself. Not surprisingly, this mode of control is most common in complex kinds of work which do not lend themselves to deskilling and programming. The workers generally have lengthy apprenticeships – formal or informal – during which they build up a knowledge of tools, techniques and cases, and apply that knowledge and experience in their work. This sometimes raises problems of control for management, since the quality of work and the effort expended lie largely in the hands of the workers themselves. This may often not matter, since such workers frequently develop a kind of self-policing system whereby standards of work are collectively guaranteed. Besides, they usually derive satisfaction from their work and hence are motivated to do a good job. Nevertheless there may still be problems in that workers and management may differ in their view of what constitutes good work; this is especially common where people-work is involved. One response of management to this situation is to regulate such work through monitoring of results (often facilitated by information technology) and gearing of pay to performance indicators. Nevertheless, management may have to pay relatively high wages as part of the bargain to persuade such workers to be 'responsible'. This approach differs radically from Taylorism, which sought to wrest control from skilled workers by breaking their work down into simple operations, and automating where possible; but for many kinds of work, deskilling may be counterproductive.

Trends and tendencies

Towards human resource management?

One of the enduring questions of industrial sociology is why people work so hard, even when they are not under surveillance. It needs to be remembered that workers often gain self-respect through their work, and want to appear competent in the eyes of their peers if not their superiors. Those whose work brings them directly into contact with the public may feel under additional pressure to maintain 'face' through being efficient and competent. They may also feel that the client's or customer's needs are legitimate and want to meet them. Recently, sophisticated strategies of human resource management have attempted to develop this sense of pride in work and competitiveness among workers through combinations of exhortation and individual rewards, encouraging workers to identify with their firm and product. While this includes responsible autonomy strategies, it goes beyond them by attempting to influence workers' attitudes to work and the informal norms of the workplace. One of the main conditions for firms to be successful and adaptable is effective communications between individuals, horizontal as well as vertical, both within companies and with their suppliers and customers. Consequently companies are increasingly emphasizing communication skills in their employee recruitment and training programmes. These strategies have been tried out mainly in leading large firms and on their higher-level employees, including managers themselves. Among manual workers, direct control tends to have increased (Gallie et al. 1998). It is not yet clear how successful these management methods are in producing results, though it is probable that workers may comply with them in their

Greeting the customer	Yes	No
1. There is a smile.		
2. It is a sincere greeting.		
3. There is eye contact.		
Other:		

Taking the order	Yes	No
1. The counter person is thoroughly familiar with the menu ticket. (No hunting for items.)		
2. The customer has to give the order only once.		
3. Small orders (four items or less) are memorized rather than written down.		
4. There is suggestive selling.		
Other:		

Assembling the order	Yes	No
1. The order is assembled in the proper sequence.		
2. Grill slips are handed in first.		
3. Drinks are poured in the proper sequence.		
4. Proper amount of ice.		
5. Cups slanted and finger used to activate.		
6. Drinks are filled to the proper level.		
7. Drinks are capped.		
8. Clean cups.		
9. Holding times are observed on coffee.		
10. Cups are filled to the proper level on coffee.		
Other:		

Presenting the order	Yes	No
1. It is properly packaged.		
2. The bag is double folded.		
3. Plastic trays are used if eating inside.		
4. A tray liner is used.		
5. The food is handled in a proper manner.		
Other:		

Asking for & receiving payment	Yes	No
1. The amount of the order is stated clearly and loud enough to hear.		
2. The denomination received is clearly stated.		
3. The change is counted out loud.		
4. Change is counted efficiently.		
5. Large bills are laid on the till until the change is given.		
Other:		

Thanking the customer & asking for repeat business	Yes	No
1. There is always a thank you.		
2. The thank you is sincere.		
3. There is eye contact.		
4. Return business was asked for.		

Figure 4.1 Management observation checklist used to evaluate the performance of counter staff in a fast-food restaurant
Source: Morgan 1986, p. 21

behaviour while being privately sceptical about their rationale (P. Thompson and Findlay 1999).

As an illustration of the way in which different management methods can be combined, in this case direct control and an emphasis on communication skills, figure 4.1 is a copy of a management checklist used for evaluating the performance of counter staff in a fast-food restaurant. It demonstrates how a labour process involving communication can be highly scripted and rationalized and subjected to direct control.

Towards flexibility?

Flexibility has been one of the most popular buzzwords of the last two decades, both as a description of new kinds of economic organization and as a prescription – from politicians and business people – for how things should change. The pursuit of flexibility has been encouraged by the difficult and uncertain economic environment of the last three decades of the twentieth century. In the face of uncertainty firms have sought ways of becoming 'leaner' and more flexible, so that they can cope with downturns in demand. A general tendency for increased flexibility has been claimed in several aspects of production: in technology and products, jobs and employment.

Technology and products   The most radical technological innovations of the last thirty years of the twentieth century have been in computerized information handling or information technology. Consequently huge volumes of complex data can be retrieved and manipulated rapidly, accurately and cheaply. Businesses have not only been able to reduce the amount of labour needed for handling information but can cope with larger amounts of more complex information. Information technology has produced both major time economies and increases in flexibility. A simple and familiar example can be seen at the supermarket checkout, where price and product descriptions are read by bar codes (thereby deskilling the cashier's job) and the customer is given an itemized bill. This is part of a point-of-sale system which gives continuous feedback to management on the rate of depletion of stocks of each of thousands of products, and can even automatically reorder them from company warehouses and suppliers. This also allows the rationalization of stocks so that no excess space is taken up by slow-selling items.

Information technology has also affected manufacturing, by enabling computer-aided design and by improving co-ordination of tasks and flexibility. Programmable machines allow production to be switched quickly between different product specifications. They reduce the need to produce in large volumes to get economies of scale, and make small batch production more efficient than hitherto, thereby allowing a more differentiated range of products. The increased number of variants of each model of car, in terms of colour schemes and options like gearboxes and sunroofs, is a good example. However, this increased technological flexibility should not be exaggerated. Most machines can still only perform a limited series of operations, resulting in a greater number of variants of particular products rather than a range of radically different products. Machines can change within a limited, programmed range with great speed and accuracy, but people are more flexible; they can change more radically, albeit more slowly, in response to unanticipated situations.

Jobs and employment Flexibility here takes two main forms – functional and numerical. 'Functional flexibility' refers to the ability of workers to perform a variety of tasks, switching between them as necessary. In British manufacturing before the 1980s it was common for there to be narrowly specified job descriptions and for each job to have its own pay scale. Demarcation rules prevented one worker doing another worker's job, and often different trade unions would defend different jobs in the same workplace. These inflexible working practices have since been eroded, most dramatically by non-unionized firms or by firms operating with a single union in order to avoid divisions within the workforce. By abolishing restrictive job descriptions and putting different workers on the same pay scale, it has become possible to increase functional flexibility. For example, many manufacturing firms which used to have dozens of different job categories in production work, each with its own pay and conditions, have now simplified them to two or three categories. This also allows time economies, because when work stops in one area workers can be moved onto other tasks instead of waiting for the work to restart. Again, the increase in flexibility should not be exaggerated; functional flexibility is clearly limited by the skills of the worker, and in practice the 'multi-skilled' worker is usually doing a range of tasks involving a fairly low level of skills and is only allowed a limited increase in discretion. It is therefore only a partial shift away from Taylorism towards responsible autonomy.

Numerical flexibility involves adjusting the number of workers to the volume of work required at any point in time. It can be achieved by restricting the number of permanent workers to those who can be fully occupied throughout the year, and by either hiring temporary workers (often part-timers) for shorter periods when needed, as demand fluctuates, or subcontracting out activities for which there is insufficient demand on a permanent basis. It may be cheaper, for example, to contract out maintenance, cleaning and catering work than to provide these in-house. On the whole the subcontractors and suppliers tend to be relatively small firms. Some of the services may be supplied by workers who have become self-employed and have to seek business from many firms instead of being employed by one. Firms therefore often develop networks of suppliers and subcontractors on which they can draw at short notice. This allows major firms to use small suppliers as shock absorbers when the market fluctuates, so that job security in the latter is often low.

Note how increasing flexibility can mean greater insecurity. While the pursuit of flexibility is arguably a response to economic uncertainty, it also inadvertently leads to greater insecurity and uncertainty for many. Information technology can allow much faster response times to changing economic situations and hence allow resources to be switched rapidly – or flexibly – among alternatives. The clearest example is in financial services, where money can now be switched around the world in fractions of a second as opportunities change. By reducing inertia, insecurity is increased.

Eighteen per cent of male and 25 per cent of female workers have flexible working patterns. Clerical and secretarial occupations – highly feminized jobs – make most use of flexible working hours. Among part-time workers – again overwhelmingly women – term-time working is the most common form of flexible working, involving 10 per cent of the UK's part-time female workforce (*Social Trends* 1998). Formally, in terms of employment security, part-time work is considerably less secure than full-time work. Nevertheless, in practice, many part-time jobs have remained secure, perhaps because many of them are located in the public sector, where conditions are more stable (Gallie et al. 1998).

Towards post-Fordism

There have been many attempts to sum up recent changes in the organization of the formal economy. One of the most popular has been the idea of a shift from Fordist to post-Fordist labour processes (see table 4.3). The former are based on mass production of standardized products within highly hierarchical firms. The labour processes are characterized by Taylorist direct control, and the deskilled workers come to share a common proletarian condition.

| TABLE 4.3 | Ideal types of production system |

	Fordist	Post-Fordist
Technology	Fixed, dedicated machines	Micro-electronically controlled multi-purpose machines
Product	For a mass consumer market Relatively cheap	Diverse specialized products High quality
Labour process	Fragmented Few tasks Little discretion Hierarchical authority and technical control	Many tasks for versatile workers Some autonomy Group control
Contracts	Collectively negotiated rate for the job Relatively secure	Payment by individual performance Dual market: secure core, highly insecure periphery

Source: Warde 1989, p. 12

Post-Fordism offers a different prospect. To some extent it entails upskilling and an increase in the autonomy and discretion of workers, especially core or permanent workers. Flexible organization and working practices entail the abandonment of technical control. Post-Fordism is associated with an alleged contraction of mass production and, some authors suggest, a significant change in patterns of consumption as new products, designed to suit special tastes or needs, are made available. It also signifies the end of secure full-time employment for a substantial proportion of the labour force.

This account is increasingly recognized as seriously inadequate, if not misleading. Mass-production labour processes never accounted for more than a minority of workers, though the pursuit of economies of scale and standardized products were seen as the best route to efficiency by many firms not involved in mass-production. Mass production continues, although on a more automated and flexible basis, and much of it has shifted to countries like Japan and Korea. Witness the continued success of mass-produced goods like VCRs, CD players, and of course cars. Small-batch and customized production has been common throughout the history of capitalism, in large firms as well as small.

Conditions of employment have altered since the late 1970s, with some increase in functional flexibility and many more insecure jobs. Employment figures show a decline in unskilled manual work and an increase in white-collar occupations. Subcontracting has increased somewhat. There has also been a considerable increase in the number of small businesses and self-employment. However, these changes may have causes other than attempts by firms to develop flexible accumulation. Temporary contracts are more prevalent in the public sector than in the private sector, contrary to the logic of competitiveness invoked by many accounts of flexibility. This suggests that changes in employment conditions may have more to do with state policy than capitalist reorganization. Indeed, it might be proposed that, in Britain at least, what we have seen since the late 1970s is a consequence less of advanced technology and new products than of a change in the balance of power between employers and unions. Declining union membership, the loss of legal immunities, unemployment and fewer jobs in traditional manufacturing sectors with high union density have swung the balance of industrial power significantly in favour of employers (see section 4.1).

Summary

1   Different jobs give different rewards and satisfactions. Those offering variety and allowing the worker discretion over how to carry out tasks tend to give most satisfaction.
2   Contrary to the expectations of Braverman, deskilling has been limited, and in recent times there are signs of a modest upskilling of work.
3   While technology is an important influence on work and changes therein, the way it is designed and deployed reflects power relations between management and workers.
4   The experience of work is strongly affected by the nature of the job and the kinds of control that management can exercise over it. Direct control, technical control, bureaucratic control and responsible autonomy are major types of managerial strategy. The ones that are dominant in any situation depends heavily on the kind of work involved.
5   During the 1990s, management in larger, leading firms has tried to influence the way managers and higher-level workers identify with their work and their firm in order to improve motivation, and has placed increasing emphasis on communication skills. As yet, there is little clear evidence of the results of such initiatives.
6   Flexibility – both functional and numerical – has become more common, but may owe more to the changing balance of power between management and workers than to a new way of organizing production.

4.3   Trade unions and industrial relations

Trade unions are the most important and visible organizations for the protection of employees' interests in the workplace. The study of industrial relations is primarily devoted to the relationship between unions and management. Current academic debate in this area revolves around evaluating the significance of changes since the 1970s, when the union movement had considerable industrial and political impact.

Trade unions are well-established voluntary associations which still have a vast membership: 7.9 million in 1996, or 30 per cent of employees. However, the comparable figures for 1979, the point of greatest strength, were 13 million and 55 per cent. They are organizations which support and protect their members against powerful adversaries, employers. This inevitably involves them in a degree of conflict with management. There is a general conflict of interests between employer and employee concerning both control at work and payment. At the same time, however, that conflict is usually covert and limited. Mostly, in practice, unions seek not to undermine employers so much as to secure, within the existing framework, a 'fair' deal for the members – a customary and adequate wage, some security and some dignity.

Arising from the inequality of power between management and workers, industrial relations are always ones of potential conflict. As Fox (1974) described it, industrial relations are relations of 'low trust'. Bargaining and negotiation are the normal forms that the relationship takes. Worker representatives negotiate with management about the so-called effort bargain. Occasionally negotiation breaks down and open conflict emerges. Strikes and lockouts are the most publicized forms of conflict, but there are other forms of industrial action by means of which workers collectively resist managerial authority. Overtime bans and working to rule are common forms of industrial action.

There are considerable costs for both sides in engaging in sustained open conflict. Management generally seeks a co-operative workforce, for strikes, work limitation, sabotage and the like reduce the productivity and income of the enterprise. Management therefore tends to seek to reduce the arena of mutual conflict. This may be achieved in a number of ways: refusing to recognize trade unions at all; persuading employees that there are no grounds for hostility and that their interests are compatible with management's; and establishing procedures for negotiations over issues which cause grievance to workers. Trade unions usually have no wish to escalate conflict either. Unions exist primarily to protect the economic interests of their members by securing satisfactory conditions for workers within a firm or industry. They are thus concerned with the exchange bargain, under which workers sell their labour power: pay, hours, security of employment and safety at work are their immediate concerns.

Unions, politics and the law

Political parties and governments have a stake in industrial relations because the balance of power between employers and workers is a pivot of British political life. Trade unions are connected to the Labour Party, through direct affiliation of members and indirectly through the Trades Union Congress (TUC). Employers individually, and through their collective organizations like the Confederation of British Industry (CBI), are closely identified with the Conservative Party. Because this political alignment exists, economic policy and the laws concerning industrial relations alter with changes of government.

Conservative governments between 1979 and 1997 attempted to alter the balance of political and industrial power in favour of capital and employers. Three means were used: reducing the national political influence of unions; introducing legislation to diminish the operational effectiveness of unions in workplace disputes; and exerting much tighter discipline over its own state employees.

The unions played a prominent and direct role in national politics in the 1960s and 1970s. The TUC was widely involved in routine consultation about economic and social policy and was for a time responsible for delivering wage restraint in exchange. Moreover, individual unions had used industrial action in order to influence government policy. TUC involvement was severely curtailed by the Conservative governments. On the national political stage, the union movement was rarely consulted.

Second, various pieces of legislation regarding the organization and activities of unions reduced their operational effectiveness. Eight major Acts of Parliament were passed between 1980 and 1993, all seeking to restrain union power. These outlawed the closed shop, curbed picketing, narrowed the definition of a lawful trade dispute, made all secondary industrial action illegal, imposed the use of secret and postal ballots in most aspects of union decision-making, abolished restrictions which protected weaker employees and rendered unions liable to be sued for a wide range of unlawful activities. These measures made recruitment and the conduct of disputes more difficult.

The government's third line of attack on union power was to exert influence over decisions made by public agencies. Since the public sector was highly unionized, intervention in the levels and processes of pay settlements was a means of directly confronting unions. In addition, the privatization of nationalized industries, the closure of parts of others, such as coal mines, and the restructuring of welfare services like the NHS all impacted on unions. Industrial relations in the public sector became increasingly adversarial as unions reacted against government policies. The bitter, year-long, miners' strike of 1984–5 (see plate 4.2) demonstrated that unions were unable to match through industrial action the concerted power of the state: a resolute government had limitless resources for sitting out the conflict and was able, also, to deploy considerable physical force through the policing of the dispute. The public sector was the scene of most of the industrial conflict in the 1980s, but the defeat of the miners was especially symbolic. Government encouraged the reassertion of managerial prerogatives in the public sector generally. Wages continued to decline relative to the private sector, and by the early 1990s government was imposing wage controls on state employees. Nevertheless, union density in the public sector declined little and bargaining procedures remained broadly intact.

At the beginning of the 1980s, many opinion polls recorded a widespread conviction that trade unions had too much power. By the end of the decade this belief was much less commonly held, since when trade unions have received more popular approval than at any time since the 1950s. This suggests that people thought that the government had been successful, even perhaps overzealous, in its policies.

Scarcely anyone denies that the trade union movement is now significantly weaker than it was in the 1970s. The legal status and political influence of unions are much reduced, with little likelihood of the Labour government elected in 1997 reversing the trend. Indeed, the most likely legislative support for unions comes from the European Union. This was not, however, simply the effect of state legislative measures. For much of the time since then *economic conditions* – particularly high unemployment and industrial restructuring – were so unfavourable to employees that, even if the new legislation had been completely ineffective, unions would still have been in a weakened position.

Plate 4.2 | Police confronting miners during the strike of 1984–5
Source: Network

For these are circumstances which reduce the size of union membership, a second indicator of union decline.

Trade union organization and membership

There were, by 1996, 245 trade unions in Britain, representing 7.9 million members. Mergers have resulted in unions being fewer than before: in 1960 there were 650 unions; by 1980, 438. The largest nine unions in 1997 represented two-thirds of all union members. The largest was UNISON, with 1.4 million members. Among the largest ten were several that recruit primarily non-manual workers, including two representing schoolteachers, the Royal College of Nursing and the Manufacturing, Science and Finance Union.

The size of trade union membership is one measure of strength. In 1979, 53 per cent of the working population were members of a trade union or a staff association. That figure, referred to as union density (i.e. the proportion of people eligible for membership who actually join), was higher than at any time in British history. Union membership increased slowly between 1954 and 1969, whilst density remained constant at a little above 40 per cent. In the next decade, 1969–79, membership and density grew significantly. Since 1979 there has been an annual fall in membership. In 1979 there were about 12 million employee members in Great Britain. By 1987 the number had fallen to just over 9 million, about the same number as in 1969. By 1996 membership was lower than at any time since 1945.

Explanation of the varying volume and density of union membership may be considered from two points of view. First, why in general do people join unions? Second, what factors operate to produce variations in membership for different groups of workers?

Why join trade unions?

People join unions primarily because collective action is the most effective way for workers to defend and promote their occupational interests. Unions try to modify and regulate the conditions under which labour is sold by using their collective organizational strength to offset the power of employers. Individual workers have few effective sanctions at their disposal: when faced by an employer, a worker alone cannot prevent wages falling, insist on improving working conditions, or protect jobs during an economic recession. The market situation of most occupational groups depends upon collective solidarity.

Strength of numbers is important, since the larger the organization of workers, the more difficult it is for employers to replace the labour force. Unions are generally weak in small firms because, unless the workers are very highly skilled, the replacement of a handful of them is relatively easy. Unionization is effective in the sense that better-paid employees are generally well organized. Organization does not guarantee high rewards, but is an important contributory factor. McIlroy (1995, p. 1) notes that 'the average wage premium for members over non-members is around 10 per cent.' Unions also help to maintain workers' control over the labour process, and offer legal and political representation and social benefits.

What affects trade union membership?

If it benefits workers to be union members, it might be asked why there are many occupations with very low levels of unionization and why there has been a steady decline in membership. There are several factors which affect levels of membership besides government policy, which we look at briefly in turn, including:

- the general economic environment;
- the size, ownership and economic position of the employing establishment;
- the typical social characteristics of the labour force;
- employers' attitudes to unionization;
- union bargaining and recruitment policies.

Unions tend to decline in size in periods of high unemployment and when real wages are increasing. Both conditions were true of the 1980s. However, during the recession at the end of the 1980s membership continued to fall, suggesting that other factors were also operating. Changes in labour contracts associated with greater flexibility might be one such additional factor (see section 4.2).

The size of an enterprise is important. Small firms are weakly unionized; large, bureaucratically organized firms, especially those with centralized personnel management, can scarcely function in the absence of unions, which transmit grievances and bargain on behalf of employees. This size-cum-organization effect is one reason why state-owned industry, where most employment is in large organizations with centralized management and centralized bargaining procedures, has higher levels of unionization. Union density is over 60 per cent in the public sector, but only 20 per cent in the private sector (see Cully and Woodland 1998). Large firms in the private manufacturing sector are, however, also subject to the same pressure of size. In private services, by contrast, firms are smaller, and densities in hotel and catering and the distribution sectors are very low (8 per cent in 1997). This is in part because such firms operate in a competitive environment where wages comprise a substantial proportion of costs. Since the 1980s, industrial structure has changed in such a way that establishments where high levels of unionization were normal (private manufacturing and public agencies) have become less prevalent. Workplaces have tended to become smaller. More important, employment contracted most sharply in traditional manufacturing industry and public bodies after 1979, which meant that jobs in enterprises with high levels of unionization disappeared fastest. For example, the National Union of Mineworkers had 250,000 members in 1979 but only 8,000 in 1993. A larger proportion of remaining jobs was in privately owned firms in the service sector of the economy.

The composition of the labour force is a third important factor. Full-time workers are more likely to be members than part-time, and associatedly, as figure 4.2 shows, men are slightly more likely to be members than women. About 32 per cent of male employees, compared with 28 per cent of women, were members in 1997. This is not because men and women behave very differently when in the same industrial situations. Women in full-time employment are as likely as their male counterparts to be union members. Part-time workers, the vast majority of whom are women, are less well unionized. Ethnic minorities are unionized to the same extent as the white population. Though different in the past, the same proportion of all members is in white-collar as in manual occupations. The best unionized now are professional and semi-professional workers, with skilled manual workers next. As figure 4.2 also confirms, membership has declined in all the different circumstances.

Employer recognition of a union for the purposes of collective bargaining is the primary precondition for attracting and retaining members. Some employers are more ready to offer recognition than others. During the 1960s and 1970s state industries positively encouraged unionization, and their membership remains very high. In private services, by contrast, employers are more reluctant to recognize unions. During the 1980s very few employers actually withdrew recognition from unions, but new firms, particularly in the early 1980s, proved very hesitant to grant recognition to any union. Employers, sensing government encouragement and a new balance of power in industry, avoided making agreements with unions. Simultaneously, other establishments sought to use new human relations management techniques, which they imagined might circumvent the need for union representation by fostering the co-operation and commitment of individual employees.

Trade unions as organizations thus faced a range of adverse structural circumstances in the 1980s and 1990s. In response, they revised their recruitment strategies, devoting effort to trying to attract new people in expanding job areas, including women in part-

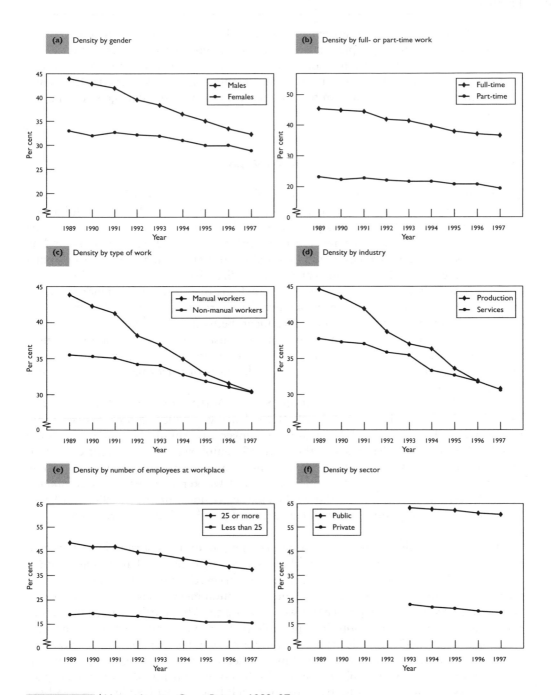

Figure 4.2 Union density, Great Britain, 1989–97
Source: Cully and Woodland 1998, p. 356

time work. As yet, the union movement has not halted the decline. There is a constant turnover of members, as people leave jobs and move workplaces: for example, 25 per cent of members of USDAW, the shopworkers' union, are new every year. Such unions thus need to recruit heavily even to maintain membership levels. Nevertheless, some unions (in the public sector and in telecommunications in particular) grew during the 1980s.

Workplace bargaining

The main function of unions is to bargain about wages and conditions. Bargaining occurs at national, company and plant levels in Britain. National bargaining had replaced local and workshop bargaining between 1920 and 1970, both increasing the sense of solidarity of union members (because the outcome of a wage claim is binding for workers in London, Lancaster and Llandudno) and preventing employers deserting high-wage regions for lower-wage regions. Centralized bargaining became almost universal in state administration and services. However, one of the main trends since the late 1970s has been the re-emergence of workplace bargaining in manufacturing industry, especially in private firms. Localized agreements between management and workforce, concerning productivity and bonus payments for instance, have become increasingly prominent. So too have arrangements which bypass unions altogether, where wages and salaries are negotiated individually or on the basis of performance, or simply not negotiated at all.

A large Workplace Industrial Relations Survey (WIRS), the third of its kind, was carried out in 1990 (Millward et al. 1992). Evidence was collected for just over 2,000 workplaces, all of which had 25 or more employees. (It should be noted that union membership is much greater where there are 25+ employees – 38 per cent compared with 16 per cent in 1997: see figure 4.2.) Senior management, mostly from personnel departments, completed 2,550 questionnaires and worker representatives completed 1,466. Questions were similar to those asked in the previous surveys of 1980 and 1984. Together these surveys offer systematic evidence of trends in industrial relations over a decade.

The 1990 study throws further light on declining union membership by reporting a significant fall in the proportion of workers covered by collective bargaining arrangements. In 1990, 36 per cent of all the workplaces surveyed contained not a single union member. The proportion of employees who were union members in all the workplaces surveyed fell from 58 to 48 per cent between 1984 and 1990, partly spurred by legislation to abolish the **closed shop**. It is possible to be a union member employed in a workplace where one's union is not recognized for bargaining purposes; and, conversely, it is possible for a worker to be covered by a collective bargaining agreement without being a union member. As table 4.4 shows, in the establishments surveyed the proportion of workers covered by collective bargaining fell from 71 per cent in 1984 to 54 per cent in 1990. Decline in the public sector was almost entirely due to the withdrawal of bargaining rights for schoolteachers. Union density in private manufacturing declined in particular sectors in engineering (especially among small firms) because industry-wide bargaining involving many employers ceased in 1989. Low union recognition was most characteristic of firms in the private services sector.

TABLE 4.4 | Proportion of employees covered by collective bargaining, 1984 and 1990 (percentages)

Sector	All establishments		Establishments with any recognized unions	
	1984	1990	1984	1990
All establishments	71	54	89	80
Sector				
Private manufacturing	64	51	82	76
Private services	41	33	82	78
Public sector	95	78	96	84
Union density, all sectors				
None	1	–	–	–
1–24%	30	15	52	29
25–49%	63	54	67	62
50–74%	87	75	88	80
75–89%	92	84	93	87
90–99%	97	91	97	93
100%	98	94	99	99
Base: all establishments				
Union density, private sector only				
None	–	–	–	–
1–24%	27	12	51	27
25–49%	58	47	64	55
50–74%	80	77	82	80
75–89%	86	84	88	88
90–99%	94	94	95	94
100%	93	(100)	97	(100)
Base: all private-sector establishments				

Source: Millward et al. 1992, p. 94

WIRS (Millward et al. 1992) confirmed that the presence of trade unions improves relatively both pay and working conditions. Table 4.5 indicates the factors affecting the incidence of an employer paying very low wages (less than £3.28 per hour in 1990). The more employees covered by union recognition, the fewer there were who were badly paid. The table also shows that the smaller the firm, and the more part-time and women workers in the workforce, the more prevalent is low pay. Influences considered relevant to determining the last pay settlement by personnel managers are shown in table 4.6. A cost-of-living calculation is the most important factor in all establishments. However, differences are apparent between the public and private sectors and between unionized and non-unionized firms. In the public sector, limits imposed by higher authority (i.e. primarily the government) are particularly germane, whereas economic performance is considered more relevant in the private sector. Within the private sector, non-unionized firms reward people much more widely on the basis of individual performance. The extent to which this makes possible the exercise of arbitrary managerial power is indicated by Millward et al.'s (1992) summary of the characteristics of 'union-free' workplaces in 1990 (see box 4.2).

TABLE 4.5 | **Proportion of establishments in the private sector with any lower-paid employees, 1990**

Establishment	Any lower-paid employees (%)	Unweighted base	Weighted base
All private sector	27	1346	1306
Manufacturing	22	618	418
Services	29	728	888
Number of employees at establishment			
25–99	28	473	1021
100–499	25	501	261
500–999	10	169	17
1,000 or more	15	203	7
Percentage of workforce part-time			
41 or more	49	165	191
6–40	32	338	447
0–5	17	832	662
Percentage of workforce female			
71 or more	46	174	221
31–70	29	453	444
0–30	17	563	561
Ownership			
Independent establishment	30	228	391
Branch of larger organization	26	1019	858
Head office	13	99	57
UK owned	28	1086	1160
Foreign owned	13	214	133
Union representation			
No recognized union	32	576	809
1 or more recognized unions	19	770	497
Coverage where recognized unions			
1–49%	32	122	113
50–79%	26	173	114
80–99%	13	297	142
100%	9	178	129
Number of competitors			
None	27	113	76
1–5	22	376	347
More than 5	31	590	702
Capacity utilization			
Full	26	465	414
Somewhat below full	27	434	339
Considerably below full	24	64	54

Base: private-sector establishments reporting typical pay and hours for at least one of five occupational groups

Source: Millward et al. 1992, p. 244

| TABLE 4.6 | Factors influencing the size of the most recent pay settlement according to managers, 1990 (percentages) |

	Manual employees			Non-manual employees		
	Private sector		Public sector	Private sector		Public sector
		Non-			Non-	
Factor	Union[a]	union[b]		Union[a]	union[b]	
Cost of living	56	47	50	57	47	44
Labour market	29	39	13	40	30	25
Recruitment, retention	6	11	1	6	8	9
Economic performance	36	36	12	38	35	9
Economic performance, ability to pay	32	34	7	34	34	5
Productivity increases	5	3	5	6	2	4
Linked to other settlement	15	14	13	8	12	13
Other influences	13	29	32	17	39	41
Limits set by higher authority	3	1	15	5	2	15
Individual performance	2	23	4	4	32	4
Strike threat, union bargaining power	2	–	6	2	1	13
Not stated	6	4	16	11	4	10
Base: establishments with employees named in column heads where most recent pay settlement determined at establishment or higher in the organization						
Unweighted	701	511	433	507	859	565
Weighted	403	708	345	260	1075	464

[a] Establishments with recognized unions for employees named in column heads
[b] Establishments with no recognized union for employees named in column heads
Source: Millward et al. 1992, p. 238

Generally, workplace procedures themselves did not change radically during the 1980s. Where collective bargaining arrangements were already established, little altered, though there is evidence that discipline is becoming more strict and employees are working harder. Rather, the main change was the declining coverage of employees by collective bargaining agreements. For these, an increasing proportion of workers in the private sector, employment conditions were often inferior and more precarious than for the rest.

Industrial conflict

The strike is the ultimate sanction available to a union in a dispute with an employer; the possibility of workers collectively withdrawing their labour is fundamental if unions are to have any influence over the behaviour of employers. But resistance may take many forms. High rates of absenteeism and lack of effort, for example, both present themselves as problems for management, and thus may be used by workers as ploys in negotiation. Especially in establishments where unions are not recognized, these may be the only possible ways of registering dissatisfaction. However, such

---

Box 4.2   The characteristics of 'union-free' workplaces compared with unionized, private-sector establishments

Without the constraint of union negotiations, pay levels were set unilaterally by management, generally managers at the workplace. In a minority of cases management at head office or some other level in the enterprise took responsibility for setting levels of pay for a group of workplaces. Only in rare cases was pay set by statutory minima. However, managements in around a fifth of non-union workplaces claimed to consult employees or their representatives about pay increases. Labour market and commercial and financial considerations dominated managements' thinking on the size of pay settlements to a much greater degree than in the unionized sector. Pay was more a matter of individual performance, with formal job evaluation being rare. Again reflecting the lack of union influence, differentials between the highest and lowest earners in non-union workplaces tended to be relatively wide. Lower-paid employees were more common.

Managers generally felt unconstrained in the way they organized work. Opposition from employees to changes in working methods was rare, and the lack of skills which managers in unionized workplaces often cited as a problem was also rare. Greater use of freelance and temporary contract workers was another aspect of the greater flexibility of labour in the non-union sector. Workforce reductions were no more common, but they were much more likely to be achieved by compulsory redundancies than by less painful measures such as natural wastage. Dismissals (other than those arising from redundancy) were common, nearly twice as frequent per employee as in the union sector. (Millward et al. 1992, pp. 363–4)

---

practices are much less effective in applying pressure upon management, for although high rates of labour turnover may create difficulties for management – new workers have to be trained, worker morale is likely to be low, etc. – quitting a job is a weak form of 'resistance'.

Industrial action has declined sharply since 1984–5. In 1997 only 235,000 working days were lost, more than a hundred times fewer than in 1984 (see table 4.7). Stoppages were mainly about pay, with the issues of redundancy, staffing and work allocation the other most common causes. About half of all disputes lasted one day or less. Lower levels of action can be accounted for in terms of an uncongenial economic and political environment. Fewer members, working in smaller establishments where conflict has traditionally been minimal, afraid of unemployment in a period when incomes have tended to grow for those in work, are conditions working against militant industrial action.

Summary

---

1   Industrial relations are mostly a matter of routine negotiation and bargaining between trade union representatives and management: industrial conflict in Brit-

TABLE 4.7	Stoppages in progress, 1977–97

Year	Working days lost (000s)	Working days lost per 1,000 employees[a]	Workers involved (000s)	Stoppages	Stoppages involving the loss of 100,000 working days
1977	10,142	448	1,166	2,737	12
1978	9,405	413	1,041	2,498	7
1979	29,474	1,272	4,608	2,125	15
1980	11,964	520	834	1,348	5
1981	4,266	195	1,513	1,344	7
1982	5,313	248	2,103	1,538	7
1983	3,754	178	574	1,364	6
1984	27,135	1,278	1,464	1,221	11
1985	6,402	299	791	903	4
1986	1,920	90	720	1,074	2
1987	3,546	164	887	1,016	3
1988	3,702	166	790	781	8
1989	4,128	182	727	701	6
1990	1,903	83	298	630	3
1991	761	34	176	369	1
1992	528	24	148	253	–
1993	649	30	385	211	2
1994	278	13	107	205	–
1995	415	19	174	235	–
1996	1,303	58	364	244	2
1997	235	10	130	216	–

[a] Based on latest available mid-year (June) estimates of employee jobs
Source: Davies 1998, p. 300

ain is *institutionalized*. Nevertheless, conflict between workers and management is endemic to industrial relations, taking many forms and occurring unevenly in time and across industries.

2   Currently about 30 per cent of all employees are members of a union, density having fallen from a peak of 55 per cent in 1979. People join a union because collective organization is necessary to protect their occupational interests. The rate at which workers join unions is affected by a number of factors including the macro-economic climate, the nature of the workplace, the character of the workforce, employers' attitudes towards unions, government policy and union recruitment strategies.

3   In the 1980s the political influence of trade unions subsided dramatically. Where they still maintained collective bargaining agreements, workplace industrial rela-

tions were little altered. However, unions have experienced a severe and continuous decline in membership and industrial coverage since 1979.

4.4   Professional occupations and associations

Government statistics refer to some occupations as professional. Among the 'higher' professions are included doctors, solicitors, judges, university teachers, architects and top-ranking civil servants. The 'lower' professions include schoolteachers, nurses, librarians, physiotherapists and social workers. Overall, professional work has increased substantially in the second half of the twentieth century (see section 6.4). People in these occupations are relatively privileged. Professionals on average earn more than most other groups of employees. Professional jobs also carry a considerable degree of prestige: people may scorn bureaucrats, trade unionists and shopkeepers, but professionals are rarely considered anything but worthy. Given the financial and status rewards associated with being a 'professional', it is unsurprising that many occupational groups attempt to get themselves recognized as professional. (There are parallels with the strategies of manual workers to have their jobs described as 'skilled'.) Since practising a profession is merely taking part in some of the tasks generated by the complex modern division of labour, the question arises: what is distinctive about these jobs which makes them so well rewarded?

It is impossible to list a set of characteristics which will determine unambiguously whether or not an occupation is a profession. Various sociologists have tried to identify the distinctive 'traits' of a profession, but they have not agreed upon which should be included; nor have such approaches helped in the explanation of professional privileges. This is partly because professions, like other occupations, change over time. This classic model of a profession is an ideal type based on the nature of a few elite occupations in the nineteenth century. The 'classic' model, contrasted with the model of proletarian occupations, is illustrated in box 4.3.

It should be stressed that these are ideal types and that rarely has any occupation had all these characteristics. Moreover, today, very few professionals work under the conditions described in the ideal type. People at the higher levels of legal, medical and architectural occupations approximate most closely to this type: barristers and consultant doctors in private medical practice, for example, are defined in official statistics as 'independent'/'self-employed professionals'.

Occupational control

The basis of professional privilege is power to shape and influence the social organization of work. That power is maintained through collective organization in professional associations. Power derives from high degrees of occupational control – control by practitioners themselves over various aspects of the occupation, including payment, recruitment and working practices.

Consider, for example, doctors. Medical doctors are one of the highest-paid occupational groups in Britain. They derive their income from two sources, salaries paid by the National Health Service (NHS) and fees paid by private patients. Though some doctors

---

Box 4.3   Two ideal types of occupation: proletarian and professional

The following summary is of *ideal types*, that is, artificial constructions of character-istics which do not always occur together in reality. The classic professional model finds its closest approximation in reality among lawyers, doctors and the clergy in the late nineteenth century.

Characteristic	Classic model of a proletarian occupation	Classic model of a (collegiate) profession
System of reward	Wages paid by employer: workers are wage-labourers	Paid fees, by a client in exchange for services; workers are self-employed
Training and education, recruitment	No credentials required and usually very limited training	Higher qualifications (a degree) and special practical training
Content of work	Routine, mindless and fragmented work	Specialized theoretical knowledge: combines conception and execution
Authority relations at work	Subordinate in a hierarchy of authority: no control over work	Self-regulating and self-directing: controls own work
Occupational organization	Organized, if at all, by a trade union which bargains with employers on behalf of members	Organized by professional association, of which membership is compulsory, which regulates entry and standards of practice, and which is a body of equals
Status	Low	High
Ideological image	Casual, irresponsible	Expert, responsible

are entirely reliant on one of these sources, most have some income from both. Private practice is more lucrative, NHS work more secure.

The main professional association for doctors is the British Medical Association (BMA). It had 78,000 members in 1985. Specialists – surgeons, physicians and the like – have their own associations, the Royal Colleges. The professional associations negotiate sala-ries with the state and establish levels of fees. They are in a powerful position regarding levels of payment because entry into the profession is highly restricted. All doctors have to be registered with the General Medical Council (GMC). The GMC officially licenses doctors on behalf of the state: it is illegal to practise medicine unless you are on the register of the GMC. While some members of the GMC are lay people nominated by the state, the majority are doctors. The GMC thus maintains a monopoly in the market for medical services, and monopolies, of course, can easily inflate charges. In order to become a doctor, it is necessary to obtain certain qualifications: a degree and a period of practice in hospital are required, taking seven years of training in all. Medical education is largely controlled by the GMC and the Royal Colleges, and they decide on the content of education and how many doctors should be trained in any given year. The GMC and the professional associations are also responsible for controlling working practices. The GMC and the BMA discipline doctors, dealing with complaints about malpractice. So groups of doctors effectively decide among themselves what is good and what is bad medicine. The professional associations are thus very powerful, being exclusive, self-recruiting and self-policing. The professional associations exercise a high degree of control over the occupation on behalf of their membership.

Doctors as individuals in the work situation also exercise control, both over patients and over other workers in health services. Doctors lay claim to expert knowledge, which is inaccessible to patients, and they decide on treatment. Both of these conditions give doctors considerable power over their patients. In hospitals, doctors also exercise power over other workers. Nursing staff, radiographers, pharmacists, etc., themselves lower professionals, are subordinate in the hierarchy of authority to doctors. The question which this raises is: how have doctors achieved such a powerful occupational position, from which their privileges flow?

Doctors themselves would probably justify their own privileges in terms of training, knowledge, responsibility, the importance to their clients of good health, the inconveniences of the job or the public service which they provide. Others would argue that these are merely self-legitimating reasons, a claim supported by the fact that far less privileged occupations have these qualities too. Rather the doctors' advantages derive from their overall high degree of occupational control. That control is achieved by collective exploitation, through an effective association, of characteristics of the work situation and the market position which, in turn, reinforce the power of the association. In other words, market position, work situation and collective organization are the mutually supporting props of occupational control.

Professionalization as an occupational strategy

'Professionalism . . . [is] an occupational strategy which is chiefly directed towards the achievement of upward collective social mobility and, once achieved, it is concerned with the maintenance of superior remuneration and status' (Parry and Parry 1976, p. 79). The rewards are such that many occupational groups aspire to be recognized as professional. Implicit in the medical model is a lesson for other occupations: professionalization is an occupational group strategy, a way of achieving collective upward social mobility, as Parry and Parry (1976) describe it. If successful, all workers in a particular occupation improve their social and material positions.

The strategy has been attempted by many groups. Key elements include setting up an association, getting universities to provide courses which all practitioners must attend and pass, and establishing a set of tasks unique to the occupational group and from which all other workers are excluded by law. The degree of success of such strategies is one thing which separates the lower from the higher professionals.

A number of factors determine the success of professionalization strategies. First, success depends on when, historically, the strategy is embarked upon. Because exclusiveness is a basis of control, professionalization is competitive between different occupational groups. If doctors have exclusive rights to sign death certificates or sick notes (both important prerogatives), then nurses are barred from those tasks. Indeed, the rise of the modern medical profession was at the expense of groups like nurses and midwives, whose opportunities for collective upward social mobility were blocked.

Second, the origins and characteristics of the personnel of occupational groups are important. One reason why the older professions were invested with considerable exclusive powers (like the BMA monopoly) was because they were originally recruited from among the sons of the upper and upper-middle class. Such men were considered reliable and could be given state-guaranteed powers. The higher-class origins of judges, army officers and doctors remain strongly visible even today.

Similarly, it is not accidental that many of the higher professions are staffed by men. In 1991 there were six male self-employed professionals for every one woman. Witz (1991) shows that patriarchal power was used both to exclude women from the higher professions and to ensure that occupations filled by women were rendered subordinate. In the late nineteenth century, women were not permitted to take university degrees in medicine in Britain, and hence were ineligible for professional accreditation. Instead, women, who traditionally had been principal carers for the sick, were forced into auxiliary and lower professional occupations like nursing and midwifery, where they could obtain training. Collusion between groups of upper-class men, in hospitals, universities

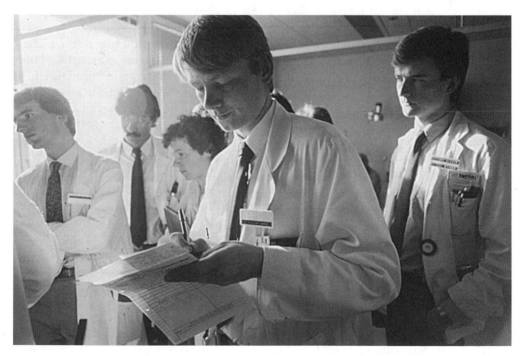

Plate 4.3 | Male doctors
Source: Network / Homer Sykes

and state departments, operated a process of occupational closure against potential women doctors.

The history of medical professionalization also demonstrates the central role of the state. It is the state that grants the monopoly to practise. The British state has probably been more sympathetic to professional claims than its continental counterparts, and consequently professional men have had more influence in British society than in some others. By the same token, governments can rescind the powers of professionals and in the 1980s some attempts were made to reduce occupational monopolies.

Third, professionalization strategies are likely to meet with resistance from potential customers. Generally speaking, professional occupational control is against the interests of the purchasers of services. Where there are few potential customers, or where the customers are organized, professionalization is difficult to secure. For example, as almost the only employer of teachers, the state has the power to oppose the extension of occupational control. Indeed, many of the lower professions are almost entirely dependent upon the state for employment – social workers, nurses, executive-grade civil servants, etc. By contrast, the higher professions are generally those where potential customers are many and there are opportunities for the professional to be self-employed in private practice. Generally, being an employee, whether of the state or of a large corporation (company lawyers and accountants, etc.), tends to reduce the professional's control.

Pharmacy: a case study of a contemporary profession

There have been several recent studies of pharmacists (Hakim 1998; Crompton and Sanderson 1990; Randle 1996; Hassell, Noyce and Jesson 1998). Pharmacy is a well-rewarded occupation and most practitioners (82 per cent) are allocated to the highest category in the Goldthorpe class scheme, the higher service class (see section 5.4). Pharmacists work in community practices, in big retail chains of chemists, in hospitals and in pharmaceutical companies. Pharmacy requires a degree and a year's on-the-job-training in order to qualify. Only qualified pharmacists can dispense NHS prescriptions, an important monopoly right. Also there must be a pharmacist in attendance whenever drugs are sold or prescriptions dispensed, which entails much temporary relief work where locums substitute for pharmacists on holiday, off sick and so forth. There was a shortage of pharmacists in the 1990s and good opportunities for those who were qualified, as owners of small businesses, in large companies and on a temporary basis.

In recent years many more women have entered the higher professional occupations, a process commensurate with their greater presence in university education. Credentials, equal opportunities legislation and the perceived benefits of a career have meant that restrictions on access for women have been removed. Some of the higher professions now have as many female as male practitioners. There were 37,000 qualified pharmacists recorded at the 1991 Census. In 1991, 48 per cent of all occupied pharmacists were women, compared with only 15 per cent in the 1950s. However, despite equal qualifications, the typical rewards and career paths of men and women diverge. Table 4.8 indicates that 29 per cent of male pharmacists owned small firms which employed others, compared with 3 per cent of women. Women were much more likely, if self-employed, to work alone. Women were also more likely to be employees and to work less than 30 hours per week, while it was mostly men who were working more than 46

TABLE 4.8 | Job characteristics of pharmacists (percentages)

	All	Men	Women
Higher qualifications held			
Two or more	51	55	48
(a) Higher degree	8	10	7
(b) First degree	87	87	86
(c) Below degree level	?	2	2
Other	3	1	5
Hours worked (excluding overtime and meal breaks)			
Overtime 46+	16	28	6
Full-time 37–45	58	68	50
Reduced 30–6	6	2	9
Part-time 11–29	13	2	22
Marginal 1–10	7	–	13
Travel-to-work patterns			
Percentage of people who work			
At home	2	3	2
No fixed place (home-based)	18	20	16
0–2 km from home	18	20	16
30+ km from home	6	7	4
Walk to work	7	6	9
Employment status			
Managers/supervisors	–	–	–
Other employees	70	64	76
Solo self-employed	14	7	21
Small firms	16	29	3
Estimated hourly earnings			
All employees	1332	1524	1167
Full-time employees (30+)	1330	1517	1114
Part-time employees (<30)	1305	–	1308
Base N = 100%	277	132	145

Source: Hakim 1998, p. 227

hours per week. The reason for this difference, Hakim argues, is unlikely to be a result of discrimination, more a matter of many women pharmacists according priority to their families and domestic obligations. As Crompton's (1995) evidence indicates, the family situations of men and women employers, managers and professionals are different. A higher proportion of professional women than men forgo marriage and children: combining family with career is made much easier for men. Still, the majority of professional women adapt their careers to the pressures of family and therefore cannot but avoid managerial and small-employer positions, which routinely entail long hours. Instead they tend to work as employees or as locums, which offers greater time flexibility. Hence, even in an occupation where there are similar proportions of women and men, equally well qualified, men fill the better-paid, full-time positions with greater power and authority.

Professional knowledge

In many respects, both established and aspiring professions behave like many other occupational groups. They organize to promote their members' interests regarding pay and control at work in the same way as do trade unions. Similar processes produce a hierarchy of rewards among all occupational groups: professions are closed-shop occupations, with effective organization and control at work. There does, however, seem to be one distinctive feature of existing professions which marks them out from other occupational groups, and that is the role of their special knowledge in securing occupational control.

It has often been pointed out that professions try to prevent the general public gaining access to their expert knowledge by making it incomprehensible to an outsider. This is partly achieved through universities, which give qualifications on the basis of the student's receptivity to a theoretical knowledge which is not made available to anyone else. But while protected knowledge is undeniably part of professional strategies of exclusivity, that knowledge is also necessary for successfully carrying out the job. Where there is no need for the flexible use of expert knowledge in the course of doing the job, workers are unlikely to be able to maintain high levels of occupational control. Where work can be subdivided or routinized, professionals, like skilled manual workers and managers, must expect that employers *will* rationalize their activities. But the one feature which survives in common among the occupations described as professions today is the high degree of discretion, or control, over work tasks retained by the worker. It is the mixture of expert, abstract knowledge and practical experience, which can be neither rationalized nor quickly acquired, that protects 'educated workers' from proletarianization.

The body of knowledge upon which a profession is based tends to have several distinct characteristics:

1   Professional knowledge must generally be considered true, which today usually means that it has scientific legitimation. The status of the clergy in twentieth-century Britain has fallen as theological knowledge has become less credible.
2   Professional knowledge must be applied successfully to practical problems and must be useful to some substantial section of the community.
3   Professional knowledge must not be too narrow or too easily expressed as practical rules for application. This is because the exclusiveness of the occupational group is hard to maintain if untrained people can quickly master the techniques involved. At the same time, however, professional knowledge has to be specialized and coherent in order to be accepted as true, effective and capable of being transmitted during a professional training course.
4   The key feature of professional knowledge, perhaps, is that it allows the profes-

sional to exercise his or her judgement in applying abstract knowledge to the client's particular case. The services of the higher professionals usually take the form of giving advice to clients in a situation of *uncertainty*, where the professional's knowledge and experience gives his or her judgement an authority which can scarcely be challenged by the client. Judgement in circumstances of uncertainty cannot be routinized or expressed as rules, and this provides an exclusive knowledge base for the professional's control in work. Occupational control is extended by preserving space for informed judgement.

One of the principal reasons why many occupations fail to achieve professional status is because they cannot carve out an exclusive sphere of activity in which they make important judgements. In addition, the greater public scepticism of much expert and scientific knowledge expressed in recent years – witness for example the growth of alternative and complementary medicine – poses a challenge to established professional authority.

Summary

1 Professions are relatively privileged occupations, being well rewarded and prestigious and having autonomy at work.
2 Professionals exercise high degrees of occupational control through exclusive professional associations. In the higher professions the extent of occupational control is very considerable, the members setting the level of their fees, being subject only to internal discipline, controlling recruitment, etc.
3 Many occupational groups seek to be recognized as professions though this is not easy to achieve. Other groups of workers and clients try to prevent this. Furthermore, only certain sorts of occupations – partly characterized by the giving of advice on the basis of knowledge inaccessible to the client – seem able to establish claims to professional status.

4.5 Unemployment

Unemployment is a condition suffered by a considerable proportion of the British population. As a consequence of structural economic changes (see sections 3.2 and 3.5), unemployment has become the most pressing social and political problem facing the member states of the European Union (EU), for the consequences of deindustrialization and technological change have had a serious impact across Europe. In this context, the British experience is part of a more general trend preoccupying several countries. In opinion polls, people persistently perceive unemployment as a serious problem and a priority political issue (Gallie and Marsh 1994). Unemployment is an unenviable condition for individuals and families because it entails both material hardship and loss of social status. Lack of money is one reason why people seek to avoid it, but there remains a motivation to work which is prompted by more than money, as evidence from many surveys has shown. Demographic change and economic restructuring are likely to keep levels high in the first decade of the twenty-first century, despite a reorientation of political strategies to combat them.

The rate of unemployment

One of the objectives of the political settlement after the Second World War in Britain was to achieve full employment and thereby eliminate the insecurity and hardship associated with unemployment. Since then, levels of unemployment have fluctuated from month to month and year to year. However, between 1945 and 1975 the overall level was negligible, the mean being about 3 per cent. Subsequently there was a rise, and a much higher plateau was reached during the 1980s, when levels approached those of the slump of the 1930s. This was partly because the Conservative governments of the period had other priorities. Figure 4.3 shows the numbers officially unemployed between 1972 and 1995.

The gradual rise from the mid-1970s escalated in the first three years of Conservative government, following the General Election in 1979, a period which saw a threefold increase in unemployment. Although this rise is often attributed to the government's emphasis on controlling inflation through monetarist economic policies, we can see in figure 4.4 that a similar increase occurred in 12 member states of the EU.

A comparative focus that considers Britain in relation to other member states in the EU demonstrates common trends in unemployment. The countries here adopted various fiscal and social policies, suggesting that the increase in unemployment owed more

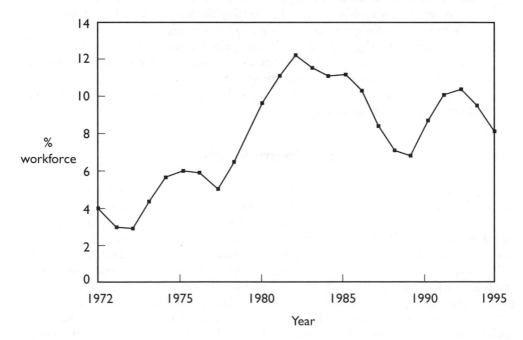

Figure 4.3 | Unemployment, Great Britain, 1972–95
Source: Tonge 1997, p. 88

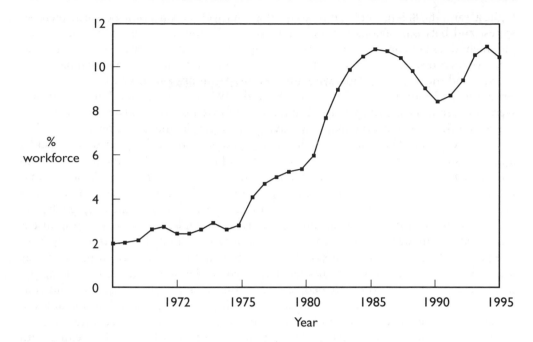

Figure 4.4 | Unemployment in the European Union (12 member states)
Source: Compston 1997, p. 7

to structural change in the global economy than to local domestic management. The mid-1970s proved to be a watershed in terms of the rates of unemployment generated by economic restructuring: an Organization for Economic Co-operation and Development (OECD) (1994) study showed a dramatic rise from 1975, so that by 1993 some 35 million persons in the OECD nations were unemployed. The rate of unemployment in the EU has fluctuated slightly in recent years but the average has remained entrenched at around 10 per cent, as table 4.9 shows.

TABLE 4.9 | Unemployment in the EU, 1992–6 (percentages)

Category	1992	1993	1994	1995	1996
Total	9.3	10.7	11.1	10.7	10.9
Men	8.1	9.7	10.0	9.4	9.6
Women	10.9	12.2	12.7	12.5	12.6
Long-term	40.6	43.2	47.4	49.2	48.3

Source: European Commission 1997

In 1998 the rate in the EU, among the (by then) total of fifteen member states, fell to 9.8 per cent, although this figure hides important variations, with Luxembourg and the Netherlands having the lowest rates at 2.2 and 3.7 per cent, whilst Spain suffered the highest rate at 18.2 per cent (Eurostat 1998). As well as variation between member states, and between regions within countries, it is important to recognize that unemployment does not constitute a static or homogeneous condition. Deacon (1998, p. 292) emphasizes a distinction between 'the *flow* of people on to and off the unemployment register and the *stock* of people who are unemployed at any one time'. For example, in Britain in a 12-month period between 1993 and 1994, an average of 3.9 million people were registered unemployed but 4.2 million had moved off the register. These people constitute the flow, with the majority leaving the unemployment register because they have found work. The evidence is that many people find work again quite quickly, although some of this work may be temporary and people may find themselves unemployed again. It is the group of those who remain out of work for more than a year that is the focus of concern for politicians and policy-makers. The numbers given in an official count are an underestimation of those actually unemployed. Some people who are seeking work are not registered as unemployed: for example, someone whose spouse is registered unemployed, or women with children who cannot demonstrate they have adequate child-care arrangements. Others may be registered as retired or ill when they are looking for work. Governments regularly change eligibility criteria for unemployment benefits in order to divert people away from unemployment agencies and thus keep the numbers down. As the criteria by which people are registered unemployed change over time, the way the numbers are counted changes, making accurate comparisons difficult (Gallie and Marsh 1994). Although the figures have to be treated with caution, it is nevertheless possible to identify a general trend in unemployment rates.

Personal and social consequences of unemployment

The unpleasant consequences of unemployment have been demonstrated in many studies. A substantial proportion of those unemployed live in poverty, surviving only on minimal state benefits. The longer unemployment lasts, the deeper the poverty. This is illustrated by the expenditure patterns of the unemployed. Households whose head has been unemployed for less than a year are clearly poorer than the average household, but a fair amount better off than those whose head has been out of work for a longer period. Shortage of money is the most pressing problem associated with being unemployed. The relationship between poverty and deprivation was established by Townsend's (1979) seminal work, and subsequently confirmed in numerous studies of unemployment and poverty. In box 4.4 three woman give examples of the routine financial difficulties they face.

One of the defining characteristics of deprivation is this condition of mere existence from week to week, involving cutting back on food, social activities, clothing and decorating, for example, and abandoning holidays, saving, purchasing household goods or replacing worn-out or broken items. Callender (1992, p. 143) details how one study found that:

> The women cashed in insurance policies and used their savings and redundancy money. They cut down on cigarettes, food, heating and lighting, and stopped buying clothes and presents. Little or no monies were allocated to maintaining their worker status – they could not afford special trips to the Jobcentre or to visit factories, a finding echoed in more recent research.

> ## Box 4.4   Poverty and unemployment
>
> 'You tell the kids they can't have this and they can't have that. And they want to know why . . . 'cos the other children have got them and why can't they have this and why can't they do this . . . it's hard, it's really hard on them. The children would come in, perhaps their friends are going to the pictures, and sometimes I'd cry because I know mine can't go. Whereas before, when I was working, I could give it to them. But not now and they don't understand.'
>
> 'The telephone bill came, it was only £24. Well it was either that or stuff for the kids. You can't see the kids without so he [husband] let it be cut off. Of course to have it put back on would cost another £9 extra. With his leg and one thing and another it does make a difference having a 'phone . . . Now it's like robbing Peter to pay Paul, you're not living, you're just existing.'
>
> 'You do get a lot of tension trying to make ends meet . . . and the worst part of being unemployed is having to be always broke . . . thinking over where's the next money going to come from.' (Callender 1992, pp. 143, 144)

Both men and women who are unemployed for long periods find a steady reduction in the activities they can pursue, and it is this factor that has led to the high profile that the concept of social exclusion has attained in British and EU political institutions. Exclusion from the labour market is linked to more widespread exclusion from many activities and networks available to those in employment, to the extent that a range of mechanisms contribute to a gradual detachment from social life that others take for granted (Gallie, Gershuny and Vogler 1994). This situation is defined as one of social exclusion, and it is at the forefront of the agenda of all institutions of global governance such as the United Nations, European Commission and the OECD, for example.

Yet whilst there is great concern amongst policy-makers to move those unemployed back into work (see below), research studies reveal that most people of working age are desperate to avoid unemployment and, if unfortunate enough to lose a job, make strenuous efforts to find another quickly. It is not only the financial hardship that causes problems. Those who are unemployed are likely to be less healthy than those in employment. They are also more likely to get divorced: increased conflict between husband and wife is regularly reported by those unemployed, quarrels arising partly because of worries about money, partly because of the demoralization that unemployment brings. Boredom, sickness, sleeplessness, isolation, anxiety and loss of self-confidence are among the main complaints normally associated with a period of unemployment (Gallie, Gershuny and Vogler 1994). There has been some debate about whether these distressing features affect men more than women, but research reported by Gallie, Gershuny and Vogler (1994) and Callender (1992) suggests similar impacts. One important reason for the distress is the loss of social identity and self-esteem experienced by those jobless. In societies where work is of central significance both in terms of the social value attributed to it and as a means of structuring time, the loss of a job can mean the loss of purpose as well as the loss of a meaningful source of identity. Consider the comments in box 4.5.

Box 4.5   The experience of unemployment

A man in his fifties reflects on his experience of unemployment after being made redundant:

> It affected me a lot when I was unemployed. I didn't think I was going to get another job. It was very depressing and got worse the longer I was unemployed. It wasn't so much the money or the way I felt. It was degrading – in the dole office or when people asked me what I was doing. People would say – 'are you still unemployed?' 'Are you not looking for work?' I was looking. It was very degrading. I have worked all my life and got angry. People who have never been unemployed don't know what it is like; they have never experienced it . . . When you are unemployed you are bored, frustrated, and worried, worried sick: at least I was. Of course it is worse for the man who has got a family: he has got responsibilities. So you worry for the wife and the bairns. (Sinfield 1981, p.41)

A woman contrasts her feelings of independence, pride and self-worth when she was employed and after she became unemployed:

> I think you feel more of a person because you're independent. I loved that. You are more independent, you're contributing, not only helping and doing in the home but you're bringing in some money as well. You're not entirely dependent on your husband. And I think you have much more confidence, you're bound to, mixing with people. As I say, you feel more of a person. (Callender 1992, p. 145)

Both men and women recount time after time feelings of shame, frustration, worthlessness and boredom. Not only is there stigma attached to unemployment, but people miss the companionship of colleagues at work and the social interactions employment brings, as well as the independence. For some women this will be the independence that comes from not having to rely financially on husbands and partners. But for both men and women it will also be independence from state support and the stigma associated with it.

Independence and social status are also important to the experience of young people who are unemployed. The language in which they describe their experience reflects the distress it causes. In Allatt and Yeandle's (1992) study of working-class families in northeast England, unemployed young men and women spoke of feeling sick, fed up and depressed. Also, like invalids, they withdrew from family situations, often to bed. Ironically, one of the main sources of irritation among other family members was that those without work stayed in bed in the mornings. While kin felt pity for those unemployed and offered, in many cases, generous economic and emotional support, the lowly status associated with unemployment was inescapable. As many studies highlight, getting a job is a basis for the renegotiation of positions within the family, part of a transition from childhood dependence to adulthood (Allatt and Yeandle 1992; Pilcher 1995). To be employed enhances personal autonomy, gives some financial independence and opportunities for consumption, and carries some positive, moral virtue associated with earning a living. It also brings extra power within the household in negotiation with parents, conveying additional rights. The personal effects of unemployment are distressing.

The social costs of unemployment are, not surprisingly, considerable. Besides the expense of unemployment benefits and the wasting of people's skills, illness, crime and family breakdown create severe social problems. Given how unpleasant it is to be unemployed, more resistance to the rapid increase in unemployment in the 1980s might have been anticipated. For three decades after 1945 it was believed that no government could survive with unemployment rates much above 3 per cent because neither the electorate nor the unemployed themselves would tolerate mass unemployment. Yet, despite public opinion polls regularly identifying unemployment as the most pressing political issue, and notwithstanding a series of inner-city riots in the 1980s and 1990s, the political response has been negligible.

Political consequences of unemployment

The absence of political unrest may be attributed to a number of factors, which themselves tell us more about unemployment.

First, there has been a significant, and apparently successful, campaign by government to reduce popular expectations about what can be done to alleviate the situation. Unemployment has been presented as both an inevitable outcome of recession and a consequence of an underskilled workforce. The increased emphasis on skills in the 1990s had the effect of individualizing a problem experienced by literally millions of people in Europe – a collective problem. Combined with a welfare discourse in the 1980s of a culture of dependency, which suggested that those claiming benefit suffered from a psychological apathy not present in the working population, the structural dimension of unemployment – that there are insufficient jobs in the economy (see figure 4.5) – was translated into the problem and responsibility of the individual affected.

However, as unemployment struck more and more in the middle-management sector of the workforce this discourse became increasingly implausible, and the emphasis shifted more to skilling and reskilling individuals for rapid changes in work. At the same time, economic globalization and recession are presented as forces of nature over which governments have little control. The effect is that of depoliticizing what is an intrinsically political issue, for the neo-liberal policies of deregulation, liberalization and privatization followed by successive governments since 1979 have contributed significantly to the development of a particular path to economic development. Underpinned by a belief that free-market economies provide the only natural and inevitable means of social reproduction, these policies attain a status that disallows serious consideration of alternative policies.

Second, and partly connected to this, is the lack of political organization of unemployed people since the 1930s. This is partly because unemployment is, for most people, a temporary experience, as well as one stratified by gender, ethnicity and 'race', age and other divisions. In the 1980s at least, people were unlikely to identify themselves as belonging to a permanent social category with common political interests. Many people flow onto the unemployment register and off again quite quickly. Relatively few people in percentage terms are unemployed for a long period of time. Older people become discouraged, defining themselves as ill, or settling for early retirement. Young people

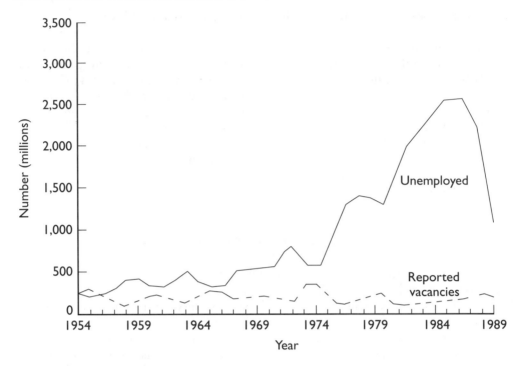

Figure 4.5 | Unemployment and vacancies, 1954–89
Source: Gallie and Marsh 1994, p. 3

shift in and out of casual and temporary jobs. Those with family responsibilities spend their time urgently seeking a new position rather than considering their political options.

Third, those most susceptible are likely to have had repeated experiences of unemployment. Risk varies depending on previous job. The chances of unskilled manual workers being unemployed at any time, or for long periods of time, are higher than for any other social group. People lacking skills are most vulnerable. As Daniel (1990) has shown, in periods of recession, if skilled workers lose their jobs, they reason that any job is better than none and are therefore mostly prepared to accept less skilled and poorer paid employment. In competition for available work they are preferred by employers, who get a skilled worker for the price of a semi- or unskilled worker, thus reducing employment opportunities for the latter groups. The customary problems of irregular and temporary work for the less skilled are exacerbated, but not changed in nature, in times of recession.

Risk also varies with age and gender. The young and older men are most likely to be unemployed, with young British African-Caribbean men, in particular, being disproportionately affected (see chapter 8). Table 4.10 shows the numbers among different age groups between 1990 and 1997. In 1997, 13.6 per cent of young people aged 16–25 years were unemployed; and the rates remained high throughout the 1990s. These figures comprise young people participating in employment or training programmes and will certainly be an underestimation of those actually unemployed. There is some

TABLE 4.10 | Standardized unemployment rates, 1990–7 (percentages)

Category	1990	1991	1992	1993	1994	1995	1996	1997
Total	6.9	8.5	10.0	10.6	9.9	8.9	8.5	7.4
Male	7.0	9.2	11.7	12.6	11.6	10.2	9.8	8.3
Female	6.7	7.4	7.7	8.0	7.7	7.2	6.7	6.2
Youth	10.0	13.5	15.5	17.3	16.1	15.3	14.8	13.6
Vacancy rate	6.0	4.1	4.1	4.5	5.5	6.4	7.9	9.8

Source: Adapted from OECD 1998, p. 184

variation by gender, but this may be a statistical artefact of the refusal to count married women. Table 4.11 gives a more specific breakdown of youth unemployment for 1998 and records lower rates for women. It is unlikely that young women aged 16–17 years are married and, even taking into account the fact that young people aged 16–18 years are ineligible for benefit unless participating in a training scheme, it may be that the lower rates for women reflect the increasing number of women in further and higher education, as well as their increasing employability. Whilst employment opportunities for unskilled men have declined, many service-sector jobs are filled by women.

Fourth, the impact of unemployment is uneven regionally and locally. For example, in September 1998 the rate of unemployment in the south-east was 2.6 per cent, less than half that of Northern Ireland at 7.6. There are even more extreme variations within regions. In Greater London some boroughs had a rate of below 10 per cent whilst others reached over 25 per cent. Areas of high deprivation, such as Brent, Tower Hamlets and Haringey, exist alongside wealthy areas, including Kensington and Chelsea and, in outer London, Richmond-on-Thames and Kingston-upon-Thames. The geographical concentration of unemployment does find some political expression, in that areas of high unemployment often elect Labour MPs. But regional differences do tend to be divisive.

Thus, despite some attempts to organize those unemployed during the 1980s, responses were limited because people who are unemployed comprise a diverse collection of individuals, many of whom consider their condition temporary and pursue a personalized solution of looking for another job. For most this is attainable, although for an unknown number the job might lead to a deskilling rather than reskilling. For others it might represent an interesting change. For yet others the new job may itself be temporary, or otherwise insecure. There is evidence (Burchall 1994) that the unhappiness

TABLE 4.11 | Youth unemployment by age and gender (percentages)

Gender	16–17 years	18–24 years
Male	19.5	13.2
Female	16.9	10.2

Source: Labour Market Trends 1998, p. 534

experienced by most unemployed people is similarly experienced by those in insecure work. Unemployment is, then, a socially complex and individually upsetting condition.

Summary

1   The rate of unemployment was constant and low from 1945 to 1975. From the mid–1970s, it began to rise sharply in continental Europe as well as Britain.
2   The turnover within the unemployed population is high with a relatively small number of people being unemployed in the long term.
3   There is a strong association between unemployment and poverty. Unemployment also causes other problems including ill-health, divorce and depression.
4   The unemployed tend not to be organized because their condition is often short term and they are a diverse group of people.

Related topics

Incomes from work are considered in section 5.2. Information on changes in the occupational structure over time appears in section 5.3. Conditions of work in different institutional settings can be found in passing in sections 6.3 and 6.4 on the working and middle classes, 4.4 on pharmacists, 11.6 on artists and performers, 14.2 on teachers and 15.6 on deliverers of health services. Material on domestic labour can be found in sections 7.3 and 9.5. Industrial and class attitudes and behaviour are examined in section 6.3 for manual workers and in section 6.4 for routine white-collar workers. Further information on women in employment is in section 7.2 and on ethnic minorities in section 8.4. Material on media presentation of unions and industrial relations can be found in section 12.2. Further discussion of government economic policy and its connections with political and class conflict appears in section 13.2. The class position of professionals is discussed in section 6.4 on the middle classes. Information on unemployment among ethnic minority groups is in section 8.4.

Further reading

For a summary of the labour process debate see Thompson (1989). For an up-to-date empirical analysis of changes in work see Gallie et al. (1998). For a comprehensive analysis of developments in trade unions see McIlroy (1995). On the professions, see Johnson (1972) for the best short overview of the topic. A good survey of sociological issues surrounding unemployment is White (1991).

Cross-references to *Readings in Contemporary British Society*

Gallie et al. on changes in skill, occupations, organizations, managerial strategies, flexibility and unemployment; **Savage** on self-employment and occupational careers; **Devine** on the underclass debate, inequality of income, poverty, unemployment and multiple deprivation; **McDowell** on managerial and organizational cultures in banks in the City of London; **Morris** on unemployment, polarization and the underclass; **Acker** on teaching as a professional occupation; **Soothill** on professional crime as an occupation.

5 Patterns of Inequality and Social Mobility

Introduction

    5.1   *Discusses sociological approaches to inequalities of income and wealth.*

Income and wealth

    5.2   *Describes the distribution of income and wealth in Britain and considers the prevalence and effects of poverty.*

Explaining inequality

    5.3   *Considers how well class differences explain patterns of inequality.*

Social mobility

    5.4   *Considers social mobility – the movement upwards or downwards in the class structure.*

5.1   Introduction

One consequence of the fact that rewards for different jobs are unequal is an uneven distribution of income across the population. Some people and some households are very affluent, others very poor. These inequalities arise from the operation of labour markets and from unequal distribution of wealth – property, shares, savings, etc. Levels of inequality alter over time, Britain having recently become more unequal. The character and causes of inequalities have always been a major topic of sociological analysis, partly because they determine standards of living and quality of life, partly because material inequality has been perceived as a basis of social injustice. The poor often make claims for redress against the rich.

Sociologists typically approach the unequal distribution of scarce resources as a study of stratification. There is an implicit geological metaphor involved, implying the layering of categories of persons. The term 'stratification' refers to the fact that there is inequality of resources between aggregates of people, and that these form a structured, or systematic, hierarchy. As a matter of fact, on average, men have more resources than women; property owners more than employees; professional workers more than unskilled manual workers; white people more than black; older people more than younger ones; etc. Sociology is interested in questions like: to what extent is this the case? Why is it so? Is it changing? Are such inequalities fair or just? What are their consequences?

During the nineteenth and most of the twentieth centuries, claims that the unequal distribution of income and wealth was unjust were often formulated in terms of class. It was observed that households dependent upon similar types of employment tended to share common material circumstances. Conditions of employment had a determining influence on where, in a hierarchy of privilege, a particular household was located. Importantly, the household rather than any individual was considered the unit of analysis. This was based on an assumption that the major proportion of the income of most households derived from the wages of an adult male, sometimes supplemented by earnings of wives and children, and that that income determined equally the standard of living of all household members. Changed circumstances have rendered this set of assumptions less tenable: more generous welfare payments contribute to subsistence in the light of needs; married women have joined the labour force in far greater numbers; and households have become smaller because children no longer expect to live in the parental home until the point of their marriage, and living alone has become a more normal option. Hence the connection between household membership and material circumstance has loosened. Interpretations of the importance of these tendencies vary. Some consider it now more appropriate to consider inequalities as occurring primarily between individuals rather than households and along dimensions other than class.

There are two analytically distinct senses in which inequalities might be considered unjust. The first concerns the disparity of material and social rewards going to different positions – do corporate executives and large landowners deserve incomes which are hundreds of times greater than those of personal service workers? The second concerns the extent to which access to highly rewarded positions is restricted. If members of privileged social classes can ensure that their own offspring obtain good positions, to the exclusion of the children of people from lower social classes, then the latter will have reason for resentment and discontent. The study of social mobility provides evidence on the openness of access to privileged positions and the consequences for the reproduction of privilege.

This chapter first describes inequalities of income and wealth. It then reflects on how these might be explained, particularly exploring the extent to which these might be attributed to the existence of a class structure. Then studies of social mobility are reviewed, introducing the debate about the extent to which privileged positions in the division of labour are open to all.

5.2   Income and wealth

In this section we consider how income and wealth are distributed in the population, by examining the results of a report commissioned by the Joseph Rowntree Foundation and compiled by John Hills. This comprised a systematic review of existing research on inequalities in income and wealth, which was published as a report on inequalities in the 1990s.

The distribution of income

Although it might seem a relatively straightforward matter to measure an individual's income, it is not so. Do we, for example, count individual or household income? Is it to be measured before or after tax? Is it just that derived from a job or should it include welfare payments of various kinds? One solution to these problems of measurement is to present data on income calculated in different ways. We can, for example, differentiate original income, gross income, disposable income and post-tax income. Original income refers to the original total received by households from employment, occupational pensions, investments and other sources. Additions to this original income of social security benefits and retirement pensions give gross income. Disposable income

TABLE 5.1 | Composition of household income, 1992 (£000)[a]

Income	Poorest	2	3	4	5	6	7	8	9	Richest	All
Wages and salaries[b]	0.7	1.2	2.2	4.9	8.5	11.5	15.1	18.7	22.4	32.7	11.8
+ Self-employment	0.3	0.2	0.5	0.8	1.0	1.4	1.6	2.0	2.2	6.4	1.6
+ Occupational pensions	0.1	0.3	0.5	0.8	0.9	1.2	1.3	1.2	1.6	2.2	1.0
+ Other market income	0.3	0.3	0.5	0.7	0.8	1.2	1.2	1.6	1.9	4.7	1.3
= Total market income	1.5	2.0	3.6	7.2	11.2	15.2	19.1	23.5	28.1	46.0	15.8
+ Retirement pensions	1.1	1.8	1.8	1.5	1.1	1.0	0.7	0.5	0.5	0.5	1.1
+ Means-tested benefits[c]	1.8	1.9	1.4	1.1	0.6	0.4	0.2	0.1	0.1	0.1	0.8
+ Other cash benefits	0.9	1.1	1.1	1.3	1.2	1.1	0.9	0.7	0.5	0.4	0.9
= Gross income	5.3	6.8	7.9	11.0	14.2	17.7	21.0	24.8	29.2	47.0	18.5
− Direct taxes	0.8	0.7	1.0	1.6	2.4	3.3	4.1	5.0	6.3	10.7	3.6
= Disposable income	4.5	6.1	6.9	9.4	11.8	14.4	16.9	19.8	22.9	36.3	14.9
− Indirect taxes	1.7	1.6	1.6	2.2	2.8	3.2	3.6	3.8	3.9	5.2	3.0
= Post-tax income	2.8	4.5	5.3	7.2	9.0	11.2	13.3	16.1	19.0	31.1	12.0

Header: Tenths of households (by equivalent disposable income)

[a] Income totals shown are not adjusted for household size.
[b] Includes fringe benefits.
[c] Income Support, Housing Benefit and Family Credit.
Source: Hills 1995, p. 16

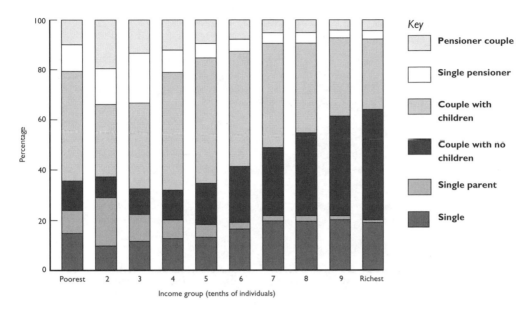

Key

Pensioner couple

Single pensioner

Couple with children

Couple with no children

Single parent

Single

Figure 5.1 | Family type by income group, 1990–1
Source: Hills 1995, p. 13

consists of gross income minus income tax, national insurance contributions and council tax. Deducting indirect taxes such as VAT yields post-tax income.

Table 5.1 shows the composition of household incomes for one year, 1992, and the effect the tax–benefit system has. There are large differences in original income: it is 30 times more for the richest tenth than for the poorest, a ratio of 30:1. When social security benefits are added to the calculation the ratio of gross incomes drops to 9:1. Direct taxes have a greater impact on high incomes, and we can see that when the calculation takes direct taxation into account the ratio falls again to 8:1. But indirect taxes have a greater proportional impact on low incomes, so when they are included in the calculation the ratio of post-tax incomes goes up to 11:1. This ratio is considerably less than the original 30:1 ratio, and we can see here that the tax–benefit system has a redistributive effect, producing a more equal structure of incomes than the original income distribution (Hills 1995, pp.16–17).

We should note that there are various inequalities in the distribution of income, for example between family types, as figure 5.1 shows. Those with children are concentrated at the bottom of the income distribution. Thirty-eight per cent of couples with children are found in the poorest tenth, whilst more than five-sixths of lone parents are in the bottom half, with nearly half in the poorest fifth. Couples without children, or without dependent children, are over-represented at the top. If we consider the distribution of income by age, we find the oldest and the youngest, pensioners and the under-16s over-represented in the bottom half, with the middle-aged predominating at the top and younger adults too showing a somewhat weaker representation in the higher levels.

Figure 5.2 shows the changes in household shares of disposable income between 1977 and 1993. We can see here that in this period the income share of the poorest fifth of

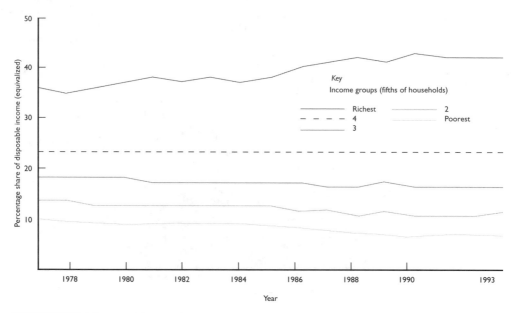

Figure 5.2 | Shares of disposable income, 1977–93
Source: Hills 1995, p. 24

households fell from nearly 10 per cent in 1978 to 7 per cent in 1990, whilst the richest fifth increased their share from 35 per cent in 1978 to 42 per cent in 1993. The drop in the incomes of the poorest and the rise in that of the richest is particularly pronounced from the mid-1980s. This relatively rapid growth in inequality constitutes a reversal of a historical trend towards greater income equality, as we shall see in the next section.

Changes in the distribution of income since 1949

The Royal Commission on the Distribution of Income and Wealth (1979) showed an apparent increase in the equality of the distribution of pre-tax *personal* income in the years 1949–77. The share taken by the top 1 per cent was more than halved and that accruing to the top 10 per cent was also reduced. This was not, however, reflected in any significant increase in the share taken by the bottom 50 per cent. What had happened, therefore, was that there had simply been a redistribution amongst those individuals in the top 20 or 30 per cent of income earners. As a whole, the income distribution showed a remarkable stability from year to year, as figure 5.3 shows. As far as personal income *after* tax is concerned, there was a small increase in the degree of equalization in the mid-1960s to early 1970s. In the mid-1970s the share of the bottom 20 per cent was at its greatest. However, by 1984–5 the richest fifth had a 43 per cent share, higher than at any other time since the Second World War (Hills 1995, p. 23). Overall then, we can see a narrowing of the gap in the distribution of income until the late 1970s, when there begins a significant reversal in the process of equalization.

Explaining this shift in income distribution is a complex exercise, as many factors

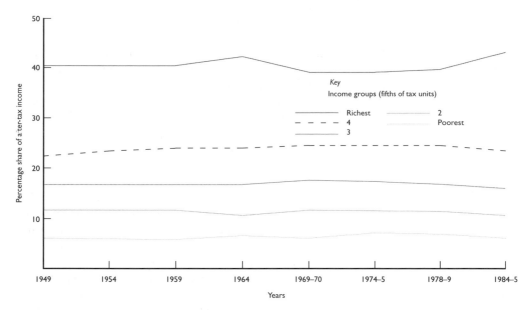

Figure 5.3 | Shares of income 1949 to 1984–5
Source: Hills 1995, p. 23

affect the relationship between changes in the distribution of individual or household earnings and the overall distribution of income. Hills (1996, p. 7) states that:

> . . . there are several intervening stages between the two. Not only are there other sources of income, such as self-employment, investment income or pensions, but an important role is played by the way in which income from these sources is associated. For instance, investment income may become more equally distributed between those receiving it, but if its receipt becomes more closely correlated with high incomes from other sources, the ultimate result may be a widening of the overall income distribution.

Several explanations have been put forward to account for both shifts in individual earnings and the overall growth in inequality of earnings since the mid-1980s. The growth of unemployment, changing forms of work, the decline of the male 'breadwinner' and the increase in women's labour force participation, the decline of trade union influence and national collective bargaining structures, and changes in the taxation and benefit systems are amongst the factors that have influenced the rapid growth of income inequality in Britain (Hills 1996).

The distribution of wealth

In many ways, wealth is more important than income from employment. Wealth often includes assets which can yield income in the future and it can be a more secure form of income than that which is earned. Even more than income, however, wealth is difficult to measure.

Problems of Measurement

One may readily think of someone's wealth as comprising stocks and shares or building society accounts. But should one include his or her house or valuable personal possessions, or even the capital value of an occupational pension scheme? The best way of dealing with these difficulties is to investigate the distribution of the different types of wealth. In particular, we should distinguish marketable from non-marketable wealth. The first refers to those assets that could potentially be sold, like houses or shares. The second includes assets, such as pension schemes, which cannot be sold but which may represent significant future income.

Another difficulty in measurement is that wealth is rather more concealed than income. People do, after all, have their income assessed on an annual basis by the Inland Revenue, but there is no equivalent set of procedures for wealth. There are two main methods for determining how much wealth someone holds. First, the size of an individual's estate may be estimated from the account of her or his assets that has to be made for probate purposes when he or she dies. Second, one can conduct a survey and determine the distribution of wealth simply by asking a randomly chosen set of people what they own. There are clear difficulties with both of these methods. The first, that it only deals with wealth left behind by individuals when they die, tells us nothing directly about the distribution of wealth amongst the living. Furthermore, rich individuals tend to distribute their assets among members of their families precisely to avoid the higher taxes that are payable when they die. The estates method may thus seriously underestimate the extent of the wealth of the rich. Lastly, many people do not leave enough to qualify for taxation at probate, and the Inland Revenue does not therefore provide very good data on poorer people. The second method, which depends on questionnaire survey, also has its drawbacks. Most importantly, many people will refuse to reveal details of their wealth to interviewers, and a high level of non-response calls the representativeness of such surveys into question. It is also, clearly, very difficult to check that answers to a questionnaire of this kind are accurate.

The changing distribution of wealth

It is important to bear these difficulties of measurement in mind when assessing the evidence of the distribution of wealth. In presenting data, we will try to show the effects of different assumptions about what wealth is and different ways of measuring it. Some recent figures derived from the estates method are presented in figures 5.4 and 5.5.

Figure 5.5 (on p. 122) shows the composition of total personal wealth. We can see here that personal wealth nearly doubled in the period between 1977 and 1992. As Hills notes, this growth was much faster than the growth of incomes. The biggest growth was in shares and insurance policies, followed by occupational pensions and then residential property (net of mortgages). Looking at marketable wealth (excluding pensions and tenancy rights but including consumer durables), the unequal distribution of wealth over time is shown in figure 5.4. Box 5.1 summarizes the changes.

The proportion owned by the richest 1 per cent declined until the 1970s, since when there has been little change. Any redistribution which has taken place has not benefited the poorer half of the country. We can also see that the wealthiest 10 per cent still

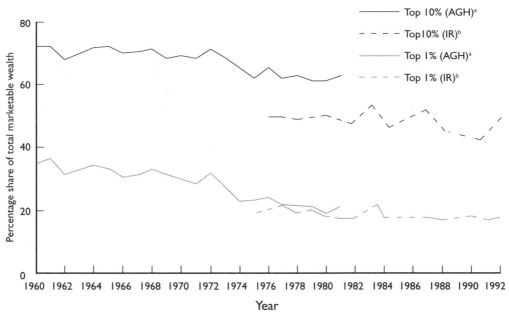

a AGH = Atkinson, Gordon and Harrison 1986
b IR = Good 1990; Inland Revenue 1994

| **Figure 5.4** | Distribution of marketable wealth, 1960–92
Source: Hills 1995, p.96 |

owned around half of marketable wealth in 1992. If one defines wealth as including occupational pension schemes and state pension rights, which cannot be sold but which do constitute an asset of a kind, then the inequalities of wealth distribution are less sharp, with the top 10 per cent taking 35 per cent and the bottom 50 per cent 17 per cent.

Box 5.1   The distribution of wealth over time

In the 1920s, the top 1 per cent of adult wealth-holders owned over 60 per cent of marketable wealth in England and Wales, and the bottom nine-tenths only 11 per cent. Until the 1970s, this distribution narrowed rapidly: by 1971 the share of the top 1 per cent was down to 29 per cent, which took it below the share of the bottom nine-tenths. The most recent figures ... suggest that this narrowing had stopped by the 1980s: on the latest Inland Revenue estimates, the wealthiest tenth of adults owned fifty per cent of personal wealth in 1976, and still owned 49 per cent in 1992 (provisional figure).

This distribution is much more unequal than that of income. For instance, the wealthiest 5 per cent owned 37 per cent of marketable wealth in 1992, but the top 5 per cent by income received 16.5 per cent of total income in 1990/1991; the 49 per cent share of the top ten by wealth compares to a 26 per cent share of the top ten by income. (Hills 1995, pp. 95–6)

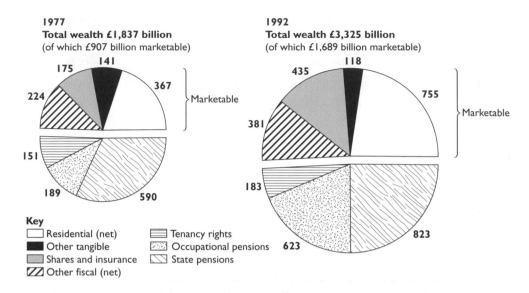

Figure 5.5 | Composition of total personal wealth, 1977–92
Source: Hills 1995, p. 94

What view one takes of these data depends at least partly on the definition of wealth and, specifically, whether or not pension rights are included. Townsend (1979), for example, argues that occupational pensions should be included on the grounds that they usually have some cash value even if surrendered early, but the state pensions should not since they cannot be cashed. Trends for the different types of wealth show some increase in equality until the mid-1970s, at least amongst the top 50 per cent, followed by a flattening out in the 1980s. These conclusions reached by the estates method are roughly confirmed by studies based on the survey method. However one defines wealth, it is very unevenly distributed, and more so than income. Where there is redistribution, it is from the very rich to the not quite so rich. The diffusion of wealth does not extend very far.

The twentieth century saw attempts to redistribute both income and wealth. The evidence suggests that these attempts have made little impact. Wealth is still very concentrated and it is still relatively easy, especially with good professional advice, for a wealthy person to pass it on to other members of his or her family. An unequal distribution of income and wealth is not achieved by accident; it requires active social processes to create and maintain it. Townsend (1979, p. 365) made an important point when he argued that:

> Riches are not only inherited or made: to be riches, they have to be unavailable to the vast majority of the population. A theory of riches depends not only on theories of acquisition – how much wealth is inherited, accumulated by entrepreneurial effort or by the exercise of scarce skills. It depends also on theories of denial of access to wealth – through selective succession, testamentary concentration, limitation of entry to the professions, monopolization of capital and property or at least severe restriction on the opportunity to acquire land and property.

Poverty

So far we have seen that changes in the distribution of income and wealth are confined largely to the richest 20 per cent. We turn now to look at what that might mean for the bottom 50 per cent and, specifically, at the incidence of poverty in contemporary Britain. It seems reasonable to say that there is a difference between being relatively deprived by being in the lower half of the income distribution and being in actual poverty. There is an apparent distinction, in other words, between being badly off by comparison with others and having a standard of living below some fixed level.

A measure of relative poverty might be where people receive an income substantially less than the average for the society as a whole. Absolute poverty might be assessed by reference to a level of income deemed to be the minimum necessary for survival, a sort of Plimsoll-line conception of poverty. Measures of relative poverty are often objected to on the grounds that they ignore the possibility that the whole society is affluent and, hence, even very poor people are well off by comparison with, say, the majority in the least-developed countries. The difficulty with absolute measures, on the other hand, lies in deciding where the Plimsoll line is to be drawn. In practice, any definition of poverty depends on the values of the society concerned and on its view of what count as the necessities of life. Consequently, there is room for a great deal of disagreement about where to put the poverty line. Government ministers, especially those of recent Con-

Plate 5.1 Poverty in the 1990s: living conditions and especially accommodation remain highly problematic for some households
Source: Network

servative governments, have a tendency to put the line very much lower down than do ministers in the Church of England, for example. In practice, therefore, the difference between absolute and relative poverty is very blurred.

The most commonly used method of measuring poverty adopted by the European Union (EU) and the British government's series *Households Below Average Income* counts those whose income falls below 50 per cent of average income. But whatever measure is adopted, poverty in Britain in the 1990s was widespread and had increased substantially throughout the 1980s. On the *Households Below Average Income* measure, poverty increased from 9 per cent of the population in 1979 to 24 per cent in 1995/6. This significant growth in poverty has many causes, including the increased numbers of workless households, that is, working-age families without anyone in work; rises in housing costs, alongside decreases in housing allowances in the benefit system and lower wages at the bottom end of income distribution; and widespread reductions in the levels of and eligibility for benefits, particularly pronounced since the implementation of the 1986 Social Security Act in 1988.

Hardship Britain: a case study

> It is a very depressing thought to think that we might have to spend maybe the next five years on Social Security. It is a very disheartening, depressing thought, to bring your new baby into the world, because when I had him, do you know one of my first thoughts was 'Isn't he beautiful . . . oh I'm so happy, oh God, how am I going to manage to bring him up and keep him fed and clothed decently?' That sums it up for me. (quoted in R. Cohen et al. 1992, p. 59)

Many studies of poverty use quantitative or survey evidence on which to base their conclusions. The *Households Below Average Income* method has been criticized because, in taking average wages as a benchmark, as wages rise or fall so do the numbers in poverty, leading some critics to argue that it is a measure of inequality rather than poverty. At the same time some critics propose that, if wages are high overall, then those at 50 per cent need not be poor necessarily, only relative to the more wealthy. Thus some researchers take the level of benefit specified in income support rates and calculate how many people are living on an income at or below that amount. In order to include those in work that are poor, it is customary to define those with incomes of up to 140 per cent of income support as living on the margins of poverty. But it is frequently argued that poverty is a phenomenon that cannot be grasped simply by measuring numbers, and thus other surveys examine the impact of poverty through qualitative studies of the experiences of those who are poor (Bradshaw and Holmes 1989). As Alcock (1997) points out, quantitative studies cannot capture the processes and experiences of poverty, an important dimension of research.

Qualitative studies reveal the relentless and stressful struggle involved in managing on a very limited income. Many people run out of money before their next payment day and debt is common. In the income support system, all claimants receive the same personal allowance whether or not they are responsible for running a home. Over one half of a claimant's income goes on three items: food, fuel and housing costs. Yet often the housing benefit does not completely cover the cost of housing, and the income support total does not cover fuel and food adequately. Many claimants report fuel bills as the most worrying, and arrears for heating costs are not uncommon. Food is regarded as the most flexible item of domestic expenditure, to be cut back when other pressures overwhelm. As J. Stewart (1997) notes, in 1991 the National Children's Home study, *Poverty and Nutrition*, found that 1 in 5 parents and 1 in 10 children had gone without food in the previous month because they could not afford it. Claimants are the most likely group to have metered heating, lighting, TV or water, despite their being more expensive, and to have had their water, electricity or gas switched off. Single parents and those unemployed for some time tend to be the very worst off, with less savings, more credit and more debts, and, often, being unable to buy basic clothing or household items. This pattern of hardship has remained the same over three decades of social surveys into poverty. The book *Hardship Britain* (R. Cohen et al. 1992) is a study that relies on in-depth interviews with people who live in poverty and claim income support, on what their *experience* of poverty is like.

The book concentrates on changes to the social security system since 1988, when supplementary benefit was replaced by income support, and the social fund, which provided loans (rather than a grant) for large items, was introduced. In the view of many of the interviewees this new system made an already intolerable system worse. They had to cut down on food, and particularly fresh fruit and meat. As one interviewee said of her husband, who suffered from stomach ulcers:

> The doctor told him he needs fish and chicken regularly but we can't afford it . . . We seem to live off chips and potatoes . . . He should have low-fat meat every day . . . when we cook anything we have to use twice the gas . . . We only have a cooked meal three times a week to cut down on gas. (p. 89)

Heating has to be reduced, whatever the consequences. As one mother said:

> With him (the child) being asthmatic we should have the electric heating on in the bedroom . . . we can't do it which is why he is like he is now . . . he's chesty all the time. (p. 16)

The lack of food and heating are but two consequences of too limited a budget. The result is a constant battle to make the money stretch, a battle often lost, with the consequence of going into debt. Some of these debts are commercial, to shops for instance, and would place a further burden on the weekly budget. Families or friends might help, which imposes other sorts of burden. A mother borrowed money from her mother for children's shoes:

> As long as she took back the money it'd be OK but my ma tends to say sometimes it doesn't matter and I feel guilty, with her being a pensioner, I feel I'm taking it out of my ma's pocket, you know what I mean, she needs it herself. But I'd need to be really desperate before I'd go. (p. 46)

Living in poverty is clearly in itself stressful, and poverty can be destructive of relationships. Their lack of money makes many parents, for example, feel inadequate in their care of their children, who are deprived of many things, such as new clothes or toys, that those from better-off families take for granted. One mother complains:

> I have actually had to swallow my pride 'till it hurts . . . It makes me feel like a complete failure because I had such high ideals . . . I wanted to give my children the best, not to the

point of spoiling them, but just so they could, you know, have confidence in themselves. So when I can't do that it makes me feel I'm failing. (p. 72)

This feeling of failure is accompanied by shame, for despite the widespread incidence of poverty there is a social stigma attached to being poor that results in many people trying to hide their situation. As one person explained at a conference attended by people in difficult financial circumstances:

Nobody wants to be poor. It's not something we want everyone to know. Some people don't want to tell others they are poor or even admit it to themselves. (quoted in Alcock 1993, p. 212)

Who is poor?

Some sections of the population are much more vulnerable to poverty than others. The figures provided in the *Households Below Average Income* survey (DSS 1998b) confirm our discussion in the section on the distribution of income; those in the bottom fifth of income distribution are families without employment, pensioners, lone parents and those who are sick or disabled. Almost three in ten children were in the bottom fifth of the overall income distribution, around seven in ten Pakistani and Bangladeshi people were also in the bottom fifth, and single women pensioners were more likely to have low incomes than single men. Breaking this down by region, we see that people from Wales and all English regions from the Midlands northwards were over-represented in the bottom fifth, with London being particularly divided in that a higher proportion of individuals were over-represented in the bottom and at the top of the income scales. In London, between 1990 and 1996, claims because of unemployment rose by over 100 per cent, from 160,000 to 365,000, with 43 per cent of the claimants having been unemployed for more than a year. A quarter of the total number were aged below 25. In 1994, more than half of the schoolchildren in Lambeth, Hackney, Southwark and Tower Hamlets were from families whose incomes were so low that they were eligible for free school meals. The unequal distribution of income can be seen from the concentration of unemployment in particular boroughs, with 20 per cent of unemployed people living in the 10 most deprived wards compared with 5 per cent in the 10 least deprived (London Research Centre 1996, p. 3).

Those who fall into the bottom fifth of the income scale are often referred to as an underclass, a term which came into widespread use in the 1980s. It derives from the poverty debates in the United States, where commentators such as Murray (1990) claimed to have identified a class of mainly black, unemployed and lone-parent welfare claimants whose position was sufficiently similar to merit the description 'underclass', caught in a situation where the existence of state benefits saps the incentive of individuals to provide for themselves. It is doubtful whether this term is of any use in talking about poor people in the United States or in Britain, because, as we have seen above and in section 4.5, the poor comprise a very diverse range of people with little in common other than a lack of resources. Those vulnerable to poverty simply have low incomes, either from work or because they are largely dependent on benefit payments of various kinds from the state because of ill-health, old age or unemployment. Furthermore, various social trends and aspects of government policy are likely both to increase the numbers of people in poverty and to alter the distribution between the various groups at risk. For example, the age structure is changing in such a way that not only is there an increasing proportion of the population aged 65 or over, but also the numbers over 75 years are increasing rapidly. Government policy affects the rates of benefit, which in turn affects the standard of living of vulnerable people who are in very low-paid jobs. The steep increase in unemployment in the 1980s was also partly a result of government policy.

Summary

1   Since the beginning of the twentieth century, there has been some redistribution of income in Britain, but the distribution has not changed much since the Second World War. In the period from 1945 to the mid-1970s, there was a small degree of equalization, involving mainly those households in the top half of the income distribution. In the 1980s there was a significant increase in inequality of income distribution.
2   Wealth is more unequally distributed than income. As with income, what redistribution there has been has involved only the more wealthy half of the population.
3   However one measures poverty, a substantial proportion of the population are in poverty.

5.3   Explaining inequality

Much of sociological analysis is an attempt to understand and explain the existence of social groups with distinctive patterns of behaviour, shared conventions and common aspirations. This entails an examination of both what members of groups have in common, and how one group differs from another. Sociologists study all sorts of groups, but particular attention has been paid to ones that express major and persistent social divisions, because they constitute actual or potential sources of conflict. Class is one of these because, in capitalist society, important divisions revolve around the fact that groups are differently endowed with material resources or the powers to secure such resources.

Until very recently most sociologists would have agreed with Karl Marx and Max Weber regarding the fundamental role of property ownership and employment in determining the differences in people's standards of living. Ownership confers wealth and profits; occupations generate salaries and wages. According to Parkin (1971, p. 18):

> The backbone of the class structure, and indeed of the entire reward system of modern Western society, is the occupational order. Other sources of economic and symbolic advantage do coexist alongside the occupational order, but for the vast majority of the population these tend, at best, to be secondary to those deriving from the division of labour.

This might be demonstrated by reconsidering the evidence on poverty. Deprivation is almost always associated with having insufficiently rewarding paid employment – being retired without an occupational pension, being very poorly paid or being unemployed. Position in the division of labour, either as property owner or wage earner, is the principal means of access to the primary scarce resource of contemporary societies, money. The source (and to a lesser extent the volume) from which people derive their means of subsistence is the basis of the commonality of condition identified by the concept of class. This is one reason why sociological analysis of inequality has focused on class and why typically sociology has used occupation as the primary category for classification. All attempts to map the class structure group together occupations in order to draw class boundaries. There have been many technical arguments about how the drawing of boundaries might best be done (see box 5.2), but most agreed that there was some sense in which the conditions of work and levels of remuneration (called 'work situation' and 'market situation' in Weberian approaches) were basic means to allocate individuals to economic classes.

Class has never been the only source of inequality. Gender, age, ethnic origins and region have always been dimensions along which inequalities might be identified. How these dimensions relate to one another is an important question and one that has come to command more attention recently, partly because many sociologists have argued that class is losing its central differentiating power. Thus there has been extensive debate about the extent to which class continues to structure economic and social opportunities independently.

Arguments about 'the decline of class' have many facets. It is helpful to distinguish those which refer primarily to the effectiveness of class as a concept for understanding economic inequalities and those which refer to its usefulness in explaining political and cultural change. Three of the arguments advanced for considering class as less important in explaining material differences deserve immediate attention. There is some truth to each, though they are often overstated. First, it has been claimed that work and its rewards are no longer central to people's lives, partly because scarcity of basic income has been eliminated (Offe 1985; Beck 1992). Evidence from section 5.2 suggests occupation and work have not declined in importance in determining life chances. Moreover, even if welfare benefits offer a safety net against total destitution, there is an increasing proportion of the British population for whom scarcity of income is a major cause of severe deprivation. Second, it is maintained, for instance by Pahl (1988), that significant differences in condition between manual and non-manual workers have disappeared and that the class structure looks like a diamond rather than a pyramid, all but a small minority of the population belonging to a 'middle mass' with roughly similar conditions and prospects. Although the differences are not as sharp as they were fifty years ago, there are still features which distinguish manual working-class from non-manual workers (see section 6.3). Classes can still be distinguished and economic differentials between them have not diminished. Arguably, class divisions still occur at similar points in the economic hierarchy (though they are, of course, blurred at the edges), and can be mapped quite effectively in terms of the probabilities of many important personal and social outcomes, like security and level of income, educational achievement of children and prospects of good health. Nevertheless, the concept of class was almost certainly made to do too much work in the past, its sociological precision compromised by its intense political associations (see section 6.3). The potentially misleading conse-

---

Box 5.2   Operationalizing the concept of class

Most empirical measures of 'objective' class position depend on manipulating answers to questions about occupations. Occupation is what a worker does and is identified by the label given to a particular job: radiographer, crane driver, typist, etc. There are thousands of such jobs. Notice that the occupation refers to what a person is described as doing at work. No reference is made to the industrial sector in which the person is employed. One can be a crane driver at the docks, or in the construction industry, for example. ('Industry' is defined by the final product or service.) For most purposes of sociological analysis it is desirable to group occupations together to talk about aggregates of people who have roughly similar occupations, and thus similar material resources and working conditions. There are many ways to group occupations together. Reid (1989 pp. 52–74) provides an extensive list of the ways in which different social surveys (conducted by sociologists and by government departments) have combined occupational groupings into social classes. Advertising agencies and opinion poll surveys use a scale whereby a person is allocated to a category (A, B, C1, etc.) largely on the basis of estimates of the prestige of her or his occupation. British official statistics use a class schema that is built on a combination of employment status and occupation (sometimes in terms of the Registrar-General's social class categories, sometimes as socio-economic groups). Sociologists scrutinize such categories closely because of the need for precision in describing the class structure. Formidable technical problems are associated with the questions of how many classes there are and where their boundaries lie.

---

quences are identified by a third argument, that other social characteristics, most obviously gender and ethnic origin, are at least as consequential as class position in determining the pattern of inequality. Undoubtedly there continue to be substantial differences in income and wealth between men and women (see section 7.2) and members of some ethnic groups are materially severely disadvantaged (see section 8.4). What is debatable is whether these divisions reduce or replace class differences, or whether instead they simply coexist with them.

The persistence of class as the basis of inequalities of income, life chances and power is strongly argued and documented by Westergaard (1995). Inequality is still a function of class position. He examines data, similar to that reviewed in section 5.2, about inequality, viewed in the context of changes in welfare state provision since the end of the Second World War. He notes a reversal of trends towards equalization of wealth as a result of high salaries in the corporate sector and substantial reductions in higher rates of taxation in the 1980s. He stresses the continued power and wealth of a very small elite (probably 1 per cent, and certainly no more than 3 per cent, of the population) whose privilege is largely a function of their ownership of property. It is the possession of massive amounts of capital as property in land, buildings or shares that identifies the very wealthy. Westergaard also shows that most of the benefits of economic growth between 1979 and 1992 went to the richest 30 per cent of the population, with the gap between them and the rest increasing significantly. These other main beneficiaries of increased incomes in the period were those in 'careers', which he distinguishes from 'jobs'. Careers offer salaries, which are higher, more likely to increase over time and more secure than the wages deriving from jobs. Careers are a prerogative of those with managerial and professional occupations and comprise, he estimates, about 30 per cent of all employees. The remainder of the population, irrespective of whether they do manual or non-manual work, are in less secure, less autonomous and less well-rewarded positions. Although the proportions of the workforce in these categories have changed, the system of distribution of material reward remains much as before. So, Westergaard concludes, the unequal distribution of rewards maps onto class positions. There are significant differences in the circumstances of different classes, with ownership of property and access to careers generating significant privilege. Hence, he maintains, sharpening inequalities are consistent with a comparatively stable, pyramid-shaped class structure.

Westergaard also contests directly several versions of the 'decline of class' thesis. He dismisses the idea that there is now a middle mass, because there are significant boundaries between aggregate groups. He shows that neither the life-course trajectory nor women's employment undermines the importance of class structuration. He says that:

> with respect to employment earnings and retirement provision alike, [gender divides] in a pattern of occupational disparities among women which roughly parallels that among men. Gender is a dimension of inequality distinct from class; and it has long been so. But its effects . . . are to compound class differences rather than to neutralise them. (Westergaard 1995, p. 140)

This is primarily because women living with a partner who joined the labour force since the late 1970s tended to have partners in more secure and better-rewarded positions, thus making such households better off overall. Westergaard concludes that the contemporary pattern of differential distribution of material resources is not significantly different from that of earlier decades. Hence the structure of inequality can still be portrayed in terms of class.

There is another sense in which sociologists use the term 'class', to refer to the transmission of privilege between generations. Inheritance of wealth and access to comparatively high levels of resources, both financial and cultural, during childhood and early adulthood are sources of advantage. A fourth variant of the 'decline of class' thesis maintains that the tendency for families to pass on privilege over generations has dissipated (Pakulski and Waters 1996). Such a change would be extremely significant, since substantial inequalities of reward might be felt justifiable if privileged positions were equally available to everyone on the basis of open competition. If individuals could be said to deserve their success as a consequence of their personal attributes and efforts, rather than because their parents gave them exceptional financial, cultural or social support, grievances about unequal outcomes might be less persuasive. This second reason for contesting material inequalities is, then, a matter of fair access rather than of differential rewards. The most informative sociological approach to access is through studies of social mobility, which allow estimation of the probability of parents' position determining those of their children.

Summary

1 There is considerable debate about how best to define class and the importance of the concept in explaining inequality.
2 Some sociologists suggest that class is no longer of much practical or political relevance while others argue that class inequalities continue to be structured in the same ways as a generation ago.

5.4 Social mobility

Social mobility refers to movement up and down a system of hierarchically ordered economic and social positions. British studies have always defined this hierarchy as a system of classes. For such purposes, social mobility is the process by which people move from one class to another. Social mobility should not be confused with geographical mobility, which refers to people moving their place of residence. In modern society, nobody is prevented by religious, political or legal regulations from moving between classes: entry to classes is not closed. At the same time, though, there are barriers to movement into some class positions. In practice, entry into the upper class is limited by birth or access to wealth. There are also effective limits to access to the more prestigious positions in the professional middle class. To be a doctor requires a degree in medicine, and only a small proportion of the working population have that qualification. More interesting, though, is what kind of people are allowed into medical school to get that qualification. Most are the children of higher professionals; few are from unskilled, manual backgrounds. This raises the question of fairness, usually as an issue of equality of opportunity. Since some groups of occupations provide better rewards, better conditions and more work satisfaction than others, it is a matter of concern on what grounds those positions are filled and whether most citizens have a reasonable chance of obtaining such posts. Studies of social mobility assess those chances.

Social mobility bears upon another central social process – that of class formation and class solidarity. It has usually been thought that high degrees of social mobility would reduce class conflict. There are several plausible reasons for this. People believing that they have a fair chance of joining the higher social classes may feel little resentment on the grounds that privileges are deserved: talent is being rewarded. If there is a lot of movement between classes then solidarity and common identity will be hard to sustain. People may pursue individual rather than collective solutions to their discontents, preferring further education to trade union meetings. Also, the cross-class contacts built up by socially mobile people might reduce the sense of the exclusiveness of social classes and the hostility between them. Indeed, ultimately, if there was perfect fluidity between positions, social background having no influence on occupational achievement, one key basis for identifying social classes – shared chances of social and economic success in life – would be removed. The nature and degree of social mobility in Britain are, therefore, interesting from the point of view of class politics.

The concept of social mobility

Social mobility concerns movements between social classes. It is usually estimated by reference to occupational positions. Movement may happen within an individual's lifetime, called intra-generational mobility, as for example the cases of the promotion of a clerk to a manager or a manual worker obtaining qualifications permitting access to a profession. Or the movement may occur between generations, children coming to fill places in a different occupational class to their parents, which is called inter-generational mobility. Examples would be the child of a train driver who becomes a solicitor or the child of a solicitor who becomes a train driver. The former would be an example of upward social mobility, the latter of downward social mobility. It is assumed that occupational classes can be graded in a hierarchy of prestige, and that the criterion of mobility is to shift across a class boundary. It should be noted that people also obtain new jobs without crossing a class boundary, moving sideways so to speak.

Deciding what are relevant class boundaries is bound to be contentious. For many people, upward mobility used to be associated with a move from blue-collar to white-collar occupations. However, since many routine white-collar jobs now pay less well and are less satisfying than skilled manual jobs, that boundary may well be thought less meaningful. The most authoritative and comprehensive study of mobility in Britain concentrated on movement into and out of the service class (composed largely of professional and managerial occupations), on the grounds that for most people since the middle of the twentieth century upward mobility has been achieved by entering professional and managerial occupations. It is to the finding of this study, the Nuffield Mobility Study, reported by Goldthorpe, Llewellyn and Payne (1980), that we will turn next. To make sense of the findings of this study, however, it is necessary to be familiar with the class categories being used.

The definitions of the seven occupational classes used by Goldthorpe, Llewellyn and Payne, are listed in figure 5.6 For many purposes, these seven classes are grouped into three – the service class, the intermediate class and the working class. For Goldthorpe, Llewellyn and Payne, the 'service class' includes higher and lower professionals and middle management. It was initially called the service class primarily because it rendered expert services to owners of capital. In exchange for the responsibility associated with such positions, and because employers had to trust such personnel to take decisions in the interest of the company, the service class was well rewarded. This class is also sometimes referred to as the salariat (those who receive salaries rather than wages). The intermediate class comprises routine white-collar workers, small proprietors and supervisory workers. The working class is defined as manual workers without positions of authority. Importantly, although Goldthorpe, Llewellyn and Payne study movement between all seven occupational classes, they consider only movement into and out of the service class as socially meaningful mobility.

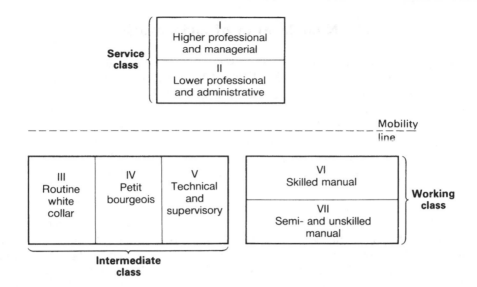

Occupational classes

  I Higher-grade professionals; higher-grade administrators and officials;
     managers in large establishments; large proprietors.

 II Lower-grade professionals and higher-grade technicians; lower-grade
     administrators; managers in small establishments; supervisors of non-
     manual workers.

III Routine non-manual workers (largely clerical) in administration and commerce;
     sales personnel; other rank-and-file employees in services.

 IV Small proprietors, including farmers and small-holders; self-employed
     artisans; other 'own account' workers (except professionals).

  V Lower-grade technicians; supervisors of manual workers.

 VI Skilled manual wage-workers.

VII All manual wage-workers in industry in semi-skilled and unskilled grades;
     agricultural workers.

Figure 5.6 Goldthorpe et al.'s (1987) model of the British class structure (Nuffield Mobility Study)
Source: Goldthorpe, Llewellyn and Payne 1987, pp. 39–41

Note: the currently dominant way of measuring class in British sociology is that of Goldthorpe and is based primarily on the employment relation. Thus, the study of class structure by Marshall et al. (1988), the electoral studies of Heath et al. (1985, 1991) (see section 13.2) and the study of educational opportunity by Halsey, Heath and Ridge (1980) (see section 14.4) all use a version of the class model developed by Goldthorpe for the investigation of contemporary social mobility. The rationale for the schema is that it groups together occupations which are similar in terms of employment relations, contracts of employment (including source and size of income and degree of job security) and working conditions. Occupation is the primary indicator of the employment relationship.

The Nuffield study of social mobility

Goldthorpe, Llewellyn and Payne (1980) discovered more inter-generational mass so-cial mobility in Britain since the Second World War than might have been expected. Previous studies had suggested that classes in Britain were largely self-recruiting. Sons would usually end up in the same class as their fathers. (Regrettably, almost all mobility studies, including the Nuffield one, only analyse the movement of men.) It was believed, on the basis of a survey in 1949, that there was a lot of short-distance but little long-distance movement, that the elite was highly self-recruiting, and that the blue/white-collar boundary was a major barrier. Goldthorpe, Llewellyn and Payne painted a different picture.

Consider table 5.2. This is an 'outflow' table, showing the class destination of sons, which indicates the extent to which opportunities are equal. If classes were perfectly self-recruiting, every son would be in the same class as his father and the diagonal boxes would all register 100. What we observe is, rather, much movement between classes. Consider, for example, the row of fathers in class VII – semi-skilled and unskilled manual workers and agricultural labourers. Of sons of such fathers, 6.5 per cent were in class I occupations (higher management and professional) in 1972; another 7.8 per cent were in the lower professional grade, class II. However, 34.9 per cent of such sons were, like their fathers, in class VII; and a further 23.5 per cent were in the other class of manual workers – class VI, skilled manual. In effect, then, about 6 out of 10 became blue-collar workers.

It is to some degree a matter of judgement whether you will be impressed by the number of sons who were upwardly mobile, or by the number who remained in class VII. But whatever your judgement, the table does show different degrees of self-recruitment. Looking at the diagonal boxes you can see that only one in eight of sons of routine white-collar workers (class III) were to be found in that class in 1972. The sons of such workers were, in fact, fairly evenly distributed across all occupational classes. By contrast, class I fathers were the most likely to pass on their class positions to their sons. Nearly one in two class I sons had class I jobs. It is this capacity for privilege to be transmitted intergenerationally that arouses suspicion about the social significance of the, undeniably large, absolute amounts of mobility. Clearly, the class into which a man was born did not determine his class destination; lots of men were upwardly mobile in the period 1928–72. But the chances of ending up in class I were weighted heavily in favour of those with fathers there already.

Issues relating to class formation are best illustrated by considering an 'inflow' table, table 5.3 (p. 136). Based on exactly the same data as the previous table, this shows the composition of social classes in 1972, in terms of the class origins of sons. Reading down the columns you can see who has arrived in which classes. Compare class I and class VII. Class I, which comprised about one worker in eight (13.6 per cent) in 1972, had drawn its members from all social classes. Although one in four members also had fathers in class I, the rest came more or less equally from the six other classes in Goldthorpe, Llewellyn and Payne's classification. Class I in 1972 was, then, very het-erogeneous (i.e. of very mixed origin). Of class I, 28.3 per cent were sons of manual workers. Class VII, by contrast, was largely composed of sons of manual workers (69.6 per cent). Only 2 per cent of class VII had fathers in class I. Skilled manual workers had similar origins. Thus Goldthorpe, Llewellyn and Payne proposed that Britain now has a

| TABLE 5.2 | Inter-generational occupational mobility of men aged 20–64, England and Wales, 1972, outflow (percentages, by row) |

Father's class when son aged 14 years	Son's class (1972)							Father's sample	
	I	II	III	IV	V	VI	VII	No.	%
I	45.2	18.9	11.5	7.7	4.8	5.4	6.5	688	7.3
II	29.1	23.1	11.9	7.0	9.6	10.6	8.7	554	5.9
III	18.4	15.7	12.8	7.8	12.8	15.6	16.9	694	7.3
IV	12.6	11.4	8.0	24.8	8.7	14.4	20.5	1,329	14.1
V	14.2	13.6	10.1	7.7	15.7	21.2	17.6	1,082	11.5
VI	7.8	8.8	8.3	6.6	12.3	30.4	25.9	2,594	27.5
VII	6.5	7.8	8.2	6.6	12.5	23.5	34.9	2,493	26.4

Class distribution of sons by the class of their father when son was aged 14 (a measure of equality of opportunity)
For definitions of classes see figure 5.6.
Total number of respondents = 9,434
Source: Goldthorpe, Llewellyn and Payne 1987

'mature' working class, alike in its origins, and therefore capable of exhibiting considerable solidarity. If they are correct, being in the same class for two or more generations does suggest the existence of a solidaristic working class and considerable fragmentation among the other occupational classes.

Given the very considerable movement between classes, it might be imagined that Britain had become less dependent on class origins. In an important sense, though, this is a misleading impression. Much of the upward mobility into the service class was merely a consequence of changes in the occupational structure. The number of positions in the service class increased sharply in the period examined by Goldthorpe, Llewellyn and Payne. Men occupied in service-class occupations rose from around 1.2 million in 1931 to 3.5 million in 1971. Compare the proportions of fathers in the service class (classes I and II) in Goldthorpe, Llewellyn and Payne's sample – 13.2 per cent (see table 5.2) – and the proportion of sons – 25.1 per cent (see table 5.3). What Goldthorpe, Llewellyn and Payne point out is that the service class increased in size to such an extent that, even if every son of a service-class father had obtained a service-class job, there would still have been more men with origins in other classes in the service classes of 1972. This can be seen in table 5.4 (p. 137), which summarizes information on movement across the boundary of the service class. Boxes A and D are percentages of men inter-generationally stable; box B is the percentage downwardly mobile; box C is the percentage of men upwardly mobile. The upwardly mobile vastly outnumbered the downwardly mobile. Put another way, the service class of the previous generation did not breed fast enough to fill all the new service-class occupations made available in the long boom after the Second World War. A large amount of upward social mobility was inevitable.

This fact led Goldthorpe, Llewellyn and Payne to try to separate absolute mobility, of which we have seen there is a great deal, from relative mobility, which is a measure of whether class differentials have narrowed. In other words, if there had been no change in the occupational structure, would there still have been an expansion of opportunities for the lower classes? Answering such a question is fraught with difficulty, not least

| TABLE 5.3 | Inter-generational occupational mobility of men aged 20–64, England and Wales, 1972, inflow (percentages, by column) |

Father's class when son aged 14 years	Son's class (1972)						
	I	II	III	IV	V	VI	VII
I	24.2	12.0	9.1	6.0	3.0	1.9	2.0
II	12.5	11.8	7.6	4.4	4.9	3.0	2.2
III	12.0	10.0	10.2	6.1	8.3	5.4	5.3
IV	13.0	13.9	12.2	26.5	10.6	9.6	12.3
V	12.0	13.5	12.5	9.5	15.6	11.4	8.6
VI	15.7	21.0	24.8	19.2	29.2	39.4	30.3
VII	12.6	17.8	23.6	18.5	28.5	29.4	39.3
Sons in sample							
No.	1285	1087	870	887	1091	2000	2214
%	13.6	11.5	9.2	9.4	11.6	21.2	23.5

Class composition, by class of father when son was aged 14 (a measure of class formation)
For definitions of class see figure 5.6
Total number of respondents = 9,434
Source: Goldthorpe, Llewellyn and Payne 1987

because the occupational structure is always changing. However, it is an important question because the 'upgrading' of the occupational structure, which would allow the service class to continue to expand, cannot continue indefinitely. It will, then, matter to what extent exclusive class privileges can be maintained from generation to generation. Goldthorpe, Llewellyn and Payne suggest that, relatively speaking, the capacity of service-class fathers to transmit privilege did not decline between 1928 and 1972. The simplest indication of this is the low rate of downward mobility from, especially, class I. Look at table 5.2 again. Of class I sons, 64.1 per cent ended up in the service class; only one in three moved down; and this may be an underestimate given the nature of intra-generational mobility. It seems, then, that a use of material or cultural resources accumulated by fathers in lucrative careers and a capacity to secure high educational qualifications for their children has ensured that sons of the service class are heavily protected against downward mobility.

Evaluation of the Nuffield study

The Nuffield study has been subjected to extensive evaluation in the years since its first publication. Four reservations are pertinent for understanding mobility in Britain today. First, the most exclusive of social groups, which lies at the very top of the economic hierarchy and which is more highly self-recruiting than any other, received no attention. Second, the mobility experiences of women were largely ignored. Third, its implicit and political moral condemnation of restricted opportunities in Britain has been challenged. Finally, the evidence was collected 30 years ago.

TABLE 5.4	Inter-generational social mobility into and out of the service class, men aged 20–64, England and Wales, 1972 (percentages)

	Son's class (1972)		
Father's social class when son aged 14	Service (I–II)	Other (III–VII)	All
Service (I–II)	A 7.7	B 5.4	13.1
Other (III–VII)	C 17.4	D 69.5	86.9
All	25.1	74.9	100.0

Total number of respondents = 9,434
Source: tables 5.2 and 5.3

The elite and mobility

The Nuffield Mobility Study examined mass mobility. It would be false to imagine that the existence of considerable mobility into the service class meant that *all* top positions were equally accessible. While the son of a manual worker may become a solicitor, he is very unlikely indeed to become a high-court judge. The evidence concerning recruitment to the upper class is considered in detail in section 6.5. People at the very top of the hierarchy tend to have impeccable upper-class backgrounds. To take just a single example, of those bank directors listed in *Who's Who* in 1970/71, 45 per cent also had fathers listed in earlier editions of *Who's Who*. This is 300 times greater than chance. It does not leave much space for others to be upwardly mobile into top banking jobs! No complete understanding of social mobility can afford to ignore this upper class. However, as Goldthorpe readily conceded, sample surveys like the Nuffield one could never pick up a sufficient number of these kinds of people to allow effective analysis because elites are small. Other techniques of investigation are required.

Women and mobility

The Nuffield study examined only men, as did most early studies of social mobility. However, women's experience of social mobility is significantly different from men's. Because of occupational sex segregation (see section 7.2), women fill disproportionately few higher professional, skilled manual or petit bourgeois positions, and therefore many women experience downward occupational mobility when compared with their families of origin. There is more absolute downward occupational mobility for women than for men because, while fathers have the same number of sons and daughters, the labour market places available strongly favour men. This is clear from table 5.5, drawn from a study providing evidence from 1991 (Marshall, Swift and Roberts 1997), which shows class origins and destinations for men and women separately.

| TABLE 5.5 | Mobility patterns for men and woman, 1991: distribution of respondents by class of origin and destination, by sex (percentages by column) |

	Men		Women	
Class	Class of origin	Destination	Class of origin	Destination
I, II	21	41	24	25
IIIa[a]	4	5	4	30
IV	12	12	13	9
V, VI	33	20	36	10
VII, IIIb[a]	31	22	22	27
	101	100	99	101

N = 1,319

[a] This was an international comparative study which used the extended version of the Goldthorpe classificatory scheme, which distinguishes between IIIa (routine white-collar occupations) and IIIb (personal service workers). The latter are, for some purposes, often considered on a par with unskilled manual workers. Class of origin and destination: higher and lower salariat (I and II); routine non-manual (IIIa); small proprietors (IV); skilled manual (V, VI); and unskilled manual (VII, IIIb).

Source: extracted from Marshall, Swift and Roberts 1997, p. 42

There was little difference in the distribution of the occupational class of fathers of men and women in the sample, and that would be attributable mostly to sampling error, but the class destinations of men and women were very different, indicating the different labour-market opportunities available to men and women in contemporary Britain.

Any suggestion that these differences might simply be a consequence of men investing more in the development of skills and competences is denied by the further demonstration that possession of similar levels of educational qualification does not bring equal rewards for women. Thus table 5.6 shows that men with low qualifications (less than GCSE) are three times more likely than their sisters to obtain higher service-class jobs. And with the highest qualifications, at least a university degree, they have rather more than twice the chance. A further study by Savage and Egerton (1997) indicates that service-class sons with low measured ability and who perform badly at school have much better chances of retaining a middle-class position than their sisters. The advantages that service-class daughters have over other women are almost entirely a consequence of their obtaining better credentials within the education system, whereas sons seem to have access to other sources of compensation for educational failure.

Absolute rates of upward occupational mobility are, thus, lower for women than for men. However, what little information there is on relative mobility for women suggests that chances are skewed by class of origin in much the same way as for men: daughters of service-class fathers are about five times more likely than those of working-class origin to obtain service-class occupations themselves, odds which are the same for the relevant men.

Women's material circumstances are profoundly affected by marriage. They marry men who, on average, have a higher occupational position than their own. Using the conventional measure of class, based on the male head of household's occupational position, women experience what is sometimes called marital mobility. Though partly

TABLE 5.6 | **Class distribution in Britain, by educational attainment and sex: respondent's class determined by reference to own employment (percentage by row)**

Educational level[a]	Sex	Class destination[b]					
		I	*II*	*III*	*V / VI*	*VII*	*N*
1 Low	Male	6	10	4	28	53	664
	Female	2	6	18	11	63	687
2 Ordinary	Male	14	19	9	39	19	788
	Female	5	12	48	5	30	738
3 Advanced	Male	35	26	11	18	9	427
	Female	13	45	30	3	10	357
4 Degree	Male	57	36	3	1	2	319
	Female	24	57	14	1	3	184

This study categorized educational level (using the categories of the CASMIN project of Erikson and Goldthorpe 1992) to facilitate international comparison, and an extended version of the Goldthorpe classificatory scheme (see note to table 5.5 above).

[a] Definition of educational level:

1 Low	1a Inadequately completed general elementary education
	1b General elementary education
	1c General elementary education and basic vocational training
2 Ordinary	2a Intermediate vocational qualification
	2b Intermediate general qualification
3 Advanced	3a Higher (secondary school) education – maturity examination
	3b Lower tertiary (including vocational) certificates
	3c Higher education: upper-level tertiary certificates
4 Degree	

[b] Class destination has five levels: higher salariat (I); lower salariat (II); routine non-manual (IIIa); skilled manual (V, VI); and unskilled manual (VII, IIIb)

Source: Marshall, Swift and Roberts 1997, p. 83

an artefact of class measurement, it has a real and substantial influence on their personal material situation. When a husband's occupation is used as the measure of his wife's class, then women in the 1980s, on aggregate, experienced neither more nor less downward social mobility than men of their own generation. Marital mobility also appears to influence strongly women's class behaviour and attitudes, to the extent that wives come to share many of the class perceptions and practices of their husbands. Though women's more complex occupational biographies might be expected to reduce the strength of their class identification, marriage encourages a household perception of class position and class interest defined by the husband's occupational circumstances.

Unequal but fair?

Some sociologists have objected to particular interpretations of the data, particularly about relative mobility, Peter Saunders (1996) being the most notable. Saunders challenges the sociological consensus that patterns of social mobility indicate that the distribution of rewards is unfair and determined by class of origin. Saunders (1995) argued that the high level of upward and downward mobility in Britain was consistent with its being a meritocracy, that sociologists had underestimated the degree of fluidity (particularly because of artificial measures to express the unequal chances of working- and service-class men), and that sociologists had systematically ignored the role of differences in motivation and ability in generating unequal outcomes. Developing the position, Saunders (1996) used evidence from the National Child Development Survey (NCDS). This is a panel study of all children born between 3 and 9 March 1958, 17,414 of them, who have been interviewed on five occasions, with their parents and later partners where appropriate, the last being in 1991 when all were 33 years old, at which point contact was made with 11,397 of them. This is a big cohort study with opportunities for examining the meritocracy thesis, because it contains information about many of the things that might affect success: education test scores at 5, 11 and 16; parental class and background; aspirations of both parents and children; questions about motivation at various stages; as well as type of school attended and qualifications obtained. It therefore provides some measures of variables that Saunders accuses other sociologists of ignoring – particularly motivation and measured ability – and makes it possible to see how much they affect success in the labour market.

Saunders argued that the evidence suggests that the differential chances of working-class and service-class children getting service-class jobs are significantly less than reported by Goldthorpe. Saunders's analysis indicated that ability test scores (measured by scores on maths and English tests at 5, 11 and 16 and an IQ test at 11) and motivation (measured by attitude scales administered during schooldays, absenteeism, and 'job commitment' at age 33) explained far more of the variation in occupational attainment by age 33 than did social class of parents, parents' educational achievement, gender, measures of social deprivation like overcrowding, or type of school attended. While all these social variables were significant, they had less effect than ability and motivation. From this he concluded (1996, p. 72):

> If we are interested in identifying those factors which play the most important role in determining the social class positions that we all end up in, then we should be paying far more attention to factors to do with individuals themselves – especially their ability and their motivations – and we should be worrying much less than we have done about the effects of the social situations into which they are born and within which they grow up. It does make a difference whether your father is an unskilled manual worker or a well-paid professional, whether your mother left school at the minimum legal age or stayed on to do exams, whether your parents encouraged you in your school work or showed no interest in your education, whether they tried to motivate you with their ambitions for you . . . etc. . . . – but in the end, what matters most is whether you are bright, and whether you work hard. This is precisely what the thesis of meritocracy is all about, and for this reason, the conclusion which surely now has to be drawn from the evidence we have reviewed is that Britain is, to a large extent, a meritocratic society which allocates people to occupational class positions mainly on the basis of ability plus effort.

In essence, Saunders does not deny that rewards from the labour market are unequal, but maintains that because ability and effort determine who shall fill the privileged positions then existing distribution can be said to be fair, the outcome of meritocratic competition.

The acceptability of Saunders's view depends partly on the definition of the term 'meritocratic'. As one critical account (Marshall, Swift and Roberts 1997) indicates, much depends on contested concepts of fairness and social justice, for, as Saunders acknowledges, meritocratic arrangements are necessarily neither just nor efficient. Marshall, Swift and Roberts concede that social mobility studies have probably paid too little attention to issues of ability and motivation. However, whereas Saunders considers these attributes as belonging, as it were intrinsically or 'naturally', to individual children, Marshall, Swift and Roberts point out that ability is nurtured, ambition instilled and work motivation imbued. Parents of different classes probably do this to different degrees. Therefore, high achievers cannot easily be said to 'deserve' success; they had the good luck, rather than being personally responsible, to have been born into a higher social class, where parents encouraged and developed talents which gave them advantages subsequently in the competition over children from other classes.

The case for the injustice of current arrangements is bolstered by the evidence of class-based inequalities of access to privileged labour-market positions. Savage and Egerton (1997), re-examining the same data from the NCDS, show that low-ability service-class sons (especially sons of professionals) obtained service-class positions in more or less the same proportions as high-ability working-class boys. This ability of households containing service-class fathers to prevent their low-ability sons from slipping down the social hierarchy is a primary objection to the meritocracy thesis. The fact that high-ability service-class children do a good deal better than high-ability people of working-class origin is another.

Change since 1972?

There has been no subsequent study as comprehensive as that of Goldthorpe, Llewellyn and Payne. However, secondary analysis of surveys collected for other purposes has permitted systematic investigation of changes since 1972. Overwhelmingly, the evidence covering the period to the early 1990s is that nothing of significance had altered. Patterns of movement between class of origin and class of destination remain the same. Social mobility is not increasing. Studies comparing industrial societies suggest that Britain exhibits fluidity near to the average, with Sweden more open, the Irish Republic and Poland more closed. Also, Scotland is a little less open than England or Northern Ireland (see Erikson and Goldthorpe 1992; Savage 1994; Marshall, Swift and Roberts 1997).

Mobility and class formation

One reason why mobility chances are important is because they govern allocation of people to positions with different levels of rewards. The other reason is that the degree of mobility affects levels of class formation. What the Nuffield study showed, from its inflow tables, was that British social classes were differently composed, in such a way that working-class men in 1972 almost all had working-class fathers, whereas service-class men had arrived from many different classes of origin. This, Goldthorpe, Llewellyn and Payne argued, affected the process of class formation.

The importance of the mobility data for understanding class relationships is harder to interpret. Only the working class is inter-generationally stable, being composed of predominantly sons of manual workers, in a ratio of 30.9 per cent with fathers from classes VI–VII to 13.8 per cent with fathers from classes I–V (see table 5.7). Whether that 30 per cent, or 3 men in 10, do constitute a 'mature' working class in the political arena remains to be seen. Voting behaviour until 1979 bore this out to some extent. A. Heath (1981) showed that working-class men with working-class fathers and working-class fathers-in-law are more likely than any other category to vote Labour. He, indeed, showed that men at every level of the class hierarchy who had working-class connections were more likely to vote Labour than those without. This corresponds to information on the friendship and leisure patterns of the upwardly mobile. Such patterns provide strong evidence that men who are inter-generationally stable, whether in the service class or the working class, have social contact with people of their own class. As might be expected, a man upwardly mobile is more likely to have working-class friends and associates than a man born into the service class. However, there seem to be few problems for the upwardly mobile in becoming assimilated into their new class position. (It used to be thought that such men might be isolated or unwelcome, but such problems have probably been overcome through the sheer volume of the upwardly mobile.) The upwardly mobile have sociable relations across classes.

The third, intermediate, class seems to exhibit relatively little continuity between generations. With the exception of sons of men in class IV, the petite bourgeoisie, who because they inherit property are relatively likely to continue in the same line of business as their fathers (see table 5.3), the other intermediate classes spread out across the class structure almost at random. This is, in important part, due to the typical patterns of intra-generational mobility in the period. Men tend to pass through jobs in the intermediate classes. Hardly any men spend their entire working life in occupational classes III or V. Stewart, Prandy and Blackburn (1980) showed that young men who were routine white-collar workers would, before they reached 35 years of age, either be promoted into managerial occupations or leave to try other jobs, usually manual ones. The other main group of male, routine white-collar workers were older men, over 50, who had been promoted from the shop floor, often because they were no longer physically capable of manual tasks. These are both instances of changes which can be understood in terms of careers. (It is important to bear in mind that many people's social and political behaviour may be oriented to their anticipated future rather than to their current situation.) People may be mobile during their lifetime, intra-generationally.

TABLE 5.7 | Inter-generational social mobility into and out of the manual working class, men aged 20–64, England and Wales, 1972 (percentages)

Father's social class when sons aged 14	Son's class (1972)		
	Other (I–V)	Working (V–VII)	All
Other (I–V)	34.1	13.8	47.8
Working (VI–VII)	21.2	30.9	52.1
All	55.3	44.7	100.0

Total number of respondents = 9,434
Source: Tables 5.4 and 5.5

Again, Goldthorpe, Llewellyn and Payne demonstrate a considerable amount of intra-generational mobility among men. In their survey, they asked for a man's first full-time job and for the job he held after 10 years of working life. A very considerable proportion (73 per cent) of those aged 35 and over in the service class in 1972 had had first jobs in other classes. Moreover, there was no evidence that this route into the service class was closing up. (It used to be thought that increased numbers of people getting qualifications in higher education would block channels of upward mobility within firms and organizations.) Another interesting feature of intra-generational mobility is that, while sons of service-class fathers often have first jobs in other social classes, after 10 years of working life they have secured service-class posts. Only 27 per cent of service-class sons were direct entrants into service-class occupations, while a further 36 per cent had first jobs elsewhere.

Ultimately the understanding of class formation depends upon a grasp of the experience of class in contemporary society. This is not as well researched as it used to be. We know that people can talk about class, but we do not know whether they much care about it, whether it much affects their lives, whether they are conscious of it as part of their daily lives. Hence in the next chapter we intend to look at the existing, sometimes dated, sometimes sketchy evidence regarding differences in the material conditions and ways of life of people belonging to different social classes.

Summary

1 There have been relatively high levels of absolute, inter-generational social mobility in Britain since the Second World War, much of it being upward mobility into an expanded service class. As a result, the service class consists of men of mixed-class origins.

2 The high rate of mobility can be attributed to the upgrading of the occupational structure – rapid growth in service-class positions has occurred. This has permitted low levels of downward mobility. Thus, sons of service-class fathers have usually secured service-class positions for themselves. It also follows that most of today's manual workers had working-class fathers.

3 The degree of self-recruitment is highest in the upper class, elite positions being filled by men of exclusive social-class background.

4 There is much dispute about how meritocratic the existing system is, and social mobility data are a vital tool of interpretation.

Related topics

Other aspects of the ownership of wealth as capital are discussed in sections 3.2 and 3.3. Further information on employment and the occupational structure can be found in sections 7.2 for women and 8.4 for ethnic minorities. The political and cultural consequences of class structure are the topic of chapter 6, and the debate on the decline of class is explored further in section 6.2. The Nuffield study included an examination of the relationship between education and mobility, which is examined in section 14.4. On elite recruitment, see section 6.5. Further discussion of the careers of clerical workers is to be found in section 6.4.

Further reading

The best up-to-date and accessible summary of changes in income and wealth is Hills (1995). A good review of the debates about understanding inequality can be found in Scott (1994). A. Heath (1981) is an accessible and interesting analysis of social mobility.

Cross-references to *Readings in Contemporary British Society*

Wilkinson on the relationships between health and poverty; **Westergaard** on the consequences of inequality of income and wealth for class differences; **Savage** on social mobility; **Skeggs** on working-class women and class identity.

Social Classes

6

6.1   Introduction

Class has been something of an obsession in British social science, not least because it proved an incisive analytic tool for understanding inequality, social division and political change. For much of the nineteenth and twentieth centuries, family background, main source of income, place of residence, cultural tastes and political affiliations were closely associated, and class position condensed information about these major aspects of social differences. It was possible to characterize neighbourhoods, cultures and political movements in terms of the class positions of the people affiliated to them. Class linked together and summarized empirical description of many aspects of any individual's life. The likelihood of prosperity, work experiences, current and long-term consumption (and health) opportunities, the future trajectories of children and collective institutional culture, that is to say most key aspects of social existence, were held in common among aggregates of people who shared an economic position. Economic circumstances generated visible and recognizable shared social experiences. Economic differences were clearly expressed in cultural and political practice. Given that class could be understood theoretically in terms of the way that the economic system of capitalist production was organized, this simple operational measure of social location was descriptively powerful and a basis for a moral critique of inequality which had immense political relevance. Commentators of most political persuasions typically agreed that differentiation of social positions was primarily generated by the allocation of people to different economic positions in society. All typically would use the concept of class to describe economic inequalities, implying a hierarchy of privilege and identifying economic origins of systematic social inequality. This was partly because, since the start of the twentieth century, political activity in Britain has been organized consciously around the notion of class – a common political term which served as a basis for asking people to join a political party, a trade union or a social movement. Indeed, much political speculation was concerned with the role of the working class in instigating revolution or reform of the social system. Much of sociological interest (and indeed of the state's interest in funding social research) was in the behaviour of a category of person (the working class) which was an unknown quantity to most middle-class personnel, including those with a concern for maintaining social order.

Simplifying greatly, there was, until recently, widespread consensus among sociologists that some version of a materialist model was applicable as a basis for understanding class inequality and social change. The model had three main features:

1   Classes are founded in a shared material position which arises from the nature of people's work and the rewards received for labour.
2   Shared material position is a basis for group identity, similarity of experience leading to both similarity of outlook and a sense of common condition.
3   Such identity may be expressed in terms of shared interests which provide a basis for political organization and action.

The link between (1) position in the mode of production, (2) social identity and (3) political action is the original core of sociological interest in class. A good deal of time has been spent by historians and sociologists in examining the operation of this model as it applied to different social classes in different societies. As a model it has proved a very serviceable filter for understanding European politics over the last 200 years. One of its main attractions is that it has served as a way of exploring social change. It linked key features of the capitalist organization of economic life with some expectations about the nature of social participation and future-oriented strategies for political transformation. The model might be summarized as in figure 6.1.

Increasing scepticism of this model of class has fuelled the debate about the declining importance of class.

The collective structural level

Class structure → Class consciousness → Class action

The individual level

Class position → Class identity → Political mobilization in class movements

Figure 6.1 | Model of the causal effects of class

This chapter deals next with some evidence about the extent to which the British population is aware of class and uses it as a source of identity. Then it goes on to examine some of the ways in which class is experienced, focusing on differences in the conditions of working-, middle- and upper-class lives.

6.2   The decline of social class?

Class has probably been more important in the UK than in some other Western societies for several reasons. Britain was the longest-established proletarian society, where economic differences had come to the fore earliest and comparatively unchallenged by other complicating divisions like ethnicity, nationality and religious affiliation, which were either comparatively muted or spatially concentrated in peripheral regions. The model above thus applied very effectively, because it held for most of the population, men and women alike, and was visible because social power and wealth were in the hands of identifiable groups of people. There were strong class-based cultures, visible from clothing, audible from accent and embodied in mannerisms.

It is often proposed that social class is no longer as important as it was even in the late 1960s. The arguments in support of the 'decline of class' thesis with respect to inequality were reviewed in section 5.3, but there are various others which relate to the political and cultural outcomes. They include:

- that the economic underpinnings to social differences are being eroded as 'post-materialist' concerns about quality of life and the environment take over (Offe 1985);
- that distinctive cultures based upon class have dissolved (Waters 1993; Turner 1988);
- that political action no longer revolves around class organizations or class interests (Pahl 1993).

Even if the concept of class was previously overworked, it could nevertheless easily and effectively be applied to British society. Britain comprised a specific, delimited population, not characterized by other major mobilized social cleavages, with limited inward migration, relative stability of marriages organized around a male breadwinner wage, the prevalence of occupational communities and a hierarchical cultural system, all of which consolidated class differences. The application of the concept of class in British sociology was at its height in the 1950s and 1960s, when these conditions were not only met, but also being actively addressed through welfare state reforms. By the end of the twentieth century, some of the social implications of economic divisions had become less salient than before. Also, the effect of class has grown more opaque because of the impact of processes of individualization, of social structural change, particularly readjustment of gender relations, of changes in the occupational structure, and of the loss of political momentum of popular movements based upon class identification.

Nevertheless, even in these respects there is still considerable evidence that class remains socially important. For example, awareness of class is still diffused throughout society. In an opinion poll in July 1998, in response to the question 'Overall, do you think Britain is classless or class ridden?', 68 per cent of people said class ridden, 21 per cent classless and 11 per cent did not know (*Guardian*, 6 July 1998), suggesting a high level of awareness of divisions along class lines.

The claim that class differences are, empirically, much the same as before and that the consequence for social life of class position is as strong as ever has been put most succinctly by Goldthorpe and Marshall (1992), who argue, with respect to a number of areas central to sociological investigation (voting behaviour, educational opportunity and social mobility), that the best available empirical research shows very little change in the statistical relationship between class position and the behaviours examined. There is no demonstrable decline in the association between class and other social practices. Sociologists arguing decline theses are misled, and are not, as they ought to be, consulting the best-established facts.

Support for the view that class differences remain strong in the UK comes from the most comprehensive recent study of the British class structure, that of Marshall et al. (1988). Marshall and colleagues provide evidence that class identity remains strong. They interviewed 1,770 people of working age in England, Scotland and Wales during 1984. They conclude:

> There is no obvious lack of class awareness among the population of modern Britain as a whole. Sixty per cent of our sample claimed that they thought of themselves as belonging to one particular social class and well over 90 per cent could place themselves in a particular class category. The proportions who refused to do so, or stated that they did not know to which class they belonged, were very small. Almost three-quarters (73 per cent) of the respondents felt class to be an inevitable feature of modern society; 52 per cent thought that there were important issues causing conflict between social classes (only 37 per cent actually disagreed with this; and, perhaps most strikingly of all, half of the sample agreed with a question [Question 25a]* which was formulated so as to invite respondents to disagree with the judgment that today, as in the past, there is a dominant class which largely controls the economic and political system, and a lower class which has no control over economic and political affairs. (Marshall et al. 1988, p. 143)

> [* Q.25(a) was as follows: 'In the past there was a dominant class which largely controlled the economic and political system, and a lower class which had no control over economic or political affairs. Some people say that things are still like this, others say it has now changed. What do you think, has it changed, or stayed the same?']

On the face of it, then, there was still considerable class awareness in the mid-1980s. More recent opinion polls suggest that this is still so. Nevertheless, there have been some criticisms of the findings in terms of the probability that people responding to a questionnaire about social class are likely to be encouraged to think in class terms by the interviewer. Certainly it is possible that class awareness might be less significant in everyday life, for one could easily know about social classes but not act in such terms. But other findings bolstered the case. Table 6.1 is interesting in that when asked 'Is there any other major group you identify with?' besides class, not many competing answers were forthcoming.

TABLE 6.1 | **Sources of social identity other than class**

Source	N	% of responses	% of cases
Business or professional group	85	23.9	26.8
Religious group	66	18.5	20.8
Ethnicity or race	41	11.5	12.9
Lifestyle grouping	24	6.7	7.6
Pressure group	22	6.2	6.9
Political party	20	5.6	6.3
Gender	20	5.6	6.3
Unemployment	16	4.5	5.0
Age group	14	3.9	4.4
The lower paid	13	3.7	4.1
Respectability	7	2.0	2.2
Trade unionism	5	1.4	1.6
The self-made	4	1.1	1.3
Others	19	5.3	6.0
Total	356	100	112.3

Valid cases = 317
Source: Marshall et al. 1988, p. 148

The study equally challenged the view that class is of declining significance because paid work is no longer so central to people's lives. In response to a question 'Is your present job just a means of earning a living, or does it mean much more to you than that?', only 34 per cent said it was just a way to get by. And when the respondents who said it was more than that were asked what the job meant to them they gave the answers in table 6.2.

When, after having been asked some questions about their leisure activities, respondents were faced with a question of whether any of those activities were more important than work, 73 per cent said 'no' (Marshall et al. 1988, p. 212).

The empirical evidence from this study implies class awareness and identity have changed less than some commentators would suggest, though a number of criticisms are worth considering:

| TABLE 6.2 | The meaning of work | | |

Way in which job is more than just a means of earning a living	N	% of responses	% of cases
Rewarding, fulfilling, worthwhile, enjoyable	634	37.0	81.6
Human contact, being with colleagues, getting out of house	279	16.3	35.9
Using or developing my skills	183	10.7	23.6
I enjoy working for the present organization	167	9.8	21.5
Job allows use of initiative	144	8.4	18.5
Variety in the work	128	7.5	16.5
Work is central to my life	85	5.0	10.9
Value of my work to country	56	3.3	7.2
Work fits in with my family/I do it for my family	16	0.9	2.1
It is better than being unemployed	8	0.5	1.0
Other	12	0.7	1.5
Total	1712	100.0	220.3

(Valid cases = 777)
Source: Marshall et al. (1988) p. 208

1   The first concerns the method of data collection. The ways in which the questions were worded and ordered seem likely to have led respondents into expressing stronger awareness of class than would otherwise be the case.
2   We might be wary of claims about demonstration of persistence of class attitudes, identity and consciousness because the survey uncovered the views of the British population at a particular point in time in 1984–5 – the period of the major strike of coalminers – which itself might have sharpened senses of class difference and class identity.
3   Other critics argue that the class schema employed by Marshall is defective; or at least that there are more enlightening ways of thinking theoretically about class. Both Crompton (1993) and Savage et al. (1992) express reservations about considering class solely in occupational terms, arguing that explaining class formation is the primary purpose of class analysis. That is to say, it is the active organization of people into behaving as a class that matters most, so that using a questionnaire about attitudes, which entails dealing with people outside of their local social context, is mistaken. Savage in particular is keen to go back to examining class relations as locally situated social relations. Class is an outcome of everyday social life, not simply of occupational position, and it is therefore largely invalid to examine it by surveying individuals.

Summary

1   Until recently, sociologists agreed that the concept of social class – linking together positions in the mode of production, social identity and political action – was critical to the analysis of British society.

2   Since the 1980s arguments have been advanced that class is no longer of much significance, but there is considerable evidence for the continued significance of class-based inequalities and class identity and awareness in the UK.

6.3   Working-class experience

The character of the working class remains a contentious issue in contemporary sociology. The debate is hard to appreciate without recalling Karl Marx's view of the revolutionary role of the working class in capitalist society. Marx thought that the logic of capitalist accumulation would turn the vast majority of the population into proletarians, that is, workers who relied on wages for their subsistence because they lacked any other means of livelihood. Lacking property and increasingly deprived of control over their own labour, the working class would come to share a common (homogeneous) economic position. Uniformly degraded work and poor pay would characterize the workers and distinguish them from a small, privileged social class of property owners. In such circumstances, Marx expected the workers to unite politically, on the basis of their common class position, to abolish capitalist domination.

The working classes of the Western world have rarely been revolutionary. Since the mid-nineteenth century, however, the main force behind social and political change has come from organizations of the working class – trade unions, socialist and social-democratic parties. Such organizations have been 'reformist': they have pressed successfully for improvements in pay and working conditions, for the extension of political rights like the vote, and for social rights like health care, education and social security benefits. These are achievements of labour movements on behalf of the working class, but they have not undermined capitalist economic relations. Indeed, with the collapse of the communist regimes of Eastern Europe after 1989, any expectation that labour movements might be agencies of revolutionary change has disappeared. However, since this reformist politics is universal in Western societies, except where it has been suppressed by dictatorships, it might be anticipated that it will continue as a form of working-class opposition to capitalism.

Differences over the way in which class conflict might be expected to develop have formed the background to sociological debates since the late 1960s, and have revolved around interpretations of how social changes have affected manual workers. Two issues have been central. The first is whether the position of the working class has changed relative to other classes, and particularly whether manual workers remain a *distinctive* class. The second concerns changes in the internal structure of the working class, especially whether or not it is becoming more *internally divided* and hence less prone to acting politically in a united, or solidaristic, way.

We look at these issues with respect to various aspects of working-class experience in contemporary Britain: class position (employment relation), lifestyle and culture (consumption and social participation), and political practices (class consciousness, voting, and membership of political organizations). In each case, we look at changes in circumstances and assess (1) whether these changes make the working class less distinctive, and (2) whether they affect the internal unity of the working class. Throughout the rest of this section we provide evidence and argument to help resolve the two main issues – the distinctiveness of the class and its internal divisions.

Class position

When British sociologists talk of the working class, they are usually referring to people currently or formerly employed in manual occupations and to their dependents. Thus, heads of households in manual jobs, retired or unemployed former manual workers, and housewives and children not in employment are considered members of the working class. This definition is problematic. It is not always easy to decide whether a particular job is 'manual' or 'non-manual'. As the debate about the proletarianization of office work (section 6.4) indicates, the contractual situation and working conditions of many non-manual jobs have developed characteristics very like those of traditional manual occupations. Furthermore, there are a substantial number of households in which the husband is a manual worker and his wife is in non-manual employment. In the past it made sense to distinguish between manual and non-manual workers because the work experience and social lives of these two groups differed significantly. Now, some sociologists, for example Savage (1995), suggest that that social boundary is no longer of significance.

In this regard, one important aspect of change has been the declining size of the manual workforce. In 1951, there were 15.6 million manual workers, constituting 72 per cent of the workforce (Routh 1987, p. 38). By 1991, according to the Census, there were no more than 9.8 million, 42 per cent of all people in employment (OPCS 1994, table 14). The majority of employees are no longer manual workers.

Contractual situation

Manual workers are better off than ever before. Real wages have risen over time, which is to say that the actual purchasing power is greater than it used to be. Also, various Acts of Parliament have improved some of the fringe benefits of manual work. Longer statutory holidays are an improvement; so too is the introduction of redundancy payments to remove some financial insecurities. On the other hand, the source of manual workers' incomes and their opportunities for promotion are probably the same as they were in the late 1940s. However, the general improvements in market situation alone are insufficient for us to resolve either of our two controversial issues: whether the working class remains distinct from other social classes, and whether the working class is internally divided.

Plate 6.1	Best-paid and worst-paid male manual workers
	Source: Format / Joanne O'Brien; J. Allan Cash

The distinctiveness of the contractual situation of the working class

Some recent changes have tended to reduce the differences between manual and other workers. During the twentieth century, the average male manual wage, especially of semi- and unskilled workers, has increased relative to that for routine white-collar work. The 1998 *New Earnings Survey* showed that the average full-time male manual wage was £307 per week, whilst the average for clerical and related work was £292 per week. The average non-manual wage for men was much higher at £425 per week. The convergence of the weekly wage of clerks and manual workers nevertheless obscures differences.

First, manual workers work longer hours. The average working week for a male British manual worker in 1998 was 44.1 hours; non-manuals worked 38.1 hours. (Incidentally, working hours are longer in Britain than in other major European countries.) This follows from the fact that high earnings from manual work usually depend upon lots of overtime: on average, overtime was 4.7 hours per week, and 13 per cent of gross weekly earnings derived from it.

Second, manual workers have a less attractive profile of earnings over their lifetime than non-manual workers with career structures, in which promotion and/or regular salary increments increase income until fairly late in their working lives.

Third, manual workers suffer from greater insecurity of employment. They are more frequently unemployed (see section 4.5). They may experience short-time working and temporary lay-offs. They are rarely entitled to sickness pay, are unable to take time off with pay to deal with family emergencies, and usually have pay deducted for lateness. Office workers suffer few of these indignities and insecurities: and the higher up the managerial hierarchy one goes, the better are fringe benefits and conditions of employment. It is probably, in the end, the degree of insecurity which most strongly distinguishes manual work. Most manual workers will experience unemployment at some time, making periods of considerable hardship part of the normal life course.

Thus, the contractual situation of manual workers is distinctive and inferior in certain respects, though the differences compared with the more routine white-collar occupations are diminishing.

Internal differentiation of contracts within the working class

There is considerable variation among manual workers. Different jobs in different industries pay different wages. The best-paid manual workers in 1998 were rail engine drivers and their assistants and telephone fitters, where the average full-time male wage was £469 per week. By contrast, male kitchen porters, the most lowly rewarded of occupations recorded by the *New Earnings Survey*, earned only £171 per week on average.

The most systematic difference, perhaps, was the gap between pay for men and women. One in three full-time women manual workers earned less than £160 per week; only one in five earned more than £250. Although there has been some slight improvement since the late 1980s, women manual workers earn only 63 per cent of men's wage even when employed full-time. Many women are part-timers and are even less well paid.

The inferior position of women is often analysed in terms of dual labour markets (see also section 7.2). Women, and to an extent men of ethnic minorities, cluster in the secondary, lower, sector of the labour market, where wages are poorer, jobs less secure, firms smaller and more precarious, and conditions worse. The market situation of women is one source of division among manual workers.

On the other hand, wage differentials between skilled and less skilled manual workers have declined, for both men and women. Though differentials continue to cause conflict between unions, with skilled workers seeking to maintain their relative privileges, the range of incomes within the class has narrowed. However, readily identifiable differences along the dimensions of gender or ethnicity might, therefore, create deeper political divisions than before, especially where trade unions protecting white males can be seen as contributing to the inferior position of women and ethnic minorities.

Working conditions

Work situations – especially the relationships of authority in the labour process – of manual workers have been discussed at length in section 4.2. It was concluded that many workers had little control over their work, as control had been wrested from them by management. This was the essence of the process of deskilling, one which had had a very considerable impact on manual work and was also spreading to routine clerical work. Most manual workers, other than craft workers, have little discretion over their own working practices. Equally, manual workers, except for a small percentage of foremen or forewomen and supervisors, exercise no authority over other workers. Rather, in general, they are in subordinate occupational positions. (Even fewer women than men held positions of authority.) Consequently, most manual workers have an instrumental or 'economistic' attitude towards work: their principal concerns are with pay and job security rather than with intrinsic features of the work. These attitudes often foster co-operative, or solidaristic, relationships among manual workers themselves.

There is a degree of convergence between manual and non-manual jobs. The working conditions of some routine white-collar workers and some lower and middle managers have deteriorated. Nevertheless, even among these jobs, conditions of work are usually more pleasant: they are less dangerous and less noisy, for instance. However, the main contrast in work situations between classes lies in the superior conditions experienced by professionals, senior managers and owners of businesses.

There remains considerable variation within the manual working class in work situation, depending upon the type of industry, the nature of managerial control, and the degree of discretion which the worker has over the work process. This is not, however, a feature of working-class experience which in itself creates serious internal divisions. A man who is a process worker is not likely to feel hostile towards either a worker on an assembly line or a farm labourer just because of the difference in type of work.

Working-class culture

The degree of prestige attached to manual jobs, and the social status of the incumbents of those jobs, suggest that manual employment is generally held in low esteem. When people are asked to rank occupations in terms of their desirability, there is a fair degree of consensus. In that hierarchy, manual jobs come at the bottom, though there is some degree of overlap between white- and blue-collar occupations. This suggests a persistent separation in most people's minds between manual and non-manual employment, which carries over into estimations of the social status of manual workers.

In the past there was comparatively little social interaction between members of different classes. Separation between manual workers and others continues to be apparent in patterns of sociability and friendship. Almost all studies show that the friends and acquaintances of manual workers are themselves predominantly working class. Hence there is little reason to think that differences of prestige attached to manual jobs cause serious internal divisions. Even supervisory workers in manual occupations, like foremen in the London docks, associate more with manual than non-manual workers. Patterns of sociability continue to be classbound, which contributes to the separation of one class from another.

Women's perceptions of class are particularly revealing. Some women seem very conscious of class differences, particularly those from middle-class backgrounds and with middle-class cultural credentials. In samples of teenage girls at school, it is middle-class girls who show the sharpest awareness of class (Frazer 1988). Other women seem more likely than men to dismiss class as unimportant, or to be embarrassed or hesitant about talking in terms of social class (Charles 1990). However, if there are a disproportionately high number of working-class women in the latter category, this does not necessarily mean that their attitudes and behaviour are not deeply coloured by their sense of class. This is powerfully demonstrated in a study by Skeggs (1997).

On not being working class: a case study

Skeggs, in *Formations of Class and Gender: Becoming Respectable*, explores the experience of working-class women. She asks how their socialization affects them in the transition to adulthood, how they deal with a sense of powerlessness and potential lack of public esteem, and what consequences this has for their sense of class, femininity, sexuality and political identification. Starting in 1980 and using ethnographic techniques, she contacted 83 young women enrolled at a further education college on courses in community care, pre-health care and pre-social care, training them for jobs as care assistants in hospitals and homes for the elderly. These were working-class girls with low levels of educational qualifications, who were inducted into an occupational culture of caring in which they learned to be responsible for others to whom they would offer personal care. This process partly transforms their identities as the courses tend to appeal to a model of nineteenth-century middle-class womanhood. *Respectability* was its motif: emphasis is put upon being caring, in many different senses of the word, being responsible, becoming married, and conforming to particular prescriptions of appropriate sexual behaviour. Such a model has never fitted the experience of poorer, lower-class women.

Skeggs suggests that these young women, whom she talked to repeatedly over a 12-year period, during which they joined the labour market and started families, 'disidentify' with the working class. They do not talk about class, but they experience its effects. They refuse the label 'working class' for themselves, as indeed they might given their responses (during interviews in 1992) to the question 'What is working class?':

> To me if you are working class it basically means that you are poor. That you have nothing. You know, nothing. [Sam]

> They're rough. You can always tell. Rough, you know, the women are common as muck you know, always have a fag in their mouths, the men are dead rough, you know. [Andrea]

> The ones who batter their kids. [Pam]

> It used to be you were working class if you worked on the railways say and it didn't mean you had no money, but now it's changed. Now it means you don't work, like it's not those with the good jobs now it's those without jobs, they're the real working class. [Lisa]

Skeggs suggests that the young women have a particular way of seeing themselves and others, which is common to the group in this particular position in the social and occupational structure, which involved trying *not* to be working class. They pursued strategies for 'improvement', but despite many attempts at 'passing' as middle class they always remained anxious and insecure, apologizing for their taste, never certain that they had succeeded, whether in terms of body management, dress or interior design. Because they had not the ingrained and much-practised confidence that develops from a middle-class cultural background, they were doomed to fail. Hence, Skeggs (1997, p. 74) surmised that 'Class was central to the young women's subjectivities. It was not spoken of in the traditional sense of recognition – I am working class – but rather, was displayed in their multifarious efforts not to be recognised as working class. They disidentified and they dissimulated.'

We are not invited to feel sorry for these women as individuals, except in so far as they seem to be aspiring towards, or holding an ideal of, a particular form of conduct which is extremely hard for them ever to attain. Their particular passage through life has restricted their opportunities and channelled them into particular sorts of social as well as occupational slots. They are operating within categories and norms more appropriate to another social group with greater resources; it is the world of the middle class which is culturally and socially legitimate, denying the young women more satisfying forms of adaptation to their own circumstances. Therefore they live as partial failures in their own eyes because they view themselves through the low estimations accorded them by middle-class women. Skeggs (1997, p. 95), concluding that 'Class is still a hidden injury', observed that:

> They attempted to display their distinction from being classified as working class through a variety of methods. To do so they made investments in their bodies, clothes, consumption practices, leisure pursuits and homes. Their investments indicated a strong desire to pass as middle class. But it was only an imaginary middle class that they wanted to be. They did not want to take on the whole package of dispositions. Their responses to classification were informed by fear, desire, resentment and humiliation.

The overall effect is to be persuaded that these women have shared experience, living under the sway of a set of powerful institutions which structure their world, their sense of self and their identities. As Skeggs (1997, p. 89) notes, 'All display a knowledge that there is another more highly valued way of doing things which they have yet to achieve.' Thus we see the power of a system of social classification in which people are made to know their place in relation to others. These would not be called class identities, because these women do all they can to forget, ignore or reinterpret their class location. There is no solace for them in being identified as a working-class woman. Whereas working-class men do have the option of adopting a heroic model of self – cast in the image of masculine strength associated with hard manual labour – there is no glorious equivalent for women. Being regarded as responsible and respectable is the greatest accolade that can be bestowed upon them. Ultimately, their shared experience was not of the kind likely to lead to any sort of positive identification with any social class.

Consumption

Experiences outside work affect class solidarity and political action. For example, the neighbourhood in which a worker lives affects his or her voting behaviour. One aspect of the changing lifestyle of the working class which has attracted special attention recently is consumption patterns. Consumption patterns emerge from the choices made about how money is spent.

Rising real incomes mean that manual workers now possess consumer goods which were previously accessible to only a small minority of the population. Working-class households are increasingly likely to own durable goods like cars, fridges and washing machines, and to have a telephone and central heating in their dwellings. Perhaps the most remarked-upon change is, however, the growth of working-class house ownership. In 1996, 77 per cent of skilled manual households, 56 per cent of semi-skilled and

38 per cent of unskilled either owned outright the house in which they were living or were in the process of purchasing it on a mortgage. This represents a considerable expansion of owner-occupation for, except in a few regions of Britain, manual workers usually used to rent housing from private landlords or the municipal council. It has frequently been assumed that these new consumption patterns would have lasting structural effects on the working class. Indeed, the embourgeoisement thesis (the idea from the 1960s that everyone was becoming middle class) was based on observing the spread of the goods associated with a middle-class lifestyle.

The consumption patterns of different classes

One weakness of the argument that affluence leads to assimilation of workers to a middle-class lifestyle is the fact that consumption patterns remain markedly unequal between classes. Table 6.3, taken from the *Family Spending* survey, shows that in 1996–7 household spending varied depending on the occupational class of heads of households. Households of professionals spent on average £138 per week more than skilled manual workers and £243 per week more than unskilled manual workers. Routine white-collar households spent about £50 less than skilled manual workers. However, when expenditure per person is calculated, a different, and more pertinent, impression is obtained. Clerical workers' households are smaller than those of manual workers, so that the level of consumption of each member is actually higher.

TABLE 6.3	Expenditure of households by occupation of head of household, employees

	Average weekly household expenditure	Average weekly expenditure per person
Professional	486	181
Employers, managers	502	171
Intermediate non-manual	385	154
Junior non-manual	293	127
Skilled manual	348	113
Semi-skilled manual	268	100
Unskilled manual	243	90

Source: ONS 1997, table 3.2

Table 6.4 shows expenditure per head of household of different occupational classes, expressed in relation to the pattern of a skilled manual worker. A number of points emerge:

- Expenditure on food and alcohol varies least across households: expenditure on household services, transport and leisure varies most.
- Non-manual household members consume more than their manual counterparts; this applies to routine white-collar workers as well as professionals.
- Unskilled workers are relatively deprived compared with other groups, especially with respect to leisure, transport and domestic services.

TABLE 6.4 | Expenditure per person on various services and commodities for certain occupational groupings of head of household as proportion of skilled manual households

	Occupation of head of household			
Commodity or service	Professional	Junior non-manual	Skilled manual	Unskilled manual
Total number of households	257	416	792	135
Housing (net)	188	137	100	87
Food	138	109	100	89
Alcoholic drink	103	95	100	87
Household goods	136	113	100	71
Household services	209	128	100	78
Transport (motoring and public)	178	113	100	67
Leisure goods and services	186	102	100	71
Total expenditure per person (£)	181.37	127.24	112.80	90.25
Total household expenditure (£)	485.52	293.33	348.22	243.33

Expenditure per person has been derived by dividing the household expenditure for each commodity or service by the average number of persons per household. These figures have then been expressed as proportions of the equivalent figures for households whose head was a skilled manual worker.
Source: *Family Spending* 1996–7, table 3.2

- Non-manual workers are most distinctive in the amounts of money they spend on services and housing.

More detailed studies of taste have also provided evidence of the continued distinctiveness of the manual working class. For example, Warde (1997, pp. 111–12) examined expenditure on food purchasing and showed that there was a distinctive manual working-class diet, characterized by a greater proportion of expenditure devoted to bread, sausages, cooked meats, beer, fish and chips, sugar and tea. Studies of cultural consumption show that working-class people are considerably less likely to visit museums or art galleries or to go to classical music concerts than are their middle-class counterparts (see table 6.5). Indeed, there is some evidence that the cultural repertoire of the working class is generally more restricted, they having experience or knowledge of fewer types of music, cuisine, literature and leisure pursuits. Though this is at least as much an effect of educational experience as occupational position, it is none the less evidence of the existence of a distinct working-class culture.

Internal differences: consumption cleavages?

Some authors argue that new patterns of consumption, especially of houses, divide the working class internally. Consumption cleavages have arisen between households with predominantly private access to housing and transport and those which depend on pub-

| TABLE 6.5 | Participation[a] in selected leisure activities away from home: by social grade,[b] 1996 (percentages) |

Activity	AB	C1	C2	D	E	All adults
Visit a public house	74	69	64	66	48	65
Meal in a restaurant (not fast food)	87	73	58	45	36	62
Drive for pleasure	54	47	48	46	38	47
Meal in fast-food restaurant	48	44	42	43	29	42
Library	59	43	31	30	31	39
Cinema	47	42	35	30	21	36
Short-break holiday	41	33	28	22	18	29
Disco or night club	26	29	27	31	20	27
Historic building	41	31	17	15	10	24
Spectator sports event	30	25	23	18	7	22
Theatre	35	26	17	11	7	20
Museum or art gallery	36	24	14	11	12	20
Fun fair	14	13	19	16	10	15
Exhibition (other than museum/ gallery)	24	18	13	7	4	14
Theme park	14	11	14	12	10	12
Visit a betting shop	5	6	11	12	12	9
Camping or caravanning	8	9	11	9	5	9
Bingo	2	5	8	10	14	7

[a] Percentage aged 16 and over participating in each activity in the three months prior to interview
[b] Social grade categories are based on the occupation of the chief income earner of his or her household as follows:
    A: higher managerial, administrative or professional
    B: intermediate managerial, administrative or professional
    C1: supervisory or clerical and junior managerial, administrative or professional
    C2: skilled manual workers
    D: semi- and unskilled manual
    E: state pensioners or widows (no other earners), casual or lowest grade workers or long-term unemployed
Source: Social Trends 1998, table 13.12

lic provision (i.e. council housing and public transport). In 1988, 64 per cent of manual workers were owner-occupiers and 68 per cent owned a car. House ownership, in particular, may create differences of status and of material interests within the working class. Most owner-occupiers have benefited financially since the 1960s because house prices have risen faster than inflation and because of tax relief on mortgages. The gains are, relatively, at the expense of tenants in rented housing, who by 1990 were almost entirely working class (see table 6.6). There was also some prestige attached to owner-occupation, and perhaps some sense of greater control over one's life arising from ownership of property. Certainly the sale of council houses to sitting tenants was a very popular policy and many, predominantly working-class, people bought their dwellings. Indeed, survey evidence shows that about 90 per cent of the British population prefer owner-occupation to renting. However, it is doubtful whether a change in tenure causes

TABLE 6.6 | Socio-economic group and economic activity status of head of household by tenure, Great Britain, 1988 (percentages)

Socio-economic group and economic activity status of head of household[a]	Owner occupied			Rented				Total
	Owned outright	With mortgage	With job/ business	Local authority/ new town	Housing association/ co-operative	Unfurnished private	Furnished private	
Economically active heads:								
Professional	3	9	10	0	1	1	10	5
Employers and managers	8	27	34	3	3	6	12	15
Intermediate non-manual	4	12	9	2	5	6	13	7
Junior non-manual	3	7	7	3	1	5	11	5
Skilled manual and own-account non-professional	12	29	16	17	13	17	14	20
Semi-skilled manual and personal service	4	8	20	11	10	7	9	8
Unskilled manual	1	1	2	5	3	2	1	2
Economically inactive heads	65	7	2	60	65	57	28	38
Base = 100% (no.)	2393	4018	166	2600	222	419	22	10043

[a] Excluding members of the armed forces, full-time students and those who have never worked.
Source: *General Household Survey* 1988, p. 242

Plate 6.2 Aesthetic change occurring when council houses become owner-occupied
Source: Nick Abercrombie

people to alter other aspects of their behaviour.

Saunders's (1990) study of Slough, Derby and Burnley (see also section 10.3) was concerned to investigate whether owner-occupation encouraged privatization. Privatization has been defined as 'a process . . . manifested in a pattern of social life which is centred on and, indeed, largely restricted to, the home and the conjugal family' (Goldthorpe et al. 1969, p. 97). Saunders found some evidence for home ownership reducing neighbourhood relations (see table 6.7). Mutual aid and neighbourhood life were, overall, stronger on council estates. However, this was probably due to different rates of geographical mobility: 79 per cent of council tenants, compared with 56 per cent of owner-occupiers, had never lived in any town other than their present one, and thus had had plenty of time to cement their social networks. In addition, tenants had lived in their existing houses longer on average.

TABLE 6.7 | **Housing tenure and neighbourhood relations**

	Home owners		Council tenants	
Neighbourhood relations	No.	%	No.	%
At least one close friend living in the neighbourhood	89	35	56	56
At least one close friend living in the town	112	44	57	57
At least one close friend met through the neighbourhood	82	35	44	50
At least one close friend known since childhood	71	31	77	90
Has lived in three or more dwellings since first set up home	182	50	60	46
Always lived in the same town since first set up home	205	56	101	79
Thinks neighbourhood is friendly or very friendly	216	60	77	60
No favours or aid for or from neighbours	100	29	37	30
Regular help by or for neighbours	38	11	23	19

Totals differ for each item owing to missing data.
Source: Saunders 1990, p. 285

Working-class owner-occupiers were, by contrast, more involved than tenants in formal organizations. Nor did Saunders find any relationship between tenure and whether people go out for entertainment: mortgagees were not so heavily burdened by debt that they had to stay at home. He found scarcely any examples of people who consciously changed their behaviour and became home-centred as a result of acquiring their own home. He therefore finds the argument that owner-occupation encourages privatization refuted.

Saunders's results are largely corroborated by the national survey of Marshall et al. (1988). This shows little difference between classes in terms of privatization. Working-class leisure is slightly more likely to be undertaken in the home, and those with friends at work are slightly less likely to meet them socially outside work (see table 6.8). But in most respects – for instance, whether leisure is taken with family or friends – class differences are insignificant. The working class is not especially privatized and no more so than the service class. Devine (1992) drew the same conclusion from her in-depth study of Luton manual workers in the 1980s.

TABLE 6.8 | **Work-based friendships by Goldthorpe class (percentages)**

(a) Proportion of his or her friends whom respondent works with at present

	Class						
Proportion	*I*	*II*	*III*	*IV*	*V*	*VI*	*VII*
None	38	45	49	76	37	34	46
1–10%	38	28	30	14	31	37	30
11–50%	17	15	12	5	19	18	13
51–100%	7	12	9	5	13	11	11

N = 1,178
Source: Social Trends 1998, table 13.12

(b) Does respondent with friends at work see these people socially outside work?

	Class						
Response	*I*	*II*	*III*	*IV*	*V*	*VI*	*VII*
Yes	91	90	86	89	88	77	67
No	9	10	14	11	12	23	33
Total (no.)	69	117	120	27	57	95	144

N = 629
Source: Marshall et al. 1988, p. 217

Working-class politics

In many respects, the debates about the working class are aimed at resolving questions about political consciousness and action. Do workers identify themselves as a class having shared class interests? To what extent does this lead them to support particular political organizations?

Class awareness and identification do not seem to have altered much in recent times. It continues to be the case that the subjective class position of many manual workers (i.e. which class they consider themselves as belonging to) does not entirely correspond with their objective class position. Those manual workers who *do* consider themselves 'middle class' tend to be those with extensive social contacts with non-manual workers and/or those who live in predominantly middle-class areas.

It used to be argued that the working class had a distinctive conception of social and political conflict which sustained their support for the labour movement. Thus, traditional proletarians had a dichotomous image of society, distinguishing sharply between 'them' (the rich, the owners, the bosses) and 'us' (the workers). From this arose both a class identity and a sense of politics as class conflict. It was reported frequently in the 1960s, for instance, that manual workers voted consistently for the Labour Party because it was the party of the workers, of 'people like us'. Despite many claims to the contrary, recent sociological evidence suggests that this imagery and awareness remains predominant and is the only pattern consistently found among manual workers.

The dichotomous image of class is actually widespread. In Marshall et al.'s (1988) study, 63 per cent of the sample 'agreed that the *main* social conflict in Britain today was between those who run industry and those who work for them' (p. 151). Differences of view between classes are mildly apparent on issues of distribution. Table 6.9 shows that the working class (classes VI and VII on the Goldthorpe scale) are most likely to find the distribution of income unfair. However, most of the evidence suggests that manual workers in general are not highly distinctive in their views of social structure.

Respondents to questionnaires show no decline in awareness of class. The vast majority of British people (in most surveys more than 90 per cent) recognize the existence of social classes and will see themselves as belonging to one such class. There is a good deal of variation in the way people describe those classes, and little consensus on how many classes there are or precisely what it is that determines which class a person belongs to. Class remains something which they can observe and which they experience, and through which they view aspects of both politics and everyday life. Consider, for example, table 6.10. Every so often Gallup Polls, in their regular monthly opinion polls, ask a question about the importance of 'class struggle'. The answers to the same question posed at different times since 1964 show a very substantial increase in the percentage of respondents who consider there to be a class struggle; in July 1991, 79 per cent said there was. Although the validity of the figures may be questioned, the trend in answers to the question is remarkable.

The evidence, then, suggests that working-class people do still feel some sense of class identity and consider that it affects their lives. This is probably the result both of living in a political environment which is structured by class interests, and of the experience of class in everyday life. Table 6.10 implies that members of other classes have of late increased their class awareness. However, class identity sustains a radical, alternative political value system among only a minority of manual workers and is not often translated into class-based political action.

TABLE 6.9 | Attitudes to distributional justice by Goldthorpe class (percentages)

(a) Is distribution of wealth and income fair?

Class	Yes	No
I	31	69
II	34	66
III	28	72
IV	44	56
V	24	76
VI	25	75
VII	22	78
All	29	71
Total (no.)	368	914

(b) Why not?

	Class						
	I	*II*	*III*	*IV*	*V*	*VI*	*VII*
Distribution favours those at the top							
Gap between haves and have nots is too wide	57	59	63	64	55	63	63
Pay differentials are too wide	21	19	19	19	26	21	19
Too much poverty, wages too low, too many reduced to welfare	13	17	20	16	13	17	18
Some people acquire wealth too easily (unearned income, etc.)	31	16	13	13	20	10	9
The higher paid are not taxed severely enough	9	15	11	9	12	20	16
Welfare benefits are too low	6	5	6	2	8	9	6
The lower paid or working class are taxed too severely	2	3	3	5	3	0	2
Inequalities of opportunity (in education, for jobs, etc.)	2	2	2	0	0	1	2
Unequal regional distribution (of jobs, income, etc.)	4	3	3	0	2	1	2
Distribution favours those at the bottom							
There are too many scroungers around	6	5	12	9	15	8	10
Pay differentials are too narrow	5	4	1	3	4	4	4
The higher paid are taxed too severely	4	2	3	8	3	3	3
Other reasons							
Inequality of wealth and income inevitable	1	4	4	2	7	2	2
Key groups of workers can hold the country to ransom	1	1	0	0	0	0	0

Percentages in the 'Why not?' columns are based on respondents answering 'no'. Valid cases = 899
Source: Marshall et al. 1988, p. 186

Perhaps the most distinctive feature of the working class is its lack of political partici-pation. Although there are no accurate figures, individual membership of the Labour Party fell from about 1 million to 311,000 between 1950 and 1990, and in the process the *proportion* of manual workers (26 per cent in 1990) has probably reduced (Seyd and Whiteley 1992, pp. 16, 33). Parallel to that is the fall in the proportion of manual workers who are selected as candidates for the Labour Party at elections. The indica-tions are that as involvement in Labour politics declines, working-class people cease to participate in party politics, except to vote (see section 13.3). Disillusionment with party politics and with governments among the working class is a process widely identified. Marshall et al. (1988) discerned an 'informed fatalism': most people thought that gov-

TABLE 6.10	Class struggle: replies to the question 'There used to be a lot of talk in politics about the "class struggle". Do you think there is a class struggle in this country or not?', 1964–91 (percentages)

Date	Is	Is not	Don't know
1964 July	48	39	13
1972 June	58	29	13
1973 January	53	33	14
1974 February	62	27	11
1975 April	60	29	11
1981 March	66	25	9
1984 March	74	20	6
1986 February	70	24	6
1991 July	79	16	4

Source: Gallup Political Index Report 1991; Moorhouse 1976

ernment could, if determined, rectify distributional inequalities and social injustice, but were resigned to the fact that it would not in practice.

As we have seen, the working class is internally differentiated. While there never has been a homogeneous working class in Britain, arguably the class is more fragmented now than in the past. This is probably mostly because of the changing composition of the working class, the reorientation of the institutions of working-class politics, and the process of cultural incorporation:

- The main body of politically active workers used to be white males. Today, not only is the number of white male manual workers declining, but a larger proportion of all manual workers (close to 50 per cent) are either women or black people. Gender and ethnic differences create some distinctive political interests which have recently been the focus of political action. To the extent that these interests are in competition with those of white men, disunity follows.
- Trade unions and the Labour Party were two institutions that appealed for solidarity on the basis of class position and class interests. There was always competition between unions, which tended to inhibit co-operation, and the Labour Party was always ambivalent about being seen as a party only of the working class. Nevertheless both made extensive use of the rhetoric of class, constantly bringing it to public attention. The reduced political prominence of trade unions and the creation of the 'New Labour' programme, which neither proclaims nor prioritizes working-class interests, mean that one previous source of a sense of solidarity has declined.
- Mass consumption, the seductiveness of the products of commercial producers, and the time and organization required to pursue material comforts have probably diluted the distinctiveness of working-class culture. Sources of solidarity that arose from the daily patterns of social interaction within working-class communities, particularly those based on mining, heavy engineering, shipbuilding and the like, have contracted.

Whether these internally divisive processes justify bidding farewell to the working class is largely a matter of judgement. It seems unlikely that there will be any imminent revival of the kinds of working-class politics that characterized much of the twentieth century. Indeed, the political consequences appear to be becoming insignificant as the conditions of the working class deteriorate without any current signs of political resistance, partly because of the restructuring of political institutions, the weakness of trade unions and reforms within the Labour Party, the reduced size of the manual labour force, its increasing heterogeneity, and the immiseration of the least secure section of the class.

Summary

1   Manual workers are a declining proportion of all workers; and an increasing proportion of manual workers are either female and/or from ethnic minorities.
2   Manual workers in aggregate remain socially distinctive, particularly in respect of their economic circumstances, their status situation, their consumption patterns and their political imagery. However, there is overlap especially with workers in routine non-manual occupations.
3   In some respects, especially of working conditions and of privatized lifestyles, manual workers are indistinguishable from routine non-manual workers.
4   There is considerable internal differentiation within the manual working class. This has always been the case, but it may be increasing, creating political divisions within the working class along lines of ethnicity, gender, region and union membership.
5   The effects of these divisions on working-class political movements for social change are uncertain, but it seems unlikely that the social bases exist for any imminent revival of the organized and centralized politics of the working class.

6.4   The middle classes

The growth of the middle classes

The starting point of any sociological analysis of the middle class is the growth of certain kinds of occupation in the twentieth century (see table 6.11). The most noticeable shift in the period 1911–81 was the steep decline in manual occupations and the relative growth in non-manual jobs. Of the non-manual groups, only those employed as sales assistants showed any decline. The white-collar categories themselves did not all gain equally. The higher-professional group increased in size by five times, managers increased almost fourfold, while those in clerical employment increased between three-fold and fourfold. The rate of growth of white- collar occupations has also varied over time. The growth in the clerical grade, for example, was at its highest in the years 1911–21, while the higher-professional category increased most quickly from the 1950s onwards.

| TABLE 6.11 | Occupied population by major occupational groups, Great Britain, 1911–81 (percentages of total occupied population) | | | | | | | |

Occupational groups	1911	1921	1931	1951	1961	1966	1971	1981
Employers and proprietors	6.7	6.8	6.7	5.0	4.7	3.4	–	–
Non-manual workers	18.7	21.2	23.0	30.9	35.9	38.3	44.3	52.3
Managers	3.4	3.6	3.7	5.5	5.4	6.1	9.8	13.7
Higher professionals	1.0	1.0	1.1	1.9	3.0	3.4	3.8	4.8
Lower professionals and technicians	3.1	3.5	3.5	4.7	6.0	6.5	7.7	10.6
Foremen, forewomen and inspectors	1.3	1.4	1.5	2.6	2.9	3.0	3.0	4.1
Clerical and related employees	4.5	6.5	6.7	10.4	12.7	13.2	14.2	14.5
Sales employees	5.4	5.1	6.5	5.7	5.9	6.1	5.7	4.6
Manual workers	74.6	72.0	70.3	64.2	59.3	58.3	55.7	47.7

Source: Price and Bain 1988, p. 164

There are gender differences in these occupational movements. For both men and women, there has been a shift out of manual work into white-collar occupations. Significantly, disproportionate numbers of women have moved into clerical and related occupations. As far as the other categories of non-manual work are concerned, however, the increase in the numbers of male managers, and of higher and lower professionals, is considerably greater than for their female equivalents. During most of the twentieth century men tended to go into the higher white-collar jobs and women into the more routine ones.

Further light on these differences is thrown by table 6.12, which describes the occupational structure as it was recorded by the Census in 1991. It shows the size and gender composition of major occupational groupings. About 16 per cent of all workers are employers and managers, and about 3 in 10 of these are women. The higher-professional categories (s.e.g. 3 and 4) remain overwhelmingly male. In the lower professions about 60 per cent of workers are female, the proportion being even greater among junior non-manual workers, of whom three-quarters are women. Fifty-five per cent of all workers are in the unambiguously non-manual categories (s.e.g. 1–6) compared with 25 per cent in 1911 and 35 per cent in 1951 (see table 6.11). Of the self-employed (s.e.g. 12), four-fifths are men. Thus the proportions of professional and managerial positions continue to increase, as do lower professional, intermediate and routine white-collar ones. Though women are increasing their proportion of the higher positions, the process is slow. Women still cluster very heavily in the less prestigious and less well-rewarded non-manual jobs.

Not only have there been significant movements between classes, but there have also been important changes within them. Within the higher professions, for example, the numbers of engineers increased by 17 times from 1911 to 1981, while scientists were 15 times as strongly represented, and accountants 7 times as numerous. The traditional professions – law, medicine and the military – only doubled their numbers, while the number of clergy actually declined. The lower professions are dominated by government service, teachers and nurses constituting over half. Social welfare workers and

| TABLE 6.12 | Occupational structure socio-economic groups: working population: all persons, men and women, 10% sample, Great Britain, 1991 |

Socio-economic group (s.e.g.)	All	% of all	Men	% of men	Women	% of women	Women as proportion of all workers (%)
1	114,534	4.9	81,797	6.2	32,737	3.2	29
1.1	705	0.03	562		143		20
1.2	113,829	4.9	81,235		32,594		29
2	245,980	10.5	168,763	12.9	77,217	7.5	31
2.1	68,268	2.9	49,694		18,574		27
2.2	177,712	7.6	119,069		58,643		33
3	22,701	1.0	19,695	1.5	3,006	0.3	13
4	91,427	3.9	74,664	5.7	16,763	1.6	18
5	319,131	13.6	131,240	10.0	187,891	18.2	59
5.1	295,362	12.6	121,629		173,733		59
5.2	23,769	1.0	9,611		14,158		60
6	495,479	21.1	120,100	9.2	375,379	36.3	76
7	106,249	4.5	19,121	1.5	87,182	8.4	82
8	47,260	2.0	39,562	3.0	7,698	0.7	16
9	298,583	12.7	271,389	20.7	27,194	2.6	9
10	247,477	10.6	154,116	11.7	96,361	9.3	39
11	125,463	5.3	51,518	3.9	73,945	7.2	59
12	150,856	6.4	121,451	9.3	29,405	2.8	19
13	9,396	0.4	8,064	0.6	1,332	0.1	14
14	10,418	0.4	9,005	0.7	1,413	0.1	14
15	17,774	0.8	12,568	1.0	5,206	0.5	29
16	19,964	0.9	18,464	1.4	1,500	0.1	8
17	22,531	1.0	13,984	1.1	8,547	0.8	38
Total	2,345,223	100	1,312,501	100.4	1032722	99.7	44

Classification by socio-economic groups was introduced in 1951 and extensively amended in 1961. The classification aims to bring together people with jobs of similar social and economic status. The allocation of occupied persons to socio-economic groups is determined by considering their employment status and occupation (and industry, though for practical purposes no direct reference is made since it is possible in Great Britain to use classification by occupation as a means of distinguishing effectively those engaged in agriculture).

The socio-economic groups are

(1.1) Employers in industry, commerce, etc (large establishments)
(1.2) Managers in central and local government, industry, commerce, etc (large establishments)
(2.1) Employers in industry, commerce, etc (small establishments)
(2.2) Managers in industry, commerce, etc (small establishments)
(3) Professional workers – self-employed
(4) Professional workers – employees
(5.1) Intermediate non-manual workers – ancillary workers and artists
(5.2) Intermediate non-manual workers – foremen and supervisors non-manual

(6) Junior non-manual workers
(7) Personal service workers
(8) Foremen and supervisors – manual
(9) Skilled manual workers
(10) Semi-skilled manual workers
(11) Unskilled manual workers
(12) Own account workers (other than professional)
(13) Farmers – employers and managers
(14) Farmers – own account
(15) Agricultural workers
(16) Members of armed forces
(17) Inadequately described and not stated occupations

Source: Census 1991, table 14

laboratory technicians increased by some 20 times in the same 60 years, while the number of teachers and nurses only quadrupled, an increase which included a striking growth in the numbers of male teachers and nurses.

The impressive growth in the number of persons employed in white-collar jobs concentrated in newer occupations rather than in traditional middle-class occupations such as lawyers, doctors or clergymen. This raises the question of whether to interpret the occupational shift out of manual employment as a significant alteration in the class structure towards the creation of a larger and more solid middle class. An answer must address two considerations. First, where should the boundary of the middle class be drawn? In the light of the employment conditions of white-collar work, is it still appropriate to take the boundary between blue- and white-collar occupations as a major dividing line? Second, are the conditions of occupational groups within the middle class broadly similar, or are there significant differences between, say, managers, professionals and the self-employed?

After 30 or more years of sociological debate about these matters, there is increasing agreement that in Britain there are major differences in the life chances of different groups of white-collar workers. Most scholars agree that there is a significant divide at the point identified by the Goldthorpe schema, between the service class of managers and professionals and the remainder. Controversy continues about whether managers and professionals constitute separate fractions of that class, but their superior salaries and comparative autonomy in the workplace make them the most privileged of all employees. There is also agreement that most *routine* white-collar workers – clerks and secretaries, but especially personal service workers and sales assistants – have few of the distinctive advantages of the service class and in many respects are in material circumstances which scarcely distinguish them from manual workers. Whether they should then be considered part of the working class, as Westergaard (1995) might contend, or as part of the intermediate class, where Goldthorpe (see section 5.4) allocates most of them, remains a matter of dispute. Finally, the expansion of self-employment in the period since 1981 has caused sociologists to think again about the fate of the petite bourgeoisie as a class, since people in this category have, in the past, had typically distinctive forms of behaviour. These considerations make possible several different interpretations of the nature of the contemporary middle class. Each implies a different view of the structuring of class, the size of classes, and the likelihood of expressing mutual solidarity among middle ranking groups. Let us, therefore, examine some of the evidence regarding conditions of existence and experience associated with different positions within the white-collar workforce.

Routine white-collar workers

A good deal of attention has been paid to the question of whether a substantial part of the middle class is being subjected to a process of proletarianization. If it can be shown that much white-collar work is, in most respects, similar to manual work, then any expectation of the consolidation of a large and cohesive middle class or middle mass is greatly undermined. This question has been addressed mostly through investigation of the condition of clerical workers, starting with the classic study of Lockwood (1958) and continuing with studies of employees of the civil service, local authorities, banks, insurance companies and so forth (Kelly 1980; Crompton and Jones 1984). However, it has become increasingly unsatisfactory to consider clerical occupations as typical of routine white-collar work, much of which no longer occurs in offices. Sales assistants in shops, personal care assistants and the waiting staff in restaurants face circumstances very different from Lockwood's 'blackcoated workers'. While there is some continuity and equivalence between clerks and current-day secretaries, many of the new and expanding jobs are in more factory-like conditions, as with typing pools or telephone call centres which, according to Scase (1998), now employ about 1 per cent of the total workforce. Market and work situations vary by industry, by type of organization and, most importantly, for men and women.

Evidence about earnings shows a well-marked gap between average manual and non-manual earnings which has remained remarkably constant since the First World War or so. This apparently persistent difference is reinforced by continuing differences in earnings over the career as a whole, fringe benefits of different kinds, and job security. However, comparisons of this kind can be misleading for, if one breaks down the larger categories, there are substantial overlaps between non-manual and manual occupations. The market situation of *some* non-manual occupations is inferior to that of manual occupations. Kelly (1980), for example, in his study of civil servants, found that management grades had, more or less, held their own, but among clerks 'a very definite decline in salaries *vis-à-vis* manual workers has occurred' (p. 131). Nor had clerks actually preserved an advantage in their total career earnings, which followed a similar pattern to those of manual workers. However, in respect of hours of work, fringe benefits, pensions schemes, sick pay schemes and job security, routine white-collar workers remain generally better placed.

A more subtle way in which the market situation of routine white-collar workers may differ from that of manual workers is in the greater promotion prospects enjoyed by non-manual workers in general. A. Stewart, Prandy and Blackburn (1980) showed that half of all men starting as clerks will be promoted. Most of the rest will leave white-collar work. Few men remain clerks for life. Stewart and colleagues (1980) believe, for various reasons, that promotion is likely to be long range: once started in the hierarchy, clerks can travel far. That clerical work represents an occupational category through which men pass on their way to management positions is given some support by the data from the Nuffield Mobility Study (see section 5.4) and from Fielding (1995; see also box 6.1 and tables 6.13 and 6.14).

However, the situation for female clerical workers is quite different. As we argued at the beginning of this section, one of the most striking features of the white-collar occupations is the way in which women have moved into the routine jobs, while not greatly improving their position in the higher reaches. Routine white-collar work (junior non-manual jobs) occupied 3.75 million women, 36 per cent of all women in the labour force, compared with 9 per cent of men. Rates of pay for these jobs are overall low and, as we showed in section 5.4, slightly lower than for manual work even among men. Moreover, promotion prospects for women in routine white-collar jobs are limited, certainly more limited than those for young men in the same occupations.

While there are also better-off and worse-off sections among routine white-collar workers, none is very prosperous and many are among the most poorly paid employees in Britain. Esping-Andersen (1993), in a comparative study of workers in the service industries in six Western economies, concluded that uniquely in Britain there was evidence of a 'post-industrial proletariat', a substantial category of workers in the service industries who were very poorly paid and who had very little chance of escaping into better jobs. So whereas the USA and Canada had just as many irregular and part-time jobs which required almost no training and which were typically filled by young people, these were held only temporarily en route to more rewarding ones. In Britain such workers were trapped for long periods of their lives.

A number of features including mechanization, bureaucratization, and changing relations of authority have had an impact on the work situation of routine white-collar workers. The computer may represent a particularly dramatic way of reorganizing of fice work but other machines have also replaced particular traditional skills. Duplicators, photocopiers, dictating and addressing machines and, more recently, word processors have all had a big and growing impact in large offices. Automation can produce conditions of work that appear to be similar to those enjoyed (or rather not enjoyed) by manual workers. Office work becomes more routine, involves a smaller sphere of decision and responsibility, is more subject to managerial control, involves less skill, and takes place in organizations that are larger, more bureaucratized, and characterized by a minute division of labour. Or take an example from retailing: EPOS (Electronic Point of Sale) machinery in supermarkets, which records the rate at which checkout staff process each item, is a prime example of computerized managerial surveillance and control.

Plate 6.3 | Shop assistant at work
Source: Format

However, though most office workers and routine white-collar workers have very little control over the pace, purpose or design of their job, they do not complain of being deskilled. As Marshall et al. (1988) record, most interviewees across all social classes did not think that their jobs required any less skill than previously. Those who did note some deskilling were primarily concentrated in the manual working class. Deskilled women appeared in both manual and routine white-collar occupations. However, Marshall et al. point out that the routine white-collar group is actually composed of two parts – clerical workers and personal service workers (including shop assistants, receptionists and supermarket checkout staff). The former group did *not* report deskilling, while a proportion of the latter did. The same conclusion can be drawn from an examination of the levels of autonomy at work reported by interviewees, measured by such questions as whether the worker can initiate new tasks, decide on day-to-day tasks, work on his or her own initiative or decide the amount and pace of work. Clerical employees – both men and women – had a good deal more autonomy at work than manual workers. Sales and service workers, on the other hand, were very close to manual workers in the low degree of control they had over their work lives.

In other aspects of life, routine white-collar workers as a whole show some significant differences from manual workers. While the total volume of their expenditure is not very different from that of the manual workers, the pattern of consumption is more like that of the service class. Regarding class identification, Marshall et al. (1988) asked respondents which social class they placed themselves in. Roughly half of both male and female white-collar workers placed themselves in the working class. Membership of trade unions and voting Labour are often taken as indices of working-class identification. Taken as a whole, routine white-collar workers are less likely to be union members than the manual working class. But again a difference between clerical and personal service workers reappears. The latter were just as likely to belong to trade unions as skilled manual workers. As far as voting is concerned, routine white-collar workers were significantly more likely to vote Conservative than manual workers.

Overall, it seems that the market, work and status situations of the more senior clerical workers are different from those of the manual working class, while the circumstances of other routine white-collar workers, like personal service workers and sales assistants, are very similar.

Managers and professionals: the service class

If there are differences within the routine white-collar worker category and between occupations within that category and the manual working class, there are even greater differences between routine white-collar workers as a whole and other fractions of the middle class. The conditions of employment of members of the service class are advantageous. Generally, they are paid more and can expect promotion through a career. In addition, they have better holiday entitlements, sick pay and pension arrangements. Even more important, the work situation of the service class gives them considerable freedom from control. Indeed it is more usually they who do the controlling (see section 4.4 on the occupational control exercised by professionals). This provides a sphere of autonomy within which it is possible to organize and pace work as one likes, taking responsibility for the work done. Professional and managerial work is also relatively

Box 6.1   Degrees of control at work

Crompton and Jones (1984) studied white-collar workers in three organizations: a local authority (Cohall), an insurance company (Lifeco) and a bank (Southbank). The data in the table are presented for clerical grades and for administrative grades by the kind of task that each grade performed. The authors distinguished tasks that required the worker:

- to exercise no control, that is the tasks were governed by simple rules such as data punching;
- to exercise no control, but where the rules were quite complex, like checking errors;
- to exercise discretion and self-control, for example writing non-standard letters.

Clearly, administrative personnel tended to perform the third kind of task and clerical workers the first or second. Only 10 per cent of clerks had self-control in their work, while only 13 per cent of administrators had jobs dominated by simple rules. There were, however, substantial differences between the organizations, differences that reflect the degree of mechanization and division of labour. In the bank, for example, three-quarters of the clerks worked at the lowest level of skill. Supervisors were most self-directed in the bank and the local authority. In general, then, the more mechanized and rationalized the organization, the greater was the difference between clerks and managers.

Organization and grades	No control, simple rules (%)	No control, medium complex rules (%)	Self-control (%)	Total workers (no)
Cohall				
Clerical	39	41	20	64
Administrative	0	33	67	15
Lifeco				
Clerical	32	60	8	60
Administrative	23	50	20	20
Southbank				
Clerical	79	21	0	58
Administrative	5	26	68	19
All				
Clerical	50	41	10	182
Administrative	13	37	50	54

Grades have been standardized across the three organizations to allow for comparison. Programmers, systems analysts and certain higher grades have been excluded.
Source: Crompton and Jones 1984, p. 62

more skilled, less subdivided and less mechanized. An illustration of the greater skill and control exercised by managerial grades is given in box 6.1.

To set against these superior work and market situations, there is some evidence that the processes of mechanization and division of labour affecting routine white-collar work are also having an impact on middle management and, especially, the lower professions. For example, after mechanization and reorganization of offices, the power to make decisions passes up the hierarchy to top management or to the new specialist groups. Computers, for instance, can make many of the more routine decisions previously made by local bank managers. Computer programming, which originally included the whole process of software preparation and demanded the involvement of highly skilled professionals, has become subdivided and rationalized into sets of less skilled tasks. Crompton and Jones (1984) presented evidence that many middle- to lower-level managers spend very little of their time exercising what are commonly thought of as managerial functions. Indeed, the content of their job may differ little from that of their alleged subordinates. Moreover, as part of strategies of corporate restructuring in recent years, downsizing and delayering have reduced the number of positions with managerial and supervisory authority.

Even if some elements of the service class are losing skill and autonomy, the class as a whole is becoming increasingly important in British society. At the end of the 1990s about 30 per cent of the occupied population of the UK worked in service-class occupations. Savage et al. (1992), in a recent study of the middle class, argue that membership is based on the ownership of three kinds of assets. *Organizational* assets are those advantages that accrue from being employed, as a manager or professional, in large organizations which offer career opportunities for promotion to posts very well rewarded and very much under the employee's control. *Cultural* assets refer to those elements of lifestyle, taste and educational qualifications that can function as markers of class membership. These lifestyles are learned, most importantly, from prolonged periods of education. As far as the third asset, *property,* is concerned, this has become more important for the service class than previously. The spread of owner-occupation, combined with a rise in the value of houses, has disproportionately benefited the service class and allowed the transmission of significant amounts of wealth between generations. Favourable occupational pensions and, for some, options on company shares give additional advantages.

Individual members of the service class may combine these three assets in different ways, although for Savage et al. these constitute the primary bases of three sections of the middle class – managers, professionals and the petite bourgeoisie, each largely based on one of the assets. As we shall see, the petite bourgeoisie is distinctive in many respects. There is, however, disagreement about whether the differences between managers and professionals is a division with repercussions for the social unity of the service class.

Savage et al. explore the question of likely changes in the structure of the three types of assets and consequent changes in the internal divisions of the service class. The different assets convey different advantages. Property assets can easily be stored and transferred to other family members, especially children. Cultural assets, similarly, can be stored and transmitted through education. Organizational assets, on the other hand, cannot be passed on because they are dependent on a position in a specific organization. Furthermore, Savage et al. argue, the salience of organizational assets is declining. Most particularly the structure of employing organizations is changing. Business organiza-

---

**Box 6.2   Movement within the middle class, 1981–91:
spatial and social mobility**

The OPCS Longitudinal Study follows a sample of 1 per cent of the population from Census to Census. From this Fielding (1995) showed much about contemporary middle-class careers in England and Wales. He confirms the tendency for the position of manager, that is those with organizational assets, to be less secure than that of professional. As table 6.13 shows, of those who were in professional positions in 1981, and who were still in the labour market in 1991, 69 per cent remained in a professional position. The equivalent figure for a manager was 51 per cent. More than one in three managers experienced downward (intra-generational) mobility. As table 6.14 shows, this difference was much more pronounced for women than for men. Fielding also shows that patterns of social mobility were related to patterns of spatial mobility. Professionals and managers were much more geographically mobile than were, for instance, petits bourgeois; small business owners were highly immobile. There was a tendency for service-class personnel embarking on their careers to move through the south-east of England. Some would stay there for ever, but many moved back out to the provinces at later stages in their careers. This has the effect of making the south-east 'an escalator region', a region where careers, especially managerial careers, are established. This also means that there is a disproportionate number of young service-class workers in the region, which affects both the culture of that region and where they develop and consolidate tastes and preferences. The experience of inter-regional mobility prompts Fielding to contrast their more cosmopolitan orientations with those of other classes, who are much more likely to remain fixed in local communities. As Fielding notes (1995, p. 186):

> migration is of crucial importance in the formation of the three middle classes, and in shaping their characteristics as political and cultural entities: 17.2% of those who were professionals in 1991 had been interregionally mobile in the previous ten years; the figure for managers was only slightly lower at 14%. The equivalent figure for the blue-collar working class was 4.8%. Not only does this have implications for social cohesiveness and class consciousness, it also influences the nature of regional and cultural relations.

---

tions are becoming flexible, less hierarchical, and smaller as tasks are subcontracted out (see section 4.2 for further discussion of organizational change). The net effect is that being a manager in an organization is not such a secure asset as it once was. Faced with this, Savage et al. argue, service-class managers will try to convert their organizational assets into other assets. For example, they will make sure that their children are very well educated and hence will acquire cultural assets. The result is that the children of managers become professionals rather than managers. As the authors say:

TABLE 6.13	Social class transitions for the total population for England and Wales, 1981–91 (1.096 per cent sample)

	Social class in 1991[a]						
Social class in 1981	PRO	MAN	PB	PWC	PBC	UE	TLM
(a) Absolute numbers							
Professionals	14,868	2,930	733	1,244	1,177	595	21,547
Managers	2,132	7,575	1,634	1,655	1,151	683	14,830
Petite bourgeoisie	445	738	7,272	614	1,192	554	10,815
White-collar	3,346	5,340	2,083	21,086	4,796	1,728	38,379
Blue-collar	2,466	3,131	5,446	4,063	35,875	4,859	55,840
Unemployed	809	611	1,366	1,467	3,780	3,366	11,399
Education	8,971	4,949	2,483	18,431	15,477	9,960	60,271
Other	2,328	1,175	1,531	8,603	5,335	1,364	20,336
Total	35,365	26,449	22,548	57,163	68,783	23,109	233,417
(b) Percentages							
Professionals	69.00	13.60	3.40	5.77	5.46	2.76	100.00
Managers	14.38	51.08	11.02	11.16	7.76	4.61	100.00
Petite bourgeoisie	4.11	6.82	67.24	5.68	11.02	5.12	100.00
White-collar	8.72	13.91	5.43	54.94	12.50	4.50	100.00
Blue-collar	4.42	5.61	9.75	7.28	64.25	8.70	100.00
Unemployed	7.10	5.36	11.98	12.87	33.16	29.53	100.00
Education	14.88	8.21	4.12	30.58	26.68	16.53	100.00
Other	11.45	5.78	7.53	42.30	26.23	6.71	100.00
Total	15.15	11.33	9.66	24.49	29.47	9.90	100.00

[a] PRO = professionals (s.e.g. 3, 4 and 5.1 plus 1.1); MAN = managers (s.e.g. 1.2 and 2.2); PB = petite bourgeoisie (s.e.g. 2.1, 12, 13 and 14); PWC = low-level white-collar workers (s.e.g. 5.2, 6 and 7); PBC = blue-collar workers (s.e.g. 8, 9, 10, 11 and 15 plus 17); UE = unemployed; TLM = total in labour market
Source: Fielding 1995, p. 171

Indeed, more children of managers become professionals than managers: 23 per cent of managers' children become professionals compared with 19 per cent who become managers. And this is a crucial issue: managers' children are still advantaged over the children outside the middle classes, but in order to retain a place in the middle classes it would appear that they have to 'trade in' their organization assets for educational credentials and entry to professional work. (Savage et al. 1992, p. 148)

Another sign of the difference between professionals and managers is the strategies which women and ethnic minority workers have used when entering the service class. They are less well represented in the higher echelons of management than in professional positions. Where successful, they tend to have pursued advancement through use of professional qualification and expertise. They are better represented in specialist professional niches. Crompton (1996, p. 119) sums up the research on women in banking, an industry which has seen a rapid increase in women managers – they were only 8 per cent of people on managerial grades in 1986, but 24 per cent by 1996:

TABLE 6.14	Social class transitions for men and women, England and Wales, 1981–91 (percentages)

	Social class in 1991[a]						
Social class in 1981	*PRO*	*MAN*	*PB*	*PWC*	*PBC*	*UE*	*TLM*
(a) Males							
Professionals	63.45	18.63	4.01	4.04	6.56	3.31	100.00
Managers	13.91	54.16	11.58	7.41	8.12	4.82	100.00
Petite bourgeoisie	3.58	6.70	70.67	2.27	11.15	5.63	100.00
White-collar	12.09	23.67	7.96	38.12	12.39	5.76	100.00
Blue-collar	4.39	6.17	11.23	3.73	65.23	9.26	100.00
Unemployed	5.52	5.25	14.43	5.16	35.91	33.72	100.00
Education	13.90	8.30	6.08	16.50	35.90	19.32	100.00
Other	12.13	10.99	11.11	14.34	33.33	18.10	100.00
(b) Females							
Professionals	77.40	5.99	2.48	8.39	3.80	1.93	100.00
Managers	16.52	36.83	8.41	28.50	6.10	3.64	100.00
Petite bourgeoisie	7.03	7.51	48.41	24.38	10.33	2.34	100.00
White-collar	7.24	9.65	4.32	62.30	12.54	3.95	100.00
Blue-collar	4.55	3.18	3.35	22.66	60.00	6.26	100.00
Unemployed	11.78	5.68	4.70	35.78	24.98	17.07	100.00
Education	16.06	8.10	1.80	47.28	13.55	13.21	100.00
Other	11.39	5.31	7.21	44.81	25.60	5.69	100.00

[a] PRO = professionals (s.e.g. 3, 4 and 5.1 plus 1.1); MAN = managers (s.e.g. 1.2 and 2.2); PB = petite bourgeoisie (s.e.g. 2.1, 12, 13 and 14); PWC = low-level white-collar workers (s.e.g. 5.2, 6 and 7); PBC = blue-collar workers (s.e.g. 8, 9, 10, 11 and 15 plus 17); UE = unemployed; TLM = total in labour market
Source: Fielding 1995, p. 180

although the proportion of women managers has increased within the industry, women have not simply moved into what were once 'male' jobs. Rather, as the nature of the work in the industry has itself been radically transformed, so women have tended to move into female 'niches' within management. These tend to involve the provision of specialist services (that is they are 'skill' and 'expertise' jobs rather than 'control' jobs), or the supervision of other women. In general, therefore, women do not hold the positions with the highest power.

Similar circumstances characterize the medical profession.

Evidence about political partisanship also suggests some differences between professionals and managers, though the picture is complicated. A. Heath and Savage (1995) used data from the British Social Attitudes Surveys between 1983 and 1990 on party identification. Respondents were asked whether they identified with a political party and if so which one. The patterns of party identification for many occupational groups within the middle class are indicated in table 6.15. Among the interesting features are:

- almost half the middle class identifies with the Conservative Party but only a fifth with the Labour Party;

- owners (the bourgeoisie) and the security forces have overwhelmingly partisan leanings towards the Conservative Party;
- among only a very few groups was Labour the preferred party – among trade union officials, higher education lecturers, artists, social workers and junior civil servants;

TABLE 6.15 | **Party identification by middle-class group, 1983–90 (percentages)**

Middle-class group	Con	Lab	Lib	Other	None	N
1 Judges and legal professionals	57.1	19.0	16.7	2.4	4.8	42
2 Accountants and financial professionals	60.9	10.9	16.7	0.6	10.9	174
3 Personnel and industrial relations managers	43.7	23.0	17.2	1.1	14.9	87
4 Systems analysts and computer programmers	39.4	19.7	22.5	–	18.3	71
5 Scientists	31.4	22.9	21.4	4.3	20.0	70
6 Marketing managers and sales representatives	61.0	16.9	11.3	0.5	10.3	195
7 Local government officers and professionals	37.7	21.7	17.4	2.9	20.3	69
8 Senior civil servants	53.3	20.0	26.7	–	–	15
9 Higher education lecturers	27.3	39.4	23.2	2.0	8.1	99
10 Teachers	39.0	24.8	22.9	2.8	10.5	459
11 Social workers	30.5	41.8	14.9	0.7	12.1	141
12 Clergy	26.7	26.7	26.7	–	20.0	15
13 Doctors and dentists	44.7	19.1	19.1	2.1	14.9	47
14 Nurses	40.0	21.0	18.0	–	21.0	100
15 Health professionals not elsewhere counted	47.9	18.3	19.0	1.4	13.4	142
16 Authors, writers, journalists	32.4	32.4	17.6	5.9	11.8	34
17 Artists, designers, photographers	37.5	28.1	18.8	1.6	14.1	64
18 Actors, musicians	23.5	44.1	14.7	2.9	14.7	34
19 Civil engineers	50.0	16.7	11.1	2.8	19.4	36
20 Mechanical engineers	45.0	15.0	17.5	–	22.5	40
21 Electrical and electronic engineers	46.9	16.3	24.5	2.0	10.2	49
22 Engineers not elsewhere counted	45.2	24.7	12.3	2.7	15.1	73
23 Laboratory technicians	40.0	14.1	18.8	3.5	23.5	85
24 Architects	43.5	17.4	17.4	–	21.7	23
25 Surveyors, property and estate managers/agents	58.0	17.3	8.6	2.5	13.6	81
26 Air pilots	68.4	–	–	5.3	26.3	1
27 Professionals in management roles	59.5	7.1	21.4	–	11.9	42
28 Production managers	56.8	15.8	13.7	–	13.7	146
29 Building and mining managers	49.0	23.5	9.8	–	17.6	51
30 Transport and distribution managers	46.6	31.5	6.8	1.4	13.7	73
31 Office managers	61.3	11.8	11.3	1.4	14.2	212
32 Wholesale and retail managers	51.4	20.4	4.9	2.0	21.2	245
33 Service and leisure managers	41.2	20.6	11.8	1.5	25.0	68
34 Security forces, etc.	78.6	2.9	4.3	–	14.3	70
35 Junior civil servants	28.9	36.8	23.7	2.6	7.9	38
36 Clerk supervisors	50.7	20.2	9.2	0.8	19.1	357
37 Trade union officials	–	75.0	25.0	–	–	4
38 Draughtspeople	45.5	22.7	7.6	–	24.2	66
39 Bourgeoisie	78.4	3.9	7.8	–	9.8	51
Total	47.7	20.9	14.8	1.5	15.0	3687

Source: A. Heath and Savage 1995, p. 281

- occupations strongly represented in managerial, marketing and financial aspects of private-sector business were particularly likely to support the Conservative Party.

Hence, it would seem that it is only a minority of professionals, predominantly in cultural, social and educational services, who had anti-Conservative leanings, suggesting that at least in political matters the service class was not sharply divided between managers and professionals.

The petite bourgeoisie

There is one further group, rarely mentioned yet, which is also conventionally considered middle class. The petite bourgeoisie consists of the self-employed owners of small businesses and people working on their own account. This group is typified by shopkeepers and traders, but also includes independent business consultants, farmers and self-employed plumbers. Overall, the petite bourgeoisie contains disproportionately older men, who tend to be married, living in the south-east or south-west of England or in Wales, who had fathers who were employers or managers and who obtained apprenticeship qualifications (Burrows 1991). Many of these people are in a paradoxical position, for their market and work situations diverge. On the one hand, they have some control over their work lives, being able to regulate and pace their tasks and deploy considerable skill. On the other hand, their pay and conditions often approximate to those of clerks or skilled manual workers. Many of the small shopkeepers studied by Bechhofer and Elliott (1968) were earning little more than many manual workers. This relatively low income was earned by very long hours of work in poor conditions. The average working day was 10.5 hours, with the two most numerous groups – grocers and newsagents – exceeding this figure. Moreover, turnover was very high, most going out of business within five years.

The distinguishing asset of the petite bourgeoisie is property, owning privately and controlling the means to make a living. In the terms of Savage et al. (1992) this allows easy transmission of assets to the next generation, and indeed the Nuffield mobility study showed that sons in this class were particularly likely to follow in their fathers' footsteps. Fielding's study (see table 6. 13 above) shows that more men were in this class position in both 1981 and 1991 than any other (70 per cent). Women were less stable in this regard.

The prior long-term decline in self-employment was reversed during the 1980s. The proportion of self-employed in the workforce increased from 7.7 per cent to 13 per cent between 1979 and 1995 (Burrows and Ford 1998). As Edgell (1993, pp. 63–6) notes, it is still too early to decide whether this is a temporary or a more lasting development. The former view might be supported by observations that the Conservative governments of the period encouraged small businesses, that there is a tendency for self-employment to grow in periods of recession and high unemployment, and that current management theory which stresses the benefits of subcontracting tasks to small firms and consultancies may well go out of fashion. On the other hand, small businesses flourish where start-up costs are low. Much commercial service provision is labour intensive, requiring people rather than expensive machinery, so entails limited initial

financial investment and is not as susceptible to competition from organizations prepared to invest large amounts of capital. New miniaturized technologies, like personal
computers, are relatively cheap and as effective for most purposes as bigger machines.
In addition, many people like the idea of working for themselves, the freedom and
control it offers: Hassell, Noyce and Jesson (1998) demonstrate, for instance, that it is
more the desire for independence than avoidance of discrimination that persuades ethnic minority groups to prefer ownership of retail pharmacy businesses to jobs in hospitals or industrial management. As Edgell concludes, probably we should not expect
much further growth in this class, but nor should we anticipate its imminent contraction.

Conclusion: divisions and fluidity among the middle class

Overall the picture is complex. There is significant differentiation among the middle
class; there is considerable movement, social and spatial; and there are marked gender
divisions. This is not a homogeneous class. But it is aware of class and class matters. It
contains some rich people, but most are comfortable and share in a high level of mass
consumption which is also marked by different styles of life. Geographical location and
housing type symbolize cultural differentiation; gentrification, suburbanization and re-
treat to the countryside are available, acceptable and affordable options. There is, then,
a basis for imputing increasing fragmentation.

   Nevertheless, we conclude that the category of occupations conventionally identified as
middle class contains a small number of identifiable, potentially cohesive fractions whose
members share many conditions. The service class, still expanding, holds an advantageous
position in most respects. Despite its internal differences it stands apart from other fractions, comprises perhaps 30 per cent of the occupied population, and shows no sign of
relinquishing its privileges. Its lower ranges overlap with the routine white-collar group
beneath, which has neither the control over work nor the rewards of higher managers and
professionals. Lower management, parts of the lower professions, and technicians nevertheless still have better market and work conditions than clerks or shop assistants. The
conditions of routine white-collar workers are also varied, but while the best-rewarded of
them have advantages over manual work, the differences are reducing. The petite bourgeoisie is set apart, distinctive in its economic, social and cultural orientations, but despite
its recent growth it has limited power and its privileges are precarious. Some independent
small proprietors, particularly those selling cultural and professional services, prosper
greatly, but others in traditional avenues like shopkeeping and the building trades are
unlikely to be much better off financially than skilled manual workers.

Summary

1   There has been a substantial growth in the proportion of people employed in
    middle-class occupations, with women holding a disproportionate share of the
    least attractive of these.

2   The middle class can be divided into three parts. The upper section comprises the service class. The bulk of the remainder, intermediate and routine white-collar workers, consisting predominantly of women, have varied levels of income but comparatively little autonomy. Lower-grade routine non-manual jobs are inferior in rewards to most manual occupations. There is also a petite bourgeoisie, a class of the self-employed and owners of small businesses.

3   Routine white-collar workers have very much poorer work and market situations than service-class workers. Their pay, hours of work, holidays and pension arrangements compare unfavourably. The promotion possibilities for male clerks are, on the other hand, fairly good, but for women, who form the bulk of the occupation, they are not. More junior white-collar workers and personal service workers have conditions very similar to those of the manual working class.

4   Service-class occupations, through their ownership of assets of various kinds, have a good market situation and their work situation is such that they have considerable control.

5   Junior management and the lower professions have a better market situation than routine white-collar workers but their work situations are threatened by mechanization and greater bureaucratic control.

6   The petite bourgeoisie has grown recently, but it is not yet clear whether this will prove to be only a temporary response to particular economic conditions.

6.5   The upper class

In the previous section on the middle class we distinguished a service class from the petite bourgeoisie and from a routine white-collar group. Although the service class *appears* to merge with the upper class, and there is no absolute point which separates small employers from large, actually the upper class is distinguished by a number of important features, which may be summarized as property, networks and power. The upper class is very small, too small to appear in many sample surveys. It is, none the less, very important because of its economic, political and social power.

Property and wealth

The most obvious point to make is that the upper class is wealthy. In section 5.2 we have shown how unequal is the distribution of income in Britain and how even more unequal is the distribution of wealth. In this century there has been a long-term trend to greater equality of wealth. Thus the share of personal marketable wealth held by the top 1 per cent of the population fell from three-fifths in the 1920s to one-fifth by 1979, while the proportion owned by the next richest 4 per cent stayed at about one-fifth throughout that period. This trend was halted in the 1980s and the position has remained roughly stable since. So in 1993 the most wealthy 5 per cent owned 36 per cent of all marketable wealth; and if the value of dwellings is discounted, the top 5 per cent owned half of such wealth. Whatever the longer-term equalization of wealth, the absolute amounts of wealth held by the very rich are very large, as table 6.16 indicates.

TABLE 6.16 | **Britain's rich, 1990**

Family	Estimated wealth (£m)	Main source of wealth
1 The royal family	6700	Land and urban property
2 Grosvenor (Duke of Westminster)	4200	Land and urban property
3 Rausing	2040	Food packaging
4 Sainsbury	1777	Food retailing
5 Weston	1674	Food production and retailing
6 Moores	1670	Football pools, retailing
7 Vestey	1420	Food production
8 Getty	1350	Oil
9 Maxwell	1100	Publishing
10 Feeney	1020	Retailing
11 Hinduja	1000	Trading
12 Livanos	930	Shipping
13 Goldsmith	750	Retailing and finance
14 Swire	692	Shipping and aviation
15 Ronson	548	Urban property, petrol
16 Barclay[a]	500	Hotels and urban property
17 Branson	488	Music and aviation
18 Cadogan (Earl Cadogan)	450	Land and urban property
19 Jerwood	400	Trading
20 Portman (Viscount Portman)	400	Land and urban property
21 Thompson	400	Food processing, property

[a] Not the family associated with Barclays Bank
Source: J. Scott 1991, p. 83

TABLE 6.17 | **Britain's highest-paid directors, 1998**

Director	Company	Annual salary (£)
Sam Chisholm	BSkyB	6,808,000
Jan Leschly	Smith Cline Beecham	2,410,000
Larry Fish	Royal Bank of Scotland	2,249,000
Sir Richard Sykes	Glaxo Wellcome	1,723,000
Peter Sedgwick	Schroders	1,464,000
Sir Clive Thompson	Rentokil	1,455,000
Sir George Mulcahy	Kingfisher	1,372,000
Greg Hutchings	Tomkins	1,359,000
Malcolm Williamson	Standard Chartered	1,156,000
Richard Brown	Cable & Wireless	1,117,000
Sir Peter Bonfield	BT	1,101,000
Robert Wilson	Rio Tinto	1,051,000

Source: Guardian, 22 July 1998, p. 24

Income is much more equally distributed. J. Scott (1994) estimated that by 1974 the top 1 per cent of income earners took only 6.2 per cent of total income before tax, 4 per cent after tax. However, since the 1970s there has been a dramatic rise in the income of the higher earners. The absolute levels of earnings of company directors, for example, can be very high indeed. As table 6.17 indicates, a dozen executives earned over £1 million in 1997. (For more detailed treatment of the distribution of income and wealth see section 5.2.)

Since wealth is at least *potential* income, its concentration is the key to the market situation of the upper class. Changes in the way that wealth is taxed in this century may have led wealthy individuals to disperse their wealth more widely in their families during their lifetime. Very importantly, therefore, we are talking not only of wealthy individuals in the upper class, but of wealthy *families*. In this context, inheritance is of great significance. In general, individuals or families are wealthy because their fathers were also. As one detailed study concluded, inheritance is the major determinant of wealth inequality: 'The regression analysis attributed some two-thirds of the inequality in the distribution of wealth in 1973 to inheritance. The proportions of top wealth leavers since the mid-fifties who were preceded by rich fathers was shown . . . to be in excess of 60 per cent' (Harbury and Hitchens 1979, p. 36).

Property confers income and a favourable market situation. It also gives *control*. The upper class, in other words, is not merely passive in the luxurious enjoyment of continuous leisure; it also actively *uses* property to its advantage.

In section 3.3 we reviewed changes in the pattern of ownership and control in Britain. The most important conclusions were:

- The ownership of land is more dispersed.
- Through takeovers and mergers, many businesses have grown larger.
- Ownership of individual businesses no longer typically lies wholly in the hands of families but is relatively more dispersed via share ownership, particularly to various financial institutions.
- Wealthy families no longer have their assets concentrated in particular areas such as land or individual businesses but have them dispersed over various fields of activity.

One of the consequences of these changes is, as J. Scott (1991) points out, the creation of a unified 'propertied class in the twentieth century, a class moreover which had to use its capital actively to perpetuate its privileged position. Class advantages derive from the benefits which accrue from property and from involvement in the processes through which it is controlled' (p. 64). In turn, the propertied upper class depends on a core of those actively involved in the strategic management of business concerns. Scott argues that this core comprises about 0.1 per cent of the adult population, about 43,500 people, and it has been estimated that these people held 7 per cent of the wealth in 1986, worth then about £740,000 each. The members of this core occupy positions of leadership in large businesses in Britain, although they will have different ways of deriving their income and wealth. Members of the core can be involved either in one or in many business enterprises. At the same time, their involvement can be either as owner of the enterprise or simply as a director of it. Figure 6.2 puts together these two dimensions of involvement.

| | | Nature of involvement | |
		Property ownership	Directorship
Number of involvements	Single	Entrepreneurial capitalist	Executive capitalist
	Multiple	Rentier capitalist	Finance capitalist

Figure 6.2 Capitalist economic locations
Source: J. Scott 1991, p. 66

There are four groups within the active core of the upper class. The entrepreneurial capitalist has direct and immediate control over all aspects of business operations. The rentier capitalist is essentially passive by contrast, but has ownership stakes, though not complete ownership, in a number of enterprises. The executive capitalist is involved exclusively in the strategic management of a concern but frequently does not have a controlling block of shares. The finance capitalist also will not have significant blocks of shares but will occupy directorships in several enterprises. By contrast with the executive capitalist, the finance capitalist does not have an active involvement in any one concern.

In sum, the upper class consists of wealthy families rather than individuals. Wealth is not passively enjoyed but is actively used. In this process, a small core of the upper class, involved in the strategic control of large business, perpetuates its privileges. This mention of strategic control, incidentally, shows how the upper class's work situation differs from that of the service class discussed in section 6.4. Members of the service class are essentially managers who carry out day-to-day technical, professional and administrative functions. Although their role in modern business is clearly important, they do not have *strategic* control over the enterprise. That control – decision over investment, new markets, relations with other companies, for instance – lies with the senior executives who belong to the core of the upper class. Of course, many members of the service class are very highly paid – senior lawyers or accountants, for example – and that *might* make the line between the upper class and the service class difficult to draw. However, it is not at all easy to build up substantial wealth from earned income alone without any assistance from inheritance. That fact in itself makes it difficult to cross the class line.

Networks

We have already argued that discussion of the upper class should focus on families rather than on individuals and that the relationships between entrepreneurial, rentier, executive and finance capitalists are important in the strategic control of large British businesses. These points imply that the *networks* of relationships between members of this very small class will be significant.

There are different kinds of networks between members of the upper class. There are marriage or kinship relations, friendship or the 'old boy network', business and financial relationships, and the whole area of common background formed, amongst other things, by school and university. We have already referred to the way that the wealth of upper-class individuals largely derives, by inheritance, from family connections. Members of the upper class also tend to marry other upper-class individuals, giving the class a unity based on kinship and marriage. This has, of course, always been the case. In the nineteenth century, when individual families controlled large businesses, there was extensive inter-marriage, as for example between the Quaker families which owned large food firms.

Connections of kinship and marriage are further extended by the ties of friendship and acquaintance which are often summarized in the phrase 'old boy network'. To a large extent, this network is social. It is based on individuals seeing each other regularly, not only in the way of business but also socially.

Social contacts of this kind are possible partly because of common background. Members of the upper class associate together easily because they have the same tastes, atti-

Plate 6.4 Upper-class lifestyle
Source: Network

tudes and inclinations, formed by being brought up in the same kinds of family and going to the same kinds of school and university. As J. Scott (1982) argues: 'The integrative role of the public schools concerns their ability to mould the ideas and outlook of their pupils and to ensure frequent and easy interaction among them' (p. 160). Members of the business core of the upper class do, indeed, have a public school background. For example, three-quarters of clearing bank directors in 1970 were from public schools, and one in three were from Eton. In addition, between half and three-quarters of these directors had been to either Oxford or Cambridge university. Or, to take a different case, Otley (1973) found that, in 1971, 75 per cent of senior army officers (lieutenant-general and above) had been to major public schools.

A common background in family, school and university gives a common culture to members of the upper class which enables them to interact freely. It also serves as the path of recruitment into the upper class by giving the required qualifications. The result is that the class has a high degree of self-recruitment and social closure. What this means is that current members of the upper class are likely to be the offspring of wealthy individuals, and their sons and daughters are also likely to remain in the same social position.

Studies have investigated the social origins of those in elite positions not only in the business core, but in the civil service, the army, the judiciary and the church. Boyd (1973), for example, found that no fewer than 45 per cent of bank directors and 30 per cent of judges listed in *Who's Who* also had fathers listed (Heath 1981). We have to conclude that entry to the upper class is 'sponsored' in the sense that upper-class individuals have to have the 'right' sort of background; it is not a competitive process. The upper class is relatively closed to outsiders.

One last issue in the formation of the upper class as a network deserves mention. We have referred to the way in which the business core of the upper class can mix its business and social contacts. Business relationships may, however, be cemented in a much more solid way via the networks of interlocking directorships. This is an issue discussed in more detail in section 3.3, but an illustration is provided by J. Scott (1985) in a study of the directorships of large companies. In 1976, 11 people had a total of 57 directorships in the top 250 companies and had many others in smaller companies. The directorships of 9 of these 11 can be linked together in the chain shown in figure 3.8; a mere nine people linked together 39 very large companies. Interlocking directorships provide a powerful network linking firms, but they also cement the connections of members of the upper class.

Prestige and power

So far we have argued that the upper class, and especially its business core, forms a relatively closed, coherent and self-recruiting elite. Coherence, combined with great wealth and the effective control of very large businesses, gives great power. However, that represents only one channel of the upper class's influence. The business core is also connected with other members of the upper class at the top of other fields like politics, the civil service and the professions.

We have already looked at the recruitment patterns of certain upper-class occupations. There is overwhelming evidence that those in such positions come disproportionately from upper-class families, from public schools, and from Oxford and Cambridge universities. They have, in other words, common backgrounds and a common process of education and training. Of the 1987 intake of Conservative MPs, for example, 65 per cent had been to public school, including 6 per cent to Eton, and 42 per cent had received an education at Oxford or Cambridge (Baker, Gamble and Ludlam 1992). One might have expected the 1990 Cabinet, headed by a woman who had attended a local authority school, to have a more even representation. Of its 23 members, however, 21 had been to private schools and 16 to either Oxford or Cambridge university.

The same pattern of education predominates in the higher reaches of the civil service; two-thirds of senior civil servants in 1970 had attended public schools. Senior churchmen and members of the judiciary are also recruited disproportionately from public schools and Oxbridge and, in addition, have a strong tendency to come from families also in high-ranking positions in the church and the law.

The common origins, common education and common experiences of the holders of a variety of elite positions lead many commentators to refer to the 'establishment'. The members of the establishment constitute a coherent and self-recruiting body of men who are able to wield immense power. A similarity of outlook and day-to-day contact between civil servants, politicians, businessmen, churchmen, professionals and the military give the upper class political power to add to the power given by wealth. The argument carries a great deal of conviction. However, common origins and common education do not of themselves necessarily mean common interests or common action, and little is known about how holders of elite positions actually do interact in the use of power.

The coherence, wealth and power of the upper class are reflected in its prestige. Doubtless, in the past, some of the prestige of the upper class derived from a flamboyant and luxurious lifestyle conspicuous to all. To some extent, this lifestyle continues to exist; it is, after all, one of the privileges of wealth. The doings of the rich continue to be displayed and even celebrated in the press and television. It could also be argued that an upper-class lifestyle is frequently presented as desirable and as something that everybody should seek. Despite all this, however, upper-class people probably display their lives less conspicuously than they used to do; in this sense the class is becoming more invisible. It may also be that the status and prestige of the upper class are not quite such unitary phenomena as they once were. Instead of there being a single set of status symbols denoting a unified upper-class status system, there are now intersecting and overlapping status circles in the upper class, each with rather different symbols of prestige. It may also be that rank and title command less respect than they once did. New hereditary peerages are not now generally created. Nevertheless, periodically, an honours list is announced which will include knighthoods and life peerages as well as hosts of lesser awards. These higher honours largely go to those who have rendered 'public service', which is defined in such a way that honours will be given to individuals who are, in our sense, upper class. Apart from anything else, the system of nomination for honours ensures that only those who are relatively well connected in public life are likely to be nominated. There are, however, some indications that the honours list is losing its prestige in the wider community, and the government has indicated that it will be changed. The appearance of each list is almost routinely greeted by a chorus of disapproval, based largely on the notion that the ideal of public service is being debased.

Summary

1   The upper class is distinguished by its wealth, its coherence and its power.
2   Members of the upper class are very wealthy. The top 1 per cent of wealth hold-ers own one-third of the nation's wealth.
3   We should see the upper class in terms as much of families as of individuals. Wealth is distributed widely in families, and family origin and influence are im-portant in gaining upper-class positions.
4   The core of the class consists in those actively involved in the control of large businesses.
5   The upper class is very coherent, being bound together in a network of kinship, similar education, friendship and business contacts.
6   This coherence gives power which is reinforced by the fact that those of upper-class origin occupy powerful positions, not only in the business world, but also in politics, the civil service, the military, the church and the judiciary.
7   An upper-class style of life still carries a certain prestige, though that may be declining.

Related topics

Other aspects of the 'decline of class' thesis are presented in section 5.3. A few of the more important sections which give greater understanding of the circumstances of the working class are: 4.2 on work; 4.3 on trade unions and industrial relations; 4.5 on unemployment; 5.4 on social mobility; 7.2 on women and employment; 8.4 on ethnic disadvantage; 14.4 on inequalities in education; 11.2 and 11.5 on leisure; and 13.3 on voting. Section 4.2 gives detailed consideration to the nature of managerial occupa-tions. Further discussion of professionals is to be found in section 4.4. Section 3.3 presents some arguments about ownership and control and the question of interlocking share-holdings amongst the upper class. Section 5.2, reviewing income and wealth distribu-tions, gives some account of upper-class wealth, while section 5.4 analyses social mobility and social closure. Class differences in social participation are examined in chapter 10, and those in consumption and leisure in chapter 11.

Further reading

The best account of occupational change in Britain in the twentieth century is Routh (1980). Among general textbooks about class analysis, Saunders (1989), Crompton (1993) and Edgell (1992) are among the best. A good general account of the empirical evidence about the British class structure is Devine (1997). Marshall et al. (1988) is still the most authoritative and comprehensive source of information. For arguments on both sides of the debate about the 'decline of class' thesis see Lee and Turner (1996). More specialized important recent studies of class, which also put Britain in comparative perspective, include Marshall, Swift and Roberts (1997) and Erikson and Goldthorpe (1992). Savage et al. (1992) is the most interesting book on the service class, and the essays in T. Butler and Savage (1995) give the most detailed up-to-date material. Skeggs (1997) is good on working-class women. On the upper class, the best available source is still J. Scott (1982).

Cross-references to *Readings in Contemporary British Society*

Warde on class differences in consumption habits; **Wilkinson** on the relationship between health and inequality; **Westergaard** on class inequalities, the decline of class and cross-class marriage; **Savage** on the middle classes, geographical mobility, self-employment and changes in careers; **Devine** on the underclass and its relationship to the working class; **Skeggs** on working-class women, respectability and distinction; **McDowell** on middle-class women working in the City of London; **Sanders** on partisanship and class dealignment in electoral politics; **Mac an Ghaill** on young middle-class rebels; **Gewirtz et al.** on the effects of the marketization of schooling on the prospects of children in working-class families.

7

Gender

7.1   Introduction

The changing social relations between men and women in contemporary Britain are the focus of this chapter. Gender is the social aspect of the differentiation of the sexes. Sociological discussion in this area recognizes that social rather than biological processes are the key to understanding the position of women (and of men) in society. Notions that a woman's biology, such as her capacity to bear children, determined the shape of her life have been replaced by complex debates as to how different social processes interact to produce a great variety of patterns of gender relations. The emphasis has shifted towards understanding the diversity of the social practices which constitute gender in different ethnic groups, nations, classes and generations. New concepts have been developed to analyse gender relations which capture the interconnectedness of the different aspects of gender inequality. One such concept is patriarchy – the system of social relationships in which men exploit, dominate and oppress women.

The position of women is often considered to have improved during the last few decades. There is, however, considerable debate as to the extent of change and the reasons for it. Some writers, pointing for instance to the formal legal equality that women have with men, suggest that women are now fully emancipated, and have no need for any further changes. Others, focusing on issues such as the inequality in the wages paid to men and women or violence against women from men, argue that there is still a long way to go before relations between the sexes are equitable and fair. Yet others suggest that the diversity of forms of gender relations mean that it is hard to say which practices give rise to greater gender inequality than others.

This chapter will inquire whether the conditions under which women live have improved, as the first set of writers suggests; are unchanged, as the second school of thought has argued; or are too diverse for such an evaluation.

Some theories of gender relations: inequality and difference

Debates on the analysis of changing gender relations can be divided into two major kinds, focusing on either inequality or difference.

Theories of inequality

Four perspectives can be identified:

- radical feminism,
- liberal feminism,
- socialist feminism,
- dual-systems theory.

Radical feminists argue that gender inequality is one of the most significant forms of inequality. They maintain that men's exploitation of women is not a by-product of other forms of inequality, but forms a system in its own right. So while forms of inequality based on ethnicity and class are important, they do not alter the fundamental nature of patriarchal power. The system of patriarchy is sometimes seen as a seamless web in which all aspects of society are part of a system of male domination. Other accounts focus on specific social institutions including: men's systematic violence towards women, as in rape, wife beating and sexual harassment; the power relations involved in contemporary forms of heterosexuality; or men's control over women's work, especially in the home as unpaid housewives.

A *liberal feminist* approach does not use such concepts of systematically interrelated patriarchal structures. Rather the forms of gender inequality are seen as a result of lack of equal opportunities for women in specific situations. There is a tendency to a substantive focus on education, employment and electoral politics. Examples are the lack of encouragement for girls to take training in technical and engineering subjects in schools and colleges; prejudicial stereotypes of women in employment; and the unsocial hours of the House of Commons, which make it hard for mothers of young children to become Members of Parliament. While this small-scale level of analysis has its place, its focus on detail can mean that it fails to see the broader picture, the extent of the interconnections and the systematic exclusion faced by women. Nevertheless, the detailed studies can contribute towards building up a picture.

Socialist feminist writers, like the radical feminists, take a more structural and systematic view. The substantive focus is usually, though not always, on women's work either in the home or in the labour market. In the labour market women are more likely to be cheap, flexible, disposable workers than men. Employers or capital take advantage. Within the home women are also workers, engaging in domestic labour, doing housework and child care for little material reward. This means that children are raised and wage-labouring husbands taken care of at little cost to employers.

Dual-systems theorists have attempted to combine the best of the radical and socialist feminist perspectives so as to be able to incorporate both class and gender inequality into the analysis on equal terms, rather than prioritizing one over the other. The analysis of gender inequality as a system of patriarchy is combined with an analysis of capitalism.

Theories of difference

Theories of difference are inspired by the postmodern impulse in contemporary social thought. They draw on the cultural turn in sociology and emphasize the construction of meaningful social relations. They start from a critique of the alleged sweeping nature of some of the theories of social inequality discussed above. They ask whether we can really generalize in this way about gender relations. Are not the differences *between* women too great to warrant such theorizing? The strongest ground for this critique concerns the question of 'race' and ethnicity. The differences in the form of gender relations between ethnic groups, and the impact of racism on gender relations, mean that generalizations should be made only with caution. Conceptual debates centre on:

- essentialism,
- equality versus difference.

Essentialism   Do generalizations about divisions between men and women rest upon hidden assumptions about eternal and essential biological characteristics? By speaking of men as a group and women as a group, does this inevitably mean falling back onto biological rather than social categories? Do concepts such as patriarchy necessarily invoke such essentialism, or can they be sufficiently sensitive to issues of difference to shrug off such criticisms? Since there are gendered social structures which have shown enormous resilience over time, extreme versions of the postmodernist denial of the possibility of generalization should be rejected.

Equality versus difference   Is the route for equity and justice for women to be found through seeking equality with men, or through respecting difference – both between women and men and between women? How far are conceptions of equity and justice based upon different culturally specific patterns, and how far are they universal? Does a demand for equality mean accepting a male norm, or can it imply changing the norm itself?

Bearing these issues in mind, we examine the position of women in modern Britain considering gender relations in paid employment, the household, sexuality, welfare, education, violence and politics.

7.2   Women's employment

Inequalities between women and men can be clearly seen in the area of employment, where men on average tend to earn more than women and to have jobs regarded as more skilled and conveying more power. There is also diversity on the basis of class, age and ethnicity.

Wages

The gap in the earnings of men and women is one of the more obvious indicators of gender inequality. Women working full-time earned only 81 per cent of men's hourly rate in 1997, according to the *New Earnings Survey* (see figure 7.1). Considered on a weekly basis the gap widens further, because men are more likely than women to work long hours, to obtain overtime pay, to get premiums for working night shifts, and to be awarded a variety of bonus payments. The gap increases still further when part-time women workers are included, since they earn only 59 per cent of men's hourly rates.

The implementation of the Equal Pay Act between 1970 and 1975 reduced the wages gap a little. In 1970 women earned only 63 per cent of men's hourly rate, and only 55 per cent of men's gross weekly pay. The size of the gap has been closing steadily for those working full-time, but not for those working part-time (figure 7.1).

The increasing integration of Britain into the European Union (EU) has affected the legal regulation of labour markets in the UK. Article 119 of the Treaty of Rome, which is the foundation treaty of the EU, lays down that there must be equal treatment of women and men in pay issues. This principle has been operationalized and developed through a series of legally binding Directives which not only have an impact on domes-

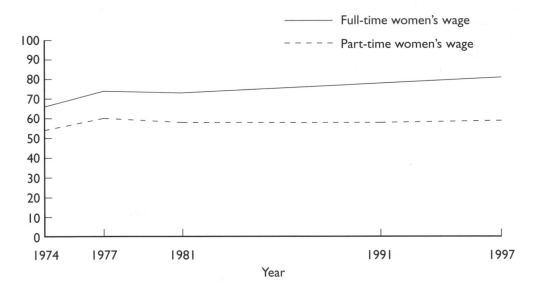

Figure 7.1   Wages gap in hourly earnings of men and women, 1974–97
Source: Calculated from *New Earnings Survey* 1974, 1977, 1981, 1991, 1997

tic legislation but, more importantly, have direct effect on all EU citizens. EU law overrides domestic law on these issues of equal opportunities in employment. The principle of equal opportunities between the sexes is even more strongly articulated in the Treaty of Amsterdam of 1998, reaching into many policy arenas. Yet the implementation of equal treatment has been the subject of prolonged legal and political disputes, so the impact has been uneven in member states of the EU. In the UK at least, European directives have been important in establishing a legal framework underlying what are now often taken-for-granted policies for equal opportunities by employers.

There are two main explanations of the wages gap between women and men: first, discriminatory labour market structures and practices; second, the division of labour in the household. The former includes direct and indirect forms of discrimination. Direct discrimination is when men consciously act to prefer men to women, because of prejudiced beliefs that women are less capable, which has been illegal in employment and related areas since 1975. Indirect discrimination is found where practices which disadvantage women are reproduced unknowingly. This includes treating part-timers less favourably than full-timers (for example, providing fewer fringe benefits such as pensions and redundancy pay), which has an adverse affect on women because they are disproportionately found among part-time workers. Indirect discrimination, also illegal, is often a consequence of deeply entrenched practices within social institutions (see the sections on part-time working and occupational segregation below).

The second major explanation of women's disadvantaged position in the labour market focuses on the impact of the household. It is argued that men get paid more because women's domestic responsibilities adversely affect their involvement in paid work. Women are too busy looking after children, husbands and elderly relatives to participate fully in the labour market. Women do not work the long hours considered necessary to earn the higher rates of pay, do not invest as much time in training, do not possess the skills to get the better jobs, and do not take opportunities for higher-paid work, because of the time and effort they expend on the care of other people and their homes. Disadvantage is thus attributed to women's greater commitment to family and caring. However, an explanation based on the household alone has limits. In particular, children can be cared for in ways other than by a mother at home. For instance, in Scandinavia there is much greater public provision of child care together with higher rates of female employment and a smaller wages gap between women and men. State policy can improve the nature and pattern of women's employment.

Gender composition of employment

Women are less likely than men to be in paid employment, but the gap has closed steadily over recent decades (table 7.1). Women's employment has continued to rise whether or not the economy has been in recession. The proportion of those in employment who are women rose from 38.1 per cent in 1971 to 49.6 per cent in 1995. The proportion of women among those who were economically active was 44 per cent in 1998, a slightly lower figure because fewer women than men were self employed. The number of men employed has declined since the late 1980s or so, closing the gender gap in employment. This has been particularly marked among older men, who are retiring earlier (sometimes for reasons related to ill-health), and among younger men, who have high rates of unemployment.

TABLE 7.1 | **Employees in employment, Great Britain, 1971–95 (thousands)**

	1971	1981	1991	1995
Female	8,224	9,108	10,467	10,584
FT female	5,467	5,290	5,764	5,645
PT female	2,757	3,818	4,703	4,939
% FT female of all (M + F)	25.3	24.7	26.5	26.4
% PT female of female	34.0	42.0	45.0	47.0
% PT female of all	13.0	18.0	22.0	23.0

PT = part-time; FT = full-time; all (M+F) = male and female employees in employment. These statistics are based on the quarterly Employment Department survey of employers. They do not include the self-employed, those on government training programmes or those in the armed forces. They are based on a count of jobs, not persons. Percentages for 1991 and 1994 are for June and seasonally unadjusted.
Source: Employment Gazette 1987a, table 1.1, 1987b, table 1.1, 1995, table 1.1; Labour Market Trends 1996, table 1.1

The UK has higher rates of female employment than many other countries in the EU, with the major exception of the Nordic countries. Nevertheless, an increasing rate of female economic activity is common across most of the EU, as can be seen in table 7.2, and the rest of the industrialized Western world. This is a consequence partly of parallel processes in these countries, and partly of increasing interlinkages between countries, a feature of globalization.

TABLE 7.2 Women's economic activity rates, EU, 1991–6 (percentages)

Country	1991	1996
Belgium	37.5	40.6
Denmark	61.1	58.7
Germany	44.4	47.8
Greece	32.6	36.6
Spain	31.9	36.2
France	46.2	48.6
Ireland	35.1	41.6
Italy	35.5	34.6
Luxemburg	35.5	37.0
Netherlands	44.3	49.3
Austria		48.8
Portugal	49.1	49.3
Finland		54.6
Sweden		57.4
UK	51.6	52.8
EUR 12[a]	42.6	
EUR 15[b]		45.3

[a] EUR 12 = all EU (12 member states)
[b] EUR 15 = all EU (15 member states)
Austria, Finland and Sweden are recent members of the EU so are not included in EUR 12 in 1991
Source: Eurostat 1991, 1996

Life-cycle changes

The main reason that women leave paid employment is to bear and look after children. Women usually return to employment later. The impact of children on women's working lives has changed dramatically since the late 1970s or so. The period that women spend out of the labour force for child care has been steadily reducing. In 1996, 53 per cent of women with children under 5 were economically active as compared with only 27 per cent in 1977–9; by the time their youngest child was 10, mothers had approximately the same level of economic activity as women who had no dependent children (see table 7.3).

TABLE 7.3 Economic activity of women of working age, Great Britain, 1973–96 (percentages)

Children	1973	1996
Youngest child 0–4	25	53
Youngest child aged 10 or over	68	78
All with dependent children	49	65
No dependent children	71	75
Total	60	70

Source: Derived from ONS 1998b, table 5.12

In earlier decades child care led to a decline in women's economic activity rates from their mid-20s to mid-30s, when they were most likely to have young children, but this is no longer the case (table 7.4).

TABLE 7.4 | Economic activity of women, by age, 1975, 1985, 1994 (percentages)

Age	1975	1985	1994
16–17	66	65	63
18–24	71	75	72
25–34	55	61	72
35–49	68	72	77
50–59	60	56	64
60–64	29	18	26

Source: *Living in Britain* 1994

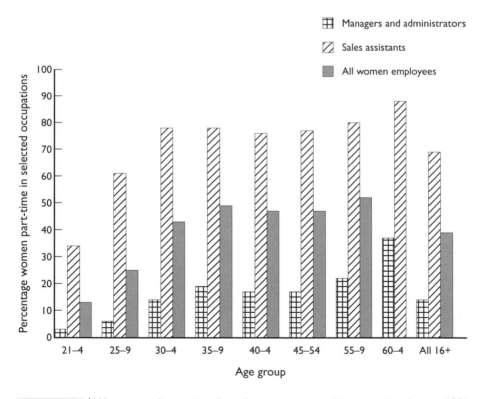

Figure 7.2 | Women employees, in selected occupations, working part-time, by age, 1991 (percentages)
Source: Calculated from 1991 Census, table 5

Part-time work

Most of the increase in women's employment has been in part-time work. The proportion of women working part-time has increased steadily, from 34 per cent in 1971 to 47 per cent in 1995. While British women have comparatively high rates of employment, they are also more likely to work part-time than those in other countries. Women with small children are more likely to work part-time, though part-time working is not confined to those with dependent children, it being common also among older women.

Part-time workers are on average comparatively poorly paid (see figure 7.1 above). They typically have few fringe benefits, such as pensions and redundancy payments. In 1996, 75 per cent of men working full-time were in an occupational or personal pension scheme, but only 65 per cent of women working full-time and 33 per cent of women working part-time (*Living in Britain* 1996). These poor conditions are partly a result of these jobs being in the less skilled sector of the labour market – for instance, most cleaners and shop assistants work part-time – and partly because employers can easily take advantage of their weak bargaining power. The concentration of part-time workers among older workers and in poorer-paid and less skilled occupations such as sales work rather than top jobs such as management is illustrated in figure 7.2. Indeed, in 1995, in recognition of such gendered exploitation, treating part-time workers worse than full-time workers was declared to be illegal discrimination under European equal opportunities law.

Ethnicity

Racism and cultural difference produce significant disparities between ethnic groups in the extent and level of participation in paid employment (see table 7.5 and also section 8.4). The differences in women's employment associated with ethnicity are more marked than those between men. Women of Pakistani/Bangladeshi descent are less likely to be economically active than others. Ethnic minority women have several times the rate of unemployment of white women.

TABLE 7.5 | **Economic activity by ethnic group, 1993 (percentages)**

| | Men 16–64 | | Women 16–59 | |
	Economic activity rate	*unemployment*[a]	*Economic activity rate*	*unemployment*
White	86	12	72	7
Black[b]	80	34	66	20
Indian	81	14	61	11
Pakistani/Bangladeshi	72	31	25	29
Mixed/other origins	76	17	59	17

[a] Unemployment by ILO definition
[b] Includes 'Black Caribbean', 'Black African' and 'Black-Other', but not 'Black mixed'
Source: Derived from *Employment Gazette* 1994, table 2

Occupational segregation and job hierarchies

Women workers are concentrated within a very narrow range of occupational groups, although there have been some significant changes in this recently (see table 7.6). Over 40 per cent of full-time women workers are to be found in clerical employment. A very few further occupational groups account for most of the rest of women. In contrast, men are spread through a much wider range of occupations. This segregation of the

TABLE 7.6 | Occupational orders for women and men, Great Britain, 1981–91

Occupational order[a]	1981			1991			
	Men (10s)	Women (10s)	% women	Men (10s)	Women (10s)	% women	% increase in women
1	77,823	20,137	21	103,181	51,310	33	155
2	66,774	126,468	65	68,654	154,120	69	22
3	15,987	8,821	36	17,835	13,609	43	54
4	92,993	9,042	9	96,266	15,517	14	72
5	180,783	53,118	23	196,993	85,782	30	61
6	104,006	298,636	74	84,159	304,719	78	2
7	60,040	85,941	59	54,704	91,126	62	6
8	50,086	5,601	10	44,160	5,962	12	6
9	56,371	203,660	78	56,499	200,840	78	−1
10	32,396	5,571	15	24,501	5,768	19	4
11	123,059	57,034	32	98,704	41,358	30	−27
12	281,394	16,050	5	194,791	11,142	5	−31
13	58,425	41,078	42	44,036	30,743	41	−26
14	93,608	597	1	74,562	856	1	43
15	155,653	9,521	6	120,311	8,633	7	−9
16	48,516	4,924	9	19,161	2,690	12	−45
17	54,757	41,059	43	139,984	8,547	38	−79
Total	1,552,671	987,888	39	1,312,501	1,032,722	44	5

[a] 1 Professional and related support in management and administration
   2 Professional and related in education, welfare and health
   3 Literary, artistic, sports
   4 Professional and related in science, engineering, technology
   5 Managerial
   6 Clerical and related
   7 Selling
   8 Security and protective services
   9 Catering, cleaning, hairdressing and other personal services
  10 Farming, fishing and related
  11 Processing, making, repairing and related (excluding metal and electrical)
  12 Processing, making, repairing and related (metal and electrical)
  13 Painting, repetitive assembling, product inspecting, packaging and related
  14 Construction and mining
  15 Transport operating, materials moving and related
  16 Miscellaneous
  17 Inadequately described

sexes in paid employment may be considered to have both a vertical and a horizontal component. Women are confined both to lower-grade jobs (vertical segregation) and to different jobs (horizontal segregation):

- *vertical segregation* Women are to be found in the lower grades in large numbers but are much less common as the grades go up, until at the highest grade there are almost no women at all.
- *horizontal segregation* This is the separation of women and men into different occupations. In most occupations there is a clear majority either of women or of men: very few occupations have an even proportion. Segregation, both by occupation and into specific industries, is one of the reasons that women generally earn less than men. Women are concentrated in sectors of the job market which pay the least, whether or not they are skilled. If women were evenly distributed across the spectrum of employment, their pay levels would be closer to those of men.

The pattern of segregation has changed significantly over recent years. At the top end of the hierarchy the number and proportion of women in the managerial and professional grades have substantially increased. These categories of job have grown overall in recent years, but men have taken a smaller share of the increase than women. The women entering these 'top jobs' in management and the professions are typically young and highly educated and also significantly less likely to have children. By contrast, the bottom end of the hierarchy, part-time and less skilled work, which has grown faster than any other over the last two decades, is disproportionately peopled by older women with few educational qualifications.

Understanding continuity and change in employment

The position of women in employment has transformed itself in recent years, though there remains considerable inequality and the picture is not one of simple progress. Simultaneous expansion at the top and bottom ends of the labour market is generating new patterns of inequality between women. It is important to recognize these differences. If the figures on women had been simply averaged, then many of these changes would have been hidden, for the average has changed much less than have the positions at the top and bottom of the labour market. Younger women have obtained levels of educational qualifications similar to those of their male peers and are beginning to enter the professions and better-paying occupations, while older women returning to the labour market take up work in the poorly paid, part-time sector. There is, therefore, increased polarization among women as labour-market and educational opportunities have changed.

The changing structure of the family and the household economy in which women spend less time on housework, the increased ability of women to have their interests heard within politics and the law as evidenced in the equal opportunities legislation, and the increase in women's education have contributed to this change in women's employment and the gender regime more broadly. These changes mesh with an altered balance between capital and labour. The growth of part-time work can be seen partly as a result of employers' desire for flexibility in the utilization of labour and their ability to create this at a time of higher unemployment. However, it cannot be understood outside the context of the new availability of women for work as a result of the changes in the gender regime.

Summary

1 Women are disadvantaged in the labour market by comparison with men.
2 There are major changes, as young educated women enter 'top' jobs, and older women take less-skilled part-time work.
3 Differences between women, including of age, are important.
4 The EU has been an important source of legally based regulations to support equal opportunities.

7.3 Households

While traditional sociologists used to write of 'the family', it is now widely recognized that there are many different forms of families and households. The traditional view was that 'the family' was composed of husband, wife and their children. Today we recognize many variations in the ways in which people live together in households, organize their intimate relations and care for each other. Diversity has always been present, but has increased recently. Households always changed over the life-cycle, related to the birth, care and growing up of children. There is also a renewed appreciation of the multiethnic and multicultural nature of British society, which has been host to waves of migration over centuries. What is relatively new is the decline in the popularity and the increased instability of marriage. But do we now have postmodern families and households?

The most striking recent change is the increased likelihood of families being formed of only mothers and children. The number of lone parents increased from 8 per cent in 1971 to 21 per cent in 1996, and the vast majority of these are women. The number includes women who have never married, though the majority are either divorced or separated. This is a diverse group with a temporary status, since they may re-partner or re-marry, and of course the children grow up. One of the most significant features of one-parent families is their tendency to live in poverty, leading to many forms of social exclusion. The poverty largely results from the lack of a male income into the household, but is compounded by the lower propensity of lone mothers to be in employment as compared with married mothers. Despite the poverty and isolation, lone parents do report positive aspects of their situation, largely those of independence and autonomy (see box 7.1).

As the population ages, and because women tend to live longer than men, the number of women living alone as widows has increased.

Box 7.1   Best and worst things about being a lone parent according to lone parents

These tables show what lone parents reported as the best and worst aspects of their situation.

Very best thing	%	Very worst thing	%
Independence	60	Loneliness	48
Freedom	31	Financial difficulties	45
Ability to make decisions for children	21	No one to discuss problems with	30
Peace of mind	15	Lack of adult conversation	12
Atmosphere in house	13	Miss being part of a couple	12
Money (coping/regular/having own)	12	Socially hard	12
More time for self/children	10	Worrying as child grows up	10
Generally like it	9	Child needs other parent figure	8
More self-confidence	8	Security (at night)	6
Nothing/don't know	13	Nothing/don't know	6
Other	13	Other	12

Source: Adapted from Bradshaw and Millar 1991

There are significant differences between ethnic groups in the form of households and the sexual division of labour. Women of South Asian descent are the most likely to live in large families with husbands and people of other generations, while women of African descent are most likely to live without husbands and extended kin. White families range between these two models. Half of all mothers of West Indian or Guyanese origin are lone mothers, as compared with 14 per cent of white mothers and less than 10 per cent of Indian, Pakistani and Bangladeshi mothers.

The traditional conception of class divisions, where the 'bourgeois' wife and mother stayed at home and working-class women had to work, has been inverted. Today, the higher her qualifications and class position, the more likely is a woman to have paid employment, while those with the fewest educational qualifications and lowest class position more frequently stay at home. Among women from a professional or managerial background 85 per cent are in paid work, while among women from an unskilled manual background only 59 per cent are (*Living in Britain* 1996).

Although it is more usual to think of the home as a place of rest, much *work is* performed in caring for others. This includes the tasks of cooking, cleaning and child care and caring for the emotional needs of others. The 'reconciliation of working and family life' has become a major theme in debates in the EU, at the core of which are alternative ways of looking after children. Although they are currently increasing, the UK has lower levels of publicly funded child care than most other countries in the EU. More children of working mothers are taken care of by relatives and child minders than by formal nurseries.

Care of the elderly is of growing importance. As people live longer, increasing proportions of the population become frail. Only a small proportion of the elderly enter
residential care, most continuing to live in their own homes. The extra care needed for
living in the community is provided in various ways by paid care workers and by relatives. Who should care for the frail elderly – and who should pay – is increasingly
controversial. In particular, there is the question of how older people are enabled to
retain dignity and control over their lives while gaining such support.

Financial considerations are insufficient to grasp the full nature of the resource issues
at stake because caring involves dimensions which are not fully articulated through
the market place. Shortage of time is a key constraint when trying to balance work
and home. Professional households with two parents working full-time can be 'work
rich but time poor' in comparison with households where paid employment is scarce.
Hochschild (1997) suggests that 'timebinds' are becoming increasingly common as more
women expect to have jobs as well as children. Men have not increased the time they
spend on housework and caring to the same extent as women have increased their time
in employment. Hochschild suggests that some workplaces have improved treatment of
women workers to such an extent that women can feel as happy at work as at home;
indeed in some instances, home is more tiring than work because of the range and
extent of domestic demands. Yet workplaces are also demanding of the time of employees, sometimes with a 'long hours culture'. Some women feel reluctant to take advantage of new 'family-friendly' policies designed to help them to balance home and work
more effectively, fearing that if they did so they would lose their place in the workplace
hierarchy. Hence the timebind.

Changing housework?

Is there less housework to do as a result of the development of technology for the home?
Has the increase in the number of household goods, such as washing machines, fridges,
freezers, food mixers, vacuum cleaners and non-stick pans, reduced the amount of housework that women do? Domestic production goods have certainly become more common, as table 7.7 shows.

These technological innovations have been interpreted in different ways. On the one
hand, they might free women from household burdens and might facilitate women tak-

TABLE 7.7 | Proportion of households with domestic production goods, 1979 and 1996
(percentages)

Goods	1979	1996
Deep freeze	40	91
Washing machine	74	90
Tumble drier	19	51
Dishwasher	3	20
Central heating	55	88

Source: Derived from *Living in Britain* 1996

Plate 7.1 | Will men ever learn to do housework as well as women do?
Source: J. Allan Cash

ing up paid work. On the other hand, it may make little overall difference to women's lives since, as one household task is reduced or eliminated by advances in technology, then others are added to the list and standards are raised. Furthermore, some tasks are not affected by the provision of household appliances, in particular the supervision of children and the elderly.

The investigation of this issue tests sociological ingenuity since it is hard to observe the activities in a household without affecting its members' practices. Among respondents to the *British Social Attitudes* survey, when asked who was mainly responsible for general domestic duties, 82 per cent said that the woman was responsible and only 12 per cent that it was shared equally (SCPR 1988). However, while 16 per cent of men said that tasks were shared equally, only 9 per cent of women did so. The most egalitarian attitudes were to be found among couples where both were in full-time employment, though even here only one in five said that there was equal sharing.

A different method is to ask members of a sample of households to keep diaries of actual activities, noting what they are doing at all times of the day. These time-budget studies reveal that the time that full-time housewives spend on housework and caring, about 50 hours per week on average, has not significantly changed for several decades. However, the proportion of women who are full-time housewives has dropped significantly during the post-war period and, since married women in paid employment spend less time on housework than those without paid work, there has been a significant overall decline in the time spent by the average woman. However, married women typically spend more time on housework than their husbands, even if they also have paid employment. There are complex variations: women with young children put in the greatest number of hours of total work, and women with neither young children nor paid jobs the least.

Do all members of a household share equally in the same standard of living? This might seem to be the case since they live in the same household; in particular, since men and women who are married to each other have the same standard of living. However, it may be doubted whether women have the same access as men to ostensibly shared resources. For instance, husbands are more likely to have control over the use of the family car and use of family income for their leisure pursuits.

Summary

1   Households and families take diverse forms.
2   There is an increase in the proportion of households in which women live without men, especially as lone parents.
3   Significant inequalities between men and women in the household remain in both the amount of housework performed and the level of consumption.

7.4   Culture and sexuality

Femininity and masculinity

Different practices and symbols mark the distinction between the genders. Within a country as complex as Britain, masculinity and femininity are constructed and experienced differently between cultural and social groups. For instance, the form of masculinity considered appropriate varies between men who are young or old, who are black or Asian, middle class or working class, gay or heterosexual. The traditional understanding of masculinity and femininity has been through a socialization perspective which links sociology and social psychology. This took as its main topic the processes through which people learned and internalized gender stereotypes. A more recent theoretical development considers femininities and masculinities as discourses, drawing on the conceptual vocabulary of Michel Foucault, the French social theorist. Recent work within a discourse perspective has shifted the issue to that of understanding the varied content of femininities and masculinities, not simply how individuals learn to adopt these identities. This latter perspective has developed through an analysis of various kinds of media, especially television, magazines and film.

Socialization

That boys are supposed to be aggressive and outgoing, strong and demanding, while girls are neat and tidy, gentle and obedient, is central to stereotypes of masculinity and femininity. Such differences between the genders are encouraged from an early age by a variety of rewards and punishments. These patterns of behaviour are absorbed through the reading materials of children, the toys they play with and the roles they see acted out in television programmes. While the 'Janet and John' type of book, used to teach children to read, portrays slightly less stereotyped roles than 20 years ago, there is still a clear distinction between the activities of males and females in the stories. People are socialized into the forms of behaviour deemed appropriate for their sex, thereby learning to become gendered subjects. Once children have adopted a gender identity they may seek to reinforce this by seeking out what they learn to perceive as appropriate behaviour.

Although femininity is often a problem for women seeking equal treatment with men – in that it is easier to take advantage of people who are gentle than of those who are aggressive and pushy – its positive aspects in terms of openness, emotional expression and human warmth are also important. Indeed, this latter aspect of femininity is emphasized by some recent writers on masculinity, who protest that the social pressures on men to contain rather than express their emotions are oppressive and restrictive, stunting their full emotional development. However, this tends to overlook the extent to which masculinity is bound up with the power and privilege from which men usually benefit.

Discourses of femininities and masculinities

Women's magazines recognize the experiences of women and, especially, the difficulties of balancing the expectations held by others – in particular husbands and boyfriends –

with their own hopes and desires. Stories in the magazines re-create the dilemmas that women face, exploring various options but with a final resolution in a traditional direction. Comparisons between different women's magazines show the variety of forms of conduct which can be called feminine. The femininity of *Woman*, with its emphasis on the role of wife and mother, is very different from that of *Cosmopolitan*, where the feminine woman is encouraged to be adventurous in catching the most sexually desirable man, retaining him for as long as he is interesting, and getting a super career at the same time. While the images of successful femininity vary between the two magazines they also share some elements, such as an emphasis on a sleek appearance (although that is obviously differently expressed also).

If there is not one form of femininity but several, the same applies to masculinities, which vary especially by age, marital status, class and ethnicity. For instance, working-class forms lay more emphasis on physical prowess than those of the middle classes, where appropriate career is more important because masculine status is defined in terms of success as husband–father and breadwinner. Images of femininity and masculinity vary significantly by ethnicity. Most obviously, different dress codes denote masculine and feminine genders. More significantly, the greater participation of Afro-Caribbean than white women in paid employment means that the cultural notion of the dependent domesticated housewife is a white rather than a universal stereotype.

Essentialism?

Gender identities are ways of life, multifaceted and sometimes contradictory. Yet they are usually perceived in terms of a fundamental dichotomy, an insuperable barrier between the lifestyles of women and men. Those who have emphasized the differences between men and women have sometimes been accused of essentialism by others focusing on the diversity of forms of representation of femininity and masculinity. The concept of essentialism posits simplification of diversity, creating a dichotomy, feminine/maculine, which is reductionist. 'Reductionism' in this context suggests a false linkage between a social distinction and a fundamental biological (or sometimes psychological) basis. However, it can be argued on the contrary that sociology's task is precisely to simplify a complex world through conceptual developments which increase our understanding via appropriate forms of abstraction.

The work of Gilligan (1982) has been a focus of debate in this area. She argued that men and women typically used different forms of moral reasoning. Men were more likely to draw on abstract universal principles to underpin their notions of justice; for instance, that in order to be fair it was necessary to draw on principles that applied to all cases everywhere. Women, by contrast, were more likely to take into account the detailed, specific circumstances of the moral dilemma in order to assess the correct course of action, examining the relationships involved in the specific context. Gilligan studied actual moral reasoning in a small group to provide some empirical support to her thesis. She maintained that there was more than one adult form of moral reasoning and that women used different, but no less valid, criteria of moral reasoning.

Gilligan's work stimulated the debate about essentialism. If the patterns of reasoning of women and men overlapped then there could be no simple dichotomy. Were there not differences among women, and among men, so that it was inappropriate to generalize about women and men in this way? Was not the reduction of complex patterns to a simple dichotomy reductionist and essentialist?

Gilligan's position can be defended in a number of ways. There is empirical evidence of differences between men and women, on average, within the culture about which she was writing (although there is some contradictory evidence). Identifying averages and typicality does not deny complex patterns of variation. There may be *social* bases to different patterns, arising from the typically different lives of men and women which result in the different forms of moral reasoning, so dichotomies are not inevitably biologically rooted, but may have social origins.

Sexuality

Giddens (1992) argued that there has been a 'transformation of intimacy' in recent years. It is widely suggested that women have made great advances towards equality with men in the area of sexuality. Does the evidence support such a contention? Has the sexual double standard, whereby non-marital sex was acceptable for men and not for women, disappeared? The evidence suggests that the double standard is less strong, in that young men much less often say that they want to marry only a virgin, yet women are still more often criticized than men for engaging in non-marital sexual activity. For instance, studies of youth culture suggest that young women may still be assessed as either 'slags' or 'drags'. Are intimate relations now sites of democratic practice? Are people sophisticated and self-reflexive about their sexual relationships? Are gay and heterosexual preferences regarded as equally valid today?

Images: 'choice' and power   Are the images of women and girls in magazines and other mainstream media empowering or restrictive? (See box 7.2.) Do successful women pop stars such as the Spice Girls and Madonna represent 'girl power', a positive representation of women enjoying and in control of their sexuality, which enhances the self-esteem of other young women? Or do images of such women, and of models who are untypically slim, feed a concern and indeed personal dissatisfaction over body shape which can contribute to obsessive dieting?

The increased freedom to create and distribute images can be seen as immensely positive. Indeed the growth of consumer culture has been seen by Nava (1992) as a source of an increased sense of autonomy and entitlement for women. But are some representations sources of creative imagination for one group of people at the expense of another? For instance, what are the implications of pornography? Pornography appears to be both growing in its availability, and becoming more violent in its content. New media, like video, represent violent sadistic sexual fantasies. Not only are these images unpleasant for women in their own right, but perhaps such representations encourage men to play out fantasies of power over women through rape, sexual harassment and other forms of sexual molestation of women. The evidence here is complex and mixed, but suggests that such images do have some impact.

Contraception and abortion   The much greater availability of contraception and safe abortion has made one consequence of sex, unwanted children, much less likely. Indeed, some writers have suggested that the development of cheap, fairly reliable and

---

Box 7.2   Femininity and sexuality

Adkins (1995) argues that women in the tourist industry are required to deploy their sexuality as a requirement of their jobs. They have to maintain a feminine appearance in order to get and keep their jobs. An appearance of heterosexuality was not a form of power or choice, but one that they were obliged to exhibit. The display of sexuality at work was not emancipating but constraining. It was a result of unequal power relations – the women had to present and behave in these ways whether they liked it or not. For instance, the handbook for workers at a theme park contained the following instruction: 'Use your mouth! A smile, especially when greeting a customer, can be the greatest customer relations exercise of all' (p. 116). Women workers at this leisure park were regularly reprimanded if they did not wear their uniforms in an appropriate way, or if other aspects of their appearance, such as their make-up or hairstyle, were considered out of line with the employer's view of what the customer would prefer. In the large hotel studied, women workers were given strict guidelines on how they should wear their hair, make-up and uniforms, so as to ensure that their 'entire appearance [was] attractive, clean and fresh' (p. 122). Men, by comparison, were not asked to 'look attractive'.

Adkins argues that even though some of the women said that they liked to look sexually attractive, this does not mean that they were not subject to power relations and to male domination. For Adkins, 'power' not 'choice' is the crucial issue.

---

fairly safe forms of contraception, together with the liberalization of the laws on abortion, have been among the most important gains to women in recent decades. British laws make it possible for women to get abortions if they are in the early stages of pregnancy and can persuade two doctors that they meet certain criteria. These criteria are open to interpretation, but mean that a woman can get an abortion if either her physical or her mental health is deemed to be at risk. Some NHS doctors have interpreted this broadly, since an unwanted pregnancy can be catastrophic to the life of a woman, so that abortion is granted to any woman who considers this to be the case. Where the interpretation is more restrictive, non-profit-making abortion clinics have stepped in to fill the gap.

Gay, lesbian and heterosexual relations   There has been greater acceptance of a wider range of sexual practices, such as gay and lesbian relationships. There has been the development of open gay and lesbian subcultures with their own public spaces, such as clubs and bars; there has been a lowering of the age at which sex is legal for gay men; and public figures no longer have to be closeted in order to retain public confidence. However, the extent of the change has been limited by the reaction against gay men as a result of the AIDS crisis, and is qualified by the difficulty some lesbian mothers have in retaining the custody of their children.

Theories   Traditional analyses of sexuality drew upon a Freudian conception of sexuality as a biological drive. Recent changes in sexual practices have highlighted the malleability of human sexuality, challenging Freudian ideas of a relatively fixed sexuality. Explanations of sexuality patterns in terms of biological drives have been largely replaced by ones emphasizing social and cultural factors. Contemporary analyses of sexuality draw upon Foucault's concepts of discourse, which emphasize the social construction of sexual practices. However, Foucault tended to underestimate the significance of gender relations and the unequal power between men and women in shaping sexuality. Sexuality is constructed in the context of gender relations and power is embedded in discourses, though not in simple ways.

Summary

1 Discourses of masculinities and femininities are represented in the media and other cultural institutions. These take highly diverse forms.
2 There has been a transformation of intimacy, in complex ways, with greater acceptance of diverse sexual practices, simultaneous with the continuation of aggressive practices towards women.

7.5   Inequality and welfare

Access to housing, health care and welfare are important components of social citizenship. Full involvement in contemporary society requires a basic floor of income provision and social services. Access to some services, especially good housing and pensions, depends on earned income, which disadvantages women who spend part of their lives caring for others rather than in employment. Access to others, like the National Health Service (NHS), does not depend on entitlements derived from income or employment, and greater gender equity prevails. Thus two key factors affect equality of access with men: first, whether they have the same employment record, which is rarely the case; second, whether being a resident or citizen of the UK is sufficient qualification.

'Rolling back the state' – reducing intervention and expenditure – has often been seen as a class project, but it is also a gendered project, since women are more dependent on state welfare provision because they spend more of their lives caring for others than earning money. Depending on yourself rather than on the 'nanny state' usually means depending on your own employment record, which is problematic especially for older women.

Changes in the level of welfare benefits thus disproportionately affect women because more of them head single-parent households and more live to pensionable age. Women in old age are particularly vulnerable to the risk of poverty. Those with only a state pension will be very poor, and this is a disproportionately female group. Occupational pensions offer superior benefits but are less common among women. Those who follow a typical male employment pattern gain the best welfare benefits. The current system is one which routinely disadvantages those who devote their lives to unpaid caring work for others.

Access to housing is primarily determined by income. Britain has a higher proportion of people who own the house they live in, rather than renting, than many other countries. Paid employment is thus key to good housing in the UK.

Until the late 1970s the ownership of a house in which a married couple lived was usually held by the husband, the woman having little direct legal claim to it. Today spouses are more likely to own their home jointly, and building societies organize mortgages with this as the presumed norm. Further, wives' legal access to the marital home has been improved by the recent practices of divorce courts, which have more often allowed the wife to claim possession of a portion of the marital home even if her name did not appear on the title deeds. Nevertheless, there remain substantial inequalities in the relative access because men are more likely to have an income sufficient to support a mortgage or high rent. This places non-married (divorced, separated, widowed and single) women at a serious disadvantage on the housing market.

Health

Access to health care under the NHS depends on citizenship determined by residence rather than on insurance contributions, which is common in other countries. Consequently, women have formally equal access to health care. Indeed, since women usually live longer than men, health would appear to be one area of life in which women have an advantage. Men die more frequently from occupationally related diseases, such as lung diseases as a result of mining, as well as heart disease. However, some of the diseases commonly found among men are treated with greater concern and more expensive medical treatment. For instance, attention has recently been drawn to the inadequate provision of screening for cervical cancer, despite the fact that this service could provide the means of identifying early forms of the disease before it reaches its incurable and lethal stage.

The development of the new reproductive technologies also raises questions about the gendered nature of medical research. New techniques enhance women's fertility by a series of intrusive medical interventions. The most famous is that of *in vitro* fertilization (IVF), in which eggs are taken from the woman's ovary and fertilized outside the body with the man's sperm before being replaced in the woman's womb. Its advocates claim that it significantly enhances women's lives in enabling otherwise infertile women to conceive, while its critics counter that it is a disruptive and uncomfortable procedure with such a high failure rate that it benefits experimental medical scientists more than the patient.

The care of frail elderly people is an issue at the borderline of health and social care. Women are disproportionately found among the very elderly. If the work of looking after the frail elderly when they need it is counted as health care, then this is free under the NHS and thus women have equal access with men. However, if this work is counted as social care, then it is either paid for by the person in need (thus better provision goes to those who have substantial pensions or savings) or available only at a basic level after a means test. The boundary between health and social care might appear unclear or irrelevant, but it matters for purposes of payment. For example, if a frail elderly person needs help in order to have a bath this can be regarded as either health care or social care, but if classed as health care help will be free, if social care it must be paid for. New kinds of gendered inequalities are thus developing at the intersection of gender, age and welfare provision.

Summary

1　Different levels of access to social provisions such as pensions, state benefits, housing and health care, which are important for effective social citizenship, can introduce inequality.
2　For those welfare provisions for which access depends on a full record of employment, women are disadvantaged.

7.6　Education

Education has seen a transformation of the position of girls and young women. In schools, not only has the traditional gender gap in examination performance been closed but girls have overtaken boys; while in higher education the gender gap is closing steadily.

Girls do better than boys in the exams taken by pupils in school and further education colleges at 16. In 1996 girls were awarded significantly more of the higher-grade GCSEs than boys and were also more successful at A-level (see tables 7.8 and 7.9). These are very significant and recent changes. As recently as 1985–6, 66,000 boys but only 61,000 girls obtained two or more GCE A-levels and Scottish Highers.

TABLE 7.8　School qualifications by sex, 1995–6 (thousands)

Qualifications	Boys	Girls
GCSE: 5 or more grades A–C	151	180
A level: 2 or more passes	95	109
No graded results	25	26

Source: DFEE 1997, table 4.1

TABLE 7.9　A-levels by sex, 1985–94 (percentages)[a]

Pupils	1985–6	1990–1	1993–4
Male	10	14	14
Female	9	14	16

[a] School pupils gaining three or more A-levels by sex 1985–94, England, Wales and Northern Ireland (percentage of those aged 17)
Source: DFEE 1995, table 31

In higher education, the gap has also been declining (see table 7.10). As higher education has expanded, the numbers of men have increased, but most of the increase has been in numbers of women. In postgraduate study, the gender gap still favours men, but as table 7.10 shows it is closing rapidly: whereas in 1975 women comprised only a quarter of full-time enrolled postgraduates, they accounted for 42 per cent by 1995.

TABLE 7.10 | Full-time enrolment, home and overseas, 1975–95

Year	Undergraduate			Postgraduate		
	Male (000s)	Female (000s)	% female	Male (000s)	Female (000s)	% female
1975–6	141	77	35	37	13	25
1980–1	157	101	39	34	15	31
1985–6	148	108	42	37	17	31
1990–1	167	138	45	41	24	37
1991–2	178	150	46	46	28	38
1992–3	191	166	46	48	31	40
1993–4[a]	398	355	47	62	43	41
1994–5	422	390	48	68	49	42

[a] The figures from 1993–4 onwards are larger because of the exclusion previously of the former polytechnic sector from this statistical series, which ceased on their acquisition of university status.
Source: Calculated from DFEE 1995, table 25

Plate 7.2 | Is this the future?
Source: Lucy Day

There continues to be some segregation of women into certain fields of educational endeavour. However, even this has been subject to change and the extent of gender specialization should not be overstated. In the mainstream subjects such as maths, science, English and French the exams were attempted by about the same numbers of boys and girls in 1995–6. Traditional gender streaming seems to be concentrated in the more vocational subjects such as craft, design and technology, where girls are only one-fifth of examinees, and home economics, where boys are one-sixth (see table 7.11).

TABLE 7.11 | **GCSE/SCE (S grade) attempts in schools, by sex, 1995–6**

Selected subject group	Males (000s)	Females (000s)	% female
Biology	32.8	34.7	51
Chemistry	37.5	28.3	43
Physics	40.0	22.1	36
Single science	43.1	43.1	50
Double science	232.2	232.2	50
Maths	344.7	342.3	50
Computing	17.0	11.1	40
Craft, design and technology	87.6	20.7	19
Home economics	15.3	82.7	84
Social studies	8.3	17.3	68
English	337.8	329.6	49
English literature	231.3	253.2	52
French	184.1	211.6	53

Source: Calculated from DFEE 1997, table 4.2

Gender segregation at university level is more marked than that in schools, but again has declined recently. Women are now 52 per cent of those studying medicine and dentistry; and men are 47 per cent of those studying humanities. However, women comprise only 15 per cent of engineering students, and only 29 per cent of those studying languages are men (DFEE 1998).

These radical changes in the educational success of young men and women mean that there is much less inequity in qualifications among young people than among older people (see table 7.12). In the future women will be better qualified than men. Potentially this has enormous implications, not only for education in its own right, but also in access to good jobs.

Increasing success in the formal educational system is one of the most dramatic improvements in the position of women in society. These changes refute some of the earlier explanations of women's lack of success in education. It was variously held that early socialization into femininity was incompatible with educational success; that early upbringing and/or the structure of the brain meant that women could not think mathematically as well as men; that orientation to a domestic role would lead to women dropping behind in school at puberty, since they 'wanted' a boyfriend/husband more than a job. These theories are contradicted by the evidence of women's superior educational achievements today.

| TABLE 7.12 | Highest selected qualifications by age and sex, Great Britain, 1996 (percentage of population) |

Age and sex	Degree (or equivalent)	A-level (or equivalent)	GCSE, O-level (or equivalent)
16–19			
Men	0	19	43
Women	0	18	45
20–9			
Men	14	23	29
Women	14	19	33
30–9			
Men	16	16	25
Women	12	11	31
40–9			
Men	18	15	18
Women	9	8	23
50–9			
Men	10	10	15
Women	5	6	17
60–9			
Men	10	5	13
Women	1	3	12
Total			
Men	13	14	21
Women	8	10	24

Source: Adapted from *Living in Britain* 1996, table 72

One reason for the change is a legal one, though its significance should not be overestimated. Discrimination against women in education was made illegal in the 1975 Sex Discrimination Act, helping to lead to the removal of the quotas against women in some university subjects, such as medicine, and the abolition of compulsory streaming of girls out of technical subjects in schools. A more important reason was the increase in the opportunities for women in the world after education as the labour market gradually opened up. A further contributory factor might be the changing orientation to marriage, which, given the rise in the divorce rate, is less likely to lead to a financially secure lifelong future. The context of cultural changes and the increasing diversity of acceptable forms of femininity under the impact of the feminist movement also played a part.

These changes in education have potential implications for other aspects of gender relations. Since access to good jobs has some (though not a perfect) relationship to educational qualifications, women might anticipate taking a higher proportion of top jobs. It may also have an impact on wages, in so far as lack of qualifications, rather than discrimination, was a reason for women's poor rates of pay.

Summary

1 There are inequalities between men and women in housing, welfare benefits and health which affect women's access to a full social citizenship.
2 Girls in school and women in university now achieve better formal educational qualifications than boys and men. However, there still remains some gender segregation.

7.7 Gender, power and politics

Violence against women

Power takes many different forms. This section looks at the force some men use against women and the forms of resistance adopted by women. Definitions, concepts and forms of measurement of violence against women have been highly contested. Underlying these ostensibly definitional disputes have been quite different explanatory perspectives.

Male violence takes many different forms, including rape, sexual assault, wife beating, sexual harassment, stalking and child sex abuse. Official statistics reveal only a relatively small number of violent incidents, yet many women are sufficiently convinced of their prevalence to organize their lives quite carefully in order to avoid the possibility of exposure to such violence. For instance, many if not most women are reluctant to walk by themselves at night.

As public awareness of the prevalence of male violence has grown, more kinds of violence have been recognized and named. Rape and battering are one end of a continuum of aggressive forms of behaviour by men. This continuum includes flashing, sexual assault and sexual harassment. High-profile court cases have been widely reported in the media, raising and redefining the categories of violence. For instance, stalking has only recently been identified in court as a form of threatening violence. These forms are often considered to have links with exploitative forms of sexuality, such as prostitution and pornography. Of course some of the violence against women comes from other women and there is some violence by women against men, though much of this latter is thought to be primarily in self-defence.

Traditionally women who have suffered violence from men have been considered 'victims' in recognition of the unmerited and unwanted horrors that they have undergone. However, the use of the term 'survivor' is now more common, as a result of the argument that the term 'victim' inappropriately represented such women as totally passive, while in fact most women have actively resisted the violence in some way or other.

Social scientists have varied in their explanations. Some have taken official statistics at face value and assumed that such violence is the infrequent action of a few psychologically disturbed men. However, these explanations of violence against women are not consistent with the evidence of the extent of the violence, or of its continuity with other forms of male conduct towards women. Others have argued that the official statistics are inadequate and seriously underestimate the extent of such violence, which renders it inexplicable in terms of mental illness.

The British Crime Survey estimates that nearly half a million women are subject to domestic violence during the course of any one year (Mirrlees-Black 1995). This survey shows that nearly half of the violent incidents take place within the domestic sphere, especially done by someone who is a husband or a current or former partner. When asked whether they had ever experienced violence from a partner, 11 per cent of women who had lived with a partner said that they had at some point in their lives. Among women who had previously separated from a partner 37 per cent reported physical violence. This survey itself is likely to underestimate the extent of domestic violence, since women are often loath to disclose such events, and an interview in the context of a general crime survey may undercount incidents which the women did not see as 'crime'. Further, the survey did not ask detailed questions about other forms of violence against women, especially sexual violence. Nevertheless, the extent of the violence reported is enormous.

Evidence to support the view that violence against women is an endemic part of patriarchal society can be found in the historical reluctance of the police and criminal justice system to intervene to protect women. The relative neglect by the police force of women's complaints of rape, domestic violence and other forms of physical and sexual abuse is well documented. The relatively limited response of some law enforcement agencies is taken as evidence that the state should be considered a patriarchal institution rather than a neutral body. Harsh treatment of women during rape trials and the relatively low rate of conviction of alleged rapists add to this view. Judges are overwhelmingly male and have been widely criticized for the way that they conduct trials and their sometimes critical comments on the behaviour of women who have been assaulted. The response by the criminal justice system to violence against women, though very varied, has changed significantly as a result of feminist pressure since the late 1970s. There are now serious, if uneven, reforms, such as trained officers and specialized departments at police stations. The number of incidents of rape recorded by the police has been increasing steadily. But whether this means that women are now more likely to go to the police as a result of changes in police procedure, or that there is more rape, is impossible to say on the available evidence.

Some writers are critical of the view that violence against women can be explained in terms of unchanging male power. Nevertheless, structured gender inequality must remain a crucial part of the explanation. There are significant changes in the nature of patriarchal society as a result of a number of social forces, not least of which has been feminist action. Violence against women is implicated in complex ways with gender inequality in various domains of society, from the household to the state to the media. Further, domestic violence appears to be particularly common among poorer households, suggesting a link between this type of violence and socio-economic inequality as well.

Politics and citizenship

While women now have the same formal political and legal rights as men, there remains a striking absence of women from positions of public power and authority. This raises questions about the nature of, and routes to, participation in political decisions.

Members of Parliament

Access to formal political citizenship and democratic rights for women has been won over the last 100 years or so. In 1918 women over 30 who possessed some property won the right to vote, followed in 1928 by all women over 21. Having won the vote, women were able to make good their claims to sit on juries and take up seats in Parliament.

Though formally equal, women do not have effective equality in access to public positions. Women MPs make up only a very small proportion of the total number. In the 1997 general election, women won 18 per cent of the seats in the House of Commons. This is much higher than in previous years, but Britain still has one of the lowest proportions in its national elected legislature in Western Europe. For example, in Sweden 40 per cent of nationally elected representatives are women. There are some differences between the parties, with the Conservatives having a lower proportion than the Labour Party. There is a slightly higher proportion of elected women representatives in local than in central government.

Explanations for this low number of women elected concentrate either on the nature of the electoral system or on the circumstances of women. The UK national electoral system is based on the 'first past the post' system. Other electoral systems take voters' second preferences into account and allow voters to elect more than one representative for a constituency. These latter systems tend to elect higher proportions of women. The

Plate 7.3 | Will these women make a difference?
Source: Popperfoto

explanation for this correlation is debated, but is linked to the greater fluidity and responsiveness of these systems to new political constituencies. In particular, having a slate of candidates rather than one may lead to greater friendliness to diverse candidates rather than those rightly or wrongly perceived as 'safe' – typically middle-aged men from the dominant ethnic/national group in the first past the post system. An alternative explanation focuses on the domestic constraints of women which allegedly make involvements in public activities difficult. Evidence in support of this is the correlation between rates of female employment and proportions of female representatives in various national parliaments. Thus, the highest rates of female representation in the world are to be found in the Scandinavian countries, which also have the highest rates of female employment. Probably both types of explanation have some validity.

Women in public life

Women hold a very small proportion of other public offices. There are very few women who sit as judges or on the boards of nationalized industries, are chief constables, or hold senior military positions. The Equal Opportunities Commission (EOC) noted in 1991 that, despite 79 per cent of the NHS workforce being female, only 17 per cent of its unit general managers and 4 per cent of district and regional general managers were women.

TABLE 7.13 | Women in trade unions, 1990 (percentages)

Women's representation	NUPE[a]	NALGO	GMB	USDAW	TGWU
As members	71.3	53.1[b]	30.8	61.7	16.9
On national executive committee	46.1	42.0	29.4	31.3	7.7
Among delegates to annual conference	33.3	–	17.4	27.1	–
On TUC delegation	36.1	41.7	19.8	26.9	20.6
As full-time national officers	38.5	31.6	11.8	20.0	3.4
As full-time regional officers	11.0	13.4	3.6	18.6	–
Women members (no.)	430,000	398,660[b]	267,371	251,371	210,758

[a] NUPE = National Union of Public Employees; NALGO = National and Local Government Officers' Association; GMB = general workers' union; USDAW = Union of Shop, Distributive, and Allied Workers; TGWU = Transport and General Workers' Union.
[b] 1989
Source: Snyder 1992, p. 370

Among trade unions, the picture is little different. Table 7.13 shows that women's percentage of the leadership positions is much smaller than their proportion of the membership, even in unions where women are the majority of the members. However, some trade unions now have special women's committees to assist the representation of the views of their women members, in an effort to ameliorate the problem.

The EU

The EU has been an important source of pressure on the British government to improve its sex equality legislation. The EU declared that the 1975 Sex Discrimination Act (which incorporated the 1970 Equal Pay Act) did not come up to European standards, and that the British government had to make it stronger. The then Conservative government was obliged to enact the 'equal value amendment', which means that a woman seeking equal pay can compare herself with a man doing work of similar value, rather than the more stringent condition of a man who is actually doing exactly the same work. This has been followed by an energetic development of equal opportunities policies by the EU which are binding on member states. The loss of British sovereignty in the context of the increasing powers of the EU has facilitated the strengthening of equal opportunities regulations. The changing relationship between the UK and the EU thus has had significant implications for the regulation of gender relations in the UK.

Feminist movements

Feminist responses to gender inequality have taken a variety of forms and have mobilized women in varying ways. Feminism is not a new social movement but one with a long history. The 1970s was the second wave of feminism in the twentieth century, the early one being instrumental in winning political citizenship for women. Many of the feminist ideas of the 1970s which had been considered outrageously radical when first expressed are now widely accepted. For instance, male violence is now recognized as a significant problem and the subject of serious discussion by the police as well as feminists. Equal pay for equal work is likewise an early feminist demand now accepted into mainstream policy initiatives such as Opportunity 2000. Indeed some of these issues are now so mainstream that they are barely recognized as feminist. There has been an extensive institutionalization of many feminist concerns into a wide and diffuse set of voluntary organizations, professional associations and other institutions. For instance, while there is a network of explicitly feminist organizations supporting women who have suffered male violence, such as the Rape Crisis Federation and Women's Aid, key aspects of such policy agendas are incorporated in bodies such as the Young Women's Christian Association, an organization not usually described as 'feminist'. Further, there are now state-financed quangos to take forward parts of the original feminist agenda, such as the EOC.

It has been argued that women are to be found less often in public life because of their domestic responsibilities, which take so much of women's time, together with a socialization into gentle rather than assertive behaviour. However, the extent to which women have been politically active renders these accounts problematic. While women have been slow to obtain formal political positions, there is none the less an extensive mobilization of women within civil society.

Gender politics is not exclusively represented by feminism. Some women have argued that women's interests are best protected by supporting traditional forms of family life. This underlies some of the concerns which have been raised by the new right, but these have not been popularly received in contemporary Britain. There has, however, been a development of some political responses against feminist successes, such as those around rights for fathers over children following divorce.

Today the dominant perspective in gender politics is that represented by equal opportunities, to which a wide range of politicians and activists of otherwise divergent views subscribe. Gender issues are broadly diffused within civil society as well as the formal elected political arena in a variety of forms.

Summary

1   Male violence against women is a serious problem which is under-recorded in the official statistics. There is too much violence for it to be explained as due to mental illness.
2   There is increasing attention being paid to violence against women in public policy, as a result of feminist pressure.
3   Women have achieved parity in formal legal and political rights, but this has not yet led to equal numbers of women in public positions, in Parliament or in public bodies.
4   Feminist concerns are taking new forms, increasingly influencing mainstream politics, and becoming embedded in the associations of civil society.

7.8   Overview

This overview of the relations of the genders has demonstrated extensive inequality. While some dimensions of gender inequality have reduced in recent years, especially in the field of education, the basic pattern of inequality remains in most aspects of the social structure, from paid work to the household division of labour, from sexuality to violence.

The inequality, and the extent to which the different aspects of this are interconnected, mean that it is appropriate to use the concept of patriarchy to describe this set of social relations. Patriarchy is a social system through which men dominate, exploit and oppress women. It is the interconnectedness of the different aspects of this which makes the concept of patriarchy particularly appropriate. However, inequality takes many different forms, especially in different ethnic groups, and among people of different ages and classes.

One way in which gender, ethnicity and class have been seen to fit together is as a consequence of capitalist social relations: women are exploited in the workplace because of the direct benefit that employers derive from this, and in the home because employers need to have a new generation of workers produced as cheaply as possible. Some of the evidence of the earlier part of this chapter supports this view. Women are paid less than men, and employers do benefit from this. However, other data suggest that this is an inadequate explanation.

Within paid employment, male workers benefit from their ability to keep the best and most skilled jobs for themselves; they are beneficiaries of occupational segregation by gender. Men also gain from the unequal division of labour within the home, in which women do disproportionate amounts of housework. Further, the physical and sexual abuse of women, much more widespread than is popularly believed, cannot be under-stood in terms of anything other than patriarchal relations.

There is considerable diversity in the forms of gender relations, often deriving from other cross-cutting forms of social relations – including class, ethnicity, religion, age and generation, and sexuality – which relate in complex ways with gender. The extent and significance of these differences between women and between men mean that it is often not appropriate to make simple statements about all women or about all men. As regards change, inequality has reduced in some areas, while new inequalities have devel-oped elsewhere. In particular, those young women who obtain high levels of education and jobs will have significantly greater opportunities than older women.

Related topics

Discussions of gender relations will be found throughout the book. Accounts of various aspects of women's work are to be found in sections 4.2 and 4.4. Section 9.5 is con-cerned with gender relations within the household. Women's access to health care is dealt with in section 15.6. Their exposure to male violence is examined in section 16.3 and their treatment by legal institutions in 16.4. Section 14.3 examines the implementa-tion of equal opportunities policies in schools, and 14.4 treats the educational disadvan-tages of women and includes material on femininity and masculinity among school pupils.

Further reading

More complex accounts of changes in gender relations can be found in Walby (1990, 1997). A useful source of data on the inequalities between women and men in employ-ment and related arenas is *Women and Men in Britain,* an annual publication from the EOC.

Cross-references to *Readings in Contemporary British Society*

Smart on conceptions of motherhood and fatherhood; **Roseneil** on a women's protest movement; **Finch and Mason** on gender differences in discharging obligations to family members; **Gillespie** on Punjabi boys' and girls' reactions to soap opera; **Gallie et al.** on changes in women's employment, flexibility and polarization; **Devine** on poverty, lone parenthood and deprivation; **Skeggs** on the cultural ambivalence of working-class women and their search for respectability; **McDowell** on gender divisions and women managers in the City of London and their encounters with masculinities and femininities; **Morris** on sexual divisions of labour, gender divisions, lone motherhood and the limits of wel-fare provision; **Lury** on shopping, domestic divisions of labour, gender divisions and femininity; **Norris and Lovenduski** on political representation, party organizations and the small number of women members of parliament; **Acker** on gender divisions, labour market segregation and equal opportunities for women teachers; **Mac an Ghaill** on masculinity, peer-group subcultures, youth and sexuality; **Thompson** on moral panics, homosexuality and AIDS; **Worrall** on gender and the criminal justice system.

Ethnicity and Racism

8

Introduction

    8.1   *Looks at the way in which race and ethnicity are studied in sociology.*

The structure of minority ethnic communities

    8.2   *Deals with the structure of minority ethnic communities.*

Ethnic identity

    8.3   *Gives an account of the ways in which different ethnic groups form their own identities.*

Ethnic disadvantage

    8.4   *Considers the ways in which ethnic minorities are disadvantaged, especially by their position in the labour market.*

Discrimination and racism

    8.5   *Looks at the role played by discrimination and racism in the disadvantaged position of ethnic minorities.*

8.1   Introduction

Contemporary Britain is a multicultural and multiethnic society. The British population is a mix of people with different regional and national origins and allegiances. According to the Census, it is made up of many ethnicities including white, Indian, black Caribbean, Pakistani and Bangladeshi. On the surface, it seems a relatively straightforward task to distinguish between these groupings and to measure the experiences and life opportunities that they have. However, there are two problems that need to be taken into consideration. On the one hand, many people do not fit neatly into these categories – many of us have relatives and forebears with different national backgrounds and ethnic characteristics. 'White', for example, covers, at least, Welsh, Irish, Scottish, English and European ethnicities. The British population has been built up through successive waves of migration around the British Isles and through immigration from several European and non European countries. On the other hand, it can be difficult for individuals to identify with clarity which ethnic or national category applies to them. There is no straightforward relationship between country, colour or culture and ethnic identity, for example. Ethnicity, it can be said, comprises a mix of characteristics. 'Race', on the other hand, is often placed in inverted commas to highlight the fact that there are no pure, genetically different races. We are all mongrels. In this chapter we have concentrated on the ethnic categories provided in two recent, large-scale surveys of British society. The categories in these surveys distinguish between white and non-white peoples. This disguises the ways in which whiteness is ethnically differentiated, so that Irish, Polish, Scottish, Welsh and English people, for example, can be divided by ethnicity as much as united by common characteristics. It is important to bear in mind, then, that while this chapter is primarily concerned with minority ethnic groups from the ex-colonies, the general points made apply equally to all ethnic groupings that find themselves in a minority.

Sociological interest in ethnicity and 'race' has a long pedigree, especially as an issue of immigration. The Chicago School of Sociology, for example, developed a research programme around migration to the USA in the first half of the century which laid the foundations for much British research from the 1950s to the 1970s. Briefly, until the late 1960s, sociology's approach to questions of ethnicity and 'race' was dominated by 'assimilation' and 'integration' models of immigration. These models suggest that ethnic and racial tension arises from the ways that immigrant populations disturb the social equilibrium of the host society. Ethnic and racial differences, as social problems, are seen as temporary phases in the gradual incorporation of immigrant groups into dominant norms and lifestyles (Richardson and Lambert 1985). More recently, research has developed around structures of ethnic inequality and the ways that British institutions (the police and education system, for example) collude in reproducing social inequalities of ethnicity and race. Research has also developed into the cultural variety of multiethnic societies: the intersection of many different styles of music, dress, writing, cinema and so on creates a rich reservoir of voices, perspectives and myths. Finally, research has developed too around the ways that individuals identify themselves, or are identified by others, in ethnic or racial terms. Here, the sociological focus is on the meaning and effect that ethnicity has for people in their everyday lives: how the experience of ethnicity is grounded in the day-to-day routines and beliefs of different individuals.

Sociologists study ethnicity, 'race' and racism, then, for a number of reasons, which include:

- the need to understand social relationships in a complex and ethnically rich society and how the interaction between people from diverse backgrounds fosters social change;

- the need to map the social divisions that characterize such a society and to learn how those social divisions affect people's life-chances;
- the need to understand how people identify through (or against) the beliefs and practices of their culture.

In this chapter we highlight some of the sociological issues that are raised by the study of ethnicity as well as describing aspects of ethnic identity and ethnic inequality in contemporary British society.

8.2   The structure of minority ethnic communities

There are two primary sources which give particularly useful data on the structure of minority ethnic communities and their situation across a range of areas of social and economic life. These are the 1991 Census and the Fourth Survey of Ethnic Minorities carried out in 1994 and published by the Policy Studies Institute (PSI). The 1991 Census provides a wealth of detail on the structures of minority ethnic communities, albeit with limitations, which we examine later in this section. For the first time since the Census was introduced in 1801, a question concerning the ethnic origins of the British population was included in the 1991 Census (see box 8.1). Although asking such a question may seem straightforward, its inclusion represented the outcome of fifteen years of debate, extensive consultation, and development through pilot trials. This lengthy period and the disputes surrounding the possible inclusion of a question concerning ethnic origins are a marker of the difficulty encountered by any sociologist working in the field of 'race' or ethnicity, which is the difficulty of separating out the sociological from the political issues surrounding the subject matter of this field of study. Many sociologists argue that such a separation is undesirable, because Britain's imperial and colonial history results in the experiences of the whole population, as well as the social structures and institutions that people from minority ethnic groups routinely encounter in their daily lives, being embroiled in the effects of this history, as we discuss later in this chapter.

The introduction of the question on ethnicity was important because it generated a significant number of new demographic and socio-economic data on the structure and characteristics of minority ethnic populations. It also provided official acknowledgement that successive waves of immigration in the post-war period have transformed Britain into a multicultural society. This recognition of Britain's multicultural status can be seen in the context of a more recent movement towards equal opportunities for disadvantaged social groups. The question on ethnicity provides data that enable analysis of the degree of social integration and the extent of discrimination experienced by minority ethnic groups, thereby providing a basis for policy development at local and national levels. The purpose of the Census is to provide information that can inform planning and practical initiatives, and previous surveys and research had already demonstrated considerable disadvantages experienced by minority ethnic groups (Coleman and Salt 1996a). The data from the Census suggest that such policies and programmes need to take account of the diversity of minority ethnic communities and the different life trajectories both between and within particular groups, because the experiences and circumstances of people from minority ethnic populations differ depending on, in par-

> ### Box 8.1   The official justification for the ethnic question in the 1991 Census
>
> The official justification for the inclusion of the ethnic question in the 1991 Census, set out in the Census White Paper of 1988, notes that the rectification of the disadvantaged position of ethnic minorities is a matter of general public welfare and is additionally important for the favourable development of race relations. The unique comprehensiveness and coverage of the Census, it claims, are needed to provide data on the housing, employment, educational qualifications and age-structure of each group so that resources can be appropriately allocated and special needs met. The information would help Government and local authorities carry out their responsibilities under the 1976 Race Relations Act and serve as a benchmark for employers to measure the success of 'equal opportunities' policies. These policies include various programmes targeted at Commonwealth immigrant and minority ethnic populations, to overcome difficulties in schools, to encourage training and enterprise and provide social and cultural facilities directed at specific immigrant communities, and many local authority initiatives aimed at specific minority ethnic communities. Comprehensive programmes directed at 'equal opportunities' depend upon ethnic 'targets' which will now use the 1991 Census data for their base. (Coleman and Salt 1996a, p. 9)

ticular, an individual's class position and gender. For the moment, we concentrate on the numbers of people from different ethnic origins resident in Britain in 1991, before moving on to examine the limitations of the Census data.

In 1991 there were approximately 3,869,000 people of minority ethnic origin in Britain, just over 5.5 per cent of the total population, compared with perhaps 100,000 in 1950. As we can see from table 8.1, there is a considerable diversity of ethnicities represented in the Census. Approximately 53 per cent of the total minority ethnic population were born outside Britain, including roughly 75 per cent of Asian and Chinese people, and nearly two-thirds of Bangladeshis. On the other hand, over 50 per cent of the black Caribbeans and 84.5 per cent of the black other group were British born, paralleling immigration patterns (Salt 1996, pp. 132–3).

The increase in the numbers of people from minority ethnic groups represents a profound change in the constitution of British society – a change largely dependent on the British economy's demand for labour. After the Second World War, migration into Britain was regulated partly by a work permit scheme which did not apply to British Commonwealth citizens. The British economy was expanding, providing an increased demand for labour which could not be filled from the pool of labour available in Britain. These were the days of full employment, when workers in Britain had a far greater range of employment opportunities than exists now, and a number of job vacancies needing filling, mostly in the least desirable occupations. A recruitment drive was launched by British Rail, London Transport and the National Health Service (NHS), amongst others, to recruit workers from the colonies and ex-colonies. During the late 1940s and

| TABLE 8.1 | 1991 Census population by ethnic group, adjusted for estimated undercoverage, England and Wales, thousands |

Ethnic group	Total	Men	Women
White	57,935.4	33,389.1	24,546.3
Indian	856.5	436.5	419.9
Black Caribbean	518.5	252.5	265.9
Pakistani	474.4	247.9	226.5
Other-Other	293.1	153.5	139.5
Black African	220.6	113.1	107.5
Other-Asian	200.0	96.5	103.5
Black-Other	184.1	91.7	92.4
Bangladeshi	167.6	88.5	79.1
Chinese	152.4	76.5	75.8

Source: Adapted from Simpson 1996, pp. 68–9

1950s, following the 1948 British Nationality Act, an 'open door' policy extended to a large number of citizens of the empire and New Commonwealth, as well as displaced persons from Europe (Salt 1996). At this time, the largest numbers were coming from Caribbean countries, where direct recruitment in the former British West Indies took place, following a pattern established during the war years, when labour was recruited from the Caribbean countries to help in the war effort, particularly in the armed forces and munitions factories (Peach 1996a). As mass migration from the Caribbean took place earliest, it also ended first. This migration was unusual in that women came relatively early and often independently of men. The length of residence in Britain has resulted in Caribbeans being the group most integrated into white social patterns and society, particularly when measured in terms of mixed marriages and relationships. In the 1970s and 1980s, after migration from the Caribbean had slowed down considerably, there was a wave of migration from the Indian subcontinent, with men migrating first to seek employment – mainly in unskilled jobs such as those in Midlands engineering companies and the textile mills in Yorkshire and Lancashire – and being joined by families at a later date. Indian people completed migration of families earlier than those from Pakistan, whilst those from Bangladesh were relative latecomers (Owen 1996a, p. 111).

Although the bulk of post-war immigration has been prompted by labour requirements, a significant minority has been for purposes of education or asylum. Daley (1996, p. 45) points out that migration for educational purposes had been important during the period preceding independence in the 1950s and immediately following it in the 1960s. For example, the Colonial Office and British Council were instrumental in establishing educational opportunities in Britain for African people after the African colonies won their independence from Britain. This was because the absence of a settled white population during the colonial period in West Africa resulted in a number of vacancies in high-status positions requiring advanced education. Since then migration for educational purposes remains important, as a number of political and economic crises in African countries have resulted in an elite group seeking education in Britain, as well as refugees and exiles seeking asylum.

The enthusiastic recruitment of labour in Britain's colonies and ex-colonies had, by the early 1960s, given way to increasing pressure for control over immigration. Acts of 1962, 1968 and 1971 restricted immigration from Commonwealth countries but, because the entry of dependent relatives was not restricted, the total number of migrants continued to grow throughout the 1960s. Since the 1971 Act most immigrants have needed work permits, and these have been granted mostly for work in those industries, like the health service and hotels, where there has been a shortage of domestic workers. The number of work permits issued has fallen as unemployment in Britain has risen. It seems likely that permits are increasingly granted for specialized professional occupations, which tends to favour the white inhabitants of countries such as the USA and South Africa. The 1971 Act also effectively discriminated against black and Asian workers by the introduction of the concept of 'patrials', which was intended to give the right of residence to persons with close ties to Britain but not others. In practice, the majority of overseas patrials have been found in the 'white' Commonwealth of Canada and Australasia.

The combination of successively restrictive immigration laws and the end of the years of economic expansion has meant that mass migration has run its course, and that any future migration is likely to be relatively small, comprised of dependants joining relatives, those taking up jobs where a shortage of labour exists, such as doctors in hospitals, and those seeking asylum from war-torn countries or repressive political regimes. The majority of those entering Britain for work purposes in the late 1990s were from the European Union (EU) countries. The majority of growth in the minority ethnic populations will be amongst those born in Britain, as indeed is already the case. The Census data are therefore important in establishing numerous demographic and socio-economic indicators which enable the planning of, for example, health and social services, to meet the needs of different constituencies. The considerable differences between various groups in terms of age and sex distributions, religion and family structure point to the need for different categories of services, such as nursing or child care, schools or home helps, that are sensitive to cultural differences.

Although the age structure of minority ethnic populations is generally youthful, we can see from figure 8.1 that there are considerable differences between the age structures of men and women in some ethnic groups. For example, women outnumber men in the Other–Asian and Black Caribbean groups, with women in the latter group outnumbering men by around 25 per cent in the 15–29 age group, and by over 32.6 per cent in the 45–59 age group of the Other-Asian population. Emphasizing the complex age and sex structures of minority ethnic communities, Warness (1996, p. 151) explains that:

Many in the 1950s migrant cohorts, mainly from the West Indies, are now around or approaching the statutory retirement age: for the next few decades there will be substantial increases in the population of elderly minority ethnic people. In addition, the decline in fertility in some ethnic groups (that will be marginally reinforced by improvements in longevity) has produced a tendency for 'demographic ageing'. . . . More importantly for the family and social situation of minority ethnic elderly people, over a period of several decades there will be a reduction in the proportions who came to this country late in life, with neither the English language nor a knowledge of our health and welfare institutions, and who as adult migrants found themselves with an attenuated social network of siblings, cousins and juvenile acquaintances. On the other hand, there will be an increase in the proportion who have raised families in this country, have full citizenship in legal and practical terms, have extended kin networks here and associates from all stages of life.

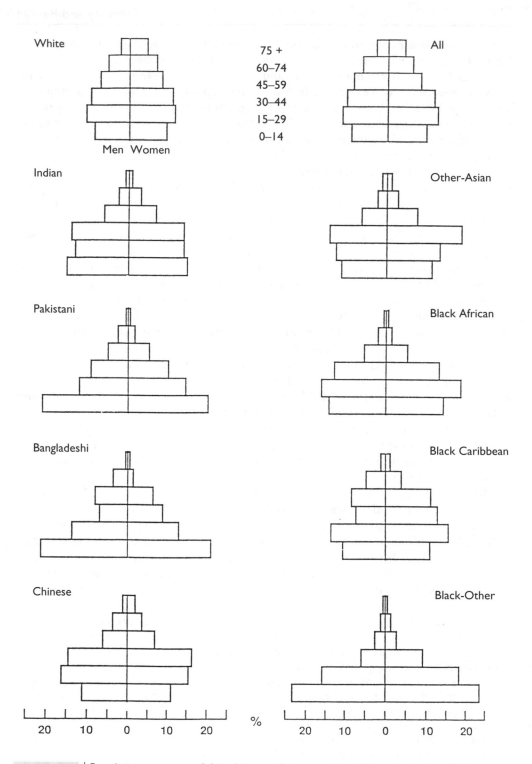

White

75 +
60–74
45–59
30–44
15–29
0–14

Men Women

All

Indian

Other-Asian

Pakistani

Black African

Bangladeshi

Black Caribbean

Chinese

Black-Other

20 10 0 10 20 % 20 10 0 10 20

Figure 8.1 | Population structure of the white population and the ethnic minority populations
Source: Warness 1996, p. 157

The structure of minority populations is, then, both heterogeneous and dynamic. Existing health and social services have not recognized either of these factors, so that adequate services are very limited, although recent initiatives in health and social care have resulted in comprehensive exercises to establish a range of services that can take into account the different religious, cultural and practical needs of minority populations. The structure of families and households is an important aspect of these initiatives, and the Census demonstrates great diversity here too, with significant differences in regard to the size of family or household, cohabitation patterns, trends in marriage, and cultural attitudes to marriage between generations. For example, Asian communities are characterized by multi-generational households, with those from South Asia having above average size households, mainly because of younger age structures and larger numbers of children, marrying younger, and rarely divorcing or cohabiting. In contrast, black households are below average size, lone parenthood is more common, and in the Black African and Black-Other groups marriage tends to be at a later age (Coleman and Salt 1996a, p. 5; Berrington 1996; Murphy 1996).

Limitations of the Census

One of the limitations of the Census data was an undercount of people from minority ethnic groups. There are several reasons for this. First, there is evidence that people are more likely to fail to register in areas with a high density of multi-occupancy dwellings and single household residency, mostly because such areas are populated by single, mobile young people. Second, there is a tendency to omit the registration of young infants, and to miss out elderly people in nursing homes. Third, in 1991 there were widespread fears that the Census would be used to check against the Poll Tax register, and the unpopularity and resistance to the Poll Tax was such that there was avoidance of the Census, particularly among young people (Bulmer 1996, pp. 54–5).

Whilst the undercount limitation is strictly a question of numbers, more significant is a conceptual, or definitional, problem. A major difficulty with the ethnic group classification was that of arriving at the classifications. There are significant dilemmas in separating out understandings and definitions of racial, national and ethnic categorizations. For example, White and Black African can be understood as racial categories, but encompass people born in many different countries and differentiated by many ethnic characteristics. As Peach points out (1996c, p. 5) the category 'White' suggests a 'racial' designation, but encompasses Welsh, Scottish, Italian, Cypriot, American and Greek people, for example. The category 'Indian' could point to either nationality or ethnicity, but within this category exist major religious and linguistic differences that render the category meaningless as a description of a social group. Different definitions and classifications are used in different surveys, leading to divergent pictures of population characteristics. Thus we can say that the categories we use construct the populations under investigation, rather than reflect a pre-given reality. The categories are *artefacts of the methodology used in the census* instead of representations of social groups.

These difficulties in categorization reflect the ambiguities surrounding ethnicity, in particular the relationships between ethnicity and identity. Ethnicity is not a static and pre-given category, but shifts according to context. Peach (1996c, p. 5) draws attention to the way in which:

> One may be Welsh in England, British in Germany, European in Thailand, White in Africa. A person may be Afro-Caribbean by descent but British by upbringing so that his or her census category might be either Black-Caribbean or Black-Other. Similarly, a person may be an East African Asian, an Indian, a Sikh or a Ramgarhia. Thus ethnicity is a situational rather than an independent category. The Census Quality Validation has indicated confusion about which category to claim, especially for those of mixed ethnic background.

We can see, then, that ethnic identity is contextual and situational. The ethnic question represents not an actually existing objective reality, but rather *a process of identification*. This can refer to self-identification, as when those of mixed parentage decide on what category they might be inserted in. For example, which category might someone with one white and one black parent fit into? The Black-Other category contains many people of mixed parentage, and 84.4 per cent of those in this category were born in Britain (Owen 1996b). As Al-Rasheed (1996, p. 206) writes:

> Racial categories such as White and Black are confusing especially for people whose skin colour is neither. The Arab population of Britain is one of these groups . . . The majority of Arabs regard themselves as Whites and many did tick the box 'White'. Those who are aware of the meaning this word implies in Britain, moved to the category Other-Other and wrote Arab while still convinced they were Whites.

Of significance here is that one can regard oneself as White in terms of skin colour, but not in terms of white European culture – not in cultural terms. Al-Rasheed (1996, p. 208) illustrates the confusion that can arise when classifying minorities with the anecdote recorded in box 8.2.

Box 8.2   Colour and identity

During my fieldwork among the Iraqi Assyrian Christian community in West London, I encountered many Assyrians, some born in Iraq and others in Britain, who asserted their Whiteness. Community leaders resented the fact that as an immigrant community they had been classified as Blacks by their local authority when they tried to get Council funds in the process of establishing a community centre in the 1980s. Many Assyrians are in fact White, some have natural blond hair and blue eyes. This also applies to the Kurds, especially those who have been living in the mountains of Kurdistan. (Al-Rasheed 1996, p. 208)

Al-Rasheed notes that possibly half of those recorded in the census in the Other-Other category are of Arab or Middle Eastern origin, yet many others from these locations are recorded as White. Ethnic identity can also be a highly political issue. For example, some Muslims consider the identity of Muslim more relevant than one based on nationality. Peach (1996c, p. 4) reports that the Islamic Secretariat of the UK campaigned among Muslims to reject the ethnic group question in the Census and record themselves as Muslim instead, even though this was not an official designation. It is difficult to grasp the importance of ethnicity in political terms without an appreciation of the complex politics of the Indian subcontinent, particularly after it was partitioned following independence from British rule in 1947, a separation that resulted in Pakistan becoming a homeland for Muslims, but riven with internal ethnic divisions (Ballard 1996, pp. 121–2), for example between Punjabis, Pathans, Sindhis and Muhajirs. The national category 'Pakistani' does not signify much to those who identify themselves as belonging to one of these groups, nor to those who see Islam as a political movement transcending both ethnicity and nationality, and whose preferred identification is 'Muslim'.

Similarly, Daley (1996, p. 44), discussing the 213,362 persons classified as Black African, draws attention to the importance of Black as a political category, resulting in over 2,000 people who were born in the Caribbean classifying themselves as Black African, a category that encompasses 53 potential countries of origin and various social classes. Africa has a very heterogeneous population and complex colonial and post-colonial residency patterns, with most of those of African origin residing in Britain originating from countries with a British colonial past (Daley 1996, p. 64).

This diversity within ethnic groups, and the different meanings attached to ethnicity, mean that defining categories is an exercise fraught with difficulty. Ethnicity is entangled with questions of identity in highly complex ways, and in the context of the multicultural character of British society has led to a growing sociological focus on issues of identity and difference.

Summary

1   Britain is a multicultural society with half of the minority population having been born in this country.
2   Different ethnic groups have very different demographic characteristics; for example, of household, age and gender structure. They also define themselves in different ways.

8.3   Ethnic identity

Cultural difference

The cultural differences characterizing post-war British society were first considered a problem of how numbers of people from minority groups were to be incorporated into British society. The assumption was that the cultural and social customs and practices that immigrants brought with them should be shed as quickly as possible and that immigrants should assimilate into the host, British culture. This view was sharply criticized because it assumed the existence of a single, homogeneous British culture into which incomers could be assimilated. This was not the case, Britain already being composed of different ethnic and class cultures. The view was also criticized for its wholly negative attitude to all aspects of immigrants' cultures. This was a time when, for example, the curry dishes cooked by immigrants were sneered at and rejected. Now curry is part of everyday British food, available in supermarkets and restaurants all over the country.

In response to criticism, a shift to an approach known as the immigration-integration model occurred. Integration here was a concept concerned with overcoming the social exclusion of minority ethnic groups from social and economic institutions. Attention was directed to the ways in which cultural differences involving language, religion, education and family life, for example, hindered the integration of immigrant groups into mainstream British life. In investigating these factors, researchers began to record the ways in which widespread racism impeded integration and perpetuated the marginalized and disadvantaged status of minority ethnic groups.

This and similar models were severely criticized for still retaining an underlying assumption that cultural differences were undesirable and inferior to the host culture or, even where negative judgements were not implicit, that integration required that the cultural identity of immigrant groups should be surrendered. Instead, attention turned to promoting multiculturalism and establishing racial harmony. This approach was itself subsequently criticized for depoliticizing issues of racism, and a shift took place towards examining how equality of opportunity and of rights could be effected, involving detailed studies of discrimination in housing, employment, education and other areas of social life.

More and more evidence was accumulated of the unequal status of ethnic minority groups, and sociologists turned to the study of racism and racist practices, such as the relationship between racism and nationalistic beliefs widespread in British society that emerge at particular times, as in the debate over membership of the EU in the early 1990s. These attitudes are revealed in the relationship of the English to minority ethnic groups who are visibly different in skin colour, but also to Irish, Welsh, Polish and others. All the racist attitudes and beliefs have in common a fearful, and often hostile, view of some social group defined as different. In its most extreme form, nationalism is the basis of neo-Nazi groups that react to multiculturalism with violence and hostility. However, it is discrimination based on prejudice against social differences that operates most commonly in day-to-day life (see next section).

Cultural difference and identity

Since the late 1980s, the study of cultural difference has shifted yet again to examine the relationships between cultural differences and identity. Keith (1993, p. 27) writes of the way that 'A name denotes a place and connotes a history.' Cultural difference is related to ethnic identity in ways which have in recent years become increasingly politicized. This politicization is complex and linked to different levels of social and political life, but has an important relationship to cultural processes in everyday life. Modood (1997a, p. 290), the author of a large-scale, longitudinal study of ethnic identities, comments that:

> There is an ethnic assertiveness, arising out of the feelings of not being respected or lacking access to public space, consisting of counterposing 'positive' images against traditional or

dominant stereotypes. It is a politics of projecting identities in order to challenge existing power relations; of seeking not just toleration for ethnic difference but also public acknowledgement, resources and representation. Moreover, these identities are of different sorts, and not stable.

Modood's study is aimed at unpacking the meaning and importance of identity in relation to a multicultural society. It offers a way of understanding some of the relationships between cultural difference and identity in contemporary British society. Modood's survey focused on ethnic minority groups and was used to investigate 'some of the components of ethnic identity, how they vary between and within ethnic groups, and how they may be changing, especially across generations' (1997a, p. 291). His work confirms some of the points we made in discussing the Census categories: identity categories are fluid, rather than fixed, and respond both to situational factors and to wider social currents impacting differently on ethnic groups. Table 8.2 summarizes responses to a question about self-definition. Respondents were asked to say how they would describe themselves, on the telephone, to a new acquaintance in another country. The variable of gender was omitted deliberately as a way of simplifying interpretation of the responses.

TABLE 8.2 | Elements of self-description (percentages)

Response	Caribbean	Indian	African Asian	Pakistani	Bangladeshi	Chinese
These would tell a new acquaintance something important about me:						
Nationality	81	78	69	74	63	77
White, black, Asian, etc.	76	68	60	56	64	74
Country your family came from	63	67	62	67	76	65
Age	61	57	50	65	57	50
Job	56	57	65	64	54	61
Education	47	49	60	57	53	54
Height	31	30	26	26	26	13
Colour of hair or eyes	30	25	24	26	19	13
Level of income	16	19	17	19	14	6
Father's job	10	14	15	19	7	7
Weighted count	765	606	290	297	141	183
Unweighted count	580	595	361	538	289	101

Source: Modood 1997a, p. 292

We can observe from these responses that self-definitions in terms of nationality and broad ethnicity are deemed, on the whole, to be slightly more revealing than self-definitions in terms of occupation, education or income. They also outweigh self-definitions in terms of personal attributes – height, or colour of hair and eyes, in this example. We can note, then, that certain collective factors – especially national and cultural ones – tend to play a larger role in self-identification than individual factors.

At the same time, the responses are based on a hypothetical situation – where the new acquaintance lives in another country. As Modood points out, the self-definitions might be very different were respondents describing themselves to another British person: British Caribbeans and British Asians appear to find it easier to identify as British when abroad than they do when in Britain. Writing of the second generation Modood (1997a, p. 330) explains:

> We found that most of the second generation did think of themselves as mostly but not entirely culturally and socially British. They were not, however, comfortable with the idea of British being more than a legal title, in particular they found it difficult to call themselves 'British' because they felt that the majority of white people did not accept them as British because of their race or cultural background; through hurtful 'jokes', harassment, discrimination and violence they found their claim to be British was all too often denied.

Such distressing experiences of rejection form the backdrop to the lives of many minority group members. However, there are important differences between ethnic minorities in their identification with individual and collective identity categories. Modood illustrates this by comparing the responses to categories of religion and skin colour as sources of self-identification. The results are summarized in table 8.3.

TABLE 8.3 | Religion and colour in self-description (percentages)

	Caribbean	Indian	African Asian	Pakistani	Bangladeshi	Chinese
These would tell a new acquaintance something important about me:						
Religion	44	73	68	83	75	25
Skin colour	61	37	29	31	21	15
Weighted count	765	606	290	397	141	183
Unweighted count	580	595	361	538	289	101

Source: Modood 1997a, p. 293

Whereas 83 per cent of Pakistani respondents felt that religion was an important indicator of who they were, less than half of Caribbean, and only a quarter of Chinese, respondents felt the same. On the other hand, 61 per cent of Caribbean respondents but only 31 per cent of Pakistani respondents felt that skin colour defined an important part of their self-identity. Unpacking the importance of religion in some of the responses provides an insight into how collective identity categories form a part of everyday practice. Jacobson's (1997) qualitative study of young, second-generation Pakistanis found an increasing differentiation between ethnic and religious self-definitions. Whereas many scholars treat religion as a component of ethnic identity, Jacobson argues that these comprise alternative and sometimes contradictory forms of self-identification. Jacobson's respondents (1997, p. 243) often unfavourably compared the customs and/or the state of Pakistani culture with the principles and doctrines of Islam: 'Religion is constant, it was sometimes said, whereas culture is inevitably, even inherently, open to change.'

For many of the young people in Jacobson's research, Islam provided a source of identity that crossed over different cultures and ethnicities: 'As Muslims, we are one', said one young man, whilst another claimed that 'Islam is important . . . because it is about how you think, not what country you are from.' (1997, p. 245). Jacobson describes the way that Islam provides a reliable guide to conduct in an uncertain and unstable world. It is a code which encourages identification across national boundaries and provides foundations not merely for a system of beliefs but for a way of life in a non-Islamic society. It impacts on diet and worship, dress and behaviour, and acts as an important source of self-definition not only in religious terms but also in terms of everyday routines and practices. However, not only Islam but many other religions form an important part of the lives of minority group members, including the black-led New Protestant churches that are a growing area of religious worship in Britain (see section 10.4).

Like the category of 'religion', the category of 'skin colour' is also not a clear component of ethnicity. For example, 'skin colour' was ranked as important by twice as many Caribbean respondents as Pakistani respondents. In exploring this reported difference in self-identification, Modood examines the circumstances under which South Asians consider themselves as 'black' and concludes that 'For some Asians identification with blackness is not just a product of the suspicion of discrimination and explicit racial abuse, it is also produced by the experience of being made self-conscious about being Asian' (1997a, p. 297). The issue of identity and skin colour is highly complex. Skin colour is not socially neutral – the experience of being black varies in different contexts. It is a component both of everyday experiences and practices and of wider social rights, expectations and perceptions. Similarly, responses to the complex experiences of being both visibly different from a majority but of the same nationality vary. Modood (1997a, p. 330) discusses the four strategies of self-identification proposed by Hutnik's (1992) study (see box 8.3).

Using Hutnik's classification of strategies Modood found that the majorities in all ethnic groups except the Chinese adopted the acculturative strategy (see table 8.4).

Box 8.3   Strategies of self-identification

The dissociative strategy: where self-categorisation is in terms of ethnic minority group membership and not in terms of the majority group dimension of their being.

The assimilative strategy: where self-categorisation primarily emphasises the majority group dimension and denies the ethnic minority roots.

The acculturative strategy: where the self is categorised approximately equally in terms of both dimensions.

The marginal strategy: where neither dimension is important or salient to self-categorisation. Here, the self may be categorised primarily in terms of other relevant social categories: student; squash player, etc.; or there may be a conscious decision not to choose an ethnic identity or majority group identity. (Modood 1997a, p. 330)

TABLE 8.4	Strategies of self-identification (percentages)						
	Caribbean	Indian	African Asian	Pakistani	Bangladeshi	Chinese	All
Dissociative	32	30	21	26	29	51	30
Assimilative	9	4	5	4	6	6	6
Acculturative	57	65	72	69	66	43	63
Marginal	2	1	2	1	0	0	1

Source: Modood 1997a, p. 331

Modood's study demonstrates great complexity in the construction of identity and sources of ethnic identification. The way in which self-identification develops is mediated by social class, gender, generation, educational qualification, rural or urban backgrounds and more. The strategies described above depict ideal types and are usually found in a mixed form. In this respect, minority cultures are in a process of continuous change, fusing elements of minority and majority cultures, and in so doing changing the majority cultures too. However, there is also a further category of self-identification distinguished in other studies that is of significance in understanding the importance of ethnic identity in contemporary society. That is the category of 'defensive' or 'reactive' identity formation that we turn to below.

Ethnic identity and political action

The intricacies of relationships between ethnicity and identity can be seen in the many forms of politics that are about how to act for, or against, social change in a world whose economic, social and political structures have altered rapidly in the post-war period. The geographical mobility of people, the effects of European decolonization, the break-up of the Soviet Union, the dispersal of people of all nationalities and ethnicities around the world, the instant communication possibilities afforded by the global media and new communications media like the internet and e-mail, all contribute to a significant transformation in social life. Such enormous changes break up cultural and social norms, and provoke many forms of political conflict. Below are three examples of areas in which ethnic identity can be seen as an important resource in political action:

1   at the local and national levels where social and religious groups are set up which promote the politics and political tensions of the country of origin. An example here is the Pakistani welfare groups that exist in many localities, each affiliated to a different local political party – Labour, Liberal Democrat or Conservative – and often displaying intense rivalries based on ethnic and political divisions in the country of origin.
2   religious identities that transcend regional or national identities and link with a complex global politics. The Muslim identity is one example here, where Islam is an important political as well as religious movement.
3   the more hybrid and cosmopolitan identities displayed in the cultural politics of youth and popular culture, particularly in fashion and music such as hip-hop, or

Plate 8.1	Political protest by ethnic minorities
	Source: Network/Andrew Wiard

fusions of traditional Indian music with Western rock and roll. In many areas of popular culture there is a hybrid mixing of different cultural influences, a series of collective urban youth cultures that mingle elements of different cultures and, in so doing, transform them.

These different levels of action contain different understandings of ethnic identity which are rooted in distinct class and generational experiences, socio-economic processes, and relationships to the individualism and secularization of Western societies. In the first example above can be observed a clearly patriarchal form of politics associated with an older generation. The emphasis is on adapting to changing circumstances and upheavals in the life course by recreating and reproducing the values and practices of the region and country of origin to the extent that this is possible. Ethnic cultural and political practices conjoin to equal opportunity and local authority politics as groups try and improve their situations by obtaining ethnically sensitive welfare provision lacking in existing services.

The second example is of political movements that cut across generations. Castells (1997) has described these movements as mobilized around a 'reactive-resistance identity': reactions to aspects of change, providing resistance through autonomous sources of meaning. Islam is an example of such a movement, one which is successful in crossing over differences in nationality, gender (to the extent that it appeals to many women) and other ascriptions through the upholding of a transcendental set of values to guide daily life and an organizational structure of interconnected global networks. It is a growing

Plate 8.2 | Nationalist sentiments expressed by marchers
Source: Press Association

movement and popular with young men, in particular, who are otherwise stigmatized and marginalized. In this sense, all such movements are expressions of what Castells (p. 9) calls 'the exclusion of the excluders by the excluded', meaning that the defensive identity is constructed in opposition to the values and ideologies of dominant institutions. It is not surprising that Islam is a fast-growing movement in deprived areas, not only in Britain but in many European countries. It offers a source of positive identification for young people, provides an education in their history that they would otherwise lack, and arranges access to resources and opportunities. As a movement it rejects many of the permissive and liberal norms of Western democracies, viewing the individualism and secularization of Western societies with suspicion. This analysis applies to political Islam. Islam as a religion has different branches and is practised in many ways.

The third example, in contrast, sees a rejection of the traditional values and practices of both majority and minority cultures, associated with youth. In popular culture young men and women are developing a politics that aims to challenge cultural norms by substituting egalitarian, cosmopolitan and alternative values and lifestyles. This form of politics embraces the individualistic and secular orientation of contemporary life, using music, irony and other humour to subvert dominant meaning systems. In so doing, it creates alternative understandings of ethnicity and belonging. This sort of cultural politics is increasing, often among young people in the same deprived urban areas mentioned above. It is based on what Castells (1997, p. 8) calls a 'project identity', where people use cultural resources to construct new identities that redefine their position in society and aim at transforming it. In a sense, many of these young people are drawing on an ethnically specific historical experience. Gilroy (1993) has charted the centrality of music in the politics of resistance of the black diaspora – that is, the dispersion of those taken into slavery and shipped across the globe during the European empire-building period. Music has made a central contribution to maintaining opposition to oppression and to recognition that oppression operates as much in the subjective and everyday practices of life as in formal institutions. This politics recognizes the subjective dimensions of disadvantage and discrimination, and much of the cultural production stemming from it is aimed at presenting more up-beat, alternative ways of feeling, thinking, living and being. However, it can also function as a resource to build a reactive identity. Gilroy details the misogynist nature of much rap and hip-hop music and the use of music to create a Pan-African identity, for example one which links various dispersed groups around an exclusionary identity.

Recognition of the importance of cultural processes and practices in structuring not only everyday life, but economic and political processes, has been part of a cultural turn in sociology. The more recent emphasis on culture and ethnicity draws attention to the everyday world of experience and the possibilities for social change, or resistance to change, existing in people's daily lives. Cultural difference has been studied primarily within the sociology of identity. It is in this area of research that recent analyses of ethnicity and identity have demonstrated their importance as a source of political action. But they are not the politics of the 1980s, emphasizing equal opportunities in access to resources and status. As we see below, since the 1970s a great deal of research has documented the disadvantaged position of minority ethnic groups in British society. By establishing the extent and degree of discrimination in society this research has outlined ways to address inequality.

Summary

1   Ethnic minorities do define themselves in terms of ethnicity or religion more than they do in terms of class, education or income, but most people in these communities define themselves in reference to both the minority and the majority communities.
2   Ethnic self-definition is related to political action, though in variable and complex ways.

8.4   Ethnic disadvantage

Employment

We begin this section by examining the labour-market position of minority ethnic groups, as work is key to people's life chances and issues of economic disadvantage. Recent studies demonstrate that the distribution of life chances amongst ethnic groups has changed considerably over time. The economic positions of different social groups are not static, and research (e.g. Peach 1996; Modood 1997a) indicates that the white–black divide is no longer adequate as a description of the social division of disadvantage, because some minority groups are faring better in employment than whites. Gender divisions as well as status divisions between and within different minority ethnic groups are more significant, in some cases, than those between white and black groups. The overall picture is a dynamic one of great complexity.

If we look at the distribution of social groups in different sectors of industry, we can see that the male minority ethnic population is heavily concentrated in certain industries. As can be seen from table 8.5, Pakistani men are heavily overrepresented in manufacturing (metal goods, engineering, vehicles plus other manufacturing), whilst around a third of Indian, Caribbean, African Asian and white men work in this sector. Bangladeshi and Chinese men are overrepresented in the hotel and catering industries, and most minority groups are overrepresented in transport and communication and underrepresented in banking and finance, except for Indian and African Asian men, whose participation here matches or exceeds that of Whites. In general, each minority tends to be concentrated in a particular sector, and the overall distribution is more restricted than is the case with white men. Having said that, the pattern for Caribbean and white men is not too dissimilar, except for agriculture, forestry, fishing, energy and water supply, which is almost exclusively the preserve of white men.

TABLE 8.5 | **Male employees by industry, excluding self-employed (percentages)**

Industry	White	Caribbean	Indian	African Asian	Pakistani	Bangladeshi	Chinese
Agriculture, forestry, fishing, energy, water	5	0	0	1	1	0	0
Extractive	5	9	4	3	3	0	0
Metal goods, engineering, vehicles	11	13	12	6	12	2	2
Other manufacturing	16	14	19	20	30	11	10
Construction	6	7	7	3	1	2	3
Retail, distribution	9	6	8	23	11	6	15
Hotels, catering	2	3	2	2	6	60	23
Transport, communication	9	17	18	13	15	0	5
Banking, finance	14	5	13	17	5	1	8
Public administration	9	10	5	4	2	4	5
Education	4	4	3	2	5	1	10
Hospitals	4	5	3	4	2	2	10
Other services	6	7	8	4	8	11	7

Source: Modood 1997b, p. 109

Ethnic minority women have a distribution nearer that of the white population, except that they are considerably overrepresented in the health services and in 'other manufacturing' industries. However, there are significant differences *within* the minority ethnic population. For example, Asian women, particularly Pakistanis, are more concentrated in manufacturing than Caribbean women, but the ethnic balance is reversed for hospitals, where there is also an overrepresentation of Chinese women. In both male and female populations there is an overrepresentation of south Asian and Chinese groups in self-employment, with Black groups having the lowest rates.

TABLE 8.6 | **Female employees by industry, excluding self-employed (percentages)**

Industry	White	Caribbean	Indian	African Asian	Pakistani	Chinese
Agriculture, forestry, fishing, energy, water	1	0	0	3	0	0
Extractive	0	1	1	1	0	0
Metal goods, engineering, vehicles	2	2	5	3	0	5
Other manufacturing	6	4	21	14	20	11
Construction	1	0	0	2	0	0
Retail, distribution	17	6	13	22	11	4
Hotels, catering	5	4	4	2	9	19
Transport, communication	3	4	5	9	2	3
Banking, finance	15	9	11	15	4	13
Public administration	7	15	12	7	14	6
Education	13	9	9	4	18	0
Hospitals	21	39	12	13	8	30
Other services	8	7	6	4	14	9

Source: Modood 1997b, p. 110

Another way to consider the position of minority ethnic workers is to consider their socio-economic group, for this will show what *level* of job workers hold. Here we can see a complicated pattern of divisions, with significant differences in the socio-economic position of different ethnic groups. Using the ethnic classifications of the Census (see table 8.7) we can observe a strong representation of Black African, Indian, Chinese, Other-Asian and Other-Other groups in professional class I. At the other end of the scale we find an overrepresentation of Black Caribbean, Black-Other, Pakistani and Bangladeshi men.

Different methods of classification will produce slightly different percentages, but the overall trend remains the same. Indian, Black African, Chinese, Other-Asian and Other-Other groups have a higher proportion of professional workers. However, some groups show a bimodal distribution. That is, they have significant representations in both the manual and the managerial classes, as is the case for the White, Black Caribbean, Black-Other, Pakistani and Bangladeshi groups. This suggests that social class divisions are at least as important a variable of inequality as ethnic and racial divisions. The divisions between minority ethnic groups are important too. For example, Asian men are *generally* concentrated in higher categories than Black men, but there are variations here, with Black African men occupying more favourable positions than Pakistani or Bangladeshi men (Peach 1996c, pp. 15–22).

TABLE 8.7 | Ethnic group for men aged 16 and over, by socio-economic class, 1991 (percentages)

| Ethnic group | Occupational class | | | | | |
	I	II	III non-manual	III manual	IV	V
White	6.7	27.6	11.3	32.4	16.3	5.7
Black Caribbean	2.4	14.2	12.2	38.9	23.6	8.7
Black African	14.3	24.5	17.5	17.6	17.3	8.9
Black-Other	3.2	24.8	17.2	30.2	17.6	7.1
Indian	11.4	27.2	14.4	23.8	18.1	4.0
Pakistani	5.9	20.3	13.5	29.9	24.1	6.3
Bangladeshi	5.2	8.5	12.9	31.5	35.0	6.8
Chinese	17.6	23.3	19.3	29.5	8.0	2.4
Other-Asian	15.9	34.3	18.2	16.0	12.3	3.3
Other-Other	14.5	30.5	16.1	19.8	14.0	5.1
Total	6.8	27.4	11.5	32.2	16.4	5.7

Source: Adapted from Peach 1996c, p. 16

The picture for women is rather different (see table 8.8). Women are generally less economically active than men. Whereas over three-quarters of men are working or seeking work, the proportion of women averages out at just under 50 per cent. The Black groups have the highest rates at 60 to 65 per cent, whilst Bangladeshi and Pakistani women have the lowest, usually explained by reference to Muslim cultural norms, which militate against women working outside the home. As a population, women are overrepresented in manual occupations and underrepresented in the professions, relative to men. However, where they do enter the professions we find that in occupational classes I and II, Chinese, Other-Asian and Other-Other groups are comparatively well represented, with Black Caribbean women slightly behind them, in contrast to White, Black-Other, Pakistani, Indian and Bangladeshi women. In the two bottom occupational categories we find a higher representation of Indian, Pakistani and Bangladeshi women, with Chinese, Other-Asian and Other-Other underrepresented.

The distribution in socio-economic groups is reflected in the level of qualifications attained in various sections of the population. For example, a higher proportion of Asians than of Caribbeans is found in the professional occupations. Indeed, the proportion of many minorities who are in professional class I is higher than the white population. Interestingly, for women workers, there is rather less difference between the white population and minority ethnic groups, the latter being relatively overrepresented in semi-skilled occupations and underrepresented in non-manual jobs as a whole. A relatively high proportion of Indian and Chinese people are in non-manual occupations and are qualified to degree level. Yet interestingly, among many of these same groups there is a further aspect of employment which is significant, and that is the tendency to self-employment. Surveys in 1991 and 1994 document an overrepresentation of south Asian and Chinese groups in self-employment, in both male and female populations, with black groups having the lowest rates. However, it is worth noting that rates of self-employment have increased across all groups, with the exception of Bangladeshis, as successive recessions and the downsizing of labour forces have diminished traditional sectors of employment. The category 'self-employment' conceals a vast diversity of activities, from poorly paid homeworkers and small shopkeepers to highly paid professionals in the financial sector or media, for example. Amongst minorities it may be the case that self-employment, at least amongst some groups, is a response to racial discrimination in labour markets (see section 8.5), although it is also likely that for some minorities self-employment is the natural extension of the economic and cultural patterns of the country of origin, so that racial discrimination and cultural choices interact differently for different groups. Nevertheless, the increased earnings shown in table 8.9 for most self-employed minorities, compared with employees, suggests that this is a successful strategy for improving one's economic position.

TABLE 8.8 | Ethnic group for women aged 16 and over by socio-economic class, 1991 (percentages)

Ethnic group	Occupational class					
	I	*II*	*III non-manual*	*III manual*	*IV*	*V*
White	1.7	25.9	39.0	7.6	17.8	8.0
Black Caribbean	1.0	30.3	33.7	6.9	19.5	8.5
Black African	3.0	31.8	30.8	5.6	16.9	12.0
Black-Other	1.3	25.2	40.6	9.3	19.1	4.6
Indian	4.4	20.9	34.9	6.4	29.2	4.1
Pakistani	2.7	22.3	34.2	6.5	31.7	2.6
Bangladeshi	1.8	22.9	35.8	6.4	26.6	6.4
Chinese	7.6	28.5	31.6	13.0	13.9	5.4
Other-Asian	6.0	30.7	33.8	7.0	16.6	6.0
Other-Other	4.5	30.8	38.4	6.2	15.1	4.9
Total	1.7	25.9	38.8	7.6	18.0	7.9

Source: Adapted from Peach 1996c, p. 18

As one might expect, the socio-economic position of minorities is inextricably linked to their earnings. White men on average earn more than men from minorities, although table 8.9 shows that the earnings of white and Chinese male employees is equivalent. The earnings differential between groups of women is notably less than that between men. Hence, the picture of the 1970s which showed across-the-board disadvantage of minorities relative to whites no longer holds. The most recent Policy Studies Institute (PSI) survey of minority ethnic groups compared labour-market positions in 1982 and 1994 and confirms a general trend towards declining differentials between whites and the main minority ethnic groups, as well as a pattern of mobility from manual into non-manual work. At the same time, differentials *between* minorities may become more pronounced, with some groups continuing to improve their position whilst others remain at the lower end. The PSI survey also suggests that gender divisions in the labour market may be at least as significant as those of race or ethnicity (Modood 1997b, pp. 120–41). In table 8.9 (p. 248) we can see that the earnings gap between men and women is highest in the White, African Asian and Chinese groups, being two or more times the gap between Caribbeans and Indians. We also see that the distribution of women's earnings across ethnic groups is considerably more even than that of men. However, the emphasis on the improved position of minorities, and the recognition that class and gender divisions are equally important determinants of life chances, should not be taken as suggesting that racial disadvantage and discrimination are no longer important issues. There is evidence of a glass ceiling in the promotion prospects of minority ethnic workers, and the picture we see in this section needs to be considered in the context of other evidence concerning unemployment and education, where we find that racial discrimination continues to be an important barrier to the aspirations and experiences of many minorities.

TABLE 8.9 | **Comparison of weekly earnings of full-time employees and self-employed, 1995 (£)**

Employees/ self-employed	White	Caribbean	Indian	African Asian	Pakistani	Bangladeshi	Chinese	All ethnic minorities
Men								
Employees	336	306	287	335	227	191	336	296
Self-employed	308	347[a]	361	321	232	238[a]	466[a]	327
Combined	331	311	302	331	229	198	368	303
Women								
Employees	244	267	252	254	–	181[a]	287	259
Self-employed	242	349[a]	370[a]	219[a]	–	251[a]	249[a]	290
Combined	244	270	268	251	–	189	274	262

[a] Indicates small cell sizes
Source: Adapted from Modood 1997a, p. 121

Unemployment

Considering the position of minority ethnic groups who are in employment, there has been not inconsiderable progress made in the life chances of many groups, both men and women, with a decrease in differentials between minorities and whites. But paradoxically the unemployment figures show a persistence of considerable disadvantage experienced by minorities relative to whites. As figure 8.2 shows, rates of unemployment for minority ethnic groups are higher than those for the white population. Black Caribbeans experience an unemployment rate that is double the national average, and the rate for Black Africans is three times greater. Pakistani and Bangladeshi rates climb as high as 29 and 32 per cent respectively. Peach (1996c, p. 17) points out that once these figures are disaggregated by age and gender, the rate is higher for men than for women, with exceptionally high rates among young black men.

Longitudinal research on unemployment suggests that minority ethnic groups have consistently higher rates than the white population, and that these display a hyper-cyclical pattern. Modood (1997b, p. 88) explains:

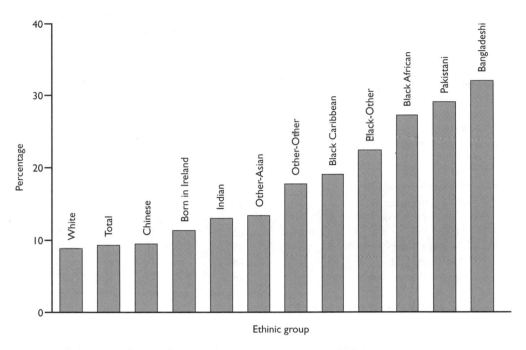

Figure 8.2 | Percentage unemployment by ethnic group, Great Britain, 1991
Source: Peach 1996c, p. 17

That is to say, when the economy is contracting, ethnic minority unemployment rises much faster, and to a higher peak, than does white unemployment. Similarly, when the economy begins to expand, unemployment among ethnic minorities falls at a higher rate than white people.

What this means is that in times of economic downturn minorities experience much steeper unemployment than whites. Those most likely to be unemployed are new entrants to the labour market and those who move in and out of jobs. As more young people, defined as those aged under 25 years, fall into these categories, they are more at risk of unemployment. The higher rates of minorities than whites are also more pronounced because the minority ethnic population tends to be younger than the white population. In the 16–19-year-old group, Caribbean, Pakistani and Bangladeshi males experience unemployment rates of over 50 per cent. The rate for all minority ethnic females in this age group is just under 50 per cent, double that of their white counterparts. If we consider the 20–24-year-old group, we find little difference in rates amongst men, but amongst women there is a fall, and it is particularly remarkable among Indian and African Asian groups where the rate drops by more than half, and is in fact lower than for whites. In explaining these differences two factors in particular need to be taken into account. One is that counting and interpreting figures is a difficult process. For example, a Youth Cohort Study found a much higher rate of Asian unemployment than Caribbean. It explained this as a result of a high rate of Asians in full-time education, so that those who were looking for jobs were poorly qualified, and therefore more likely to be unemployed. This brings us to the second factor. It is not surprising to find that school leaving age and level of qualifications affect employment prospects and the risks of unemployment (see tables 8.10 and 8.11).

TABLE 8.10 | Rate of male unemployment, by highest British qualification (percentages)

Age group	White	Caribbean	Indian/ African Asian	Pakistani/ Bangladeshi
All ages				
None	19	42	20	46
O-level or equivalent	11	31	20	36
A-level or higher	12	23	12	17
Under 35 years old				
None	19	61	18	45
O-level or equivalent	13	28	20	43
A-level or higher	15	28	18	15
All under 35 years old	15	34	20	37

Source: Modood 1997b, p. 91

TABLE 8.11 | Rate of female unemployment, by highest British qualification (percentages)

Age group	White	Caribbean	Indian/ African Asian	Pakistani/ Bangladeshi
All ages				
None	13	19	13	54
O-level or equivalent	10	16	10	42[a]
A-level or higher	7	16	12	18[a]
Under 35 years old				
None	36[a]	36[a]	21	65[a]
O-level or equivalent	14	16	13	45[a]
A-level or higher	8	22	14	20[a]
All under 35 years old	13	24	15	43

[a] Indicates small cell sizes
Source: Modood 1997b, p. 92

There are other explanations as well for the differences in unemployment rates between white and minority ethnic groups. The latter may work in industries particularly hard hit in recessions. One way of looking at the effects of the kind of industry they work in is to see whether minorities and whites living in the same area – inner cities, for example – have similar rates of unemployment. In fact, although the differences between them are much reduced in these areas, they do not disappear entirely.

Housing and health

Racial disadvantage extends to other areas of social life. For example, the quality of housing occupied by minority ethnic groups is generally lower than that occupied by whites. Properties are older and more likely to be terraced houses or flats; they have fewer rooms but more people per room; and they are less likely to have a garden. As with other areas, global comparisons between minority ethnic and white populations hide differences within the former.

TABLE 8.12 | Housing tenure (percentages)

Tenure	White	Caribbean	South Caribbean/ White[a]	South Asian/ White[a]	Indian	African Asian	Pakistani	Bangla-deshi	Chinese	All ethnic minorities
Owner-occupier	67	50	58	70	85	84	79	48	54	66
Council tenant	20	33	29	10	7	10	13	35	19	20
Housing association	3	13	7	3	2	2	2	10	5	6
Private tenant	9	4	6	17	7	5	6	8	22	7

[a] Households of mixed ethnicity
Source: Lakey 1997, p. 199

Asians and Caribbeans, for example, favour very different types of accommodation (see table 8.12). The proportion of Asians who are owner-occupiers is higher than amongst Whites. Caribbeans, on the other hand, have a lower rate of owner-occupancy and a high rate of tenancy of council accommodation compared with the white population. These different tenures mean that Asians and Caribbeans have different housing problems. It remains true, however, that when compared with the white population minority ethnic groups have worse housing conditions.

Disadvantage is similarly evident in risk of poverty and ill-health, and health care. If we look at measures of poverty we find minority ethnic groups significantly disadvantaged compared with whites. One way of measuring poverty is to look at the numbers of households who have an income below the national average. Table 8.13 shows that on this measure all minority groups are worse off than whites, and Pakistani and Bangladeshi households particularly badly off. Berthoud's (1997) survey of income and standards of living shows this to be the case whatever the method of measuring poverty. A variety of reasons explains this high level of poverty; Pakistani and Bangladeshi men have high rates of unemployment, and women a very low participation in the labour force. Those in employment earn low wages, as we saw previously. These two groups also have large households, and more children per family than other ethnic groups. However, Berthoud (1997) states that none of these factors can account entirely for the extent of poverty in these groups. The other group whose financial problems are severe are Caribbeans, who as a group have low household income and exceptionally high levels of rent arrears.

As we show in chapter 15, there are also strong differences in health and illness

TABLE 8.13 | Households below average income (percentages)

Income	White	Caribbean	Indian	African Asian	Pakistani	Bangladeshi	Chinese
Below half average	28	41	45	39	82	84	34
Between half and one and a half times average	49	47	43	46	17	15	44
Above one and a half times average	23	12	12	15	1	2	22

Source: Berthoud 1997, p. 160

between social classes. Because of their employment – or unemployment – prospects, one would expect most, if not all, of the minority ethnic population to suffer the ill-health of the white working class. Indeed they do so, but even more extremely. For example, with the exception of Other-Asian and Chinese groups, all ethnic minorities experience considerably more chronic illness than the white population (Luthra 1997). Women in minority groups show a higher rate of illness than men, although it may be the case that women's illness shows up more than men's because women are generally more likely to consult a doctor. Young Caribbeans have a disturbingly high rate of illness. As the Caribbean population has a general socio-economic profile that matches that of the white working class, this group forms a good standard of comparison, and shows the disproportionate experience of illness compared with whites.

Summary

1   Regarding employment, the differences between whites and other groups are closing, but discrimination continues on promotion prospects and the lower rate of pay for minority groups with qualifications equal to those of whites.
2   Whilst gender and class inequalities remain important, some groups of women are in a better position than men.
3   Racial disadvantage is especially evident when considering vulnerability to unemployment.
4   Ethnic minority groups suffer disproportionately the effects of poor housing, poverty and ill-health.

8.5   Discrimination and racism

Explaining ethnic inequalities

In the previous section we saw that minority ethnic populations are diverse and that generalizations are difficult to make. However, we can say that the socio-economic position of many groups is improving, whilst others are considerably disadvantaged. In some areas, such as unemployment and chronic illness, minorities are systematically disadvantaged relative to whites. Interpreting these data of ethnically based inequality is a complex exercise. What are the factors involved in producing this situation? The essential problem is whether the explanation of racial disadvantage lies in the nature of the British class structure or in the racism, and its associated practices of racial discrimination, which pervade British culture. But there is also the question of the ways in which gender inequalities cross-cut those of class and ethnicity (see chapter 7). Here, we begin by contrasting accounts of class and racism as explanations for racial disadvantage.

Class explanations of racial disadvantage

One type of approach examines ethnic disadvantage as essentially a function of the class structure in capitalist societies. British society is unequal, with those at the bottom of the hierarchy having many overlapping disadvantages. Immigrant groups form part of this class structure, often having jobs which tend to place them towards the bottom. They, therefore, share class disadvantage with many white people. The demands of the capitalist economy for workers during the post-war reconstruction resulted in those from the colonies and ex-colonies being employed in working-class jobs and, in times of unemployment, forming a reserve army of labour that functions to keep wages low and discipline those in work by constituting a pool of potential workers who will take any work available. From this perspective, the class position of ethnic minorities is functional to the requirements of the capitalist socio-economic structure.

Other commentators who examine class from a liberal position consider that although some immigrant cultures may result in a separation from white communities, the children of immigrants will gradually become assimilated into white society, into the wider working class and some, by upward mobility, into the middle classes. To the extent that minority ethnic groups are not assimilated into white society, the obstacle will be the way that they preserve a separate cultural identity. For example, if they refuse to allow their children to attend British schools, do not learn English, or insist on forming ethnically based work-groups, their assimilation will be impeded. The sociological questions become, then, how minority ethnic groups are integrated into white society and what effect their separate cultural identity has on the rate of integration and mobility. Clearly, there are policy implications of this view. The suggestion seems to be that integration is desirable and mobility possible if the obstacles put in place by the minority ethnic culture are removed. The problem, in other words, is caused by the ethnic minorities themselves, a view implicit in much newspaper and television coverage.

White racism as an explanation of racial disadvantage

This view essentially starts from the proposition that the problem is caused by whites, and the disadvantages suffered by members of minority ethnic groups are the result of white racism and the discriminatory practices that flow from it. White racism keeps ethnic minorities in a disadvantaged position and excluded in many areas of social life. In no meaningful sense are minority ethnic groups part of the British working class. Widespread racism within working-class groups and institutions such as trade unions serves to prevent any common experience of class location. Such racism is very profound, going to the roots of British society. It is highly visible in racial attacks or the activities of the British National Party, but it also exists in subtler forms at all levels of society in Britain. It is even present in much sociology, which, so proponents of this view would claim, is implicitly racist in treating minority ethnic groups as deviants from the British norm. Indeed part of the prevalent culture is the belief that minorities have no culture of their own or that what there is will impede their attempts to 'get on' in white society. The sociological implications of this view, that racism produces ethnic disadvantage, are that attention should focus on the history and mode of operation of racism and discrimination rather than the way in which minority ethnic groups do or do not adapt to British society. The political implication is that people from minority ethnic groups should be self-assertive and proud of their identity and not rely on well-meaning attempts to assimilate them into white society.

The 'culturalist' perspective discussed in section 8.3 approaches questions of racism and discrimination through investigations of how assumptions about Britishness, the use of stereotypes, language and writing, for example, serve as resources in reproducing racist and discriminatory practices. Racism is seen as a set of practices that change over time, and how these are maintained in daily life is one area of investigation. The sociological implications here are that there is not one monolithic racism but many racisms existing in society.

Explaining disadvantage in education

The differences between these two ways of approaching ethnic disadvantage appear clearly in the case of education. The former view would see education in at least one of two ways. Education can be seen as a means of instilling the disciplines and values that the future workforce and administrators of society need. Inasmuch as most children from ethnic minorities are educated in the state sector and comprehensive schools, their position is seen as part of the process through which a working class is maintained for industry. Alternatively, consideration might be given to education as one of the most important means by which members of minority ethnic groups become integrated into the mainstream of white British life. As the children go through the education system, they not only learn to speak English but also gain qualifications, which help them with jobs, and acquire familiarity with broader British cultural practices, which enable them to assimilate and move up the class scale. It is, therefore, a question of minority ethnic children fitting into the educational system, and the sociological problem would be to explain any failure to integrate. Thus, failure may be due to reluctance to speak English, to a situation in which children might be caught between two cultures, or to the manner in which some families do not encourage educational success.

From a perspective which focuses on racism as the cause of disadvantage, the issue would be not 'What is it about minority ethnic children that causes them to fail?' but 'What is wrong with an educational system that produces failure and does not recognize the cultural distinctiveness of minority ethnic people?' In this view, the fault lies not with minority ethnic communities and children but with white teachers who label children as failures and operate on stereotypes; for example, that Caribbean boys are only good at sport and music, or that Asians will become small shopkeepers. The point here is that explanations of disadvantage lead to different sociological research priorities.

Although, in fact, minority ethnic children are making significant progress in acquiring qualifications, this progress is greatly uneven. Some groups have high proportions of people who cannot speak English, whilst others have higher qualification levels and staying-on rates after compulsory education ceases than white people, and this division can be found within the same ethnic group. Indians, African Asians and Chinese groups have qualification levels comparable to whites, and better at degree level. This is particularly marked for young women from minority ethnic groups, with Caribbean women, for example, having twice the qualification level of young Caribbean men. Pakistanis and Bangladeshis are the groups with the largest proportions of those without qualifications. Despite the general progress, though, concern has been expressed at the negative experience of schooling affecting some groups; for example, the numbers of school exclusions of Caribbean boys (Modood 1997c).

Recent research into the disadvantages experienced by minority ethnic groups has looked in detail at racist beliefs and discriminatory practices operating across many spheres of social life.

Racism and discrimination

British culture can often be fiercely nationalistic. The British way of life may be thought best and the ways of foreigners inexplicable. Furthermore, the nationalism is anxious. We mean by this that alien or foreign ways of life are treated not only as odd, but also as very threatening. Nationalistic feelings of this kind are often kindled by war, but they also emerge easily in other circumstances, as in dealings with the EU, for example. Nationalism is also closely related to racism (Gilroy 1987). So, ideas of what it is to be British are used against people who are defined as foreign and can be identified as belonging to a particular ethnic group. In fact, the British Isles contain representatives of a large number of different cultures; there is no such thing as a single *British* way of life.

Now, it is, of course, true that many countries exhibit fearful nationalistic reactions of this kind. An example from recent history is the treatment of Jews in Germany in the 1930s. However, white British people probably have reasons for reacting to minority ethnic people in this way. Britain, after all, was an imperial nation. Until relatively recently, the British benefited greatly from lordship over large numbers of people in many different countries, most of whom were black. For the past 300 years, first as travellers to places deemed exotic, and later as imperial masters, the British have learnt to identify darkness of skin with inferiority, strangeness, and allegedly repellent or primitive religious and cultural practices. The colonization of far-off places was not known as the 'civilizing mission' for nothing: the phrase represented British views of their own superiority. The decline of empire has only made these deep-seated attitudes more pronounced. The loss of the colonies and the lessening of Britain's position in the world goes hand in hand with the independence of black nations. Immigrants from the New Commonwealth arrived just at the time that Britain lost an empire and with it the country's position in the world.

Surveys of attitudes tend to confirm this general racism. In a 1993 survey, almost half of the white people sampled disagreed with the statement 'Immigration has enriched the quality of life in Britain' (*Independent on Sunday*, 7 July 1993). Racism of this kind is constantly experienced by black people at all levels of society, even if it takes the more

Plate 8.3 | New Commonwealth immigrants in the 1950s
Source: Hulton Getty

subtle form of simply being treated differently. For example, compare these three statements. The first one is a south Asian woman speaking of her experience at work in the 1970s:

> I had been allocated to a new machine; you see we are moved around every two or three weeks and one morning I was allocated to a new machine. The machines are quite big with a large conveyor belt, one person has to sit in the centre, the idea is to check the cleanliness of the sugar. That day I had to sit in the middle. But soon after I went in, another woman on the machine – quite an elderly woman – started saying 'Smelly! Smelly! Smelly! . . . I went up to ask her what the matter was. Then she began to push and poke at me. . . . Then she went and got a spray of air freshener and started spraying it at me. All the other women on the machine – about eight of them – joined her in following me and mocking me. (Roberts, Davies and Jupp 1992, p. 175)

Here is a black middle-class man speaking of his experience:

> Professional blacks are treated as rare specimens by most of their white colleagues. I am no exception. Generally speaking, racist humour is used to make simple conversation and reactions to these jokes generally leaves us, the black individuals, feeling guilty that we have challenged them. It is a continuous process that those blacks like myself, who have moved up (in a manner of speaking) in society, have very often to contend with the labels that not only do we carry 'chips on our shoulders', but we are over-sensitive to racial issues . . . Making it in Britain is simply a dream for many whites let alone blacks. My colour, my cultural norms and me – a person – will always be viewed through white coloured lenses with all their distortions. (Husband 1987, pp. 196–7)

More recently, a black police officer describes a not unusual encounter in his working day:

> I remember being sent to a job, domestic dispute, different part of the patch and of course the door opened and this guy says, 'What do you want nigger?' And I said, 'Domestic dispute, come to sort it out for you, what's your problem?'. He said, 'I don't want a nigger policeman dealing with my family, send me a real policeman'. So I said, 'OK'. (Holdaway 1997, p. 74)

These sorts of experiences testify to the widespread racism existing in British society. Recent surveys document a range of different prejudices and beliefs based upon a variety of stereotypes, leading many academics to talk about different forms of racisms. Whilst all groups that are visibly different are targets of racism, particularly strong anti-Muslim attitudes have been identified, perhaps as a reaction to the revival of Islamic confidence. Yet, at the same time, a high proportion of whites report support for equal opportunity policies and race equality laws (Modood 1997d).

Racism and discriminatory attitudes can be reflected in – perhaps fostered by – media treatments of issues like immigration or racial attacks. For example, a conception of the black community as a particularly crime-prone group took hold in the 1970s in press treatments of attacks on, and thefts from, innocent people in the street; these attacks subsequently became known as 'muggings'. It became widely accepted that the attackers were predominantly black and the victims predominantly white, although there was little evidence for this belief. This effectively defined black people in the street, especially young people, as potential criminals. Not surprisingly, in view of the public pressure relayed through the media, the police responded by adopting routine tactics of stopping and searching black people in the street, especially in areas where muggings were thought to be commonplace. This situation continued into the 1990s, with young black men in particular being the focus of 'stop and search' policing. This stereotypical view of black men as criminals was reported in Holdaway's (1997, p. 73) study. An Asian policeman described how 'It was an us-and-them situation against blacks. With black people they [police officers] saw them as trouble-makers, drug-dealers, robbers and nothing else.' This sort of victimization of minority ethnic men by the police has been identified in several inquiries as an important factor in occasional riots that have broken out in urban areas, and remains a constant source of anxiety for parents of young men from minority ethnic communities, who are never sure, when their sons step outside the house, if they are going to meet with racial harassment from those who represent the laws they try to teach their children to respect. In fact, discrimination against people from minority ethnic groups is systematically evidenced at all stages of the criminal justice system, from methods of policing to sentencing. This is an area where there has perhaps been the least change since the late 1980s.

Racism and policing

Ethnic minorities are much more likely, in fact, to be the victims of crime than white people. Furthermore, many of these crimes are racially motivated. The table below is compiled from the British Crime Survey of 1988 and 1992, and estimates a significantly higher rate of victimization of ethnic minorities for most categories of offence.

TABLE 8.14 | **Differential risks of victimization: victimized once or more, by ethnic origin (percentages)**

Crime	White	African Caribbean	Asian
Household vandalism	4.3	3.5	6.2
Burglary attempts	5.8	11.1	7.8
Vehicle crime	3.0	6.7	4.6
Vandalism	9.1	10.0	11.6
All thefts	19.1	27.3	21.0
Assault	3.4	5.9	4.0
Threats	2.5	3.3	4.5
Robbery/theft from the person	1.3	3.2	3.1

Source: Adapted from Aye Maung and Mirrlees-Black 1994, p. 7

There is a problem in compiling statistics of racially motivated attacks in that the designation of motivation depends on the perception of the person attacked, so that, for example, African Caribbeans were less likely, and Asians more likely, to think that offences were racial in 1992 than in 1988. However, many such incidents remain unreported because it is believed that the police will not be interested and will not follow up a complaint. This belief has recently been highlighted in the inquiry into the police investigation into the tragic murder of a young black man, Stephen Lawrence, one of several recent victims of racially motivated murder. In 1993 this young man, an A-level student, was waiting for a bus in a suburban street when he was stabbed to death by a group of white youths, who first hurled racist abuse at him. Five suspects – known to hold extremist racist views and to have a propensity for weapons such as Gurkha knives, scabbards and swords – were eventually arrested and subsequently acquitted of his death. His parents documented a series of failures on the part of those police investigating his death, amongst them a reluctance to accept the murder was racially motivated, failure to follow up witnesses properly, and delay in gathering evidence. After five years of campaigning, Stephen's parents were successful in forcing a public inquiry into their son's murder, and in this case extensive media coverage kept in the public arena the catalogue of police failures identified in the inquiry. This inquiry became a catalyst for debate over the extent of racism in the police force, revealing widespread racism against victims from minority ethnic communities. In this context, it is little wonder that much racial harassment and attack goes unreported.

Racial harassment

Hesse et al.'s (1992) book, *Beneath the Surface: Racial Harassment*, is a study of racially motivated harassment in the London borough of Waltham Forest from 1981 to 1989. It is clear from their work that harassment of many different kinds is a fact of life for most minority ethnic groups throughout the country. In the Waltham Forest area, racial harassment involved constant verbal abuse or physical assault in the street, the daubing of graffiti on homes and schools, missiles thrown through windows at night, and, most terrifying of all, the fire-bombing of houses. Although there were many incidents of arson of this kind, the most notorious involved the Khan family in July 1981. Mrs Khan and her three children were burned to death after petrol was sprayed into the hall of their house and ignited while they slept. Mr Khan jumped from a window and was saved, but died of a heart attack some time afterwards.

In reporting incidents of racial harassment, people from minority ethnic groups in Waltham Forest faced the problem that the police had difficulty in interpreting attacks as racially motivated and preferred other explanations or no explanation at all. Furthermore, complainants not infrequently found themselves suspected. The authors illustrate this point:

> In April 1982 a Black youth, Emile Foulkes, and his mother, Esme Baker, were assaulted by police officers from Leyton division. Emile was sitting on a wall near his home on Priory Court estate, Walthamstow, when police officers from an Instant Response Unit arrived, accused him of taunting white youths and called him a 'black nigger'. When Emile's mother tried to intervene she was grabbed and both of them were forced into the police van. They were charged with threatening behaviour and assaulting the police, but were subsequently acquitted. In August 1982 the Sadiq family eventually left their home in Lawrence Road, Walthamstow, after several arson attacks. The police, however, did not accept these were racial attacks. Three months later in November Mr Hussein's home in Walthamstow was burgled. He called the police, but when they arrived ninety minutes later, they took no interest in the crime, preferring instead to search his briefcase and examine the family's

passports. In the same month, a Black youth, Phillip King (15), was on his way home when a white youth racially abused him. He chased the white youth. Plain clothes officers in the vicinity, however, confronted Phillip in Hoe Street, Walthamstow, and assaulted him. He was taken to Chingford police station, his parents were not informed, no doctor was called and he was subsequently charged with burglary. He was later acquitted. (Hesse et al. 1992, p. 20)

The local council, particularly the housing, education and social services departments, was also drawn into the debate about racial harassment. Like the police, the council was slow to recognize these as cases of racial harassment and did not make a solution a very high priority. These examples are from the early 1980s. Yet sadly little has changed since. Recently, the press has reported the case of Mr Hussein, a Pakistani who lives above his shop on a council estate in the north-west of England. Mr Hussein is suing his city council for negligence, following inaction by the council and police force after over 1,500 documented incidents of harassment that have involved Mr Hussein and his partner being constantly threatened with stones, guns, knives, fire-bombs and death threats over a seven-year period (*Observer*, 28 March 1998, p. 10). Other tenants on the estate who are from minority ethnic groups have had faeces smeared on their front doors and put through the letterbox, graffiti scrawled on their houses, and verbal abuse shouted at them. Many report harassment from the local police force.

Virdee's (1997) report of the extent of racial harassment revealed by the PSI study confirms that all these examples continue to represent the experience of people from minority ethnic groups in Britain. The underreporting of racial harassment persists along with the frequent failure on the part of the police to record those incidents that are reported as racial crimes. As well as highlighting a number of brutal assaults, including 15 deaths between 1992 and 1994 from what are believed to be racially motivated attacks, Virdee documents the extent of persistent 'low-level' harassment, which is particularly significant in creating a lasting climate of insecurity amongst victims (Virdee 1997, p. 264; see table 8.15).

TABLE 8.15 | **People who were subjected to some form of racial harassment in the previous 12 months, 1993–4 (percentages)**

Harassment	Caribbean	Indian	African Asian	Pakistani	Bangladeshi	Chinese
Racially attacked	1	1	1	1	1	0
Racially motivated property damage	2	2	3	3	1	1
Racially insulted	14	9	12	11	8	16
Any form of racial harassment	15	10	14	13	9	16

Source: Adapted from Virdee 1997, p. 266

The racist culture of police forces cannot but prevent victims of such harassment from seeking help. At the same time, racism affects those from minority groups within the police force. In 1998 the Metropolitan Police were at the centre of allegations of institutionalized racism against officers from minority ethnic groups. Yet, with some 19 tribunal actions in progress, one involving a detective inspector who claimed his promotion was denied because of his colour, the Metropolitan force is not alone in exhibiting racism towards, and discrimination against, ethnic minorities. In response to evidence of widespread and entrenched discriminatory practices, the Home Office set up a National Black Police Advisory Group to advise it on combating racism (*Independent on Sunday*, 26 April 1998, p. 5).

This situation, combined with a lack of concerted effort on the part of housing, education and social services departments, local authorities and police forces to identify and respond to racial abuse and harassment, reinforces an institutional racism, in which the problem is not recognized as a racial one, responses are greatly delayed, and there is a tendency to blame the victim.

Discrimination in employment and housing

Just as racism has been shown to permeate the experiences of people from minority ethnic groups both as victims of crime and as police officers, so also is it widespread in other key areas of social life, such as employment and housing. Studies of discrimination in employment have investigated the extent of different treatment of majority and minority ethnic groups. One way of establishing the degree of discrimination in employment is to arrange for equally qualified white and minority ethnic workers to apply for the same job. The method is for, say, an African Caribbean to pretend to apply for an advertised job and then to be followed by a white person applying for the same job. These experiments generally show that there is discrimination against minority ethnic candidates in the sense that the minority actor is not given the job, or is told it is filled, while the similarly qualified white actor is given the job. An early study pioneering this method of research (D. J. Smith 1977) found that the white actor was preferred ten times more often than the black one. Similar tests were devised for white-collar jobs by applying for advertised posts by letter in the name of fictitious minority ethnic and white applicants, again with similar qualifications, but making it clear what the applicants' ethnic origins were. In this case, the test of discrimination was whether the applicant was invited to interview. This is a weak test, because an invitation to interview is only the first stage of selection and discrimination is even more likely actually at interview. However, interesting examples of blatant discrimination have been uncovered using this method, as in the case of an identical letter of application from two applicants who each had identical qualifications. The name of the applicants made it clear that one was white and one Indian. The white applicant received an invitation to interview, whilst the Indian received a letter informing him that owing to the oil crisis the position had been withdrawn. These and similar tests continue to be carried out with similar results, indicating that at least a third of employers discriminate against minority ethnic groups (Modood 1997b). Thus, although there is evidence of diminishing prejudice in employment there is, paradoxically, evidence also of continuing discrimination. Discrimination on the grounds of colour or ethnicity is not a sufficient explanation of the persistence or decline of racial disadvantage, though. Modood (1997b, p. 149) emphasizes that:

> There is a general agreement that the most important fact is of economic restructuring. The
> changes in job levels for the minorities, no less than for the majority population, are above

all a consequence of the continuing loss of jobs in manufacturing especially those that require low level of skills, in favour of the service sector, which has seen a continuous growth in higher level jobs and lower level part-time work.

Thus, whilst discrimination in employment persists, the greater disadvantage is caused by structural changes in employment opportunities, changes that affect both minorities and the majority.

Discrimination in housing has been established using tests similar to those described above. Here it is shown that at least one-third of landlords discriminate against minority group members on grounds of skin colour. However, the private renting of accommodation is no longer as important as it once was; owner-occupancy and council renting are now the most significant sources of housing available. Evidence of discrimination in these sectors is less easy to obtain. Up until the 1980s one area of discrimination was in the provision of finance by building societies and banks for owner-occupation, where whites obtained conventional mortgages from building societies whilst minority ethnic groups were more dependent upon more expensive bank loans and mortgages. Since then there has been a considerable decline in this disparity. However, a number of studies have shown that the allocation of council housing is likely to be discriminatory. Minority ethnic groups can be denied eligibility by rules which were originally drawn up for completely different purposes; property let to ethnic minorities tends to be of a lower quality than that allocated to the white population; and Asian families, which tend to be larger, may not find council accommodation large enough for their needs. Lakey (1997), in reporting ways in which disadvantage is manifest in the provision of housing, points out that since the 1980 Housing Act, which offered local authority tenants the right to buy their accommodation at subsidized rates, the stock of council housing has reduced considerably, with the poorest stock, in the least desirable areas, remaining for rent. Because of their economically disadvantaged position, many minority ethnic tenants were left in the worst accommodation, particularly lone parents.

We have seen that not only throughout the police force, but also in labour markets and the provision of housing, there exists discrimination. Much research undertaken in other institutions, such as social services, health services, leisure facilities, courtrooms and elsewhere, confirms similar patterns of discrimination. It is often argued that the racism manifested by the central institutions of British society is actually due to the activities of a few individuals. However, the major research programmes carried out since the 1970s indicate that discriminatory attitudes and practices are so pervasive as to be part of the everyday, routine cultures of social institutions. Yet despite this, many minority ethnic groups continue to improve their position, particularly in education and employment. The conclusion of the PSI report suggests that 'Britain has undoubtedly made some progress towards developing multiracial equality in the last three decades' (Modood 1997d, p. 358). It is certainly the case that Britain has avoided the social and geographical racial segregation found in much of the United States. So whilst the situation of ethnic minorities is varied and diverse, so that generalizations are difficult to make, it is important to note the improvements in many areas of social life, alongside the disadvantages.

Summary

1 Racism is widespread in British society and leads to discrimination against ethnic minorities in employment, policing, housing and the social services.
2 Discrimination may be part of the explanation for the disadvantaged position of some ethnic minorities. A further part of the explanation lies in the operation of the class structure.

Related topics

Further information about the demographic structure of other sections of the British population can be found in section 9.2. To situate evidence on unemployment see section 4.5, and on gender differences in employment see section 7.2. For further detail on patterns of religious belief and practice of majority and minority populations see section 10.4. On associated types of political movements and cultural resistance see section 10.5. Material on inequality in education is presented in section 14.4 and in health care in section 15.6. Ethnic minority vulnerability to crime and relations with the police are further explored in section 16.4.

Further reading

Modood et al. (1997) is a detailed and largely statistical study of the position of ethnic minorities in Britain, while Fryer (1984) is an account of their recent history. Mason (1995) and Skellington with Morris (1992) are introductory books on race and ethnicity.

Cross-references to *Readings in Contemporary British Society*

Bennett on the appropriation of black music by white youth in Newcastle; **Gillespie** on the meaning given by young Punjabis to television soap opera; **Virdee** on racial harassment; **Hetherington** on societal reactions to travellers; **Mac an Ghaill** on youth, ethnic divisions and national identity.

9

Families, Households and Life Courses

9.1 Introduction

This chapter has three recurring concerns: the life course, families and households. It also contains an exploration of the social and cultural practices and relationships which underlie and underpin life courses, families and households. The main themes include the UK population, childhood, youth and adolescence, families, household formation and dissolution, and old age. Not all aspects of all these themes are closely related to both families and households. Especially for children and adolescents, it is likely that their social realities and practices are to some extent independent of families or of the households in which they live. For adults, families may or may not be a major element in their lives, though households are likely to be so; even one individual living alone constitutes a household.

Because the family seems to be such an enduring feature of our social and cultural lives, there is a tendency both to think of it as natural and as a 'good thing', and to imagine that it is central to everyone's lives. However, none of these needs be the case – family forms have changed dramatically since the nineteenth century and are likely to change even more in the twenty-first century. The extended family of several generations sharing residences or living in close geographical proximity, as noted by sociologists in the 1950s in many working-class areas, is much rarer now. So, too, is the stereotypical nuclear family of two adults and dependent children living in the same household. What are the reasons for this? Changes in employment, including a massive decline in heavy manufacturing industries that employed many men, and a rise in service and retail industries involving women, are one factor. Another is changes in the percentage of young people entering higher education away from their parents or leaving home for employment reasons. Finally, different expectations of marriage and new ideas about what parenthood means as a set of social and cultural practices are also relevant to changes in when and if people marry (and how long they stay married), whether they have children, and how they bring up those children.

Families and households: life-cycle and life course

The two terms 'family' and 'household' overlap to some extent, but whereas a family may also sometimes constitute a household, a household does not necessarily involve a family. Whilst members of families have some legal or kin relationship to each other, members of households need have no such relationship.

A definition of a family is: a kinship grouping of adults or adults and children, who may not necessarily have a common residence (for example, your grandmother is still part of your family, even if you and she live in separate houses). By contrast, a household is merely a residence unit, such as a single person living alone or a group of people, who may or may not be related, living temporarily or permanently at the same address but with common housekeeping. Thus a group of students sharing a flat constitutes a household, even if the common housekeeping largely consists of keeping their lager in the same fridge and refusing to clean a shared bathroom. However, the residents of 12 self-contained studio flats in the same block do not constitute a household, since they share only a building and not their domestic arrangements.

During the course of any one individual's life, she or he may become a member of more than one family and household. Experiences of families may include living in a family of origin or with adoptive parents. It may also involve a step-family, where, for instance, the father divorces and remarries and the children acquire a stepmother with whom they live, whilst retaining a relationship with their own mother who now no longer lives with them. Other possibilities include the family of someone's spouse, and (if a couple have children) perhaps in time the families into which their children marry. Individuals may also live in several different households during their lifetimes. These might include, in childhood, adolescence and early adulthood, the household of their family of birth, a shared student flat, a house-share with other single people, and a residence-share with a cohabitee or partner. In adulthood, households might also include a house or flat shared with a husband or wife and perhaps children too, a house alone or with dependent children after divorce or death of a partner, a house shared with a dependent relative, and perhaps finally a room in a residential home for the elderly. From this we can see that the life course of individuals, their family or families and their household arrangements are closely linked together, though not necessarily coterminous.

Another pair of terms that require careful definition are 'life-cycle' and 'life course'. At one time it was common for sociologists and others to refer to something called the life-cycle. Such a term assumed that there were fairly similar stages that most people went through at similar points in their lives, such as childhood, adolescence, marriage, becoming parents and old age. Gradually, it became clearer that such experiences were widely variable, socially and culturally constructed rather than closely tied to physiological factors such as biological age, and defying deterministic or rigid formulations about life stages. People's lives do differ considerably, even for those of the same gender or ethnicity or social class, and there are no set age limits to particular experiences, even though there are patterns and collective experiences (such as unemployment) which will affect whole social and cultural groups. Some people have children at 17, others in their late 40s, still others not at all. Some individuals feel old at 60 while others do not at 85. Thus the term 'life course' has gradually taken the place of 'life-cycle'.

The notion of a life course is more flexible than that of life-cycle and concerns the differences as well as the similarities in people's lives. It is closely associated with families and households since life courses themselves will involve and implicate one or both of these at many different points. The concepts and transitions linked to ideas about the life course are in themselves social and cultural constructions and hence subject to variations in meaning and in length as well as significance. Thus, for some young people (for instance, schoolgirl mothers, or carers for chronically sick parents), adolescence (in the sense of a time with no responsibilities) may end long before they are even 16 years old. Old age may be relative to the life chances of those concerned, with sheltered housing and Saga holidays available to the over-50s but 80-year-olds running marathons. Furthermore, not everyone goes through key life events at the same time or even at all. Some may not experience all of the events (e.g. parenthood, higher education, leaving home), whilst others go through these events more often than others (e.g. marriage and remarriage, births of several children).

9.2 The British population

In the 1940s and 1950s sociologists were very interested in demography – literally, the study of population changes – especially in relation to social class, life expectancy, marriage, divorce and other forms of family formation or dissolution, numbers of children born (and to what age parents), and geographical and social mobility. They were interested because such data helped them to understand what changes were taking place both in British society as a whole, and to groups within it (for example, social class groups and upward or downward mobility, or the age and marital status of mothers of first-born babies). This information also formed the basis of sociological theories about social systems and institutions in Britain and other societies. Demographic information continues to provoke sociological research. For example, sociologists and social policy analysts concerned with migration and with citizenship and human rights are interested in who lives in Britain. This raises questions of who has the right to come to the UK and why, who decides this and on what basis. Since the 1980s, the number of people leaving the UK has been less than the number entering, but during the 1960s and 1970s there was a net loss of population. This has the potential to tell us a considerable amount about employment possibilities, immigration policies, employment opportunities and people's social and cultural satisfaction with life in the UK. Changed patterns of inward and outward migration also reflect, to some extent, the effect of membership of the European Union (EU) and the so-called mobility of labour of people across EU member states. Box 9.1 gives some basic facts about the UK's population.

Box 9.1   The UK population now

Some basic facts about the population:

- In 1996 there were nearly 59 million people in the United Kingdom (including Northern Ireland).
- By far the largest group of these (49 million) lived in England, with 5 million in Scotland the next largest.
- The largest population concentration in the UK was in Greater London, with 4.5 thousand individuals per square kilometre there, compared with 8 people per square kilometre in the Scottish highlands.

The age of the UK population and the demographic time bomb

The UK population is an ageing one, as can be seen from figure 9.1. Between 1961 and 1996 the number of people aged 85 and over trebled to reach over 1.1 million.

The ageing of the UK population is sometimes referred to as the demographic time bomb, implying that some disastrous consequences lie ahead if the age structure remains as it is. The assumption behind this is that, in an ageing population, those of

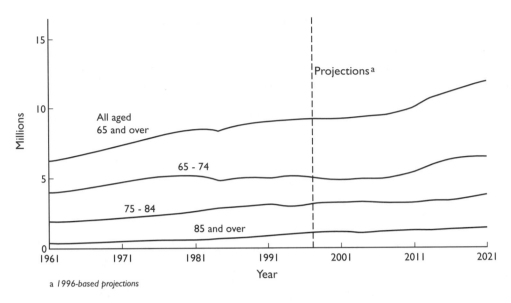

a 1996-based projections

Figure 9.1 | Population aged 65 and over: by age
Source: Social Trends 1998, p. 33

retirement age will be dependent for their survival on those still in employment and that this will become an intolerable burden for adults of working age. In an absolute sense this is probably so, if trends in population continue as at present (though this might not be so over the medium term), and if UK society remains as it is, without adequate arrangements for everyone of retirement age (in respect of pensions, housing, medical care, transport, part-time employment, leisure facilities), and in the absence of positive cultural attitudes towards those over 65.

However, the picture is complicated by different patterns of retirement, social class and gender. The age at which people retire now varies widely, from late 40s to late 60s or older. Some people in their 70s or even 80s may remain in or find new, part-time employment. Some will have adequate finance for their retirement and others will not. This same variation applies to people's health and fitness. So we cannot make any simple statements about the relationship between age and dependence. For those who do have adequate pensions and are fit and healthy, any period of dependence on others may be a long way off, as Carroll's (1998) study of a small number of retired female physical education/dance lecturers and teachers shows. Using diaries, interviews and written narratives in which the women concerned wrote about their present and past lives, Carroll shows how these women, who had good pensions and owned houses, were extremely active in retirement in a range of pursuits and interests for which their jobs had previously left little time. They walked up fells, ran fun runs, swam, read books, took foreign holidays, visited the theatre and cinema, entertained, and were involved in a range of voluntary organizations. As consumers, such relatively affluent older people may be eagerly sought after by manufacturers and service providers, as they are in the United States, where the term 'grey power' is sometimes used to refer to the consumption habits and patterns of those over 65 years of age. Of course these women are not typical of all older people. First, social class differences continue into retirement. Lifestyle and taste differences and the impact of different occupations as well as different forms of housing tenure persist. Second, ill-health is also gendered, with men more likely to experience it at an earlier age (see chapter 15, table 15.1).

The kinds of job people have over their lifetimes, other aspects of their social class (for example, leisure interests, lifestyles) and their gender are important in shaping their lifestyles and health in retirement, and also affect how much pension or other retirement income they will receive. Men in professional and managerial jobs are likely to have more money and better health in retirement than male counterparts who have done manual jobs. The same is roughly true of women in managerial and professional jobs, though their pensions will tend to be lower for two reasons. First, women will tend to have lower final salaries, since they are more likely to have been employed in the public sector than men and less likely to have held a senior position. Second, as women are likely to live longer, their annual income from their pensions will tend to reflect this.

There are at least four reasons why women's incomes in old age will tend to be lower than those of men. One is that women's expectation of life is greater than men's (see table 9.1). If we take 89-year-olds, there are currently three women to every one man of that age in the UK. So, women's pensions are differentially calculated from those of men, as they are likely to draw on pension funds for longer and hence cost more. Second, parenthood usually affects women's pensions in a way it does not affect men's. Mothers who have taken time out of employment to have children are particularly likely to have breaks in their pension contributions. Third, equal pay for work of equal value still does not exist fully in the UK despite changes to the equal pay legislation in 1984. There are many more women in part-time jobs than men, and, although part-time workers are now legally entitled to join a pension scheme rather than rely on the state pension, this is a very recent development and still not widely complied with by employers (see table 9.12). In the past, part-time employees were often excluded from pension schemes.

Finally, many married women who become mothers, especially if they have had long breaks from full-time employment, have tended to rely partly or entirely on their husbands' pension arrangements, although this may be changing now as women become more aware of issues concerning pensions. Relying on a husband's pension makes women highly economically (and by implication socially) dependent on those husbands. Furthermore, all such shared pension rights have previously been lost on divorce. There is now provision for divorce settlements to involve splitting the pension rights of partners, but this is very recent and may still not provide divorced women with an adequate income.

The existence of many more single-person households, and the trend towards members of the same family living miles away from each other, mean that it is increasingly unlikely that the care of those older people too poor or too frail to care for themselves will involve younger family members either financially or in other ways. Hence, the implications of the demographic time bomb are more likely to lie in making adequate pension arrangements available to all and in finding ways to fund the higher health-care costs of older people. There is also the question of provision of pleasant and affordable residential homes and sheltered housing, as well as arrangements allowing older people to stay in their own homes as long as possible. In addition, if changes to family size and a decline in the number of children born to each woman are an effect of employment

TABLE 9.1 | **Employees who are members of pension schemes: by socio-economic group, Great Britain, 1994–6[a] (percentages)**

Group	Occupational pension			Personal pension			Any pension		
	Women		Men	Women		Men	Women		Men
	Full-time	Part-time	Full-time	Full-time	Part-time	Full-time	Full-time	Part-time	Full-time
Professional	66	51	75	24	24	27	79	67	89
Employers and managers	63	43	68	24	24	33	78	59	88
Intermediate non-manual	68	41	72	20	16	21	80	53	85
Junior non-manual	51	25	62	19	11	21	65	34	75
Skilled manual[b]	41	17	48	21	13	32	56	30	72
Semi-skilled manual[c]	30	16	46	17	8	23	46	23	64
Unskilled manual	28	11	39	12	5	20	39	16	54
All socio-economic groups	54	23	59	20	10	27	67	33	77

[a] Combined years 1994–5 and 1995–6
[b] Includes own-account non-professional
[c] Includes personal services
Source: Social Focus on Women and Men 1998, p. 49

and other economic trends towards a time-poor, work-rich society for those in employment (especially the middle classes), then a reversal of people's social, economic and cultural priorities could produce a reversal in family size. As Schor's (1992) study of time/money choices by workers in large corporations in the United States found, many of them did work longer hours (hence increasing their disposable income while reducing their leisure hours) than strictly required by their jobs. This included men as well as women. However, a sizeable proportion said that they would have preferred to work fewer hours, if they had thought it would not affect their future job and promotion prospects. Though this study was not done in the UK, it is likely that workers here make similar choices. Whilst the hours worked (rather than what is accomplished) remain the important indication of job commitment used by employers, such trends are unlikely to change. This is despite media hype about middle-class couples with a lot of savings 'downshifting' their lifestyles to have more leisure time and less income. Such a choice is rarely available to those who do not own expensive houses or flats and whose earnings in full-time work are low to begin with. Should employer expectations of employees change (for example, in response to government demands for family-friendly policies such as shorter hours and time off for the care of sick children), so might other social phenomena. The demographic time bomb is only a time bomb if we assume that its implications are inevitable and cannot be altered by our social actions or a change in our cultural priorities.

Family size

As figure 9.2 shows, families are growing smaller; young women are having fewer children than in the past and marrying later, if at all. There were half the number of first marriages in 1995 as in 1970 and one-quarter of all 18–49-year-old women are currently cohabiting, though a high proportion of these have already been married to a previous partner. Thirty-year-old women in 1996 had an average of 1.3 children, as compared with the average of 1.9 born to 30-year-old women in 1966.

This fall in the number of children born reflects a number of social, cultural and economic changes. First, there has been an improvement in the reliability of contraception and greater legitimation of its use (even amongst religious groups supposedly opposed to contraception). Second, a larger proportion of mothers with dependent children participate in the paid workforce. This reflects an actual shift in employment patterns of women with children, brought about both by demands for labour and by economic need in households, as well as (in some cases) a desire by mothers to continue in employment. Third, this shift in employment patterns is also underpinned by a cultural change in people's ideas about whether mothers of dependent children should be employed. Surveys of public opinion in the 1960s showed wide disapproval, whereas surveys from the mid-1980s indicated much greater acceptance. These attitudes continue to change, as table 9.2, comparing 1987 and 1994, shows. Interestingly, the actual changes in employment patterns and practices almost certainly came about before more relaxed ideas about them appeared widespread.

Fourth, paradoxically, when both fathers and mothers are part of the paid workforce,

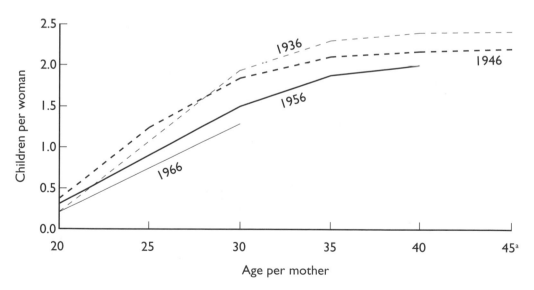

Figure 9.2 | Average number of liveborn children per woman: by age, and year of birth, of woman, England and Wales
[a] Includes births at ages 45 and over achieved up to the end of 1996
Source: Social Trends 1998, p. 35

TABLE 9.2   Attitudes towards women working, Great Britain, 1987 and 1994 (percentages)

	1987		1994	
	Women	Men	Women	Men
A husband's job is to earn the money; the wife's job is to look after the home and family				
Agree strongly	21	26	5	5
Agree	22	26	17	22
Neither agree nor disagree	19	19	17	16
Disagree	12	14	40	42
Disagree strongly	25	15	20	15
All	100	100	100	100
A job is all right, but what most woman really want is a home and children				
Agree strongly	12	15	5	7
Agree	19	27	18	21
Neither agree nor disagree	20	23	23	25
Disagree	23	19	38	34
Disagree strongly	25	15	16	13
All	100	100	100	100

Source: Social Focus on Women and Men 1998, p. 40

this enables more support for children simply because there is more money in the household, but it may also reduce the number of children born in or cared for by an individual household. More parents in paid work means less time for child care and domestic work, and not everyone can afford paid help with these tasks. Research on middle-class married couples, which focused on their attitudes towards and practices with regard to domestic labour (Gregson and Lowe 1994), suggests that where neither women nor men are willing or able to carry out some of the domestic work needed in a household, paying others to do it is one solution, albeit one probably not available to working-class parents. Fifth, there is also an argument advanced by Giddens and others that parents in contemporary society want to give more emotional attention to a smaller number of children (Giddens 1998). There may, of course, be other parents to whom care for more than one or two children is seen as an economic burden they cannot contemplate.

The idea that children might be a burden rather than a benefit, or certainly so in large numbers, began in the nineteenth century amongst middle-class parents who were worried about their ability to maintain their standard and quality of life if they had a large family. Such couples thus made use of available means of contraception. Historical research on the limitation of family size by family planning shows that by the time of the 1930s' economic depression in the UK, when many working-class people were unemployed, hardly able to feed and house themselves, the use of contraception and the view of children as an economic burden began to spread to working-class households too (Banks and Banks 1964). After the Second World War, the development of a welfare state, including comprehensive and free medical care, also began to affect infant mortal-

Plate 9.1 Changing family sizes between the nineteenth and twentieth centuries
Source: Hulton Getty; Format/Sally Lancaster

ity rates, so that parents could be much more confident that children would grow up to be adults and not die in childhood.

Large families in the past, particularly in working-class households, were produced not only by social and cultural customs, and ignorance of, or moral principles against, contraception, but also by the fear that many liveborn children would not survive into adulthood. Today other factors may also be affecting the numbers of children born to households and families. These include women's desire for men to be more involved in child care, concern about the possibility that women will become single mothers through separation, divorce or widowhood, and increasing awareness on women's part (especially middle-class women) of their rights to enjoy leisure time and sport as well as engaging in paid and unpaid work.

The ethnic composition of the UK population

The ethnic composition of the UK population (see box 9.2) is also important, as are shifts in the extent to which members of ethnic minority groups have been born in the UK as opposed to being first-generation migrants. These facts are significant not just in relation to which cultural and ethnic majority and minority groups live in the UK, but also because they form a backdrop to race relations in the four countries of the UK (see chapter 8), and because they may help to explain differences in family size, marriage practices and household composition across different ethnic groups.

Box 9.2 Ethnic composition of the population

The 1996 General Household Survey found that 94 per cent of respondents described themselves as white (which of course does not preclude ethnic minority membership, since it may include, for example, those who are Irish or Italian). Of those describing themselves as non-white and aged under 25 in 1996, nearly 80 per cent were born in the UK; if we look at those aged 25 and over, then this percentage of UK-born individuals is much lower for some groups than others (e.g. only 8 per cent of those describing themselves as Pakistani/Bangladeshi were UK born).

The ethnic composition of the population raises some concerns. First, often the term 'ethnic group' is used to apply only to non-white groups, whereas sociologists have noted that we all have an ethnicity of some kind, whether it is made explicit or remains implicit. Mac an Ghaill's (1994) work on the subcultures and identities of young people in secondary education shows that black and Asian young people are concerned with their ethnic identities. His work also demonstrates that some white groups, such as those who are first- or second-generation Irish, also want to express their ethnicity in their identities. Even for those white people who do not explicitly express some kind of ethnic identity (e.g. Englishness, Welshness), the notion that whiteness is a cultural identity is still an issue. Second, the patterns of migration into the UK over the latter part of the twentieth century, particularly from Commonwealth countries which once formed part of Britain's imperial power grouping, have been such that many non-white as well as white people, whose parents or grandparents came to the UK from another country, are now UK passport holders and regard themselves as British. Third, the UK is increasingly becoming highly multicultural but, at the same time, the presence of white and non-white ethnic minority groups raises issues about social and cultural tolerance of difference and diversity, whether in education, housing, employment or sport. There is still evidence of continuing discrimination against some ethnic minority groups by majority ethnic groups.

Summary

1 Considerable changes are taking place in British society, including changes to the age of childbearing and the number of children born to any one mother, more elderly people living for longer, and rises in the number of couples cohabiting, as well as changes in ethnic composition.
2 Any one person's life is both highly individualized and lived out in relation to wider demographic changes, as well as being related to social class, gender and ethnicity.

9.3 Childhood

Although childhood may be seen principally as a stage of family life, there is also a need to focus on children as children, not as dependants of their parents. This involves recognizing differences between children in respect of gender, ethnicity, social class and possible disabilities. Childhood, like adolescence, when viewed sociologically, appears as a mix of individual life-course experiences and those marked by legal prescriptions such as the onset of compulsory schooling or legal rights. The individual rights of children were specified, for example, in the 1992 Children's Act for England and Wales.

The way in which childhood is regarded has changed a great deal over the last two centuries. In the mid-nineteenth century, it was considered normal for children from working-class families to work full-time, but routine for upper-class boys of the same age to remain at school and girls to spend their time acquiring social accomplishments (such as playing music or embroidering). The way that children are regarded by their parents has also changed over time. For example, research on historical archives and artefacts such as paintings relating to working-class families shows that the perception of a child has gradually moved away from the nineteenth-century idea of the child as wage-earner to the child as school pupil and family dependant (Hendrick 1997). Now there are legal restrictions on paid employment for under-16s (though these are sometimes broken) and all 5–16-year-olds must be educated, usually in school.

Socialization and gender/ethnic stereotyping

Children seem to acquire stereotypes at a young age. Connolly's (1995) work on observing the talk and behaviour of a group of young boys (5 years old when he began the research at Manor Park, a working-class inner-city infant school in the UK) suggests that ideas about both gender and ethnicity are evident quite early:

PC [Researcher]:	What about the girls in your classroom, do you play with any of them?
All:	No-oo! No!
Daniel:	Some are Indians!
PC:	Are they? What, do you play with Indian girls then?
Stephen:	NO-WAY!
Daniel:	Jordan kisses um!
Jordan:	NO! I'm West Indian!
PC:	Eh?
Jordan:	I'm West Indian – I'm English and I'm half-white ain't I?
Paul:	Yeah but if you say that – d'you know what – you're an Indian!
Jordan:	No! . . . Are you still my friend then?
Paul:	Not if you talk like India! No talking like an Indian.
PC:	Which girls do you like to play with the best?
Paul:	Nicky and Emma!
Daniel:	and Emma!
Stephen:	I like Natasha and Marcia and Samantha. I like, I've got fourteen girl friends.
	. . .
Paul:	How you going to sex 'em then?
Stephen:	I'll put all of them on top of each other and when I've done one – put her over there, then when done another one put her over there. (Connolly 1995, pp. 180–5)

Children and families

Children exist in their own right and develop specific social and cultural practices, but at the same time are also parts of families and households. Some of the changes in household size referred to in section 9.2 have meant that the social, emotional and cultural importance of individual children to individual households has increased, now that there are fewer children born to families. The time devoted to child care seems to have gone up, even though there are fewer children in each household, more labour-saving devices, and mothers as well as fathers likely to be in employment (see table 9.3).

The time spent and the tasks undertaken when looking after children are extremely important. However, it is also important to look at the changing social and cultural meanings attached to families and to parenting. Irwin (1995) points to the changes which have taken place in families. These include particularly the disappearance of the predominance of the male as a sole breadwinner and the increasing tendency for women to be in paid employment. Irwin considers arguments about the greater individuation of adults within families (and also outside them, such as the rise in people not marrying even if they have children), with social ties having less significance than before. She

TABLE 9.3 | Time spent looking after children, women and men aged 20–60, 1961–85 (minutes per average day)[a]

Adult and children	1961	1975	1985
Women			
Full-time employed			
Pre-school children	19	28	107
Schoolchildren	9	7	12
Part-time employed			
Pre-school children	44	57	73
Schoolchildren	34	12	22
Non- or unemployed			
Pre-school children	95	81	137
Schoolchildren	31	24	37
Men			
Full-time employed			
Pre-school children	11	14	44
Schoolchildren	3	4	8
Non- or unemployed			
Pre-school children	48	37	37
Schoolchildren	25	4	11

[a] The figures given in this table are for time spent looking after children as the person's main activity. Looking after children while doing other things – cooking a meal, shopping, housework and so on – is not included. *Source*: Hewitt 1993, p. 61

suggests that although we may be seeing a new kind of what some call a market family, whose fortunes are largely determined by what happens to individuals in the labour market or outside households, this trend towards prioritizing employment (so that caring for dependants is a hindrance) can be exaggerated. Many women and men are still choosing to have children.

As Smart's (1999) study of 60 divorcing parents over a two-year period shows, mothers and fathers do not necessarily have the same view of parenting and both may find that divorce brings significant changes in the mothering and fathering relationships. She bases some of her arguments on Backett's (1987) work, which suggested that fatherhood, even in families where both parents live in the same household, tends to be mediated through the behaviour of mothers and does not often constitute an independent relationship to children. Definitions of fatherhood were not made in terms of how much care fathers provided and few fathers whom Backett (1987) interviewed wanted to spend more time with their children. Even in situations where fathers had a lot of contact with their children, Backett found that they often relied on mothers to interpret their children's moods and needs. As Smart says, if this is so when couples live together, when they divorce then fathers may find that they have lost the basis for their relationship with those children:

Les Holt: I hadn't really thought about it. We were still living in the house together for about a year . . . It was a case of I'd always worked really hard, I'd come home, gone up into the study and the children were there. My role as a father was to go out to work, to bring the money in, to try and look careerwise and the children were young and it was a case of just saying 'hello, sit on my knee, then off to bed'. And I was just there and I probably didn't pay them much attention at all. *It was only when I realized that they might not be part of my life that gave me a real shock and it made me more aware.* (Smart 1999, p. 103; italics in original)

Mothers also find problems after divorce because they may no longer feel able to trust their former partners with their children:

Linda Hewitt: . . . I also discovered . . . a few months ago that he was letting David go round to some shops and cross a very busy road which I was amazed at and said so. (Smart 1999, p. 106)

For their part, some fathers themselves may want the parenting relationship to be as it was before and refuse to accept responsibility, for example by taking time off work if a child is ill:

Stella Drew: Ralph was ill and he was with Nick the day and night and I said to him 'If he's ill tomorrow are you going to sort something out?' and he just went mad with me on the phone. 'I am not prepared to accept that level of responsibility, it is up to you to sort that out, that is not my responsibility.' (Smart 1999, p. 107)

Children from one-parent families (which in 1996 accounted for 21 per cent of all households with children) are often popularly supposed to be disadvantaged relative to those from two-parent families, but this depends considerably on the circumstances, as many single parents devote a lot of attention to their children.

Concentrating on children within the context of the households, however important, has limitations. Researchers looking at the social and cultural consequences of age have noted that the very young and the very old may be regarded somewhat similarly – both are seen as dependent on others and lacking self-determination, autonomy and choice. Children and older people may be treated as though they cannot be expected or trusted to make any decisions for themselves, and indeed their opinions may not even be asked for, let alone taken into account, by those dealing with them. The power relations involved in these perceptions and associated attitudes are extremely important, particularly since they include inter-generational struggles.

Children as active agents

Recently, researchers have drawn attention to the failure of many sociologists to examine childhood in its own right as a set of social practices distinct from, and not a preparation for, adulthood. Children are more often studied by sociologists in the context of their households or their schools rather than as active agents in their own right, able to reflect on their own actions.

Connolly's (1995) study of masculinities amongst young boys, which was quoted earlier, is unusual in concentrating on the boys' own views and perceptions of phenomena such as racism and sexism, rather than on the features and characteristics of their families and surroundings. S. Scott, Jackson and Backett (1998), in setting out a research agenda about children and risk, focus on the theme not via parents but through children's construction of realities as well as their social relations with adults. As they note, children are the subject of much anxiety on the part of parents and others with respect to avoiding or protecting them from risk, whether road traffic accidents or child molesters. The actual and imagined dangers do not always match up. Hence, although statistics show that for children over one year old there is a much greater likelihood of being involved in an accident (including at home) and of being attacked or abused by a member of their family or household than there is risk of attack or abuse from a stranger, it is the latter which forms the focus of adults' advice to children. It is often assumed that children, unlike adults, are unable to assess risks and vulnerability and hence need protecting. Their own actual judgements and how they make them are rarely considered. Nor have researchers looked at the ways in which adults' attempts to manage children's risk avoidance shape those children's own actions, thoughts and attitudes. These three researchers note how adults both fear for and also express fear of children. 'Within this landscape of risk, sexuality is a prominent feature, figuring both as a threat to children, and where imputed to children themselves, as symptomatic of a dangerous precocity' (S. Scott, Jackson and Backett 1998, p. 691). Thus researchers have not often considered how children themselves make sense of parental advice on avoiding risk, which is informed by adult views and fears of sexuality rather than children's views.

Summary

1   Children are sociologically significant both in their own right and as part of households and families, but the latter perspective has dominated sociological research until recently.
2   Children have lives which are socially and culturally constructed in complex ways and often autonomously from adults. Gender, ethnicity and sometimes social class have an effect.
3   Though some attention has been paid to children's rights as opposed to legal constraints on children, in the main even the 1989 Children's Act tends to construct children's rights in relation to adults rather than as individuals with some autonomy.
4   Childhood should not be seen as the mechanical progress of a stage of life but rather as an important aspect of social and cultural life in its own right.

9.4   Adolescence and youth

Like childhood, adolescence is sociologically significant from the vantage point of adults who are in positions of authority in relation to teenagers (parents, teachers, youth workers), from the perspective of inter-generational power struggles, and from the viewpoint of young people themselves, as active agents in shaping their own destiny. Whilst adolescence involves physical changes to the body, it is as much, or more, the social and cultural interpretations of these which are important. The concentration on children, which is one of the hallmarks of the contemporary family but is nevertheless an attempt to minimize the autonomy of children, becomes even more contested and problematic for families with adolescents. Yet here, government intervention (for example by disallowing benefits to young people not in employment, or by ending free tuition in higher education) has tended to increase the length of time during which adolescents are dependent on their parents. The extension of education and training has lengthened the period prior to independent living and full-time employment. In turn, this may have increased adolescent determination to break free of households and parents in other ways, whether expressed through drug taking, alcohol, clubbing or clothing styles.

It should not be assumed that in the past all teenagers moved away from home on taking up their first job. This was rarely the case for working-class young people from the 1950s to the early 1970s. D. Leonard's (1980) work on young people in south Wales in the 1970s showed just how much they relied on their parents' resources, even during extended periods of heterosexual relationships. Though the young people concerned did not feel they lacked independence or a social life, it was not expected either by them or by their parents that they would live anywhere else than in the parental home until they married. It was often marriage which led to moving out of the parental home – sharing of flats and houses with unrelated individuals was much less common, and even middle-class students in higher education were often encouraged to live in halls of residence rather than flats if aged under 21.

Debates about youth cultures in general suggest that some of the distinctive features of post-1945 subcultures – gangs and groups sharply differentiated by style, taste, music, class, as in punks, rockers, or teddy boys – are less apparent in the 1990s than previously. The reasons given for the changes are usually to do with arguments about postmodern societies having more globalized economic trends (e.g. multinational companies and homogenization of taste, as in McDonald's), less certainty about the future (economic instability, environmental disaster fears), fragmentation of social class groups, and the disappearance of stable communities with inter-generational households living together or in close proximity. However, not all the commentators accept that these changes are radical. Some argue for the continued importance of class, gender and ethnicity. Others suggest that there is more of a merging of social groups amongst young people (e.g. students and working-class youths alike attend clubs, drink and take drugs).

Whilst some researchers identify new groups such as lager louts, football hooligans, new fascists, New Age travellers, gangsta rappers and ravers, others suggest that it is now much harder to identify distinctive groups like those studied in the classic youth-culture ethnographies. This may well be so for those groups not based on lifestyle and life course. While New Age travellers may live in benders (a kind of tent) on bits of waste land, eking out a living from various part-time jobs or dependent on benefits, this is different from the experiences of some other groups. Thus, though lager louts may drink a great deal of lager and be badly behaved in certain contexts, it is probable that they do not behave like this in every context, and they are unlikely literally to live in a pub or club. Indeed, research on environmental protest indicates that groups may be issue-based rather than continuing on a long-term basis as did previous subcultures,

Plate 9.2	Young people out on the town
	Source: Network/Barry Lewis

whilst also eschewing traditional voluntary organizations, whether youth organizations or environmental pressure groups.

Changes in the youth life course itself are only part of the story of young people, families and the life course. Changes in family life and parental expectations will also affect young people, as box 9.3 shows.

Box 9.3   Changes in family life and parental expectations

As Mann (1998) points out in her analysis of life histories of 17-year-old working- and middle-class girls, family lives are now very complicated, with parents living away from grandparents, families split by divorce, and the growth of step-families and one-parent households. Mann got her respondents, who were studying for A-levels, to write about their educational experiences and choices so far. She notes that, despite changes in family life, the young women she researched, especially those from working-class backgrounds, were ambivalent about high levels of academic achievement and expressed doubts and anxieties. Thus more traditional ideas may persist about gender roles, especially for working-class teenagers. Whilst some mothers clearly hoped that their daughters might achieve things they did not, grandmothers might have different ideas:

> Gran wants me to be a straight A student, setting an example as the eldest grandchild but she says a woman's job after schooling is to get married and have lots of children. (p. 47)

Mothers too were not immune from this uncertainty:

> Mum says go to college – and then changes her mind. I don't know what she thinks really. (p. 48)

For middle-class girls, by contrast, the previous educational achievements of their families were important for their own experiences and aspirations:

> All the women in my family have careers – thanks to Grandma. My mum says 'You're no good without that piece of paper' – the same message she got from her own mother. (p. 49).

On the other hand the middle-class girls felt that as a result they experienced more pressure to achieve from their families:

> I was following in the footsteps of my two successful sisters. This has always put me under quite a bit of pressure to succeed like they've done and when I've failed to reach their standard, I've always felt a failure to my parents and teachers. (p. 50)

Thus whilst working-class girls found themselves having to seek educational advice outside their families, middle-class girls got such advice and interventions but at the expense of feeling themselves more controlled by their families.

The lives of parents are themselves in transition – with male working hours much longer than those of women and indeed the longest in Western Europe (see table 9.4).

TABLE 9.4   Usual weekly hours of work of employees,[a] winter 1997–8 (percentages)

Hours per week	Women	Men
10 or under	9	2
11–20	18	3
21–30	16	2
31–40	38	35
41–50	16	39
51–60	3	14
Over 60	1	5
All employees	100	100

[a] Women aged 16 to 59, men aged 16 to 64
Source: *Social Focus on Women and Men* 1983, p. 33

Many women, as well as men, work unsocial hours, often with worries about job security – so that contact between adolescents and adults may be rushed and infrequent. One of Mann's working-class respondents, Vicky, the daughter of a Nigerian father and English mother, makes some of the social and cultural effects of this rushed contact evident:

> When it comes to my Pop there's a big gap in my mind. I hardly ever see him because he's at work all day. In the mornings I'm out of bed before he's awake, to go to college. When I get home he's at work. When he gets home I'm in my room (making a very poor effort to revise for exams). He sits downstairs. (p. 54)

Youth, leisure, consumption and schooling

The long period over which adult rights are granted (see table 9.5), in conjunction with the extension of education and of absence from the labour market, may encourage a view of adolescence in which, like children, teenagers are seen as being in a state of preparing for adult life. This is in contrast with a view of adolescence which sees it as a set of socially and culturally constructed practices in its own right. Yet adolescence is a time for complex identity shifts and attempts at peer alignment, for coping with sexual orientation, gender roles, racism and other potentially challenging or traumatic situa-

TABLE 9.5 | **Ages for adulthood, Great Britain**

Age	Context
10	Age of criminal responsibility (8 in Scotland)
13	Minimum age for employment
14	Own an air rifle
	Pay the adult fare on public transport
16	Leave school
	(Heterosexual) age of consent to sexual intercourse
	Buy cigarettes
	Marry with parental consent
	Hold a licence to drive a moped
	Eligible for full-time employment
17	Hold a licence to drive a car
18	Vote in elections
	Buy alcohol
	Watch films and videos classifed as '18'
	(Homosexual) age of consent[a]
	Marry without parental consent
25	Adult levels of income support
26	Adult in housing benefit rules

[a] In February 1994, the homosexual age of consent was lowered from 21 to 18 following a vote in the House of Commons.
Source: Pilcher 1995, p. 62

tions and issues. Conformity for some, whether in terms of assuming heterosexuality, or in relation to clothes, music or thinking it not 'cool' to study, is an important way in which identity crises and uncertainties are solved. Others, for example young people with disabilities, may find this conformity is denied them. If children are avid consumers, teenagers are much more so, even if their financial situation makes this difficult. Whilst some will pay for music, drink, and entry to clubs from money earned in part-time jobs or provided by rich parents, others resort to theft and deception in order to acquire material goods. Social, economic and cultural changes in society have had a big effect on young people. This is so both in school and out of it. The passage of the life course for adolescents prior to school leaving age involves school, their families and their communities.

We might assume that school and leisure are sharply divided, just as it was once assumed that work and leisure were separate spheres. However, some of the research on youth cultures in school indicates that a range of other activities and aspects of consumption apart from academic performance and motivation may also be important in the development and maintenance of those cultures. These include clothing, music, sexuality, dance, smoking, alcohol and drugs. Some of these take place in school, whether legally or illegally, and whether in class or outside class. This suggests that schooling, consumption and leisure may occur in the same spaces.

Research on boys' underachievement suggests that some boys may see school as an opportunity to relax and have fun with their mates rather than work. However, Sewell's (1998) work on African Caribbean boys at Township School in inner-city London suggests that, even within a single ethnic group, the extent to which boys are prepared to mess around in class and put their education at risk varies. Thus he identified conformist boys such as Kelvin, who avoided certain other pupils on parental advice:

TS [Researcher]:	Do you belong to a gang or posse?
Kelvin:	No, because my mum says I shouldn't hang around students who get into trouble . . .
TS:	What students in this school do you avoid?
Kelvin:	They are fourth years, you can easily spot the way they walk around in groups, they are mostly black with one or two whites. They're wearing base ball hats and 'bopping' (black stylized walk).
TS:	Don't you ever 'bop'?
Kelvin:	Sometimes for a laugh but it's really a kind of walk for bad people. (Sewell 1998, p. 113)

Sewell also identified innovators, who accepted the goals of schooling but rejected the means and thus rebelled to some extent against their teachers. The source of their pro-school values was often their parents, which led them to be frequently chastised by those parents for behaving badly, but it was peer influence as well which sometimes caused them to reflect, as Frank, a pupil several times excluded from school, said:

Frank:	He (Dad) says it would be harder for me to get a job than a white man. He's always talking about this . . .
TS:	Do you think it is worth coming to school?
Frank:	Yes, I have some friends who are about 21 and they're just loafing around. I just want to go to college to do a B.Tec National. (p. 117)

Other pupils, termed retreatist by Sewell, reject both the goals and means of schooling. They may spend time at school outside class, which is considered boring, but they do not hang around with gangs of other rebelling students. Finally, other pupils are more openly rebellious but, instead of siding with other pupils, seek links with the wider black community outside school:

TS: How important is it for you to own your own business?

Calvin: It is important for black people to make money because white people don't take us seriously because we're poor. (p. 123)

Here it is apparent that a group of adolescent boys with similar ethnic backgrounds are responding in a variety of different ways not only to school but also to their parents, their friends and the wider society. All but the conformists see school as a place to enjoy themselves, but the extent to which this is combined with bad behaviour or an attempt to do well at school work varies.

Research on girls' friendship patterns also indicates that those friendships may involve talking about leisure or 'doing' leisure in school as well as outside (Griffiths 1995; Hey 1997). The research suggests that girls form friendships both in school and out of school and may use their time at school to cement and develop those friendships. Like Sewell's Afro-Caribbean boys, girls have a variety of responses to school, based on parental views, friends in school and friends outside school. Social class is also relevant to this, though, as you can see from section 14.4 on gender inequalities in education, boys from middle-class homes who attended private schools with the aid of a state bursary did not necessarily work as hard as their parents wanted them to do.

Some schools explicitly think that it is part of their role to prepare pupils for leisure as well as employment. Thus Scraton (1992), in her research on girls and sport in secondary schools in one local education authority in England, found in observing physical education lessons (PE) that a lot of girls seemed to hate PE and regarded it as an unpleasant activity they would never freely choose. By contrast, some of the PE teachers to whom Scraton talked thought that teaching sport and PE was a way to help pupils to prepare for their future leisure time:

> We aim to give them an interest in sport in general, something they'll enjoy doing so that they'll want to carry on in something when they leave school.
> I'd like to think that when they left they had found one activity that they enjoyed enough to keep up. (Scraton 1992 p. 73)

The leisure patterns of young people do vary by class, gender and location. Some researchers question whether class is still as important an explanation of differences in leisure behaviour between young people as it once was, arguing that consumption patterns and preferences now outweigh social class factors. Thus Roberts, quoting unpublished research by Hollands on the leisure of young people in Newcastle, notes that this showed students and young people in employment attending the same pubs and clubs. In 1994, Roberts used data from a large survey of young people done in the late 1980s to suggest that some social class differences in leisure continued, with middle-class young people more leisure active, having closer relationships with their friends and being more enthusiastic about out-of-home leisure (K. Roberts and Parsell 1994). Nevertheless what Roberts argued in 1994 was that working-class young people had themselves begun to participate in similar forms of leisure to middle-class young people. The late 1980s also showed that gender differences in leisure persisted, though less sharply demarcated than in the 1970s, but particularly marked by girls' lower interest in sport and in other out-of-home activities.

Young people living in rural areas may have fewer leisure and socio-cultural choices than those living in urban areas. Prosser (1995) studied two locations, Waterside and Hillside, small towns with few leisure facilities for people of any age, in order to examine drug use by teenage girls. Prosser spent much of her research time in two youth clubs in the towns. She noted the particular constraints that not being old enough to drive or go to a pub and having virtually nowhere else to go placed on the lives of the teenage girls. Hanging around a local park, woods or town centre was something some of them did frequently, both out of and sometimes in school time. The dance floor in the clubs was largely used by the girls, in contrast to the sport facilities in the local park, which tended to be used by boys for football or rugby. Most of the girls could not even get part-time jobs because public transport went only to the nearest larger cities and not to the local areas surrounding the two small towns.

Summary

1 'Adolescence' is shorthand for the complex set of social and cultural practices of young people between 11 and 21.
2 The teenage years raise questions not only about what young people do – in school, in their leisure time, in their relationships and in the wider community – but also about their relationship to adults and in particular to parents.
3 Shifts in the labour market and economy and in state interventions in connection with schooling and welfare benefits, as well as wider cultural shifts, all affect adolescents, and adolescence in turn has a profound effect on the rest of society.
4 Though sometimes seen as a series of transitions, adolescence may have more permanent impacts on and connections with social relations and cultural life. It is no longer as distinctive a part of the life course as it once was, despite the recent attempts to keep young people in education and training for longer and longer periods of their lives.

9.5   Families and family practices

The state and the family

The state has intervened significantly in families for a considerable length of time, whether by providing support (such as family income credits for those earning low wages and with dependent children) or in overseeing the bringing up of children (if social workers think this is not being done properly then children may be put temporarily or more permanently into the care of the local authority). This interference has not lessened – indeed as politicians and the media have come together to discuss what they see as the

Box 9.4   The 1998 government green paper on families

In this paper the government outlined how it wanted to strengthen the family. The focus of the paper was on marriage and care for children. This is how the Home Secretary, Jack Straw, introduced the green paper in November 1998:

> This document [the green paper] is not about lecturing people about how they should live their lives or nagging them about how to bring up children. . . . I've been divorced myself. I was raised by a single parent . . . however the evidence is that children are best brought up where you have two natural parents and it is more likely to be a stable family if they are married. (*Guardian*, 5 November 1998, p. 4)

The paper's proposals, published early in November 1998, included:

- the creation of a National Family and Parenting Institution offering advice, support, research, and a 14-hour-a-day advice line for parents;
- prenuptial marriage agreements (e.g. about money, children, etc.) to become legally binding on those drawing them up;
- the ending of quick, 24-hour-notice weddings, with 15 days' notice required for all marriages;
- an enhanced role for registrars, including not just their present roles of registering births and deaths and presiding over marriage ceremonies, but also offering advice and counselling to those about to be married, and holding naming ceremonies for babies whose parents do not want a religious ceremony;
- an enhanced role for health visitors attached to general practitioners' surgeries, who currently carry out home visits to the mothers of very young children, especially those with newborn babies, and who will provide advice to the parents of older children and those in early adolescence, dealing with everything from settling 4- and 5-year-olds into school to advice on drugs and young people;
- more parenting education in schools;
- encouragement for parents to provide more help with their children's school and informal learning;
- encouragement for grandparents to offer more help with grandchildren;
- offering mediation to those considering separating in order to save more married couples from divorce;
- more help for those affected by domestic violence;
- reform to the tax system in increased child benefit and a working families tax credit, so that it is more friendly towards families with children;
- a New Deal for single parents, including help with finding employment;
- encouragement to firms/employers to be family friendly, by establishing national awards for this. Other measures would include a maximum 48-hour week for those in full-time employment, and ending discrimination against part-time workers.

decline of the family, so the extent of that interference has increased. Box 9.4 gives one example, the government green paper of 1998.

These proposals are not untypical of the kinds of things politicians want to change in families, marriage and parenting. They make many assumptions:

- that the state has a right and a duty to intervene in the family;
- that families are homogeneous in form and activity and so can all be helped or changed by a single set of proposals;
- that parents welcome help with their parenting skills;
- that experts such as health visitors and officials such as registrars of births and deaths are qualified to give advice to families about children;
- that parenting can be explicitly taught;
- that employers want to help the families of employees;
- that there is a clear economic link between families and the labour market.

Just how much the state still imagines it can intervene in the family is evident in the work of Giddens on the family and the Third Way (1998). The Third Way is supposedly a new centre/left set of political ideas which builds on the rejection of both social democracy (on which the welfare state is based) and neo-liberalism (political ideas emphasizing markets and choice for public services). Giddens differentiates between these three positions in relation to the family as follows:

- Social democracy argues that the family is the rock of society, helped by the welfare state but on the basis of a male breadwinner/female housewife model and the encouragement of dependency on the state in times of trouble (e.g. unemployment).
- Neo-liberalism sees families as the little platoons of civil society, and is concerned to protect the traditional nuclear family. It is opposed to the welfare state and wants families to make choices about former or currently publicly provided services such as schools, health and housing. Neo-liberals are in favour of making divorce harder, and do not want to offer state support of any kind to unorthodox families (such as single mothers, or gay and lesbian couples).
- The Third Way approach to the family is to recognize it as the meeting point of many current social trends, such as increased equality between the sexes, more women in the labour force for more of their lives, changes in sexual behaviour, and a changing relationship between home and work.

Giddens outlines the policies which a Third Way approach might imply. These include ending the inequality between sexes inside and outside the family, making after-school child-minding services available to mothers and fathers, ensuring that the family is free of violence, and making efforts to maintain the relationships of formerly married parents and to help men keep in contact with their children. Giddens's analysis is based on a recognition that the traditional family had serious drawbacks. For example, it was based on inequality between men and women. Children had few rights. There was a double sexual standard which claimed that married women were virtuous but there was no need for men to be so.

The division of labour within families

Part of the image of the family in our society depends on assumptions about the relationships of men and women inside the home. The nuclear family stereotype assumes that the man is the breadwinner and the woman is responsible for domestic tasks including child care, cleaning and cooking. Men make the large-scale decisions affecting the family, while women control only those areas that are strictly 'domestic'. There is, in other words, a division of labour within the home.

This image may well have borne some relation to reality between 1850 and 1950, following the process of industrialization which took men out of the home to work in factories and offices, though, of course, it should be remembered that in the nineteenth century many working-class women were in employment even after marriage and childbirth. What does the division of labour look like in the contemporary family?

The symmetrical family?

Young and Willmott (1973) argued that, in modern Britain, a new family form, the symmetrical family, which did not require a domestic division of labour, was slowly emerging, one in which the roles of men and women were less differentiated. A whole series of factors combined to produce the change from families with a high gendered division of labour to those in which domestic tasks are more equally shared. These included the rise in the proportion of married women in paid work, the trend towards smaller families, the privatization of the family, and changing social attitudes about the roles of men and women. It has also been claimed that changes in patterns of employment may alter the balance of domestic work. For example, if the wife is employed full-time, one might expect that the husband would carry out more of the domestic tasks.

For Young and Willmott, the symmetrical family had three main features. First, the married couple and their children are very much centred on the home, especially when the children are young. Second, the extended family counts for relatively less and the immediate nuclear family for relatively more. The third and 'most vital' characteristic is that the roles of men and women have become less segregated and more balanced. Young and Willmott's detailed empirical study found that in poorer and older families there was still a considerable gendered domestic division of labour but that, none the less, the great majority of married people in their sample formed the newer symmetrical family (1973, p. 94).

A much more recent study offers support for this proposition. Gershuny (1992) aimed to measure changes in the domestic division of labour by reanalysing a set of studies, done at different times, all of which look at the use of time in the household. He investigates the 'dual-burden' hypothesis which states that, even as wives enter the labour market and take on full-time jobs, they continue to carry the burden of domestic work; 'women remain housewives even when they become breadwinners' (p. 73). Gershuny concludes that this hypothesis is only partially correct. Figure 9.3 shows the amount of work, paid and unpaid (domestic), carried out by husbands and wives. The critical point for Gershuny is that over the period 1974/5 to 1987 the proportion of domestic work carried out by husbands has risen in a context of increased paid work by wives and increased total work by both spouses.

It could be argued that the growth in men's domestic work is actually not in the core tasks of cleaning and cooking but rather in odd jobs, repairs and decorating. Again, Gershuny argues that his evidence does not bear this out. Over the period from 1974/5 to 1987, husbands of full-time employed wives doubled the amount of time they spent in cooking and cleaning. Gershuny concludes that, although women still carry the principal burden of domestic work, there is a lagged adaptation to their increasing paid work as men take on more household tasks.

In Gershuny's account, as in many others, a crucial feature in the domestic division of labour is the way that the husband and wife are involved in paid work. A study of the Isle of Sheppey also contributed to this. Pahl (1984) constructed an index of the division of domestic labour composed not only of 'female' tasks such as cooking, clothes washing or child care but also of 'male' jobs such as house repairs, car maintenance or beer-making. One of his most striking findings was that the more hours a woman was

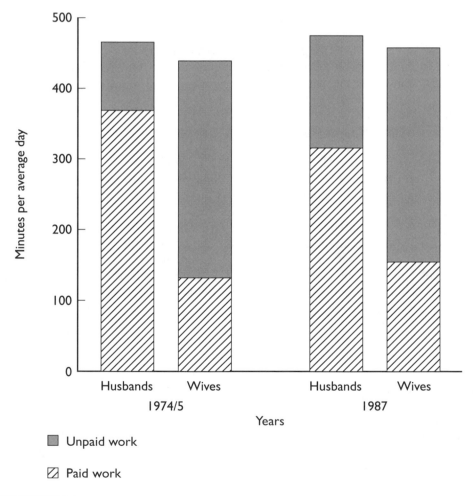

Figure 9.3 | Changes in couples' work patterns, 1974–5 to 1987
Source: Gershuny 1992, p. 78

employed, the more domestic work was shared. However, it is not quite as simple as that. Although households in which both partners are employed do manifest a more equal division of domestic labour, women still do the bulk of the domestic work; more equal certainly does not mean absolutely equal. Furthermore, the balance of the domestic division of labour did not seem to be related to the work done by men. It did not matter if the man was full-time employed or unemployed; the balance of domestic work was still determined by the woman's employment status.

Later researchers have shown that it is not as straightforward as this. Morris (1990) carried out a study of the relationship between male working-class unemployment and domestic work. She argues that women do not take over from their unemployed partners as the main breadwinners, and unemployed men do not take over the housewife role. Traditional gender roles are relatively unaffected. For good measure she adds, as against Gershuny, that 'married women's employment does not prompt a significant rise in domestic involvement on the part of husbands' (p. 189). It is worth adding that, in another study of the relationship between men's unemployment and the domestic division of labour, Wheelock (1990, p. 3) comes to the opposite conclusion: 'Amongst the thirty couples interviewed there was a marked shift towards a less traditional division of household work, with men undertaking more domestic work and childcare when they became unemployed.'

Research by Gregson and Lowe (1993) on middle-class couples found that it was not women entering employment which affected the household division of labour so much as the kinds of attitude which women have towards domestic work. Thus those who thought that it was a woman's responsibility tended to think this when in employment. In their book, Gregson and Lowe note the extent to which middle-class couples are able to buy in domestic help, whether this is child care (for example, by employing a nanny) or housework. This is a strategy not normally available to working-class couples, though it was noted by Gregson and Lowe that those employed were usually working-class women themselves. Thus buying in domestic help still perpetuates the belief that this is women's work. Data collected in 1994 show that many household tasks are still the responsibility of women (see table 9.6).

TABLE 9.6 | Division of household tasks,[a] Great Britain, 1994 (percentages)

Tasks	Always the woman	Usually the woman	About equal or both together	Usually the man	Always the man	All couples[b]
Washing and ironing	47	32	18	1	1	100
Deciding what to have for dinner	27	32	35	3	1	100
Looking after sick family members	22	26	45	–	–	100
Shopping for groceries	20	21	52	4	1	100
Small repairs around the house	2	3	18	49	25	100

[a] By married couples living as married
[b] Includes those who did not answer and where the task was done by a third person
Source: Social Focus on Women and Men 1998, p. 64

It is important, however, to distinguish ordinary domestic labour (cooking, cleaning, washing, shopping, etc.) from the kind of caring functions discussed earlier in relation to family obligations. As Smart and Neal (1999, p. 20) note, 'Caring is qualitatively different from housework because it involves negotiations with others and responsiveness to others' needs; it is both a form of labour and of love.'

Summary

1   Families remain both intensely private and a source of concern to politicians and the state. State interventions in family life and practices are becoming, if anything, even more intrusive. The so-called Third Way seems to include moral, legal and a range of other obligations and duties that families are supposed to provide for the state, employers and other third parties.

2   Debates about the privatization of families continue. Though there is evidence of smaller family size, there are also indications that wider kin networks continue in importance as before and that family obligations may even outlive divorce by some of the parties.

3   It has been argued by some that families are becoming more symmetrical, with domestic work being more balanced between men and women. Recent evidence indicates that, although there may be such a tendency, it is still not very pronounced and is not necessarily being shifted much by women's increasing involvement in the labour market.

9.6   Household formation and dissolution

It might be useful at this point to refresh our memories about two definitions used at the beginning of the chapter. A definition of a family is: a kinship grouping of adults, or adults and children, who may not necessarily have a common residence. A household is merely a residence unit with common housekeeping and may not involve individuals with any kin relationship to each other. Some other definitions may also be useful. 'Marriage' refers to a legally married heterosexual 'couple', whereas the term 'couple' can be used to mean two heterosexual, gay, lesbian or other individuals living together in the same place or conducting a close relationship with each other. Thus it is easy to see how confusion may exist about what constitutes a family as opposed to a couple. Is an unmarried, heterosexual couple with dependent children to be considered a family or not? There is no right answer to this question, but it seems likely that many people in the UK would regard it as a family even if an unconventional one. Similarly, a household containing one parent and dependent children is usually referred to as a (one-parent) family. As several writers have pointed out, the term 'family' itself is far too homogeneous to be used unselfconsciously to refer to a wide range of household formations, couples and kin relatives. Thus Morgan (1996) suggests that we might instead think of family practices. This is fairly consistent with the use of 'life course' as an alternative to 'life-cycle'.

There have been, as mentioned in sections 9.1 and 9.2, some very profound changes in the formation, variety and dissolution of households over the past few decades. Between 1961 and 1997, the number of households consisting of one person has doubled and the number of households comprising an adult heterosexual couple plus dependent children, which in 1961 accounted for 38 per cent of all UK households, fell to 25 per cent or one-quarter of all households. Yet over 70 per cent of the population still live in households headed by a couple. The number of single-parent families (the vast majority headed by mothers) almost trebled between 1971 and 1996 (to 21 per cent of all families with dependent children). Cohabitation either instead of or as a prelude to marriage has dramatically increased.

The different attitudes to marriage come from a variety of sources. The greater economic and social independence of women may make some of them less willing to get married or want to delay marriage, particularly if they are more aware of the potentially oppressive power relations which may exist in marriage or know that the domestic divisions of labour and wider caring responsibilities for other kin may not be equally shared. Nutt (1998) in a study of the social networks of 25 heterosexual women aged 30–50, all without children, noted that along with those who wished to escape motherhood despite disapproval from relatives, there were also those who, in addition, objected to conventional notions of coupledom, domestic labour expectations and becoming a wife. In some cases, this came out of experiencing marriage once, or of resisting pressure to be a mother. In other cases, there was a dislike of what was involved in marriage:

Fay: They [in-laws] think it's really odd and they say things like 'it's not right you know, that you don't have children, I mean we had to have them'. (p. 140)

Zoe: I've had one boyfriend . . . and I think that was out of curiosity (laughs), then I thought 'no' I think it's just too much . . . effort . . . you have to compromise an awful lot. (p. 144)

Deborah: I mean I didn't marry my husband because he could support me, at all, and the fact that I could barely support myself, didn't stop me leaving him either. (p. 156)

Though avoidance of motherhood, marriage and being a conventional wife were sometimes linked in the experiences of some of Nutt's respondents, they do represent different phenomena. We need also to remember two other things. First, women's economic and social independence is a relative concept (as most women, even those in full-time employment, still get paid less than men) and is significantly mediated by ethnicity and social class. It does not apply to all women. Second, as Smart and Neale (1999) note, marriage and families are analysed by some sociologists in such a way that they block out other relationships which these practices imply: 'There are no mothers-in-law, no cousins, no grandchildren, step-grandparents and so on. The field of intimacy seems very empty of players. . . . Even if we accept that relationships with wider kin are now negotiated rather than governed by strict rules . . . it does not mean they are insignificant' (p. 19).

There have also been changes in men's lives. For working-class men in particular, the disappearance of much heavy manufacturing industry and the replacement of it by service industries has meant quite different life courses and much more experience of unemployment or insecure employment. In conjunction with other changes to men's role, this may have affected men's willingness to marry or to marry at a young age. Furthermore, with the advent of agencies like the Child Support Agency (which pursues absent parents for maintenance payments) and the extension of children's rights in the 1989 Children Act, men may be more aware than previously that if they have children then those children cannot just be forgotten when a marriage ends.

Changes in youth cultures and social policies as applied to young people may also be important. Young people are more anxious to experience at least some independent living (and the consumption of goods and services that this implies) before getting married. Furthermore it may be, despite widespread indications of continuing prejudice against gays and lesbians, that there is now slightly more tolerance of sexual relationships which are not heterosexual. Lastly, there may be more anxiety and cynicism about marriage as a social practice, perhaps directly related to the greater incidence of divorce and the uncertainties of modern social life.

However, one can overemphasize the extent of decline in marriage. Many people do still marry eventually. For those who marry at some point, however, a first marriage is clearly not necessarily a permanent arrangement. The UK divorce rate is now the highest in the EU, and twice as many children are now affected by the divorce of their parents as in 1971. In the 1991 Census half a million children were living in step-families, and by 1996 one child in every 65 could expect to experience the divorce of their parents during that year. The effects of high divorce rates on the adults and children concerned are also important and a number of these have already been explored in sections 9.3 and 9.4.

Smart and Neale (1999) interviewed some 60 parents drawn from 60 different families. They did this in order to look at households with children where divorce or separation of parents had occurred after the implementation of the 1992 Children's Act and to examine what they called 'households in transition'. Fathers responded in different ways to the break-up of their former households. Some resented it and were concerned about the injustices they felt were occurring as a result and were more interested in their rights than in the quality of the relationship to the mother of their children:

> *Anthony Dart*: I've been discussing schools since he was two. I said 'Don't shut me out.' And I made her aware of the legal standpoint. I says 'You have a duty as a caring parent' which is a joke 'to inform me of his schooling and medical records.' I says, 'By statute.' And I throw the law at her. (p. 129)

By contrast some parents were much more aware of the importance of maintaining a good relationship with their former partners, even if they themselves were struggling to do this:

> *Meg Johnson*: I think when you start to resent – I know I am starting to resent his contact so that, and the communication itself, I mean, I suppose that's part of the care isn't it, because if you're communicating you're caring about how things are. (p. 131)

So far the concentration has been on gender, and on changes to families in a general sense. Ethnicity also has some important effects on household size and formation. In 1996–7, 28 per cent of white households consisted of a single person, and 34 per cent of black households were single-person, but only 5 per cent of Pakistani and Bangladeshi households were composed of single people. Pakistani and Bangladeshi families have on average larger household sizes (4.4 and 5.0, respectively) than white or black families, and often the former will have more than one family living in the same household. This is not only the effect of different attitudes to the family and sometimes of low incomes, but also reflects different cultural and social practices with regard to family life.

Summary

1   There have been considerable changes to household structures and family forms since the late 1970s. These both reflect and have affected individual practices and attitudes towards domestic labour and child care, as well as attitudes towards marriage and other forms of coupledom.
2   There is no evidence that families have become any more individuated than previously, and kin networks are often extended rather than narrowed by divorce.
3   Class and ethnic differences in household form continue to exert some influence on domestic labour and on family sizes.
4   Though the form of families has changed quite dramatically in recent decades, with increased incidence of divorce and single-parent households, family practices survive.

9.7   Older adults

The rising proportion of older adults relative to younger ones is one of the striking features of contemporary societies. In the UK in 1961, only 12 per cent of the population were 65 years of age or older, with a mere 4 per cent aged 75 or more. In 1996, 16 per cent of the UK population was aged 65 or older, and 7 per cent were 75 or older (see table 9.7). Current projections suggest that by the second decade of the twenty-first century, those over 65 will outnumber those aged under 16.

However, the proportion of over 65s to under 16s is only one feature of the demographic changes. The distribution by gender is also notable, as figure 9.4 shows. Whereas at age 40 men outnumber women, from age 45 onwards there is a change in the distribution. At age 89 there are three women to every one man. This has consequences for the kinds of households that older people live in (often if living independently, they live alone) and also for the kind of social relations characteristic of older people. Some of the social and economic consequences of the skewed age distribution of the population have already been considered in section 9.2. Here the focus is more on the extent to which older people are of sociological significance.

Until recently, few researchers were interested in older people except as social problems, but recently the emphasis has begun to shift and the notion of old age as a diverse set of social and cultural practices has begun to be studied in more detail. Of course, seeing the lives and experiences of older people as a varied part of the life course does not in any way mean that what happens to those who become ill or frail is no longer of any interest. It is important to realize that this is not the totality of the experiences of older women and men.

TABLE 9.7 | Population: by age, 1961–2021 (percentages)

	Under 16	16–24	25–34	35–44	45–54	55–64	65–74	75 and over	All ages (= 100%) (millions)
Mid-year estimates									
1961	25	12	13	14	14	12	8	4	52.8
1971	25	13	12	12	12	12	9	5	55.9
1981	22	14	14	12	11	11	9	6	56.4
1991	20	13	16	14	11	10	9	7	57.8
1996	21	11	16	14	13	10	9	7	58.8
Mid-year projections[a]									
2001	20	11	14	15	13	10	8	7	59.6
2011	18	12	12	14	15	12	9	8	60.9
2021	18	11	13	12	13	14	11	9	62.2

[a] 1996-based projections
Source: Social Trends 1998, table 1.8

In later life, men and women and those from different social class backgrounds may have very different experiences and it is here that a number of features of changes to family practices and in life courses which we have previously discussed may be relevant. First, women may be more used to giving care than receiving it. A not inconsiderable amount of the data found in Finch and Mason's (1993) work on the negotiation of family obligations refers to the care of older parents and other relatives, in terms of both the changing balance of support and how to negotiate this tactfully. Here a daughter, Sarah, whose mother for some time has done the washing and ironing for Sarah's house-

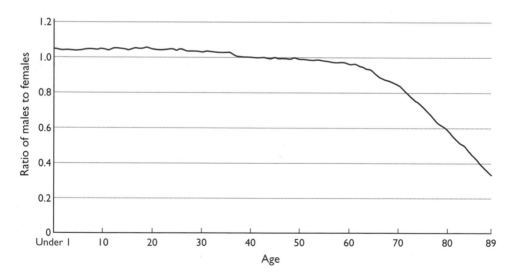

Figure 9.4 | The gender ratio: by age, 1996
Source: Social Trends 1998, table 1.6

hold, is realizing that this support is about to change, as her mother starts to require help herself:

> *Sarah*: She's developed angina. So now I'm going to have to be very careful what I do with her because a) I don't want her to think that she's an invalid because that'll make her worse, er a lot of people her age get angina, it's not unusual, and b) I've got to cut the washing down or how she does it . . . without her being hurt. (Finch and Mason 1993, p. 72)

Older women and men without children may not find support so easily. Wenger's (1994a, 1994b) longitudinal research on older women argues that some older childless women lack support networks and are hence likely to have to find alternative means of care. The implication here is that women who have not been mothers do not develop the same kind of support and wider kin networks that mothers tend to acquire. Wenger found that friendship, marital status and social isolation also affected social networks. It is also likely that the ethnic group affects these too. Nutt's (1998) research on younger childless women showed that such women had quite broad networks and, despite their relatively young age, some of them had already given thought to how they would deal with their care in old age, should they need it. Much of the research concentrates on older women as there are fewer men in the same age cohort (see figure 9.5). Furthermore, it is likely that much of the caring work involving men will be carried out by women.

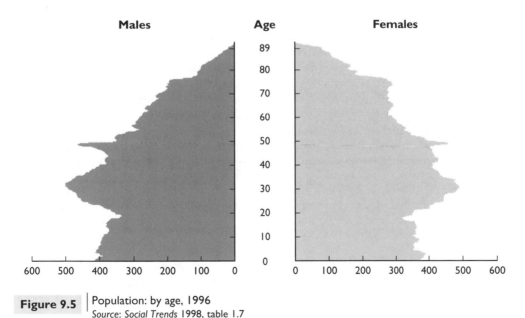

Figure 9.5 | Population: by age, 1996
Source: Social Trends 1998, table 1.7

Older people tend to lack social status. As Pilcher (1995) and others note, the withdrawal of older people from the labour market is one reason for their lack of social status. However, some social analysts have begun to realize that older people are important in their own right, both as consumers and as those whose tastes, lifestyles and values are as socially and culturally interesting as those of younger people. Thus Carroll's

(1998) work on the life histories of seven reasonably affluent women aged between 68 and 78, all of whom had working lives in physical education and dance, shows the way in which older women blend together their present and past to construct full and enjoyable life. Of course their relative wealth helps:

> *Gwen*: I mean I'm so lucky that I've got enough money to do what I want to do. (p. 296)

Others saw their retirement as a chance to do things that there was no time for when they were in employment full-time:

> *Marjorie*: Since our arrival in Cumbria I have joined a walking group and enjoyed weekly outings with a small number of people of like interest. (p. 312)

This does not mean that the women concerned were unaware of their age; as Harriet says:

> So you could just go on living and enjoying life as it is. But I am kind of conscious that most of life is gone so there can't be a lot left, which is unfortunate because there are still quite a lot of books left to read and pictures to paint. (p. 355)

Of course, not all older people are as fortunate as the women that Carroll researched. Clough's (1996) work on the lives of older people living in residential homes demonstrates the still widespread belief that as people age, so their autonomy and independence may be taken from them, especially if they lack the economic, cultural and social capital of the group studied by Carroll. Thus, people may find themselves sharing a room with a stranger and not allowed to leave the home when they want or to eat food that they like at a time that suits them. Even those who are middle class may find that this is insufficient to protect them if their income and health start to decline:

> Sissy Crowther, a middle class woman in her eighties, had come to Highfield House to try to be 'independent' and 'make her home' in the institution. Sharing a room with Ada Brown, a mentally handicapped working class woman, Sissy remarked, 'Do you know I pay eighty six pounds a week to stay here. And I have to share a room with her!' Ada objected to Sissy's use of a heater saying 'Have you got that bloody heater on again?' Sissy said afterwards, 'Well I'm not used to that sort of thing. Language like that. I don't know what my nephews and nieces would say if they knew. Well I wouldn't tell them.' (Hockey 1990, quoted in Hockey and James 1993, p. 155)

Hockey and James (1993, p. 31) note that for many older people on low incomes, becoming older means losing their independence and being patronized by younger people:

> A new resident must, for example, hand over their pension book, valuables and medicine to Matron. Control of possessions is placed in 'adult' rather than 'elderly' hands. Medicines, labelled 'Keep out of reach of children', are doled out to them at set times by care staff: £5 of their pension is returned to them as 'pocket money'.

Patronizing attitudes may exist whether older people are living in residential homes or not. Age, however, does not only influence the views of adults over statutory retirement age – it also affects younger adults, with ageism in the workplace widespread and prejudice against employing even those as young as their late 30s. Thus, ironically, at a time of increasing life expectancy, older people in the UK may find themselves more discriminated against on grounds of age. Younger and older workers are seen as in competition for jobs, sometimes on the unproven assumption that older workers will find difficulty working with younger people, especially when the latter are in positions of authority. Perhaps this is another aspect of the demographic time-bomb discussed in section 9.2.

Summary

1   Age is as much a cultural and social construct as it is a physiological process. Like childhood, it is a diverse set of social practices.
2   The UK population is becoming older, with women outnumbering men from their middle 40s. It is often to other women that the care of older people falls, whether as relatives, friends or paid care workers.
3   Ageism in society affects both attitudes towards and the employment of older people, even though as a group they often have considerable purchasing power and are as much a part of the consumption society as adolescents.
4   Older people who are frail or otherwise unable to look after themselves may find that they are regarded like children and their autonomy is limited, especially in residential care.
5   Gender and social class, as well as ethnicity, continue to affect people's experience of the life course even in older age.
6   Whereas with adolescents whose concern with individuation and establishing identities through consumption is both expected and encouraged, for older people it may be assumed that individuation is no longer important.

Related topics

Extensive evidence about the ethnic composition of the British population is presented in section 8.2. Youth culture is examined in relation to consumption in section 11.3 and the experience of young people in the educational system is addressed in section 14.3. Relations between non-resident kin are examined in section 10.2. Additional material on gender relations within the household, including the domestic division of labour, can be found in section 7.3. There is further discussion of housing policy in section 13.4. Patterns of mortality and morbidity are reviewed in relation to health care in section 15.3.

Further reading

Morgan (1996) is a readable and comprehensive book on family practices, while Bernades (1997) introduces family studies. An introduction to age as a cultural and social practice is Pilcher (1995). A good book on youth is Furlong and Cartmel (1997). On old age try Arber and Ginn (1995). A different perspective on family relationships is given by Jamieson (1998).

Cross-references to *Readings in Contemporary British Society*

Irwin on changing family structure; **Smart** on fatherhood after divorce; **Roberts** on youth, leisure and identity; **Finch and Mason** on kinship and obligation; **Gillespie** on family, ethnicity and gender in Punjabi young people's response to television; **Morris** on household formation, sexual divisions of labour and lone motherhood.

Associations

10

10.1   Introduction

In this chapter we consider those social relationships – or associations – that are outside the immediate family and are not primarily to do with paid employment. The kinds of association we consider include wider kin, friendship groups, rural and urban communities, various religious groups, and social and political networks.

These associations are elements of what is often called civil society. This can be understood as all those thousands of social groupings into which households are embedded. These associations lie outside both the economy and the state. Civil society consists of associations which people join voluntarily. People are not forced to join them and so they are not like one's family, with whom we have ascribed relationships. Nor are they like the state, which necessarily organizes the society from the centre. These associations are joined for various reasons: for friendship, the exchange of services (babysitting, do-it-yourself), to organize leisure time, spiritual enlightenment, and to organize politically to challenge aspects of British society. One argument that we examine is that the web of associations is in decline. People, it is claimed, are spending less time with their friends and wider family and participating less in voluntary organizations than they used to in the late 1940s. Instead, they are retreating into their immediate family, spending more time in the home and being more involved in relationships with children and partners.

It should also be noted that these associations are not formed equally by all social groups, but are partly determined by class, gender and ethnicity. These associations are affected by these social divisions in three senses. First, there are very different resources available to different social groups and this affects the capacity of groups to join or to form such associations. Even friendship depends upon resources of time to travel and money to pay for entertaining. Second, different social classes, genders and ethnic groups prefer different kinds of associational activity; to some extent social groups express their social identities through the kinds of association which they form and sustain. Third, the network of associations that people form will be of benefit to them. They constitute what is sometimes called social capital. Family and friends, for example, are sources of support in times of difficulty, but these and wider associations can also be of assistance in furthering careers. If the argument noted above – that the network of associations is in decline – is true, then the total volume of social capital in Britain is diminishing. In addition, different social groups may well have different amounts of social capital to the extent that they have different patterns of association.

10.2   Families, kin and friends

Family privatization

One sociological argument developed in the 1950s ran as follows. Before the industrial revolution in Europe, the predominant family form was extended; people had regular and extensive contact with their wider kin. Industrialization through the nineteenth century, however, changed that. With the requirement for greater geographical mobility, people lost contact with their extended family and families shrunk to the minimal, nuclear size. Emotional and personal needs would be met within this smaller unit rather than by a wider family network. So the nuclear family 'fits' into industrial society while the extended family is more characteristic of pre-industrial society.

This argument was shown to have certain deficiencies. First, it was argued by historians (Laslett 1965) that the family in pre-industrial England was not in fact extended. A low expectation of life, high infant mortality, relatively low fertility, and late marriage combined to produce small households that were not multi-generational. Grandparents living in the household were rare and the population anyway was relatively youthful. On Laslett's estimate, only 1 household in 20 contained more than two generations. Family structure, in other words, conformed closely to the nuclear form.

A second line of argument maintained that the industrial revolution did not produce a nuclear family form through the disruption of rural communities. Rather, the reverse was true. M. Anderson (1971) suggested that there was actually an increase in extended households in urban areas in the nineteenth century. Parents lived with their working, married children and provided child care in exchange for receiving assistance and support in old age.

In addition, a number of sociological studies of the 1950s and 1960s suggested that the isolation from wider family of the nuclear family had been exaggerated. Young and Willmott (1957) found that people in the heart of London, in Bethnal Green, lived near their kin and had frequent contact with them. Of particular strength was the tie between mother and daughter.

However, at the time, Bethnal Green was an area of great residential stability; a lot of the people interviewed by Young and Willmott had lived there all their lives. Not all regions of the city have this kind of stability. Young and Willmott also investigated a new housing estate to which some East-Enders had moved. They found that the people living on the estate did not have such intimate contact with their extended kin. The nuclear families were instead relatively enclosed and inward-looking.

By the late 1960s a new version of this argument was developed; that although families were not being totally severed from contact with wider kin, a variety of pressures was causing them to be more inward-looking, more concerned with the home and with children. This argument was described as family privatization by Goldthorpe et al. (1969) in their study of affluent workers in Luton in the 1960s. They define privatization as a process 'manifested in a pattern of social life which is centred on, and indeed largely restricted to, the home and the conjugal family' (1969, p. 97).

The primary reason for the adoption of this lifestyle was the attitude to the economic rewards of work. The Luton workers valued the high incomes that they could earn; they were involved in a 'quest for affluence'. This meant that they had often moved to their present jobs away from their previous connections of kin and friends. Furthermore, the jobs themselves left little time and energy for sociability outside the home because they involved both overtime and shift work. The Luton families studied did not have much free time left after work, given the multifarious activities required to maintain a house, garden and car. What free time there was available was devoted to household leisure pursuits such as watching television. Of all the spare-time activities reported by affluent workers and their wives in the few days before being interviewed, 62 per cent were located in or about the home itself. Three-quarters of all activities were carried out by the husband or wife alone or together with other members of the family household. Almost a quarter of the couples engaged in no activity with people from outside the family.

Although the main reason for this apparent privatization of family life is the instrumental orientation to work, it is not the only one. Apart from the constraints of work life, many of the affluent workers preferred their home-centred lives. For example, even those who did live near their kin did not see them especially often. Respondents would emphasize the central place that their immediate family played in their lives. These 'familistic' values were also demonstrated in the limited leisure-time involvement by husbands with their workmates.

However, there are some difficulties with this family privatization argument. First, there are different dimensions of the phenomenon of privatization. It can refer to an increased interest in the home; to a conviction that families should be the main focus of activity; to a greater sharing of domestic and child-rearing tasks between husband and wife; to a generalized tendency to treat the home as the focus of leisure and consumption activity; to a concentration on children on the part of both husband and wife; or to a neglect of wider social relationships of family and friends. Not all of these different ways of measuring privatization necessarily run together. A family may be privatized on one dimension but not on others.

Second, comparative data over time are difficult to obtain. This should make one wary of talking about changes in family life since evidence about the degree of privatization of families in the recent past is not available. There is a tendency to see the past as a golden age, a time of mutual aid, neighbourliness and extensive, warm and supportive relationships with wider family and friends. In fact, what evidence there is suggests that privatization has a history dating back at least into the nineteenth century. There is nothing very new about wanting to spend time at home with one's immediate family (Devine 1989; Saunders 1990).

Third, an interest in home and family does not necessarily imply that modern British families are inward-looking. Home-centredness can still go with a measure of sociability with family and friends. It can also go with participation in collective activities. In his study of those who own their own homes, Saunders (1990) shows that such home-owners, who one would assume are likely to be home-centred, are more inclined to join organizations for the collective good than are council tenants, as shown in table 10.1.

TABLE 10.1 | **Housing tenure and organizational activity**

| | Housing tenure | | | |
| | Home owners | | Council tenants | |
Organizational activity: belongs to	No.	%	No.	%
At least one local organization	209	56	45	34
Residents' organization (all)	39	11	5	4
Residents' organization (where available)	39	50	5	10
Trade union or other work-based association	117	33	23	18

Source: Saunders 1990, p. 287

Fourth, the degree of privatization will vary with stage in the life-cycle. For example, couples may be more home-centred when they have young children, and less so when their children leave home. The experience of privatization will also vary between social classes and even more significantly between men and women. It should also not be assumed that because households spend a lot of time watching television they are necessarily privatized and separate from what is happening across the globe. In chapter 2 it was suggested that television may play a crucial role in developing a sense of global connectedness.

We now consider in more detail some of the personal relationships that British people form outside their nuclear family, both with kin and with friends.

Wider family

We have seen that there are sociological arguments that suggest that the immediate family is becoming disconnected from the wider family of parents, sisters and brothers, uncles and aunts, and cousins. There are also suggestions in the press and by politicians that too many people are neglecting their responsibilities towards their elderly parents, becoming absorbed in their work and their immediate family. Are these claims correct?

There are various ways of measuring a family household's involvement with their wider family. McGlone, Park and Roberts (1996), for example, show that members of such wider families are less likely to share a house than they once were. In 1986, 20 per cent of mothers lived with their adult children, while in 1995, 14 per cent did so. There were similar falls in the proportions of adult children living with their parents and adult siblings living together. These changes are directly related to the rise in the proportion of single-person households. The same authors also analysed how close people lived to members of their wider family and how often they saw them. As can be seen from table 10.2, a high proportion of family members do in fact live geographically close to wider kin.

TABLE 10.2 | Journey time to the home of a relative, 1995 (percentages)

Relative	Less than 15 minutes	15 minutes to 1 hour	1 to 3 hours	3 hours or more	Base[a]
Mother	31	34	17	16	1026
Father	28	30	17	18	822
Adult sibling	23	37	19	20	1702
Adult child	30	36	14	10	812
Other relative	30	36	17	15	1796

[a] Bases exclude those without the relative in question, as well as those who live with this relative.
Source: McGlone, Park and Roberts 1996, p. 56

Between a quarter and a third of people live within 15 minutes of a relative and the majority live within one hour. But these proportions have declined since the mid-1980s. In 1995, 65 per cent of adults lived within an hour of their mother's house, while the corresponding figure for 1986 was 70 per cent. It should be noted that the mobile phone is most commonly used by young men to keep in touch with their mothers, many apparently ringing every day!

Geographical proximity does not, of course, necessarily mean that family members actually see each other. Table 10.3 describes the frequency with which people come into contact with their wider family. A very small proportion of people never see their relatives – but that proportion is exceeded by those who see a relative every day. Weekly contact is common. Again, however, McGlone and colleagues note a decline in the period 1986 to 1995. For example, while about one-half of people saw their mother at least once per week in 1995, the figure for 1986 was 60 per cent. However, this fall is not because people are seeing more of their friends and less of their kin, since, strangely, face-to-face meetings with friends have also fallen over the same period.

TABLE 10.3 | **Frequency of seeing non-resident relatives/friends, 1995 (percentages)**

Relative/friend	Daily	At least once a week	At least once a month	Less often	Never	Base[a]
Mother	8	40	21	27	3	1026
Father	6	33	20	29	9	822
Adult sibling	4	25	21	45	4	1702
Adult child	10	48	16	18	1	812
Other friend	3	31	26	37	1	1796
'Best friend'	10	48	22	17	–	1768

[a] Bases exclude those without the relative/friend in question, as well as those living with this relative/friend.
Source: McGlone, Park and Roberts 1996, p. 57

These data indicate that, although there has been some decline in involvement with wider family, the social network created by kinship is still strong. It also shows the importance of the tie between parent and child. The strongest relationships are between adults and their parents, rather than those between siblings or those with other relatives. Indeed it would be more precise to say that what is strongest is the mother–child tie, since relationships with fathers tend to be weaker. Some 9 per cent of people, for example, never see their father, while 48 per cent see their mother at least once a week or daily, compared with 39 per cent who see their father daily or weekly.

The importance of the parent–adult child tie spills over into the relationship of grandchildren to grandparents. A much extended expectation of life since the Second World War means that parents are potentially also grandparents for a much longer period of their lives. Whether children then grow up having much contact with grandparents depends on all sorts of factors – geographical proximity, the grandparents' ages, whether the grandparents are still in paid work – and there is a very wide degree of variation in the amount of involvement that grandparents have with their grandchildren. However, it is clear that grandparents do provide a good deal of practical assistance. Kiernan and Wicks (1990), for example, show that grandmothers provide a significant amount of the child care needed by their working adult children.

So far, we have looked at overall measures of a household's involvement with their wider family without considering differences by gender, age or social class. Gender differences are particularly relevant since women are more likely to maintain social networks based on kinship. For example, when asked what were the most significant events of the past year, women are more likely than men to cite family matters (Buck et al. 1994). McGlone, Park and Roberts (1996) found that 53 per cent of women saw their mother at least once a week compared with 42 per cent of men; an adult child was seen at least once per week by 62 per cent of women and 53 per cent of men.

This picture is, however, more complex if we take full-time work into account. As table 10.4 shows, men in full-time work in 1995 were just as likely to see their mother once a week as were women in full-time work. Thus it seems that the overall differences between men and women in relationship to the maintaining of kin ties result from the high rates of kin contact of those women not employed full-time.

TABLE 10.4 | Seeing non-resident mother at least once a week, 1986 and 1995

	1986		1995	
Men/women	%	Base	%	Base
Men				
All	50	308	42	450
In full-time work	49	266	46	314
Women				
All	65	335	53	576
In full-time work	64	97	45	177

Source: McGlone, Park and Roberts 1996, p. 59

The position is still more complex if we compare 1995 with 1986. We have already noted the decline in contact over this period. Table 10.4 shows that all men and women including those in full-time work saw their mother less frequently in 1995 than they did in 1986. One should note, however, that the decline is sharper for women than for men, and is extremely sharp for women in full-time employment. It would appear, therefore, that there are two factors responsible for this decline – a general transformation in women's behaviour towards their wider family and a changed impact of women's full-time work upon their lives. We might also note the much more widespread availability of the telephone and even e-mail, which allow virtual contact with wider kin. We need to be cautious in interpreting these findings; they describe changes within a single decade and may relate to particular short-term developments.

There are also class differences. Young and Willmott (1973) found that those lower down the occupational scale were more family-centred than the professional and managerial classes. The professional class saw fewer relatives but many more friends. Some care should be exercised, however, in interpreting these contact rates. A lower contact rate may say nothing about the quality or duration of the meeting, but can be due to the physical separation from kin caused by the relatively greater mobility of the middle class.

The vitality of relationships with wider family members is not, of course, just measured by the frequency of contact. Families are also agencies of support. McGlone, Park and Roberts (1996) asked their respondents to whom they would turn for help in various situations (see table 10.5). Spouse or partner turns out to be the major source of help in most situations, except, unsurprisingly, with marital problems. Parents are the next most used source except for marital problems and depression, when friends are more important. Kin outside the immediate family are most called upon when practical help is required and friends when the support is for an emotional problem. The following case study looks at these issues in more detail.

TABLE 10.5	Support from family and friends, 1995 (percentages)				
Source of support	Household job	Help while ill	Borrowing money	Marital problems	Depression
No one	1	1	7	8	3
Spouse/partner	58	61	21	9	47
Parent	8	13	20	15	8
Child	13	11	6	17	7
Sibling	4	3	4	12	6
Friend	7	5	2	27	21
Bank	n.a.	n.a.	32	n.a.	n.a.

Base = 2077
n.a. = not applicable
Source: McGlone, Park and Roberts 1996, p. 61

Family responsibilities: a case study

Finch and Mason (1993) carried out a study of the sense of responsibility and obligation and the flows of assistance within families. They show that many members of family groups are connected by a web of assistance of many different kinds. This web, however, is not sustained by a rigid set of rules of obligation. Instead, there exists a series of guidelines within which negotiations are conducted. These guidelines concern reciprocity and the balance of independence and dependency. They also serve to protect the reputations of giver and receiver; it is important to be seen to be generous as a giver and not grasping or ill-deserving as a receiver. What makes the web of assistance particularly strong is that exchanges are as much moral as they are material. They confirm the importance and permanence of family relations and function as a kind of social cement.

Though important, this web of assistance is also very variable. There are no well-understood rules shared by everyone about who should look after whom in what circumstances. So Finch and Mason did not find any general agreement that the family should be the first port of call for any family member who wants or needs help. For example, in response to the proposition 'Children have no obligation to look after their parents when they are old', 58 per cent of the sample thought that there was such an obligation and 39 per cent thought that there was not. There was even less agreement about what kind of help should be given. For instance, in responding to a slightly different proposition concerning responsibilities towards parents who had been injured in a car accident but lived several hundred miles away, 33 per cent suggested a move near the parents, 24 per cent favoured having the parents to live with them, and 25 per cent would offer only financial help.

Despite the lack of agreement in principle about precisely what obligations should exist in families, kinship relations remain very important. Almost everyone in the sample had given or received financial help. About half the women – and only slightly fewer of the men – said that they had helped to look after a relative who was ill or otherwise incapacitated. A whole range of other kinds of help is involved as well – practical assistance, looking after children, emotional support. In general, then, the experience of helping, and being helped, is very widespread in families.

So far, we have seen that there are extensive contacts and flows of support between members of the wider family, even if this involvement on a face-to-face basis is declining. This conclusion is supported by examining the attitudes that people appear to have towards their family. McGlone and Cronin (1994) showed that most people agreed that one should stay in touch with family members, including aunts, uncles and cousins, even when they do not have much in common. Most people also believed that one's family is more important than friends. Women and older people tend to express more family-centred attitudes than do men and the young. It is unclear whether age-related differences arise as people get older or because there are generational differences.

However, these expressed attitudes are in fact more family-centred than are people's actions with regard to their kin. There is considerable evidence that people select the family members with whom they will maintain important contacts.

Friendship networks

In sociological literature and public debate, friendship is seen in one of two ways. Either it is viewed as something that is threatened by the much greater absorption of people's time, energy and enthusiasm into the immediate family. Or, on the other hand, friendship is seen as threatening family commitments already weakened by geographical mobility, family instability and more demanding work lives, especially with the rapid increases in women's activity rates and hours of work. Some of the discussion in the previous section simultaneously indicates the importance of friendship in our society and illustrates the tension between these two views of friendship. We have pointed out that friends are an important source of emotional help and people tend to see their best friends more often than they see members of their wider family (table 10.3). At the same time, friends are not replacing family, and the general decline in the social network outside the immediate family is at the expense of both friends and wider family members. Other theorists (e.g. Sennett 1986; Giddens 1992) see friendship and immediate family relationships as examples of intimate modern relationships, to be contrasted with the more diffuse relationships of the wider family or community.

Frequency of contact with friends is an unreliable indicator since it cannot represent the quality of the relationship or its purpose. In table 10.5 we described the extent to which friends gave practical or emotional support. In fact, friends are not valued for the support that they actually give, which is, for most people, relatively little, even if people do like to think of their friends as potentially providing assistance in time of need. Thus, in a sample of married women, O'Connor (1992) found that only a tiny minority of friends provided practical help, while more than two-fifths provided a sense of security, that is, the feeling that they could help. Friends – particularly women friends – also act as confidants. O'Connor's study found that half of the very close friendships that she studied were characterized by the exchange of intimate confidences. Of course, friends are also companions, people to go out with, share activities with, or simply talk to. As people grow older, this aspect of friendship becomes especially important. For the elderly, friendship is an important source of social integration. As Jerrome (1981) says in her study of the friendships of older women:

> A widespread feature of the friendships I have encountered has been the emphasis, in practice, on pleasure, on pleasure as opposed to help or the exchange of confidences ... the main need seems to be for companionship in an enjoyable activity, 'someone to do things with'. (p. 192–3, quoted in O'Connor 1992, p. 122)

The ways in which people conduct their friendships, even what they mean by friendship, vary considerably. Women and men appear to have different friendship practices, having their origin in childhood and continuing into adolescence. Male children tend to play outdoors, in large groups that take up a lot of space. Girls, by contrast, tend to stay indoors and play in pairs or very small groups. In adolescence, girls tend to subordinate their friendships to heterosexual relationships while boys organize their heterosexual relationships around their friendships (Jamieson 1998). In adulthood, men tend to form their friendships around specific activities of one kind or another (often sports-related). This provides a source of sociable enjoyment, but the relationships are not particularly intimate since personal worries and anxieties are rarely discussed.

Many writers relate the differences between men's and women's friendship patterns to the manner in which men's lives have been historically more involved with work.

Plate 10.1 | Older women friends
Source: Network/Homer Sykes

Men have inhabited a public sphere and women a private world. In the public world too much disclosure of the self is not encouraged and may actually be dysfunctional. In the private world intimacy is closely related to the nurturing role. However, this difference, even if once only partially accurate, is likely to change as men's and women's economic activity rates are now more or less equal (see section 7.2). Indeed, some writers warn against the tendency to exaggerate these differences between men and women in the formation of their friendships.

A number of studies indicate differences between middle- and working-class people in their patterns of friendship. Allan (1979) found that not only did the middle class have more friends, but also they were drawn from a greater variety of social settings and from a much wider geographical area. Allan argues that these class differences result from different ways of organizing friendship:

> Briefly, whereas the working-class respondents tended to restrict interaction with their friends (and with their other sociable companions) to particular social contexts, the middle-class respondents developed their friendships by explicitly removing them from the constraints imposed by specific settings. (Allan 1979, p. 49)

Middle-class friendships start in particular settings, such as at work or at a club. However, people only truly become 'friends' when the interaction is continued outside that specific setting. So someone met initially at work may be brought home to a meal, or arrangements may be made to go out to a concert. The point is the transfer of friendship outside the original setting. The meaning of middle-class friendship is given not by the original place of meeting but by the individuality of the people concerned, who can now interact in various situations.

The same is less true of working-class people, whose social contacts are more confined within particular settings. In this case, people met at work or in the pub will not be asked home or invited to go to a concert. Sociability is confined to the original setting. Allan's working-class respondents, therefore, experienced their social contacts in terms of their setting: there were workmates, people in the pub, or neighbours, but not friends whose relationship transcended the original setting. Part of the consequence of this was that working-class respondents were often unwilling to use the term 'friend', being unsure if they were using it appropriately. They preferred instead to use the designation related to the setting – neighbour, for example. They also tended to see their social contacts as unplanned. For example, although they might see the same people every night in the pub, that was not a planned attempt to see those people but an unplanned consequence of being there. In sum, Allan suggests that middle-class sociability involves a 'flowering out' of friendship while, for the working class, there is a confinement of social contact to particular settings.

Summary

1 Wider kinship relations are still of great importance, particularly the ties between adult children and their parents, which are actively sustained by visiting and telephone calls and by the exchange of support and help.

2   Friendship is also important and is oriented more towards security and companionship than as a source of practical help.
3   The relationships between the nuclear family and kin and friends are differentiated by class and gender. Middle-class and working-class people, and men and women, appear to have somewhat different friendship patterns.

10.3   Rural and urban communities

We now consider some of the different kinds of wider communities within which families and kin have lived. Up to the sixteenth century, most people lived in the countryside. Towns were relatively small and of little importance. They were mainly market centres containing few public buildings except perhaps a corn exchange and some churches. Towns were dominated by the countryside, where family wealth and power were concentrated.

This situation began to change so that by 1700 the population of London had expanded to over half a million people. There was an extraordinary growth of world trade controlled by merchants and financiers living in London. From the time of the Tudors and Stuarts onwards (the sixteenth and seventeenth centuries), London was the centre of culture and commerce in England, with elegant houses and multiple entertainments, including the theatres where Shakespeare's plays were first staged.

However, it was outside London that the most significant change for the whole development of modern societies took place: the industrial revolution from the late eighteenth century onwards. This revolution involved not just new kinds of work but also new sorts of town and city, organized around mining and manufacturing industry. Many of these were very small at first, located close to where coal was mined. They were generally settlements that either were entirely new or had been small towns relatively free of control by medieval guilds. They grew at a tremendous rate in the nineteenth century. In 1801 only one-fifth of the population of England and Wales lived in towns and cities; by 1901 it was four-fifths. In such industrial towns and cities there were dreadful levels of ill-health, overcrowding and social deprivation (see plate 10.2).

London too grew extremely rapidly, having a population of 6 million by the end of the nineteenth century. It was easily the largest city in the world. However, its wealth was based not on industry but rather on finance, government, the professions, transport and trade. Nevertheless what was the world's largest and richest city contained the world's most extensive slums at the time.

For the first half of the twentieth century there was an accelerating physical expansion of large towns, which had an increasing influence over the surrounding countryside. Four million houses were built between the two world wars. However, there was a slowdown in the rate of population growth in the industrial areas in the north of England, Scotland and Wales. Towns and cities in the southern half of Britain increased in population. The area around London grew rapidly in population, and it also acquired higher proportions of people (mainly men) with professional and managerial jobs. Suburbs rapidly expanded, although most work remained concentrated in town and city centres. There was an increased separation between the place of work and the home. This led to the development of widespread commuting, to the need for improved public transport, and to increased isolation for the housewife less able to escape from her suburban home.

Plate 10.2 | An industrial town
Source: Camera Press / Ray Green

More generally over the past two decades, the largest urban areas have suffered economically and lost population, while smaller towns and rural areas have prospered and attracted industry, services and population. In the 1960s and 1970s there was extensive growth in manufacturing employment in the more rural parts of Britain. This was an aspect of counter-urbanization, the tendency for large cities to lose population and for smaller settlements to acquire population.

There has been some reversal of this in the 1980s and 1990s. Two processes have been involved. First, a number of inner-city areas were increasingly thought to contain attractive Georgian and Victorian terraced houses that could be gentrified and made suitable for middle-class occupation (such as Tony Blair's Islington in north London). Second, the collapse of employment in British ports and docks made a large amount of land and property available. Some of this has resulted in new housing in the docklands of London, Liverpool, Cardiff and so on. This rediscovery of some inner-city areas by middle-class professionals has resulted from a changing valuation placed on living in cities as opposed to living in suburban and rural areas (Savage and Warde 1993, ch. 3).

The countryside

There has been a long-standing debate about whether the associations of urban life are different from those of rural life. Urban life is thought to be characterized by large size, a high density of population, a heterogeneity of social groups, anonymity, distance and formality between people, and the need for people's associations to be formally regulated by law. By contrast the rural way of life is set out in box 10.1.

Box 10.1   Patterns of rural life: ideal-typical features

The ideal-typical features of rural life are as follows:

- Rural life is organized as a community with people frequently meeting together and being connected in lots of different ways.
- People have close-knit social networks; as a result one's friends know each other as well as oneself.
- Most inhabitants work on the land or in related industries. There is a high proportion of jobs that overlap and there is a relatively simple division of labour.
- Most people possess an ascribed status fixed by their family origin. It is difficult to change the status through achievement. People are strongly constrained to behave in ways appropriate to their status.
- Social inequalities are presumed to be justified, often in terms of rural tradition.

These patterns of urban and rural life are, however, deceptive. The 'countryside' in fact changes enormously. It is not something that is fixed. Even the 'olde English village' (plate 10.3) is relatively recent, resulting from the eighteenth-century enclosure movement and improvements in agriculture. The model of life in rural society represented in box 10.1 was more or less true of parts of rural England in the early years of the twentieth century. It would never have fitted highland Scotland, which experienced huge rates of depopulation as those living on the land were cleared off it during the infamous Highland Clearances of the eighteenth and nineteenth centuries.

Life in the East Anglian countryside: a case study

In the nineteenth century most land in Britain was owned by a few landowners. This was leased by tenant farmers, who in turn employed large numbers of agricultural labourers. Newby (1985) shows that since the beginning of the twentieth century three main changes have occurred in this ownership pattern within England and Wales.

First, there has been a large increase in owner-occupation so that about three-quarters of farmland is now farmed by its owners. Second, there has been a substantial increase in the ownership of agricultural land by large institutions, especially those based in the City of London. Third, there has been an irreversible rationalization of agriculture. It is much less a way of life and more a business. There has been the development of agri-business, where large food-processing companies control and direct the output and product quality of individual farmers. Agriculture has been industrialized.

Plate 10.3 | A typical English village
Source: J. Allan Cash

One aspect has been the increased mechanization of farm work. This has dramatic-ally reduced the workforce employed on farms. About one-half of all farms employ only one worker and many employ none. The reduction in the numbers of farm-workers has weakened the basis of agricultural trade unionism, the peak membership of the National Union of Agricultural and Allied Workers being in 1948. The reduction has also helped to lessen the social distance between farmers and their workers.

Newby also shows that the connections between farmers and their workers have been strengthened by the large influx of people from towns and cities, urban newcomers who live permanently in the countryside or buy cottages for the weekend. To some extent the rural community is organized around the farm and farming in opposition to these urban newcomers. Farmers and their workers come to form a community within a community. This has reinforced a nostalgia for the past, when rural societies were thought to be relatively undivided communities. It is believed that the newcomers do not appreciate or recognize the value and nature of agricultural work. It is also thought that such newcomers seek to preserve quaint and inappropriate aspects of rural charm, what has been called 'the village in their mind'. This has given rise to considerable social tensions, since newcomers will often oppose new shopping developments or council houses that would be of particular benefit to farm-workers:

The newcomers often possess a set of stereotyped expectations of village life which place a heavy emphasis on the quality of the rural environment . . . many newcomers hold strong views on the desired social and aesthetic qualities of the English village. It must conform as closely as possible to the prevailing urban view – picturesque, ancient and unchanging . . . [this has led] many newcomers to be bitterly critical of the changes wrought by modern farming methods. (Newby 1985, p. 167)

Considerable conflicts also arise over leisure activities. Local farmers and their workers often support and participate in field sports including hunting, while urban newcomers frequently try to prevent such 'uncivilized' activities. Indeed rural areas across most of the UK are now important sites for leisure, especially for those visitors from elsewhere who travel in and through the countryside by car (see Urry 1995). About one-quarter of the population are frequent countryside visitors; those with service-class jobs are twice as likely as skilled or unskilled workers to visit; white Britons are more frequent visitors than those from various ethnic minorities; and those with cars are much more likely to be visitors than those without.

From the 1980s onwards farmers have been responding to this strong demand by developing leisure-related sources of income. This has also stemmed from the fact that some farmland is being taken out of agricultural production under European Union (EU) policies. Rural areas are partly moving into a post-productivist phase. Interestingly, newcomers will often campaign against some of these developments, since it is believed that too many 'tourists', as opposed to those who have bought property in the village, will destroy the 'true' character of the village. Those expressing such a view are articulating a ruralist ideology.

Rural life is often seen in terms of the existence of community-type associations, with close relationships between inhabitants that are in turn reinforced by family ties. In recent research in England and Wales it was shown that people moving into the countryside often used notions of community to explain why they were drawn into such areas (Cloke, Phillips and Thrift 1995). Implicit within such notions is a critique of the city and of the higher rates of crime and forms of ethnic diversity that characterize at least some cities. We now consider whether similar 'communities' do exist in urban areas – something that undermines simple contrasts between country life and city life.

Urban communities

Research conducted in the 1950s and discussed in section 10.2 did indeed suggest that 'urban villages' can develop in certain enclaves within large cities, most famously in Bethnal Green in the East End of London (see Young and Willmott 1957). At the time Bethnal Green was a relatively compact borough of about 50,000 people concentrated within a small area of about 2 square miles. No major roads ran through it. Almost three-quarters of the male labour force were manual workers and most of those who were not ran shops or pubs. Although there was no single dominant industry in the area, it was an overwhelmingly working-class locality. There was a distinctive pattern of social life; Frankenberg (1966, pp. 185–6) summarizes:

One consequence of . . . immobility is that everyone is surrounded by people very like himself, most of whom he has always known. Bethnal Green has many points of similarity with a village, or rather with a whole series of overlapping and interlocking villages. The opportunities for close, long-term relationships are greater than is usually the case in a large, metropolitan, residential area. The likelihood of an inhabitant having neighbours who are strangers, or whose way of life is very different from his own, has, until recently, been very slight. This immobility also makes it essential for him to be on good terms with his neighbours, as they are likely to be there, for better or worse, for most of his life.

There are, however, large parts of many British cities that are now nothing like this. People living in many inner-city areas do not stay there because they are attracted by feelings of 'community'. On the contrary, they cannot escape: they are unable to rent or buy a house or flat elsewhere, and often they do not possess the qualifications or appropriate skills to move. In certain areas, a large proportion of the local population is in this position, and this reinforces the sense of decay and despair found in many inner-city areas. Various measures are used to assess which inner-city areas are suffering particularly high levels of deprivation: population loss; high levels of unemployment; high proportion of long-term unemployed; large number of lone-parent households; high proportion of people over pensionable age; significant number of houses without an inside toilet; large proportion of people without higher degrees or diplomas; high ratio of people with unskilled or semi-skilled jobs; and high rates of drug use and related semi-criminal activity.

Three processes have particularly contributed to the worsening of the condition of such inner cities during the 1980s and 1990s. First, there has been the reduced availability of affordable housing. Few houses are being built for the poor, and one-quarter of council houses have been sold off by local authorities. And yet semi-skilled and unskilled workers mostly do not buy their own houses but have to rent them. The 1980s and 1990s have seen a remarkable growth in homelessness and of council estates turning into sink estates devoid of most services and facilities.

Second, there have been major changes in the location of industry and employment. Many plants in central urban areas have closed. Less than 15 per cent of employment in most large cities is now to be found in manufacturing. One factor contributing to this has been the process of acquisition by which firms get taken over and merged into larger companies (see sections 2.3 and 3.3). These larger companies often own plants in different regions of Britain as well as in other countries. They are able to pursue a global strategy that often involves closing older plants in inner-city areas.

And third, many inner-city areas are centres for various kinds of crime, mostly against property but not entirely. This in turn can make areas unsafe and unattractive, so much so that people can be unwilling to leave their homes for fear that they will be broken into.

These characteristics are also found on various 'outer estates' of major cities. These areas of council housing and new industrial estates have suffered catastrophic economic and social collapse. Meegan (1989) describes Kirkby and Speke, located on the edge of Liverpool. The effects of economic decline have been devastating: social polarization between those in work and those without jobs; large numbers of long-term unemployed, with many young people never having worked; huge reductions in household income: increasing reliance upon the state; and increasing numbers of households with rent arrears.

Meegan, though, suggests that this has not resulted in fatalism about the future.

Apart from the famous Liverpool humour, which involves a lively scepticism towards authority, the unemployed people on these estates do not seem to have formed themselves into a separate underclass. He notes the 'confidence of local unemployed people in their own abilities to organize a collective response to their situation' (1989, p. 229). People living in these outer estates seem to demonstrate a great attachment to their locality. Meegan describes 'strong attachments to the area by local residents, the family-based support networks and the refusal of some of the unemployed to be marginalised in the social life of the locality' (1989, p. 230).

Thus those living in areas of rented housing in Britain can suffer acute social problems. This argument has been extended by Saunders to suggest such problems could be avoided by most family households in Britain becoming home-owners.

A nation of home-owners: a case study of privatization

Saunders (1990) argues that privatized consumption is of increasing social importance. There is a new division of interest between those able to purchase products and services individually on the market, and those who are forced to rely on state provision. This new division or cleavage leads to the decline of social class and its replacement by consumption as the main axis of social conflict.

Increasing standards of living have enabled people to meet most of their consumption needs through individual purchase (even if subsidized) rather than through standardized state provision. This results in further decline in state-provided services, which has been found on many council estates as we have just seen. This results in social polarization, in which most people consume privately and only those who have no choice resort to the state.

For Saunders the private ownership of housing is not merely one alternative amongst several, but is superior to both private and public renting. This is because, first, it enables considerable capital gains to be achieved, as house prices, until the early 1990s, kept well ahead of the rate of inflation. Second, it gives much greater control to the owners, who are able to change and develop their properties, so deriving considerable satisfaction. And third, owner-occupation provides people with a sense of identity and security. He argues that since people's identities are increasingly formed not at work but from what they consume, the shift to the private purchase of housing is profoundly important. It gives people a really significant stake in 'Britain'.

However, there are various criticisms to be made of this argument. First, it applies more to England and especially the south-east. Scotland and Wales have always had higher rates of council house renting and some of the estates are popular and well maintained.

Second, many of the capital gains made from home ownership in the 1980s were lost in the collapse of house prices in the early 1990s. Those people with negative equity – a mortgage higher than the current value of the house – can experience neither capital gains nor security. Indeed much of the argument ignores the often very high cost of borrowing (through a mortgage if one is lucky) that can be involved in house purchase.

Third, Saunders attempts to generalize from the case of housing to other spheres of consumption, such as health or transport, where he also argues that private provision through the market is desirable. However, this is dubious since housing is a peculiar commodity. One can buy (if one is lucky) a whole house but not a whole hospital or bus. In the latter cases all one can purchase is a service, which cannot be resold to make a capital gain. Furthermore, the housing market in Britain is not a pure market but has been structured by specific policies, especially that of maintaining tax relief on mortgages and encouraging council tenants to purchase their homes through 'right to buy' legislation.

Gentrification

There is no doubt though that many areas in British cities have been transformed through what is often called gentrification. This involves older properties or derelict land in what were often working-class areas being converted into fashionable brick or stone houses for owner-occupation for middle-class households. Some gentrification has assisted in slowing down the depopulation of some cities and the more general process of counter-urbanization.

There are two main forms of gentrification: an episode of collective action by a number of individuals moving into and remaking an area; and a process of major investment by large developers engaging in large housing construction projects (see Warde 1991). In his study of Hackney in the late 1980s and early 1990s, Butler (1995) concentrates upon gentrification in the first sense.

Butler describes how the area was initially lived in as an element of the post-1968 counterculture. Young men and women, often organized in what were at the time unconventional households, moved into the area. They were attracted by its down-market and unsmart appearance, as well as by the availability of cheap yet improvable eighteenth- and nineteenth-century housing. These groups, initiating such a gentrification, can be termed 'pioneer' gentrifiers. They were then followed by more mainstream gentrifiers during the 1980s and 1990s.

Butler's survey of these mainstream gentrifiers suggests the following characteristics:

- There was a higher than usual proportion living as single persons and with partners rather than as husband/wife.
- In almost all the two-person households, both partners were in full-time employment.
- A remarkably high proportion of both men and women had attended private schools and university (80 per cent).
- Most were in well-paid professional and administrative jobs similar in status to those of their parents. Men were more highly paid than women.
- Few of the households had moved to Hackney from outside London. Most had been brought up in prosperous London suburbs.
- Despite the high incomes and high-status jobs, there was long-standing support for the Labour Party and generally for progressive political causes.
- Gentrifiers of this sort constitute a distinctive fraction of the middle class, working in media, arts, education and advertising, politically radical and anti-Conservative, and attracted by living in places that previously housed the working class.

So far we have considered the kinds of social life within particular areas of Britain, but we have not considered the mobility of family households between different parts of the UK. This process of geographical mobility is explored in box 10.2 with regard to the service class.

Finally, households look to towns and cities to provide them with a wide array of services, sometimes concentrated in particular places. Examples include financial serv-

---

Box 10.2   The service class and geographical mobility

Savage and his collaborators (1992) investigated the general connections between the formation of social class and geographical mobility between different regions. In particular they explored the role of the south-east, which they describe as an 'escalator region'.

In the 1980s the south-east of England came to play a particularly important role within the overall British economy (as just seen in the growth of Hackney). There was an exceptional growth of companies producing services, both for consumers (such as hotels, restaurants, bars and leisure centres) and for producers (such as lawyers, accountants, advertisers and bankers). Many of these firms contained very significant numbers of service-class personnel (for a definition of the service class see pp. 174ff). The south-east attracted a large number of potential recruits to the service class, especially from those attending higher education institutions in the region. There was a great deal of mobility between firms and occupations for those young service-class recruits in the south-east. Many of these people were rapidly promoted into positions of authority within these firms.

But then as their careers matured a proportion of these people left the south-east. Hence, the service class outside the area contained a high proportion of people who were 'southerners' or had been 'southerners'. The south-east thus functions as an 'escalator region', one in which young people destined for the service class are often trained and where they initially work, but from which they may move away as their careers develop. So although the south-east appears to be overrepresented in the service class, quite a significant proportion will in fact leave to pursue their careers in other regions across the UK. This also means that some of the social and cultural practices associated with the service class in the south-east are widely disseminated.

Savage et al. thus suggest that there may be a process of national homogenization of the service class as a result of these mobility patterns. Interestingly, though, many such people become particularly keen on conservation, either of rural or of urban areas (such as the De Beauvoir area in Hackney). Some reduction in the mobility of the service class, especially of those over their mid-30s, means that they become particularly interested in what happens to their locality and, in many cases, very keen to prevent new developments (as we saw in the case of urban newcomers in the countryside). So the service class is 'nationalized' but also increasingly involved in local issues. Processes of social class formation are thus importantly geographical and not simply social.

ices in London, entertainment services at Blackpool, cultural services within Edinburgh, educational services within Cambridge, sports facilities in Sheffield, heritage in the north-west of England, and so on. These services are moreover important in attracting new residents and visitors to different places. There is a process of competition, and in part British towns and cities are competing with places abroad, especially in Europe. The designation of Glasgow as the 1990 European City of Culture is a good example of an effort by a British city to refashion itself, to participate in a competition between what have been called 'European city-states'. Part of this competition involves many towns and cities trying to develop their range of leisure, cultural, entertainment and sporting services so as to be increasingly attractive to tourists. This was one of the fastest grow-ing areas of investment and employment in the 1980s and many local authorities have seen it as one of the few sources of jobs and income.

Many of these towns and cities have sought to present themselves as 'historical' or as 'heritage cities'. This has involved the conservation of many old buildings constructed in the local vernacular style, including factories, mills, workers' cottages, alleyways, docks, warehouses and inns (as we saw in the case of Hackney). Often this preservation first occurred because of campaigns by members of the service class. But this conserved environment can then be turned by a mixture of public and private interests into a set of townscapes suitable for what one may term 'visual consumption'. This is achieved by associations forming to clean up the environment to produce a 'heritage effect', decorat-ing it with suitable street furniture, and then encouraging the private sector to establish appropriate shops, restaurants, bars, leisure clubs and so on. See section 10.5 below.

Summary

1 The kinds of rural and urban places that one lives in or which one visits are strongly affected by historical notions of the nature of the countryside and how they contrast with towns and cities.
2 British countrysides are very diverse and subject to conflict and change, especially over the organization of different kinds of leisure activity.
3 British towns and cities have been subject to many economic and social changes that transform the associational activities that are possible within them.
4 Contemporary towns and cities are becoming important sites for consumption.

10.4   Religious communities

Religion in Britain is a paradox. On the one hand, formal religion appears to be in decline. Unlike in the USA, only a small and declining minority of the population regu-larly attend religious worship or are members of the major religious associations. On the other hand, there is considerable religious activity. Certain faiths, chiefly non-Christian or evangelical Christian ones, are growing. The clergy, whether Anglican or Roman Catholic, are listened to and their pronouncements can generate considerable controversy. The ordination of women has been a major public issue in many churches.

Further, while people are not publicly religious, they continue to have private religious beliefs. In this section we explore this paradox.

Church adherence

Table 10.6 shows that there has been a steady decline in the membership of most Christian churches. In 1994 only 13.9 per cent of the population were active members of a Christian church. If the historic rate of decline is projected forward to 2005, this figure will fall to 12.2 per cent. It is, however, important to note that church membership is dynamic. Even those churches that are in decline are recruiting new members; it is simply that rather more people leave. Only the Pentecostal, New and Orthodox churches have shown a net growth in membership and these are all relatively small.

TABLE 10.6 | **Membership of Christian churches, 1975–2005**

Church	1975	1980	1985	1990	1992	1994	2000	2005
Anglican	2 297 871	2 179 458	2 016 943	1 871 977	1 812 492	1 760 070	1 604 450	1 491 550
Baptist	235 884	239 780	243 051	230 858	228 199	229 276	230 010	229 276
Roman Catholic	2 605 255	2 454 253	2 279 065	2 198 694	2 087 511	2 002 758	1 830 865	1 685 650
Independent	240 200	227 782	225 634	221 444	214 246	210 200	201 300	194 260
Methodist	576 791	520 557	474 290	443 323	434 606	420 836	379 825	355 550
New churches	12 060	25 250	80 494	125 869	149 556	164 317	200 300	233 000
Orthodox	196 850	203 165	223 721	265 968	276 080	283 897	309 565	331 960
Other churches	137 083	131 510	126 127	121 681	120 609	119 453	115 988	113 970
Pentecostal	101 648	126 343	136 582	158 505	169 071	183 109	210 600	232 000
Presbyterian	1 589 085	1 437 775	1 322 029	1 213 920	1 172 011	1 120 383	995 496	889 174
Total	7 992 727	7 545 873	7 127 936	6 852 239	6 664 381	6 494 299	6 078 399	5 756 390
Of which *free* churches	1 303 666	1 270 862	1 286 178	1 301 680	1 316 287	1 327 191	1 338 023	1 358 050
Percentage total is of adult population	19.5	16.9	15.5	14.7	14.3	13.9	12.8	12.2

Source: Adapted from Brierley and Wraight 1995, p. 240

Membership may, however, be an unreliable guide to the number of people who take their religion seriously. The individual churches define what membership means for them and are responsible for submitting the returns that form the basis for tables such as 10.6. Definitions vary between the different churches. In addition, membership figures may be inflated because they do not entirely reflect turnover; that is, they include people who have lapsed from membership, and this may be particularly true of the smaller churches. Moreover, people who are members of churches may not frequently attend acts of worship. Thus, although one in seven adults in Britain is a member of the Anglican church, only one in ten goes to church each week, although the proportion rises for less frequent worship.

Other indicators of participation show the same numerical decline. Within the Anglican church, for example, infant baptisms have declined from 672 per thousand births in 1950 to 275 in 1990. Confirmations of young people similarly fell from 191,000 to 84,500 between 1960 and 1982 (Davie 1994). The number of ministers dropped from 13,543 in 1975 to 12,211 in 1994 and the number of churches from 19,795 to 18,799 in the same period (Brierley and Wraight 1995). While 60 per cent of marriages took place in a Christian church in 1971, the proportion had dropped to 53 per cent by 1989.

It is frequently said this decline in active membership and participation in religious associations constitutes a general process of secularization. In the past, the argument runs, there were many more churchgoers and Britain was more devout. The twentieth century brought with it a greater secularism. The comparison is usually made with the mid-nineteenth century, since there was a religious census conducted in 1851 and churches kept good records. It is certainly true that this comparison does show a steady process of secularization, whether one considers membership, attendance at worship, Sunday School attendance, baptisms or confirmations (Currie, Gilbert and Horsley 1977). Finke and Starke (1992), for example, calculate church membership in Britain was 16.7 per cent in 1850 and 18.6 per cent in 1900, certainly higher than the 12.2 per cent in 1994.

However, the late eighteenth and nineteenth centuries manifested a pattern of religious growth that was historically unusual. By contrast, in the medieval and early modern periods there is evidence that church attendance was low (Finke and Starke 1992). As with many historical comparisons, it all depends what point in the past is selected for comparison. Compared with the nineteenth and early twentieth centuries, modern Britain is more secular. But if the comparison is with the eighteenth century or earlier, then the position is less clear cut.

There are various reasons for this twentieth-century decline in what we can call institutional adherence – participation in the formal associations of the Christian churches. The state has grown in power and the Church of England is not so involved in the political process. Science and the institutions of scientific work have grown in importance and claim to solve problems, such as those of health or the origins of the universe, which previously were the province of religious institutions. Many of the welfare and charitable functions of the churches are now also performed by other agencies.

It is worth noting, however, that this decline in institutional adherence is uneven. Women are markedly more religious than men. Similarly, elderly people are more religious than the young, although it is unclear whether this is because of a steady process of historical secularization or because people become more religious as they get older and get closer to their own death.

There are also substantial regional variations within the UK. Church membership and attendance at worship are much higher in Northern Ireland and Scotland than in England. In England about 11 per cent of the population are church members while in Northern Ireland the corresponding figure is around 70 per cent. The 'Celtic Fringe' – Wales, Scotland and Northern Ireland – is more devout than England (Greeley 1992), although even in England some individual parishes, especially in rural areas, are growing.

The overall decline in institutional adherence does not, however, necessarily mean that Christianity – or religion in general – is a spent force in Britain. There are three further factors that have to be considered: those religious associations that continue to maintain their vigour, the importance of civic religion, and the importance of private religious beliefs.

Vigorous religion

Although a large proportion of the population regard themselves as nominally Anglican and an even larger proportion see themselves as Christian, these faiths are not now so typical of the religious experience of the whole British population.

First, some movements in Christianity have shown great vigour. As we noted from table 10.6, some smaller Protestant churches, Pentecostalism and the evangelical new churches, have been growing in membership. The House Church movement within the group of new churches, for example, increased its membership from an estimated 100 in 1970 to around 120,000 in 1995. The Pentecostal movement, which is growing more slowly, is composed of a large number of small and usually locally based churches such as the Beneficial Veracious Christ Church or the London Happy Church. Pentecostalism is particularly favoured by those with an Afro-Caribbean background.

More striking still is the importance of non-Christian faiths, as table 10.7 shows. Except for Judaism all these non-Christian religions increased their membership from 1975 to 1995, and are projected to continue to do so. This religious growth partly derives from the continued effects of past migration from the Indian subcontinent (see also section 8.2). Particularly noteworthy is the increase in membership of the Muslim community, so that by 1990 there were more Muslims than Methodists. Britain is becoming much more diverse in its religious associations. Multi-faith Britain is, however, geographically uneven. Members of non-Christian faiths are almost all concentrated in large metropolitan centres, while there are extensive areas of the country, especially rural areas, with very few Muslims, Sikhs, Hindus or Jews.

TABLE 10.7	Membership of non-Christian religions, 1970–95 (thousands)					
Church	1970	1975	1980	1985	1990	1995
Hindus	80	100	120	130	140	145
Muslims	130	204	306	435	495	586
Sikhs	100	115	150	160	250	350
Jews	120	115	111	105	101	96
Others	24	35	46	61	75	94

Source: Derived from Brierley and Wraight 1995, pp. 282–3

The transformations in the religious map of Britain are summarized in figure 10.1.

New religious movements

The Christian and non-Christian faiths that are growing are vigorous, not only in an increasing membership, but also in the religious commitment that their members display. Acts of worship are often more dramatic, noisy and enthusiastic than those held in orthodox Christian churches. This is even more the case with new religious movements (NRMs). The members of such associations are so committed to their faith that their

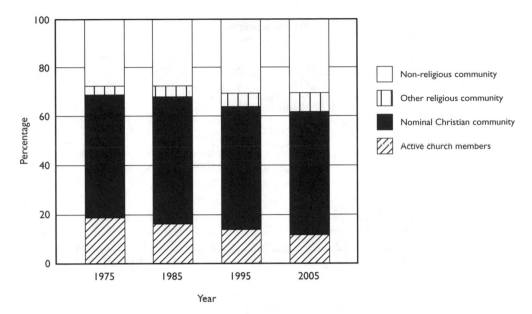

Figure 10.1 | Religious components of the population, 1975–2005
Source: Brierley and Wraight 1995, p. 284

everyday lives are inextricably bound up with it. Since the late 1970s or so, much public attention has concentrated on these new religious associations.

Such movements (often called cults) have also attracted considerable sociological interest. By contrast with orthodox faiths, almost all involve a conversion experience and provide some insight into how conversion occurs. They all involve conviction and hence illustrate how values more generally are formed and transformed. Most of them excite controversy and thus demonstrate how society defines deviant groups. And such NRMs have been formed internationally, especially demonstrating the influence of the cultures of the 'East' over those of the 'West'.

There are a very large number of new religious associations or movements; possibly 500 in Britain (Barker 1989). Most prominent are the Unification Church (the Moonies), the Hare Krishna movement, Transcendental Meditation and Scientology. It is tempting to treat these as rather similar since they are undoubtedly new and religious and, above all, seem to inspire their believers with a degree of commitment and dedication missing in many older churches. However, these NRMs are in fact diverse. Wallis (1984) proposes a typology of new religious movements. There are three types: world-rejecting, world-affirming and world-accommodating. These relationships are shown in figure 10.2, although of course many NRMs actually fall between these types.

World-rejecting movements tend to be exclusive, being based on the importance of the community as against the individual. Converts are expected to renounce their past lives and emotional ties, including those of their family, and the outside world is seen as threatening. The virtues of sharing money, clothes and affection are emphasized in contrast to individual possession. The submerging of personal identity is sometimes

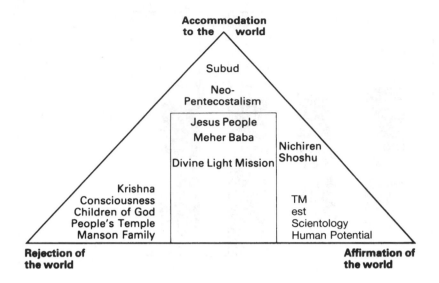

Figure 10.2 | Types of new religious movement
Source: Wallis 1984, p. 6

reflected in the similarity of appearance or dress or in the way in which converts may take new names. Conversion to the world-rejecting movements tends to be sudden, involving a sharp break with the convert's previous life. These movements recruit relatively young people in their early or mid-20s, disproportionately of middle-class origins and highly educated. Wallis (1984) suggests that these recruits are, in addition, socially marginal, perhaps having dropped out of higher education. World-rejecting NRMs appeal to those who have found little satisfaction in the conventional world but who nevertheless hold high expectations.

World-affirming movements see the prevailing social order as having certain virtues. Humankind is seen not as essentially evil but as perfectible and having powers that can be released by participation in the given movement. These may well be part-time movements without acts of collective worship or precise theologies. By contrast with the collective orientations of world-rejecting movements, world-affirming NRMs are individualistic, aiming to unlock the hidden powers latent in each person. The sources of unhappiness, in other words, lie not in the society outside but rather within oneself. There is no rejection of the world involved but an attempt to relate to the world more effectively. Recruitment can be a more gradual process and one that uses existing networks of friends and relatives. World-affirming movements recruit from socially integrated people, not necessarily middle class, with an average age of about 35 and who may be successful, but could be even more so.

World-accommodating movements contrast with both of the above. For world-accommodating movements, religious experience is not social or collective but is personal and individual. It is the importance of individual religious experience that is at the

heart of these movements, such as the growing charismatic, evangelical, renewal movements within Christianity. Acts of worship are enthusiastic and vital, providing participants with a spirituality within their lives which appears to be lacking in the more
orthodox Christian churches.

Many of the new religious movements are very small in membership amounting to a few
hundred. Some argue (Robbins 1988) that there has been a slowing down in the growth
of these NRMs. This may indicate that there are intermittent bouts of religious association growth in modern societies.

The small size of these cults makes it difficult to understand the ferocity of public
reaction to some of them. Societies do sometimes react violently to the presence of strange
and unfamiliar groups in their midst. This reaction tends to vary with what Beckford
(1985) has called the 'mode of insertion' of such cults into society. Those cults that are
world-affirming and are more integrated with the wider society attract less controversy
than the world-rejecting NRMs. One possible explanation for societal reaction to world-
rejecting movements such as the Moonies lies in the centrality of family life in modern
societies. The accusations of brainwashing stem from the sudden and apparently inexplicable way that people are converted and move away from their families. This sudden
cessation of 'normal' family ties seems unnatural and, not surprisingly, the relatives of
Moonie converts often become extremely distressed about it. Ultimately, societal reaction
is determined by the definition of a certain pattern of family relations as natural, right and
proper; deviations from this norm are considered abnormal or even wicked.

Civic religion

Despite the decline in institutional adherence to the major Christian churches, they are
integrated into the dominant English culture, where the Church of England has played
a pivotal role. Many national events – or civic rituals – have a religious component. The
Archbishop of Canterbury, for example, presides at coronations, royal weddings and
funerals, and services of national thanksgiving. Children are brought up in a religious
culture at school, and there are many schools administered and controlled by religious
bodies in which religious instruction is taken seriously. Religious broadcasting is popular and continues to attract significant audiences. Churchmen frequently pronounce
on issues of importance, they are invited onto television to air their opinions, and
their words are widely reported and carry influence. This is particularly so when the
issues are ones of morality on which the churches are deemed especially qualified to
speak. This influence can have definite political impact. For example, the proposal to
lower the age of consent for homosexuals, debated in Parliament in the summer of
1998, was defeated in the House of Lords partly because of the Anglican bishops. The
Christian churches, in short, still have a considerable amount of power and political
influence.

Church influence does not operate only at the national level. Major events in the lives
of people are often commemorated within religious settings. For example, many births,
marriages and deaths are solemnized in church or chapel. We indicated earlier that the
number of people getting married in church was declining. None the less, more than
half of weddings in Britain do still take place in church.

So far, in describing ritual observances which have a religious or more narrowly Anglican character, we have concentrated on fairly formal events. There are less formal, but none the less very significant, events which have a religious or quasi-religious character. Recent examples include the outpouring of popular grief after the Hillsborough football stadium disaster in 1989 and the death of the Princess of Wales in 1997. These involve suspensions of the routines of everyday life, in which a very large number of people have what can only be described as a spiritual experience. Furthermore, this experience has a clear ritual character in that a substantial part of the population travels, often a considerable distance, to participate. In both of the examples cited, it is estimated that one million people took part in memorial services. The Church of England is actively involved, the event is suffused with religious imagery, and the memorial services are conducted by religious leaders, who are normally from the Anglican church.

Private religion

The limited institutional adherence to the major Christian churches does not necessarily mean that people are no longer privately religious. Berger (1968), for example, argues that religion in modern societies is pushed increasingly into the sphere of the family or even the individual. Religion becomes a question of private feeling rather than of public worship or even public morality. There is some evidence that, in Britain, religion does flourish in the private sphere, even when its public significance is in decline. According to a recent survey of religious beliefs and attitudes (Greeley 1992), 69 per cent of the population believe in God, 55 per cent in a life after death, 45 per cent in religious miracles, and 28 per cent in the devil. Forty-three per cent described themselves as religious, 28 per cent had had an intense religious experience, and 27 per cent prayed at least once a week. Women are consistently more religious in their beliefs and private practices than men. For example, 76 per cent of women believe in God compared with 60 per cent of men.

There is, however, some controversy as to the meaning of these findings. For example, Abercrombie et al. (1970) found a large reservoir of beliefs that are non-scientific or spiritual. Many respondents engaged in superstitious or luck-bringing practices such as touching wood or throwing salt over the shoulder. 'It seems that for many people, probably the great majority, religious beliefs and practices merge almost indistinguishably with superstitions of all sorts, to be summoned only in special situations of crisis and anxiety' (Abercrombie et al. 1970, p. 113). Private prayer, or even a belief in God, may be more like magic than any formal Christian religion. Thus contemporary religious beliefs form more of a continuity with the magical beliefs of medieval and early modern Europe. Formal, institutional adherence to religious associations may thus be a minority phenomenon that is laid on top of a much larger set of mundane beliefs and practices that enable people to cope with the demands and uncertainties of everyday life.

A further point that adds some weight to this conclusion is the confusion between magical, spiritual and religious matters that many people appear to feel. For example, if people have their belief in the existence of God further investigated, a complex picture emerges. Asked to identify which statement comes closest to their beliefs about God:

- 11 per cent said they 'do not believe in God';
- 11 per cent 'do not know if God exists and cannot find evidence for God's existence';
- 12 per cent 'believe in a higher power of some kind';
- 12 per cent 'believe sometimes';
- 23 per cent 'doubt but believe';
- 21 per cent believe that 'God exists, but with doubts' (*Social Trends* 1997, p. 193).

This pattern does not indicate a confident belief in God, but rather a series of doubts and confusions. But at the other end of the spectrum, Greeley (1992) shows that non-believers in God are similarly confused. For example, many of those who say that they do not believe in God actually report having had an intense religious experience, praying at least once a week, or supporting religious worship in schools.

The relationship between religious belief, church attendance and church membership in 1990 is summarized in figure 10.3.

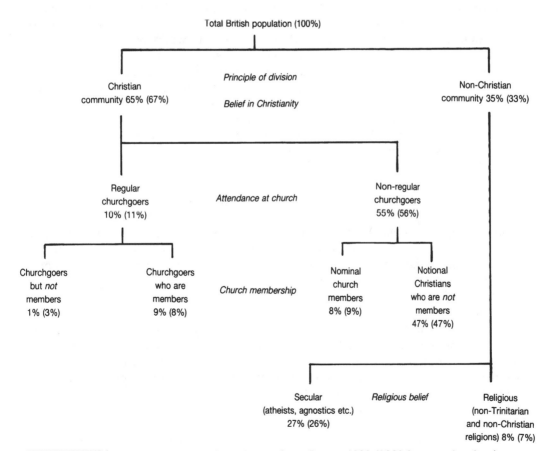

Figure 10.3 | Religious structure of population, Great Britain, 1990 (1980 figures in brackets)
Source: Brierley 1991, p. 203

Summary

- There is a decline in institutional adherence to the main Christian churches although they continue to be important in public life.
- There is, however, growth in various religious associations in Britain, in some branches of Christianity and especially in non-Christian faiths and movements.
- Many people express private religious beliefs although it is not altogether clear in what sense these are religious.
- The position of the majority of the British population may be summed up in Davie's (1994) phrase, 'believing without belonging'.

10.5   Social and political networks

In this section we consider some further 'communities', some of which are connected to the rural, urban and religious movements we have already discussed. We are concerned here with organizations which are joined out of choice, to which people may dedicate substantial amounts of time and which are the focus of working together for a common purpose. Such voluntary associations include organizations dedicated to world peace, groups organized around particular medical conditions, familiar charities such as the British Red Cross, fan clubs, associations dedicated to particular hobbies, self-help groups, animal rights organizations and countryside organizations. For the purposes of our discussion they may be divided into three groups: traditional voluntary organizations, newer movements often organized around protest, and enthusiasms.

Voluntary organizations

Voluntary organizations, which are very frequently constituted as charities, have been part of the British social landscape for many years. Over time, some kinds of organization grow while others decline. For example, the membership of many traditional and women's organizations has fallen during the post-war period. Between 1971 and 1990, the Mothers' Union declined from 308 thousand members to 177 thousand, the National Union of Townswomen's Guilds from 216 thousand to 105 thousand, and the women's section of the Royal British Legion from 162 thousand to 112 thousand. On the other hand, during the same period, organizations broadly to do with the environment increased in membership. The National Trust, for example, had 278 thousand members in 1971 but more that 2 million in 1995, the Royal Society for the Protection of Birds' membership increased from 98 thousand to 890 thousand, while the World Wildlife Fund for Nature moved from 12 thousand to 219 thousand (*Social Trends* 1992, 1997).

Despite variations of this kind, overall it is likely that there is growth in membership of voluntary organizations that exceeds population growth (P. A. Hall 1998). Since such a conclusion refers only to those organizations that have been in existence for some time, it will understate the vigour of the voluntary sector, as large numbers of new such organizations are created every year (estimated at some 3,000–4,000). Looking at membership from the point of view of the individual produces the same result. Hall reports that the average number of memberships per member of the population was 1.12 in 1990 compared with 0.73 in 1959. In 1992/3, about one-quarter of the population had been involved in voluntary activity of some kind. Of these, half had spent 20 or more days per year in that activity (*Social Trends* 1996).

In sum, a substantial proportion of the population are members of voluntary organizations to which they dedicate much of their time and energy. Even this understates the degree to which people engage in associations with others, since there are newer forms of association including vegetarian groups, spiritual/therapy groups, festivals, road protests, dance culture, direct action organizations, community groups ethnic groupings, women's groups, travellers, gay/lesbian groups and environmental pressure groups. Maffesoli (1996) refers to the emergence of these groups in almost all Western societies as reflecting the 'time of the tribes'.

Networks of resistance

It is argued that one effect of an individualized and marketized society is to generate social networks that in part evade the logic of the market, through establishing various forms of gift-giving, voluntary work, self-help networks and friendship. These acquire value as ways of resisting the global market place. Many voluntary associations are organized around the idea of resistance. These resistant networks 'defend their spaces, their places, against the placeless logic of the space of [global] flows characterizing social domination in the Information Age' (Castells 1997, p. 358; see section 2.4).

Hetherington (1998, ch. 4) argues that these networks should be characterized as bunde. The bund involves community, but a community that is conscious and freely chosen on the basis of mutual sentiment and emotional feeling. Affective commitment to the bund is conscious, rational and non-traditional. Such bunde are not permanent or necessarily stable. They produce self-enclosed worlds with a particular code of practice and set of symbols. Bunde involve the blurring of the public and the private spheres of the lives of their members.

Bunde point to the important role of relatively informal and overlapping networks which are culturally defined. Bunde are normally joined out of choice and people are free to leave. Indeed people rapidly enter and leave such associations. They remain members in part because of the emotional satisfaction that they derive from common goals or shared social experiences. These associations enable people to experiment with new kinds of living together that are often temporary. They may empower people, providing relatively safe places for identity-testing and the context for learning new skills, such as organizing meetings, using the internet or speaking in public.

Mckay has recently elaborated the main features of some such bunde in Britain (see box 10.3).

Box 10.3   Mckay's 'cultures of resistance since the sixties'

Mckay (1996) concentrates upon those bunde that since the 1960s have resisted many features of the wider society, such as promoters of free festivals, New Age travellers, punk musicians, developers of the rave culture, road protesters and those opposing the Criminal Justice and Public Order Act of 1994. He emphasizes three features of these bunde.

First, there is the way in which such groupings construct their own spaces. Normally these spaces convey some sense of the previous forms of building or element of 'nature' that occurred in that particular place, such as fairs, markets, houses, woods, workshops, rivers and so on. Such spaces are often defined against those of the rest of society. These places of 'alternative ordering' are characterized by unsettling and often shocking juxtapositions of unlikely objects.

Second, the dwellings of such bunds are often impermanent. They are characterized, according to one participant, by 'their shared air of impermanence, of being ready to move on . . . re-locate to other universities, mountain-tops, ghettos, factories, safe houses, abandoned farms' (quoted in Mckay 1996, p. 8). There is a sense of movement, as happens in the case of a peace convoy. Their spaces are constituted through various route-ways rather than the permanent forms of dwelling. Emotionally intense communion through likeness and friendship takes place within specific places at particular moments in the year.

Finally, groupings form a 'loose network of loose networks', such as those involved in free festivals, rural fairs, alternative music, hunt saboteurs, road protests, New Age travellers, rave culture, Poll Tax protest, peace convoys, animal rights and so on. These networks are reinforced by various patterns of travel in which there is a mapping of key events and places. A member of the Donga tribe, which first came to prominence at the protest against the building of the M3 across Twyford Down, well expresses both the impermanent and changing nature of the Dongas:

> The Tribe itself has grown and diversified in that time with some people now working full-time in the grassroots protest movement which has sprung up, or in related areas such as tree-planting and permaculture. A small group continues to live a nomadic lifestyle, moving from hillfort to hillfort with horses, donkeys and handmade carts to transport personal and communal possessions. We remain in close contact and meet up often at major seasonal celebrations and feel bound together through our experiences and shared vision. (quoted in Mckay 1996, p. 143)

One particular network consists of the travellers, self-styled groupings of young people who choose to spend at least some of the year moving irregularly in convoy through the countryside (Mckay 1996, ch. 2; Hetherington 1998). Such travellers live in brightly painted, makeshift lorries, buses and caravans which constitute their places of dwelling. But they also dwell in irregular movement, their timetable being constituted through various free festivals, sacred sites and special routes. Such travellers thus form bund-like communities, joined and left out of choice, impermanent and mobile.

Particularly intense hostility can be expressed against such travellers, who might dwell for a while in the midst of attractive English villages. Hetherington summarizes the response to such an 'invasion': as 'has been the case with Jews and gypsies down the centuries, the "New Age travellers" are hated not because they are always on the move but because they might stay and "contaminate"', particularly because they almost use dirt as a mode of resistance against what they see as the oppressive society (Hetherington 1992, p. 91).

Enthusiasms

Some bunde can also be conceptualized as 'collective enthusiasms' (Hoggett and Bishop 1986). Such enthusiasms carry out a great deal of 'work' that is normally done in what is people's apparently formal 'leisure' time. These leisure activities are often more engaging than people's actual (paid) work experiences. The members of the enthusiasm work through reciprocity and mutual aid. Members of such leisure associations are self-organized and particularly resentful of outside experts instructing them how to act or to manage themselves. Much emphasis is placed upon acquiring through networks arcane forms of knowledge and skill. And there is often strong resistance to the products or the forms of labour involved being turned into commodities.

Many outputs are produced by such enthusiasms, including those that are artistic, written, sporting, spoken and visual. These outputs are mainly consumed by the members themselves or by their families and friends (Hoggett and Bishop 1986, p. 42). People's activities within such enthusiasms are not passive and individualistic but involve communication, networking and moments of emotional satisfaction at particular events, which they will travel to and which are timetabled at particular moments within the yearly calendar. There are obviously tens of thousands of such enthusiasms within advanced societies, ranging from fan organizations which are very much connected with the media, through various cults, to the purer collective enthusiasms such as 'hot-rodding', soccer or tropical fish.

Moorhouse suggests that an enthusiasm like hot-rodding will be characterized by a core of professionals, amateurs and 'intellectuals', surrounding which are the interested public and then beyond that the general public (1991; and see Abercrombie and Longhurst 1998). The intellectuals of hot-rodding particularly emphasize the values of community, hard work and skill – these are seen as opposed to the values of the market place. They point especially to the dangers of commercial interest, and to how professional hot-rodders depend upon the existence of large numbers of amateurs who have been responsible for many innovations within this enthusiasm. There is a collective production and consumption of the outputs of hot-rodding. This sense of community is reproduced through magazines, videos and intermittent race meetings.

One popular set of enthusiasms is concerned with 'heritage'. Normally what is remembered as heritage is that of national elites. In England, it is the houses and estates of the mostly agrarian-based landed class living in the south that have been 'saved for the nation' by the National Trust and other preservationist organizations (Samuel 1994, pt III). But recently, many other groups have actively sought to save 'their history' as opposed to the history of national elites. Examples include enthusiasms to preserve railway engines, canals, industrial archaeology sites, docks, ancient languages, trees, steam traction engines, cottages, mills and derelict coal mines.

Since the early 1960s there has been a proliferation of many new heritage sites, which have often been started and run by enthusiasts who in a sense are helping to extend and elaborate civil society. Samuel notes that there are now nearly 13,000 designated ancient monuments, new museums open once a fortnight, there are 78 museums devoted to railways, and 180 water- and windmills are open to the public (1994, pt II). Samuel cites some telling examples within Britain of such collections resulting from social associations of heritage: a mustard museum in Norwich, exhibitions celebrating the inter-war semi-detached house, the Trerice museum of lawnmowers, the Victoria and Albert exhibition of inter-war wirelesses, and a museum memorializing the glories of polystyrene (1994, pp. 151–4).

Samuel summarizes the new democratic, familial, workerist, feminine, consumerist and domestic heritages which these collective enthusiasms have documented, laid out for display, and sought to bring in visitors to see, touch, hear and remember:

> the 'heritage' which conservationists fight to preserve and retrieval projects to unearth, and which the holiday public or museum visitors are invited to 'experience', is in many ways a novel one. Though indubitably British . . . it departs quite radically from textbook versions of 'our island story'. It has little to do with the continuities of monarchy, parliament or

---

Box 10.4   Gaelic heritage

Enthusiasts established the Aros heritage centre on the Isle of Skye in Scotland (see Macdonald 1997). Its two founders had been involved in various projects, such as setting up playgroups, primary school projects, community history initiatives, festivals, television broadcasting and so on, all based on reviving the use of the Gaelic language within Scotland. They thought that establishing such a centre would further strengthen Gaelic language and culture and prevent its imminent disappearance.

The founders of Aros use the concept of 'cultural tourism' to indicate that they are trying to provide tourism 'for the people' of Skye, partly by presenting an alternative to the romanticized English-heritage account of Scottish history. In this alternative account it is claimed that Gaelic is the national language for Scotland, although this is historically controversial.

Aros is interestingly a centre with relatively few 'authentic' exhibits – it mostly consists of reproductions of Gaelic history and culture. More important than the exhibits is the story that the centre tells, a story which links together the decline of Gaelic culture with the history of resistance of the people not only to the English but also to the Scottish clan chiefs. So Aros developed out of a collective enthusiasm for preserving the Gaelic language and for telling a different story of how social life developed and mutated within the Scottish Highlands. The establishment of Aros is viewed by this association of alternative, upwardly mobile Gaelic speakers as compatible with commercial enterprise and not in contradiction to it.

British national institutions . . . It is the little platoons, rather than the great society, which command attention in this new version of the national past. (1994, p. 158)

In box 10.4 we consider a recent example of how a resistant enthusiasm of the 'little platoons' in the Isle of Skye led to a commercially successful heritage centre being established.

Summary

1   There are very many associations that engage people in their leisure time, often providing skills and interests greater than they find at work.
2   Some of these involve a kind of resistance to aspects of British society and to the nature of the market place. These can best be understood as bunds.
3   Some bunde emerge around enthusiasms that are also defined in part in opposition to aspects of commodification. One important set of enthusiasms is concerned with preserving many different kinds of heritage, not just that of the national elites.

Related topics

On relations with immediate family see sections 9.5 and 9.6. Further material on the significance of tourism to the countryside and the city appears in section 11.4. More on the consumption patterns of the fraction of the middle class involved in gentrification is in section 6.4. The role of religion in the social identity of ethnic minority groups is discussed in section 8.3.

Further reading

Chapters in Jamieson (1998) and Buck et al. (1994) explore aspects of relationships with family and friends. Allan (1989) deals with the topic of friendship. See Savage and Warde (1993) on the urban. A good guide to contemporary religious practice, largely Christian, is Davie (1994). A recent book on new religious movements is Heelas (1996). On political and social networks, see Hetherington (1998), although some of this is difficult. On heritage enthusiasms, see Samuel (1994).

Cross-references to *Readings in Contemporary British Society*

Hetherington on the social relationships of travellers; **Finch and Mason** on relationships with the wider kinship network.

Leisure

11.1   Introduction

It is widely argued that Britain has become a leisure society. More people have more time and more money to indulge leisure pursuits, whether these be watching television, going on holiday or day trips, playing sports or going to the theatre. This growth in leisure is related to wider social trends, which are examined in this chapter and in the rest of the book. On the one hand, the great bulk of leisure time is spent in the home. This contributes to a tendency to family privatization – to the withdrawal into the home and family. On the other hand, much leisure provision is commercialized and can therefore be seen as part of the growth of consumer society. Also, access to leisure pursuits is unevenly distributed in the population. The professional classes are, for example, much more likely to engage in active leisure pursuits outside the home than the unskilled.

11.2   Leisure, work and non-work

The definition of leisure

Since the Second World War, there has been much public discussion about the leisure society. People have spent less time in paid employment and, as a consequence, have had more time for themselves and for their leisure activities. At the same time, leisure has become a specialized area of human activity. A lot of time is spent thinking about it or planning it, there are magazines devoted to various ways of spending leisure time, and, importantly, whole industries have grown up to service leisure needs. Furthermore, in future years, it seems likely that the population of the UK will spend less time at work and will have more time and money to devote to their leisure pursuits. Many pundits argue that leisure will be the priority of the future, not work, and the problem will be to find enough creative and absorbing leisure activities for the population.

These statements imply that leisure is defined in terms of work. That, indeed, is how our society sees it. Leisure is the opposite of work. It represents choice, freedom, fun and pleasure while work is seen as constraining, limiting, dull, grinding and boring. There are, however, obvious difficulties in defining leisure in this way. First, it misrepresents the nature of *work*, for many people at least. For those in non-routine or professional employment, work can be creative and pleasurable and is a realm of human experience characterized by freedom and choice rather than by constraint. Even for those who have relatively routine jobs over which they have little control, while the work itself is not a source of creativity or pleasure, it none the less gives social contact which is pleasurable. For example, in her study of a clothing factory, Westwood (1984) notes that, for the women employees, work is repetitive, unskilled and hard and they are closely controlled and monitored. Yet in the women's response to work the friendships are crucial:

> this was a cultural response which emphasized friendship and solidarity and which was oppositional, energetic and potentially very powerful. Women on the shopfloor attacked life with great energy and verve; there was nothing to suggest defeat or submission or that they were cyphers or puppets. (p. 90)

Second, the definition of leisure in terms of work may misrepresent the nature of *leisure*. Some people, indeed, seem to fill their leisure hours with the same grim determination that they bring to their work. This has led some writers to argue that it is wrong to see leisure as activities that have been freely chosen and which represent an assertion of individuality (see Rojek 1985, 1989). According to their account, what passes as leisure in modern Britain is just as highly organized and constraining as work. Thus leisure pursuits often have to be planned and regulated; they are often seen as compelling (e.g. DIY, caring for a neighbour); they are measured (particularly in sports); and they are commercialized.

Third, many people in our society do not have paid work with which their leisure can be contrasted. The young or those in full-time education, the retired and elderly, the unemployed and long-term sick, and parents at home caring for children may have part-time work, but they do not have an all-embracing paid occupation. All these points suggest that some care should be exercised in defining leisure in terms of work and that at times it may be positively misleading to do so; they are not separate phenomena (Moorhouse 1989). For the purposes of this section, however, we will continue to see leisure time as that time free of what the participants define as work or that set of activities in which they have little choice, whether paid or not. For women at home, for example, leisure activities are contrasted with domestic work, caring for dependent relatives, or part-time paid work. The same is true for large numbers of elderly and unemployed. Again, many young people see their lives in terms not of work but of leisure, even if that perception only lasts a few years.

To talk of a leisure society, therefore, is to say that more people, certainly over their lifetime, have more time free of what they define as work and have more money to devote to leisure pursuits. This is not to say, of course, that this generalization is true of everybody and, as we shall see later, different social groups will have very different amounts of resource, whether of time or money, to give to their non-work lives. Since the start of the twentieth century the number of hours actually worked (including overtime and short-time) has steadily fallen. For example, manual workers in most industries worked an average of more than 55 hours a week at the beginning of the century. This had fallen to 50 hours by 1943 and less than 43 by 1985. Martin and Mason (1994) estimate that the total amount of leisure time available to the British population rose by an average of 0.5 per cent per year from 1982 to 1992, although there are signs that, more recently still, this trend has slackened or even reversed. In considering the relationship between work and leisure time for the population as a whole, it is important to keep three points in mind. First, there are large differences between sectors of the population. As we have already indicated, many people do not have paid work at all either because they are unemployed or because they are too young or too old. At the same time, those who are employed work very different amounts; there has, for example, been a substantial increase in part-time working among women since the late 1940s. Second, even if working hours fall over time, the pattern of work may change in such a way that the opportunities for leisure are not thereby increased. Thus, greater flexibility of work, involving overtime and/or shift work, may make it more difficult to engage in leisure activities which involve others. One in six employees now works in the evening and one in two working men and one in three working women work for some or all of Sunday. Third, the British work longer hours than their continental European counterparts (see section 6.3).

TABLE 11.1	Time use by employment status and gender, May 1995 (hours)						
	In full-time employment		In part-time employment		Retired		All adults
	Males	Females	Males	Females	Males	Females	
Weekly hours spent on							
Sleep	57	58	62	60	67	66	61
Free time	34	31	48	32	59	52	40
Work, study and travel to work	53	48	28	26	3	4	32
Housework, cooking and shopping	7	15	12	26	15	26	16
Eating, personal hygiene and caring	13	13	13	21	15	17	15
Household maintenance and pet care	4	2	6	3	9	3	4
Free time per weekday	4	4	6	4	8	7	5
Free time per weekend day	8	6	8	6	10	8	8

Source: *Social Trends* 1996, p. 216

Table 11.1 shows in more detail how a sample of the population used their time in 1995. For those in full-time work, sleep was the activity taking up most time in the week. Work, study and travel to work was close behind. There are clear differences between men and women. For all employment statuses, women have less free time than men because they spend so much more time in domestic labour of all kinds (see sections 7.3 and 9.5). Not surprisingly, for both men and women, the more paid work one does, the less free time one has available (though note the very small differences between full-time and part-time women). In the next section we look at the patterns of the use of free time in more detail.

The manner in which people can avail themselves of leisure time clearly depends on the money that they can spend. Since the beginning of the twentieth century, and especially since the Second World War, as people have become more affluent, so expenditure on leisure has increased. Table 11.2 shows that the proportion of household leisure expenditure rose from 13.4 per cent to 15.6 per cent between 1981 and 1989.

The patterns of leisure

The patterns of leisure seem to be changing in that there appears to be an increasing tendency to spend leisure time within the home. There is a variety of indices of this trend. For example, compared with the position in the late 1960s, people are spending a higher proportion of their budget on alcohol consumed at home and less on cinema visits. As with the expenditure of money so also with the expenditure of time. There is, in other words, less involvement in 'public' spheres of recreation. It is not only that people participate less in public events such as religious festivals, processions, fairs and carnivals (or 'public' holidays). It is also that there is relatively less involvement in lei-

TABLE 11.2 | **Average weekly household expenditure on selected leisure items, 1981–9 (£)**

Items	1981	1986	1989
Alcoholic drink consumed away from home	5.39[a]	5.93	6.92
Meals consumed out[b]		4.38	5.51
Books, newspapers, magazines, etc.	2.00	2.73	3.31
Television, radio and musical instruments	3.26	4.85	5.65
Purchase of materials for home repairs, etc.	1.57	3.06	2.89
Holidays	3.08	5.39	7.76
Hobbies	0.08	0.06	0.09
Cinema admissions	0.14	0.10	0.16
Dance admissions	0.12	0.12	–[c]
Theatre, concert, etc. admissions	0.17	0.29	0.35
Subscription and admission charges to participant sports	0.43	0.71	0.85
Football match admissions	0.06	0.08 ⎫	0.20
Admissions to other spectator sports	0.02	0.04 ⎭	
Sports goods (excluding clothes)	0.26	0.37	0.62
Other entertainment	0.24	0.41	0.70[c]
Total weekly expenditure on above	16.82[d]	28.52	35.01
Expenditure on above items as a percentage of total household expenditure	13.4	16.0	15.6

[a] Including home consumption
[b] Eaten on the premises, excluding state school meals and workplace meals
[c] For 1989, 'Dance admissions' have been included with 'Other entertainment'.
[d] The total for 1981 is not comparable with later years since the figure for the category 'Meals consumed out' is not available.
Source: Social Trends 1992, p. 187

sure activities outside the home. In 1995, both men and women spent about two-thirds of their free time in leisure pursuits at home. So there were fewer visits to the pub or cinema in favour of more drinking at home and a greater dedication to watching television. There was also an increasingly wide range of devices which service home-based leisure. For example, in 1996, 82 per cent of households had a video-recorder, more than double the 38 per cent which owned one in 1986. This process is described more fully in box 11.1.

Many sociologists have seen this as a relatively recent phenomenon, dating perhaps from the Second World War, and as part of a growing tendency to privatization, which consists in a greater involvement of people with their immediate family, a changed pattern of domestic relationships and a greater interest in the home – in furnishing and equipping, interior decoration, gardens and, indeed, in home ownership (see section 10.3).

Tables 11. 3, 11.4 and 11.5 give some idea of the chief leisure activities measured by the amount of time spent on leisure and the frequency of participation in leisure

Box 11.1   The privatization of leisure

The privatization of leisure is a long-term trend in Britain. It is a product of a more mobile population, the decline of local neighbourhood communities, and the rise of the relatively independent nuclear family. The spread of car ownership has accentuated privatization: families with cars can even go out in private. Radio and television have strengthened the home's position as most people's main leisure centre. In recent decades home-centred lifestyles have been further strengthened by the spread of home ownership. Two-thirds of Britain's dwellings are now owner-occupied. This has helped to promote the various forms of do-it-yourself. Home repairs, decorating, car maintenance and gardening are now the nation's main hobbies.

In the 1980s more time than ever is being spent at home, partly as a result of the declining proportion of lifetime claimed by employment. In addition, however, more money is being spent on home recreation, and this spending is mainly by the employed sections of the population. Britain's main growth areas in leisure spending in the 1980s have been on sound and vision reproducing equipment, telecommunications, and computer technology.

The proportion of employment in service sectors has increased, but much of this employment is in producer services such as banking and insurance. The proportion of consumer spending on services has actually declined. There has been a trend towards purchasing goods which are then used for self-servicing. Transport is a prime example. We are buying more motor cars to transport ourselves instead of purchasing bus and train journeys. For entertainment we are purchasing televisions, videos and music centres instead of attending live performances.

Participation has declined in most forms of out-of-home recreation that can be replicated or closely substituted by in-home entertainment. Cinema and theatre audiences, and paid admissions at spectator sports events, are in long-term and continuing decline. In Britain they have now been joined by out-of-home drinking. We are consuming more alcohol per capita than during any previous period in twentieth-century history, but there is less drinking in public houses and more off-sales for home consumption. Drink, film and sports producers have survived by gearing to increasingly home-centred markets. Most films are now made for television and video distribution rather than cinema performances. Live sport is played to tele-viewing audiences. Commercially successful sports promotion now depends on television coverage. The presence of the media attracts sponsors, and attracting the media requires top-level performers. Hence the changing structure of professional sports occupations. Stars command astronomical fees while the rank and file must be motivated primarily by the slender prospect of joining the elite.

Lifestyles are generally home-centred in all social strata, but homes vary tremendously in their comforts. Individuals in employment, who spend least time at home, can best afford large and well-equipped dwellings. Home has different connotations for most of the unemployed and retired, many of whom have become trapped in home-based lifestyles by poverty, and as a result of local community facilities – cinemas, sports teams and pubs – either declining or disappearing completely. (Roberts 1989, pp. 52–4)

TABLE 11.3 | Leisure outside the home, 1961 to 1983–4 (minutes per average day)

Activity	Men, full-time employed			Women, full-time employed		
	1961	1974–5	1983–4	1961	1974–5	1983–4
Travel	5	12	24	5	12	21
Excursions	10	5	1	9	5	0
Playing sport	4	7	10	2	1	2
Watching sport	3	3	2	1	1	1
Walks	4	5	9	4	2	4
Church	3	2	2	4	2	6
Civic duties	6	4	3	2	3	7
Cinema, theatre	4	2	1	6	2	2
Discos, dances, parties, bingo	2	17	5	3	17	7
Social clubs	4	8	5	1	6	2
Pubs	4	14	13	0	3	10
Visiting friends	19	21	18	24	27	21

Source: Adapted from Gershuny and Jones 1987, pp. 38–9

pursuits. The first two tables demonstrate the importance of home-based leisure. In 1983, for example, both women and men spent about 70 per cent of their total leisure time in the home. Within that context, television is, by a very long way, the most significant form of leisure although there are signs that the dedication to television has been falling off in recent years (see section 12.2). At the same time, there are differences within the population in the pattern of leisure activities. Men watch more television and play more sport than women, for example, while women are more likely to spend time talking to people and engaging in voluntary activities of various kinds. The most marked difference, however, is that employed women simply have less leisure time than men. As the discussion in chapter 7 makes plain, employed women still carry out the bulk of domestic work and that necessarily erodes their free time.

In some ways, gender differences in leisure activities are more obvious than those of class. A study by Young and Willmott (1973) showed few class differences between married men, except in certain areas like active sports, reading or gardening. The sharpest class differences are between unskilled or semi-skilled men and other classes taken together. In almost all areas of leisure, whether at home or as active or spectating participants in sports, the professional and managerial classes do more than any other class. This is a finding very much in line with other evidence about non-work activity patterns and it must reflect, amongst other factors, the greater financial resources available to the professional and managerial classes. We should also note that, although Young and Willmott do not show great class differences in most leisure activities, this may in some respects be misleading. For example, the 'quality' of leisure activities will vary across classes. So, even if people of all classes go out occasionally for a meal, professionals may well eat better than the unskilled (see Warde 1997). Professionals, for example, are able to spend 17.7 per cent of their income on leisure goods and services while the unemployed can only manage 11.9 per cent.

TABLE 11.4 | Leisure inside the home, 1961 to 1983-4 (minutes per average day)

Activity	Men, full-time employed			Women, full-time, employed		
	1961	1974–5	1983–4	1961	1974–5	1983–4
Radio	23	5	3	16	3	2
Watching TV	121	126	129	93	103	102
Listening to music	1	3	1	1	1	1
Study	0	1	3	0	0	2
Reading book/papers	28	19	24	13	13	20
Relaxing	20	31	16	27	31	14
Conversations	2	7	14	1	7	21
Entertaining	5	6	6	5	10	7
Knitting, sewing	0	0	0	14	8	7
Hobbies, etc.	8	7	12	3	7	11

Source: Adapted from Gershuny and Jones 1987, p. 42

TABLE 11.5 | Participation in home-based leisure activities: by gender, 1977 to 1993–4 (percentages)

Activity	1977	1980	1986	1990–1	1993–4
Males					
Watching TV	97	97	98	99	99
Visiting/entertaining friends or relations	89	90	92	95	95
Listening to radio	87	88	87	91	91
Listening to records/tapes	64	66	69	78	79
Reading books	52	52	52	56	59
DIY	51	53	54	58	57
Gardening	49	49	47	52	51
Dressmaking/needlework/knitting	2	2	3	3	3
Females					
Watching TV	97	98	98	99	99
Visiting/entertaining friends or relations	93	93	95	97	96
Listening to radio	87	88	85	87	88
Listening to records/tapes	60	62	65	74	75
Reading books	57	61	64	68	71
DIY	22	23	27	29	30
Gardening	35	38	39	44	45
Dressmaking/needlework/knitting	51	51	48	41	38

Source: Social Trends 1997, p. 215

Finally, there are age differences of a kind that one might expect. Younger age groups spend less time in leisure pursuits at home and markedly less in specifically domestic activities such as gardening, sewing or DIY. As Abrams (1995) argues, the elderly would appear to have a great deal of free time but they do not, on the whole, use it for active leisure, since they are constrained by a relative lack of money, ill-health, lower educational levels than the rest of the population, social isolation and a fear of going out.

Although the bulk of leisure time is spent in the home, the data presented in tables 11.3 and 11.4 do not show any great movement, in the twenty years covered, towards a further concentration on home-based leisure. If there has been a privatization of leisure it has taken place over a longer time-scale and, as Allan and Crow (1991) point out, is likely to be associated with the greater tendency of *men* to spend time in the home in the company of their families. It is also worth noting that, since, over the last one hundred years, the *amount* of leisure time has been increasing, any increase in home-based leisure is not necessarily at the expense of leisure outside the home. In sum, in the medium term there has been a privatization of leisure, while, more recently, the trend has stabilized or even, by some measures, been reversed.

Summary

1   Care should be taken when defining leisure in terms of paid work.
2   Since the late 1940s, most people have had more leisure time.
3   The bulk of that leisure time is spent in the home and the most important leisure activity there is watching television.

11.3   Lifestyles and consumer culture

The concept of lifestyle

Lifestyles are sets of attitudes, values, ways of behaving, manners and tastes in everything from music, art and television to gardening and house furnishing. Lifestyles are not the idiosyncratic properties of individuals however much everybody believes that she or he has freely chosen her or his lifestyle. Rather, elements of a lifestyle hang together in some way and are held in common by a number of individuals. Social groups, in other words, are often constituted by the possession of the same lifestyle.

The concept of lifestyle suggests, then, that individuals adopt a stylized approach to life. It is *important* to them that they like Barry Manilow, eat Thai food, stencil their wallpaper, or believe in entertaining in their homes rather than simply meeting in the pub. Many sociologists see this interest in style, certainly as a mass phenomenon, as modern (see, for example, Chaney 1996; Lury 1996). It is since the start of the twentieth century that people have seen the conduct of their lives almost in aesthetic terms. The idea that people adopt lifestyles, take a stylized view of life, implies that they conceive of their lives almost as an artistic project. The various components of their beliefs and practices form a coherent whole in which characteristics that are essentially artistic play an important part; there is a process of the aestheticization of everyday life. It can be further argued that, in this process of stylization, the mass media, as they have become more significant since the beginning of the twentieth century, play an important part. Advertising, television, popular music and magazines provide a stream of images of potential lifestyles. These images then allow people to imagine, and then construct, a lifestyle that pleases them (see chapter 12).

These issues of lifestyle and the aestheticization of everyday life can be illustrated by a consideration of how youth cultures are formed (see section 9.4). In modern Britain, young people have become a focus for attention. It is assumed that being young is somehow special; it is a state that requires public notice from the middle-aged and the old. Obviously, a wide variety of attitudes are mixed up in this, including fear, envy, dislike and even sympathy. Whatever the attitude, however, the young are seen as *different*.

To some extent, sociological analysis of youth culture (or cultures) has adopted the common-sense view of young people as a problematic category, focusing on spectacular youth cultures. These are cultures that construct themselves as spectacles; it is as if they are meant to be looked at. Participants dress flamboyantly and distinctively, are noisy and demonstrative in public places, and appear to behave defiantly in such a way as to attract condemnation. Critical to this spectacularity is the adoption of a particular *style*. Each youth culture has its own particular style, a blend of special tastes in music, clothes, hairstyle or even body language. Furthermore, young people are creative in putting together elements of style drawn from quite different sources; punk style was a case in point. Despite these disparate sources, the elements of youth cultural styles do fit together. Different styles separate one culture from another, give members an identity, and enable them to recognize themselves and others. The post-war period in Britain has seen many examples of spectacular youth cultures differentiated by style: teddy boys, mods, rockers, skinheads, punks, hippies, ravers, crusties, travellers.

Of course, such spectacular youth cultures represent an extreme adoption of style. One study (Willis 1990) found that only 13 per cent of young people questioned claimed to belong to a spectacular youth culture. However, an interest in creating a style is common to almost all young people. We can say that a generalized youth culture has three main features. First, it is a culture of leisure rather than work; the primary focus of attention is on non-work life, and that provides the best means of self-expression. Second, the social relationships of youth cultures are organized around the peer group; they are as much collective as individual. Lastly, as we have already pointed out, youth groups are characterized by a strong interest in style. It is this interest in style that enables us to talk simultaneously about youth culture and youth *cultures*. There are many youth cultures; each is differentiated from the others by its own distinctive style, even if they blend into one another at the boundaries. However, it is also possible to speak of a youth culture that is differentiated from other age cultures in our society by the three features just mentioned. A number of studies have pointed to the ways that young people are creative of their style. In box 11.2, for instance, Willis points to the mechanisms of that creativity.

While youth cultures may provide an obvious example of the use of style, older age groups also engage in lifestyle projects. For example, Savage et al. (1992) conducted a study of the lifestyles of members of the middle class by analysing the results of a market research survey into the habits of 24,000 individuals. They conclude that there are three major middle-class lifestyle groupings, each with a distinct social base. An ascetic style concentrates on healthy pastimes, including exercise and sport, combined with an interest in high-culture pursuits, such as visiting art galleries and going to concerts. People with this orientation tend to be recruited from public-sector professionals like teachers.

Plate 11.1 Different youth culture styles (above and opposite)
Source: Camera Press/Ray Green; Format/Ulrike Press

Box 11.2   Symbolic creativity

Clothes shopping has been a central part of post-war youth cultural consumerism. As a cultural practice, however, shopping has tended to be marginalized in much of the writing about youth, style and fashion. Shopping has been considered a private and feminine activity and part of the process of incorporation into the social machinery.

But young people don't just buy passively or uncritically. They always transform the meaning of bought goods, appropriating and recontextualizing mass-market styles. That appropriation entails a form of symbolic work and creativity as young consumers break the ordered categories of clothes, the suggested matches and ideas promoted by shops. They bring their own specific and differentiated grounded aesthetics to bear on consumption, choosing their own colours and matches and personalizing their purchases. Most young people combine elements of clothing to create new meanings. They adopt and adapt clothing items drawn from government surplus stores, for example, or training shoes, track suits, rugby shirts, Fred Perry tops from sportswear shops. They make their own sense of what is commercially available, make their own aesthetic judgments, and sometimes reject the normative definitions and categories of 'fashion' promoted by the clothing industry.

While many of the young people we spoke to obtain their ideas about clothes from friends or from simply observing how clothes looked worn on other people, many also use the media to understand and keep up with the latest fashions. They get ideas about clothes from sources such as television programmes, like *The Clothes Show*, fashion and music magazines, or from the personal dress styles of particular pop artists. Aspects of the clothes and outfits worn by pop groups like Bananarama and Amazulu, for example, were taken up *en masse* by young women in the early and mid 1980s, particularly items such as haystack hairstyles, dungarees and children's plimsolls.

Since the early 1980s, media and marketing attention has shifted towards the employed with high salaries such as the 25–40 age group and the 'empty-nesters'. Changing economic circumstances, particularly the growth in youth unemployment and the start of what will be a long-term decline in the youth population, have made the 16-to-24-year-old market far less attractive and lucrative. This has meant that there now exists a substantial block of young people for whom the retail boom has provided few benefits. With many working-class youth now denied the sources of income which financed the spectacular subcultures of the 1960s and 1970s, the right to 'good clothes' can no longer be automatically assumed.

The young unemployed especially find it difficult to develop their own image and lifestyle through purchased items. For these young people, using clothes to express their identities, stylistically, is something of a luxury. With social identities increasingly defined in terms of the capacity for private, individualized consumption, those who are excluded from that consumption feel frustrated and alienated.

For many working-class young people, impotent window shopping is a source of immense frustration. One young woman said that she would not go window shopping for this reason:

I don't like window shopping very much. Especially if I don't have the money . . . 'cause if you see something and you want it, you can't afford it. So I don't go window shopping unless I have money.

Remarkably, however, even young people with limited spending power still often find ways to dress stylishly and to express their identities through the clothes they wear. Young women and men still manage to dress smartly and make the most out of slender resources, buying second-hand clothes or saving up to buy particular items of clothing. For some the emphasis on presenting a smart or fashionable image is a priority above everything else and results in quite disproportionate amounts being spent on clothes. One young woman said that she bought a clothing item every week, but sacrificed by going 'skint' for the rest of the week. Her rationale was that quality was better than quantity:

I'd rather buy things that'll last me than cheap things what won't, and you don't get the quality in them, do you? . . . I feel better in myself if I know I've got summat on like expensive, instead of cheap. (Willis 1990, pp. 85–7)

Managers and administrators in the public and private sectors, on the other hand, have an undistinctive culture; there are no pastimes, pursuits or attitudes that particularly mark them out. Private-sector professionals and specialists adopt a third lifestyle that Savage et al. call postmodern. This lifestyle is apparently paradoxical in that it combines an interest in health, exercise, sport and fitness with a dedication to high living, manifested in champagne and foreign eating styles. In the postmodern style, the traditional boundaries and distinctions between cultural pursuits have broken down. The postmodern style is gaining influence, partly as a result of the growing importance of professional and specialist workers in the private sector. Savage et al. also note that the adoption of lifestyles is interwoven with gender, age and regional factors. A young, male, London-based advertising executive, for example, is particularly likely to adopt a postmodern lifestyle.

Lifestyles, identity and social structure

Sociologists often understand the social structure in terms of categories like social class, gender, ethnicity or age. Some of the force of these categories is that they say something about the sense of belonging individuals have, their sense of *identity*. If a person is a woman or a professional worker those characteristics are very much part of who she or he thinks she or he is. These people *identify* with other women or professionals; they *belong* to those groups. The same would seem to be true of the idea of lifestyles; the lifestyle that people adopt is part of their identity. Indeed, some writers argue that life-style is now the most important source of identity. As Chaney (1996) puts it:

> There does also seem to have been a change in the later years of the modern era in the primary social base of identity. There is now a widespread feeling that whereas tradition-ally work or occupation determined social class and thus an individual's way of life, in the second half of the century leisure activities and/or consumer habits are being increasingly experienced by individuals as the basis of their social identity. (p. 112)

It matters what clothes you wear, what kind of carpet is on the floor, or what taste in music you have. It is clear that, under these circumstances, identity in modern societies is a complex phenomenon. To some extent, the senses of identity given by class, gender, age and lifestyle, for example, will cross-cut. But also, to some extent, they coalesce. So, as in the Savage et al. study discussed above, lifestyle is closely related to social position, especially occupational position.

Inasmuch as lifestyles are one of the means by which individuals construct their iden-tities, they also function to position the individual in a hierarchy of prestige and status. The consumer goods that people buy to establish their lifestyle give them a position in society in other people's eyes; they are positional goods. As Lury (1996) puts it:

> With what are sometimes called luxury objects, it is the fact that such goods are only affordable by an elite group of consumers which gives them their value. In the case of so-called cult objects it is not the limited availability arising as a result of economic cost that is the source of value, but the fact that certain items have limited appeal. In both cases, acts of consumption are actively carried out by consumers to indicate social status, good taste or simply 'being in the know'. (p. 46)

Consumer society

It will be clear from the discussion so far that, in part, lifestyles are formed by the acquisition, or intended acquisition, of goods and services of various kinds; leisure and lifestyles are crucially, though not exclusively, to do with *buying* things. Individuals use consumer goods to indicate their lifestyle, their position in the social world, and their membership of particular social groups. While this construction of a lifestyle out of consumer goods may seem to be a demonstration of individual choice, it is actually socially patterned.

As a result, there is a flourishing industry producing goods and services for people's leisure. As table 11. 6 shows, expenditure on leisure has increased since 1971 faster than basic household necessities like food or housing. Very big firms like the Rank Organization, the Grand Metropolitan Group, or the big brewing groups provide for leisure activities across the social spectrum. This commercialization of leisure provision does not extend only to activities outside the home. Many home-based forms of leisure are obviously commercialized – from video-recorders to home improvements. The leisure sector is becoming a big employer. From 1979 to 1992 employment in all sectors in the UK fell by 6 per cent but employment in the service sector rose by almost 15 per cent. However, in the same period, the leisure industry increased its employment faster than the service sector generally. For example, restaurants, cafés and snackbars provided 59 per cent more jobs, pubs and bars 30 per cent, and nightclubs 19 per cent (Cooke 1994).

TABLE 11. 6 | Household expenditure, 1971–96

		Indices at current prices				£billion (current prices)
	1971	*1981*	*1986*	*1991*	*1996*	*1996*
Leisure						
Alcohol	100	132	171	194	219	81.5
Tobacco	100	89	74	71	59	11.8
Other goods and services	100	121	163	218	238	92.9
Non-leisure						
Transport and communication	100	132	171	194	219	81.5
Housing	100	119	136	147	155	74.7
Food	100	104	109	115	124	52.0
Recreation, entertainment and education	100	153	191	240	300	49.7
Household goods and services	100	115	143	166	197	29.9
Less expenditure by foreign tourists, etc.	100	152	198	181	257	−14.3
Household expenditure abroad	100	193	229	287	379	14.4
All household expenditure	100	121	144	165	183	464.1

Indices: 1971 = 100
Source: Adapted from *Social Trends* 1998, p. 110

Many writers use the term consumer society in describing the way that lifestyles are formed and commercialized in modern society. Box 11. 3 describes the main features of consumer society.

The notion of consumer society therefore implies that consuming things, including leisure goods, becomes a central life interest, and shopping a major national preoccupa-

---

Box 11.3   The main features of consumer society

These features are as follows:

1 The availability of a large (and constantly increasing) number and range of types of consumer goods.

2 The tendency for more and more aspects of human exchange and interaction to be made available through the market. One instance of this is the contemporary shift away from state or publicly provided services to their marketization. Examples include housing and education – so, for example, it is often said that Britain is now a home-owning nation and that students are consumers of education.

3 The expansion of shopping as a leisure pursuit. In the United States, shopping is the second most popular leisure pursuit – six hours per person a week – after watching television (Nicholson-Lord 1992).

4 The increasing visibility of shopping, from mail order . . . to shopping malls to car boot sales and second-hand shops.

5 The political organization by and of consumers. Examples include so-called green consumption . . . and the use of consumer boycotts, as well as the growth and popularity of consumer organizations such as the Consumers Association . . .

6 A growth in the visibility of the consumption of sport and leisure practices. This involves not simply the broadcasting of sports events, including snooker, cricket and football competitions and the Olympics, but their reorganization (for example, one-day Test matches) to suit the requirements of commercial sponsors.

7 The lifting of restrictions on borrowing money and the associated change in meaning of being in debt. During this century, for example, there has been a shift from the dubious respectability of the 'never-never' through the anxieties of hire-purchase, to the competitive display of credit cards – to a situation now in which an Access card is your 'flexible friend' and a gold American Express card is a symbol of elite exclusivity.

8 An increase in sites for purchase and consumption, such as the spread of shopping malls . . . the growth of retail parks . . . and leisure complexes and their stylization, from the increase in 'themed' pubs to the building of Disneyworlds.

9 The growing importance of packaging and promotion in the manufacture, display and purchase of consumer goods.

10 The pervasiveness of advertising in everyday life.

11 The increasing emphasis on the style, design and appearance of goods.

12 The manipulation of time and space in the simulation of 'elsewheres' and 'elsewhens' to promote products, as in the case of, for example, the company 'Past Times' . . .

13 The emergence of a range of so-called consumer crimes – credit card fraud,

shoplifting and ram-raiding – and consumer surveillance technologies – the remote video camera and the itemized financial records of banks, telephone and telecommunications companies.

14 The impossibility of avoiding making choices in relation to consumer goods, and the associated celebration of self-fashioning or self-transformation in the promotion of lifestyle as a way of life.

15 The increasing visibility of so-called consumer illnesses ... whether it be addiction to alcohol, food or shopping ...

16 The interest in the personal and collective collection, cataloguing and display of material goods, whether these be artworks, stamps, antiques, music tapes or photographs. (Lury 1996, pp. 29–39)

tion. Consumption becomes overwhelmingly a question of *personal identity* (but for a contrary view see Warde 1997):

> People have increasingly turned to commodities to differentiate themselves as individuals, to imbue themselves with a distinctive style and create for themselves an identity perceived as lacking elsewhere. Products of all kinds – particularly clothes, but also electrical appliances, cars, beverages and food – have come to signify *who* their wearers are. Consumption has ceased to be purely material or narrowly functional – the satisfaction of basic bodily needs. Today, consumption is both symbolic and material. It expresses, in a real sense, a person's place in the world – his or her core identity. (Gardner and Sheppard 1989, p. 45)

This idea is taken up in a study by Lunt and Livingstone (1992). They found that the involvement with consumer society permeates every aspect of people's lives. People live their lives in relation to the consumer objects around them. For example, in an extended life history, a respondent's story 'is peopled with those who try to deter him from his chosen path, and each time he overcomes them. His connected self is experienced only in relation to his wife, as a cohesive unit they face the world and get what they want from it. Emotional and financial investment in objects go hand in hand to construct an identity' (p. 73).

Although people may construct their identity partly in relation to the pressures and pleasures of consumer society, Lunt and Livingstone also found that their respondents were ambivalent about its advantages. Consumer society might indeed give freedom and choice. However, interviewees frequently compared it with a previous time, which may have been hard, limited and oppressive but was also secure, moral and authentic. It should be noted that Lunt and Livingstone (1992, p. 118) found too that the different generations respond differently: 'It seems that younger people find a pleasure in acquiring objects, seeing this process of acquisition as relevant not only to their material lives but to other aspects of their lives also. The material and the immaterial – spiritual, intellectual, emotional – have become interlinked.' Older people, on the other hand, have a rather more moral attitude and are suspicious, for example, of anything that involves borrowing.

The ambivalence that Lunt and Livingstone detected in their interviewees is reflected in the sociological literature. Sociologists have evaluated the appearance of a consumer society and the commercialization of leisure in different ways. Some see these social changes as destructive. The consumer, it is suggested, is fed with ready-made leisure – at a price and making a profit for someone – which serves to divert attention away from real problems by giving spurious pleasure. This cultural influence is all the more pervasive because it is brought right into the home. Others argue that consumer society provides opportunities and the freedom to choose a lifestyle.

Summary

1 In contemporary Britain, lifestyles are important and the particular lifestyle adopted is part of an individual's identity.
2 The way in which lifestyles are formed is very much bound up with buying things – with consumer society.

11.4 Tourism

The importance of tourism

One very significant component of the idea of the consumer society concerns travel and tourism. Going away on holiday has become a major feature of people's lives as consumers. The holiday industry offers wide choice, many apparent freedoms and the opportunity to purchase a huge variety of associated goods and services. The idea of the consumer society is taken to its extreme in periods of intense holidaymaking.

Until fairly recently sociologists did not have much to say about tourism. But in the last decade this has changed (see Urry 1990; Sharpley 1994). The array of industries and activities that we call 'tourism' is now seen as especially important. This is so for three reasons.

First, it is the largest industry in the world in terms of trade and employment. The receipts worldwide are growing at 9 per cent per annum, while the numbers of international visitors are growing at 5 per cent per annum (WTO 1997, pp. 14–15). In Britain today there is scarcely a town or city that is not endeavouring to develop its tourism potential – some towns and cities that have recently become significant tourist sites include, perhaps surprisingly, Birmingham, Bradford, Cardiff, Glasgow, Liverpool and Wigan.

Second, tourism is an industry with high levels of organizational and technological innovation. Box 11.4 sets out some of the innovations that have occurred within the British tourist industry.

Third, in most countries holidays have been centrally bound up with the culture of that society. Images and symbols from holidaymaking are integral to how we think of other places. Examples include the café and boulevard in France, the chalet, ski-lift and cleanliness in Switzerland, driving along the 'open road' in the USA, and the quaint Mediterranean fishing village in Greece. Holidaymaking has helped to form different modern societies and their particular cultures.

<hr>

Box 11.4   Innovations in the British tourism industry

These include:

- the mid-nineteenth-century development of the packaged trip by Thomas Cook, who was more or less the first ever travel agent and tour operator;
- the late nineteenth-century growth of specialized seaside resorts for the industrial working class;
- the mid-twentieth-century development of the luxury holiday camp by Billy Butlin and others;
- the growing use from the 1960s onwards of cheap charter flights in developing international mass tourism;
- the early use from the 1960s onwards of computers so as to deal with the huge amounts of information involved in organizing mass travel;
- the widespread growth of highly efficient and rationalized fast-food outlets, theme parks and leisure complexes;
- the early use of the internet in the 1990s to provide increasing amounts of information and resources for holiday bookings.

The history of British tourism

At the time of the Second World War seaside holidays had become the predominant form of holiday within Britain. Brunner claimed that seaside resorts were 'essentially native to this country, more numerous and more highly specialised in their function as resort than those of any other land' (1945, p. 8). There was extensive investment in such resorts, as well as the passing in 1938 of the Holidays with Pay Act that guaranteed paid holidays. By the Second World War there was widespread acceptance of the view that going on holiday was good for one, that this was the basis of personal replenishment. Around that right developed an extensive infrastructure of specialist services, particularly in the seaside resorts along the English coastline (see Walvin 1978; Urry 1990).

In the immediate period after 1945, rationing ended, austerity ceased and the tourist industry at home boomed. The holiday abroad was still the preserve of the few and overseas package tours had not developed. The traditional or organized pattern of holidaymaking continued, with whole towns moving to the seaside in a given week. A central role in sustaining such patterns was played by the railway. British Railways organized many specials or excursion trains, taking visitors to the resorts that they traditionally visited. Major new investments were planned, although most visitors still stayed either in traditional hotel or bed-and-breakfast accommodation (which was unlicensed), or in the holiday camps that grew greatly in the 1950s.

The holiday experience was remarkably regulated. The holiday was based on the time period of the week and it was almost impossible to book mid-week. Visitors knew when they were to eat, what they would eat, and exactly how long they were to stay. If people were staying in a holiday camp then much else was organized, and indeed: 'from one camp to the next the mix was identical – the same pattern of entertainment, the same diet, the same type of accommodation, the same weekly routine' (Ward and Hardy 1986, p. 63).

However, these patterns began to change dramatically in the 1960s. The seaside resort no longer seemed to contain the extraordinary sites with which to entice prospective visitors. Piers and towers were much less exceptional; indeed piers were frequently washed out to sea. Likewise competition developed from new-style amusement and theme parks not normally located at the seaside but with an attractive rural location close to the motorway network (such as Alton Towers). Apart from Blackpool Pleasure Beach, the pleasure parks at seaside resorts struggled to compete.

Most such resorts had contained holiday camps. Compared with the typical hotel or guesthouse, holiday camps provided luxurious facilities, with extensive on-site amusement, good-quality food, high-class entertainment and modern sanitation. In 1948, 1 in 20 of all holidaymakers in Britain stayed at a Butlin's camp. Their heyday was in the post-war period up to 1959, when the BBC television series *Hi-de-Hi!* was set (see plate 11.2).

However, during the 1960s these camps too became very unfashionable. Ward and Hardy suggest that:

Holiday camps are something of a period piece . . . new concepts of holidaymaking have been developed . . . Package holidays to exotic places, coupled with more individualistic

Plate 11.2 | A Butlin's holiday camp
Source: Network / Barry Lewis

off-season breaks, increase the difficulties of the camps . . . Much about the holiday camp is now commonplace. (1986, p. 152)

Furthermore from the 1960s onwards, British resorts had to contend with a new form of competition, the package holiday, that led first to a Europeanization of the holiday market and then to its globalization. The development of overseas package holidays stemmed from a number of factors. First, amongst the fashionable upper and middle classes in the inter-war period there was a cultural reaction against having a pale skin. In resorts like Biarritz and Cannes it became fashionable to be tanned, partly because of the presumed spontaneity and 'natural' sensuality of black people. It was thought that sun-bathing brought one closer to nature. This cultural shift was then diffused down-wards in the social order so that it became desirable within all social groups to have a sun-tanned skin. The effect is that many package holidays nowadays present the activity of getting tanned as *the* reason for going away. Many north European resorts came to be seen as much less fashionable since they were unable to guarantee the effectively tanned body.

Second, in the 1960s there were extensive areas of coastline in the Mediterranean region, away from the already fashionable and expensive French resorts, which were ready for development. The two most 'successful' countries have been Spain and Greece, which offered the appropriate climate and potential coastline but with a much cheaper cost of living than France. In 1997, UK residents made nearly 9 million visits to Spain (ONS 1998a, p. 103). Package holidays have subsequently been developed in most of the countries in the Mediterranean (such as Turkey and Tunisia) and then in most pre-viously poor countries across the globe (such as India and Indonesia). Nevertheless, France is still the most popular country for UK citizens to visit, with 12 million visits in 1997 (ONS 1998a, p. 103).

Third, the package holiday industry developed early within Britain. The tour opera-tors were innovative in seeing how to take advantage of the new technologies of jet planes and computers, and of new ways of organizing holidays through an inclusive booking, often with a vertically integrated company. The British tour operators have sold their package holidays at a cheaper price than in comparable European countries. They thereby attracted larger numbers of less affluent people to go abroad. Package holidays democratized the foreign holiday. Their expansion has been accompanied by a considerable degree of economic concentration of the industry.

Contemporary British tourism

We will consider first some contemporary travel patterns. There has continued to be a significant increase in the number of tourists coming to the UK. There were about 12 million visits in 1976 and about 25 million in 1997 (ONS 1998a, p. 18). But at the same time there has been an even more marked rise in the number of visits abroad. The number of visits by UK residents has grown from 11 million in 1976 to 46 million in 1997 (ONS 1998a, p. 19). So while the inward and outward visits more or less co-incided in the mid-1970s, by 1997 there were nearly twice as many outward.

These figures include all visits. Specifically with regard to what is defined as a holiday (staying four nights or more), about 8 million holidays were taken abroad in 1971. By

1995 this had grown to 26 million (*Social Trends* 1997, p. 213). In any year about 60 per cent of Britons go on holiday (abroad or at home), while 40 per cent take no holiday. This last figure ranges from 18 per cent of the professional and managerial classes to 57 per cent of semi- and unskilled workers (*Social Trends* 1997, p. 213). Many affluent people now will go on a number of holidays each year. Social class significantly affects the ability to go away.

Nevertheless the package holiday has meant that going abroad is no longer distinctive. If anything, travelling to Spanish and Greek resorts has become somewhat unfashionable. People are tending to move away from the standardized package and seeking out a wider variety of leisure activities, including independent travel. There has been a marked increase recently in seats-only flights. Many commentators suggest that from the 1980s onward the switch to independent travel is partly a reaction against package holidays, which are no longer viewed as fashionable or smart (see Barrett 1989).

This has led to a number of developments. First, there has been the campaign for so-called 'real holidays'. Barrett (1981, p. 1) argues that the 'rise and rise of the package holiday has imposed on travel the same problems that mass production has inflicted on beer, bread, ice cream and many other things'. A real holiday has two main features: it will involve getting away from other people, especially mass tourists, to be off the 'beaten track'; and small specialist agents/operators rather than one of the mass tour operators will be used. The latter are sometimes described as 'delicatessen' agents who specialize in travel for the supposedly more discriminating, independent-minded clientele (travel which of course in the twenty-first century will include holidays in space).

Second, a partly related development has been the increased attraction of the British countryside. About three-quarters of the population make at least one visit to the countryside each year. This is most common among the professional and managerial class. In 1990, the 15 per cent of people with such jobs made 21 per cent of all countryside visits. Those who were unemployed not surprisingly made disproportionately fewer visits. The countryside also tends to be disproportionately visited by white people, by car-drivers and their passengers, and by older people who like going on country walks (Sharpley and Sharpley 1997, p. 57). The countryside is visited because it is *thought* to embody a lack of planning and regimentation, a vernacular quaint architecture, winding lanes and generally labyrinthine road system, the virtues of tradition and the lack of social intervention. However, in fact, rural areas in Britain have been subject to a wide range of modernizing processes – large-scale agriculture, land-use planning and extensive private-sector rural and housing developments. It is hard to get away from it all, in at least the English countryside.

Third, a related development is that of green tourism, which is concerned to ensure the conservation of rural areas, including the look of the landscape, local forms of agriculture, other traditions of life and the area's biodiversity (see Sharpley and Sharpley 1997). The development of such a novel tourism stems from a repudiation of aspects of modernity, especially modern forms of transport, energy, and industrial and agricultural production. Particular hostility has been shown to the 'modernized' planting of extensive forests of conifers, by the Forestry Commission and by private landlords. Such forests are thought to have deleterious environmental and social consequences. Green tourism normally involves small-scale developments based on local techniques and vernacular traditions that have minimum impact.

Fourth, there has been an extraordinary development of preservation in recent years, resulting in a veritable 'heritage industry' (Hewison 1987; Samuel 1988). It seems that a new museum opens every week or so in Britain. Almost everywhere and everything from the past may be conserved. In Lancashire, environmentalists have sought to preserve the largest slag heap in Britain. There are now 500,000 listed buildings in Britain, as well as over 5,500 conservation areas. Large numbers of people visit such places. More people visit museums and galleries in Britain than the cinema. The proportion of the professional and managerial class visiting museum and heritage centres in any year is about three times that of manual workers. This development of the heritage industry resulted from the remarkably rapid deindustrialization in the late 1970s and early 1980s. This created a profound sense of loss, both of certain kinds of technology (steam engines, blast furnaces, pit workings) and of the patterns of social life that had developed around those technologies. Further, much of this industry had been based in inner-city Victorian premises, large numbers of which became available for alternative uses. Such buildings either were immensely attractive in their own right (such as the Albert Dock in Liverpool), or could be refurbished in a suitable heritage style for housing, offices, museums or restaurants. This process of deindustrialization occurred when many local authorities were developing a strategy for tourism, and saw in urban and industrial tourism a means to generate jobs both directly and through more general publicity about their areas.

Finally, there has been a more general globalization of tourism, with over 600 million international arrivals each year across the globe. In 1995 the most popular destinations worldwide were France, the USA, Spain, Italy and then the UK, although in terms of receipts from tourism the USA was easily the largest beneficiary of global tourism (WTO 1997, pp. 14–15). Different countries specialize in different sectors of the holiday market. Some examples of this include Spain for cheaper packaged holidays by the beach, Scotland for romantic holidays in a wild nature, Thailand for 'exotic' holidays often involving sex tourism, Switzerland for skiing and mountaineering holidays, and Singapore for shopping holidays. Britain has partly come to specialize in holidays emphasizing the historical and the quaint (north Americans often refer to Britain as that 'quaint country'). Overseas visitors to Britain tend to remain inland, rarely visiting either the coast or much of the countryside. Such visitors will normally visit only Oxford, Cambridge, Chester, Stratford-upon-Avon, York, Edinburgh and some of the sites of industrial tourism (as well as London, which is visited by over half of all overseas visitors).

One might summarize the changes in the post-war period in British tourism as involving two shifts, from the seaside to sun-worship, and then from holiday camps to heritage-history.

Summary

1 Holidaymaking is a major leisure activity; tourism is the largest industry in the world.

2 There has been a movement from mass-market holidays to independent travelling and a growth, within Britain, of visits to the countryside and to heritage sites.

11.5 Sport

Sport is important to many people. As one can see from table 11.3, men spend a considerable part of their leisure time outside the home participating in sport. At the same time watching sport, especially soccer, is a national pastime. Furthermore, sport takes up a good deal of the television schedules and television is, as we have seen, easily the most significant leisure activity in terms of time use.

Participating in sport

Table 11. 7 shows the proportion of each age group participating in the most popular sports in the four weeks before they were interviewed. Walking is easily the most popular sport. Hardly surprisingly, participation falls off markedly with age in all sports, although the decrease is less marked with walking. As always with data related to age, one has to distinguish effects due to the increasing age of interviewees from effects due to differences of behaviour between different generations. For example, the fact that 47 per cent of men aged 16–19 play soccer, while only 1 per cent of men aged 55–64 do, is almost certainly due to the older age group feeling less physically capable. But the difference in participation rates of younger and older women in keep fit and yoga is as likely to be related to different generational attitudes to these activities as it is to any perceived decline in fitness.

Men and women clearly do have different sporting preferences but the differences are perhaps not as great as might be imagined. The same four sports or games figure in the

TABLE 11. 7 | **Participation in the most popular sports, games and physical activities: by gender and age, 1996–7 (percentages)**

Gender	16–19	20–24	25–34	35–44	45–54	55–64	65 and over	All aged 16 and over
Males								
Walking	57	57	50	53	51	50	37	49
Snooker/pool/ billiards	54	45	29	19	13	9	5	19
Cycling	36	24	19	18	12	8	5	15
Swimming	18	17	17	20	10	7	5	13
Soccer	47	28	17	10	2	1	–	10
Females								
Walking	45	43	44	45	49	43	25	41
Keep fit / yoga	29	28	24	20	14	12	6	17
Swimming	23	21	26	22	14	12	5	16
Cycling	14	11	10	12	7	4	2	8
Snooker/pool/ billiards	24	17	6	3	1	–	–	4

Source: Social Trends 1998, p. 224

list of the most popular five for both men and women, and only soccer and keep fit are gender specific. Class differences, however, are much more marked. The higher the social class of a person, the more active in sport he or she is likely to be. In every sport, people from the professional classes are more likely to be participants than the unskilled. The class differences are most marked for walking, swimming and jogging, but they are there for snooker, darts, weight-lifting and soccer. For example, the proportion of professionals who swim is three times that of the unskilled, while five times as many professionals as the unskilled jog. As we noted earlier in the chapter, this class difference is present for leisure pursuits in general and is mostly related to the lack of resources possessed by the unskilled. However, there also may be an independent tendency for the higher social classes to participate in activities outside the home.

Since before the Second World War, governments have intervened in sports. Sometimes this can take the form of banning, or trying to ban, certain activities – bareknuckle boxing or fox-hunting, for example. More recently, they have also promoted sport, in the name of a healthy nation, often by providing funding for facilities through the Sports Council. Whether this promotion is effective or not, there has been a rise in participation in active sports since the late 1960s or 1970s. Gratton and Tice (1994) show that, in the period 1977–87, there was an increase of 13 per cent in those taking part in at least one outdoor sport. Much more dramatically, however, there was an increase of 60 per cent in those participating in at least one indoor sport – an increase largely due to the popularity of swimming. Not only did the percentage of adults active in sport increase but so also did the frequency of participation. Gratton and Tice point out that the old are more participant than they were. In particular, they note that the average age of participants increased in the period 1977–87 and 'the percentage of participants that were retired increased dramatically across virtually all activity groups' (p. 49). If there has been a change in the behaviour of the older members of the population, there has also been a change in the participation of women. The percentage of women participants increased in all categories except those taking part in outdoor sports alone.

Watching sport

As a leisure activity, watching a sports event is fairly popular with the British people. When asked, 22 per cent of all adults had been to a sports event during the 12 weeks before the interview. This compares with 20 per cent who had been to the theatre or a museum, 12 per cent to a theme park, 36 per cent to the cinema and 39 per cent to a library. Many of the class and gender differences that we have noted for other activities appear here too. The higher social classes are far more likely to attend a live sports event than the lower, and men are almost three times as likely to go as women. Watching sport is a peculiarly male activity; the gender difference here is much larger than it is for most other leisure activities outside the home. Going to a football match remains something that men do together; going to the theatre, the cinema, a museum or a theme park are activities that men and women do together or in family groups.

Football, of course, in general has the image of male bonding. Attendance at football matches has increased in recent years. The average attendance at Premier League (or old Division One) matches, for example, increased from almost 21,000 in 1989/90 to just over 23,000 in 1993/4. However, this follows a steep fall since the early 1970s, when attendances were averaging over 31,000.

Part of the reason for this fall lies in the conversion of football grounds from traditional terraces to seated accommodation. These conversions were prompted by a public concern for and alarm about crowd safety and football hooliganism. The latter has particularly occupied government, the media and the public. Actually, most research shows that football hooliganism is neither new nor confined to football. The game has been accompanied by bouts of spectator violence since the earlier part of the twentieth century. Over a much longer period, public events have often gone together with civil disorder. Policy prescriptions have been as diverse as the explanations offered for the phenomenon. Attempts to control aggression by the players, stiffer sentences for those convicted of violent offences at grounds, the construction of all-seat stadia, stricter crowd control by the police, involvement of football clubs in their communities, membership cards, and attempts to persuade football clubs and the Football Association to take responsibility for their fans have all been tried. As Houlihan (1991) points out, these changes in policy have often been short-term, inexpensive and not based on any of the research that has been done. That research, on the other hand, is hardly conclusive. Explanations have varied from male bonding, through ritual expressions of male aggression, to subcultural theories which argue that football hooliganism is an expression of resistance to dominant social groups. It is doubtful if there is any one cause. As Dunning, Murphy and Williams (1988) argue:

> Among the factors at work in shaping the specific character of the football hooligan phenomenon since the mid-1950s have been: social and economic policies of governments throughout the period, particularly as they have affected the material circumstances of the lower working class; the structural changes that have occurred within the 'rougher' and more 'respectable' sections of the working class and in the relationships between these sections; the rise of a specifically teenage leisure market and the various youth styles that have arisen, partly in connection with and partly independently of that fact; the increased ability and desire of young fans to travel away to matches, even abroad, on a regular basis; the ebb and flow of power relations between the sexes; the changing racial contours of British society; changes in the mass media, particularly the advent of television and the rise of a sensationalizing tabloid press; a media-orchestrated moral panic over football hooliganism and consequent pressure on the football authorities and the government to take remedial action; government inspired attempts as a result of this pressure to curb hooligan behaviour; and, last but by no means least, the recent virtual collapse of the youth labour market. (pp. 241–2).

Sport in the media

Although a fair number of people play or watch sport, most people are involved via the mass media, especially television. The population spend about 10 per cent of the time given to television watching sports programmes. On average, therefore, people are watching two hours of sport per week. This is about the same as films or news; light drama and information programming takes up about 25 per cent and 18 per cent respectively. By comparison with other types of programme, the audience for sport is dominated by men (Barwise and Ehrenberg 1988). Sports reporting is also important in selling newspapers. The *Sun*, for example, gives one-fifth of its space to sports coverage, chiefly football and horse racing.

The media do not simply report sport. Many writers (e.g. J. Hargreaves 1986) have pointed out that the way in which the media handle sport serves to construct the social world in particular ways. For example, the idea of Britishness is conveyed by the way that international competitions are reported, often by a stereotypical contrast with the athletes of other nations. Similarly, particular notions of femininity are conveyed in descriptions of women's sport. But also the organization of sport is profoundly influenced by the demands of television. Matches are scheduled at times and places which suit television production. Games of cricket are shortened so that the attention of television audiences can be retained. Entire structures of administration of a sport are influenced by the importance of the television audience, as in the creation of the Premier League. Television and the press, in other words, are an important part of the tendency for sport to be a business, to be commercialized. Some sport is organized to make a profit. Professional football is an example of this in that some clubs now have stock exchange quotations. Other sporting activities do not necessarily aim to make a profit but simply try to break even. All sports, however, are necessarily increasingly commercialized as they struggle to cope with rising costs and they look for funding from a variety of sources, whether it be sponsorship, ticket sales or merchandising.

Summary

1   There are marked differences in the degree of participation in sports activity, a difference also found in watching live sports.
2   Sport is an important constituent of the television schedules. In general, the media increasingly influence the organization and funding of sporting events.

11.6   The arts

In this section we discuss participation in leisure pursuits such as theatre-going, attendance at concerts, and visiting galleries. The arts are an important area of leisure in modern Britain. They represent a significant source of employment, are a draw for tourists and hence indirectly a producer of overseas income, and give pleasure to millions of people.

Audiences for the arts

In the mid-1990s, when asked what cultural events they attend 'these days' (*Social Trends* 1998), one-half of the population had gone to the cinema, one-quarter to the theatre or art galleries, one-eighth to classical music concerts, and less than 10 per cent to ballet, opera or contemporary dance. As one might expect, social class plays an important role in audience composition. A study of the arts in Manchester found that 39 per cent of arts visitors were from the professional or managerial classes, 17 per cent were students and only 3 per cent had a semi- or unskilled background (Wynne 1992).

For some of the arts, total attendances have been improving. This may not be because more people are attracted to the arts but rather because devotees of the arts are going more often. As table 11. 8 shows, opera, ballet, art galleries, theatre and classical music concerts all had increased attendances in the period 1986–94, while those at jazz concerts and contemporary dance decreased.

TABLE 11. 8 | Attendances at arts events, Great Britain, 1986–94 (percentages)

	1986–7	1991–2	1993–4
Opera	100	112	125
Ballet	100	111	120
Art galleries	100	102	105
Plays	100	102	105
Classical music	100	100	104
Jazz	100	82	87
Contemporary dance	100	77	86

Source: *Social Trends* 1995, p. 221

However, there are signs, that, more recently, attendances at cultural events have begun to fall off. Moreover, the data reported in table 11.8 probably conceal differences within the various categories. For example, attendances at classical concerts will include amateur events as well as professional, and the indications are that the number of tickets sold for concerts involving professional orchestras in London has been declining since the mid-1980s (*Cultural Trends* 1995). Those involved in promoting such events believe that this is because the audience is less loyal. That is, audiences are less likely to be repeat attenders and those who do attend regularly do so less frequently.

So far we have discussed audience attendances at the separate arts events, which may conceal the extent to which the same people go to concerts, ballet and opera. It might be that there are relatively few people interested in the arts but those that are dedicate themselves. While true to a certain extent, this is variable between different cultural pursuits. For example, opera lovers have the highest level of interest in other arts events, while those who go to galleries have less commitment to other arts. However, the situation is complex. As Myerscough says:

> museum and gallery goers and theatre and concert attenders would appear to represent separate market segments. The levels of cross-visiting within each segment were higher than the cross-visiting between segments . . . Museum and gallery goers . . . were least interested in other arts activities . . . play goers scored low in museum and gallery going. There appeared to be two-way linkages between concert going and attending art exhibitions, and also between concert going and opera and dance attending. People going to pop concerts had a high propensity to attend art exhibitions, but the relationship was weak vice versa. (1988, p. 31, quoted in I. Waters 1989, p. 11)

Artists and performers

It is difficult to estimate the number of people employed in the arts as we have defined it. The 'cultural industries' as a whole employ about half a million people, twice as many as the motor industry, but this category includes those who work in publishing, the recording industry, film, radio and television as well as in the arts. Perhaps between 150,000 and 200,000 people derive their income from work in the arts as defined in this section, whether they work as artists and performers or in arts venues. These people tend to be older and better educated than the national average. Not surprisingly, they are also much more likely to be self-employed. Earnings within the arts are highly variable. Clearly, some performers in theatre, opera, ballet and classical music can be very highly paid, although their incomes may largely come from recordings rather than live performance. At the other end of the scale, in the mid-1990s, the majority of craftpersons were earning less than £10,000 per annum from their artistic work, and visual artists are likely to earn less than £5000 (*Cultural Trends* 1995a, 1995b). These artists are therefore dependent to a large extent on other sources of income. This conclusion is reinforced by a study of Manchester artists which concluded that about half of the artists questioned derived less than 60 per cent of their income from their artistic activity (Wynne 1992).

The relatively low earnings of many involved in the arts are related to the prominence of volunteers in these fields. Volunteers work in arts centres, act as guides in country houses, and staff museums, as well as providing members of management committees. It is difficult to be precise as to the degree to which artistic activity is dependent on volunteer labour. However, it is estimated that some 30,000 volunteers are working in arts centres, museums and heritage sites, 38 per cent of arts festivals are run entirely by volunteers, and 80 per cent of arts centres use volunteer labour. What is more, there are signs that artistic and cultural activities are utilizing volunteer labour more than they used to.

Arts events are organized in several different ways: in public-sector organizations, in the commercial sector and by amateurs. There has been a long tradition of government encouragement of the arts, since it is recognized that participation in artistic activities is a public benefit but is also difficult to fund. As a result, central and local government offer subsidies to the arts by a number of routes, including the Arts Council, the Crafts Council, the National Heritage Memorial Fund, and numerous local initiatives. The Arts Council, for example, distributes some £250 million per year (Cooke 1994). The boundary between public and private provision – as in the commercial theatre of the West End of London – has always been unclear, but, in recent years, it has moved as governments have encouraged more private sponsorship of the arts. During the 1980s, business sponsorship of the arts almost doubled as a proportion of total arts funding including local and central government sources. A good deal of artistic provision is by amateurs, most commonly in music and theatre (see section 10.5 for further discussion of 'enthusiasms'). Many towns and even villages will have amateur dramatic or choral societies which put on shows regularly. Some even have their own performance spaces. Most notably, these are performances by the community for the community. Indeed amateur participation, sometimes aided by professionals, is the keystone of the community arts movement, defined by I. Waters (1989) as 'as much about community work as about art; they seek to raise expectations and self-confidence, putting the emphasis on active involvement, on the process rather than the product' (p. 61).

Governments have become interested in the arts for the economic impact that they can make. As we have seen, the cultural industries do employ substantial numbers of people and generate a considerable turnover. Wynne (1992) estimates that in Manchester the arts generate between £50 and £100 million per year. They can also have indirect benefits for the economy in that they can encourage tourism; people who go to arts events also spend money on other things, including accommodation and restaurants. The realization that the arts can have a significant economic impact has led to proposals that arts quarters be developed in cities. These would be areas of the city, perhaps currently run down, which would be developed to house venues, galleries and performance spaces, as well as workshops and studios for artists of various kinds. There would, in other words, be a mixture of cultural production and consumption.

Summary

1 Participation in the arts is a minority pursuit.
2 Although the arts may have a substantial direct and indirect economic impact, earnings of most of those employed by arts organizations are relatively low.

Related topics

The demands of paid work, with which leisure time is often contrasted, are reviewed in sections 4.1 and 4.2. Sections 10.2 on visiting friends and non-resident kin, 10.4 on religious participation and 10.5 on social movements refer to other activities occurring in leisure time. Sections 12.2, 12.3 and 12.4 look separately at television, popular music and newspapers, as the major activity absorbing leisure time is media use. Class differences in non-work activities are described in sections 6.3, 6.4 and 6.5. Gender and age differences in leisure, consumption and sport are considered in section 9.4 with respect to youth and section 9.7 with respect to older people. The growth of service industries is examined in section 3.5. Additional material on tourism and heritage can be located in section 10.3.

Further reading

On the idea of consumer society, see Lury (1996). Urry (1990) deals with tourism while J. Hargreaves (1986) examines sociological approaches to sport.

Cross-references to *References in Contemporary British Society*

Irwin for an account of the changing position of young people; **Bennett** on differences in the way that hip-hop is interpreted by different youth cultures; **Roberts** on the relation of changes in the situations of young people to their lifestyles and identities; **Gillespie** on young Punjabis and television; **Hetherington** on Stonehenge; **Skeggs** on working-class women and their quest for respectability through consumption; **Lury** on consumption, shopping and femininity as a space of consumption; **Warde** on food; **Bechhofer et al.** on identity in the context of national identity.

The Media

12

Introduction

12.1 *Discusses the significance of the media in everyday life and considers rival accounts of their effects.*

Television

12.2 *Looks at the ownership of television companies, the system of television production and the way that audiences make use of television programmes.*

Popular music

12.3 *Gives an account of the music industry and of those who produce and those who listen to popular music.*

Newspapers and magazines

12.4 *Discusses the newspaper publishing industry, the readership of newspapers and magazines, and the question of bias in newspaper presentation.*

12.1   Introduction

The mass media are very much part of modern life. Our everyday lives are so interwoven with the media that we are scarcely aware of them. In modern Britain, newspapers, magazines, books, radio, advertising, tape and CD players, television and video are constant features of the daily round. Drawing attention to a parallel, related development, some writers (see Miles 1988) refer to an 'information revolution' in which every household will have access to an ever-increasing flow of information and entertainment through devices of ever-increasing sophistication. To the media of mass communication mentioned above can be added the telephone and the use of fibre-optic cable, communication by satellite, and the more extensive use of computers. Major innovations are expected as telephony, computing and satellite transmissions are brought together in generating an information-rich environment. The organizations that provide the flow of information and entertainment are part of a media industry that has grown rapidly since the late 1940s. Furthermore, that growth is global as large media conglomerates look for markets in countries across the world.

The prevalence of the media in everyday life naturally prompts speculation about their effects on the audience. There are, for example, claims that the media are trivial or, more seriously, that they contribute to violence or political manipulation. Sociologists have, to a great extent, debated the last of these issues. One may identify two extreme and contrasting views. On the one hand, there are those who argue that the media present a relatively coherent view of the world which is one that, on the whole, favours the interest of the powerful. The audience does not have the ability to distinguish this as one view amongst many possible ones and is, in any case, lulled into insensibility. On the other hand, it is argued that the media present a multiplicity of views, not all media output is trivializing, and the audience is capable of reacting critically. Of course, no sociologist adopts either of these views in its entirety and most take up positions somewhere in the middle. The key to the debate lies in the view of the audience and the degree to which it is active in relation to media products. The view that we take in this chapter is that members of the audience are knowledgeable about the media and are capable of being critical about what they watch, read and hear.

12.2   Television

Television is central to life in modern society. Some 98 per cent of households in Britain own at least one television set and 53 per cent own two or more, that figure rising to 65 per cent for families with children. Eighty-two per cent have a video-recorder, while 14 per cent own two or more. At the moment about 15 per cent of households have subscribed to satellite services and 7 per cent to cable. People also commit a substantial amount of *time* to watching the television. In 1997, on average, each member of the population watched 25 hours per week of television, rising to 36 hours for those aged over 65 and falling to 18 hours for those aged between 4 and 15. That is obviously a very substantial commitment indeed. Television watching occupies more time than all other leisure pursuits combined and ranks with working and sleeping as time-consuming activities, although, as we shall see, it is by no means clear what people are actually doing while the set is on. All this implies that television reaches a very large number of people. Individual programmes and films can be seen by half the total population and *Coronation Street* regularly attracts audiences of 18 million. This implies that television is an important – perhaps the most important – source of common experience for the British people, who are otherwise divided by class, ethnicity, gender, region, personal tastes and a host of other factors. As a result, conversation about television programmes is a routine and taken-for-granted aspect of everyday social interaction. At work, in the home, in the street, in the bus or in the pub, people talk about the characters in soap opera, marvel at the latest natural history programme, and discuss the issues raised in news broadcasts or documentaries. In recognition of the importance of television in everyday life, television programmes and the doings of television personalities occupy a substantial proportion of daily newspaper coverage. Politicians realize the importance of appearing on television and presenting a good television image. When the Labour Party were debating who should be their next leader following the death of John Smith in 1994, one of the potential candidates, Robin Cook, was apparently ruled out because he would not look good on television.

The television industry

There has been considerable debate in recent years about the concentration of ownership in the media industries including television. The major reason for this is that television, radio, newspapers and magazines are the main means through which the citizens of a nation become informed about the issues of the day, and can have access to reasoned debate about them, and hence the media institutions are an important part of the democratic process itself.

Direct control of television output by an owner to serve political or economic ends is a fairly rare event. Other kinds of anxiety are produced by the concentration of ownership. Larger companies, with much greater financial resources, are more able to keep smaller competitors out of the market, especially as the costs of entering the television market are rising. More important, however, is the impact of more concentrated ownership in reducing the diversity of programmes available. Privately owned television companies actually make more or less similar programmes as they aim to maximize audience size. For these reasons we should be concerned about the ownership of television companies, but is their ownership in fact concentrated? Until recently, the companies in the commercial television networks could not take shareholdings in each other directly and it was impossible for one company to own more than one franchise. The possibilities for concentration of ownership in broadcast television were therefore limited. More recently, since the 1990 Broadcasting Act, cross-ownership of this kind has been permitted. Furthermore, it is now possible for there to be some concentration of interests between broadcast television and satellite and cable television. The chart reproduced as figure 12.1 demonstrates some of these links in the early 1990s. At that time, a number of mergers took place between commercial television companies – Meridian and Anglia, Carlton and Central, and Granada and LWT.

There is therefore some degree of concentration amongst companies involved in the supply of television in Britain, and it is likely that there will be further rounds of merger activity (for further material on concentration in British industry see section 3.3). There are almost certainly some limits to this process, and a much more important issue is the way in which ownership patterns have changed, not *within* television, but *between* television and other branches of the media. Very large media conglomerates have been formed which often bring together television, book, magazine and newspaper publishing, radio, film and video production. Some of these have taken on a high profile in public debate, often because of the entrepreneurs that direct them. Rupert Murdoch, for example, owner of News Corporation, is very much in the public eye and has extensive political connections. Figure 12.1 again illustrates the formation of media groups in

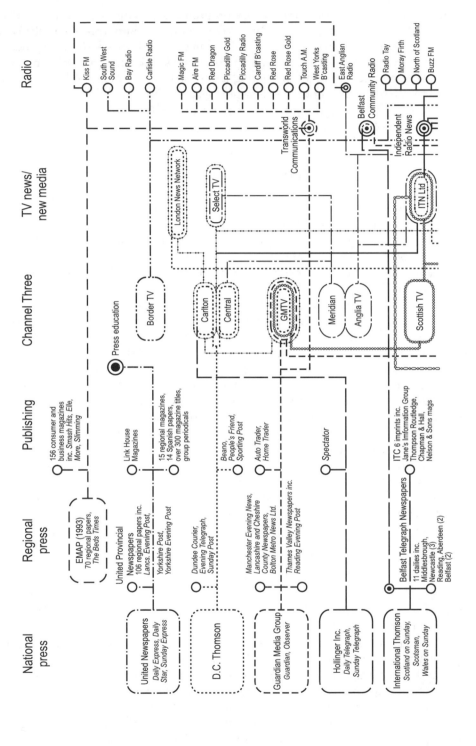

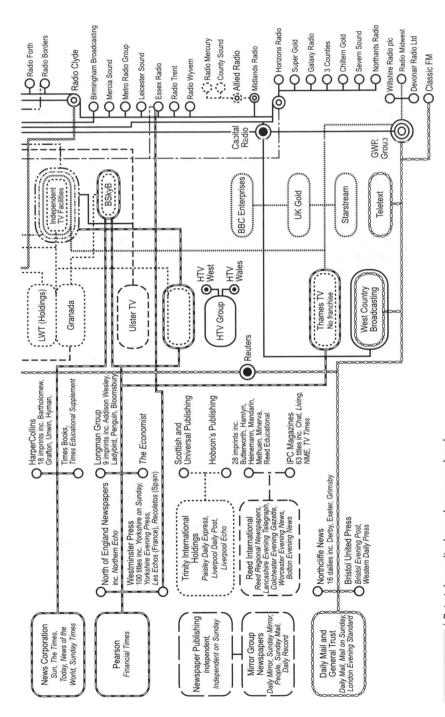

Figure 12.1 Britain's media: how they are related

Source: G. Williams 1994

Britain. The Pearson Group, for example, owns national and local newspapers, magazines, some of the largest book publishers, including Penguin and Longman, an interest in satellite via BSkyB, and an interest in television via Yorkshire/Tyne Tees TV. Similarly, News Corporation owns a string of national newspapers, including the *Sun* and *The Times*, large book publishers, and the majority interest in BSkyB as well as a small shareholding in Pearson. One must also note that this refers only to the British interests of these companies. Many of them are international and their British involvements are relatively minor.

A number of factors have combined to produce a concentration of ownership of this kind. First, companies are driven to grow in order to compete, and the fastest way to grow is by acquiring other companies or, at least, by forming alliances with them. This tendency is compounded by the cost of the new technology, and of the necessary marketing and promotion, all of which require the resources that only a large company can command. Second, the companies themselves believe that there are substantial economies to be made in owning several branches of the media. It is possible for one branch to promote the products of another, for television to advertise the appearance of a film or book, for instance. More important than these economies of marketing, however, are the potential economies in creative activity. Companies will argue that it is the same *kind* of resource that goes into producing a film, a television programme or a book and they might as well make the best use of that resource. So novels can be used as the basis for television programmes, which in turn can be issued as video-cassettes and/or audio-tapes and have extracts used in magazines

The most important motive force in the concentration of ownership in the media industries, however, is the action of governments since the late 1980s or so in attempts to introduce more competition and deregulation into the economy. In Britain, such attempts were associated with the Thatcher governments, although there have been similar movements in many of the developed countries. As far as British television is concerned, the main policy changes are: removal of restrictions on ownership; loosening of some of the rules governing the conduct of television stations; and moves towards the commercialization of the BBC. Initially, this has taken the form of the development of peripheral services which operate in the free market, and the insistence that the Corporation buy in a proportion of its programming from independent production companies. There are more radical proposals to make the BBC less dependent on licence fee income by opening subscription services or, even, by taking advertising. While these moves to commercialize aspects of the BBC's activities do not directly lead to greater concentrations of ownership in television, they may do so indirectly in that they provide further opportunities for already powerful media companies effectively to take shares in the BBC's market (by providing programming, for example).

Of all the media forms, it is television that contributes most to a sense of globalization (see chapter 2). Along a number of dimensions it has become truly international in its scope and effects. First, its *content* is international; television is, in effect, constructing a global audience. Certain events, the Gulf War or Tiananmen Square, for example, are played out in front of an audience drawn from every country. Second, television can be *received* internationally. In certain circumstances, the international scope of television transmissions can leave national governments powerless to regulate the content of the programmes that its population can receive. Third, the *ownership* of television production and distribution is becoming internationalized, a tendency driven by the same processes of government deregulation, technological changes, and the perceived econo-mies of concentration that are discussed above.

The fourth aspect of the globalization of television concerns the *trade*, the imports and exports, in television programmes and products. Britain is a net exporter of televi-sion programmes and is one of the world's largest exporters, although lagging a long way behind the United States. Britain is successful in this trade partly because the pro-grammes are in the English language, partly because they are internationally recognized as being of high quality, and partly because of the efficiency of production stemming from the long history of the industry in Britain. Fifth and last, television is *produced* internationally. Some of the processes involved here are most obvious in the production of news. A number of international news organizations have grown up, such as Visnews, which distributes raw, unedited news footage around the world, CNN, which supplies fully edited news programmes by satellite and the European Broadcasting Union, which manages the exchange of stories between its members.

Television production

In many ways the production of television is like the production of manufactured goods. It is a very complex process with a high degree of division of labour; the production process is broken up into a large number of stages, some of which may be subcon-tracted. A considerable degree of standardization is involved; the repeated use of par-ticular sets, for example. Each stage is carried out by very skilled people who specialize in that activity. This fragmentation of the work process requires active and detailed co-ordination by management.

The result of the production system is that a good deal of importance is given to the television producer, who organizes and manages, making sure that the various elements of the production system are there at the right time and that the whole process is carried out within budget. For some producers this may be a detailed, day-to-day matter, while, for others it may involve more remote control. At the same time, producers are actively involved in the creation of programmes, often responsible for the original idea and working closely with writers.

Producers in British television: a case study

These points are illustrated in a study by Tunstall (1993) which distinguishes several levels of programme decision-making in both the BBC and ITV. At the apex are the channel heads. Next down are departmental heads in the BBC and directors of pro-grammes in ITV. Below that are executive producers in the BBC and department heads in ITV. The next level down, consisting of series producers or editors, is the one that interests Tunstall most, since this is the highest level of decision-making which still has daily contact with the content of programmes. Series producers, in turn, have responsi-bility for managing producers or assistant producers.

Series producers exist in what Tunstall calls 'private worlds' defined by the genre of the programmes that they make. Producers of different genres will have very different backgrounds, images of their audience, and styles of work, and their output attracts

Plate 12.1 | A television studio
Source: J. Allan Cash

very different amounts of prestige. Producers of documentaries, for example, are usually highly educated, with university degrees, often from Oxford or Cambridge. Documentaries are expensive to make and projects can take a very long time to come to fruition. They frequently have an international orientation and are often the subject of co-production deals with other countries to cover the expense of production. The producers concerned stress the necessity of their being emotionally involved in the subjects being documented and they have a strong belief in television as an institution serving and educating the public. Perhaps as a consequence of all these features, documentary production is a high-prestige sector of television.

In this sense, as in others, documentary producers are very different from sports producers. The reporting of sports has a relatively low reputation in the television industry. It also attracts criticism in that it is claimed that sports producers have too close a relationship with sports personalities and organizations. This very close involvement with the sports that they report may contribute to the way that sports producers' private world is very private, more cut off from the rest of television than other branches. Recruitment takes a non-elite form. Only a minority of sports producers have a university degree and the majority have come up through the ranks or from sports journalism. They are all sports fans and in this sense, as in others, they are very close to their audience.

Comedy producers, on the other hand, take very little notice of audience research. They trust their judgement and back artists and programmes that make *them* laugh. Like drama producers they have a very great respect for writers; at the core of comedy are funny scripts and characters. The prestige of comedy is low in British television, although, with the rise of alternative comedy, that may be changing. This uncertainty of status may be related to the changing recruitment pattern of comedy producers. Alternative comedy producers tend to move from university into radio comedy, where they acquire script-writing experience, and thence into television. Mainstream producers are older, typically have come into television from the theatre, and then have worked their way up through the television hierarchy.

Light entertainment, including quiz shows, chat shows and game shows, has the lowest prestige of all in that it is thought to be simply the repetition of formulae. At the same time, programmes of this kind attract relatively high ratings and, of all producers, light entertainment specialists pay most attention to audience research. Programmes of this kind are also very cheap to make, requiring little or no rehearsal, and using members of the public or guests who do not charge. The major cost, indeed, is the host or presenter. Again, the backgrounds of these producers reflect the lower prestige attached to their output. Few have a university education; most have worked their way up from the technical side of television. All pride themselves on having an unusually good feeling for popular taste.

For Tunstall, despite the variations in the producer's role from genre to genre, they all have considerable power and autonomy. But their autonomy is still effectively limited by their superiors, who take *strategic* decisions. In the British system, these decisions are taken by individuals not committees. However, most of these senior posts have so far been taken by ex-producers, which has made sure that production considerations (including questions of programme quality) have remained very much to the fore. British television, in other words, is producer-driven.

So far, we have argued that television is a producer's medium chiefly because of the exigencies of television production – the volume of programming required, the speed at which it has to be produced, the tight financial constraints, and the consistency that is demanded. The more significant these constraints, the more powerful is the position of the producer.

Despite the importance of the producer, the production of television is still a collaborative exercise involving a large number of people with a very wide range of skills. Team-working of this kind can be so strong that it is not always possible to tell who has made a particular contribution. In effect, the issue of authorship has been obscured. For example, in the extremely successful 1982 series of television plays, *The Boys from the Blackstuff*, although the original script was written by Alan Bleasdale, the actual lines as delivered, or the gestures used, were arrived at by contributions from the actors, the producer and director as well as the script-writer.

The question of bias

Exposure to television news implies that many people are dependent on television for their ideas about what is going on in the world. As a source of international, regional and local news, television is more important than newspapers and radio. In a recent survey, 69 per cent of respondents mentioned television first as their main source of news (Gunter, Sancho-Aldridge and Winstone 1994). Furthermore, television is thought to be more reliable. In the same study, some three-quarters of the sample believed that television was the most complete, accurate, unbiased, quick and clear source of reporting of events of national and international significance.

The starting point for any analysis of television news is the relationship between the flow of events in the world and the news programme. The latter is constructed out of the former. It is impossible to represent on our television screens the sheer multiplicity of events that occur every day even in the immediate locality, let alone in the nation or the world. News programmes have to *make sense* of this multiplicity of events and in this way television is no different from any other news medium. This sense-making activity is a *construction*; it involves, for example, deciding what *is* news and what is not, and how to present a news item so that it can be understood by a very diverse audience. Television news filters the welter of events in the world by means of certain news values. If some happening fits in with these values, it is likely to be reported. If it does not, it is likely to be missed. It is important to stress again that the presence of these news values is a *necessary* part of any news-gathering process. It is literally impossible to cope with the flow of events without some means of separating out the important ones. But what is the connection between news values and bias?

In a series of studies, the Glasgow University Media Group (GUMG: 1976, 1980, 1982, 1985, 1993) set out to answer this question. In their view, the television news both includes and excludes. It includes certain views and information and gives those a prominent position. At the same time it excludes other, perhaps contrary, opinions and thereby makes them invisible to the viewer. This process happens in a number of different ways. Most important, the news *defines the issue*, decides what is important, and organizes its presentation in terms of those news values. For example, during the 1970s there was a public debate about Britain's poor economic performance and, in particular, the high rates of inflation. There were several possible explanations for inflation but the television news preferred one to the virtual exclusion of others. GUMG's study of the first four months of 1975 showed that statements saying that wages were the main cause outnumbered by eight to one those reports that contradicted that view. As a result, great prominence was given to the argument that the way to reduce inflation was to keep wage settlements down. In this period, there were 287 occasions when arguments that wage restraint was the proper policy were presented, as against the 17 times that contrary arguments were put. Similarly, in the late 1970s, there was extensive argument about the apparently poor performance of British Leyland, a company then manufacturing Austin, Morris, Triumph and Jaguar motor cars. There were two (at least) competing explanations of this – low investment by the company and disruptive behaviour by the workers, particularly their strikes. The television news preferred the latter explanation.

The particular definition of the issue adopted by the news will usually coincide with the official view of the matter. Official figures, whether they be company directors or politicians, are given more space and time to air their views and they are treated with more respect by interviewers than, say, employees. At times, people who may well be deeply involved are seen almost as neutral commentators giving an objective view. Official sources and official statistics have a privileged position in the television news, in part because journalists are dependent on them for information. The corollary is that dissenting or oppositional opinions do not get such exposure. For example, in coverage of an industrial dispute involving dustcart drivers in Glasgow, which left a great deal of rubbish uncollected in the street, not one striker was interviewed although ten others, largely figures of authority, were, some of them several times. Of course, people who hold other views are occasionally represented on the news. However, 'information which contradicts the dominant view, if it appears at all, exists as fragments and is never explored by news personnel as a rational alternative explanation' (Glasgow University Media Group 1982, p. 29). Alternative versions of reality are not then used to structure interviews or organize the way in which an item is presented. Figures of authority tend to be interviewed in authoritative situations, in offices for instance. Others, especially if they are strikers, will be interviewed in circumstances which scarcely lend weight to what they say, in the street for example. Methods of news presentation of this kind are reinforced by the language used. Strikers are characterized by television news as making 'demands', while the management makes (the milder) 'offers'.

GUMG's work has been the subject of fierce criticism, most prominently from two rival empirical studies, P. Harrison (1985) and Cumberbatch et al. (1986). Harrison's book is a re-study of the television coverage of the events on which GUMG based their work. It consists of an analysis of the transcripts and other documents relating to ITN News's coverage of strikes. At one level Harrison simply disagrees with GUMG about the analysis of the data. He suggests that shop-floor views are presented and background information is given. While one of GUMG's most telling points was that the news does not explain why strikes happen, and thus gives the impression that they are random events perpetrated by troublemakers, Harrison shows that the news does present the viewer with the causes of strikes. The language of television reports does not all go one way. For example, in the treatment of one strike, ITN news used the word 'threat' more often applied to management activities than labour. From this, Harrison draws the conclusion that GUMG do not make clear what yardstick is being used to make their judgements: 'One of the worst difficulties in assessing the Glasgow critique is the repeated condemnation of television in relation to standards that are never clearly specified' (P. Harrison 1985, p. 68). Without such standards of judgement GUMG's reading of the television news is just that: one partial reading among many others.

There are more fundamental issues at stake in Harrison's disagreement with GUMG, however. First, Harrison agrees with the group about the importance of news values. Of course journalists work with some sense of what is important, which determines which items are treated as news and which are not. However, Harrison's point is that these news values do not cohere in such a way as to discriminate against trade unions and in favour of management: 'It is a commonplace that news is more readily concerned with negative than positive occurrences, with events more than non-events, processes or situations' (p. 139). Trouble is much more likely to be reported than harmony. Under certain circumstances, such news values will also discriminate against management. To take a more recent example, television news in the early months of 1995 was preoccupied with the large pay rises awarded to the directors of privatized companies. Second, television news is produced under great pressure and little time is given to each item. Harrison calculates that the average time given to news items covering industrial disputes during the period of this study was 70 seconds. This does not necessarily discriminate against trade unions. More probably, it will hinder the proper understanding of all news items. The difficulty created by the speed of news coverage is not the presence of a dominant frame organizing the presentation, but the absence of a frame at all. Third, any apparent partiality of the news may be built into what is being reported. If blame is to be attached, it belongs to society rather than the television programmes that seek to describe it. For example, trade unions are, as a rule, organizations that are much more public and accessible to the media than private companies, which tend to be rather more secretive. The simple result is that their doings will be more exposed to media investigation, and this is hardly the fault of the television producers.

One possibility that emerges out of the debate between GUMG and Harrison is that the television news has certain *central tendencies*. Broadcasters have interpreted the BBC Charter commitment to impartiality in terms of the need to defend certain features of British life. The BBC does not see itself as being impartial about parliamentary democracy, or terrorism, or religious or political extremism. Instead, it has a most definite view on these matters (see Schlesinger 1978). The difficulty is that such a veneration of parliamentary institutions, however much it represents the consensus of opinion in Britain, may well have the effect of discriminating against extra-parliamentary politics of various kinds.

A second study which bears on the conclusions of GUMG is the one by Cumberbatch et al. (1986). This is an investigation of television treatment of the miners' strike of 1984 and 1985, aiming specifically to 'describe the arena of debate in which the strike took place as defined by the main protagonists on television news, and to examine the vexed issue of bias in the news' (Cumberbatch et al. 1986, p. 6). The authors did a detailed content analysis of all the BBC *Nine O'Clock News* and ITN *News at Ten* broadcasts over a one-year period from March 1984. In addition, they carried out two surveys of audience opinion in the middle of that period.

If there is any one conclusion that Cumberbatch et al. come to, it is that the issue of bias is complex and there are elements of both bias and balance in television news, depending on what measure of bias one uses. In certain respects, then, they agree with GUMG's conclusions that the television news can be biased. For example, television cameras tended to be placed behind police lines when there was any conflict with strikers. This appeared to emphasize the police point of view and gave the impression that strikers initiated violence. Interviewing was not even-handed and the miners' leader, Arthur Scargill, was almost four times as likely to be interviewed in a critical fashion as the Coal Board chairman, Ian MacGregor. In the use of statistics, television news had a tendency to bias, in that it favoured the Coal Board. In a particularly significant incident, the 'Battle of Orgreave', the television news blamed the violence on the behaviour of the pickets, when the police video showed that it was due to the use of police horses. Perhaps most important of all:

> throughout the strike there was a tendency for the news to emphasize the conduct of the strike – the epiphenomenon of union ballots, talks and negotiations and picketing violence – rather than the causes of the dispute. Thus the economics of coal production amounted to

only 2.5% of the issues raised, while pit closures and redundancies accounted for a mere 1.2%. This is hardly surprising given the event driven nature of news. As with war, it is the movement and progress of campaigns and battles that are followed. The conduct eclipses the causes as the story moves on. Violence on the picket line is easier to represent visually on the news than a pit closing down. (Cumberbatch et al. 1986, p. 135)

This conclusion, that television news privileges events over causes, is precisely that reached by GUMG. In other respects, however, the news was found by Cumberbatch et al. to be balanced. Occasions of misrepresentation, such as that following the Battle of Orgreave, were, and are, very rare. No one issue, and certainly not violence on the picket line, predominated over others. In the kind of language used there was no obvious bias. So potentially disapproving adjectives or verbs were not used any more frequently in connection with Arthur Scargill than with Ian MacGregor. Most important of all, Cumberbatch et al. did not find that the television news set an agenda for viewers in the way that GUMG suggest it does. In particular, viewers gave a quite different priority to issues from the one the news did. For example, pit closures and redundancies as an issue were thirteenth in terms of their frequency in news broadcasts, yet they were judged by viewers to be the most important issue in the strike.

The television audience

At the beginning of this section we noted the importance of television as a leisure activity. However, as table 12.1 shows, the number of hours of viewing has declined over the years. This decline is particularly significant as the amount of programming available to audiences has increased over the period. The result is that each channel commanded a smaller amount of audience time. Part of the reason for this loss of audience is the increased use of video-recorders (VCRs); currently homes with VCRs record some five hours of television per week, about half of which is played back within a week.

From a sociological point of view, perhaps the most interesting finding from the measurement of audience behaviour concerns the kinds of programme that people watch.

TABLE 12.1 | **Hours of viewing,[a] 1986–90**

Audience	1986	1987	1988	1989	1990
Social class (hours:mins per week)					
ABC1	20:47	20:54	20:14	19:48	19:31
C2	25:18	24:40	25:25	25:00	24:13
DE	33:11	31:47	31:44	30:57	30:13
All persons	25:54	25:25	25:21	24:44	23:51
Reach (per cent)					
Daily	78	76	77	78	77
Weekly	94	93	94	94	94

[a] Viewing was of live television broadcasts from the BBC, ITV and Channel 4. Percentage of UK population aged 4 and over who viewed TV for at least three consecutive minutes
Source: *Social Trends* 1992, p. 177

Table 12.2 shows that the proportions of time spent watching different types of programme are almost constant across different groupings within the audience. In many ways this is a remarkable finding. In other fields of activity, generally speaking, one finds that different social groups have different social behaviours. For example, the middle class have very different tastes and leisure pursuits from the working class; women and men tend to have very different kinds of jobs. Yet all social groups watch a remarkably similar mix of types of television (see Barwise and Ehrenberg 1988; Goodhardt, Ehrenberg and Collins 1987).

| TABLE 12.2 | Viewing of the main programme types by socio-economic background, 1985 |

| | | Percentage of time spent viewing | | | | | | |
| | | Entertainment | | | | Demanding | | |
UK adults	Average viewing hours per week	Light entertainment	Light drama	Films	Sport	Drama arts, etc.	Information	News
Social class								
ABC1[a]	23	16	24	11	9	4	18	10
C2DE	30	15	26	12	9	3	17	9

[a] Better-off and longer-educated, professional, managerial, etc.
Source: Barwise and Ehrenberg 1988, p. 26

Barwise and Ehrenburg (1988) argue that these data on television audiences indicate that television is a mass, low-involvement medium. Many of the markets for consumer goods are segmented. For example, the readership of different magazines, newspapers or books varies by social class, age, gender, and so on. Thus the *Sun* has a much more working-class readership than the *Guardian*. On average, the readership of *Bella* is younger than that for *Good Housekeeping*. Television, however, as we have seen, is quite different. Programmes do not appeal to particular social groups. For almost any programme the make-up of the audience is the same. Television is truly a mass medium.

Morley (1986) notes that current social conventions still define the home as a place of leisure, relaxation, and enjoyment, away from the rigours of employment, for the man of the household, while for women the home is a place of work, domestic work, even if they are also engaged in paid work outside the home. For many women, this means that domestic work has to be fitted in when the household is gathered round the television set. As a result, a man's characteristic mode of viewing is attentive, a woman's inattentive. This difference does not arise out of the different biological constitutions of men and women, or out of any 'natural' inability of women to concentrate, but is a socially determined difference related to the different obligations and expectations placed on the two genders in the organization of the household. For Morley, one of his major findings is the consistency of this difference between men and women:

Essentially the men state a clear preference for viewing attentively, in silence, without interruption 'in order not to miss anything'. Moreover, they display puzzlement at the way their wives and daughters watch television. This, the women themselves describe as a fundamentally social activity, involving ongoing conversation, and usually the performance of at least one other domestic activity (ironing etc.) at the same time. Indeed, many of the women feel that to just watch television without doing anything else at the same time would be an indefensible waste of time, given their sense of domestic obligations. To watch in this way is something they rarely do, except occasionally, when alone or with other women friends, when they have managed to construct an 'occasion' on which to watch their favourite programme, video, or film. The women note that their husbands are always 'on at them' to shut up. The men can't really understand how their wives can follow the programmes if they are doing something else at the same time. (Morley 1986, p. 150)

The issue of attentiveness is not simply a question of gender. It is actually normal not to pay attention to the television set. Another set of experiments conducted by Collett (Collett and Lamb 1985) involved the mounting of a video-camera and a microphone inside television sets and filming people watching the television. Collett found an enormous variety of ways of watching. Some viewers were slumped in front of the set while others were paying rapt attention, concentrating on everything going on. Still others were paying no attention at all and played the flute, wrote letters, engaged in animated conversation completely unrelated to what was on the set, did hand-stands, vacuumed the carpet – and left the room. There have been attempts to measure the degree of inattention in audiences (Barwise and Ehrenberg 1988). During commercial breaks about 20 per cent of people apparently 'watching the programme' are in fact out of the room, 10 per cent are not viewing, 30 per cent are viewing but also doing something else, and only 40 per cent are viewing only. While actual programmes are on, the proportion of people who are not attentively viewing is lower, but is still 40 per cent of the total.

Most television is watched at home. Furthermore, a very large proportion of the leisure time spent in the home is taken up with watching television. Television is also watched in families. Despite some fundamental changes in household structure, one consequence of which is a rise in the number of single-person households, television is watched by members of families together. Television interacts with domestic life in a number of ways. For example, Hobson (1982) shows how the rhythms of the household are organized around television programmes, which can regulate meal-times, bedtimes and occasions for going out. More importantly, the medium can provide for communication between family members. People will refer to television programmes in their everyday conversation and use characters and events to illustrate what they want to say. Soap opera is often used in this way. Buckingham (1987) illustrates this point in his study of youthful viewers of *EastEnders*. One 17-year old felt that television enabled him to talk to his parents about problems like drugs by presenting characters who were involved in drug use. As this interviewee said:

The other thing that it does, is that you sit there, and normally you're with your parents, and you're sitting down watching it, and you just talk . . . The conversation arises from that, and so you're talking to your parents about it, and so it probably makes you feel a bit comfortable, like if you need the backing from your parents, and the security there. (Buckingham 1987, p. 163)

Indeed, one of the critical qualities of television seems to be its capacity to provoke conversation, to encourage talk. Indeed, television often seems to be *about* talk. Television mirrors and interacts with the conversational lives of its audience.

Different social groups, however, differ in their use of television as a conversational opportunity. It appears, for example, that men talk less about television than women. As Morley (1986) points out, although women watch television less intensively than men, they talk about it more. As one of his respondents says:

> I go round my mate's and she'll say, 'Did you watch Coronation Street last night? What about so and so?' And we'll sit there discussing it. I think most women and young girls do. We always sit down and it's 'Do you think she's right last night, what she's done?' Or, 'I wouldn't have done that', or 'Wasn't she a cow to him? Do you reckon he'll get . . . I wonder what he's going to do?' Then we sort of fantasize between us, then when I see her the next day she'll say, 'You were right' or 'See, I told you so'. (p. 156)

Men, on the other hand, generally in Morley's sample, will only admit to talking about sport. It is not clear whether this is because they really do not talk about television programmes or because they are reluctant to admit that they do – and it may well be both. Certainly men do display considerable contempt for much television, particularly 'women's programmes'. In many ethnographic studies men will not admit to watching fictional television, soap opera for instance, although the survey evidence shows that they do actually do so. Men may in other words be *pretending* not to like soap opera, a characteristic which might well lead to their not admitting that they talk about it.

When people talk about what they have seen on television, they frequently relate events or characters to their own lives. For example, in discussions of soap opera, viewers will interpret the behaviour of one of the characters by noting his or her similarities to someone they know. Such a strategy enables prediction of what will happen next or some reflection on the plausibility of the character's actions. The reverse may also happen in that people may interpret events in their own lives by reference to the way that a television character behaves. Such uses of television may be termed *referential* – television refers to everyday life. There are other ways of relating to television. In particular audiences may be *critical*, applying critical methods to them, discussing the acting or sets or suggesting that characters are not behaving consistently.

Television conversations represent a more or less seemless unity between references to experience and references to the characters in the soap; people bounce effortlessly backwards and forwards between their own world and the world of the soap opera. As Willis (1990) puts it:

> the young women who watch soaps are constantly judging them and reworking the material they provide, finding echoes in their own lives and spaces which allow them to ask what would happen 'if'. TV watching is, at least in part, about facilitating a dialectic between representation and reality as a general contribution to symbolic work and creativity. The audience is not an empty room waiting to be furnished in someone else's taste. (p. 36)

Adults may make comparisons between a real-life event and one that has occurred on television in order to manage their relationships. Children may use television programmes to investigate and discuss the secrets of the adult world (Buckingham 1987). Within certain communities, television watching may be used to manage tensions of various kinds. Gillespie (1993) carried out a study of the viewing of soap opera in a Punjabi community in Southall in London. Young people within this community used their watching of *Neighbours* to understand the relationship of their community to the surrounding white society:

> While young people regularly emphasize the *differences* between the soap world and their own cultural experience, in another sense they stress strong *parallels* between the soap world and the social world of Southall . . . In certain respects, the soap opera embodies many of the characteristics of local life: the central importance of the family; a density of kin in a small, geographically bounded area; a high degree of face-to-face contact; a knowable community; and a distinctive sense of local identity . . . While young people's own families and those in their social networks provide their primary frame of reference about family life, soap families not only extend but offer alternative sets of families as reference groups by which young people can compare and contrast, judge and evaluate, and, in certain cases, attempt to critique and transform aspects of their own family life. (p. 32)

It is important to stress that, despite the way that people move between their own world and the televisual world, they also operate in critical mode and are very well aware of how television programmes are constructed. A number of writers have also argued that, from a comparatively young age, television audiences have some notion of how the programmes they watch are created and that there is some process of construction behind the fiction (Buckingham 1993). As a result, their conversation is peppered with comments about how well the actors and actresses play their roles, criticisms of the writing, and speculations about who is about to leave the serial because there has been a dispute between actor and the management. In their television talk, in the use of referential and critical framings, the audience show that they are not passive. It is difficult, therefore, to conclude that audiences are simply manipulated by television.

Summary

1   Television is a very pervasive feature of everyday life.
2   Ownership of the television industry is becoming more concentrated and global.
3   Television is a producer's medium.
4   There is a continuing debate as to whether television reporting is biased and, if so, in what ways.

12.3   Popular music

There is no clear-cut definition of popular music. Indeed, it is most often thought of by way of a contrast with 'serious' classical music (and perhaps jazz), which are often considered difficult and thus only appreciated by a minority. Such a definition is, of course, part of a more general distinction between high and popular culture, a distinction which owes more to the way that popular culture is valued in British society than to any intrinsic qualities of popular music, television, radio, film or newspapers.

Popular music is overwhelmingly recorded music. According to a 1994 study (*Social Trends* 1996) people spend four hours per week listening to recorded music, an expenditure of time on leisure at home only exceeded by watching television and listening to the radio, which, of course, themselves play substantial amounts of recorded music. Attendance at concerts, on the other hand, is a minority phenomenon. Only 8 per cent of the population had attended a classical music concert in the previous three months, compared with 7 per cent who had attended a pop or rock concert. These figures will understate the attendance at live musical performances since they do not include such events as music in pubs but, nevertheless, they indicate that the great bulk of most people's musical experience is via recorded music.

The popular music industry

The music industry as a whole is of considerable economic importance to the UK as an exporter. For example, in 1993, the total trade surplus of the industry was £571 million and British musicians were responsible for 18 per cent of recorded music. It is important to note that these earnings are not only made up of earnings from record sales; income from royalties accruing from the playing of recorded music on radio and television, from performance, and from music publishing actually constitutes the bulk of earnings. The industry is also important in the domestic market. In 1994 over £1.5 billion was spent in Britain on recorded music, almost the same as that spent on books (*Cultural Trends* 1995). In that year, each member of the British public bought an average of 3.1 albums and, in this respect, Britons were the fourth heaviest purchasers in the world. These sales are overwhelmingly of popular music of one kind or another. In 1994, only 7 per cent of sales of recorded music were of classical work, 2 per cent were of jazz and 4 per cent were of folk or country music. Seventy-nine per cent comprised popular music genres of various kinds.

Popular music is, in other words, a large business even if many performers and fans believe that it is also an art, and the contrast between commerce and art runs through the whole history of popular (and particularly rock) music. Furthermore, it is an industry dominated by a few very large, international companies – EMI, Sony, Polygram, Warner, BMG and MCA. Between them, these companies command a 70 per cent share of the world market in recorded popular music and even more in some countries (95 per cent in Britain, for example: Wicke 1990; Longhurst 1995). In turn these companies are part of even larger enterprises, which usually have interests in other branches of the media. For example, Warner is part of Time-Warner, which in the mid-1990s was valued at $18 billion, has a labour force worldwide of some 340,000 people, and is engaged in magazine and book publishing, music recording and publishing, film and video, and cable television. As with all international media companies, Time-Warner is highly vertically integrated, bringing together all the stages of the production process, thereby generating substantial economies in production and marketing. It is also horizontally integrated, owning companies operating in related media fields. BMG is a subsidiary of Bertellsman, which started life as a book publisher but has diversified not only into popular music but also into magazines and newspapers and cable television (see sections 3.3 on industrial concentrations and 12.2 for the television industry).

Despite the dominance of the large record companies, there is, of course, an independent sector in Britain. It has been argued (Peterson and Berger 1990) that there are cycles of concentration, when small companies are bought up and larger ones merge, and deconcentration, when the large conglomerates lose market share. The relationship between large and small companies is not so much antagonistic as symbiotic. In general, small companies are closer to public taste, in part because they are more locally based (see below) and are able to detect musical innovation and capitalize on it. However, the small companies depend on the greater ability of the larger to distribute, market and sell their products. In addition, if an independent company takes on an artist who subsequently becomes successful, the greater financial power of the large companies often ensures that the artist will move from the independent. As Wicke (1990, p. 125) puts it:

> Thus the rock business consists of two very different sectors which make up a functional unity: the highly centralised environment of the multinational media organisations on the one hand, and on the other the decentralised structure of the independents – not just record companies, but also small agencies and local promoters. The difference between them is the criteria according to which they work, but not their aim, which is to sell records or tickets respectively. For the one the rock business is just part of a huge commercial organisation and only of interest in terms of turnover figures, earnings calculations and profit rates, for the others it is first and foremost working in and with music – but the *music business* only arises out of the conjunction of both of these.

The tension between small, local record companies and large international ones within any one country is repeated on the global scale. The American and to some extent the British music industries dominate the sale of music throughout the world. This has led many commentators to worry that indigenous music – that coming from the special traditions of each country – will die out and be replaced with Western music in a form of cultural imperialism. While it is true that, with the growing accessibility of radio, television and tape, record or CD players, many previously relatively undeveloped countries have become rapidly expanding markets for Western popular music, there are a number of reasons for thinking that anxieties about cultural imperialism may be misplaced. First, indigenous music continues to flourish and local recording industries grow up to service it. Indeed, the large international music companies have become interested in selling local music back to those countries that originated it *and* worldwide; a world market in world music is developing. Second, as the media become truly global, creating a global mediascape (see chapter 2), new musical forms are generated out of the mixture of Western and non-Western indigenous traditions. Local musicians blend their own local music with ideas derived from other countries. Third, cultural imperialism does not necessarily follow economic imperialism. Just because Western popular music is sold and played worldwide does not mean that indigenous musical traditions are not still perpetuated in live performance. Even more, each national or local culture may interpret Western music in its own particular way. In sum, as Robinson, Buck and Cuthbert (1991, p. 227) put it in a study of popular music and global cultural diversity:

> We see internationalized music as a global music system that transcends but does not overwhelm national boundaries. Throughout the world the globalization process, as represented by the international music industry, is being countered by the production of unique musics by local musicians.

The production of popular music

In this section we consider how popular music is produced and concentrate on two aspects: the way in which musicians and bands develop and the process by which musicians get taken up by large companies and recorded.

Most musicians, when they start out, have a firm conception of their music as a serious contribution, even as an art form. Indeed, innovation in popular music frequently comes from those who find the music of their time too commercial and they look for musical forms that self-consciously reject the conventions. These contrasts between art and commerce are illustrated by a study of the connections between the art schools and popular music in Britain by Frith and Horne (1987). They show 'how, in art schools, a particular tension between creativity and commerce is confronted and how pop music works as a solution' (p. 3), and point to the striking number of innovative rock musicians that have been produced by Britain's art schools throughout the period since the Second World War. During this period art schools provided a supportive environment for people (largely men) who had been rebellious, non-conformist or drop-outs at school. In this environment it was relatively easy to get started in music. The colleges provided space for performance, and student audiences were more tolerant than others and more receptive to musical innovation and to novelties in performances:

> Our argument about this crucial period in British pop history is not that all significant British musicians were at art school but that those that were, brought into music-making attitudes that could never have been fostered under the pressures of professional entertainment. Over the next few years the art school connection became the best explanation of why some British beat groups made a successful move into the new rock culture (in pursuit of creative challenge), while others were doomed to play out their careers in performances of their old 'entertaining' hits night after night on the working men's club and cabaret circuit. (Frith and Horne 1987, p. 86)

The art school background provided the innovatory edge which, in turn, generated commercial success. At the same time as they were selling large numbers of records in the 1960s and 1970s, bands such as Cream, the Rolling Stones and Led Zeppelin believed in the *authenticity* of what they were doing: 'Rock, then, unlike pop, was to be serious, progressive, truthful, and individual, a cluster of terms whose significance lay in the Romantic self-image of the 1960s art student, and it was to be hugely successful' (p. 90).

The artists of the 1960s and 1970s could live happily with the apparent tension between their belief in their music and their commercial success, but it was the punk movement in the 1980s that solved, or even celebrated, that tension. There is little doubt that punk was new and deliberately non-conformist, not only in the attitudes expressed, but also in the willed absence of musicianship. At the same time, punk did not just live with commercialism, it actively embraced it. By celebrating consumer culture, the trivial, the artificial, punk made art into commerce and commerce into art. For Malcolm McLaren, the founder/manager of the Sex Pistols, the aim was:

> To stay sharp by burrowing into the money-making core of the pop machine, to be both blatantly commercial (and thus resist the traditional labels of art and Bohemia) and deliber-

ately troublesome (so that the usually smooth, hidden, gears of commerce were always on noisy display). (Frith and Horne 1987, p. 132)

On the whole, popular musicians start their careers by performing locally (Longhurst 1995). S. Cohen (1991), for example, studied local bands in Liverpool, bands that had, at least at the time of the study, not yet won a recording contract. She notes the importance that the bands attached to originality. They insisted on performing their own material even if it was not particularly attractive to a wider market. At the same time, however, they were very keen on recognition beyond the local milieu and obtaining a record contract.

Finnegan (1989), in a study of musicians in Milton Keynes, also shows how important music-making is to a locality:

Milton Keynes was swarming with rock and pop bands. They were performing in the pubs and clubs, practising in garages, youth clubs, church halls and school classrooms, advertising for new members in the local papers and lugging their instruments around by car or on foot. There were probably around 100 groups, each with their own colourful names and brand of music. (p. 103)

This is largely amateur music. The majority of the bands, particularly those composed of employed people, did not make any money out of their playing and did not seriously

Plate 12.2 | A rock band playing in a pub
Source: Rephoto/B. Wentzell

intend to. They were not really organized for money-making, they did not have dedicated managers and rarely used agents to arrange bookings. Rather they got great personal satisfaction from their music, a sense of comradeship, the pleasures of performance and the opportunity to express themselves. As with the Liverpool bands studied by Cohen, Finnegan's Milton Keynes musicians placed a great deal of importance on the originality of their material and on individual expression:

> Perhaps the most prominent single characteristic of the preoccupations of rock players in Milton Keynes – apart from their variety – was their interest in expressing their own views and personality through music-making: a stress on individuality and artistic creation which accords ill with the mass theorists' delineation of popular music. One need only recall the widespread emphasis on self-teaching for learning their instruments; the small-scale and independent form of rock groups, necessarily self-reliant and outside the formal organisation pattern typical of many other musical (and non-musical) groupings. (Finnegan 1989, p. 129)

While most bands had a solely local existence and wanted to keep it that way, a few clearly had wider ambitions. For example, at the time of Finnegan's study, one local band was playing two or three times per week and, although they still played locally and in relatively small venues, they were beginning to appear in clubs and large pubs and at colleges and, occasionally, in London. They had attracted media attention and had had feelers from record companies. They had begun to find that they needed professional help from agents and managers to arrange bookings and negotiate with record companies. Their aim was to get a record contract and to tour and to play to large audiences. Despite this ambition for commercial success, however, they also felt that the band provided an opportunity to communicate their own distinctive vision – both musical and ideological.

The transition from local, live performance to a recording contract is not a simple one. Record companies will want to 'brand' every band – to give it a distinctive set of characteristics that will set it apart from other bands and be instantly recognizable to audiences. Partly, marketing and promotion sell an act. Often this is done by creating an image of the band, perhaps centred on the personalities of the band members or of a star performer. It is more beneficial for the record company to emphasize the band rather than the individual record because that is a better basis for long-run sales. Partly, also, the branding is produced in the process of recording by producer and sound engineer, who aim to create, out of many recording sessions, a distinctive sound for any band. The work of producers and engineers is largely invisible. It is not simply a technical exercise. It has become as creative as the original performance, as the technology which enables manipulation of sound has improved.

With many popular music bands, especially rock bands, therefore, there is a tension between localness, creativity and originality, on the one hand, and a desire for fame, commercial success and a recording contract, on the other. Since the large record companies are constantly on the lookout for musical innovation, they can resolve that tension for a few bands, at least in the short term.

The popular music audience

People can listen to music in a variety of different ways: at live performances, from records, tapes or CDs, from the radio, or even from television, video or film. Listening to recorded music from tapes, records or CDs is a popular pastime. As we have already pointed out, on average each member of the British population spends four hours per week listening to music in this form. There are, of course, variations between different sections of the population. For example, 97 per cent of those aged 16–19 have listened to tapes or records during the previous four weeks, compared with only 54 per cent of those aged 55–64. As one might expect, there are similar differences in the record-buying habits of the population. Expenditure on recorded music has risen steadily. In 1992, the British population spent a quarter as much again as in 1985 (*Cultural Trends* 1993). Considering purchases of albums, classical music represents about 10 per cent of all sales and tends to be bought by older people and the higher social classes. Rock music is more of a male taste while pop is bought more by women. Interestingly, more pop is bought by those aged 25–44 than by younger age groups. Although the 16–24 age group buys more rock than any other, the 25–44 group is not far behind. As Longhurst (1995) points out, rock and pop are not necessarily exclusively the music of youth, and sociological research ought to give more attention to the middle-aged rock and pop fan.

The substantial amount of ethnographic research in youth cultures in recent years has shown that music plays an important part in the creation and maintenance of those cultures (see sections 9.4 and 11.3). For example, Willis (1990) argues that popular music is young people's central cultural interest:

> What is clear . . . is that young people's musical activities, whatever their cultural back-ground or social background or social position, rest on a substantial and sophisticated body of knowledge about popular music. Most young people have a clear understanding of its different genres, and an ability to hear and place sounds in terms of their histories, influences and sources. Young musicians and audiences alike have no hesitation about making and justifying judgements of meaning and value. (p. 59)

The important point for Willis is that the use of popular music by the young is not merely passive consumption but is an active creative enterprise. Music is there to be talked about, judged and evaluated, and emotionally appreciated. It has *meaning* for young people, as this quotation from one of Willis's respondents illustrates:

> It's telling people something through music, through something that most people like and enjoy. It gives you a lot of wisdom. 'Cause in your heart, you know you feel that way, and when you listen to it you know that other people are thinking on them same kind of ways, and it kind of gives you more strength. (p. 70)

The association between youth and music has often provided unfortunate ammunition for the media. A succession of musical styles from 1950s rock and roll, through 1980s heavy metal, to 1990s dance has been blamed for a variety of the ills that are supposed to affect young people, including suicide, violence and drug addiction. In the late 1980s and early 1990s, for example, the media discovered Acid House, the rave and Ecstasy (Thornton 1995; Rietveld 1993). These were associated together to create a moral panic in which serious dangers to innocent participants and bystanders were anticipated. This panic had important effects in that legislation was passed, clubs lost their licences, and the freedom to stage outdoor events was severely curtailed.

Summary

1 Ownership of companies within the popular music industry is becoming more concentrated and global.
2 Bands start their careers playing locally and being primarily interested in the music rather than commercial success. The innovation that this can generate can lead to commercial success.
3 Although popular music plays a substantial role in youth culture, the middle-aged are also significant buyers of pop and rock records.

12.4 Newspapers and magazines

Since television dominates leisure time, it might seem that media forms competing with television, especially newspapers, would be in terminal decline. There has indeed been a decline in newspaper readership over the past few decades. In the early 1950s the total of national daily newspapers was almost 17 million. By 1995 that had shrunk to about 14 million. None the less, that is still considerable and newspapers still make healthy profits for their proprietors. Moreover, circulation figures only represent *sales* of newspapers. Every newspaper that is sold has more than one reader, ranging from 2.3 readers for every copy of the *Express* to 3.5 for the *Financial Times*. As table 12.3 indicates, 56 per cent of the population – 26 million people – *read* a national daily paper and, if one adds in weekly papers, the figure rises to 80 per cent. The table also shows the dominance of the tabloids, especially the *Sun*, which alone has half as many readers again as all the broadsheets put together. It is interesting that younger age groups are more likely to read newspapers than knowledge of their other leisure pursuits might imply. The *Daily Mail,* the *Express* and the *Daily Telegraph* tend to have a readership that is relatively old, while for the other titles either young readers predominate or there is a fairly even age distribution. Men outnumber women in newspaper readership, with the solitary exception of the *Daily Mail*, but not by much.

The most popular magazines judged by readership surveys are generally TV guides or in-house magazines like the *AA Magazine*. In the list in table 12. 4, two 'women's magazines' figure in the top twelve, together with one appealing to a predominantly male audience and one which is generally read by younger girls.

In terms of circulation and readership, newspapers and magazines continue to have considerable impact. Although the evidence is by no means clear, they may also be significant sources of information and belief. Partly this influence is indirect. Politicians, for example, are very concerned how they appear in the press and they spend a lot of time trying to manipulate their image. Television itself often picks up stories from newspapers. There may be a more direct impact on readers. Although, as indicated in section

TABLE 12.3 | **Reading of national daily newspapers: by age and gender, Great Britain, 1997–8[a]**

		Percentage reading each paper							
	15–24	25–44	45–64	65 and over	Males	Females	All adults	Readership[b] (millions)	Readers per copy (numbers)
Sun	28	23	19	15	25	18	21	9.9	2.7
Mirror	13	13	14	15	15	12	13	6.3	2.8
Daily Mail	8	9	14	13	11	11	11	5.1	2.3
Express	4	4	7	8	6	5	6	2.6	2.3
Daily Telegraph	3	4	7	8	6	5	5	2.5	2.4
The Times	4	4	5	3	5	3	4	2.0	2.7
Daily Star	7	5	3	1	6	2	4	1.9	3.2
Guardian	3	3	3	1	3	2	3	1.2	3.2
Independent	2	2	2	1	2	1	2	0.7	3.2
Financial Times	1	2	2	–	2	1	1	0.6	3.5
Any national newspaper[c]	52	52	61	60	61	52	56	26.0	–

[a] Data for July 1997 to June 1998
[b] Defined as the average issue readership and represents the number of people who claim to have read or looked at one or more copies of a given daily newspaper yesterday
[c] Includes the above newspapers plus the *Daily Record*, the *Sporting Life* and *Racing Post*
Source: *Social Trends* 1999, p. 213

TABLE 12.4 | **Reading of the most popular magazines: by age and gender, Great Britain, 1997–8[a] (percentages)**

Magazine	15–24	25–44	45–64	65 and over	Males	Females	All aged 15 and over
Sky TV Guide	19	17	12	3	15	11	13
M&S Magazine	6	11	12	7	5	14	10
Reader's Digest	4	8	13	12	10	10	10
Take a Break	11	12	8	7	4	15	10
What's on TV	14	11	6	6	8	11	9
Radio Times	10	7	9	9	9	9	9
AA Magazine	3	8	11	8	10	7	8
TV Times	9	7	7	8	7	8	8
Woman's Own	8	8	6	5	2	12	7
Bella	5	7	6	5	2	10	6
FHM	21	7	1	–	10	2	6
Cable Guide	10	8	5	2	7	6	7

[a] Data for July 1997 to June 1998
Source: *Social Trends* 1999, p. 214

12. 2, television is a more widely trusted source of information, newspapers may have more influence than readers think. There is some evidence that information taken from newspapers is retained better than that derived from television (McNair 1996).

Reading newspapers and magazines

There are many prejudices about the way in which people use the media. In particular, reading is thought to be a more serious activity than looking at a television screen; reading is active while television is passive. However, some of the evidence about how people actually read newspapers and magazines suggests fewer differences between the acts of reading and of watching the television. Hermes (1995), for example, argues that magazine reading should not be thought of as a deeply meaningful activity for the participants. On the contrary, like television, it is closely integrated with ordinary life and domestic routines. People pick up magazines in odd moments between other domestic events. They skip articles or read them more than once. As Hermes says:

> Magazines may be opened or leafed through, television sets may be on, but that is hardly an indication that they are 'read' consciously, seriously or with animation. How women's magazines are read and how television is watched appear to be inextricably tied in to everyday routines. Both television and women's magazines have become such standard parts of our lives that their status is almost unquestioned. (p. 15)

Billam (1995) makes much the same point about reading newspapers. For the majority of the population, reading the newspaper is integrated with domestic life. It is read at particular times of the day when nothing else is particularly pressing, and it is the subject of sporadic domestic conversation but is not otherwise of great importance. Most of Billam's interviewees do not set out to be educated by their newspaper and consequently do not read it from front to back with great attention. As some of them said (pp. 155–8):

> I think people in general buy newspapers as comics really, don't you? To see what's going on in Coronation Street, to see what the stars are up to.

> Most people buy them just to pass time when they're having a cup of coffee. That's the only time I read it.

> Pass the time when you're on the toilet.

> I've got twenty minutes for my morning break, so I have a fag and read the paper. Twenty minutes, that's it.

Even if Hermes's and Billam's interviewees do not treat their magazine and newspaper reading as a deeply meaningful or serious activity, that is not to say that, at some level, these activities are without effect. So, Billam argues that newspaper reading contributes to what he calls a 'collective identity':

> At its broadest, I understand the term 'collective identity' as referring to the relationship between a newspaper and its (collective) readership (its audience). This relationship should

Plate 12.3 The variety of newspapers and magazines
Source: Format/Joanne O'Brien

be seen as a two-way process whereby the discourse of the newspaper is in part the product of the opinions of its readers and the overall tone of the newspaper itself, hence the use of the term 'collective'. The collective identity of a national morning newspaper is thus something which the producer (the newspaper) wishes to present and exhibit, whilst at the same time, it is also something which the consumers (the audience) wish to be associated with and belong to. (Billam 1995, p. 160)

As an interviewee said:

If I look at somebody else and they're reading a newspaper, I think that means something. It tells me something about their personality and views, and if I'm walking along with a newspaper, I'm conscious that other people will think of me what I've said myself. (p. 160)

Hermes also argues that the reading of magazines is associated with identity. In particular, magazines help women maintain and enhance their images of themselves. They provide the raw material for fantasy and day-dreaming:

the practical tips, the recipes and the advice on the one hand and the features about relationships and stories of having a child with cancer and the like on the other may temporarily empower a reader. Even if you do not do anything at all with the recipes or the practical advice, you can imagine baking a perfect pie, or managing your boss so that she or he will feel you cannot be missed. The stories that deal with the wide area of human emotion, from a discussion of secret love affairs to a sad tale of accepting the death of a child, can help you feel prepared in case such a thing happened to you, or more knowledgeable about human nature in general, which may give a satisfactory sense of being a 'wise person' or bolster your professional confidence. (Hermes 1995, p. 145)

Content and control

Accusations of bias are often levelled against newspapers. For example, for a very long time most newspapers in Britain supported the Conservative Party. Following the 1992 election that changed, with the result that newspapers like the *Sun* began to support the Labour Party. Even with these defections, however, the press is still predominantly Conservative. In this sense, the press does not represent political opinion in the electorate or, indeed, its readers. More seriously, there is the distinct possibility – about which there is continuing argument – that readers may be persuaded to vote Conservative by the newspapers that they read.

As with television, because it is necessary to select newsworthy items from the events of the day, newspapers *cannot* give a flawlessly objective presentation of the world. The choices that media personnel make are partly determined by social factors. Selectivity works in a number of different ways. First, newspapers have a marked tendency to report events as they occur rather than to give an explanation. Second, journalists operate by a set of values about what is newsworthy, what events they think the audience will find interesting. The most important factor, however, is what has become known as agenda setting. This means that the broadcasting media effectively decide what are important issues, promoting some and leaving others out. For example, in the treatment of race relations in Britain, discussions in the media have tended to establish racial conflict as the central, newsworthy issue, leaving out factors that may explain such conflicts – the multiple disadvantages that black people experience in Britain, for example. Black people, therefore, become defined as a threat, an implicit assumption which structures news reports. Agendas are constructed using a variety of methods. Particular issues are taken up while others are ignored; one viewpoint is stressed while others receive less extensive treatment; some sources are seen as authoritative and neutral while others are seen as biased; participants in a story will be treated in different ways, some being subjected to hostile interviewing; particular words will come to be associated with particular issues ('conflict' with 'race' for instance), while language used in other issues will be more neutral; and visual material is used as evidence for a written commentary when it does not provide relevant illustration.

These factors provide an account of the mechanism of selectivity but they do not explain why selectivity takes the form that it does. No one argues that the particular way in which television news is structured is the result of a conspiracy by television journalists. We have to look for other factors that account for the view (or views) of the world presented by newspapers. It is convenient to divide these into factors external and internal to the institutions in which media personnel work.

External factors

Externally, the state can influence the way that material is presented in newspapers, though not to the same extent as it can influence, and has influenced, the BBC. This is clearly not a matter of direct control, but is a more subtle process of providing briefings, formal and informal. Ministers and government departments have access to news institutions through their public relations agencies and the expression of ministerial displeasure and, hence, some measure of control can be very effectively exercised. More subtly and, therefore, probably more efficiently, governments can make their influence felt because the media portray the institutions of state as neutral and as above political controversy.

In looking at newspapers one might easily think that their ownership had something to do with control of their content. Proprietors do interfere directly with editorial policy and it would be surprising if they did not. As McNair (1996) says: 'the economic and political interests of the proprietor continue to be the most important determinant of a news outlet's editorial line' (p. 47). At the extreme, Lord Beaverbrook, for example, said that he only kept his newspapers (the *Daily Express* and *Sunday Express*) for the purposes of propaganda. To the extent that it does occur, interference by proprietors is more serious because of changes in the ownership of newspapers. Table 12. 5 shows how four – or perhaps two – groups dominate newspaper sales.

In turn these newspaper groups are also deeply involved in other branches of the media. News International, for example, has interests in television, film and book publishing as well as newspapers worldwide. Any proprietorial intervention can have an impact over a wide area.

In contemporary Britain, owners are more likely to interfere with editorial content for commercial rather than political or ideological reasons. They may, for example, want not to antagonize a particular government. More important, however, their general commercial interests are more likely to coincide with Conservative policy than with

TABLE 12.5 | **Major proprietors and share of national newspaper circulation, 1995ᵃ (percentages)**

Proprietor	Daily	Sunday
News International (*Sun, Today, The Times, Sunday Times, News of the World*)	36.7	38.8
MGN (*Mirror/Record, People, Sunday People, Independent*ᵇ)	22.6	30.0
United Newspapers (*Daily Express, Star, Sunday Express*)	14.0	9.1
Associated Newspapers (*Daily Mail, Mail on Sunday*)	12.4	12.7
Hollinger (*Daily Telegraph, Sunday Telegraph*)	7.4	4.5
Newspaper Publishing (*Independent on Sunday*)	–	2.1
Guardian and Manchester Evening News (*Guardian, Observer*)	2.8	3.0
Financial Times Ltd (*Financial Times*)	2.0	–

ᵃ Calculated on average figures for January–June 1995
ᵇ MGN holds a 43 per cent share
Source: McNair 1996, p. 11

Labour. Another source of commercial intervention is advertising. Advertisers may well want to advertise their products and services in newspapers that do not promote unpopular causes or which otherwise attract criticism in, for instance, their treatment of the private lives of politicians and other celebrities. The values, themes and topics promoted by newspapers may well fit in with those espoused by owners. One might guess that, other things being equal, owners would like to see their newspapers take a central position, leaning neither to the left nor to the right, emphasize consensus on common values, and set the agenda on items of public debate, all features described earlier. Perhaps owners do not need to intervene because they already share social values with the people who produce newspapers, and owners, journalists and audiences are bound together in a set of social values that is continually reinforced by media content.

Internal factors

This last point draws attention to factors that may constrain newspaper output that are internal to newspaper organizations. In all occupations there is pressure to conform to the particular occupational culture. Where these occupations are professionalized, these pressures can take a distinct form. While there is no recognized profession of journalism in the sense that medicine is a recognized profession, several studies note the way in which people who work in the media stress the 'professionalism' of their work. This has become so pronounced that professional values appear to take precedence over all others. In practice, an adherence to professional values means an emphasis on methods of presentation rather than content, on skill in spotting and writing stories, on being efficient and craftsmanlike, on imagining the readership and producing newspapers which satisfy it, on achieving balance and impartiality. The media generally are seen as the means by which the various voices or interests in a society may be heard and balanced. These voices, however, are not equally skilled, resourceful or even obvious, and the professional's role in merely representing them will be to include some while leaving others out. In other words, the very professionalism of journalism, the dedication to methods rather than content, will have the agenda-setting consequences that we have already noted.

Professionalism, however, also has another consequence, which might, under certain circumstances, run counter to this. The emphasis on skill, experience and efficiency enables journalists to defend themselves from interference, either from management or from the outside world. They can present themselves as impartial professionals who do a good job and have no axe to grind. Here lies one of the sources of resistance to control by governments or owners.

One final, familiar, factor of constraint on the media should be noted. Journalists – and their managers – are recruited from a relatively narrow segment of the population. Their social origins will inevitably influence the way they look at the world. Some viewpoints will seem more important than others and some topics will be altogether lost to their sight. The generally middle-class and upper-class origins of most journalists will predispose them to respect expert opinion and to treat it as unbiased, to find it easier to talk to fellow members of the middle class than to the working-class population, and to seek out other middle-class opinion – that of management, for instance. The middle-class experience of life often excludes the recognition of other experiences. It may, therefore, be quite natural for a journalist to be unaware of whole areas of working-class life, to believe that ranges of problems and difficulties do not exist and, therefore, not to represent certain voices or topics on programmes.

Summary

1   Although many people do not treat their newspapers particularly seriously, the kind of newspaper that is read is part of people's identity.
2   There is little doubt that newspapers are biased in a way that television is not, but there is continuing debate as to what effect that bias has on the readership.
3   Newspapers are typically owned by companies which also have interests in other branches of the media.

Related topics

On the globalization of media messages see section 2.1, and on the concentration of ownership and control of industry consult section 3.3. On one group of employees within the media industries – artists and performers – see section 11.6, which also discusses the audience for arts. Sections 11.2 and 11.3 discuss the privatization of leisure activity. On competing uses of leisure time see especially sections 11.4 and 11.5. Youth cultures are explored further in sections 9.4 and 11.3, and the influence of cultural consumption on the creation of identity is examined in sections 8.3 and 11.3.

Further reading

Longhurst (1995) provides further guidance on popular music, while Abercrombie (1996) is an introduction to sociological work on television. Hermes (1995) gives a particular perspective on the reading of women's magazines.

Cross-references to *Readings in Contemporary British Society*

Bennett on the different meanings given to hip-hop; **Hesmondhalgh** on the British dance music industry; **McNair** on the changing British press; **Gillespie** on the manner in which a Punjabi community interprets *EastEnders*; **Thompson** on moral panics in the mass media and the representation of AIDS.

13 The State and Politics

13.1 Introduction

There is a sense in which this book is all about 'politics'. When we consider the relationship between one social class and another, or the character of gender relations, or the nature of the police, we are dealing with matters that are in part 'political'. But in order to be clear here we distinguish between two senses of the 'political'.

On the one hand, 'politics' refers to all aspects of social life where there is some inequality of power between two or more people and there are attempts to sustain or to change that unequal relationship. In that sense, politics is everywhere; all social life is political. As the women's movement argues, 'the personal is political'. People's closest personal relationships, with mothers and fathers, brothers and sisters, wives and husbands, friends and lovers, are all political since they involve inequalities of power and attempts to sustain or to change those inequalities.

On the other hand, 'politics' refers to the major social institutions, the 'state', that in combination organize and regulate British society. The British state comprises:

- Parliament, which makes laws and sets the broad context of policy in most spheres of life;
- the civil service and local councils, which implement laws and organize a wide range of legally regulated public services;
- judicial institutions of the courts and the police, which ensure obedience to the law;
- various organizations, such as the Post Office, that provide economic services deemed to be central to British society;
- the armed forces, which protect the citizens of Britain from attack by other states.

It is this latter sense of 'politics' that mainly concerns us in this chapter (see section 9.5 above on the first sense of politics).

We have already talked of the 'state', on the one hand, and 'society', on the other. That we can make this distinction results from a revolution in people's thinking that occurred in the eighteenth and nineteenth centuries. Before then, state and society were viewed as one; the state was society, and it was impossible to think that there was something called society that might significantly 'cause' the state to take a particular form.

These present arrangements between 'state' and 'society' in Britain result from a lengthy historical development, particularly involving the reduction in the formal powers of the monarchy. In the nineteenth century, power came to reside more with the House of Commons. There were substantial extensions of the franchise (those entitled to vote in elections), and the boundaries of different constituencies were changed so that they became similar in size. Political parties also began to develop in the House of Commons, and pressure groups, such as the Anti-Corn Law League, first put pressure on Parliament to initiate or to amend legislation. It also became normal for the person chosen as prime minister to be that person with a majority of supporters in the House of Commons.

Elections greatly increased in importance and so did a need to contact voters through well-organized political parties based on mass membership, especially as voting was made secret and people could not be openly coerced to vote particular ways. People increasingly voted for these political parties and such parties developed 'programmes' of policies. Once elected, a party was expected to implement its programme and this, in turn, centralized power in the hands of the party leaders, especially the Cabinet, which had become the key element in the state by 1900. The importance of political programmes was also reinforced by further extensions to the franchise, especially to women, so that by 1928 all adults over 21 had the vote. However, it should be noted that even in the late 1990s Britain is not perfectly democratic. People in Britain are still described as 'subjects' of the monarch as opposed to being 'citizens', and (in 1999) non-elected hereditary peers in the House of Lords could block legislation which had been voted through within the House of Commons.

In the late twentieth century, British politics has come to focus upon the mobilization, organization and control of mass public opinion, particularly as expressed in support for different national political parties and their leaders. Modern British politics is a competition between two or three leading individuals, between the prime minister of the day and the leaders of the main opposition parties. This competition is largely fought out in the mass media and involves so-called 'spin doctors', who seek to manipulate and orchestrate the images of those leaders as they appear, especially on television.

At the same time, there have been large changes in the size, range and power of the British state. It has at its disposal enhanced powers of observing, recording and repressing the population (particularly through use of computer databases). It provides a wide range of services administered by large bureaucracies (both the civil service and local authorities). And it plans and acts on behalf of society as a whole, since, if matters were left to each individual, many would suffer unnecessary deprivation. There have been a number of major expansions in activities of the state, as it has intervened in pursuit of such 'collective' goals at the expense of individual interests. This expansion was most clear in the development of an extensive welfare state between 1945 and 1951, after the Labour government was elected at the end of the Second World War.

Much contemporary politics is indeed based upon divisions caused by such welfare state developments. Thus while the Conservative Party between 1979 and 1997 attempted to reduce the size of the welfare state and to lower the taxation needed to pay for it, the Labour Party in opposition was committed to maintaining significant aspects of a welfare state. Contemporary politics is substantially organized around disputes concerning the appropriate size and functioning of the state.

In the following section, we consider the British state, particularly its powers, internal organization, and recent changes in its relations with other states and organizations, especially those lying beyond the borders of Britain. We also examine how power more generally is organized in modern Britain: is it widely distributed or is it concentrated? If it is concentrated, which groups have power? In section 13.3 we consider the question of elections, analysing the factors that appear to influence the way people in Britain vote in general elections. The chapter concludes with an assessment of current changes in British politics, particularly in the area of social welfare.

13.2   Power and the state

The state

The state consists of that set of centralized and interdependent social institutions concerned with passing laws, implementing and administering those laws, and providing the legal machinery to enforce compliance with them. These institutions rest upon the state's monopoly of legitimate force within a given territory, which means that most of the time the laws of Britain are upheld. The powers of the state ultimately rest upon this threat of legitimate force. In Britain, the state comprises a diversity of interdependent social institutions, including the prime minister, Cabinet, Parliament, political parties, civil service, judiciary, police, armed forces, local government, schools, colleges, universities, National Health Service (NHS), Bank of England, Post Office, BBC, OFWAT, OFGAS and so on.

Unlike in many countries, the powers of these different social institutions are not formally specified in a written constitution. Rather, the British constitution is largely unwritten, but is nevertheless binding. As a result, changes can occur in the powers of those social institutions that constitute the state. For example, the power of the civil service has increased in recent years and that of Parliament has declined. In other words, there has been a restructuring of the state made possible by the substantially unwritten constitution.

This further means that the powers of the government of the day in Britain are extremely far-reaching, since they are not circumscribed by a written constitution that might protect individual rights. Provided the current government has appropriate authority to make and enforce certain laws, the judiciary will generally uphold them and ensure compliance. For example, in 1972 the home secretary introduced a bill in the House of Commons that retrospectively legalized various actions of the British army in Northern Ireland, actions which the Northern Ireland high court had determined were illegal. That Bill was approved by both the Houses of Commons and Lords on the day that it was first introduced. This has recently led many to propose that there should be a formal Bill of Rights.

The first and most significant power of the British state is the almost unlimited ability to make and to enforce laws. Some of these laws delegate authority to ministers to make what are, in effect, further laws (statutory instruments) without the necessity of bringing a new Bill to Parliament. No other social institution possesses such powers. There is no private company, however powerful, which is able to compel all British citizens to act in particular ways justified as being in accordance with the 'rule of law'.

People in Britain generally obey the state, not because state directives are particularly popular or just or even sensible, but because they *are* the law. About 60 per cent of people questioned in 1989 would not break a law even if they were very strongly opposed to it. The levels of sanction necessary to enforce compliance are thus less marked in Britain than in some other countries. There are proportionately fewer policemen and women, and, apart from in Northern Ireland, the police do not normally carry weapons, there is no large paramilitary force to maintain public order, and the army generally keeps out of policing work.

The second major power of the state is its ability to raise very large sums of money. Total central and local government receipts in Britain amount to just over one-third of national income (GDP). However, this ability to raise taxes is not unlimited. If the government tries to raise taxes to very high levels then this may reduce the size of the national income because it lessens the amount of business activity in Britain. The actual receipts from taxes would thus be lower than if there had not been an attempt to increase taxes in the first place. There is thus some restriction on the ability of governments to raise revenue through taxation, although there is much political dispute as to where this limit actually lies. One crucial consequence of the raising of taxes and of the expenditure of the resulting income is to alter the relative rewards for different social groups. Broadly speaking, up to the 1980s the effects of taxation in the UK had been to produce a modest redistribution of income towards the poorer income groups. The tax changes introduced by the Conservatives during the 1980s seem to have ended this period of redistribution (see Pierson 1996, pp. 109–13). One consequence is that poorer people pay a significantly *higher* proportion of their annual income in taxes of various sorts than do richer people.

The third power of the state is the ability to employ large numbers of people. In the Second World War, for example, most of the male population were conscripted into the armed forces or organized into war-related civilian employment. In the 1960s and 1970s, about one-third of the labour force was employed by the state, in providing services in education and the health service, distributing benefits through Department of Health and Social Security (DHSS) offices, and producing goods and services in the nationalized industries (railways, coal, gas, electricity, telephones and so on). However, under the Conservative governments between 1979 and 1997, the proportion of the workforce employed by the state fell to about one in five of all employees (that is about 5 million; see Pierson 1996, p. 105). This reduction mostly resulted from the policy of privatizing former nationalized industries, a policy also occurring in most countries in the world.

The fourth power of the state stems from its control over land. The state is a major landowner in its own right, owning a fifth of the UK land area in the early post-war period. It can acquire land through compulsory purchase on favourable terms, if it plans to build, say, a major new road. The state also regulates the use of land through planning legislation, and can alter the relative value of privately owned land through building the new Channel rail link, for example. And the state can establish new uses for existing land, by establishing new towns such as Milton Keynes.

Fifth, the state controls various instruments of economic policy. The state has been a major investor in, and producer of, various commodities, although this is less so now than two or three decades ago. It exercises control over the exchange rate between sterling and the major currencies and, hence, affects the relative prices of exports and imports. The state exercises some control over interest rates and hence over the supply of money; and, through taxation and public borrowing, it affects the general level of economic activity in Britain, national income, level of output, pattern of price increases, and rate of unemployment. However, it should be noted that globalization has reduced the effectiveness of some of these instruments of economic policy, especially because the flows of money in the world economy totally dwarf the resources available to a particular state, even a relatively rich one like the UK.

Finally, the state is not just an economic regulator but is a 'social regulator'. As it is less involved in the direct provision of services funded by taxation, so the British state has established a wide array of organizations which regulate the quality and forms of provision. OFWAT and OFTEL respectively monitor prices and the quality of services provided by the water and telephone industries, both of which are now privatized. Strangely, the Conservative governments elected as 'deregulators' introduced extensive new forms of regulation (see Pierson 1996, p. 107). The 1980s and 1990s have involved the 're-regulation' of industries (OFGAS), of the environment (the European Union Bathing Waters Directive), of education (OFSTED), of the railways (the Rail Regulator), of the press (the Press Complaints Council), of trade unions (the Certification Officer for Trade Unions and Employers' Associations) and so on. The European Union (EU), as we will see, is essentially a 'regulatory state', mostly involved in monitoring and regulating the policies of individual nation-states.

So far, then, we have seen that the state is a particularly powerful set of interdependent social institutions. The British state has the power to pass and implement laws, to raise taxes, to employ people, to control land, and to regulate the economy and social life more generally. No set of private institutions possesses such a range of powers. Figure 13.1 sets out the powers of the British state.

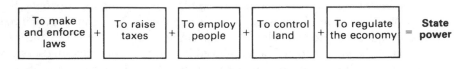

Figure 13.1 | The powers of the state

Power at different levels – from global to local

It should also be noted that the British state is divided into different levels: the national, the regional and the local. Changes occur in the relative importance of these different levels. In the past two decades there has been a steady reduction in the powers of the local level, both in the range of services provided through local authorities and in their degree of financial autonomy. Examples of the former include the 'opting out' of grant-maintained schools from control by local education authorities, and the setting up of central government institutions which operate at the local level, such as urban development corporations, but which are not locally elected. Also many local services, such as the buses, have been privatized, so they are no longer under the control of locally elected bodies. It is important to note too that the most popular service still provided by the state, the NHS, has been organized through areas and regions which involve unelected bodies appointed by central government ministers. The establishment of Trusts in the NHS further reduces the role of locally elected representatives in governing the health system. This more general development of very sizeable quangos to organize the delivery of state services represents a further way in which local people have no say in the nature of local provision.

Such a reduction of local power is of importance because this level is subject to popular representation and accountability. Local authorities still spend differing amounts on different services (such as on education per child), which suggests that they can decide matters on a local basis. The opposition to central government interference is widespread amongst local authorities. It is widely believed that there is too little local accountability. Many local councils within Britain have developed close relationships with the EU in Brussels, bypassing Westminster and Whitehall, which they feel are unresponsive to their local concerns.

Since the election of the Labour government in 1997, a regional level of government has developed within the UK. A Scottish Parliament with limited tax-raising powers and a Welsh Assembly were established in 1999. Plans for regional assemblies in England have been mooted. Changes have also taken place within the governance of Northern Ireland that involve power-sharing between Protestants and Catholics, in a new assembly that devolves power from Westminster to Belfast.

There is therefore developing what we can call a regionalization of the once unified British state. This has occurred for a number of reasons but is linked to the processes of globalization (see chapter 2). Historically, central to the British state has been the notion that there is a single, stable and exhaustive national identity; and that it is this single national identity that ensures a coherent and unified British nation-state. Smith summarizes:

Nation-states have frontiers, capitals, flags, anthems, passports, currencies, military parades, national museums, embassies and usually a seat in the United Nations. They also have one government for the territory of the nation-state, a single education system, a single economy and occupational system, and usually one set of rights for all citizens. (A. Smith 1986, p. 228)

It should be noted that the UK has never been quite like this, since Scotland has functioned as something of a separate nation within the nation-state of the UK. McCrone (1992) describes Scotland as a 'stateless nation' with quite a few symbols of what Billig (1995) calls 'banal nationalism'.

However, there is little doubt that globalization is transforming this pattern of well-established nation-states. Globalization appears to fragment single nation-states, emphasizing local, regional and subnational identities. In the UK multiple identities are developing, cross-cutting those of the British nation and hence the British state. Especially important are newly resurgent identities of Scottishness, Welshness and Irishness (and some would also say Englishness). These appear to have become much more pronounced, and campaigns have developed to restructure the British state so as to reflect such increasingly diverse and competing identities. The Conservative Party, which has most sought to maintain a single, unified and exhaustive nation-state, has lost almost all electoral support in Scotland and Wales, where there is now considerable support for much greater political autonomy. The UK no longer seems to be a single unified nation-state.

At the same time as the British state is more fragmented regionally, it is even more intertwined with various international state organizations. There is what can be called an internationalization of the British state. It plays a significant role in the American military defence system, as evidenced by its support for the bombing of camps of alleged international terrorists in Afghanistan in 1998. Britain is also part of the International Monetary Fund (IMF), which, especially in the 1960s and 1970s, dictated deflationary economic policy to a succession of British (and other) governments. There are many international conferences that involve the British government of the day signing up to international agreements that constrain future British policies. The 1992 Rio Earth Summit involved various commitments by all signatories to reduce the emission of carbon gases that are thought to produce global warming. Increasingly also, states have to develop their policies in the full glare of the world's media. Particular states therefore can often be shamed by pictures and reporting of failures, such as human rights abuses in jails in Northern Ireland.

But most importantly Britain is part of the EU, which enjoys legal authority over the British state. The EU is not a particularly large state, employing fewer than 30,000 bureaucrats. Nor does it have access to large funds (only 1.3 per cent of total EU income), although it does redistribute these in ways that have benefited some smaller countries such as Ireland. It does not therefore possess most of the powers of the British state that we noted earlier. The EU does not possess the monopoly of the means of legitimate violence and does not command major armed forces. It does not directly raise taxes from the population of Europe, and it does not employ large numbers of people. The EU is not a major landowner, although some of its regulations greatly affect the value of land in different parts of Europe (see Mann 1998, pp. 200–4). The EU is made up of a number of institutions (the Commission, the Council of Ministers, the European Court of Justice, the Parliament, and multiple agencies) which compete with each other and where the elected parliament does not exercise sovereignty over the non-elected parts. Hence the EU's so-called democratic deficit.

The EU

The EU is increasingly important in terms of economic policy, since it insists upon a range of strict 'convergence criteria' that have to be met by all those countries that are going to join the single European currency. The European Central Bank will in future be able to determine many features of the economic policy of those countries that do join the single currency (this does not so far include the UK). More generally, the EU has sought to develop the four freedoms of movement – of goods, services, labour and capital – and has intervened with national state policies to eliminate barriers to trade and competition. The EU has also pursued something of a social agenda, especially since the Treaty of Maastricht in 1992, with regard to a variety of environmental, health and safety, industrial and equal opportunity policies. In such cases European laws take precedence over British laws where they conflict, and it is possible for the actions of the British government to be declared illegal. In some cases, British laws such as those on immigration, or very weak British laws such as those preventing sex discrimination at one's workplace, have been declared illegal by the European Court of Justice.

There are three important points to consider here about the EU. First, just what sort of state is it, given its relatively small size and limited range of functions? Might it possibly provide a model of how conventional nation-states will develop in the future? That is to say, states in the future, like the EU, will not so much tax and spend as mainly act as an economic and social regulator of activities that are predominantly provided by the private sector (regulate health and safety, hours of work, equal opportunities, environmental impact and so on).

Second, just what kind of society is 'Europe' anyway? Can we envisage a time when people will consider themselves as principally European, that their principal identity will be as Europeans? Already two-thirds of those living in the EU claim to feel 'European', although few associate the EU with that feeling (M. Leonard 1998, p. 19). Thus there is an apparently increasing sense of European-ness, although the EU itself is not thought to produce that sense. However, there are clear divisions of class with regard to this, with capitalists, managers and professionals being the most European, although they are the most global as well (see Mann 1998, pp. 195–6).

Third, the question of Europe has had a major impact upon the trajectory of British politics over the past decades. In the 1990s the Conservative Party has suffered very substantial splits over the EU. Broadly speaking, the Thatcherites in the party have organized against any expansion of the powers of the EU, arguing that there is something inalienable about British national interests that has to be defended at all costs. Other sections of the party have taken a much more pro-European position. They argue that in a global world it is necessary to be at the heart of Europe, developing a single market that enables Britain and other European countries to develop their economies so as to compete successfully with the USA and east Asian economies.

Power and politics

We now consider the more general issue as to how power in Britain is distributed. In whose interests does the state operate? Do we live in a society where the state acts on behalf of most citizens, or does it act in the interests of particular social groups, and if so which are they? There are three main approaches to describing the distribution of power within the UK: the pluralist approach, the elite and the ruling-class.

The pluralist approach

Pluralists argue that power in Britain is dispersed and fragmented. There are a very large number of different groups and interests that seek to influence policy, and no particular group is able to control the state or influence policy across a wide range of different issues (see figure 13.2, and summary in Pierson 1996, pp. 71–4). Different groups influence policy on different issues and, in many cases, outcomes result from pressure from a large number of separate groups. Individuals are seen as free to join groups and attempt to influence policy. Any particular individual will be likely to have more than one interest, so that the individual's concerns will pull in different directions at different times on different issues. He or she will be 'cross-pressured'.

Pluralists further maintain that all interests may be represented and influence policy, and that no particular interest, such as trade unions or employers, is dominant within the state. Indeed pluralists object to the idea that there is some entity to be termed the state, since they focus upon specific policies and outcomes which can be observed.

The resources available to different groups are seen as widely dispersed and non-cumulative. New issues come onto the political agenda and new groups can develop. Politics is always a matter of negotiation and competition for ideas and votes. Governments are open to influence and are not systematically biased towards any particular interest. The role of government is twofold: first, to maintain the rules of the game by which this competition between different groups takes place, to be a referee; and second, to implement appropriate policies through responding to, and orchestrating, the balance of political forces on each relatively separate and distinct issue.

The main evidence supporting a pluralist view of power in Britain is as follows:

1   *Many different groups do attempt to influence policy.* Pressure-group activity is widespread; one study in the 1970s showed over 4,000 groups attempting to influence political decisions in Birmingham. Very many people are members of interest groups – for example, about 8 million people are members of trade unions, nearly 6 million are members of Christian churches, and 2.5 million are members of the National Trust. Some campaigning groups have recently grown rapidly in size and influence; between the mid-1980s and the mid-1990s Greenpeace UK grew from 50,000 to 400,000 and Friends of the Earth from 27,000 to 250,000 (Macnaghten and Urry 1998, pp. 29, 60). Increasingly, organizations operate across different societies. It has been calculated that there are over 15,000 non-governmental organizations (NGOs) operating in three or more countries (Axtmann 1998, p. 17).

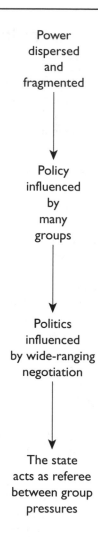

Power
dispersed
and
fragmented

Policy
influenced
by
many
groups

Politics
influenced
by wide-ranging
negotiation

The state
acts as referee
between group
pressures

Figure 13.2 | The distribution and exercise of pluralist power

2   *Groups are generally involved in only one or two political issues.* Very few are
    involved in a large number of issues. There are some conflicts where the sides
    change from issue to issue. Moreover, groups involved in policy-making enjoy
    both victories and defeats. No one group appears to be generally successful in
    getting its way. The influence of government bodies varies. In foreign policy they
    are very powerful, while on other issues, such as social policy, transport and
    environment, they are less effective. Conflicts also occur between different parts
    of the state, between those ministries concerned to expand expenditure (on new
    schools or roads) and the economic ministries (especially the Treasury) that seek
    to reduce public expenditure.

3   *There has been a marked widening of the range of individuals and groups able to influence policy*. Thus recent Conservative leaders have come from relatively less privileged backgrounds (John Major, William Hague), many prominent business people did not have elite family origins (Richard Branson of Virgin, Alan Sugar of Amstrad), there are alternative routes to fame and fortune through sport and music (Alan Shearer and Paul McCartney), and the City of London has been changed by the influx of overseas banks and the recruitment of men and women with more modest educational qualifications. Pluralists argue that these changes in elite recruitment show the relative openness of a pluralist British society.

The elite approach

The elite view of British politics is based on challenging much of the pluralist account. In particular, it emphasizes how some topics are prevented from becoming issues for political resolution at all – they are kept off the agenda. Elite approaches also emphasize that only some interests are organized and that there is a systematic bias in the political system over the long term which favours certain social groups more than others (figure 13.3).

Although many people are members of organized groups in Britain, many others are not. Far fewer than half the working population are members of trade unions. Many interests are not represented by organizations (for example, many young people or groups of consumers), or are represented poorly (for example, women members of trade unions). Some other interests by contrast, such as the City of London, are very well represented (through the Treasury, the Bank of England and the financial institutions themselves). Moreover, many campaigning groups are themselves undemocratically organized and lack participation by their membership. They are often run by self-perpetuating oligarchies.

The main evidence put forward to substantiate the claim that there are powerful elites in modern Britain is as follows:

1   *There are certain key institutions in British life; each of these is run by an elite; and each of these elites is recruited in approximately similar fashion*. In other words, it is argued that most elite members are white males who received private rather than state school education, went to Oxford or Cambridge universities (Oxbridge), frequent similar London clubs, and are connected to each other through kinship, friendship and overlapping elite membership. Until very recently, not a single senior army officer, Anglican bishop or high court judge had a manual worker as his or her father, none was black and almost none was female. There is also considerable interchange between these various elite groups. It is common for former MPs to become directors of private companies. Conservative MPs hold, on average, two chairs and four directorships of companies. One study suggested that three-quarters of elite members in government, the civil service, private companies, the armed forces, the judiciary, the media and the aristocracy all belonged to a small number of exclusive London clubs.

2   *Elite groups structure the form of political debate*. They prevent some issues coming on to the political agenda (such as proposals to abolish private property, or to

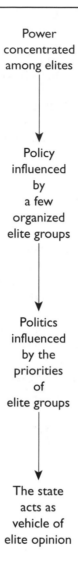

Power
concentrated
among elites

Policy
influenced
by
a few
organized
elite groups

Politics
influenced
by the
priorities
of
elite groups

The state
acts as
vehicle of
elite opinion

Figure 13.3 | The distribution and exercise of elite power

produce equality of opportunity for blacks and Asians or genuinely equal pay for men and women). Issues that are on the agenda tend to be relatively safe and do not challenge the general unequal distribution of power and privilege.

3 *Decisions made favour the interests of these elite groups.* Thus, fee-paying schools are still thriving and providing an educational route straight into many elite occupations. Likewise Oxford and Cambridge are the two most financially favoured universities in Britain. Also, there has been relatively little change in the overall distributions of income and wealth. And when tax rates on high incomes are reasonably high (as in the late 1970s), then ways are found to minimize tax liabilities and, in time, these tax rates tend to be reduced (as they were throughout

the 1980s). So over time the elite groups appear to benefit from the range of political decisions made (see J. Scott 1991, ch. 5).

4   *The British state partly operates behind the scenes as a powerful secret state not accountable to elected representatives* (see box 13.1).

Box 13.1   The secret state in Britain

The secret state consists of those state institutions that are non-elected, that enjoy considerable autonomy from Parliament and from the government of the day, and are closed and secretive in the manner in which they exercise their extensive powers (see Dearlove and Saunders 1991, ch. 5). There are two crucial points to note about the secret state.

First, there is the fact of secrecy itself. Civil servants rarely appear in public to explain or justify their actions and to be subjected to questioning or investigation. Judges maintain that their deliberations are secret and they never have to explain why particular judgements are made. The police are not really accountable to anyone apart from the home secretary. This is particularly true of the most powerful force, the Metropolitan Police, which does not even have a local police authority or committee to whom it is minimally responsible, for it answers directly to the home secretary. The security services are the most secretive of all. The three most important are MI5, which is not established by statute or recognized in law; MI6, which until recently did not officially exist; and the Government Communications Headquarters (GCHQ) at Cheltenham, which is at the centre of a worldwide network of spying, eavesdropping and communications. These bodies operate almost entirely outside the law, since there are few, if any, laws that relate to their work. All are protected by section 2 of the 1911 Official Secrets Act, which makes it a crime for anyone employed by any of these bodies to disclose any significant information learnt in the course of his or her job. It is also an offence to receive such information. Likewise the Defence, Press and Broadcasting Committee 'advises' the press not to publish what are meant to be sensitive matters of information relating to state actions and policies.

The second point is that the secret state is extremely powerful. For example, although in theory ministers control their departments of state, the permanent civil servants in fact exercise considerable control over ministers. Particularly powerful is the Bank of England, since the 'advice' given by its governor carries great weight in determining government economic policy. In the 1980s and early 1990s the Ministry of Agriculture opposed telling government ministers and the public that offal infected with BSE (mad cow disease) was entering the food chain as a result of the flouting of the regulations regarding slaughterhouse practices. Keeping secret these failures was regarded as more important than even telling ministers of the serious health risks from the failure of abattoir regulation.

Leading judges, who in theory are bound by the laws made by Parliament, are actively engaged in making the law because they are continuously involved in interpreting the existing laws. This process of interpretation, particularly through the establishment of precedents, itself creates the law. Likewise, although the social background of the police is very different from that of the other groups considered here, the force similarly attempts to limit its accountability, particularly to local authority representatives. The police are powerful because they have the scope to exercise discretion. Amongst the millions of law-breakers, the police decide whom to stop on suspicion, and they do so in terms of a number of crude stereotypes of possible criminals. The security services also enjoy a very high degree of autonomy in their operations and operate largely outside the law. The elected parts of the state have little idea of the activities of the security services, or of the scale of their operations. On occasions, even the prime minister has not been aware of the scale of operation of the secret security forces.

The ruling-class approach

The ruling-class analysis of British politics maintains that there is a centrally significant class structure in Britain. This consists of those who own 'property for power', which gives control over the lives of others who do not own significant property of this sort (see J. Scott 1991, p. 65). This view further argues that politics and the state both reflect and maintain this dominant class structure (figure 13.4). Elite theorists, although correct in criticizing pluralism, inadequately analyse this most fundamental feature of British society. It is not, the ruling-class model asserts, merely a question of there being a number of elites in a variety of social institutions. Rather, it is the class structure that lies at the very heart of British society, and the state is, to a considerable extent, the instrument of the capitalist employing class (this class is of course increasingly European and global).

Much contemporary politics, including voting patterns, is relatively unimportant compared with this more fundamental set of economic and social relations. Parliamentary politics is mainly significant 'ideologically', in implying that people can significantly affect political outcomes. Ruling-class theorists assert that the major political parties are 'capitalist', since all are concerned to run the capitalist economy as efficiently as possible and hence to maximise the rewards accruing to the capitalist class. The main political differences only concern how that capitalist economy is to be run.

The evidence to support this thesis is as follows:

1 *No elected government in Britain has sought to abolish the capitalist economy based on private ownership.* The most radical Labour government was in power from 1945 to 1950. Although there was considerable nationalization of economic resources, this mainly involved industries that were at the time unprofitable when in private ownership (for example, railways, coal). Nor has any government seriously tried to reorganize industry so that firms are managed by their workers. Nor has any government in Britain extended the welfare services so that they provide adequate provision for *all* the population, from the cradle to the grave.

2 *Business interests are not merely one group amongst a number, but are the best organized.* Business interests are the wealthiest of all groups and were able, as in

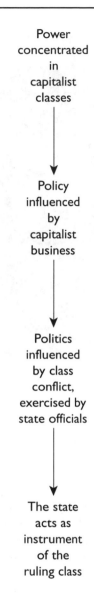

Power
concentrated
in
capitalist
classes

Policy
influenced
by
capitalist
business

Politics
influenced
by class
conflict,
exercised by
state officials

The state
acts as
instrument
of the
ruling class

Figure 13.4 | The distribution and exercise of power by the ruling classes

the early 1970s, to mount extensive newspaper campaigns against the national-ization of the banks in Britain. They are also able to derive support from most MPs, very many of whom are employed at some time by corporations. The legal system is extremely expensive and so companies can use the libel laws to prevent criticism of their activities (as with the huge American company Monsanto, which uses the UK libel laws to prevent criticism of its genetically engineered food-stuffs). Indeed, more generally, the state is dependent upon private industry to

Plate 13.1 The City of London: the driver of the British state?
Source: J. Allan Cash

provide both employment and taxation revenue. Any radical government would not be able to finance large increases in public expenditure unless private industry continued to employ most of the working population, to pay them reasonable taxable salaries, and to provide some taxation themselves.

3 *The best-organized social grouping within Britain is finance capital, popularly known as the City of London.* This comprises commercial banks (such as NatWest), merchant banks (Hill Samuel), insurance companies (Guardian Royal Exchange), Lloyds insurance, pension funds, finance houses, the stock exchange, foreign currency dealers and the Bank of England. These institutions have been exceptionally important in the British economy, providing high levels of what are known as invisible exports. British economic policy has been mainly devoted to protecting finance capital through keeping a strong value of the pound sterling, enabling these institutions to invest abroad on a massive scale, and ensuring that foreign confidence in the City of London is maintained by the pursuit of safe economic policies. By contrast the British state has not developed strong ties with industrial companies or developed the capacity for detailed support, planning and subsidy of industry that has occurred in some other countries, such as Japan (although see J. Scott 1991).

How then should we evaluate these different models? Each has its strengths and weaknesses. The pluralist model highlights the sheer diversity of interests and groups that surrounds the contemporary British state, a state operating within a remarkably open environment which no single interest can simply control. Its weaknesses are the way it ignores the empirical data pointed to as supportive of the elite and ruling-class models. The elite model well describes the kind of secret and oligarchic way in which major social institutions are organized. But it neglects to consider whether the shaping of state policy is more systematic than is implied by the claim that there is simply an elite as the top of each institution.

This leaves the ruling-class argument, but this too makes an overstated claim, namely that the British state is the instrument of finance capital. First, economic policy in Britain has never been able to overcome the major contradictions between different objectives, such as full employment, stable prices, a healthy balance of trade, rising productivity and output, and so on. All economic policy has been, in a way, unsuccessful and failed to meet the interests of the dominant social class. The state is not a successful instrument of the capitalist class. Moreover, the globalization of economic relations has reinforced this; for example, in late 1998 global crises were blamed for considerable job losses in British manufacturing industry, which the British state presumed were unavoidable and which it was unable to prevent.

Second, the state does operate partly separately from individual groups of employers. It makes a more general attempt to secure at least some of the conditions required for continued capitalist production and investment, conditions that would not be provided by individual employers. Examples include a national motorway network, a comprehensive educational system, a system of unemployment benefit, and so on. The state

---

Box 13.2   Left and right both criticize the state

One curious feature of recent British politics is that many very different social groups, from both the left and the right, have strongly criticized the British state in somewhat similar terms (this issue will be explored below in the context of 1990s developments around social welfare provision). On the left, the state has been criticized for employing unnecessarily large, bureaucratic and unresponsive ways of governing psychiatric hospitals, prisons, council estates, schools and so on, modes of governance which are alienating and repressive. New social movements have developed which have viewed the state and its often formal and secretive procedures as the problem rather than the solution. Emphases in such movements have been placed on new modes of self-government, participation and community involvement.

On the right, neo-liberal critiques, associated with Margaret Thatcher and the 1980s Conservative Party, saw the state as interfering with the ambitions and desires of individuals and families, especially to set up businesses, own their own homes, save for old age and so on. Both left and right found fault with the 'nanny state', with large-scale bureaucracies, and sought to develop alternatives. The right emphasized the ways in which the market could develop such non-statist alternatives (as with private health care, private housing, fund-holding general practitioners), while the left sought to develop neighbourhood and community projects which were separate from both the state and the market place, to extend and elaborate civil society.

seeks to ensure some of the conditions necessary for continued production because it is itself dependent upon the success of the economy to raise sufficient taxation revenue to pay for its disparate activities. There is here a state interest as well as a class interest.

Finally, the state carries out a wide range of different policies and, although some of these reflect the interests of finance capital, others relate to alternative dominant interests, especially those of men and of white people. The British state is not only capitalist but also patriarchal and racist. The patriarchal nature of the state can be seen in the failure of the police and courts to protect women from sexual harassment, rape and especially domestic violence within the family; in the ways in which the social security system has treated women as dependent upon a male breadwinner; and in the overwhelmingly male composition of the upper levels of state institutions (see section 7.7). That the British state is racist can be seen most clearly in the Immigration Acts of 1962, 1968, 1971 and 1982. After the 1971 Act, the status of Commonwealth immigrants was dramatically changed, to being that of black migrant workers who might or might not be granted citizenship after a four-year period of probation. It has also been recently recognized that racism is commonplace and institutionalized within the police and judicial system (see section 8.5).

Summary

1 The state possesses a range of powers unlike those enjoyed by any other institution within Britain. Its power of social regulation is increasingly important.
2 The British state is increasingly regionalized, partly because globalization provokes new identities. An understanding of the British state must take into account the EU as an important state crucially involved in economic and social regulation.
3 The *pluralist* account of the distribution of power points out the wide and increasing variety of interest and promotional groups attempting to influence the state, at all levels.
4 The *elite* view shows how the central and regional levels of the state and many pressure groups are undemocratically organized, often maintaining exceptional levels of secrecy.
5 The *ruling-class* analysis demonstrates how British financial interests have been extremely powerful in sustaining central aspects of British policy. But a ruling-class analysis is not altogether correct, partly because the British state is also patriarchal and racist.
6 Both the new right and new social movements have launched critiques of the state, especially of its powers and its bureaucratic and secretive procedures.

13.3   Voting behaviour

Adult Britons may vote to elect candidates to local councils, national Parliaments and the European Parliament. Elections are important because they usually determine which party will form a government and because they offer a periodic opportunity for mass participation in political affairs. Far more people vote than take part in other forms of political activity, like writing to MPs or joining demonstrations. Elections are generally seen as the most legitimate form of popular political action, equated with the valued concepts of democracy and representation. People's behaviour at elections gives an indication of their preferences regarding policies and governments, and their more abiding underlying political values and commitments.

There is no simple sociological explanation of why people vote the way they do. There has always been quite a strong statistical relationship between a voter's social characteristics and his or her choice between parties at elections. The social characteristics most closely associated with voting choice include occupation and class, ethnic group, union membership, housing tenure, religion, education and generation. Such correlations have never been overwhelmingly strong and they have fluctuated from election to election. However, in the 1960s, if a voter came from a manual household the odds were 2:1 that he or she would vote Labour; if the voter was from a non-manual household the odds were about 4:1 in favour of voting for the Conservatives. Class was thus a powerful predictor of party choice. Then, sociologists tended to be most concerned to explain exceptional behaviour, and especially why a substantial proportion of working-class people voted Tory.

The 1960s saw the height of class alignment in British elections. The possibility of predicting a person's vote on the basis of occupational class (or any other social variable) has fallen since then. The explanatory problems for psephology (the study of voting behaviour) are now quite different. The main question concerns whether or not there has been a fundamental transformation in voting behaviour since 1970. The spur for such speculation was the weak electoral performance of the Labour Party at national level for a long period, particularly from 1979. The Conservative Party won four consecutive General Elections comfortably in 1979, 1983, 1987 and 1992. The last of these, held during a recession when opinion polls suggested that the Conservatives were very unpopular and likely to be defeated, seemed particularly momentous. Some commentators thought it signified the end of the two-party system and implied that the Conservatives had become the permanent party of government. However, a massive swing against the Conservatives in 1997 (their share of the votes cast declined by 12 per cent) resulted in a huge parliamentary majority for Labour, apparently posing very different questions.

Sociological inquiry has focused on re-examining the findings of the British Election Studies. At each election since 1964 a national sample survey of voters has been asked questions about political attitudes and behaviour (party affiliation, which issues concern people most, which party they actually voted for, etc.) and about socio-demographic characteristics (occupation, age, ethnic group, etc.). This unique series of surveys, where broadly similar questions have been asked intermittently over a period of more than 30 years, gives enormous scope for rigorous exploration of trends and for heated disagreement about their interpretation. The principal current dispute concerns the adequacy of the argument advanced by Crewe and co-workers, who identified a process of dealignment, occurring after 1970, which signified a change of direction for British politics. The main alternative position, that of A. Heath and his associates, sees greater continuity throughout the post-war period, one characterized by trendless fluctuation rather than by any fundamental shift. (Crewe was responsible for the British Election Studies of 1974 and 1979, Heath for those of 1983, 1987 and 1992.)

Dealignment

Dealignment refers to the breaking down of the patterns of voters' choice characteristic of the period 1945–66. Dealignment has two aspects which are not necessarily directly related to one another. First, voters have become unwilling to vote regularly for either of the two major parties. Second, a person's occupational class gives an increasingly poorer guide to his or her party choice. These aspects are called partisan dealignment and class dealignment, respectively. Since dealignment is a process, we must look at change over time and hence at a number of consecutive elections, making a comparison with the patterns of the 1950s.

It is generally agreed that between 1950 and 1966 voting preferences had two stable elements. First, individual voters identified with, and regularly voted for, one of the two major parties, that is, either the Conservative Party or the Labour Party. This partisanship, a sustained preference for a particular political party, derived from the political socialization process whereby voters were strongly influenced by the political persuasions of their parents. Second, they tended to vote Conservative if they lived in a white-collar household, and Labour if the head of the household was a manual worker. Such regularities were explained in terms of class interest: the Labour Party, with its partly socialist tradition, was thought of as being more likely to promote the interests of the working class, and the Conservative Party was likely to favour the middle classes. These were, however, by no means *laws* of voting behaviour. Disapproval of party performance led to abstention from voting. People changed party between elections. And other social factors besides social class were related to party choice: age, region and religious affiliation affected voting and cut across class divisions.

Partisan dealignment

A partisan is someone who feels a sense of identity with, or loyalty to, a political party. Partisanship is usually measured by asking people whether they consider themselves to be a supporter of a particular party, and how strong is their attachment to that party. The assumption is that partisans will usually vote for the party with which they identify, though they will not always do so. All things being equal, the higher the extent and intensity of partisanship among the electorate the more will voters regularly vote for the same party at each general election. Three different kinds of evidence suggest that partisanship has declined since 1970.

First, election results show that after 1970 the British voter began to desert the two major parties. In the elections between 1950 and 1970, on average 92 per cent of the poll (i.e. of votes actually cast) was shared between the two major parties, Conservative and Labour. In the five elections following, those between February 1974 and 1997, this two-party share of the poll had fallen to 75 per cent. This is presented graphically in figure 13.5, which shows the rising support for other parties. These others are primarily nationalist and liberal parties. The former group includes the Scottish National Party, Plaid Cymru and the parties of Northern Ireland. In Northern Ireland neither of the two major UK parties was represented at all in elections from 1970 to 1997; votes there were cast for one of several Unionist parties, for the Social Democratic Labour Party, or for Sinn Fein. Since their formation after the 1987 election, from the amalgamation of

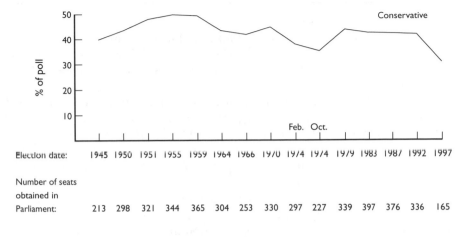

Election date: 1945 1950 1951 1955 1959 1964 1966 1970 1974 1974 1979 1983 1987 1992 1997

Number of seats
obtained in
Parliament: 213 298 321 344 365 304 253 330 297 227 339 397 376 336 165

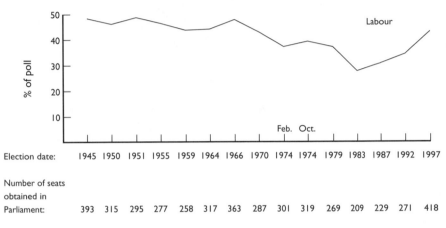

Election date: 1945 1950 1951 1955 1959 1964 1966 1970 1974 1974 1979 1983 1987 1992 1997

Number of seats
obtained in
Parliament: 393 315 295 277 258 317 363 287 301 319 269 209 229 271 418

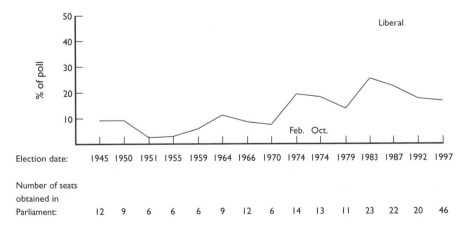

Election date: 1945 1950 1951 1955 1959 1964 1966 1970 1974 1974 1979 1983 1987 1992 1997

Number of seats
obtained in
Parliament: 12 9 6 6 6 9 12 6 14 13 11 23 22 20 46

Figure 13.5 | Share of the poll in General Elections for the Conservative, Labour and Liberal Democrat Parties,[a] 1945–97

[a] Liberal Democrat from 1992; Liberal votes in 1983 and 1987 include those for the Social Democratic Party

Source: Adapted from D. Butler and Kavanagh 1998, pp. 254–5

most members of the old Liberal Party and the Social Democratic Party (which had itself split off from the Labour Party in 1980), the Liberal Democrats were the most successful third party in the UK. Figure 13.5 shows that the Liberal Party made substantial gains in 1964, 1974 and 1983, with a tendency for its share to subside in the intervening elections.

A second body of evidence concerning partisan dealignment has been obtained by asking people whether they identify with a particular party and, if so, how strongly they are attached to that party. The number of electors who feel some attachment to a party seems to have remained fairly constant: in 1987, 86 per cent of voters volunteered that they considered themselves supporters of a party compared with 90 per cent in 1966. The intensity of their attachment has declined, though. Table 13.1 shows that in the 1964 election survey 48 per cent of voters who identified with a party said their sense of identification was very strong, but by 1987 the proportion was only 23 per cent. (Unsurprisingly, the stronger the party identification the more likely is an individual to vote for that party.)

TABLE 13.1 | Trends in strength of party identification, 1964–87

| | Identifiers who felt: | | | |
	Very strongly (%)	Fairly strongly (%)	Not very strongly (%)	Respondents (no.)
1964	48	40	12	1623
1966	48	42	11	1688
1970	47	41	13	1651
Feb. 1974	33	48	19	2162
Oct. 1974	29	52	19	2063
1979	25	53	23	1621
1983	25	47	28	3231
1987	23	48	29	3134

Source: A. Heath et al. 1991, p. 13

The reason for declining intensity of identification is disputed, but several factors may be relevant. First, there is some disillusionment with the major parties because of their failures when in government. This may have reduced commitment to them. This might also account for a slight tendency for abstentions (non-voting) to have increased recently. Second, voters may be becoming more instrumental, choosing between parties on the basis of which party they think will best satisfy their personal interests. Identification and loyalty to a party would thus become less relevant. Third, voters may now be more concerned with political issues. Before, stability of identification was the result of political socialization, party identity being passed on from parents to children and rarely being abandoned thereafter. In such circumstances it would make no difference to voters what their favourite party intended to do if it won power. If voters became concerned with particular issues and discriminated between parties in terms of proposed policies – for example, on law and order, defence, trade unions, economic regulation, or whatever – then old partisan loyalties would cease to matter. Recent evidence (Brymin and Sanders 1997) suggests that identification is much less enduring than previously thought; about one-quarter of respondents to the British Household Panel Survey changed their reported identification in a two-year period between 1991 and 1993.

Third, while some of the increased support for 'other' parties may have come from people who would otherwise have abstained, most is taken from the two major parties. This has reduced the likelihood of electors *regularly* voting Labour or Conservative, but only slightly. It might not have reduced partisanship overall if people had become attached to the nationalist parties or the Liberals instead. As a matter of fact, however, there is little sign of people becoming Liberal Democrat partisans. Liberal supporters appear to be fickle voters, rarely supporting the party at two consecutive elections. The generally increased support for Liberals and Liberal Democrats has meant that a lot of people are shifting votes between elections. However, the degree of movement, often called volatility, did not increase substantially after 1964. Until 1997, volatility in the UK was comparatively modest and well beneath the European average. Sanders (1998) interprets this as a consequence not only of partisan dealignment, but also of the reduced importance of ideological divisions along a left–right axis after the ending of the Cold War, and of class dealignment.

Class dealignment

Class dealignment refers to the declining probability that any individual will vote for the party associated with his or her social class. Whereas we would have been moderately successful in predicting how a person would vote in the 1964 election merely by knowing whether the head of the household was a white-collar or a blue-collar worker, this is no longer the case. Using conventional measures, the correlation between occupational class position and voting has fallen. Table 13.2 shows that in 1987, compared with 1964, fewer white-collar respondents were voting Conservative, and fewer manual workers voting Labour. This shift occurred in two stages. Between 1964 and 1974, it was due to an increase in white-collar support for the Labour Party. This support seems to have come from people working in the public sector, and particularly from those in welfare services. In that period there was no perceptible trend for manual workers to vote more frequently for the Conservative Party. However, in 1979 about 10 per cent more manual workers voted Conservative, and the proportion remained constant during the 1980s at around 35 per cent. In addition, after 1966 there was a fairly steady decline in the proportion of manual workers, especially skilled workers, voting for the Labour Party. However, preliminary evidence about the 1997 election suggests that the levels of manual support for Labour returned to the levels of the early 1970s, while non-manuals voted more than ever before for Labour and less than ever in history for the Conservatives.

The best way to measure the decline of class voting is disputed. Table 13.3 offers two measures. As regards absolute levels, there was a fall at the end of the 1960s and then the level remained fairly steady. The relative measure showed the same fall before 1970, but from then until 1992 there was what A. Heath et al. deemed 'trendless fluctuation'. If class did not matter at all, the ratio of relative class voting would be zero, hence the conclusion is that class still matters and only a little less than in the 1960s.

Class and vote: the political distinctiveness of white-collar and blue-collar workers, 1964–87 (percentages)

Party voted for	1964	1966	1970	Feb. 1974	Oct. 1974	1979	1983	1987
White-collar workers								
Conservative	60.7	58.2	59.3	48.9	47.0	58.0	54.6	53.4
Labour	23.9	28.5	29.3	26.9	28.3	24.6	15.7	19.4
Liberal	14.3	12.8	8.9	22.6	21.4	15.7	28.7	25.6
Other	0.9	0.8	2.5	1.6	3.3	1,7	1.1	1.5
Respondents (no.)	669	643	641	1,035	980	743	1,490	1,643
Manual working class								
Conservative	26.3	24.9	34.4	24.6	23.5	35.5	34.5	34.0
Labour	65.6	69.5	57.1	57.0	58.2	50.7	42.6	43.7
Liberal	7.7	5.2	6.1	15.1	14.2	12.2	21.3	21.2
Other	0.4	0.5	2.4	3.3	4.1	1.6	1.7	1.1
Respondents (no.)	861	900	763	921	873	744	1,486	1,418

Source: Calculated from Crewe, Day and Fox 1991, p. 19

Trends in class voting, 1964–92

General Election	Absolute class voting[a] (%)	Relative class voting[b] (log odds ratio)
1964	64	2.2
1966	64	2.0
1970	60	1.4
Feb. 1974	56	1.8
Oct. 1974	57	1.9
1979	57	1.6
1983	52	1.9
1987	52	1.7
1992	56	1.7

[a] Absolute class voting = the percentage of all voters who are middle class and vote Conservative plus the percentage who are working class and vote Labour
[b] Relative class voting = log odds ratio of the votes won by the Conservatives and Labour among members of the salariat and the working class
Source: A. Heath et al. 1994, p. 283

A. Heath et al. (1985, 1991), in their British Election Studies of the 1983 and 1987 elections, suggest that the class dealignment thesis grossly exaggerates the degree of change in voting behaviour. They argue that what is important is change in the class structure and the political climate. Thus, Labour's poor performances were the result of a cross-class decline in the party's political appeal, combined with the reduced size of the working class, rather than any process of class dealignment.

Heath and his colleagues maintain that advocates of the class dealignment thesis have used inappropriate class categories and measurement techniques. They contest the validity of grouping all manual workers together, for they show that self-employed manual workers and manual workers in supervisory positions vote in a different fashion from the mass of manual workers. The behaviour of the last group has not altered systematically between 1964 and 1987; manual workers who are not in positions of authority vote Labour in the same proportions as before. Two other things have changed, however. First, this group is considerably smaller in size than it used to be. Second, the Labour Party was very unpopular politically in the 1980s. The argument of Heath et al. that class position remains the major influence on an individual's voting behaviour is rehearsed next.

The British voter, 1964–87: a case study

It is unclear whether the election results which kept the Conservative Party in government from 1979 to 1997 indicated that voters had changed, or whether it was just that the political environment had altered. Incontestably, fewer manual workers voted Labour in the 1980s. But, as A. Heath et al. insist in *Understanding Political Change: The British Voter, 1964–87* (1991), fewer white-collar workers did too. This might be interpreted to mean that the Labour Party was simply politically unpopular in that decade, without any real implication for class preferences in the long term. Heath et al.'s sophisticated argument to this effect, regarding the period 1964–87, deserves consideration, particularly in the light of the severe shift of support registered in 1997.

Heath et al. generally maintained that there had been limited change except for the short-run events in the political sphere, with no change in voter psychology; rather, changes were due to changing political context and social structural change. Thus they argued: that there had been no real change in voter volatility since 1964; that attitudes were fairly stable, though the parties' ways of tapping those opinions were not; that the levels of political knowledge and sophistication in the electorate, as measured by the relationship between attitudes and votes, had altered very little since the 1960s; that people in the same classes behaved in much the same way as before, though of course the relative sizes of the classes altered; that Labour's poor electoral performance from 1979 was just inept political management, which, in association with increased Liberal Party competition, reduced their overall support; that both salariat and working class were internally divided and sectional, but this was neither new nor different from 1964; and that there had been limited change in popular attitudes, despite the campaigns of the Thatcher governments. In effect, they argued that recent commentators have exaggerated systemic change. Of course, they recognized some changes, particularly those due to the parties themselves having shifted in terms of ideology and programme, the emergence of wider support for parties other than Labour and Conservatives, and the emergence of some significant regional differences.

One way in which they expressed this was by estimating the size of the effects on the parties of different components of social and political change over the period 1964–87. The methods for doing this are complex and the results are speculative estimates based

TABLE 13.4 │ The hypothetical effects of social change, 1964–87 (percentages)

	Share of the vote		
Source of change	Conservative	Liberal Alliance	Labour
Class	+3.8	+0.7	−4.5
Housing	+4.6	+0.6	−5.0
Region	−0.1	+0.1	−0.1
TU membership	+0.5	−0.1	−0.4
Higher education	−0.4	+0.8	−0.5
Ethnicity	−0.7	−0.3	+1.0
Religion	−4.0	+0.1	+4.1
Combined effects of class, housing, religion, ethnicity and education	+2.7	+1.8	−4.0

Source: A. Heath et al. 1991, p. 209

on the premise that: '*associations* between [social and demographic] characteristics and voting behaviour have (with a few notable exceptions like region) remained fairly stable throughout the period, but the *proportions* with the different characteristics have changed quite substantially' (A. Heath et al. 1991, p. 202). The effects of social changes are summarized in table 13.4. Thus, the changing shape of the class structure is estimated to have decreased the Labour vote by 4.5 per cent and increased the Conservative vote by 3.8 per cent. Increased owner-occupation likewise helped the Conservatives at the expense of Labour, but decline in religious affiliation worked in the opposite direction. The overall effect of these social changes is much less than the actual shift in vote between 1964 and 1987. Much more of the variation is accounted for, according to Heath

TABLE 13.5 │ The effects of social and political change, 1964–87 (percentages)

	Share of the vote		
Source of change	Conservative	Liberal/Alliance	Labour
Social change	+2.7	+1.8	−4.0
Extension of the franchise	−0.3	+0.4	−0.1
Liberal candidates	−2.4	+6.7	−4.3
Tactical voting	+0.4	−0.4	−0.6
Formation of the SDP	−0.7	+1.3	−0.6
Ideological polarization	−2.0	+4.0	−2.0
Total predicted	−2.3	+13.8	−11.6
Actual change	+1.7	+12.8	−15.3

Source: A. Heath et al. 1991, p. 220

et al., by political changes, the strength of which is estimated in table 13.5. This suggests that it was the fact of Liberals contesting all parliamentary seats, compared with only about 55 per cent in the 1960s, that made most difference. The ideological polarization of the two main parties (though much less pronounced in the early 1990s) was also important.

The General Election of 1997

It will be several years before we have as thorough an analysis of the 1997 election results as has been possible for the period 1964–87. However, the 1997 results were so out of keeping with the recent trends that it is worthwhile examining them with the data currently available.

In 1992, the Conservatives, under their new leader John Major, won a fourth consecutive parliamentary majority. The overall majority was 21 seats, compared with 99 in 1987. Despite the Labour Party having been marginally ahead in most opinion polls just before the election, the Conservative Party obtained 42 per cent of the votes cast, the Labour Party only 34 per cent. The Liberal Democrat share of the vote fell from 23 to 18 per cent. Overall, the 1992 general election appeared structurally little different from those of 1983 and 1987, suggesting that the Conservative Party had a rather big-

Plate 13.2 The general election results, 1997: the new prime minister celebrates victory
Source: Popperfoto

ger core of support than do either of the other two large parties. Patterns of voting seemed relatively stable and the long-term prospects for Labour very grim.

The 1997 election was very different. The Labour Party obtained 43 per cent of votes cast, the Conservatives only 31 per cent (their lowest share post-war) and the Liberal Democrats 17 per cent. Labour won 418 of the 643 seats, compared with the Conservatives' 165, and gained an overall majority in the House of Commons of 192. The turn around was dramatic, clearly endorsing A. Heath et al.'s claim that a changing political environment could have an impact very much greater than inevitably more gradual social structural change.

Early commentaries on the election suggest that the unprecedented unpopularity of the government after 1992 was the main reason for such a large defeat for the Conservatives. Divisions within the party over relations with the EU, rising levels of taxation, enormous salary increases for directors (especially in the utility industries, whose privatization was unpopular), and scandal about corruption and the sexual affairs of some ministers all harmed its chances (Denver 1998). However, above all, commentators identify Black Wednesday in 1992, when Britain was forced to withdraw from the European Exchange Rate, as critical, because it destroyed the reputation of the party for competent economic management. Thus, while economic circumstances were favourable by 1997 – and it has often been suggested that an expanding economy, falling unemployment and rising incomes are sufficient to ensure the re-election of a government – opinion polls suggested that the public perhaps did not believe the spin put on the economic statistics, and certainly did not trust another Conservative government to sustain prosperity. Unusually, the British electorate thought that the Labour Party was much more likely to manage the economy effectively. This was, in part, an impression arising from reforms within the Labour Party promoted by its leaders in the 1990s. Policies to 'modernize' the party involved less tolerance of internal dissent, ideological movement towards the centre of the British political spectrum, and distancing from the trade unions. Tony Blair in particular, who was seen as a popular and authoritative young leader who would also make the best prime minister, made the party much more credible. The outcome was an apparent landslide.

Exit polls give an approximate indication of the ways in which the electorate voted. Table 13.6 shows that the Labour Party gained 9 per cent more of the total vote than in 1992, with the shifts particularly strong among younger people and among routine white-collar and skilled manual workers. Previously evident features of differential support remained. Labour got more support from council tenants than from owner-occupiers, and it was selected by a majority of trade unionists and manual workers. A tendency for the salariat and the elderly to vote disproportionately Tory persisted. The Liberal Democrats obtained their support almost uniformly from all social categories.

Curtice and Steed (1998) warn against exaggerating the extent or the consequences of the 1997 result. Despite its vast majority in the House of Commons, Labour obtained less than half of all votes cast (43 per cent) and only about 31 per cent of all those entitled to vote (turnout being a comparatively low 71 per cent).

No government in the post-war period has ever won half the votes cast. Support for smaller parties has increased over time. But except when their support is geographically concentrated, as with the Scottish Nationalist Party and Plaid Cymru, the British constituency system gives them few seats. So in 1992, the Liberal Democrats got over 18 per cent of all votes while winning only 20 (3 per cent) of seats. In 1997 the Liberal

TABLE 13.6 | **How Britain voted in the General Election, 1997 (percentages)**

	Conservative		Labour		Lib Dem	
	1997 vote (change on 1992 in brackets)					
All Great Britain voters	31	(−12)	43	(+9)	17	(−1)
Men	31	(−8)	44	(+6)	17	(−1)
Women	32	(−11)	44	(+10)	17	(−1)
AB voters	42	(−11)	31	(+9)	21	(0)
C1	26	(−22)	47	(+19)	19	(−1)
C2	25	(−15)	54	(+15)	14	(−4)
DE	21	(−8)	61	(+9)	13	(0)
First-time voters	19	(−16)	57	(+17)	18	(−3)
All 18–29	22	(−18)	57	(+19)	17	(0)
30–44	26	(−11)	49	(+12)	17	(−3)
45–64	33	(−9)	43	(+9)	18	(−2)
65+	44	(−3)	34	(−2)	16	(+2)
Home-owners	35	(−12)	41	(+11)	17	(−3)
Council tenants	13	(−6)	65	(+1)	15	(+5)
Trade union members	18	(−9)	57	(+7)	20	(+2)

Source: D. Butler and Kavanagh 1998, p. 246

Democrats got 1 per cent fewer of all votes, but 46 seats. To their supporters this was still unfair, since a system of simple proportional representation would have given them 108 seats. The discrepancy between votes cast and seats obtained for each party is partly a function of the first-past-the-post electoral system and partly of the structure of opinion in 1997. Liberal Democrat gains over 1992 were, in important part, a measure of the unpopularity of the Conservatives, since there was evidence of considerable tactical voting. In the desire to defeat the Tories, many voters selected their second preference after calculating which of the Liberal Democrat and Labour candidates had most chance of defeating a Conservative. (If this tacit alliance continues then the Conservative Party will struggle to return to government.) Thus the electoral system, based on geographically defined constituencies in which the single candidate with the most votes wins, biases the overall outcome.

The 1997 election gives some support to those psephologists who argue that electors' political opinions and attitudes are becoming increasingly important. Asking people questions like 'Which party do you think will govern best?' gives some fair indication of how they will vote. The electorate's judgement of which is the best party is influenced by both its evaluation of the policies of the parties and its assessment of how well they have been performing in the recent past. This might seem unsurprising, since people may be expected to use their political knowledge and judgement when deciding how to vote. But many studies from the 1960s suggested that people had very limited political knowledge; some voters were unable to distinguish the policies of one party from another, for example. Wider knowledge may have made issues and policies more important. One problem with such explanations is that Labour had the most popular policies in both

1987 and 1992, but was defeated on both occasions. Another is that often people adopt their preferred party's policy stances rather than decide for themselves issue by issue. Hence they maintain fairly stable ideological convictions, aligning with the party closest to their principles rather than deciding by issue. However, the last three elections suggest that a party has not only to offer attractive policies but also to persuade the voters that it is competent to implement those policies. One difference in 1997 was that the electorate had greater confidence in Labour's competence, particularly in the economic field, and did not believe that they would be materially worse off under a Labour government.

Clearly, not all voters calculate in this fashion. One of the most striking electoral trends since the late 1960s has been increased regional differences. This was very marked during the 1980s. For example, in the 1983 election, excluding the two big metropolitan counties of London and the West Midlands conurbation, Labour won only three seats in England south of Derbyshire. The Liberal Alliance won another four. The Conservatives won all the rest. Support for both the Labour Party and the Conservative Party has steadily become more concentrated geographically since 1955. The Labour Party has increasingly obtained its support from urban and northern constituencies whilst the Conservatives gained support from rural and southern constituencies.

There has always been some regional variation, but it has clearly increased, especially among working-class voters. Table 13.7 shows the size of regional differences in 1987: 69 per cent of working-class voters in Wales, but only 30 per cent in the south of England, voted for the Labour Party. Some accounts attribute such regional variation to rational calculation about likely local and regional economic prospects, with people thinking not so much about their own individual livelihood as about that of the majority of other people living in the same place. Others see it as the outcome of sustained regional cultures. Whichever it is, it remains an interesting paradox that while an individual's occupational grade is not much guide to voting behaviour, the class composition of a constituency as a whole is a sound predictor of the success of the major parties.

TABLE 13.7 | **Region and vote in the working class, 1987**

	Respondents (%)				
	Conservative	Alliance	Labour	Other	Respondents (no.)
Wales	14	13	69	4	(71)
Scotland	10	21	62	8	(92)
North	24	16	59	0	(345)
Midlands	38	23	40	0	(245)
South	44	26	30	0	(281)

Source: A. Heath et al. 1991, p. 108

The geographical basis of electoral support was starkly emphasized in 1997 when the Conservative Party failed to win a single seat in Scotland or Wales. This was not because the nationalist parties were any more generally successful in 1997 than in 1992, or because the electoral swing between parties was spatially skewed. But it does remind us of the increasing importance of the spatial aspect of governmental power. The devolution of power to Scotland and Wales introduced by Blair's Labour government, and the restoration of powers to Stormont, introduce a new and substantial level of democratic decision-making which may therefore move policy in new directions. Party alignments are likely to be more distinct than has been the case with local and European elections, which, to date, have mostly reflected the current standing of the parties at Westminster.

Summary

1 The evidence regarding changes in voting behaviour is complex. Different measures give different results and the available statistical techniques, though increasingly sophisticated, are often insufficient to discriminate between explanations. Disagreement is intense over how to interpret changes in the relationship between class and vote.

2 Accounts that suggest radical secular change in voter behaviour are probably exaggerated; there are some strong continuities throughout the post-war period.

3 The Conservative Party obtained parliamentary majorities at four consecutive elections after 1979, but were very heavily defeated in 1997. The implications of this are not yet known, but, while probably not indicating major realignment among the electorate, the effect on the party system may be to encourage continued accommodation between Labour and Liberal Democratic Parties, which could exclude the Conservatives from government for some time to come.

4 Party choice remains importantly based on anticipated material outcomes, and the past and estimated future economic performances of the competing parties are critical to the voting decision.

13.4   Welfare and the state

The term 'welfare state' was coined, following the Second World War, to denote a major expansion of state involvement in the provision of social welfare. The objectives of the welfare state were announced in 1942 by William Beveridge, the architect of the post-war welfare reforms, as the abolition of 'Want, Idleness, Squalor, Ignorance and Disease', by which he meant poverty, unemployment, poor housing, and lack of access to decent education and health care. The major planks of the welfare state were a National Health Service providing free health care to all citizens, education provided free of charge, a major slum clearance programme and expansion of local authority low-rent housing, and a comprehensive social security system providing income security 'from the cradle to the grave', in Beveridge's famous phrase, through a range of benefits from child allowances to old-age pensions. The philosophy behind the Beveridge reforms was strongly influenced by the experience of the war years, when state planning and the allocation of resources through rationing of food and clothing provided a model of successful political action to meet collective risks and needs.

These reforms were underpinned by two important assumptions. The first was that the state could maintain full employment through utilizing Keynesian economic techniques to manage the national economy. The welfare state is often referred to as the Keynesian welfare state because of the important relationship between economic and social policy that characterized it. State management of the economy was the part of the reforms that aimed to abolish the unemployment of the 1920s and 1930s. It was envisaged that, by maintaining full employment, the majority of people would not need to make claims on the social security system: claims due to interrupted employment would be short term, and married women were entitled to support calculated according to their husbands' contributions. The second assumption was that the traditional nuclear family would remain the norm. Full employment was considered to be employment for men, with women providing primary care for dependants in the home. In this sense, the Keynesian welfare state has been implicated in the construction of a formally separated male public sphere of paid work and a female private sphere of unpaid domestic and caring work.

Since the 1970s a number of economic, social and political changes have undermined these two assumptions. Changes in the global economy have seen unemployment rise and new patterns of work emerge that render obsolete the idea of a 'job for life', particularly for male unskilled workers. Social changes include the influx of women into the workforce and an increase in divorce and lone-parent families, so that the availability of women for unpaid, caring work in the home diminishes. Politically, the inability of both Labour and Conservative governments in the 1970s to stem the tide of unemployment and inflation that beset Britain in this period undermined confidence in Keynesian economic management, whilst newly influential political groupings criticized many aspects of welfare delivery. The combination of these factors led to a reorientation of social and economic policies in the 1980s and subsequent shifts following the election of a Labour government in 1997. We explain these political shifts in social welfare policy below after outlining the role of housing and social security in welfare provision.

Housing

There are two important ways in which the state is involved in the allocation and provision of housing. One is in planning and regulating the total supply of housing for the population. Here a pressing problem is the rise in single-person households caused by social and demographic change. England, in particular, has seen a major increase in numbers of people who, through choice, family break-up or longevity, live alone. In 1971, only 18 per cent of households in England were single-person households. By 1991, this had risen to just over a quarter; it is estimated that by 2016 some 36 per cent of households will have only one person living in them (*Social Trends* 1997). Roughly half of these single-person households will be made up of people over pensionable age and a considerable number will be people living alone as a result of divorce or will be younger people living alone as a consequence of a trend to later marriage. Underlying this last trend is a significant cultural shift. Until very recently the majority of younger people would live at home until they got married, with men, in particular, remaining in a household where a mother would take care of domestic tasks until a wife took over.

Younger people are nowadays much more likely to live independently: young women have considerably more economic independence and men are increasingly setting up home alone. There is an estimated growth in male single-person households of 10 per cent between 1971 and 2016. As a result of these various demographic and social changes, somewhere between 4.4 and 5.5 million new homes will have to be built. This figure is considered by many to be an underestimation, because it fails to take into account the backlog of homes needed because of the cutback in council house building in the 1980s and the poor condition of much existing housing stock.

This poses serious problems in terms of space: where are these new homes to be sited? Rural areas have more space than cities, but proposals to build in many rural areas meet with opposition from groups worried that green-belt land will disappear. In any event, rural housing will not be practical for many people. Another planning problem is that single people in need of housing represent a diverse group with different requirements in terms of indoor space and external location, so that, for example, divorced or separated people with children will require extra space for children living with them or to share custody, whilst young people may use less space and prefer to live near clubs, pubs and restaurants.

A second way in which the state is involved in housing allocation is through the direct provision of housing. After the Second World War there was a large expansion of hous-

Plate 13.3 Homelessness in the 1990s
Source: Network

ing that was rented directly from local authorities. Following the election of a Conservative government in 1979 the stock of available local authority housing was severely depleted. So whilst the problems of space and social change discussed above extend across housing sectors, housing policy has contributed to a more specific and urgent problem of people with no homes at all. Homelessness has been a steadily growing problem in the last two decades, partly as a result of unemployment, partly because of changes to housing allowances in the benefit system, and partly because of the 'Right To Buy' policy in the 1980s, which allowed council tenants to purchase the homes they rented but without the building of replacement stock. Mortgage arrears, domestic violence, and the onset of mental illness are some of the reasons for people becoming homeless, alongside physical and sexual abuse in the parental home, which accounts for much of youth homelessness. Local authorities have a legal duty to house people who meet the criteria of a 'priority need' category: pregnant women, families with children, those vulnerable because of age or disability, and those homeless because of an emergency (Lowe 1997). The system is punitive and designed to eliminate claims upon it, resulting in unknown numbers of rough sleepers, people whose only option is to live on the streets. Where people qualify for accommodation, local authorities have a duty to provide temporary accommodation, mainly, although not exclusively, in the privately rented sector, for a minimum two-year period (Lowe 1997, p. 31). There are stringent conditions governing eligibility, including a requirement that a person has not become 'intentionally' homeless. Intentionality has a very wide interpretation, so that if a person has been evicted for failure to pay housing costs because of unemployment, for example, she or he can be deemed to be intentionally homeless.

The data in table 13.8 refer only to households, not numbers of people, and of course

TABLE 13.8	Characteristics of statutorily homeless households and average estimated acceptances by local authority type, 1995					
Reason for priority need	No.	District and city councils[a] average	Metropolitan districts average	Outer London average	Inner London average	England average
Dependent children	67,100	116	469	331	450	173
Member pregnant	13,350	22	82	85	142	34
Vulnerable older person	5,950	11	32	30	54	15
Disabled person	6,470	9	33	56	96	17
Mental health problem or learning difficulty	7,250	9	47	56	101	19
Vulnerable young person	3,620	4	47	9	21	9
Person(s) escaping domestic violence	7,650	7	140	14	30	22
Other special reason[b]	4,210	4	99	19	32	15

[a] Includes new unitary authorities
[b] People accepted because of serious and/or debilitating illness, such as HIV. Some authorities accepted vulnerable categories of ex-offender and other vulnerable groups under the code of guidance to the 1985 Housing Act.
Source: Pleace, Burrows and Quilgars 1997, p. 15

they exclude those not accepted as homeless by local authorities, so that they show only the tip of the iceberg of homelessness. The pattern of acceptances between authorities indicates the extent of problems facing some areas, as Pleace, Burrows and Quilgars (1997, p. 15) point out:

> The higher overall acceptances made by large urban authorities were reflected in much higher acceptance levels of vulnerable households . . . Across England as a whole in 1995, approximately 74 per cent of acceptances were households containing children and 24 per cent were 'vulnerable' households, which are mainly lone homeless people. In the district and smaller city councils, the figures were close to this national level (75 per cent and 23 per cent) but in Outer London more vulnerable households were accepted (31 per cent) and in the Metropolitan Districts the figure rose to 33 per cent, while in Inner London it was 38 per cent. Statutory single homelessness is therefore concentrated in urban areas, especially within Inner London, which has especially high levels of acceptance of people with mental health problems compared to other areas.

Homelessness is linked to a range of disadvantages and deprivations affecting individuals, yet whilst state intervention is required to provide suitable accommodation for large numbers of homeless persons, we will see below that policy initiatives in the 1980s and 1990s shifted significantly from the post-war aims.

Social security

The social security system developed after the Second World War built on the structure of its predecessor but substantially extended it in a particular direction. The system is split into two parts. One is based upon an insurance principle whereby employees, employers and the state contribute payments to pay for unemployment, sickness and pensions, for example. The other part of the system is a means-tested safety net which provides income support for those who fall outside the insurance system, who have limited, if any, savings, and who meet stringent eligibility criteria. Beveridge envisaged that claims upon this side of the system would be relatively few as most people would be in work. Through a comprehensive nationalization of the social security system, Beveridge intended to intervene in the life course at points of high poverty risk – child rearing, old age, or interruption to earnings through sickness or unemployment – with the aim of preventing poverty rather than merely alleviating it. The relationship between social security and labour markets was central to the development of the system, for only by maintaining full employment could the insurance side of the system function as intended. The principle of state-administered insurance was important, for it symbolized a shift towards recognizing the structural causes of poverty and the value of responding through a collective responsibility for risks that could afflict anyone. The universalism of the social security system was similarly applied in health and education, representing a key mechanism of the provision of the social wage in the post-war settlement. Universalism was a means to extend citizenship rights and to build a welfare state that functioned as a mechanism of social cohesion and integration.

The reasons why people claim social security fall into five broad categories. Those who are unemployed can claim an increasingly restricted number of benefits; those in low-paid work can also claim certain benefits; those who are ill or disabled have entitlements; pensioners are eligible for state-administered pensions; and child allowances are available. The structure of the system is extremely complex, comprising a range of benefits and eligibility criteria. It accounts for a major part of public expenditure. Table 13.9 shows the amounts spent on different parts of the system.

However, the social security system has not developed in the way envisaged by Beveridge. Rising numbers of unemployed people, lone-parent families and elderly people have resulted in more of the population being dependent on the system than was imagined would be the case. Following the election of the Conservative government in 1979, the insurance principle was all but abandoned in favour of the principle of 'targeting' benefit entitlement to those 'most in need'. In practice, this diverted claimants to the means-tested side of the system, never designed to cater for large numbers of claimants, and encompassed a shift to highly individualized and prejudicial explanations of poverty and misfortune. This marked the start of an accelerated abandonment of the idea of collectively pooling resources to deal with risk, as well as of the idea that social rights to benefit were a right attached to one's status as a citizen. Instead of the language of rights and citizenship, the 1980s saw the development of a political rhetoric of the respon-

TABLE 13.9 | Income and expenditure on social security

Income/expenditure	£	%
Income		
Insured people	20,399m	20.8
Employers	24,203m	24.7
General taxation	52,863m	54.0
Other	480m	0.49
Total	97,944m	
Expenditure		
Elderly people	42,820m	44.0
Sick and disabled people	24,400m	25.0
Unemployed people	6,150m	6.0
Widows and others	2,070m	2.0
Family support	18,670m	19.0
Administration	3,818m	4.0
Total	97,929m	

Area	Staff number
Headquarters	2,748
Benefits Agency	69,183
Child Support Agency	8,103
Contributions Agency	7,521
IT Services Agency	1,935
War Pensions Agency	1,052
Total	90,542

Source: DSS 1998a

sibilities of citizenship and of negative evaluations of those unfortunate enough to depend for their income on the benefit system.

This shift was possible, in part, because of problems intrinsic to the system. The funding of its insurance side had always been problematic and levels of benefit low. The 'rediscovery of poverty' in the relatively affluent 1960s signalled a failure to prevent poverty, as opposed to simply relieving it. The complexity of the system was often too difficult for claimants and administrators alike. The system also encompassed a relationship between work and family life which came under critical scrutiny as cultural norms changed. The principal criticism concerns the racism and sexism within the Beveridge Report itself and the administrative measures flowing from it (Williams 1989). J. Stewart (1997) highlights the fact that, in part, the Beveridge plan was based on assumptions about the particular contribution which women were meant to make to the economy and family. For example, Beveridge (1942, para. 114) stated that: 'The attitude of the housewife to gainful employment outside the home is not and should not be the same as that of single women. She has other duties.' The assumption was that married women would be at home looking after breadwinners and dependants. The report continues by stating that 'maternity is the principal object of marriage'. Married women were therefore construed as dependants of their husbands and their eligibility for benefits tied to this status. Their status as mothers was particularly important as it was couched in relation to the national interest. Beveridge (1942, para. 117) explained that: 'In the next thirty years housewives as mothers have vital work to do in ensuring the adequate continuance of the British race and British ideals in the world.'

Certain lifestyles, values and economic direction were the basis of the post-war social security system. Economic globalization, the collapse of full employment, a multicultural society and changing social norms and expectations have all served to undermine the system. Since the 1980s successive governments have implemented reviews and reforms, sharing a desire to restructure social security to make it more congruent with current economic objectives, and at the same time to encourage the promotion of stable families, a reaction to increases in divorce and lone parenthood. These concerns demonstrate that social security is never simply a technical issue of administration or entitlement. It is also an important vehicle for the realization of economic modernization and normative visions of desirable social progress. We examine this in more detail below, where we look more broadly at the political dynamics in which social welfare is situated.

Political change and social welfare

The post-war consensus collapsed in the mid-1970s under the impact of recession, when the rate of economic growth became insufficient to subsidize both industrial recovery and the provision of expanding welfare services. As Pierson (1997) points out, under circumstances of recession, national product and revenue from taxation and insurance fall whilst claims upon welfare provision, particularly income support, rise. In the late 1970s this situation was often diagnosed as crisis. Political strategists, of both left-wing and right-wing persuasions, concluded that because popular demand for welfare spending was inexhaustible, pressures for more public expenditure necessarily compounded national economic problems. Governments, at first Labour, then Conservative, sought ways to alleviate the situation. The two major parties diverged, suggesting different solutions to social and economic problems. The uneasy consensus that supported the post-war settlement collapsed, challenged most fundamentally by the Conservative governments to whose policies the prime minister elected in 1979 gave her name – Thatcherism.

Reform of welfare: Conservative governments 1979–97

The distinctive character of the post-1979 Conservative administrations lay in the adoption of an interconnected set of policies on public spending, public- and private-sector employment and consumption, and trade union rights. Often described as 'anti-welfare, anti-union and anti-egalitarian', these policies marked a fundamental departure from Keynesian social and economic management. Following neo-liberal prescriptions, they were aimed at reducing the role of the state in the management of economic activity and welfare provision and increasing that of the private sectors and market competition. The key areas of innovation were economic regulation through monetary policy, sharp contraction of public ownership and public-sector employment, and reduction of public expenditure by reducing and restructuring welfare services, thereby permitting reductions in direct taxation, acceptance of high levels of unemployment, and reductions in the powers of trade unions. The relative coherence and comprehensiveness of these initiatives, together with an ambitious series of legislative programmes which exceeded that of the immediate post-war years, led many commentators to talk of the development of a neo-liberal strategy of social and economic management, the main application of which in the public and private sectors is shown in box 13.3. Jessop (1994) identified six key elements of the strategy:

1   *liberalization*, promoting the free market (as opposed to monopolistic or state-subsidized) forms of competition as the most efficient basis for economic development;
2   *deregulation*, giving economic agents greater freedom from state control;
3   *privatization*, reducing the public sector's role in the direct and indirect provision of goods and services to business and the community alike;
4   *marketization*, of the public sector to promote the role of market forces, whether directly or through internal and quasi-markets;
5   *internationalization*, encouraging the mobility of capital and labour, stimulating global market forces, and importing more advanced processes and products into Britain;
6   *tax cuts*, to provide incentives and demand for the private sector.

The strategy was justified by claims that Britain needed to create an enterprise culture in order to promote international competitiveness. In this sense one objective was to alter the values of the British population. Individualism, independence, competitiveness and self-reliance were encouraged. Welfare reforms were explicitly connected to initiatives designed to promote changes in labour markets, attitudes to entrepreneurialism and the extension of financial markets. It was said that the regeneration of the economy required work incentives, lower wages and benefits, flexibility in working practice and

---

Box 13.3   Neo-liberal regulation of public and private sectors

Public sector	Private sector
Privatization and liberalization	Deregulation
Introduction of commercial criteria	Enterprise zones and private-sector-led development; enterprise culture
Social security to support and subsidize low wages	'Flexible' working and wages
'Targeting' of welfare and restricted eligibility	Increasing social management role for private business through the growth of quangos
Dismantling of national collective bargaining; attempted introduction of performance-related pay and local pay deals	Support for workplace unions
Jobs and pay reduced and insecurity increased	Promotion of 'hire-and-fire' policy (O'Brien and Penna 1998, p. 156)

---

low direct taxation rates, with a consequently reduced public sector. The creation of an enterprise economy therefore involved deregulating labour markets in order to promote flexibility, weakening the strength of organized labour, and maintaining a punitive benefits system for those unemployed. The labour market strategy, and the increasingly residualized benefits system that accompanied it, encouraged the growth of low-paid employment and pushed many people, both in and out of work, into greater poverty.

Other aspects of the strategy included: incentives to purchase personal pensions and shares in the newly privatized public utilities; the introduction of compulsory competitive tendering in NHS and local authority social services, requiring that agencies put out to tender certain aspects of service provision; the creation in the public sector of quasi-markets and internal markets with a separation of purchasers and providers; the introduction of private-sector performance and monitoring criteria; a reduction of the full-time workforce and an increase in the use of part-time and temporary staff; and a displacement of many welfare functions to the community, voluntary organizations, charities, families and the private sector.

However, despite this major reorientation of policy, the Conservative administrations found it very hard to reduce real public expenditure on welfare. Although the state's share of all spending is lower than it was at the beginning of the 1970s, it still represents a significant expenditure. Table 13.10 shows spending on various welfare services between 1981 and 1995. The 1986 Social Security Act reduced considerably the state's commitments in income support, and public-sector contraction more generally along with privatization was consistent throughout the 1980s. Yet table 13.9 shows that although spending on housing dropped significantly as a result of the decision more or less to stop building council houses, health spending gradually rose because of the changing demographic profile of the population, the labour-intensive nature of care and

| TABLE 13.10 | Spending on welfare services, 1981–95 (£bn)[a] |

	1981	1991	1995
Social security	61	83	102
Health	26	35	41
Education	28	33	38
Public order	9	15	15
Housing	14	10	10
Total social	138	176	206
Total all	230	257	304
Social security as % of all	60%	68%	68%

[a]At 1995 prices (i.e. the increases or decreases are 'real' for 1995)
Source: *Social Trends* 1997, p. 118

the extra cost of increasingly sophisticated treatments. Social security rose more, a result of consistently high unemployment, a larger number of people receiving pensions, and an increase in the number of people whose wages were so low that they were entitled to claim top-up in-work benefits.

The dramatic increase in spending on public order is worth noting. S. Hall (1983) noted a drift towards an increasingly authoritarian state in the 1970s and 1980s, in which minority social groups were scapegoated as a source of social and economic problems, through a strategy to distract attention from the problems afflicting global capitalism. If we look at political speeches and media reporting during this period, we can observe how often welfare claimants were labelled as 'scroungers' draining the resources of taxpayers, trade unionists as communist agitators undermining the ability of the economy to modernize, and ethnic minorities, single parents and homosexuals as 'alien' elements undermining the genetic quality of the British people. There was also a huge policing effort in the 1980s. The reduction of social rights in the welfare state – the social wage – was accompanied by reductions in rights to protest against changes in working practices. Certain dimensions of industrial disputes were criminalized in the 1980s, thus requiring large increases in expenditure during industrial conflicts. The expansion of new social movement politics, particularly environmental politics, is also of significance. The direct-action tactics employed by many environmental groups posed a public order problem, as did the increases in warehouse rave parties and in New Age travellers. The Public Order Act was an attempt to police alternative, post-materialist values by criminalizing their expression in certain lifestyles and forms of extra-parliamentary protest. The effect, however, may have been to intensify protest and, by presenting a clearly identifiable 'enemy', actively to facilitate the development of a collective identity and purpose amongst a very disparate collection of groups.

The lack of a significant quantitative shift in spending should not be taken to imply that the quality of services had remained constant. Although measuring quality objectively is difficult, the quality of provision declined for certain groups: for example, social security claimants became relatively poorer, most unemployed young people between 16 and 18 years became ineligible for benefit, and the terms on which compensation for unemployment was offered deteriorated. Yet despite the drive to reduce the role of the welfare state in social protection, we have not witnessed the end of the welfare state, as some commentators feared, but rather its restructuring. Taken together, the elements of the neo-liberal strategy shifted the role of the state from a provider of services to a market or quasi-market relationship between suppliers and consumers in a decentralized and fragmented system. As Jessop (1994) observes, in contrast to the Keynesian welfare state, the welfare system became geared towards enhancing competitiveness in an internationalized economic framework. The range of private, voluntary and state institutions involved in the provision of social welfare, as well as the relationships existing between national and supranational policy-making institutions such as the EU and IMF, has led to suggestions that, instead of talking about a welfare *state*, it would be more useful to talk of welfare *governance*.

New Labour and the modernization of welfare

Despite the reforms of the 1980s, economic uncertainty and difficulty continue. The Labour government elected in a landslide victory in 1997 inherited a radically different welfare system from that existing when it was previously in office between 1974–9, as well as a number of economic problems. But several other political changes had also transformed the political environment. Social Democratic parties across Europe have been challenged for some time by new social movement politics, a politics that was manifested in debates over the welfare state (Pierson 1997). Feminists had pointed out the patriarchal character of the welfare state with its differential, gendered allocation of rights and responsibilities. Similarly, anti-racist groups had demonstrated the racist assumptions and different entitlements obtaining between majority and minority ethnic groups. Disability groups campaigned over the discriminatory and disabling character of welfare provision, and gay and lesbian groups over the lack of entitlements to pensions and other benefits, for example, for same-sex couples. At the same time, user movements, different groups of service users within the welfare system, were campaigning vigorously against the hierarchical and bureaucratic organization of welfare services and for more participative, democratic structures of welfare delivery. What these various groups highlighted was that the post-war settlement and the class compromise entailed in it nevertheless perpetuated many other forms of inequality.

The Labour government was dubbed 'New Labour' because it set out to modernize social and economic institutions through a 'Third Way' programme that aimed to transcend the neo-liberalism of the previous Conservative administrations as well as the Keynesianism of post-war social democracy. The prime minister, Tony Blair, argued that the left must 'modernize or die', and described how 'Our task today is not to fight old battles but to show that there is a third way, a way of marrying together an open, competitive and successful economy with a just, decent and humane society' (cited in Driver and Martell 1998, p. 7).

Accepting and extending the neo-liberal strategy, the Labour administration sought to conjoin it with a welfare modernization programme based on the notion of social inclusion. To overcome deepening social divisions, Labour proposed not so much a redistribution of income or wealth as a redistribution of opportunities. Whereas the Labour Party has traditionally viewed social welfare as a key means of redressing the inequalities arising from markets, New Labour accepts free-market capitalism and defines inequality as social exclusion from the opportunities it brings. Box 13.4 indicates the government's view of social exclusion as a priority issue.

Box 13.4   What is the government doing about social exclusion?

Tackling social exclusion is one of the government's highest priorities, as demonstrated by its actions since coming to office. For example, the welfare to work programme, the emphasis on school improvement and raising standards of literacy and numeracy, the national childcare strategy, the review of pensions and work on poorer pensioners, the setting up of the Low Pay Commission, the release of capital receipts to improve housing stock, the review of tax and benefits and the Task Force to hold a wide-ranging review on how to implement comprehensive and enforceable civil rights for disabled people. In addition, the Prime Minister has now set up the Social Exclusion Unit.

A Social Exclusion Unit based in the Cabinet Office and chaired by the prime minister signalled a concerted effort to develop policies to combat social exclusion through reform of welfare structures and benefits. Launched in December 1997, in its first six months the unit's work was concentrated on truancy and school exclusions, rough sleeping and the problems of the most deprived estates. Its brief is to be wide-ranging, drawing up key indicators of exclusion, and working with other government departments and private-sector and voluntary agencies. The spread of those involved in welfare governance is evident from the membership of the unit. Half come from the civil service and half from those working in welfare agencies, local government, business sectors, the police force and the probation service. Also included in the staff of the unit are researchers from the think-tank *Demos*, where policy proposals based on 'Third Way' politics have been developed (I. Hargreaves and Christie 1998).

The range of proposals to combat exclusion correspond with those of the EU (see box 13.5). They revolve around developing 'active' employment strategies that assist unemployed and insecurely employed people to cope with rapidly changing forms of work, rather than simply responding to misfortune through the 'passive' strategy of expecting claimants to sit and wait for their weekly benefit entitlement; the emphasis on lifelong learning to prepare people for the 'fourth sector' informational economy; and the recognition of the barriers posed by discrimination in the labour market.

Within the EU, social exclusion is also seen as part of a concern for modernization. The view held is that the structures of the post-war welfare state were developed to support the industrial society of the nineteenth and first half of the twentieth century. The new global economy and the social and cultural changes accompanying it require a new set of institutions to support new patterns of working and household formation. The concern with retaining the social model – adequate social welfare provision – reflects a concern that the degree of exclusion and polarization accompanying economic restructuring will cause unacceptable levels of social and political conflict. Retaining the social model is considered essential for maintaining social integration and cohesion.

> ### Box 13.5   EU strategies to combat social exclusion
>
> These strategies include:
>
> - active labour-market policies to promote flexibility;
> - a welfare-to-work programme;
> - integration of work and family life;
> - equal opportunities for women, ethnic minorities, disabled people and older and younger people;
> - lifelong learning.

Yet there is, for Britain and other EU countries, an acute and irreconcilable dilemma between retaining a neo-liberal economic strategy that demands low direct taxation rates, a shrinking public sector and reductions in public expenditure, and a social welfare system that can provide sufficient social protection to serve a politically and socially integrative function. Social welfare provision, as Pierson (1997) discusses, is caught in a set of structural contradictions between the requirements of capitalist economies for profit maximization and the requirements of the population for social protection. As those who most need welfare provision are precisely those who, for a number of reasons, do not have the means to purchase private provision, no amount of private-sector involvement will benefit them. At the same time, there is clear evidence that when welfare is not universally available and accessed by the majority of the population, the quality of service declines. In other words, services for the poor are poor services. The politics of welfare are now centre-stage in the EU, for at the heart of political debates lie competing visions of what societies ought to be like, and whether it is possible for social and economic progress to go hand in hand, or whether the latter must be achieved at the expense of the former. Underlying this political debate is another set of environmental politics, with Green activists and parties pointing out that the productivist logic underpinning social and economic policy is environmentally destructive and thus actively undermines the welfare of current and future populations.

Summary

1   The welfare state was created in the immediate post-war period, but a series of economic, social and political changes since then have produced radical alterations in welfare policy, particularly since the early 1980s.

2   The state is involved in planning and regulating the provision of housing through the exercise of planning controls and fiscal policy, but is also a direct provider of housing, although to a much lesser extent than it was in the late 1940s.

3   Although the social security budget continues to form a very large part of

government expenditure, the insurance principle that underpinned the original system has been abandoned in favour of targeting benefit at those 'in need'.

4 There is continuing political controversy over the appropriate level and form of welfare provision.

Related topics

Section 6.5 contains additional material relevant to evaluation of the elite and ruling-class views of power. On state powers of surveillance and restraint see sections 16.4 and 16.6. On the role of informal political practice and social resistance, consistent with a pluralist account, see sections 8.3 and 10.5. The political orientations of different social classes are considered in sections 6.3, 6.4 and 6.5. On the consequences of ethnic identity for political action see section 8.3. On social movements see sections 2.4 on environmentalism and 7.7 on feminism. For further material on the form and effectiveness of state welfare policies see section 4.5 on unemployment, 5.2 on poverty, 9.3 on housing, 14.2 on education and 15.6 and 15.7 on health. On gender and welfare see also section 7.5.

Further reading

The most useful single book on the British state is Dearlove and Saunders (1991). Other useful sources are Dunleavy and O'Leary (1987) and J. Scott (1991). On voting behaviour, see A. Heath et al. (1994) and Denver (1994). On debates on the welfare state, Pierson (1997) is good, as is O'Brien and Penna (1998). A. Scott (1990) is a sound text on new social movements, describing different sociological approaches.

Cross-references to *Readings in Contemporary Society*

Roseneil on a local protest movement; **Hetherington** on protests associated with Stonehenge in the mid-1980s; **Judge et al.** on changes in the National Health Service; **Bechhofer et al.** on Scottish identity; **Norris and Lovenduski** on political representation, electoral bias, political elites and party organizations; **Sanders** on political parties, partisanship, electoral volatility and class dealignment; **Gewirtz et al.** on the policy to privatize economic organizations and the quality of welfare provision in the educational sphere.

14 | Education

14.1   Introduction

Education is particularly important for three reasons. Firstly, formal education is a crucial element in the experience of almost all young people in Western societies. All children and adolescents between 5 and 16 must either attend school or be educated otherwise by parents (e.g. at home but subject to inspection by trained teachers). For young people aged 17 and over, the numbers attending further education colleges and universities are increasing, and some 30 per cent of all young people aged 18–21 now enter higher education (in the late 1970s it was well under 10 per cent). So education potentially has a major social and cultural role. Second, a significant proportion of public expenditure is spent on education in the UK, which means that education policies receive a great deal of scrutiny for their economic effects, which are often in tension with their cultural role. Third, education, and increasingly educational qualifications, play a key part in shaping not only entry to employment but also life chances and lifestyles. Qualifications provide a basis for further social, cultural and economic selection, people with a degree, for instance, being likely to have higher earnings over their adult lives than those who do not (National Committee of Inquiry into Higher Education 1997, tables 6.1 and 6.2).

14.2 Education and the state

Political debates about schools

Because of the substantial amount of public funding involved (see box 14.1), it is not surprising that each generation of politicians sees education as a proving ground for their ideas about schooling in particular and society in general. Some writers have argued that the immediate post-war period saw a consensus around education which lasted until the mid-1960s. Subsequently, controversies over educational content and institutional form have been commonplace, starting with a series of critiques of comprehensive education and school standards, published in the late 1960s, known as the black papers, and continuing until the present day. Though different political parties and groups have divergent views about education, all of them seek reform. Since the mid-1980s the education systems of England, Wales and Northern Ireland have been in almost continual transformation. The values underlying reforms have differed. The Conservative government of 1992–7 sought to introduce more diversity into education. The Labour government after 1997 had a greater commitment to ensuring consistent and uniformly high standards of schooling for children and young people. Nevertheless, in contrast to the earlier part of the post-war period, the gradual erosion of concerns about social class inequality was a common feature of almost all education policies from the 1980s onwards (see box 14.2). The curriculum and assessment methods of schools have been one object of change. Reform has also been attempted in other sectors of education, including 'early years' education (where there was a short-lived voucher system for all children aged 3 and 4), teacher training and further education.

Box 14.1 State expenditure on education

State expenditure on education in the UK is high. Indeed the amount spent has continued to rise in real terms, for example by over 60 per cent between 1971 and 1995. However, the total amount as a percentage of gross domestic product was the same in 1994–5 (5 per cent) as in 1970–1. (See table 14.1.)

TABLE 14.1 Government expenditure on education in real terms: by type (£million at 1995–6 prices)[a]

	1970–1	1980–1	1990–1	1994–5	1995–6[b]
Schools					
Nursery and primary	5,298	6,657	8,103	9,874	9,874
Secondary	6,132	8,603	9,056	9,698	9,561
Special	490	1,018	1,376	1,529	1,542
Higher, further and continuing education[c]	5,782	6,896	8,130	9,563	9,770
Other education expenditure	785	1,140	1,623	1,035	1,070
Total	18,486	24,313	28,288	31,700	31,818
Related education expenditure	3,024	3,323	2,924	3,752	3,611
VAT incurred on above expenditure	747	410	587	910	923
Total expenditure	22,257	28,046	31,799	36,362	36,352
Total expenditure as a percentage of GDP	5.2	5.5	4.8	5.2	5.1

[a] Adjusted to 1995–6 prices using the GDP market prices deflator
[b] Includes 1994–95 data for Wales and Scotland
[c] Includes universities. In April 1989 fees for polytechnics and colleges transferred to the former Polytechnics and College Funding Council.
Source: Social Trends 1998, p. 71

Organizational reform of education by the state

There have been organizational changes to educational institutions at all levels of the system. One goal of the 1979–97 Conservative administrations was to reduce public expenditure and to subject public organizations to market competition as a means of increasing their efficiency, markets being seen as a rational way of organizing the distribution of public services as well as private ones. It was intended that educational institutions should become more like private business organizations, responding to the preferences of their customers. However, parents, pupils and employers are all educational customers, not necessarily with similar concerns or interests. It was also intended that educational institutions should have some control over their finances, and that the size of their budgets would depend on their success or failure in attracting customers. This was done in several ways:

1   In 1986 legislation was passed encouraging the co-option of school governors (lay people who oversee the running of state-funded schools) from the business community.

2   In 1988 the Education Reform Act paved the way for what became known as local management of schools, whereby instead of local education authorities (LEAs) managing the finances of schools, schools themselves would be responsible for their own budgets, albeit on a formula basis (for example, primary schools get less than secondary schools). In addition, each pupil in each school would attract

---

BOX 14.2   The role of the state in education

A number of writers have examined the role of the state in education. Dale (1997), for example, suggests that all states are faced with particular core dilemmas:

- ensuring good conditions for capital accumulation (e.g. healthy, well-qualified workers with access to health care and free education);
- guaranteeing a context for the expansion of capital accumulation (by providing a stable democratic government with no incitement to public disorder);
- legitimating the state's role in stimulating the economy, including encouraging those aged over 16 and not in jobs to take training or to enrol in courses leading to educational qualifications.

However, Dale argues that in an increasingly globalized world, there are new dimensions to these core dilemmas, including:

- the more uncertain role of government in economic growth with the development of multinational organizations and supranational bodies;
- a decline in welfare provision, leading to the privileging of some groups over others;
- the more limited role of national states, which itself has meant a shift from regulation towards governance, in common with deregulation of other formerly publicly provided services like railways.

---

per capita funding, so that popular schools would have high revenues while less popular schools would have to make economies or even close altogether. This system of devolved budgeting gave schools and their headteachers an illusion of autonomy (Deem 1994), but was accompanied by increasing government surveillance and continued restrictions on spending.

3 Schools wishing to do so, after obtaining the consent of parents through a ballot, were allowed to opt out of the local authority system altogether. They would become grant-maintained schools (GMS), which then became responsible to the Funding Agency for Schools. GMS schools directly employed their teachers and owned their own land and premises. Despite financial inducements to become GMS, this policy was never overwhelmingly successful even in secondary schools (and not at all in Scotland, where they were called 'self-governing' schools). Nor was it clear that GMS schools ever differed in any important organizational or pedagogic ways from schools which remained under LEA jurisdiction. In 1998 GMS schools were returned to LEAs. By this time, LEAs had few remaining powers, so this meant mainly that their representatives would once again sit on governing bodies of former GMS schools.

Markets and parental choice

Controversy arose over the Conservatives' attempt to make schools operate under quasi-market conditions (see section 13.4). Nevertheless, the policy remained in place with the election of a Labour government in May 1997. The argument in favour of giving parents more choice of school is that this empowers the consumer rather than the producer (i.e. the teachers) of education, just as privatizing other former public services such as housing 'frees' people from dependency on the welfare state. However, as a number of researchers have shown, the amount of choice available to parents is related to where they live, their class position and their cultural capital (Gewirtz et al. 1995).

Gewirtz, Ball and Bowe (1995) researched the development of quasi-market reforms in three groups of secondary schools in the London area. Most of the headteachers who were interviewed felt that a move to a more competitive situation had not necessarily been a good idea:

> I am conscious that a number of parents who don't choose us, don't choose Parsons School for social reasons. We are more of a working class comprehensive. (headteacher, Parsons School)

> Our competitors are not the other Riverway mixed schools, so much as . . . the independent sector . . . that's a very unstable feature for us because parents might decide their businesses are at risk and they'll send their daughters to us this year and then it'll pick up and we lose them again next year . . . it does make budgeting very difficult. (headteacher, Pankhurst School) (quoted in Gewirtz et al. 1995, pp. 72, 73)

The researchers also talked to parents who were in the process of choosing secondary schools for their children but who had not yet received offers of places. The research team distinguished between three different categories of parents on the basis of social class and cultural capital:

- *Privileged and/or skilled choosers*, who value the opportunity to select between schools, are able to spend time and energy finding out about the differences between schools. They will consult not only other parents but educational professionals and employers, as well as directories of information about education. If they do not get the school they want they are confident about using the appeal system. However, the amount that these parents know can leave them judging very fine differences between schools which appear comparable in other terms. Often such parents made the final choice on the basis of their own feelings about the ethos of a school: 'The facilities . . . the feeling, it seemed a happy school as I went round' (Mrs Roding, quoted in Gewirtz et al. 1995, p. 32).
- *Semi-skilled choosers* want to engage actively in choosing a school but have fewer cultural resources (e.g. fewer informed friends, less acquaintance with pressure groups or exam league tables) to draw upon and are, hence, less confident about the process. They are less likely to appeal and are more influenced than the first group by newspaper reports and hearsay: 'a) it's received very good press, b) in the papers it always has good academic results and I talked to several people who

have children . . . (who) have already gone to senior schools' (Mrs Pritchard, quoted in Gewirtz et al. 1995, p. 41).

- *The disconnected* are parents who, while interested in where their children go to school, see schools as broadly similar and often leave the final choice to their children: 'Schools are much of a muchness really. . . . as long as there's nothing academically vastly different or better with one school then David (son) can make the final choice' (Mrs Sutcliffe, quoted in Gewirtz et al. 1995, p. 45). Such parents may also, especially if they are white, be susceptible to the ethnic composition of schools and reject them on those grounds: 'Because it's all nig nogs, isn't it? It's all Asians and it is a known fact that they hold all ours back' (Mr Tufnell, quoted in Gewirtz et al. 1995, p. 49).

Studies of parental choice generally seem to indicate that determined, articulate parents get the schools they want for their children. Less affluent parents are more likely to send their children to underfunded and unpopular (so also understaffed) schools. There is evidence of racism too, with white parents in inner cities choosing to send their offspring to schools with other white pupils, so that Asian and black pupils end up in inner-city schools with few facilities. Parents of pupils with special educational needs have not been given the same degree of choice as other parents, as work with such parents in two local authority areas of northern England has shown.

Wilkinson (1996) studied a small number of families with children of primary-school age but with special educational needs in each of two areas, one rural, one urban. She traced the progress of the allocation of these pupils to mainstream and special schools. Professionals, such as educational psychologists, LEA officers and headteachers, tended to have a bigger say than the parents, and even very determined, privileged and semi-skilled choosers sometimes found their preferences ignored or sidelined. Wilkinson also found, as have studies of secondary-school choice (e.g. David et al. 1994), that fathers are not necessarily as much involved in the process of school choice as mothers. David and her research team found that mothers not only put more effort into the procedure (for example by attending open evenings, reading school prospectuses, collecting information about exam results) but were often more interested in the process than fathers and more likely to talk to their children about it. In addition, they may anticipate greater involvement if the school their child eventually attends is a long way from home and not on a bus or train route, for it is they, rather than fathers, who are likely to act as chauffeur.

The advent of a National Curriculum was supposed to reduce the impact of attending any particular school, but in Gewirtz's (1995) study only the 'disconnected' group were convinced of this. Indeed, market rhetoric suggests, on the contrary, that schools differ considerably. Some parents, on discovering this, may be baffled and confused by differences between schools which in many respects seem similar. Since the beginning of the 1990s, researchers concerned with school improvement have tried to address questions of why schools in identical situations with similar intakes of pupils fare differently. Though some progress has been made in identifying crucial factors such as leadership qualities of headteachers, clear objectives and good communications, it remains unclear whether these can be achieved in all schools. Some sociologists have criticized school-improvement theories for ignoring social and cultural factors such as gender, power relations and the social selection role of education. The last, particularly, militates against

Plate 14.1 Different types of schooling
Source: Format/Raissa Page; Network/John Sturrock

all schools having the same effect on their pupils' future life chances. This issue is revisited in the next section.

Legislation, however, is neither simply nor easily translated into practice. There are always unintended consequences. Bowe and Ball studied the implementation of reform policies in four schools in the south of England (Bowe et al. 1992). Their research indicated that financial imperatives had had a considerable impact on activities and organizational cultures: senior staff became engrossed in intensified managerial roles and more hierarchical and bureaucratic arrangements. Competition between schools was encouraged in order to attract pupils and much more attention was paid to indicators of performance, such as exam results and truancy rates. However, there was still a great deal of room for manoeuvre, with schools implementing the policies flexibly and conditionally. For instance, the schools planned to teach the National Curriculum in very different ways, adapting it to existing practice. The specific manner of implementation of any policy depends on context – the history and development of particular schools, the variable commitment of teachers, and political conflicts within the school and in its local area. However, some recent policies, such as the literacy hour in primary schools and literacy and numeracy targets, have left teachers with no discretion, their compliance being required and reinforced by school inspectors.

Teachers and the state

One calculated effect of much government policy towards public-sector services has been to reduce the power of professional practitioners. Thus teachers in schools lost some of their autonomy through the introduction of the National Curriculum, for they could no longer decide what to teach. Similar changes were introduced into further education and there are now attempts at curricular control in higher education too, under the guise of ensuring standards, via the Quality Assurance Agency. Changes in the composition of school governing bodies, which increased parent and local business representation, reduced other channels of professional influence. Nevertheless, research on 10 governing bodies in primary and secondary schools in two LEA areas, over the four years after the introduction of the 1986 and 1988 reforms to school governance, found that headteachers were still powerful (Deem et al. 1995). Teacher governors, on the other hand, often found themselves isolated from other governors and some were reluctant to speak. Running schools as business organizations has made financial management more important than educational philosophies, in which teachers could claim special expertise. Given that teachers were also deprived of national union bargaining rights in 1987, subjected to a personal appraisal scheme and faced with increased work loads, many have become demoralized and dissatisfied. The introduction of performance-related pay for heads and deputies has caused an increasing gap in pay and conditions between senior staff and other teachers.

A study by Gewirtz et al. (1995) found that senior teachers in secondary schools developed a dual value system. This enabled heads to speak about business and finance when necessary but also to draw upon their educational values, depending on the audience:

> The idea of . . . using terms like 'marketplace', people are absolutely horrified by that. I don't think any of us are embracing that willingly but in the knowledge that . . . if we don't ensure that we're successful, we simply won't survive. (deputy head, Milton School, quoted in Gewirtz et al. 1995, p. 102)

This bilingualism, as the authors term it, was not found among less senior teaching staff. A study of the effects of the National Curriculum on the creativity of primary-school teachers also found that some teachers were able to find new outlets for their creativity despite the limitations on what could be taught (Woods 1995).

Teaching in schools has become a less popular occupation than it once was, not least because of the pay, and the ways in which successive governments have blamed teachers for the state of education and the standards achieved by pupils. Applications to become primary teachers fell by almost one third between 1996 and 1998, and applications for the postgraduate certificate of education in 1998/9, taken by most intending secondary-school teachers, also fell short of the targets set by some 2,500. Theorists point to the ways in which teachers at all levels have gradually become more deskilled, so that what they do is increasingly regulated from the outside. Instead of deciding what to teach, how to teach it and with what materials, teachers are losing autonomy over content. Materials such as textbooks or software programs may leave little room for teacher intervention, and even the methods of teaching may be prescribed.

In UK schools it is arguable that this deskilling, in so far as it has occurred, has been achieved by the introduction everywhere except Scotland of a National Curriculum and national assessment of pupils at ages 7, 11, 14 and 16. League tables of exam and Standardized Assessment Tests (SATs) tend to put blame onto teachers for poor results, even though some of the pupils themselves may be using a second language for the tests or come from materially deprived homes. There have also been attempts by government in the late 1990s to prescribe particular teaching styles, for example by recommending whole-class teaching as opposed to individualized learning using worksheets, or group discussion and activities.

Teacher training itself is also closely controlled in respect of content, and the quality of trainees is monitored by inspectors. Deskilling in further and higher education could be attributed to regular audits of teaching quality and efforts to make subject curricula more standardized. In further education, syllabuses are increasingly shaped by employers, and lecturers have to teach accordingly. Of course, teachers still have some autonomy; for example, teaching alone in a classroom or lab is still the norm. Nevertheless, unlike people in medicine or accountancy, and despite many decades of calls for a teachers' general council, except in Scotland school teachers have no control over recruitment to the profession.

Summary

1 Education policy became subject to more partisan political direction from the 1980s onwards. Changing economic conditions, the introduction of practices from private-sector business, and the end of a wider consensus about the content and organization of state education altered circumstances.

2 A National Curriculum and national assessment system were set up in three of the four countries of the UK but without removing differences between schools or reducing their role in social selection.

3 More parental choice has been introduced, especially in relation to secondary schools, but in practice this has not empowered all parents equally.

4 The state still has a key role in education, but it is now more one of governance than regulation, because educational institutions have become responsible for their own budgets and subject to local management.

14.3   Education and the economy

Nationalism, globalization, the economy and education

Halsey et al. (1997) argue that the post-war reform of education in Western societies has been profoundly affected by shifts in the relationship between education, culture, society and economy. They identify two major stages in this process:

1   *The foundation of economic nationalism, 1945–73.* In this period education was considered to play a key role in shaping the social and economic progress so important after the Second World War. National economic growth was seen as a fundamental basis of progress, with emphasis on prosperity, security and opportunity. This was emphasized by the growth of bureaucratic and Fordist organizations routinely characterized by hierarchical work relations with a highly specialized, though sometimes not very skilled, division of labour. It was also marked by the development of welfare provision, based on a notion of a stable family (with male breadwinners and women as mothers and domestic labourers) and the socialization of young people into roles appropriate to their gender and social class. In the UK, this involved the division between secondary modern and grammar schools (plus an intermediate secondary technical school) and a curriculum which was consciously gendered (although less so for middle-class pupils). However, it gradually became clear that a selective system did not maximize opportunities for young people or match the work skills required by employers. As a consequence, from the mid-1960s onwards, the UK saw a massive growth in comprehensive secondary education, which was most widespread in Scotland, England and Wales.

2   *The breakdown of economic nationalism and the shift to the global economy, 1973– present.* In the early 1970s world economic recession occurred, triggered initially by the oil crisis which raised fuel and transport costs. This in turn stimulated the growth of multinational companies and signalled a decline in heavy manufacturing industries (a major source of employment for working-class men in the UK), and the growth of new forms of economic enterprise using new technologies or oriented towards retailing and services. The mobility of multinational firms, able to switch their base to different countries depending on the location of cheap labour, weakens the power of national states. In several countries this fostered New Right ideologies, emphasizing the importance of competition and markets in both public and private sectors. In turn, welfare services were cut back and new questions arose about those areas of public policy and services that are still major areas of spending. This brought different forms of work organization, less

bureaucratic but also using more flexible forms of labour and organized in less hierarchical ways (more teams, fewer layers of managers). More workers were put on short-term contracts. Some functions (for example, personnel management or computing) were bought in rather than provided in-house, a process happening in education too. Even middle-class workers have felt the effects of such insecurity. Both single parents and mothers in dual-parent families are seen not just as legitimate members of the workforce but as requiring paid work as a matter of economic necessity. Changes in employment have led to changes in education, with more emphasis being placed on so-called key skills like numeracy and computer literacy rather than on academic subject knowledge, and the development of competency-based qualifications for those entering or in employment (National Vocational Qualifications or NVQs). NVQs assess practical skills and experience in a wide range of occupations from leisure industries to hairdressing.

Why does education matter to the economy?

Sociologists argue about the extent of the contribution of educational institutions to economic production.. Their effects are diverse. For example, universities play an important part in scientific and technological innovation, and educational institutions themselves provide a lot of jobs. However, broadly speaking, the education system has three major related and important connections to the economy: training, credentialism and selection.

Training

Schools and colleges train students in several ways:

- by giving instruction in useful skills (team working, word processing);
- by providing them with different kinds of knowledge (e.g. about biology or maths);
- by teaching the personal characteristics and social orientations required in work.

The last of these is important because, from an employer's point of view, skills – like literacy, numeracy, computer programming and cookery – are beneficial only if workers also turn up regularly and on time and do the tasks allotted to them when at work. The habits and motivations of work-discipline have to be instilled into each new generation of workers. Resistance may be encountered if young people do not internalize these forms of discipline. Social class may be vital; for whilst young graduates in employment which they sought may happily work long hours, school leavers with no or few qualifications may see work differently. Different types of workers require different social and cultural characteristics. A supermarket checkout operator and an accountant may both deal with money, but their levels of autonomy at work are not the same.

Credentials

As well as training, educational institutions also provide most of their students with evidence of their educational achievements in the form of certificates and awards. The growth of this is sometimes called credentialism, since some sociologists see it as a contagious disease unrelated to the availability of jobs. Awards include GCSEs, A-levels, higher national diplomas, degrees, professional qualifications and national vocational awards. On their own these mean little, but they may become the minimum basis for entry to certain jobs or occupational training. Qualifications may be in addition to other desirable characteristics. For example, to train as a riding instructor, it is not enough to be able to ride or to have some experience of teaching riding; people also require riding and school exams before entering training.

Selection

Educational institutions perform other selection functions as well. The very many positions produced by a highly specialized division of labour require some means of allocating people. Schools are closely involved. This occurs most obviously because schools prepare pupils for the examinations which confer qualifications. But it also occurs because there are differences in prestige between schools, for example between grammar schools and comprehensives or between independent and state-funded schools. We saw in the last section that some parents agonize long and hard over what these differences are and whether they matter. Having attended a school with a good reputation may also subsequently benefit its pupils. Processes of social inclusion and exclusion present pupils with different job opportunities whilst trying to ensure that the economy gets the differentiated workforce which it requires. However, this kind of economic planning is rarely entirely accurate and young people themselves may want to make different choices. For example, there may be many vacant jobs in teaching and nursing but working in the media may be more appealing, even if such jobs are rare.

Remember, however, that these three processes are interrelated. Schools select pupils for different kinds of training and help them to acquire certain kinds of social and cultural attributes. The training offered limits occupational choice. Also, training and forms of social selection are often in tension with other social and cultural roles of education. If education is seen to be even partly about helping young people to achieve their potential, then its parallel role in ensuring that some of them fail academically is problematic.

Vocational training

In the past neither the content of schooling nor the system of formal qualifications for middle- and upper-class children was explicitly driven by labour-market considerations, though that has not necessarily been so for working-class children. It is only in the later part of the twentieth century that educational policy-makers have thought it especially important to train young people in technical skills. For much of the nineteenth century it was thought far more important that a moral and religious education for 'citizenship' should be provided to the mass of the population. Britain's poor economic performance has increasingly been blamed on the defects of its educational system, though such analyses are often based on crude and inaccurate understandings of the relationship between economic performance and educational systems.

Protagonists in recent policy debates have recommended both that education should be more practically relevant to work and that new attitudes towards work and industry should be transmitted to students. Schools, colleges and universities are all urged to teach transferable skills – literacy, numeracy, computing and team work – though just how often these need to be taught and how transferable they will prove to be is debatable.

Training and Vocational Education Initiative

The 1980s witnessed some fresh experiments designed to extend training within schools with a view to improving Britain's economic performance. The Training and Vocational Education Initiative (TVEI) experiment was the most prominent example. Introduced in 1984, and finally abandoned in 1997, TVEI invited schools to put forward schemes for new courses of instruction for students of all abilities in the 14–18 age range. Courses designed for approval had to meet criteria overwhelmingly related to future employment. Courses had to:

- tie in with other training and job opportunties;
- include a 'work experience' component;
- be constructed in the light of local and national changes in employment opportunities;
- include technical education.

Successful schools were provided by the Manpower Services Commission (MSC) with additional resources to mount appropriate courses. Significantly, TVEI involved moving control and provision of training away from the Department of Education to the MSC, a branch of the Department of Employment which was also responsible for the Youth Training Scheme (YTS). TVEI symbolized the most marked change in priorities since the widespread introduction of comprehensive education to England and Wales in the mid-1960s. One intention was to overcome the resistance of defenders of liberal educational values in order to introduce more practical and relevant training. As Shilling (1989) described its operation, the covert rationale of the scheme was to prepare students for employment in capitalist organizations and to accept and adapt to the routines, the hierarchical social relations and some of the indignities associated with mundane jobs.

S. J. Heath's (1997) work examines the longer-term effects of TVEI, focusing on the extent to which the principle of equal opportunities, integral in the pilot phase, was realized. Her research was carried out in one local authority area, 'Masonfield', where the decline in heavy manufacturing had seriously damaged the local economy. This was so even though new jobs in the service sector (e.g. banking, tourism, etc.) had partially replaced the old ones in engineering and skilled manual work. As well as talking to teachers and education officers from Masonfield, Heath also surveyed a sample of young people a year before leaving school and then did follow-up interviews with them two years after they had left. She noted that when TVEI was introduced to Masonfield schools, there was little engagement with equal opportunities issues, not only because it was a traditional and rather conservative LEA but also because councillors and officers were worried about 'extremism'. The TVEI central co-ordinator said:

> Not only was equal opportunities not an issue, it was considered dangerous extremism to raise it, because there was a caricature of what had been going on in some authorities, with an emphasis on gay rights and lesbian rights. (S. J. Heath 1997, p. 73)

Hence Masonfield TVEI schools appeared to avoid dealing with issues related to sexual harassment and were wary of adopting controversial strategies, like single-sex setting for subjects where one gender tended to perform better than the others. Instead they tended to concentrated on 'safer' concerns like subject choice by girls and boys and career advice and planning. Furthermore, the posts in schools relating to equal opportunities were all held by women, thus reinforcing the view that equal opportunities was a matter for girls and women only. In any case, the tendency was for schools to assume that gender stereotyping came from parents, not from school:

> there's a tremendous parental influence. We find girls tend to, they've got this image that girls have babies, get married, their position is at home, full stop. The lads, they are the macho men, they go to the pub, have a beer, they have the money, wife stops at home. (TVEI co-ordinator, Seddon Park High School, quoted in S. J. Heath 1997, p. 92)

When Heath examined the curricular provision of schools, she found evidence of strong gender polarization among pupils in relation to their choice of subjects on the TVEI curriculum. Yet in her survey, less than 15 per cent of male and female respondents thought TVEI had been directed more at one gender than the other. However, some ex-pupils did not feel the careers advice available to them had been at all helpful:

> They tried to shuffle us off into jobs they wanted us to have. I said I wanted to be a draughts-man and the careers officer at the time said 'actually there's not much call for that at the moment . . . why don't you try this, that and the other'. (John, ex-TVEI pupil, quoted in S. J. Heath 1997, p. 116)

Heath found that only one in five school leavers surveyed had received advice encouraging them to think of jobs non-traditional for their gender. Such encouragement was much more marked for girls than boys. There was little attempt to get boys to consider new areas of employment, despite the changes to local employment opportunities making it likely that some young men would need to enter service-sector jobs previously thought of as female-only domains. As Heath notes, issues of equal opportunities tended to be presented as simply related to matters of individual access to jobs and ignored concerns to do with gender identity and more systematic cultural bases for gender discrimination. Of the small group with whom she did follow-up interviews two years after they left school, the majority were in jobs typical of their gender.

Like Shilling, Heath found that not all young people felt they had benefited much from their work experience placements. One young woman interested in becoming a personnel manager in retailing ended up serving in the bakery department of a supermarket. Another who wanted to be on a hospital ward spent her placement typing in a dentist's reception office and not being allowed anywhere near the surgery. However, perhaps these experiences reflect the difficulties of offering work placements to school students, who may be considered too young even to observe professional jobs, and hence are mainly introduced to less skilled and manual work regardless of whether this is a likely destination for them.

New policies for vocational training

Ultimately, schools are not well placed to pass on technical competence relevant to employment. Apart from the inclusion of information technology in the National Curriculum, job-related training in schools is very limited, though the introduction of the new General National Vocational Qualifications (GNVQs) for those staying on at school or college after 16 does attempt to include more directly job-related skills. GNVQs differ from NVQs in focusing on broad areas of employment such as tourism or the built environment rather than hotel receptionist work or bricklaying.

The UK education systems still differ considerably from those of some other European countries like Germany, where early in secondary education academic and vocational routes divide. Extended experience in real workplace situations is better suited to providing technical training – the short periods possible under TVEI, and as offered to many other secondary pupils also, are simply not long enough to do more than give some general familiarization with work routines and disciplines. GNVQs suffer from similar problems. NVQs by contrast take into account the competences which an individual employee already has: thus a hairdresser already familiar with tinting hair might provide a list of clients whose hair has been tinted, plus details of products used and the process employed. NVQs, unlike GNVQs, which are taken mostly by full-time students, tend to be taken by those already employed in the fields concerned.

Employer-provided, workplace-based apprenticeships, and later schemes under the auspices of Industrial Training Boards, were the traditional sources of male employment training. This has largely been replaced by Youth Training, introduced in the 1980s, aimed at 16–25-year-olds, with the intention of helping them acquire NVQs or other recognized vocational qualifications (see table 14.2). Though in 1990–1 more young men than women participated, by the end of 1996 there was a more even gender balance. Youth training has been overseen by locally based Training and Enterprise Councils. Other forms of work-based training have also developed. These include a system of Modern Apprenticeships (MAs) introduced in 1994, which are aimed at 16–25-year-olds too. However, MAs have the intention of encouraging those participating to gain higher-level qualifications. MAs normally include achieving an NVQ

TABLE 14.2 | **Youth Training leavers by qualification, England and Wales, 1990–1 to 1995–6 (percentages)**

	Gained any full/part qualification	Gained any full qualification	Gained any full qualification at level 2 or above
1990–1	49	39	–
1991–2	49	34	20
1992–3	47	34	23
1993–4	49	38	28
1994–5	50	39	31
1995–6	51	42	35

Source: Social Trends 1998, p. 69

level 3 (A-level equivalent) during the time of apprenticeship, and in 1997 about 104,000 young people were participating. There is also a third scheme called Training for Work, aimed at adult long-term unemployed people.

Full-time courses in institutions of further and higher education also provide elements of training. In higher education only a few subjects are actually directly relevant to work, mostly in professions like medicine, dentistry, veterinary science and pharmacy. However, higher education is currently being urged to pay more attention to job-related general skills like team work and computer literacy. Debates from 1997 onwards also put much emphasis on lifelong learning, that is, the notion that education does not stop when full-time schooling ends but continues throughout life, for work and personal development reasons (see table 14.3). To support this, a system of learning accounts has been suggested, particularly by the Kennedy Report on further education. People would, through a combination of their own, employers' and government money, build up funding for their lifelong learning. However, the debate around lifelong learning also suggests that if it were to work well, more young people would need to leave school with positive experiences of education. The social selection and exclusion roles of schools make this unlikely.

TABLE 14. 3 | **Progress towards lifetime targets: by occupation, spring 1997 (percentages)[a]**

	Lifetime target 1	Lifetime target 2
Professional	90	83
Managers and administrators	53	33
Associate professional and technical	72	57
Clerical and secretarial	29	12
Personal and protective services	26	9
Sales	26	10
Craft and related	41	6
Plant and machine operatives	19	3
Other occupations	13	3
All occupations	42	25

[a] Percentage of employed workforce in each occupation category attaining each target
Source: *Social Trends* 1998, p. 66

Discipline and the hidden curriculum

While job-skill training in schools is quite limited, schools are in a better position to try to encourage positive attitudes and motivations towards employment and sometimes (mostly in the case of women) unpaid work like mothering too. Such teaching is part of what has become known as the hidden curriculum. The concept of the hidden curriculum implies that the social knowledge which is imparted as a by-product of schooling is at least as important as the content of the visible, 'formal' curriculum – history, maths, technology, etc. The hidden curriculum teaches many things – from obedience and punctuality to gender identity and political awareness – which contribute to producing and reproducing a labour force.

Some years ago, Bowles and Gintis (1976) argued that schools are vital in the teaching of regularity, conscientiousness and obedience but that this is differentiated by social class. According to Bowles and Gintis, the personal qualities desired in employees develop because of the form of schooling rather than its overt content. They assert that there exists a correspondence between the organizational environment of the school and the workplace. Merely attending school, following its rules and routines, experiencing its hierarchical organization, instils into pupils attitudes and outlooks (e.g. about following orders) required later in the workplace. For those who will enter more middle-class jobs, this is less necessary and more initiative and ability to work unsupervised are required. In short, the main contribution of schooling, according to the correspondence principle, is that it prepares students from different social classes to be workers at different levels of organizations.

Though reproduction of both class and gender is far from being straightforward, and though different generations will have different views from those of their parents, some attitudes and beliefs about gender and class seem remarkably persistent. The role of teachers and schools in this process is far from neutral. Riddell (1992) in her study of two secondary schools in south-west England observed lessons as well as talking to pupils, teachers and parents. She focused on subject choice and explaining why, for example, girls did biology rather than physics. Riddell throws some interesting light on hidden curriculum debates. The teachers she spoke to claimed that they intervened in subject choice as little as possible and that they had a value-free view of option choice. Indeed some teachers denied that they pressured pupils to do anything in particular: 'I think to take over a child and tell it it ought to do something, that's not the business of the school' (Mr Appleyard, headteacher, quoted in Riddell 1992, p. 70).

Teachers seemingly wished not to do anything radical, or anything which involved putting much effort into advancing equal opportunities. Girls at these schools were prepared for a limited range of occupations other than marriage and motherhood. However, Riddell suggested that mothers in particular might have been more supportive of an equal opportunities approach than teachers supposed, thus raising the possibility that the social and cultural messages imparted by school are far from rigid.

Reproduction theories tend to have difficulty explaining how changes come about. Changes in labour markets are not infrequent and if the school is to be effective at preparing young people for employment then teachers have to be aware of these changes and respond to them. As we shall see in the next section, it may be these changes in labour markets for young workers which explain the more recent concern with the achievements of boys rather than girls.

Resistance, compliance and differentiation

Though the controllers of the education system might want schools to create disciplined workers, there is much evidence that this is not straightforwardly achieved. Complex processes of resistance and adjustment intercede. First, some pupils are undisciplined during their school careers, playing truant regularly, disobeying school rules or refusing to do school work. Some whose learning difficulties or behaviour are extreme may have to attend special schools or units. There are those pupils who offer only qualified co-operation and sometimes only with certain teachers. Others do not achieve what is expected of them.

Plate 14.2 | The hidden curriculum prepares children for working life
Source: Camera Press/R. Taylor; Format/Jenny Matthews

In schools of all types, pupil subcultures, hostile to schooling, develop. Contesting the authority of teachers, disobeying rules and rejecting the values of the school are characteristics of 'anti-school cultures' which flourish among groups of, usually, academically less successful pupils. Subcultures have been shown to exist in grammar, comprehensive and secondary modern schools. In the past, it was assumed that most of these pupils were male, though more recent research suggests that girls also resist schooling, though not necessarily by exhibiting the aggressive language or violent actions typical of boys.

For some time it was assumed by sociologists that girls' resistance to schooling did not involve subcultures or that the cultures when formed were more complex than those of boys. There were also suggestions that girls were less likely to be opposed to education as such. Here ethnicity as well as social class may make a difference. Work on African Caribbean girls in the late 1970s (Fuller 1980) found that black girls in the comprehensive school studied were anti-school, but not necessarily anti-education. Indeed these girls recognized that they needed educational qualifications in order to succeed in the jobs they wanted. So whilst opposed to some of the restrictions of school, they could see the advantages of nevertheless doing some school work. For the most part, girls' responses do seem to be more individualized and private. Girls sometimes remain silent in class, which may signal uninterest, lack of confidence, boredom, sullenness or just an unwillingness to co-operate with teachers. However, more recent studies suggest that girls do form subcultures.

Some writers suggest that we need to understand the complexity of the ways in which boys' and girls' school subcultures interrelate and the relevance of heterosexuality. Lees's (1993) work on secondary pupils aged 15–16 in three inner-city schools notes that boys often seemed to dominate girls in and outside the classroom. This is not just in relation to boys' more overtly noisy and disruptive behaviour but also because of the expectations boys have about girls. This is linked to different cultural assumptions as well as to different ideas about sexuality in girls and boys, a double standard which is critical of girls, whether or not they are thought to be sexually active, but which does not apply to boys:

> If we got a loud mouth, when we do the same (as the boys) do, they call us slag, or 'got a mouth like the Blackwall tunnel'. But the boys don't get called that, when they go off and talk. They think they're cool and hard. (female pupil, quoted in Lees 1993, p. 44)

This extends to sexual behaviour too, especially heterosexual sex:

> Some boys are like that, they go round saying 'I've had her' and then they pack you in and their mate will go out with you. And you're thinking that they're going out with you cos they like you. But they're not. They're going out to use you. The next you know you're being called names. (female pupil, quoted in Lees 1993, p. 45)

Though this interaction is not primarily about resistance to school or to particular conceptions of pre-employment socialization, it does put resistance in a context of complex gender power relations between boys and girls, and suggests why they might adopt different forms of resistance.

It has often been supposed that resistance is found most commonly in working-class pupils. However, this does not necessarily mean overt anti-school behaviour. Brown (1987), in a study of working-class secondary education, identified two other types of response by working-class pupils. One involves accepting teachers' definitions of schooling as directed towards educational credentials, which will lead them, via higher education, into middle-class occupations. This is often a minority response. The most common response among working-class pupils is instrumental compliance. Brown described the majority of working-class pupils as 'ordinary kids' who are unenthusiastic about school but nevertheless participate. They 'neither simply accept nor reject school, but comply with it . . . [T]he ordinary kids made an effort in school because they believed that modest levels of endeavour and attainment, usually leading to CSEs, would help them to get on in working-class terms. In the working-class neighbourhoods of Middleport [South Wales] "getting on" usually meant boys being able to find apprenticeships and girls entering clerical and personal service jobs' (1987, p. 31).

Brown argued that compliance was ensured in the past because modest qualifications and a good reference did secure the kinds of jobs that 'ordinary kids' wanted. However, occupational change and high levels of unemployment mean that many young people currently are seriously disappointed when they obtain poorer jobs than they anticipate. In some areas of high unemployment they may remain unemployed for long periods, and this may have effects on younger siblings and other young people in the communities concerned. This may be particularly so for some boys, especially white working-class boys with no or low educational credentials, for whom few jobs are available (see table 14.4). Young women with relatively few qualifications may go in other directions, perhaps becoming mothers. They may alternatively, as did the young working-class women studied by Skeggs (1997) (see section 6.3), seek to get some recognition for their caring skills through further education, even though this is unlikely to lead to well-paid jobs afterwards. Training to be a care worker or nursery nurse is still poorly paid and may involve unsocial hours, but it can serve to make the skills of 'caring', at which women are supposed to be naturally good, seem legitimate and more visible to others.

Although many studies of student subcultures are of those who have relatively low levels of academic attainment, one study looked at relatively high achievers. Blackman (1995) studied more than 120 girls and boys in a secondary school in the south of England. He observed them in and out of class and also interviewed many of them. His categorization suggested that girls, in some circumstances, form distinctive subcultural groups. He identified four major groups in the school and a variety of smaller and less distinct ones. The major ones were:

- mod boys, who were connected with the 1980s revival of 1950 mod culture. The boys, nine in all, liked particular kinds of music (soul and northern soul, Tamla motown, blue beat), wore their hair short, with neat clothing, ties, loafers, and parkas or crombie coats. They all had motor scooters. They mostly had girlfriends and part-time jobs and came from working-class homes. They trod a line between deviant and appropriate school behaviour, and were all in middle and upper streams and studying for academic and vocational exams;
- new wave girls, 10 girls who shared musical interests in new wave, punk, reggae and dub. Their clothes included black trousers and Doc Marten boots; they also wanted to disrupt assumptions about typical female behaviour and were a dis-

TABLE 14. 4 |Highest qualifications held:[a] by socio-economic group,[b] 1996–7 (percentages)

	Professional	Employers and managers	Intermediate non-manual	Junior non-manual	Skilled manual and own-account non-professional	Semi-skilled manual and personal service	Unskilled manual	All socio-economic groups
Degree	66	24	26	5	2	1	–	14
Higher education	16	19	25	6	9	5	1	12
GCE A-level	7	16	12	14	14	9	5	12
GCSE A*–C[c]	5	20	20	37	25	23	16	24
GCSE D–G[c,d]	1	6	6	16	14	12	11	11
Foreign other	4	2	3	2	2	3	2	2
No qualifications	2	12	8	20	34	47	65	25
All	100	100	100	100	100	100	100	100

[a] People aged 25 to 69 not in full-time education
[b] Excludes members of the armed forces, economically active full-time students and those who were unemployed and had never worked
[c] Or equivalent
[d] Includes commercial qualifications and apprenticeships
Source: *Social Trends* 1998, p. 67

tinctive and highly visible group. Most had boyfriends and part-time jobs, were from lower middle- and working-class homes and exhibited behaviour similar to that of the mod boys. All were studying for exams.

Blackman suggests that these two groups were based on youth cultures but the second two groups were not:

- boffin boys – three central boys plus eight others;
- boffin girls – 13 central and eight more marginal girls.

Unlike the other two groups, who had somewhat ambivalent attitudes to school, boffins were academic achievers who supported the school's values and system. Mostly they were from middle-class homes. Within the two groups there was a variety of youth cultural styles, but amongst the boys in particular there was no attempt to follow the social relations associated with those styles.

Blackman found that in the interactions of these groups, their statuses rather than their class positions were crucial in shaping different degrees of resistance and conformity. Thus the boffins invested a lot in school and in intellectual achievement but were often not conformist in behaviour. The boys, particularly, wanted to demonstrate their masculinity despite their attention to homework rather than sex. The mods engaged in more violent forms of masculinity, but 'they pursued fighting and gaining qualifications with equal vigour' (p. 254). The new wave females drew on their sexuality and their body images and exploited these, in jokes, in stories and in their actions in and out of class, but in a feminist way which put them, rather than young men, in control. Blackman concludes that it is territoriality in youth culture rather than social class resistance which explains their behaviour. (Previous studies such as that of Willis 1977 have tended to assume that class is the major determining factor.)

Mac an Ghaill (1988) draws attention to ethnicity and its role in resistance and compliance among the academically successful. He describes the Black Sisters, a group of young women of Afro-Caribbean and Asian parentage, at an inner-city sixth-form college in the Midlands, who were deeply dismissive of school and teachers, but who calculated that achieving qualifications was in their best interests. They complained that teachers held racist stereotypes and underestimated their abilities; streaming discriminated against them; they were subjected to a curriculum that ignored the history and experience of black people in Britain. Nevertheless, they pursued their studies through to higher education, mostly by dint of peer-group support and their collective determination to succeed. The women's response was one of acting mostly as they were expected to, but without any commitment or investment of self-identity in the content of their activity: their strategy was 'anti-school but pro-education'. A white male teacher's observation that the four of them in his class behaved unusually betrays, incidentally, his expectation of conformity among the academically successful:

> They are very strange. I didn't, I mean at first I didn't think that they were as clever as they undoubtedly are. Their written work is very good, at times excellent, especially Judith. But they have a strange attitude, I mean not the usual attitude for clever kids. They sit there huddled together in the class, chatting away, never directly interrupting but not fully co-operating either, if ye know what I mean. (Mac an Ghaill 1988, pp. 27–8)

The rationale for the women's practice is summed up by 'Judith':

> With me like I go into school and I listen to the teacher and I put down just what they want. Christopher Columbus discovered America, I'll put it down, right. Cecil Rhodes, ye know that great imperialist, he was a great man, I'll put it down. We did about the Elizabethans, how great they were. More European stuff; France, equality, liberty, and fraternity, we'll put it all down. At that time they had colonies, enslaving people. I'll put it down that it was the mark of a new age, the Age of Enlightenment. It wasn't, but I'll put it down for them, so that we can tell them that . . . In their terms I come from one of the worst backgrounds but I am just saying to them, I can do it right, and shove your stereotypes up your anus. (Mac an Ghaill 1988, p. 28)

Summary

1   The nature of the relationship between education and the economy is complex and made more so by the growth of multinational companies. Nevertheless most politicians still try to intervene in education to make it more responsive to the requirements of employers and the national economy.

2   New schemes of training for work are frequently introduced. Only those involving substantial work placements seem to provide actual work skills as opposed to general social and cultural attitudes favourable to work.

3   Gender, social class and ethnicity all play a part in the way students respond to work preparation and training.
4   Student subcultures, both those derived from youth cultures and those from school cultures, are important in the responses of young people to schooling. Social class may be less important than once supposed in these cultures but gender and ethnicity remain important. Subcultures are confined neither to working-class pupils nor those with low levels of academic attainment.

14.4   Inequality and selection in education

Educational qualifications are now a principal determinant of job opportunities. Employers use examination results as a way of screening applicants, usually prescribing a minimum level of qualification for any position, though they will look for other social and cultural characteristics too. Schools are thus a vital link in the allocation of individuals to places in the workforce. Even two decades ago this was not the case for school leavers entering semi- or unskilled manual work, though it was so for those entering skilled manual work apprenticeships and clerical as well as professional employment. As the number of school leavers with qualifications has increased, so the level of education expected for particular jobs has risen.

At least at age 16, girls tend to be better qualified than boys, though this advantage may not be reflected in the labour market and is not true for some ethnic minority groups such as Bangladeshi girls. Achievement is a continuous process, but is symbolized by decisions made at key stages in a young person's educational career. Not only gender, social class and ethnicity but also the type of school attended, the stream or set within the school to which a pupil is allocated, and age of leaving full-time education affect the acquisition of the certificates important in determining long-term life chances.

Levels of achievement are systematically related to the social characteristics of pupils. Thus figure 14.1 shows those in the working population with no qualifications, by ethnic origin and gender in spring 1997.

The least-qualified group were women from India, Pakistan and Bangladesh. Younger generations of all ethnic groups tend to have higher levels of qualification because educational provision has expanded rapidly in the recent past, as have the percentage of school students staying on beyond 16. Class origins are also important. The children of white-collar workers are very much better qualified than their peers from manual backgrounds, especially those whose parents are in the professions. Ethnicity and gender interact with class in the determination of educational attainment. To understand the causes of unequal attainment requires attention to all three factors.

Class inequality

Origins and destinations: a case study

One major landmark in the development of education during the twentieth century in England and Wales was the 1944 Education Act, which required that all children be provided, free of charge, with a place at secondary school. Previously most children had

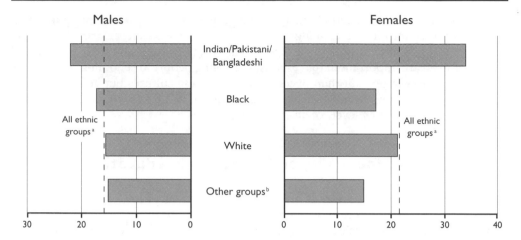

Figure 14.1 | Working-age[c] population without qualifications: by gender and ethnic group, Great Britain, spring 1997 (percentages)
[a] Includes ethnic group not stated
[b] Includes those of mixed origin
[c] Males aged 16 to 64, females aged 16 to 59
Source: Social Trends 1998, p. 67

remained in elementary education (until age 14) throughout their schooldays, as selective secondary schools, which charged fees, were available only to a minority. The 1944 Act reorganized schooling on a 'tripartite' system: with the exception of those in private education, children were to be transferred at age 11 to either a grammar, technical or secondary modern school, on the basis of their individual abilities and aptitudes. The expressed wish was that all three types of school should be accorded 'parity of esteem'; each should cater for different kinds of children by offering different training. It was imagined that this system would provide better, and more equal, educational opportunities.

Halsey, Heath and Ridge (1980) studied the workings of the tripartite system, inquiring into the extent to which inequalities in education had been reduced for boys born between 1913 and 1952 (see box 14.3). They examined the educational biographies of 8,526 men aged between 20 and 60 in 1972, a part of the national sample taken in the Nuffield Mobility Project. Besides demonstrating that class inequalities showed no sign of declining over the period, Halsey and colleagues sought to show how, and to a lesser extent why, unequal educational selection takes place. Dealing successively with the key 'decisions' which define an educational career (private or state primary school? selective or modern, private or state secondary school? when to leave school? whether to enter higher or further education?), they evaluated explanations of educational inequality.

Despite much debate, it has never been established conclusively whether the cause of working-class underachievement is material poverty or the cultural attributes of typical working-class families. Halsey, Heath and Ridge approached this question by attempting to separate out the effects of material circumstances and cultural background. They measured the former by family income, the latter by the cultural characteristics of parents (particularly their educational experiences). They found that cultural background, and specifically parental values, were of principal importance in determining the child's progress up to age 11. Whether a child went to a private primary school, and whether

Box 14.3   Main determinants of the educational careers of men born 1933–52

This model shows the *main* causal determinants only. It indicates that a child's cultural background is mainly relevant to explaining the nature of primary schooling and entry into secondary school. When considering qualifications, the material circumstances of the child's home become important, along with the type of secondary school attended. The qualifications obtained are the primary determinant of entry into the various forms of further and higher education.

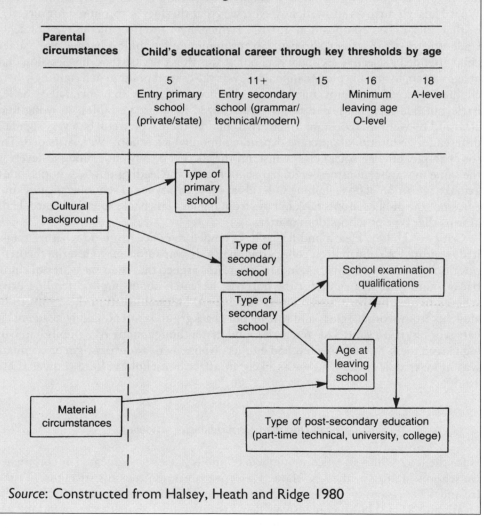

Source: Constructed from Halsey, Heath and Ridge 1980

he subsequently entered a selective secondary school, were most clearly related to cultural background. After age 11, however, material circumstances became much more important in determining at what age, and with what qualifications, a boy was likely to leave school. This reflects the financial expense of keeping a child at school, a cost more difficult for working-class parents to bear. This discovery undermines arguments that working-class children have inadequate cultural preparation for engaging in the intellectual pursuits required of academically successful children.

Success in secondary schooling was, according to Halsey and colleagues, most importantly determined by the type of school which a pupil attended. They found that it did not matter whether a child went to a private or a state primary school. However, the kind of secondary school a boy attended was considerably more important than any other factor, including the material circumstances of the family. The chance of a boy in a secondary modern school surviving past the minimum school-leaving age, or of obtaining any certificates, of course, was much lower than for a boy at grammar school. What Halsey's analysis showed, however, was that this fact is accounted for directly by neither social class composition nor IQ. Rather, it is an effect of the type of school. Under the tripartite system, survival past the minimum school-leaving age was usual if a child attended a selective secondary school. It was thus the case that the 'decision' made at age eleven, by the 11–plus examination, was the critical point in determining whether children 'succeeded' or not. Incidentally, this does not imply that social class or IQ is irrelevant. Halsey, Heath and Ridge standardized for these variables, showing that if class and IQ were held constant for any two children there would still be a very significant difference in educational outcome depending upon which schools were attended. Thus, for example, holding social class constant, the success of boys in gaining O-levels was the same in state-maintained grammar schools as in the leading public schools; but the actual proportion of boys gaining O-levels at these two types of school was quite different, since the public schools took in boys from higher-class backgrounds. Hence, Halsey affirms that type of school does matter.

Critics of Halsey, Heath and Ridge have tended to concentrate on whether the limited biographical information collected in the study was sufficient to test the theoretical positions which they evaluated. In particular, it is argued that their measures of cultural background were too crude for the purpose. Research about pupils attending private schools funded by the Assisted Places Scheme (APS), established in the 1980s to help students from working-class and low-income backgrounds attend highly academic private schools, is relevant. This research found that although many APS pupils had working-class fathers, more than a few had mothers whose own family of origin or occupation was more middle-class, which was likely to affect household culture (Edwards et al. 1989).

Social class and comprehensive schooling

Since the later 1960s significant numbers of pupils have been educated at comprehensive schools in most of the UK, though selective education remains strong in Northern Ireland. The reasons for the introduction of comprehensives were partly that, as Halsey, Heath and Ridge (1980) conclusively demonstrated, the tripartite system did not seem to ensure equal educational opportunity: the segregation of 11-year-olds into the three different types of school did not produce a meritocracy. The movement for comprehensive education also had social objectives, particularly that class divisions and prejudices might be dissolved if there were greater mixing between those social classes at school. In some areas middle-class parents felt that schools which were socially divisive were not a good preparation for adult life.

A research team recently re-examined, using historical data not available at the time, the development of comprehensive schools in England and Wales during the 1960s and 1970s (Kerckhoff et al. 1996). They drew upon 10 case studies of LEAs and data from the National Child Development Survey (NCDS). The latter is based on a longitudinal study of all children born in one week in March 1958 in England, Wales and Scotland. The children in this study first attended secondary school at exactly the point, the end of the 1960s, when comprehensive schooling was starting to become widespread. Kerckhoff et al. note that in the 1960s many LEAs did not have the resources or appropriate buildings to establish 11–18 comprehensive schools with sixth forms, and two variants of this, the junior high school (11–14) and the middle school (8–12 or 9–13), with a further tier at the end, were not uncommon. However, there were also 11–16 comprehensives established with no sixth form. In such schools, students wanting to continue their education beyond 16 had to move to another school or a further education college. The new system was therefore not as uniform as the tripartite one it replaced, especially since 'going comprehensive' also often involved mergers of grammar and secondary moderns or of boys' and girls' schools. Furthermore, the comprehensives were very recent when the study was done (1974–6) and in areas where comprehensive and selective schools co-existed most high-attaining students did not attend the comprehensives. Hence, had Halsey's study been able to look at comprehensives, deciding on the extent of their effects on social class inequality and attainment levels, it would have been much more difficult than for the tripartite system.

Kerckhoff et al.'s study, taking all schools which were comprehensive by 1970 and comparing those with remaining selective and secondary modern schools, found that the children of manual workers were much more likely to have attended a comprehensive with no sixth form. This group had lower attainment levels on entering secondary school, and even when ability levels at 11 and 16 were controlled for their exam results at 18 were lower than might have been expected from their earlier performances. Those children from higher socio-economic groups, who were more likely to attend comprehensives with sixth forms, effectively attended a different kind of comprehensive schoool. As the researchers point out, it is difficult to determine the effects such a dual system had on pupil attainment levels.

Comparing students between 1974 and 1976 from the NCDS cohort, it was found that higher-ability students did better in selective schools, and low-attaining pupils did better in the comprehensives. However, the research team point out that one should not necessarily conclude that high-attaining pupils are disadvantaged by attending comprehensive school. Rather, an alternative explanation might look at resources allocated to schools. The selective system allocated proportionately more resources per pupil to grammar than secondary modern schools. The comprehensive system allocated resources somewhat more evenly. Hence those formerly disadvantaged in resource terms did better and those formerly allocated more were no longer privileged. Kerckhoff et al. argue that an overall greater allocation of resources within a comprehensive system might be shown to have the best effects on ability levels of all students at secondary school.

Though this piece of research is not comparable to the study by Halsey, Heath and Ridge of social class mobility and secondary education, it is the most systematic attempt to analyse the effects of comprehensive education in England. The data confirm that organizational type affects pupils' achievement, and suggest the value of looking at the system in which schools exist and the resourcing per pupil by type of school.

Whether a fully comprehensive system of secondary education was ever likely to achieve its meritocratic and social goals will remain a matter of some speculation. Though in Scotland the majority of secondary schools remain comprehensive, in England and Wales policies have changed. Incentives for schools to opt out of local authority control as grant-maintained schools (GMS) or City Technology Colleges, and encouragement of independent fee-paying schools, increased the number of schools exercising some selectivity during the 1980s and early 1990s. A recent innovation is one which will allow parents in areas with grammar schools to vote to say whether they wish them to continue. However, apart from selection there is little evidence that GMS schools have particular educational advantages over other publicly funded schools, or that they teach pupils in a more effective way than other state schools (Fitz et al. 1993). The position of GMS schools at the top of the league tables for school exam results is explained more by the type of selective schools, with high middle-class intakes, which typically opted out of the local authority system. However, GMS status also allowed previously non-selective schools to select some of their pupils. Comprehensive schools figure at the bottom as well as top of league tables of exam performance since most children in England attend comprehensives.

The percentage of pupils in private schools is also relevant to the perceived success of state comprehensives. This figure increased from 5 per cent in 1976 to 7 per cent in 1990 and since then has stayed at around 7 per cent, though it fluctuates slightly according to the state of the economy. The survival of selective and private schools was clearly detrimental to the comprehensive project. It was also frequently observed that streaming and banding within comprehensive schools segregated pupils within those schools, thereby replicating the old tripartite divisions. Some comprehensive schools were internally organized in a way that facilitated differentiated treatment of pupils, permitting teachers to transmit different hidden curricula. Beachside Comprehensive, when researched, had a policy of putting children into 'bands' on the basis of their performance at primary school (Ball 1981). This resulted in the top band initially containing a disproportionate number of middle-class children. Because the bands were taught different subjects (i.e. the formal curriculum was different) there was very little movement between bands. Thus, they tended to coincide with social-class differences, and to generate different patterns of interaction between pupils and teachers as an oppositional culture emerged within the lower band. During the time that Ball was examining Beachside, the school's policy changed to mixed-ability grouping. For the first three years in the school, pupils were put into classes without reference to their academic abilities. This system seemed to prevent the emergence of an oppositional, 'anti-school' culture and to increase social interaction between pupils with different class backgrounds. Nevertheless, at the time of entry into their fourth year, the pupils' friendship networks were sharply delimited by social class and academic attainment.

The transitions from compulsory schooling of young people, aged 16–19, in the years between 1985 and 1988, were investigated by M. Banks et al. (1992). Most respondents had attended comprehensive schools. Results in exams at 15 or 16 indicated that class differences in performance persisted. Besides the fact that girls were more successful than boys, household social class and the educational levels of both mother and father were the principal social determinants of attainment. However, household class characteristics explained only a small proportion of the variance in pupil performance.

Gender inequalities in education

For many years, girls have had better overall levels of educational attainment than boys up to and including school-leaving age. Since the late 1980s girls' superiority has further increased, as figure 14.2 demonstrates (see also tables 7.8 and 7.9).

At age 18 the gap between girls and boys is less evident, and male A-level candidates tend to do either extremely well or relatively poorly, with female candidates clustering around the middle grades. By 1998 there were slightly more females than males in degree-level courses.

Greater female presence is partly accounted for by the predominance of women on nursing and teaching degree courses. By PhD level, men are again in the majority, with only 35 per cent of doctoral students being women. If we take subjects into account, there are still gender differentials in the pure sciences, languages, maths (though here women have shown massive improvements since the late 1980s), music and computing from the later years of secondary education onwards. The education reforms which have been carried out in the UK since the late 1980s or so (see section 14. 2) might be supposed to have helped girls improve their school performances, as might the much more widespread existence of equal opportunities policies in schools from the mid-1980s onwards. The existence of a National Curriculum, preventing the kind of premature option choice described in Riddell's (1992) study in section 14.3, was in itself at least a partial response to feminists wanting schools to adopt a core curriculum.

Two extensive studies were conducted in the mid-1990s, funded by the Equal Opportunities Commission. One was carried out by a team of researchers looking at England and Wales (Arnot et al. 1996), and a similar study was done in Scotland, where the education reforms took place later and have been less extensive (Turner et al. 1995).

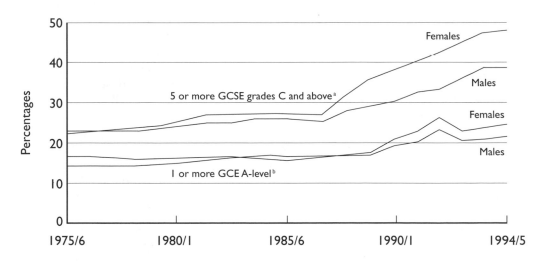

Figure 14.2   Examination results:[c] by gender, England and Wales, 1975/6–1994/5
[a] Pupils in last year of compulsory schooling
[b] Or equivalent
[c] Data for 1983/4 are for England only.
Source: Social Trends 1997, p. 55

The studies involved analysis of school exam results, postal surveys of primary and secondary state schools, and case studies of equal opportunities policies in a number of local authorities, including visits to schools and interviews with teachers and pupils. Key findings include the following:

- There are still gender-related differences in performance in exams, for instance in physics and humanities, but some gaps, for example in maths, have closed.
- Most schools have an equal opportunities policy but governors and school inspectors show little interest in these.
- LEAs no longer give high priority to equal opportunities issues.
- The strategies adopted with regard to gender differences vary widely but liberal approaches (see discussion of S. J. Heath 1997 in section 14.3) are more common than radical ones.
- Changes to curriculum and assessment and monitoring of gender differences in performance are perceived by schools to have had positive results for gender equity.
- Pupils seem to have less stereotyped views than in the past but some girls still have very narrow occupational horizons.
- School management is heavily male-dominated in secondary schools – the finance-led nature of it discourages women, and appointing committees tend to think that financial skills are more likely to be found in male applicants for headships.
- The impact of school reforms has been different in Scotland, Wales and England and seems much affected by varying cultural values and social attitudes.

Study of gender differences in subject choice suggests that inequalities within schools are related to other aspects of gender inequality, though the precise nature of such a relationship is disputed. The gender segregation of the labour market and the continued inequalities in household divisions of labour are perhaps the most important factor, since many girls will orient themselves towards occupations known to offer reasonable access for women and towards jobs that they can combine, if necessary, with bringing up children. Restricted job opportunities are compounded by conventional perceptions of appropriate gender identities. The pressure not to transgress the boundaries of femininities is one of the hardest obstacles to overcome. This is not just a matter of sexist attitudes, but is embedded in routine, everyday practice. Riddell (1992), Gaskell (1992) and M. Banks et al. (1992) show that in their teenage years young women are more closely pulled into the domestic arena than young men. Girls make substantially greater contributions to housework; they are more constrained in their leisure activities, being less mobile and highly dependent on the availability of a female 'best friend'; and the predominant form of peer-group culture revolves around the anticipation of heterosexual partnerships. This emphasizes the extent to which a gender-specific hidden curriculum interacts with the formal content of education.

Though writers such as Mac an Ghaill (1994) emphasize how fluid gender identity is in secondary schools, his data suggest that girls and boys remain groups which, despite many social and cultural contacts, remain apart. Mac an Ghaill talked to male students about their part-time jobs and found some of them seeking to reinforce gender boundaries:

Graham: where we work in the supermarkets, the boys do all the harder work like filling shelves and dragging things around the warehouse . . . .And the girls are on the tills talking to the customers and that. Like you would prefer to talk to a girl in a shop. (Mac an Ghaill 1994, p. 73)

After the researcher asked them if they thought girls chose these jobs, another student, William, said:

I don't know. But if you think of it, girls read all the girls' magazines with silly stories and that, but boys are always into video games and making things. So, they must be more interested in it, in how things work and all that. Boys are just better at these things. (Mac an Ghaill 1994, p. 73)

Levels of formal achievement of girls continue to improve. However, gender identities associated with other spheres of activity are reinforced within schools, which cannot compensate for the wider patriarchal culture. As a number of feminist writers have pointed out, sexual harassment and sexual violence by boys towards girls continue to exist in schools, whatever the academic achievements of girls.

Recently, however, the situation of boys has attracted more attention. School inspectors, teachers and politicians have begun to argue that girls' problems in schools have been solved, leaving boys beleaguered, with poor exam results and low self-esteem, underperforming against their own, their parents' and their teachers' expectations. Certainly the gap between female and male pupils in exams taken at 16 has opened up considerably over the last few years, though this is not the first time girls have exceeded the achievements of boys. There is some suggestion that girls have benefited from GCSE assessment relying more on coursework than exams, but recent changes to re-emphasize exams have not narrowed the gap. Furthermore, the Equal Opportunities Commission research discussed above (Arnot et al. 1996; Turner et al. 1995) does not indicate that radical equal opportunities policies have been in existence in most UK schools. The debate about boys' relative achievement deserves careful examination, although authoritative research on the topic is not yet available. However, the following points are worth bearing in mind:

- Some boys may have been more affected than most girls by changes to the labour market for school leavers, particularly by the disappearance of heavy manufacturing industry and its replacement by service-sector jobs in retailing, finance or the caring occupations.
- Not all boys are failing to achieve academically – at A-level, the gap is much narrower, with 23 per cent of girls and 20 per cent of boys getting two or more A-levels in 1995/6, compared with a 10 per cent gap at GCSE level. Both social class and ethnicity are relevant to an understanding of which boys underachieve, with working-class white boys being most at risk.
- Despite the long history of girls' superior performance in exams at 16, there is still a considerable gap between women's and men's earnings.
- The term 'underachievement' needs to be carefully examined. It does not mean low achievement but rather indicates a gap between expected and actual performance. Here many factors may come into play. Power et al. (1998) looked at a sample of nearly 350 students identified at age 11 as academically able students. The students are now in their 20s. The researchers were interested in the extent to

which parental involvement had affected the performance of these students: 'There seemed to be the people whose parents really pushed them . . . My parents didn't really push me that hard. I mean I was quite well behaved as a child and I was doing my homework. But I would kind of just drift along and do what I could' (Power et al. 1998, p. 166).

The researchers also noted that the cultures of the schools attended and the attitudes of the young people themselves were significant, especially for working-class students, even when their parents' aspirations for them were high: 'I used to miss a lot of lessons . . . when it got hard, I suppose the better way of coping was not going . . . I still felt I had it in me to pass exams. Because I am very good at revising . . . But it didn't pay off' (p. 172). The connection between self-image and academic achievement is hard to establish. Changes to women's roles in society may have affected boys more than girls.

Racial inequalities in education

There are some striking inequalities of attainment between and within different ethnic groups. The aggregate statistics document sharp gender divisions within different minority groups, indicating that gender and race interact with each other. Class differences likewise also exist within ethnic groups. Those Asian groups with high levels of educational attainment often contain an extensive middle class.

Ethnic minorities face some of the same obstacles to high levels of educational attainment as do white people. Inferior class position, low parental levels of education, and social and religious restrictions on female social participation all present barriers. These affect some ethnic groups more than others. Language difficulties may occur, but they apply largely to first-generation immigrants. Probably the most potent distinctive hindrance is British racism. The testimonies of students frequently record racist assumptions and treatment in school. Wright and her research team studied black male teenagers who had been permanently excluded from school for bad behaviour . Black males form a large proportion of such exclusions. These young men felt that teachers had behaved differently towards them and to white pupils: 'most of the lessons, the White kids can get up and walk around. Me, if I get up "sit down!", it's "sit down" all the time . . . 'Cos at school . . . they don't listen, unless you're white' (David, quoted in Wright et al. 1998, p. 80). Other researchers report similar findings. These include recalling racist harassment from fellow pupils, observing that teachers deploy racial cultural stereotypes, and expressing antipathy to parts of the curriculum that glorify British imperialism.

Kay Haw (1998) researched the experiences of Muslim girls in two different single-sex girls' secondary schools, City State, a state comprehensive, and Old Town High, a private school. She spent considerable time with the girls and their teachers in both schools. Though the state school had in place equal opportunities policies, Haw found that staff were often confused about how they should treat Muslim pupils, a confusion not found at the all-Muslim private school. The confusion was around whether teachers should talk about equal opportunities issues for girls and women (for example about who in a household should wash up) for fear of 'saying the wrong thing'. In addition, in the state school Muslim girls often lacked confidence (as one ethnic group amongst many). A teacher said of City State Muslim girls: 'They also tend to be the ones who've got less confidence. I think they don't aim high. I feel they are quieter and they need confidence in class to speak up because other students can be louder' (Haw 1998, p. 118). In the Muslim school, the pupils appeared to be more confident: 'I like the environment of my school and the way the teachers push you to do your utmost to make you produce the results you want . . . I like the way some teachers think of you as an individual and not a whole class. They make you work and try to build your confidence' (Haw 1998, p. 118).

Haw also noted that the private school tried to help Muslim girls come to terms with an Islamic way of life in a non-Muslim society, something that the state school did not even attempt. There was also a greater commitment to overcoming stereotypes of Muslim girls. Haw, although not uncritical of single-sex schooling and segregation of pupils by ethnicity, notes that some of the fears of non-Muslims, that girls who attend Muslim schools have narrow horizons, are not found to be supported by her evidence. Rather, she suggests that the Muslim school may be more successful in conveying the notion of equality in difference than the non-Muslim school, despite the latter's commitment to formal equal opportunities policies.

Summary

1   The study of education and social mobility suggests that although, in absolute terms, more working-class boys are taking A-levels and going on to college, their chances *relative to other classes* have not improved much since the Second World War. Indeed recent debates about boys' underachievement may even suggest some decline in this position in the last decade.
2   Sociological research showed that under the tripartite system the type of school a pupil attended was the main factor determining educational achievement. The introduction of comprehensive schooling was designed to remedy class inequalities, but the statistical relationship between class and attainment is still evident.
3   Gender inequalities in educational achievement had been almost entirely eliminated by 1990, with females performing as well as or better than males until aged 18+. However, women's continuing inequality becomes very apparent on entry into the labour market.
4   Ethnicity affects educational attainment, though it is mediated by class and gender.

Related topics

The political context and character of recent reforms of other arms of welfare provision are further examined in section 13.4. More detail about economic development and the changing division of labour appears in section 4.2. The relationship between class of origin, education attainment and job (the issue of meritocracy) is examined further in section 5.4. More material on gender inequalities in education appears in section 7.6.

Further reading

The book by Halsey et al. (1997) is the most recent text on sociology of education but contains some quite difficult articles as well as some easier ones. It is one of few recent books to discuss class. On gender, useful books are by Mac an Ghaill (1994) on masculinity, Epstein et al. (1998) on boys' underachievement and Dawtrey et al. (1995) on girls and schooling. S. J. Heath's (1997) book on attempts to inject vocationalism into the school curriculum is very readable. Worth reading on ethnicity are Mac an Ghaill (1994) on young men, Haw (1998) on Muslim girls and Mirza (1993) on black women. Trowler's (1998) book on educational policy is also useful in providing a clear background to current policies in the UK.

Cross-references to *Readings in Contemporary British Society*

Acker on school teachers and their careers; **Mac an Ghaill** on peer-group subcultures and schooling; **Gewirtz et al.** on working-class families, the marketization of education and the process of pupils transferring to secondary school.

15 | Health

15.1   Introduction

Health is an emotive and political topic. During the 1980s the Conservative government's first concern was to reassure the public that health provision was being maintained and to argue that with greater efficiency the service could be improved, even without additional resources. More than any other policy initiative during the 1980s, the reform of the National Health Service (NHS) represents the legacy of Thatcherism. Introducing market principles into the one service most valued by the public was audacious. Certainly the reforms were viewed with suspicion by the public and were strongly resisted by many NHS staff. Nevertheless, they enabled a number of long-standing weaknesses to be tackled and there is increasing evidence of some improvements in services to patients. So the new Labour government of 1997 was faced with the question of whether it would continue with the reform programme initiated by its predecessor or whether it had another agenda for health.

Governments remembered for social change have had legislative programmes which include health. Reforming governments have usually sought to remedy the shortcomings in the British health-care systems – the Liberals coming to power in 1906, the Labour Party in 1945 and the Conservatives in 1979. The National Health Insurance Act of 1911 and the National Health Service Act of 1946 are two landmarks in the evolution of British policy. The National Health Insurance Act of 1911 represented an incomplete revolution. This scheme of David Lloyd George's Liberal government applied to only a small portion of the population, and even by the 1940s a mere 40 per cent was covered by national health insurance. By 1946, there was overwhelming popular, professional and political enthusiasm for the notion that health care should be a right for all people and an obligation of the state. Aneurin Bevan, the Labour government minister responsible, later described the NHS as 'the most civilized achievement of modern government'. Now over half a century after its birth, many people remain more than willing to echo those sentiments, enthusiastically embracing the concept of a national health system largely free at the point of use. Consequently, governments tread carefully in proposing any fundamental shifts in health-care provision.

The low standards of health in Britain were vividly revealed as the population was mobilized for war – the Boer War at the turn of the century and then the First and Second World Wars. In more recent times, as was especially evident in the Conservative administrations of 1979–97, the predominant concern has been to limit state involvement for reasons of financial restraint. In fact, the 1980 government report *Inequalities in Health* (known as the Black Report after the chairman of the working group, Sir Douglas Black), which revealed the shortcomings of health care, was released quietly in the hope that the contents and recommendations would go unnoticed.

By the mid-1980s, the future of the NHS was developing as a major public issue, and by the beginning of the 1990s the Conservative government had made an important contribution in setting into place a series of significant reforms. The NHS reforms, first unveiled in the 1989 white paper *Working for Patients,* were remarkable. The aim of the government proposals was to make the NHS more sensitive both to patients' needs and to market forces. Much attention focused on the effect of the reforms on the hospitals, particularly following the Tomlinson Report (1992) on changes recommended for London. However, the reforms developed in community-care services were equally radical, although at first they received less prominence in the media. The 1990 NHS and

Community Care Act provided considerable potential to reshape services. In many respects the situation remains volatile and it will take some time to appreciate the impact fully. While further privatization and commercialization of medicine, with the accompanying demise of the NHS, are unlikely under the Labour government, the problems remain enormous.

Dealing with problems in the NHS is rather like trying to keep a rubber ball under water – you keep it down and then see it pop up elsewhere. The Labour government has had some success in keeping its pre-election promise of cutting waiting lists for operations (that is, the *in*-patient waiting lists), but only by allowing backlogs to build up elsewhere. Surgeons doing more operations are perhaps seeing fewer out-patients. The demand for more resources for the NHS seems endless.

In July 1997 the Labour government set up an independent inquiry, chaired by Sir Donald Acheson, to review inequalities in health in England and to identify priority areas for the development of policies to reduce them. In late 1998 the report was published and recognized that the inquiry was addressing a fundamental issue of social justice:

> namely that although the last 20 years have brought a marked increase in prosperity and substantial reductions in mortality to the people of this country as a whole, the gap in health between those at the top and bottom of the scale has widened. *Yet there is convincing evidence that, provided an appropriate agenda of policies can be defined and given priority, many of these inequalities are remediable.* The same is true for those that exist between the various ethnic groups and between the sexes. (p. v, emphasis added)

The Acheson Report provides an appropriate agenda for a government wishing to reverse a trend of widening health inequalities. However, health is an issue which extends way beyond the domain of the Department of Health and impinges on the work of many government departments. Indeed, the view that providing a more efficient health service would have a marked impact on the health status of the population has been increasingly challenged. Sociologists have been among the first to proclaim that the health of the nation is not simply about providing a good NHS or putting our health care in the hands of doctors.

15.2   Sociological interest in medicine

Among sociologists, concern with health and illness is comparatively recent. The tremendous feeling of satisfaction and accompanying complacency that followed the launching of the NHS in 1948 raised hopes that the benefits of health would be available to all, irrespective of wealth or position in society. The question of whether health determines your place in society, the kind of issue posed decades earlier in other fields, like the sociology of education, only began to be addressed in the early 1980s. Against this background, the political importance of (and the potential political dynamite contained within) the Black Report of 1980 can be appreciated.

The 1980s and 1990s have been an important period in the examination of health problems. Probably the most important contributions of sociologists have been to provide fresh insights implicitly challenging traditional medical assumptions. The crucial shift, which occurred towards the end of the 1970s, was to focus on issues of health and illness rather than of medicine. Subsequently, it was argued that health delivery should be more patient-oriented than doctor-oriented. In other words, we should not readily assume that what is in the interests of the doctor is equally in the interests of the patient. The wider message is that the medical profession may have a somewhat narrow or limited vision in terms of improving health.

Sociological analyses of medical-care systems provided some relevant, but mostly unheeded, messages for policy-makers. Most importantly, feminists came to identify the health-care system as one of the major arenas of the subordination of women. They challenged the male-dominated professionalism of medicine, while re-creating or reasserting female self-confidence by 'demedicalizing' (that is, taking out of the direct medical sphere) such natural female functions as menstruation, conception, pregnancy and child bearing. The issue is the definition of health and the treatment of illness.

Health and illness: medical or social conditions?

As Kelman (1975, in Mackay, Soothill and Melia 1998) has pointed out, 'perhaps the most perplexing and ambiguous issue in the study of health since its inception centuries or millennia ago, is its definition' (p. 625). Kelman argues that the definitional problem is crucial to the determination of health-care policy. Usually the problem is evaded by assuming, implicitly or explicitly, that 'health' is the absence of illness.

The first scientific approach to health originated with the development of the machine model of the human body. With this conception, 'health' came to be regarded as the perfect working order of the human organism. Kelman argues that the methodologies that developed from this view (and continue to dominate in the practice of medicine today) consider illness to be both *natural* (biological) and occurring on an *individual* basis. It then follows that treatment is pursued essentially on an individual basis, using surgical or chemical means of treatment. This approach relegates the recognition and implications of social causes of illness to secondary importance.

While an appreciation of the social basis of many diseases and ill-health has a long history, the great thrust in this direction came with the publication of the Chadwick Report in the mid-nineteenth century. The report showed that the gross inadequacy of water supplies, drainage and facilities for the disposal of refuse in big towns were the biggest sources of disease. The study of epidemics – or epidemiology – had begun in earnest. Since that time there has been a great deal of writing and research on social epidemiology, and the development of an environmentalist approach to health. However, this approach is clearly in conflict with the biological and individual orientation of the classical school, which still underpins most of modern medicine.

Some theorists take the argument one stage further by suggesting that health is primarily socially, rather than strictly biologically, determined. We cannot view 'health' as independent of the form of society in which it is studied. This insight lays the foundation of a materialist or radical epidemiology, supported by some sociologists. They argue that, since the advent of capitalist industrialization, the primary determinants of death and illness in the West have shifted gradually from infectious and communicable disease – spread by unhealthy conditions such as malnutrition, overcrowding or inadequate sanitation – to problems such as cancer, heart disease, hypertension, stroke, mental illness and drug addiction.

Summary

1   Sociological interest in this area was late to develop. Recently, it has moved its focus from studying doctors and medicine to consideration of the conditions for health and illness.
2   There is an argument over whether medical or environmental models of health are most appropriate. These models conflict over whether health is primarily determined by social, rather than strictly biological, factors.

15.3   General trends in health

Sociologists differ in their emphasis, but all recognize the dangers of complacency about the success of conventional medicine. While life expectancy continues to increase by about two years every decade, statistics collected since the late 1970s indicate that 'healthy life expectancy' (that is, living with a healthy quality of life) has not risen in parallel. As table 15.1 shows, a 'healthy life expectancy' for males in 1976 was 58.3 years and had risen to only 59.2 years by 1994; for females there had been virtually no change – from 62.0 years in 1976 to 62.2 years in 1994. So what this means is that the extra years of life gained by the elderly may be extra years with a disability or a long-standing illness – both of which may make additional demands on formal and informal health care.

TABLE 15.1 Life expectancy and healthy life expectancy at birth: by gender, England and Wales, 1901–96

Gender	1901	1971	1976	1981	1985	1991	1994	1996
Males								
Life expectancy	45.3	69.0	70.0	71.1	71.9	73.4	74.3	74.6
Healthy life expectancy	–	–	58.3	58.7	58.8	59.9	59.2	–
Females								
Life expectancy	49.2	75.2	76.1	77.1	77.6	78.9	79.6	79.7
Healthy life expectancy	–	–	62.0	61.0	61.9	63.0	62.2	–

Source: Social Trends 1998, p. 124

While death rates have been falling over the past century, from a crude death rate of 18 per thousand in 1896 to 11 per thousand in 1996 (Acheson Report 1998), we should recognize two features of Western society that are easily overlooked. First, whereas death rates have declined owing to the reduction of childhood illnesses and other infectious diseases, some kinds of premature death have increased, particularly among males, owing to conditions arising from self-destructive behaviour, such as industrial cancers, diet-related disorders and routinized stress. In fact, the main shift in life expectancy relates to a much greater expectation of childhood survival. As figure 15.1 illustrates, the dramatic decline in infant mortality has contributed to the improvement in life

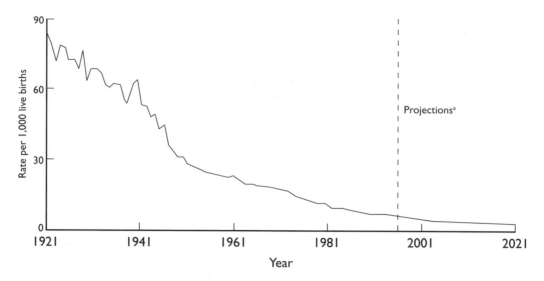

Figure 15.1 | Infant mortality: actual and projected, 1921–2021
ᵃ 1996-based projections
Source: Social Trends 1998, p. 123

expectancy at birth. The sharp decline in infant mortality during, and immediately after, the Second World War has been largely attributed to better nutrition, improved living conditions and the use of antibiotics.

Second, and equally disturbing, medicine is almost wholly ineffective against some of the new epidemics. There is a danger of focusing entirely upon what doctors manage to accomplish. As Stark (1977) argued over two decades ago, 'death is now socially constructed and distributed with barely any reference to nature or to disease in the traditional sense. It is endopolic, not endemic, the outcome of politics, not biology' (p. 686).

Since the mid-1970s there have been important reductions in death rates from a number of major causes of death, for example for lung cancer (but for men only), coronary heart disease and stroke, which for men aged under 65 are the most common causes of death. As figure 15.2 shows, the death rate from heart disease has more than halved for men – from 148 deaths per 100,000 population in 1972 to 68 deaths per 100,000 population in 1996. Death rates among men from lung cancer and stroke have also fallen to less than half their 1972 levels: in 1972 the death rates from lung cancer and stroke were 50 and 28 deaths per 100,000 population, compared with 1996 rates of 23 and 13 respectively. For women the figures are less impressive. However, women start from a lower base rate – that is, fewer women suffer premature death – and so the decline is less marked. While death rates from the two most common causes of death for women under the age of 65 – namely, heart disease and breast cancer – are falling, the situation with regard to lung cancer is worrying.

Lung cancer is one of the more preventable cancers. The Health Education Authority estimated that in 1995, 90 per cent of lung cancer deaths among men in the United Kingdom, and 78 per cent among women, were attributable to smoking. While the rate has been falling for men since the early 1970s, that for women has not really shifted, a

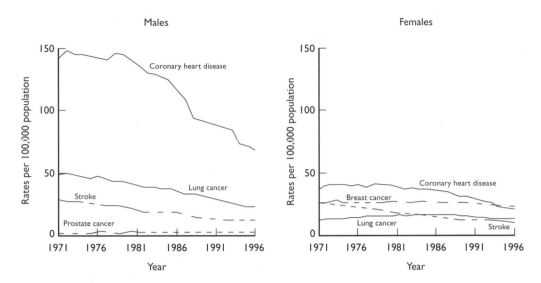

Figure 15.2 Death rates[a] for people aged under 65: by gender and selected cause of death
[a] Age standardized to the 1971 population level
Source: Social Trends 1998, p. 136

difference linked to the changing patterns of smoking. The apparent increase in smoking among young women may lead to more premature deaths in the future.

Table 15.2 demonstrates that causes of death vary considerably by age. So, for example, among 15–24-year-olds, injury and poisoning are the most common causes of death.

In terms of the causes of death for all ages (the last column in table 15.2), there is some similarity between males and females when one uses these broad categories. For example, 27 per cent of males die of cancer and 23 per cent of females. This is perhaps surprising as, while about one person in three develops a cancer at some time in their lives, the incidences of the main types are very different for men and women. Also, different types of cancers may have very different outcomes; from some cancers one has a good chance of full recovery, while for others the prognosis is dire.

Lung cancer was still the most frequently diagnosed cancer in men in the United Kingdom in 1992: men were two and a half times more likely to suffer from lung cancer than women. As figure 15.3 demonstrates, the incidence rates of lung cancer for men *fell* by nearly a fifth over the period 1981–92, while incidence rates for women *rose* by nearly a fifth over the same period. The most frequently diagnosed cancer among women is breast cancer. In 1992 the standard incidence rate of breast cancer in women in the United Kingdom was 106 per 100,000 population. The apparent rise over the previous decade indicates how cautiously one must approach health statistics. It is difficult to assess whether this really represents a rise in the disease or is the outcome of earlier and more widespread detection through the NHS breast-screening programme which began in the late 1980s.

The incidence of certain diseases is changing. One given much publicity since its recognition as a separate clinical entity in 1981 is AIDS (Acquired Immune Deficiency Syndrome). The most common causes of transmission of the virus are sexual contact,

TABLE 15. 2	Selected causes of death: by gender and age, 1996 (percentages)

Gender	Under 1[a]	1–14	15–24	25–34	35–54	55–64	65–74	75 and over	All ages
Males									
Circulatory diseases[b]	4	5	4	9	33	43	45	45	42
Cancer	1	16	7	10	28	37	33	22	27
Respiratory diseases	10	7	4	5	5	7	12	20	15
Injury and poisoning	4	30	63	51	15	3	1	1	4
Infectious diseases	7	8	2	5	3	1	–	–	1
Other causes	73	34	19	20	16	9	8	11	11
All males (= 100%)									
(thousands)	2.6	1.1	2.8	4.7	22.6	35.1	81.7	155.9	306.5
Females									
Circulatory diseases[b]	6	6	7	12	18	29	39	47	43
Cancer	1	18	17	26	52	48	36	15	23
Respiratory diseases	9	7	5	6	5	9	13	19	16
Injury and poisoning	6	23	43	28	8	2	1	1	2
Infectious diseases	6	8	4	5	1	1	1	–	1
Other causes	73	37	24	24	16	12	11	16	15
All females (= 100%)									
(thousands)	1.9	0.8	1.1	2.2	14.5	21.5	58.2	232.2	332.4

[a] Figures by cause exclude deaths at ages under 28 days
[b] Includes heart attacks and strokes
Source: Social Trends 1998, p. 135

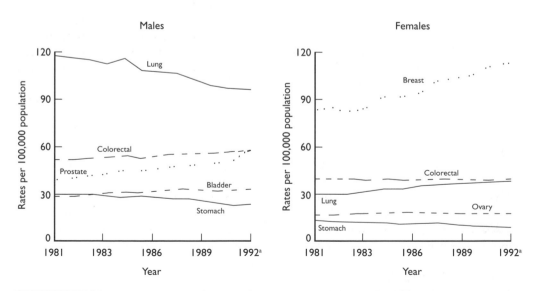

Figure 15.3	Standardized incidence rates of selected cancers: by gender, 1981–92

[a] 1992 figures are for Great Britain only
Source: Social Trends 1998, p. 128

TABLE 15.3 | AIDS cases: by year of diagnosis, EU comparison, 1986–96 (number per million population)

Country	1986	1991	1996
Spain	12.1	112.7	104.7
Italy	7.9	66.9	72.5
Portugal	3.5	30.0	51.2
France	22.3	79.4	51.0
Luxembourg	7.5	31.2	29.3
Denmark	1.5	40.8	28.1
Netherlands	9.4	29.6	18.4
United Kingdom	9.3	24.0	16.1
Greece	2.4	17.5	15.5
Sweden	6.7	15.9	13.7
Austria	3.2	25.0	13.6
Belgium	7.5	25.6	12.7
Germany	7.3	20.9	9.7
Irish Republic	1.7	20.5	9.5
Finland	1.4	5.2	4.1
EU average	10.1	48.5	38.0

Source: *Social Trends* 1998, p. 129

sharing syringes and the use of contaminated blood. The rate of new diagnosed cases of AIDS across the European Union (EU) has been declining since a peak in 1994, and in 1996 was 38 per million people (table 15.3). In the United Kingdom in that year there were 16 new cases of AIDS per million population, the lowest number since 1988. Spain has the highest rate with 105 new cases per million population in 1996 – nearly three times the EU average.

Despite concerns about the arrival of 'new' diseases, such as AIDS, and the revival of some 'old' diseases, such as tuberculosis, death rates have generally fallen overall, but what of everybody's quality of life while still alive? Are we healthier nowadays?

There are immense problems in defining and measuring health outcomes, even within individual countries where definitions and reporting conventions are relatively uniform. Studies of patterns of ill-health are handicapped by the difficulty of obtaining information on sickness and disease rates. That is why mortality rates continue to be the main focus of attention, although they may be of more limited value. The historical decline of infectious diseases like tuberculosis, and the increased incidence of chronic and degenerative diseases (like multiple sclerosis, cancers, strokes, etc.), suggest that the relationship between mortality (i.e. death rates) and morbidity (i.e. sickness rates) has changed and may now be fairly weak. Therefore, the study of mortality rates may not provide an adequate or accurate picture of patterns of ill-health: inequalities in death may not be similar to inequalities in health. This, essentially methodological, problem may be particularly serious in the case of mental illnesses, which rarely result in death yet account at any one time for around one in four NHS patients.

The relationship between physical health and mental health is a moot point. To what extent do they go together? As table 15.4 demonstrates, the Survey of Psychiatric Mor-

| TABLE 15.4 | Adults with and without a neurotic disorder: by type of long-standing physical complaint, Great Britain, 1993 (percentages) |

Physical complaint	With a neurotic disorder	Without a neurotic disorder	All
Musculoskeletal	23	11	13
Respiratory system	10	7	7
Heart and circulatory system	8	5	6
Digestive system	7	3	4
Nervous system	6	3	3
Endocrine disorders	4	3	3
Genito-urinary system	6	1	2
Skin	3	2	2
Ear	2	2	2
Neoplasms	2	1	1
Eye	1	1	1
Blood disorders	1	–	1
Infectious and parasitic diseases	–	–	–
Any long-standing physical complaint[a]	50	30	33
No long-standing physical complaint	50	70	67
All adults	100	100	100

[a] Some adults had more than one physical complaint
Source: *Social Trends* 1998, p. 130

bidity found that the prevalence of a long-standing physical complaint in adults is associated with the presence of a neurotic disorder. The relationship is complicated. Of all adults in Great Britain with a neurotic disorder in 1993, half had a long-standing physical complaint.

The proportion of people reporting a long-standing illness which limits their life has risen from 15 per cent to 22 per cent since 1975, while the proportion reporting recent illness (that is, in the two weeks previous to interview) nearly doubled, from 9 per cent to 16 per cent. Such figures are difficult to interpret. Are we really getting more ill, or do we now more readily identify symptoms as illness when previously we accepted them simply as a fact of life and did not bother to report them? Are there changing perceptions about illness (that is, what we are willing to report as illness) or are there real changes for the worse?

Summary

1   'Healthy life expectancy' has not risen at the same rate as life expectancy.
2   The dramatic decline in infant mortality has contributed substantially to the increase in life expectancy.
3   Causes of death have changed quite significantly over time.
4   The relationship between physical health and mental health is complex.

15.4   Inequalities in health

With little evidence that we were getting any healthier, there was a feeling in the mid-1970s that Britain was slipping behind comparable countries in health improvement. This led to the setting up of the Working Group on Inequalities in Health in 1977. The Black Report, presented in 1980, was described by the *British Medical Journal* and many others as 'the most important medical report since the War'; but the new Conservative government (elected in 1979) strongly rejected it. In essence, the Black Report showed considerable class differentials in health. However, the main bone of contention was about the explanation for the differences and what to do about trying to narrow the gaps. It opened the major epidemiological debate since the early 1980s between those who emphasize the importance of the lifestyle or behaviour of individuals and those who stress the importance of the socio-economic environment.

The individualization of illness accompanied the health policies of the 1980s and early 1990s. R. Crawford (1998), in a powerful article originally published in 1977 on the politics and ideology of victim-blaming, was one of the first to recognize the dangers of this kind of approach. He argued that by focusing on the individual – and, indeed, blaming the individual for his or her poor health – the ideology performs its classic role of obscuring the class structure of work. It may be the workplace which is unhealthy and this may not be the fault of those working there – or as someone provocatively put it, 'does smoking kill workers or working kill smokers'?

The individualists form an essentially conservative group, as they see the problem of health differences being solved within the existing class structure – for example, by members of the working class changing their lifestyle so that it more closely matches that of the healthier social classes. In contrast, the environmentalists generally offer more radical solutions to health differences, seeing the need for change in the way that society is structured. The conservative approach stresses the process of consumption: for example, social differences in smoking, diet and exercise. The radical group is more likely to stress the process of production; for example, social differences in exposure to dangerous work systems and industrial chemicals. In essence, the battle is about the importance of cultural versus structural factors in the explanation of health inequalities. Cultural explanation focuses on the ways that people behave, structural approaches lay greater emphasis on where people are placed within the social system (Soothill, Mackay and Melia 1998) (see table 15.5). The emphasis on the production process by some

TABLE 15.5 | Contrast between two different types of health model

Model	Main focus of concern	Main solution to health problems
Radical health model	On production process	Changing socio-economic environment
Conservative health model (also known as the lifestyle model)	On consumption process	Changing behaviour

Source: Mackay, Soothill and Melia 1998, p. 9

radical critics was somewhat undermined by the sudden increase in unemployment in the early 1990s, which shifted the focus away from the production process to the effects of unemployment. Nevertheless, the radical approach still emphasizes position in society rather than personal behaviour. Despite these disagreements, both structural and cultural factors have a bearing on the health of a population.

The Black Report recommended improving the material conditions of the lives of members of the poorer groups, especially children and people with disabilities, with a reorientation of health and personal social services. While the Conservative government quickly dismissed its recommendations as being too expensive to implement, it stimulated debate and action in many countries. Updated evidence published in 1987 under the title of *The Health Divide* (Whitehead 1992) ensured that its message remained in the public arena. The Acheson Report (1998), in espousing a socio-economic model of health and its inequalities and its call to intervene on a broad front, is a direct descendant of the Black Report. However, in recognizing the importance of lifestyle determinants as well, it provides a more complete model of health and helps to resolve some of the major battles of the 1980s. Before focusing on the Acheson Report (1998), we need to recognize that the Conservative government's emphasis on lifestyle factors, such as smoking and diet, was strategic. This strategy was espoused in the Department of Health's *Health of the Nation* (DoH 1992) documents, which set certain targets for reducing the level of ill-health and death caused by particular diseases. There was little mention of inequality. When the risk factors associated with conditions like coronary heart disease and stroke were reviewed, the focus was squarely on what were regarded as the voluntary behaviours of smoking, diet, alcohol and physical activity, with no reference to environmental factors. All this was against a backcloth of a growing body of research which suggested that individual risk factors account for relatively small amounts of the variations in health.

In an important study, *Health and Lifestyles*, based on a national survey of 9,000 individuals, Blaxter (1990) focused on issues such as measured fitness, declared health, psychological status, life circumstances, health-related behaviour, attitudes and beliefs, but especially on the question: 'Which is the more significant for health: the social circumstances in which people live, or lifestyle habits such as exercise and smoking?' Her broad conclusion was that ' "circumstance" – not only socio-economic circumstances and the external environment, but also the individual's psycho-social environment – carry rather more weight, as determinants of health, than healthy or unhealthy behaviours' (p. 233). Moreover, Blaxter shows that some behaviours, particularly refraining from smoking, *are* relevant to health. However, her important finding is that 'they have most effect when the social environment is good: rather less, if it is already unhealthy.' Or, put another way, 'unhealthy behaviour does not reinforce disadvantage to the same extent as healthy behaviour increases advantage.' The corollary to the finding that social circumstances are more important than lifestyle is that lifestyle habits may have greater positive effect among the more privileged than among the disadvantaged.

The recognition of social, economic and environmental causes of ill-health distinguished the new Labour government of 1997. In February 1998 a green paper, *Our Healthier Nation*, acknowledged social causes, but also claimed – using a familiar term in this government's rhetoric – a 'Third Way' between the 'old extremes of individualist victim blaming on the one hand and nanny state social engineering on the other' (DoH 1998, p. 5). There was a commitment not only to improve the health of the population as a whole, but also to narrow the health gap. The independent inquiry into 'the evidence base for action to tackle inequalities in health' (DoH 1998, pp. 5, 53), the Acheson Report (1998), provides a useful summary of the current state of knowledge.

A socio-economic model of health

The socio-economic model of health (figure 15.4) embraced by the Acheson Report (1998) considers the main determinants of health as layers of influence, one over another. As figure 15.4 shows, individuals are at the centre, endowed with age, sex and constitutional factors which certainly influence their health potential, but which are fixed. Beyond that, however, are layers of influence which, in theory at least, could be modified. The innermost layer represents the personal behaviour and way of life adopted by individuals, with factors such as smoking habits and physical activity which have the potential to damage or promote health. The next layer of influence shows the social context – friends, relatives and their immediate community – which make up a set of social and community influences. The wider influences on people's ability to maintain health (shown in the third layer) include their living and working conditions, food supplies and access to essential goods and services. Finally, in the outermost layer, there are the economic, cultural and environmental conditions prevalent in society as a whole.

The Acheson Report (1998) makes a powerful case that many of the determinants of health are deeply ingrained in social structure. Its list of areas for future policy development is a formidable one, including policies to reduce income inequalities (that is, poverty), to provide additional resources for schools serving children from less well-off

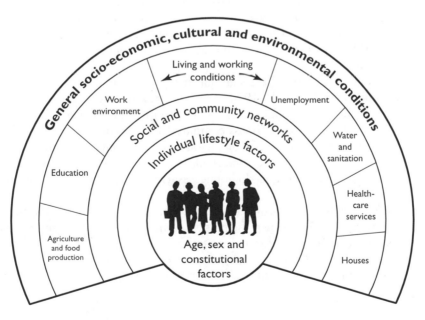

Figure 15.4 | The main determinants of health
Source: Acheson Report 1998, p. 6

groups, to extend opportunities for work (that is, to improve the health consequences of unemployment), to improve the quality of housing, to create a safe environment for people to live in, to improve transport systems and to cut the mortality and morbidity associated with motor vehicle emissions. The list is long, but it enables us to recognize how wide-ranging are the factors which may influence health.

Trends in socio-economic determinants of health

The Acheson Report (1998) culls findings from previous research rather than supplying any new material. Its overall message is that disadvantage is associated with worse health, but it goes on to point out that the actual patterns of inequalities vary by place, gender, age, year of birth and various other factors. In terms of the life chances of different social groups, we will focus particularly on gender and ethnicity. However, we will start by considering differences between social classes, which underpin much of the report.

Social class

The crucial point to recognize is that, while since the early 1970s death rates have fallen among both men and women and across all social groups, the difference in rates between those at the top and bottom of the social scale has actually widened.

Table 15.6 provides some dramatic examples. If one considers the table on 'All causes', one can see that in the early 1970s, the mortality rate among men of working age was approaching twice as high for those in class V (unskilled) as for those in class I (professional). However, by the early 1990s, although the rates for both groups had improved, the rate for class V was now almost *three* times higher. While the difference between classes I and V is the most striking, there is a steady gradient: as class position rises so mortality rates fall.

As already indicated, there is little sign that the population is experiencing less morbidity or disability than, say, in the 1970s. Socio-economic differences are very substantial. For example, in 1996 among the 45–64 age group 17 per cent of professional men reported a limiting long-standing illness compared with 48 per cent of unskilled men. Among women, 25 per cent of professional women and 45 per cent of unskilled women reported such a condition. While less marked, there are similar patterns among other age groups. However, such patterns do not necessarily hold for all kinds of health problems.

As figure 15.5 shows, major accidents among men are more common in the manual classes up to the age of 55, but then the pattern changes. Between 55 and 64, the non-manual classes have higher rates for major accidents, and thereafter are much the same. For women there is a totally different pattern; there are no differences in accident rates until after the age of 75, when women in the non-manual groups have higher rates of accident.

Figure 15.6 shows how mental health varies by social class. The patterns are not clear cut. One can see that the generalized depressive disorders and depressive episodes tend to have a gradient among women, with the lower social classes experiencing more of

| TABLE 15.6 | European standardized mortality rates: by social class, selected causes, men aged 20–64, England and Wales, selected years (rates per 100,000) |

All causes

Social class	Year		
	1970–2	1979–83	1991–3
Professional	500	373	280
Managerial and technical	526	425	300
Skilled (non-manual)	637	522	426
Skilled (manual)	683	580	493
Partly skilled	721	639	492
Unskilled	897	910	806
England and Wales	624	549	419

Lung cancer

Social class	Year		
	1970–2	1979–83	1991–3
Professional	41	26	17
Managerial and technical	52	39	24
Skilled (non-manual)	63	47	34
Skilled (manual)	90	72	54
Partly skilled	93	76	52
Unskilled	109	108	82
England and Wales	73	60	39

Coronary heart disease

Social class	Year		
	1970–2	1979–83	1991–3
Professional	195	144	81
Managerial and technical	197	168	92
Skilled (non-manual)	245	208	136
Skilled (manual)	232	218	159
Partly skilled	232	227	156
Unskilled	243	287	235
England and Wales	209	201	127

Stroke

Social class	Year		
	1970–2	1979–83	1991–3
Professional	35	20	14
Managerial and technical	37	23	13
Skilled (non-manual)	41	28	19
Skilled (manual)	45	34	24
Partly skilled	46	37	25
Unskilled	59	55	45
England and Wales	40	30	20

Accidents, poisoning, violence

Social class	Year		
	1970–2	1979–83	1991–3
Professional	23	17	13
Managerial and technical	25	20	13
Skilled (non-manual)	25	21	17
Skilled (manual)	34	27	24
Partly skilled	39	35	24
Unskilled	67	63	52
England and Wales	34	28	22

Suicide and undetermined injury

Social class	Year		
	1970–2	1979–83	1991–3
Professional	16	16	13
Managerial and technical	13	15	14
Silled (non-manual)	17	18	20
Skilled (manual)	12	16	21
Partly skilled	18	23	23
Unskilled	32	44	47
England and Wales	5	20	22

Source: Acheson Report 1998, p. 12

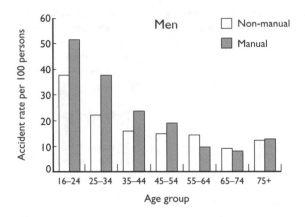

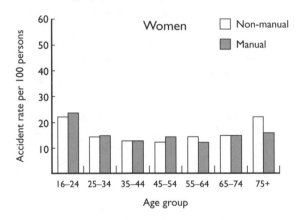

Figure 15.5 | Annual major accident rates: by age and social class, England, 1996
Source: Acheson Report 1998, p. 165

these problems, but there is not this difference for men. In contrast, there are striking social class gradients for men in relation to alcohol and drug dependence, but not for women. Rates for alcohol dependence are around 100 per 1,000 (or 10 per cent of that population) for men in classes IV and V, around double those for men in classes I and II. Women have much lower rates. Rates can vary according to the measures of health being used, but equally there may be differences in *reporting* deviant behaviour which need to be taken into account.

Ethnicity

The Acheson Report (1998) found many indications of poorer health among the minority ethnic groups in England. So, for example, the report notes that people in black (Caribbean, African and other) groups and Indians have higher rates of limiting long-standing illness than white people. In fact, those of Pakistani or Bangladeshi origin have

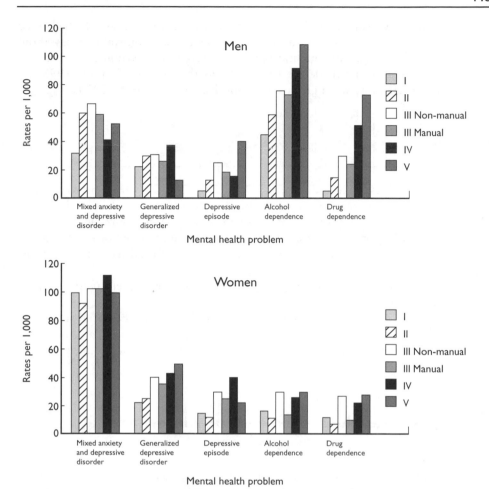

Figure 15.6 | Prevalence of mental health problems, by social class, men and women aged 16–64, 1993–4
Source: Acheson Report 1998, p. 16

the highest rates. However, the Chinese and 'other Asians' have rates *lower* than the white population.

While despairing of the sparseness of evidence, one anomalous feature of the Black Report was that in the poorer occupational classes, it seemed that men born in India, Pakistan or the West Indies tended to live longer than their British-born counterparts. This might be explained because men and women prepared to cross oceans and continents in order to seek new occupational opportunities in Britain do not represent a random cross-section of people, any more than did the Pilgrim Fathers who crossed from Britain to America in 1620.

While the study of minority ethnic groups has expanded since the early 1980s, there are still problems in interpreting some of the data. Often the country of birth is the only information (for example, ethnicity is not recorded at birth registration) and so is used as a proxy for ethnicity. Among mothers who were born in countries outside the United Kingdom, those from the Caribbean and Pakistan have infant mortality rates about double the national average. Perinatal mortality rates have also been consistently higher for babies of mothers born outside the UK. Sadly, as the Acheson Report (1998) reminds us, the differences between groups have not decreased since the 1970s.

Summary

1   The major epidemiological debate since the early 1980s has been between those who emphasize the importance of the lifestyle or behaviour of individuals and those who stress the importance of the socio-economic environment.
2   The Acheson Report (1998) espouses a socio-economic model of health and its inequalities and proclaims the need to intervene on a broad front to rectify the situation.
3   The patterns of health inequalities vary by place, gender, age, ethnicity and various other factors.
4   Health inequalities between those at the top and bottom of the social scale have widened since the 1970s.
5   There are many indications of poorer health among the minority ethnic groups in England.

15.5   Health-care expenditure: international comparisons

Comparing health-care expenditures across countries is hazardous. Countries produce data for their own administrative reporting systems, not for international comparisons. Nevertheless, strenuous efforts have been made to produce meaningful figures, and Schieber, Poullier and Greenwald (1992) have analysed health-care expenditure and utilization trends in the 24 member countries of the Organization for Economic Co-operation and Development (OECD), a Paris-based international organization whose members are the Western industrialized countries (table 15.7). The most striking finding is that the United States spends considerably more on health than other countries, both in absolute dollar terms and relative to gross domestic product (GDP). It is the only country to be spending over 10 per cent of its GDP on health.

Table 15.7 contains the estimated shares of *total health expenditure* as a percentage of GDP. In 1980, the share of total health spending in GDP ranged from 4.0 per cent in Turkey to 9.4 per cent in Sweden, with 9.2 per cent in the United States and with an OECD mean of 7.0 per cent. The United Kingdom was below average with an expenditure of 5.8 per cent and, although its health expenditure has risen, it has remained significantly below the average throughout the period. Prior to the 1980s, the OECD average had increased steadily, but it has risen at a slower rate ever since, reaching a mean of 7.6 per cent in 1990. In 1990, the shares ranged from 4.0 per cent in Turkey to 12.1 per cent in the United States, with the United Kingdom at 6.2 per cent.

TABLE 15.7 | Total and public health expenditures for 24 OECD countries, 1980–90

Country	Total expenditure (% GDP)			Public expenditure (% total expenditure)		
	1980	1985	1991	1980	1985	1990
Australia	7.3	7.7	8.2	63	72	68
Austria	7.9	8.1	8.4	69	67	67
Belgium	6.7	7.4	7.5	83	82	83
Canada	7.4	8.5	9.3	75	75	73
Denmark	6.8	6.3	6.3	85	84	83
Finland	6.5	7.2	7.8	79	79	81
France	7.6	8.5	8.8	79	77	74
Germany	8.4	8.7	8.1	75	74	73
Greece	4.3	4.9	5.5	82	81	76
Iceland	6.5	7.1	8.6	88	91	87
Ireland	9.2	8.2	7.0	82	77	75
Italy	6.9	7.0	7.7	81	77	76
Japan	6.4	6.5	6.5	71	73	72
Luxembourg	6.8	6.8	7.2	93	89	91
Netherlands	8.0	8.0	8.2	75	75	71
New Zealand	7.2	6.6	7.4	84	85	82
Norway	6.6	6.4	7.4	98	96	95
Portugal	5.9	7.0	6.7	72	56	62
Spain	5.6	5.7	6.6	80	81	78
Sweden	9.4	8.8	8.6	93	90	90
Switzerland	7.3	7.6	7.7	68	69	68
Turkey	4.0	2.8	4.0	27	50	36
United Kingdom	5.8	6.0	6.2	90	87	84
United States	9.2	10.5	12.1	42	41	42

Source: Schieber, Poullier and Greenwald 1992, p. 4

Table 15.7 also identifies *public* health expenditure as a percentage of total health expenditure. The trends for the public share of health spending relative to GDP largely mirror those for total expenditure. Health spending in the public sector accounts for about three-quarters of health spending, on average, in the OECD countries, and for more than 60 per cent of spending in all countries except the United States and Turkey. That 84 per cent of health expenditure in the UK is within the public sector suggests a high commitment to the NHS. However, with only 6.2 per cent of GDP devoted to public health the total amount spent is, comparatively, very low. Less surprisingly, the United States is well below the average in this respect. What is evident from table 15.7 is how health spending in the public sector has been relatively stable since 1980 among the Western industrialized countries.

The analysis of international comparisons of expenditures produces two important conclusions. First, the evidence suggests that the United Kingdom has been spending much less on health than many other comparable countries and so it would seem appropriate to spend more. Second, as a country where the vast majority of health expenditure is in public rather than private expenditure, despite some claims to the contrary the NHS is not profligate compared with most other industrialized countries.

Has the NHS been a success?

Spending on health care in Britain, as in other industrialized countries, has grown steadily since 1960, both in total and as a share of the gross national product (GNP). As most of the health expenditure in Britain is in the public domain, we need to consider the NHS in more detail. Those who established the NHS believed that demand would fall once a high standard of care was freely available to all. This clearly has not happened. In fact, trends in the use of the NHS are upwards. As we have asked before, does this signify increasing health problems or demand for treatment for less serious ones? The apparently simple question 'Has the NHS been a success?' needs a rather complex answer.

Leichter (1980) raised this question before the start of the Conservative programme of health reforms. He contrasted the health-care policy of four countries – West Germany, Britain, the Soviet Union and Japan – and stressed that 'the most obvious difficulty lies in the definition and measurement of the term success.' Leichter went on to illustrate this difficulty. For him, one measure of the relative achievement of the NHS would be to compare the intention and purposes of the original Act with its actual accomplishments. The purpose of the National Health Service Act was 'the establishment in England and Wales of a comprehensive health service, designed to secure improvement in the physical and mental health of the people in England and Wales, and the prevention, diagnosis, and treatment of illness'. Furthermore, it was the intention of the Act 'to divorce the care of health from questions of personal means or other factors irrelevant to it'.

Essentially – but with increasing reservations – medical care is available to all the residents of Britain, regardless of their ability to pay. In broad terms, therefore, the original objectives of the NHS have been achieved. But there are other questions that need to be asked. Are the British healthier than before? Leichter noted that, compared with the period at the start of the NHS, people today are much less likely to die in infancy, and are less likely to die from diseases such as tuberculosis, influenza and pneumonia, appendicitis, or whooping cough. In contrast, they are more likely to die from heart disease and cancer. However, Leichter stressed caution, for he noted that the general trends that appear in Britain are similar to those appearing in other economically developed countries, such as the USA, France, West Germany, the Soviet Union and Japan, over roughly the same period of time. The crucial point is that the explanation for the similarity of these trends lies less in the nature of their health-care delivery systems (that is, the way their health-care systems are organized) – which varies enormously in the countries mentioned – than in their general socio-economic conditions. So, while the overall health of the British people may well be better today, it would be unsafe simply to attribute these improvements to the NHS.

Summary

1   Spending on health care in Britain, as in other industrialized countries, has grown steadily since 1960, both in total and as a share of gross national product.
2   The spending on health in the United Kingdom has remained significantly below the average for comparable industrialized countries.
3   The similarity in trends in health care among industrialized countries are due less to the way health-care systems are organized than to general socio-economic conditions.

15.6   The NHS

Public opinion and the NHS

One of the remarkable features of the NHS is the speed with which it became 'a national institution as British as the Battle of Britain or Wimbledon. Like the Monarchy, it is at once beyond fundamental criticism and the subject of interminable complaint' (Widgery 1988, p. 28). However, the 1990s have featured discontent. The *British Social Attitudes* survey aims to monitor underlying changes over time. Since 1983 the surveys have asked people about their levels of satisfaction with the NHS in general and with specific services in particular. Between 1983 and 1990, the proportions reporting dissatisfaction with the running of the NHS nearly doubled (see table 15.8). However, the early 1990s were associated with a decline in the proportions expressing dissatisfaction. Some concluded from this that the Conservative health reforms were 'beginning to reduce the level of political conflict surrounding the NHS' (Bosanquet 1994, p. 53), but a more recent survey shows that by 1996 the proportion expressing dissatisfaction had risen to exactly one-half of the respondents (the highest ever) with just over one-third expressing satisfaction (Judge, Mulligan and New 1997).

TABLE 15.8 | Levels of satisfaction with the way the NHS is run, 1983–96 (percentages)

	1983	1984	1986	1987	1989	1990
Satisfied (very or quite)	55	51	40	41	36	36
Neither	20	19	19	20	18	20
Dissatisfied (very or quite)	25	30	39	39	46	47

Source: A. Harrison, 1992

As regards particular aspects of the health service, most dissatisfaction is expressed in relation to hospitals. As table 15.9 shows, dissatisfaction with being an in-patient trebled between 1983 and 1996, while the level of dissatisfaction with hospital out-patient work has remained consistently high since 1986. In contrast, dissatisfaction with other areas of the health service remained remarkably low throughout the 1980s.

| TABLE 15.9 | Levels of satisfaction with hospital and out-patient services, 1983–96 (percentages) |

| | *Quite or very satisfied* | | | | |
	1983	1986	1987	1989	1996
Local doctors / GPs	13	14	13	12	11
NHS dentists	10	10	9	11	11
Health visitors	6	8	8	8	8
District nurses	2	3	3	4	4
Being in hospital as an in-patient	7	13	13	15	15
Attending hospital as an out-patient	21	29	29	30	28

Source: A. Harrison 1992

Solomon (1992) has considered the apparent anomaly of the comparatively high level of dissatisfaction with the NHS as a whole and the low levels of dissatisfaction for most of the specific services reported in British Social Attitudes surveys. He suggests that respondents reply to questions about specific services primarily on the basis of their own experience. In contrast, the general questions about the NHS elicit views based more on political opinion than on personal experience. Solomon reports results from two other surveys which 'indicate that the same questions asked in a different context . . . elicit a slightly different picture of the attitudes of the public towards the NHS', suggesting more satisfaction. Nevertheless, the shift in attitudes over time remains and, whatever the 'true' figure, there are substantial levels of dissatisfaction reported in all the recent surveys of public opinion. In terms of asking about improvements in the hospital service, there are certainly differences (table 15.10). While the quality of medical and nursing care in NHS hospitals is little criticized, waiting times for treatment (both in-patient and out-patient) are the focus of widespread concern. Over three-quarters of respondents feel these times are in need of improvement. However, the trend since 1987 has been marginally downwards, indicating that the Conservative government's targeting of waiting lists achieved a modest impact (Judge, Mulligan and New 1997).

Unequal access to health care

Given that the NHS is the main source of formal health care for most people, it is important to ask whether everyone has equal access to service of a uniform quality. Traditionally there has been concern over three major problems of inequality from which the health service suffers: a geographical maldistribution of medical resources; a related social class maldistribution of resources; and irrational priorities within the medical community. On all three counts, the NHS fails to provide all sections of the British population with equal health services. The regional and social class variations inherited

TABLE 15.10	Those saying the NHS needs 'a lot' of or 'some' improvement, 1987–91 (percentages)			
	1987	*1989*	*1990*	*1991*
GP services				
GPs' appointment systems	47	45	41	45
Amount of time GP gives to each patient	33	34	31	35
Being able to choose which GP to see	29	30	27	29
Quality of medical treatment by GPs	26	27	24	31
Hospital services				
Hospital waiting lists for non-emergency operations	87	85	83	76
Waiting time before getting appointments with hospital consultants	83	86	82	71
Hospital casualty departments	54	59	52	50
Condition of hospital buildings	53	61	54	58
Quality of medical treatment in hospitals	30	36	31	36
Quality of nursing care in hospitals	21	27	24	27

Source: Judge, Mulligan and New 1997

by the service in 1948, and which were part of the rationale for developing a National Health Service, have not been remedied. The priorities of medical care continue to cause concern and dispute as resources become more restricted. We therefore consider regional, class, gender and ethnic inequalities of access and then consider the problem of priorities in the NHS.

Regional variation

In the 1970s, there was considerable regional variation in the availability of medical personnel and services. Although there were exceptions, the general picture showed that the industrial areas of northern England and Wales had fewer and older hospitals, fewer hospital beds per head of population, higher patient/doctor ratios, and inadequate specialized medical personnel and facilities. One result was higher mortality rates in the northern regions of the country than in the southern regions. Townsend, Phillimore and Beattie (1988) have focused particularly on the link between poor health and material deprivation within 678 wards in the north of England. Their principal findings were that differences in health between local populations are very considerable and 'perhaps more consistently wide than presumed in recent scientific discussion' (p. 153). There have been attempts to remedy this situation, for instance by prohibiting GPs from starting new practices or taking over existing practices in over-doctored districts. However, the NHS, through its system of funding health facilities, has tended to perpetuate these geographical inequalities. Regions which were well-off in terms of hospital beds and doctors in 1948 have been given relatively more money, while those with fewer resources have been given less. Attempts to reallocate resources to needy areas is not new, but, when resources are limited, such shifts inevitably result in a levelling down of services.

The first annual report of the NHS ordered by the Social Services Secretary (DHSS 1984), gave a breakdown of finance for each of the 14 English health regions, showing whether their level of spending was within targets to meet the Conservative government's estimate of patients' needs in those areas. Continuing to try to correct regional imbalances, while restraining spending in the public sector, helps to explain the outcry from areas where medical facilities have been traditionally well resourced.

Most spectacular was the response to Sir Bernard Tomlinson's report (1992) on health provision in London, which planned to cut London's hospital services by almost a quarter. In one respect the report was no surprise, for everyone knew that London had too many hospital beds. Apart from the expected outcry from directly interested parties, the underlying concern of others was whether enough resources would be put into alternative provision by family doctors and community health teams. Health care should not be seen in isolation from other services. For example, London has very poor provision of residential care for the elderly. An equitable allocation of resources needs to take account of a wider range of factors.

Finding a solution to London's problems was a top priority of the new Labour government of 1997. As Carrier and Kendall (1998) stress, the speed of announcing the London Review Panel just seven weeks after assuming office and the complete acceptance of the Panel's recommendations were an unusual event in British social policy. In fact, this was one of the first pieces of evidence that planning rather than market principles would be much more at the centre of decision-making in the new government's focus on health. The commitment of resources to support the recommendations, particularly the commitment to rebuild, took the steam out of a long-running conflict between the London hospital community and the government of the day.

It is difficult to interpret geographical variations in services in isolation. So, for example, information from the General Practice Database suggests that the prevalence of treatment for anxiety and depressive disorders varies regionally across England and Wales. Overall the prevalence is highest in the northern regions and East Anglia, and lowest in the North West Thames area. The rates for women are just over double those for men in all regions. Does the difference in rates between the regions mean that there is actually more anxiety or depression in some areas than others, or do these figures on treatment simply mean that such concerns are more likely to be taken seriously in some areas? Perhaps in some regions some people are more likely to admit to such conditions, while in other regions there may be a tendency to try to mask such problems.

Variation by social class

There is, of course, a relationship between the health status of people from different social classes and the regional differences we have just discussed. Some of the geographical areas traditionally starved of resources also contain a higher proportion of people from the lower social classes. The evidence suggests that the differences in health-care provision for different social classes have *not* diminished since the introduction of the NHS. Although the figures clearly show that working-class children are much more vulnerable to fatal injury and illness, their parents are less likely than those in the middle classes to take them to the doctor. This may be because they perceive the quality of care to be poor and costly rather than because they are unconcerned about illness. Health services in predominantly working-class areas are often less accessible and of poorer quality. Working-class adults may typically be more sick than middle-class adults before they seek help; their medical condition may have deteriorated. Middle-class patients tend to get better care from their GPs, not only because they live in areas which are better served, but also because they are more skilled at demanding and obtaining the care they need.

Health care and gender

While the life expectancy gap between males and females is quite marked, this is not the case for *healthy* life expectancy. Healthy life expectancy of females is only two to three years more than that of males. Women report more illness of many different types than men during their reproductive years. Since the mid-1970s, the health-care system has become more and more an area of concern for feminists. There has been the spread of direct, collective action by women, reflecting and influenced by the women's health movement in the USA. An increasing number of local women's health groups meet regularly in Britain. Indirectly stemming from this activity, the significance of medical care in women's everyday lives has been recognized. Medicine affects women to a much greater degree than it does men. The gender-role system, which relegates caring and nurturing duties to women, results in their being involved in the health-care system not only as workers but also from within the family, in a way in which most men are not.

While the vast majority of workers in the health-care system are women, they are concentrated at the bottom end of the medical hierarchy. Males dominate the highly technical and the most responsible roles in the medical hierarchy – those which also provide the greatest status and salary. In contrast, those jobs involving the greatest contact with the patient and the most practical, day-to-day, caring functions are occupied by women.

The ambivalent relationship between women and medical care has a long history. Before the rise of the modern medical profession, lay healers were traditionally female; midwives in local communities, for instance, were also skilled herbalists or 'wise women'. Gradually, during the Middle Ages, women began to be forced out of medical care by men. Eventually, women were left only midwifery, and even this came to be taken over in the seventeenth century by male barber-surgeons after the invention of forceps, which women were not allowed to use. By the eighteenth century, the medical profession had become completely male-dominated. However, the outlawing of the traditional female healer that was associated with the rise of the medical profession did not bring an end to women's traditional caring role. Women were simply relegated to the subordinate role of helpers in the increasingly technological, expanding, male medical profession.

Women are the biggest users of health-care facilities, which is largely due to their twin roles as child-bearers and child-rearers. Many women are dissatisfied with the attitudes of the health service to their health problems and needs, particularly on consultations with doctors and in the tendency to treat pregnancy and childbirth as illnesses. Indeed, the appropriateness of the intervention of the medical profession in women's lives is challenged by the women's health movement. Much of the feminist literature and practical action in the women's movement has focused, in a critical manner, on the medical control of reproduction through control of contraception, abortion and childbirth facilities, as well as the management of the supposed female 'disorders' such as the menopause. Giving birth, preventing birth, or even having an abortion are not intrinsically the concern of the medical profession. Women are not necessarily, or even normally, ill in connection with these matters, although of course they may be so. There is tremendous resistance to attempts to 'demedicalize' reproduction, because of the threat to medical specialties dealing specifically with women, for example gynaecology and obstetrics.

Feminists argue that male control over women's reproduction is central to the question of male domination and female subordination. Feminists want women to control their own health and fertility. Recent action towards this goal has taken the form of women's health groups, where women learn about their own bodies, and 'well woman clinics', where women are able to consult other women about their health. There are calls for a woman's right to choose whether or not she gives birth at home with the help of a midwife, or in hospital. At present, something like 99 per cent of births in Britain take place in hospital and home births are definitely discouraged. Furthermore, labour is often induced for the convenience of the hospital and women are forced to assume the delivery position which affords most ease to the doctor.

Since the 1970s, when a working party was set up under the Committee on Medical Aspects of Food and Nutrition Policy to review infant feeding patterns, mothers have been encouraged to breastfeed for four to six months. Other initiatives include an annual National Breastfeeding Awareness Week. The Acheson Report (1998, p. 131) argues that the impact of such initiatives has recently started to have an effect. However, the figures in terms of change over time are not impressive. Table 15.11 shows the proportion of mothers who put their child to the breast on at least one occasion. Clearly among the factors which influence the likelihood that a mother will breastfeed are the mother's social class (measured in this instance by the age at which the mother finished full-time education). Breastfeeding is much more common among mothers from the non-manual social classes.

There have been some fairly recent programmes introduced as a preventive approach specifically in relation to women's health. Breast cancer is one of the most common causes of death for women aged under 65 in the United Kingdom. To help to combat

TABLE 15.11 | Incidence of breastfeeding:[a] by age at which mother finished full-time education and birth order, Great Britain, 1985 and 1995 (percentages)

	First birth		Later births		All births	
	1985	1995	1985	1995	1985	1995
Age at finishing full-time education						
16 and under	58	59	49	47	53	52
17–18	80	78	70	67	75	72
18 and over	69	73	59	61	64	66
All mothers[b]	69	73	59	61	64	66

[a] Includes babies who were put to the breast at all, even if this was on one occasion only
[b] Includes some cases where mother's age at finishing full-time education was not shown
Source: Social Trends 1998, p. 131

this, the NHS breast-screening programme was introduced between 1988 and 1990. In 1995–6 nearly 1.5 million women in the United Kingdom were invited for screening and the uptake rate was 76 per cent. Cancers were detected in just under 6,000 women screened. The impact of this programme as a preventive measure – relating costs and possible benefits – remains under discussion. Similarly a separate screening programme for cervical cancer involved around 3.9 million women being screened in 1995–6, of whom 94 per cent were negative (i.e. no evidence of cancer), 5 per cent gave an abnormal result and 0.5 per cent were positive. Failures of procedure which have received national publicity have from time to time caused much anxiety among some women. However, these programmes demonstrate a genuine attempt to move to prevention.

Where preventive measures are the same for both males and females, there is some evidence that women look after themselves more than men. Regular visits to the dentist for a check-up help prevent tooth decay and gum disease. In 1995–6, 61 per cent of all women in the United Kingdom with some natural teeth said they had visited a dentist for a regular check-up compared with only 46 per cent of all men with some natural teeth. While there are differences between males and females regardless of social class, table 15.12 shows that the differences between socio-economic groups are much more significant than for gender. Table 15.12 also indicates that more adults than a decade earlier attend the dentist for a regular check-up; this is perhaps surprising considering the changes for dentistry payment that took place in the period, and involved charging for check-ups.

TABLE 15.12 | Adults who visit the dentist for a regular check-up: by socio-economic group[a] and gender, 1985 and 1995–6 (percentages)

	Males		Females	
	1985	1995–6	1985	1995–6
Professional	60	59	77	71
Employers and managers	54	55	70	70
Intermediate and junior non-manual	50	51	63	62
Skilled manual[b]	34	40	51	57
Semi-skilled manual and personal service	29	37	46	49
Unskilled manual	26	38	35	52
All adults[c]	41	46	58	61

[a] Married women whose husbands were in the household are classified to their husbands' occupations
[b] Includes own-account non-professional
[c] Aged 16 and over with some natural teeth, including full-time students, members of the armed forces, persons in inadequately described occupations who have never worked
Source: Social Trends 1998, p. 135

Health care and ethnicity

In the mid-1980s McNaught (1984) suggested that health authorities in areas where ethnic minorities live had not developed adequate strategies to meet their needs. The pattern of mortality and morbidity that emerges from a variety of studies is that, apart from those blood conditions such as sickle-cell anaemia and thalassaemia that have a clear race/genetic link, the health conditions that affect ethnic minority groups in Britain are the same as for the population as a whole. However, McNaught notes that the incidence of certain conditions is much higher among ethnic minority groups, and this can be linked to their socio-economic conditions in Britain, including changing patterns of diet, increased smoking and urbanization. In short, McNaught stresses that the social consequences of racial inequality are much more powerful determinants of the health status of ethnic minority groups than genetic or racial susceptibilities.

Not only do ethnic minorities suffer the general problems reflecting their class position, but also they experience additional difficulties because of language and cultural differences, or because of racial discrimination. Many people from the ethnic minorities, particularly women, either speak no English or speak it poorly as a second language. Consequently, they have difficulty in obtaining treatment, advice and guidance from health workers. Health authorities have tried to surmount this, but their initiatives have been very patchy. Cultural barriers have also created problems for the NHS. Perhaps the best known is that some Asian women insist on seeing only female doctors. This is thought to be a particular deterrent in relation to Asian women taking up an invitation for cervical cancer screening. Studies have shown that access to female practitioners is poorest in areas with high concentrations of Asian residents. Hence, Asian women have particular demands which are less likely to be met. This experience tends to endorse what the Acheson Report classes as the 'inverse prevention law' – communities most at risk of ill-health tend to experience the least satisfactory access to the full range of preventive services. While much more attention is being paid to ethnicity and health care, not everyone is confident about the appropriateness of the outcome.

Sheldon and Parker (1992) suggest that the importance of ethnicity or 'race' as a variable is perhaps overstated. Their point is that 'ethnic groups, in so far as they exist, are not socially homogeneous and may span different class locations. Therefore, analyzing studies by ethnic groups may hide wide differences in important characteristics. In brief, the concentration on ethnicity tends to displace the importance of class' (p. 109). Their argument raises the spectre of 'racialization' in the collection and use of official statistics. Discussion has largely centred on the collection of 'race' data and ethnic monitoring, subsequent upon inclusion of an 'ethnic question' in the decennial Census. Sheldon and Parker suggest that people may be increasingly encouraged to conceptualize the population along ethnic lines (the process of racialization) when other kinds of analyses and interpretation may be more appropriate. Sheldon and Parker stress elements of victim blaming, or of portraying ethnic cultures as alien, deviant, deficient and in need of change. In epidemiological studies, differences in outcome are often wrongly ascribed to racial differences. A telling example from an earlier time usefully makes the point. At the turn of the century, high mortality rates in Glasgow were attributed to the racial stock of the Irish immigrants even though mortality rates in Ireland were a lot lower. In reality, the excess was much more the outcome of the poor social conditions in which migrant labourers lived (Williams 1990). Focusing on ethnic groups usually leads to concentrating on so-called cultural differences rather than on socio-economic structure and racism. The centrality of racism in structuring black people's experience is implicitly denied.

The pathologizing of groups or cultures is perhaps most marked in psychiatry, where all black minority groups have a greater chance of being diagnosed as schizophrenic or as suffering from the more serious forms of mental illness (Grimsley and Bhat 1990). These figures are deeply contentious. Socio-biologists would perhaps suggest that these figures represent very real differences between ethnic or racial groupings. The figures may be partially explained by the severity of prejudice, but may also reflect the racist bias in the diagnostic categories and methods used by psychiatrists.

Priorities in health care

In broad terms, there has always been a tendency for the less glamorous medical care problems and medical specialties to receive a disproportionately small share of available resources. Although the 1984 NHS Report (DHSS 1984) showed some improvement, it was reported how the elderly, the mentally ill and the mentally retarded in long-stay institutions still tended to be neglected. In contrast, the medically more prestigious, acute, health-care problems attract both the more able physicians and more government resources than the areas of chronic illness. For example, it is doubtful whether the shift to community care and away from the use of long-stay institutions has been adequately resourced. Furthermore, as private medicine and the commercialization of public medicine have increased in recent years, an extra ingredient has been that the more financially rewarding medical work gets more and more attention. Sadly, Leichter's (1980, p. 194) macabre comment 'that those who are neither quick to die nor quick to recover tend to be short-changed under the NHS' still obtains.

Summary

1   The proportions reporting dissatisfaction with the running of the NHS have significantly increased in recent years. Dissatisfaction with the NHS as a whole appears to be much higher than that with the specific services it offers.
2   Access to health care in Britain is unequal. There are differences by region, by social class, by gender, by ethnicity, and as a result of decisions about priorities in allocating resources between medical specialisms.
3   Differences in access to health care do not necessarily indicate inequity in access between social groups unless these differences are adjusted for need.
4   Women, especially because of their conventional role in the family, are likely to have more contact with the health services than men.
5   Women are poorly represented among the higher ranks of the medical profession, and many feel that male medical control over women's health is unacceptable.
6   Ethnic minorities tend to suffer from the same illnesses as the rest of the population but, owing to their class position and restrictions on access to health care, they are prone to relatively high levels of ill-health.
7   The pathologizing of groups or cultures is most marked in psychiatry, where all black minority groups have a greater chance of being diagnosed as schizophrenic. The reasons for this are highly contentious.

15.7 A contemporary audit

Reforming the NHS

Both the size and the symbolism of the NHS make it a daunting target for reform. It had become the largest employer in the country and probably also in the whole of Europe. The Conservative government's rejection of the Black Report (1980) and its espousal of the importance of healthy lifestyles as the major plank for improving health heralded the view that the individual was responsible for his or her health, not the government. Nevertheless, a 'revolution' in the organization and management of the NHS had actually started. While the Labour Party, as the main opposition, focused on what it regarded as incremental privatization and increasing commercialization, the nature of the 'revolution' in the NHS was perhaps missed. The crucial feature of the NHS is the centre–periphery relationship, the fact that the NHS delivers *local services* but is a *nationally funded* organization. This has always produced a basic tension. The contradiction between moving towards the localization of priority-setting and decision-making on the one hand, and the tendency towards centralization on the other, was one aspect of developments in the 1980s in many areas of the public sector, such as education and law and order. In brief, stress on local accountability can be seen as a mechanism by which local management was to be made much more accountable to the centre.

Increasingly, the Thatcher administrations (1979–90) focused directly on good management as the major solution to the problems of the NHS. The Griffiths Report in 1983, *NHS Management Inquiry*, was concerned with the link between local accountability and central control. It successfully challenged the principle of consensus management by a team of professionals, and instead strongly advocated the appointment of chief executives or general managers at all levels in the NHS. The government required all health authorities to implement such change by the end of 1985. The changing inter-professional relationships were quickly noted by the health-care professions but only much later came into public consciousness. Austin's cartoon in the *Guardian* (plate 15.1) captured the shift at a time when a wider audience was beginning to appreciate what was actually happening. However, at the earlier stage, as far as public perceptions were concerned, the emphasis appeared to be upon achieving 'efficiency savings', which simply meant the attempt to obtain more by way of service from the same level of spending. While these savings quickly produced adverse public reaction, the process was not different in kind from the practice of cash limitation which had started under the Labour governments of the 1970s.

The Conservative manifesto for the 1987 election did not promise – or indeed threaten – much radical change for the NHS. However, as a result of increasing concern about funding, the government announced a review. The only option which everyone soon recognized as being disallowed from the outset was significantly *increased* funding, for this would have been in conflict with the primary fiscal objective of holding down public expenditure to facilitate reductions in income tax. The majority of proposals which emerged can be split into two main groups: those which sought to change the funding base of the NHS and those which sought to introduce greater internal competition and a more efficient delivery system. There was much discussion surrounding three basic models of funding: national taxation, social insurance, and private insurance. The most

Plate 15.1 | Source: *Guardian*, 10 October 1991

fundamental ideas to survive into the final draft of the review were the opt-out plan for hospitals, which would be allowed to become self-governing trusts, and the highly controversial American-inspired scheme to fund GPs to go out and buy health care for their patients. The white paper *Working for Patients*, published in January 1989, was perhaps the most important document to emerge in the 40 years since the inception of the NHS.

The implementation of the National Health Service and Community Care Act 1990, which incorporated proposals for reforming the way that health and social services were provided throughout the UK, required the creation of a competitive market. Without precedent in the UK and with experience abroad also limited, the scale of the experiment was quite remarkable. Indeed, in an editorial feature *Health Care UK 1991* suggested 'it represents a very bold venture in public sector reform, the boldest of all the many measures that the Government have taken in their 12 years of office' (A. Harrison 1992, p. 7).

The most crucial shift in setting up the internal health market was the requirement that all district health authorities should divide themselves into a purchasing arm and a providing arm. The main task of districts was to concentrate on their purchasing and commissioning functions, which involved assessing the health needs of their populations, identifying the services to meet those needs, and setting priorities when resources were insufficient to meet all identified needs. Contracts became the centre-piece of the new system. Purchasers defined by contracts what the providers were to do and the price at which they would be paid for their services.

A crucial feature of the legislation was that district health authorities were just one kind of purchaser; the Act also provided for groups of GPs to become fundholders and to establish contracts with providers in rather similar ways. The GPs involved in this scheme were to be allocated budgets out of funding previously directed to health authorities. While the GP fundholding scheme began on only a small scale, there were early signs that it did have some limited effect in improving care standards, as GPs 'shopped around' in order to get better services for their patients (A. Harrison 1992, p. 12). However, there was another side of the coin. GPs who were not fundholders began to be perceived as being disadvantaged. Furthermore, it seemed likely that the extra administration involved could well offset any possible benefits, and there was really no knowing what unintended consequences could follow.

The other shift which attracted considerable attention was the development of NHS trusts as provider units. The central presupposition behind introducing trusts was that greater independence from district management would result in better performance. While the notion of competition between different providers rapidly gained acceptance, it soon became clear that the government were unwilling to allow the trusts to be genuinely independent, particularly in the key area of capital finance. The tension between the centre and the periphery simply emerged again in another form.

While much of the media coverage since 1990 has focused on the desperate plight of some hospital acute units, there have been other, less noticed results. Described as 'the best known piece of external auditing in the 1980s' (A. Harrison 1992, p. 19), the Audit Commission's report *Making a Reality of Community Care* in 1986 identified a number of serious problems in the then existing arrangements for financing and providing care for the so-called priority groups – frail elderly, mentally ill and handicapped people. The government reacted by asking Sir Roy Griffiths to consider the issues. His 1988 report, *Community Care: Agenda for Action*:

> accepted most of the criticisms [of the Audit Commission's report] but did not fully absorb their logic. In particular, he attempted to keep a clear line between social and health care and, by emphasizing the need for joint planning rather than changes to the existing pattern of responsibilities, made no proposals relating to changes in the boundaries of health or local authorities. (A. Harrison 1992, p. 19)

However, there were still important measures for community care in the 1990 National Health Service and Community Care Act which represented radical change, opening the way for innovation, in both market and administrative behaviour. The introduction of policies for achieving better health based on prevention rather than treatment is a fundamental realignment. The initiatives of the new Labour government of 1997 (discussed below) must be seen in the context of these recent changes.

The private sector

Another important development is the expansion of the private sector in British health care. The value of privately funded acute health care provided both within and independently of the NHS was estimated at £2.35 billion in 1996 (Acheson Report 1998). It can be cogently argued that the distribution of, and access to, private health care compounds existing inequalities. Information on the private sector is sparse, and among the suggestions of the Acheson Report was that those providing private health care should be required to give the same routine information on activity and quality of services as the NHS. It seems likely that the relationship of private practice to the NHS must soon be addressed, but the government may prefer to avoid the associated political controversy.

A new vision?

When the new Labour government was elected in 1997, the NHS internal market model had been in operation for a sufficient period for the public to have realized that it did not solve problems, but actually produced a new set. Lengthy waiting lists and times, evident deficiencies in community care, and the problems of a two-tier system based on fundholding and non-fundholding GPs all contributed to a view that little had improved. As a backcloth, implicit rationing of health services and the increasing costs of the bureaucracy to run the new system were further concerns which the new government had to face.

The Labour government took some immediate action as well as planning for the longer term. There were promises of more funds going into patient care and the announcement of the largest new building programme in the history of the NHS. Also, the new government indicated its interest in public health by appointing the first ever Minister for Public Health, whose brief included the task of breaking down old-established territorial boundaries and organizational barriers which hampered development. The announcement of a number of Health Action Zones (HAZs) which aimed to bring together all those contributing to the health of a local population – local authorities, community groups, the voluntary sector and local businesses – in order to develop and implement a locally agreed strategy for improving the health of people was an associated initiative within the same kind of theme.

While much of the thrust of the last few decades has been in challenging the 'medical model' of health and widening our understanding of health determinants, interestingly the doctor remains the most powerful figure in the health-care system. This is for a variety of reasons, partly because there is a legal requirement for an individual to take responsibility for treatment, partly because the medical profession remains the most powerful occupational group, and partly because the doctor–patient interaction is still seen as the most fundamental site of health care. Nevertheless, advances taking us beyond the traditional view of health and illness have been made.

In terms of seeking health for all, there was immediate recognition that the strategy of the previous government – based on the document *Health of the Nation* (DoH 1992) and enunciating targets – was limited because of its reluctance to acknowledge the social, economic and environmental causes of ill-health. The new government's response in *Our Healthier Nation* (DoH 1998) called for action on a much wider front:

> The Government recognizes that the social causes of ill health and the inequalities that stem from them must be acknowledged and acted upon. Connected problems require joined up solutions. This means tackling inequality which stems from poverty, poor housing, pollution, low educational standards, joblessness and low pay. Tackling inequalities generally is the best means of tackling health inequalities in particular. (DoH 1998, p. 12, para. 1.12)

Plate 15.2 | Health promotion is an important part of public health
Source: Department of Health © Crown; Cancer Research Campaign © Crown

Embodied in the Acheson Report (1998) was a list of 39 major recommendations that will be a useful benchmark against which to identify the seriousness of the attempt to tackle health inequality. The first of the two general recommendations is that 'all policies likely to have a direct or indirect effect on health should be evaluated in terms of their impact on health inequalities, and should be formulated in such a way that by favouring the less well off they will, wherever possible, reduce such inequalities.' The second general recommendation suggests the most appropriate targeting: 'We recommend a high priority is given to policies aimed at improving health and reducing health inequalities in women of childbearing age, expectant mothers and young children' (p. 120). The areas covered by other recommendations – 'Poverty, Income, Tax and Benefits'; 'Education'; 'Employment'; 'Housing and Environment'; 'Mobility, Transport and

Pollution'; 'Nutrition and the Common Agricultural Policy'; 'Mothers, Children and Families'; 'Young People and Adults of Working Age'; 'Older People'; 'Ethnicity'; 'Gender'; 'The National Health Service' – provide a useful checklist of areas contributing to a reduction in health inequalities. It is perhaps salutary to note that only around 10 pages of this major report was devoted to a consideration of the NHS – the message being that the health of the nation is too important to be left to the NHS.

Carrier and Kendall's (1998) book, *Health and the National Health Service*, provides a powerful reminder that current concerns and controversies have a long-established history. The first two-thirds of their book is titled 'An Historical Audit' and the last one-third is titled 'A Contemporary Audit'. Their use of the term 'audit', from the world of accountancy and business, is no longer out of place in the world of health and medical care. Encouraged by Conservative governments since 1979, the language of market principles has entered health and social service areas. Also, health services are faced with a more demanding public backed up by politicians who are no longer afraid to ask whether they are getting 'value for money'. Governments have been interested in 'value for money' in terms of cost containment, while opposition politicians and the public have been asking whether we are gaining all we might reasonably expect from the apparent advances in health and medical care. The latter groups tend to raise expectations on health-care delivery, while the former group tries to contain expenditure.

The aim of the audit conducted by Carrier and Kendall, however, is not the usual financial audit but 'to locate health care in a series of contexts – both historical and contemporary – by which the nature and significance of . . . conflicts [in the delivery of health care] may be assessed' (1998, p. xvii). The questions of the amount of state intervention in health, whether provision should be universal or selective, the limitations of community or institutional care, and the contributions of professionals or non-professionals in health-care delivery provide us with an agenda for the twenty-first century similar to that which largely preoccupied the past century.

Summary

1 The fact that the NHS delivers *local services* but is a *nationally funded* organization has produced a basic tension within the NHS throughout its entire history.

2 The Griffiths Report (1983) successfully challenged the principle of consensus management by a multi-disciplinary team by advocating the principle of chief executives or general managers at all levels in the NHS.

3 The white paper *Working for Patients* in 1989 marked an important watershed in presenting the thinking of the Conservative government.

4 The National Health Service and Community Care Act 1990 contained the important underlying concept of the creation of a competitive market.

5 The most crucial move in setting up the internal health market is the requirement that all district health authorities should separate their purchasing and provisioning functions.

6 The new Labour government of 1997 proposed combating health inequality on a wide front, arguing that tackling inequalities generally is the best means of tackling health inequalities in particular.

7   The Acheson Report (1998) will provide a useful benchmark against which to assess policies for the reduction of health inequality.

Related topics

The context of recent reforms of welfare provision is outlined in section 13.4. The medical and auxiliary professions are discussed in section 4.4 On the physical and psychological effects of unemployment see 4.5. On the changing structure of the British population see section 9.2 and on ageing see section 9.7. Other aspects of the disadvantages experienced by ethnic minorities are discussed in section 8.4.

Further reading

Mackay, Soothill and Melia (1998) is a useful compendium of short excerpts from some of the most important articles written on health since the Second World War. A good sociological approach to many of the issues is Nettleton (1995). An excellent account of both historical and recent developments in health policy is Carrier and Kendall (1998). However, anyone wishing to keep abreast of the rapidly changing provision of health care needs to read the newspapers and professional journals.

Cross-references to *Readings from Contemporary British Society*

Wilkinson on the relationship between inequality and health; **Judge et al.** on attitudes to the National Health Service; **Thompson** on media representation of AIDS.

16 | Deviance, Crime and Control

Today, institutions fundamental to the British system of government are under attack: the public schools, the House of Lords, the Church of England, the holy institution of marriage, and even our magnificent police force are no longer safe from those who would undermine our society. And it's about time we said 'enough is enough' and saw a return to the traditional British values of discipline, obedience, morality, and freedom – freedom from the reds and the blacks and the criminals, prostitutes, pansies and punks, football hooligans, juvenile delinquents, lesbians and left-wing scum; freedom from the niggers, and the pakis and the unions, freedom from the gypsies and the Jews, freedom from the long-haired layabouts and students – freedom from the likes of you.

Tom Robinson Band, 'Power in the Darkness'

16.1 Introduction

Social problems are inherently political phenomena. Social problems in general, and deviant behaviour in particular, are not objective 'givens' of social life, but are identified and shaped in an ongoing political process. We do not all agree on what is deviant behaviour. What is regarded as a problem by one group may not be seen in this way by another group in society. We are, therefore, engaged in a controversial political process in which the values and interests of various groups are frequently in direct or indirect opposition to each other. The task – or perhaps the trick – of one group is to try to convince others that conditions which challenge *their* values or threaten *their* interests are *objectively* harmful and need to be corrected. In this sense, deviancy is created or socially constructed, it is a case of somebody defining some person or behaviour as deviant.

Social protest highlights the issue. In fact, there has been much concern about the increasing criminalization of activities that were previously considered to be legitimate forms of dissent. Since the late 1970s, civil protest, Britain's oldest democratic tradition, has been progressively criminalized. Mrs Thatcher's authoritarian trade union laws (see section 4.3) were followed in 1986 by the Public Order Act, which restricted the right to demonstrate. The 1992 Trade Union Act criminalized such activities as carrying insulting banners. The 1995 Criminal Justice and Public Order Act allowed the police to break up almost any public protest. The 1996 Security Service Act and 1997 Police Act included in their definition of serious crime 'conduct by a large number of persons in pursuit of a common purpose': peaceful protesters were thus exposed to state-backed bugging, burglary and arbitrary searches. All these Acts are responses by the state to a range of perceived problems. However, taken together they make the task of people dissenting or protesting that much more difficult. Indeed, that is much of the purpose of this recent legislation. Many campaigns, whether they be protests against the use of nuclear weapons or, more recently, about the destruction of the environment, are motivated by concern about the common good. Curiously, some people trying to change society for the better have been turned, by degrees, into criminals. Hence, understanding what is crime and who are the criminals may sometimes challenge some of the stereotypes so readily displayed in the media. In today's society, the relationship between deviance, crime and social control may be complex.

While all crime and deviance may be essentially political, there is a variation in the degree of overt political emphasis that may be observed in particular cases. At any given point in time, some issues excite considerable disagreement, while others seem to command a basic consensus.

16.2 Varieties of deviance

A Canadian criminologist, Hagan (1984), developed a framework that identifies the varieties of deviance. From the starting point of defining deviance as a variation from a social norm, he argues that we should think of deviance as a continuous variable. Quite simply, there is an obvious difference between multiple murder and adolescent marijuana use. Hagan suggests that most deviant acts can be located empirically on a continuum of seriousness between these two extremes. He identifies three measures of seriousness:

1 *degree of agreement about the wrongfulness of the act*. This assessment can vary from confusion and apathy, through high levels of disagreement, to conditions of general agreement.
2 *severity of the social response elicited by the act*. Social penalties can, of course, vary from life imprisonment to polite avoidance.
3 *societal evaluation of the harm inflicted by the act*. Here the concern is with the degree of victimization and the personal and social harm a set of acts may involve.

Hagan argues that, in most modern societies, these three measures of seriousness are closely connected. So what he is saying is that the more serious acts of deviance are those likely to evoke broad agreement about their wrongfulness, a severe social response, and an evaluation of the act as being harmful. This approach provides insights but is also contentious. Hagan portrays the situation in visual terms as a pyramid, with the less serious forms of deviance at the base and the more serious forms of deviance at the peak (see figure 16.1). This is an interesting notion, for the form of a pyramid suggests that the most serious acts of deviance in a society tend also to be less frequent, while less serious acts may be quite common. Hagan's framework provides a useful basis from which to consider the current British situation.

Hagan's major division is between criminal and non-criminal forms of deviance. In fact, he argues that the most serious forms of deviance are defined by law as criminal. This can certainly be challenged, for one of the arguments of the radical criminologists is that the powerful manage either to prevent some of their more dangerous activities being proscribed (that is, forbidden) by criminal law, or to ensure that any sanctions are ludicrously light (such as small fines). For example, environmental pollution, health and safety in factories and unethical business practices can adversely affect vast numbers in the population. However, the criminal law either is not operative in these areas or is not enforced to any significant degree.

Hagan's consensus crimes – murder, rape, robbery, etc. – are those that outrage and scare the public. One of the effects of the women's movement has been to make us all much more aware of the seriousness of the offence of rape. Many people now – not just women – think the problem of rape should be tackled much more seriously and, where appropriate, offenders should be punished much more severely than at present.

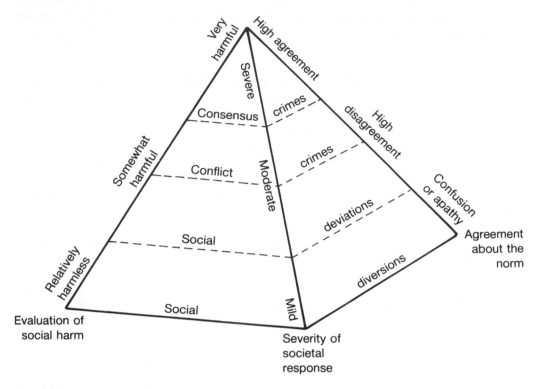

Very harmful
High agreement
Severe
Consensus
crimes
High disagreement
Somewhat harmful
Conflict
crimes
Moderate
Confusion or apathy
deviations
Social
Agreement about the norm
Relatively harmless
diversions
Social
Mild
Evaluation of social harm
Severity of societal response

Figure 16.1 | Varieties of deviance
| *Source*: Hagan 1984, p. 111

The next category, conflict crimes, is that of activities about which public opinion is more divided. Social class and various interest groups may well be the source of such conflict. These offences provide examples of how the criminal law can be used by one class or interest group to the disadvantage of another. There is a whole range of conflict crimes. Hagan includes public disorder offences (e.g. vagrancy, creating a public disturbance), chemical offences (e.g. alcohol and drug offences), political crimes (e.g. espionage, terrorism and conspiracy), minor property offences (e.g. petty theft, vandalism) and the 'right-to-life' offences (e.g. abortion, euthanasia). In many ways these contain the most interesting varieties of deviance, for, as Hagan stresses, the feature that unites these offences is the public debate that surrounds them. In short, 'we lack societal consensus on the dimensions of public disorder, the use of comforting chemicals, permissible politics, the protection of private property and the limits of life' (p. 16). While Hagan applies his framework to Canada, it is equally, if not more, true of contemporary British society. Since the late 1970s or so we have been in the midst of debates at varying levels about all these areas. The miners' strike of 1984–5, the Campaign for Nuclear Disarmament, Greenham Common women, the Irish question, Poll Tax non-payments, new road schemes, rave parties, drug use and so on have all raised issues about the use and appropriateness of the criminal law as a weapon in social conflict.

One important point that should be recognized is that persons involved in conflict crimes are less likely than those who commit consensus crimes to differ in significant ways from the general population. In brief, there is probably nothing distinctive about political criminals apart from the fact that they happen to have been identified as current or potential political threats. While those in power often try to give pejorative labels to those who oppose their policies – 'troublemakers', 'mad', 'wicked', 'evil' and so on – this is simply part of the political game of defining deviance. In contrast, a person who kills his or her mother – a consensus but, fortunately, rare crime – is much more likely to suffer from some form of psychiatric disorder that makes him or her differ in significant ways from the general population. In short, a psychological explanation is far more likely to be useful for this type of crime, while the political context is likely to be much more important than personality in considering political crime.

Criminal forms of deviance depend for their definition on the *formal* process of control – police, courts, prisons, etc. – while non-criminal forms of deviance depend for their definition on the *informal* processes of social control, such as the family, peer groups and other community groups. Hagan considers two non-criminal forms of deviance, which he terms 'social deviations' and 'social diversions'. The distinction is not precise, but examples of social deviations would be psycho-social disturbances, the violation of trust and various adolescent pranks. The crucial point is that these activities and experiences are not considered criminal but are, none the less, disreputable. In contrast, social diversions tend to be frequent and faddish activities which are not always looked upon favourably. Certain symbolic diversions (styles of dress, speech and mannerisms) are sometimes used in the development of stereotypes as indicators of more serious forms of deviance but, in themselves, are usually harmless.

Changes in definitions of deviant behaviour

Before leaving Hagan's pyramid, it is important to underline one point. As it stands, the pyramid, like the pyramids of Egypt, looks rather static. In studying deviance, however, it is crucial to recognize that there are significant shifts in what holds the centre of the stage of political debate. As Hagan stresses, probably the most important change that can occur in the societal evaluation of an act involves the movement of that act from criminal to non-criminal status. In the 1960s and early 1970s, there was much debate about and some action in decriminalizing certain activities. The so-called 'victimless' crimes were the main focus of this change, in particular abortion, homosexuality and soft-drug use. Changes in the law have undoubtedly made some difference here. Abortion is now available in a much wider range of situations than prior to the 1967 Abortion Act; homosexuality – while still more restricted by law than heterosexual activity – is no longer outlawed in the way it was prior to the passing of the 1967 Sexual Offences Act; while the penalties for the possession of soft drugs have been considerably reduced since the mid-1960s. Nevertheless, a cursory glance at newspapers or even a brief listen to neighbourhood gossip hardly suggests that such activities are totally acceptable. Having an abortion, declaring yourself homosexual or even smoking pot can still be personally hazardous.

A focus on mugging and football hooliganism in the 1970s and 1980s illustrates how interest can shift. The term 'moral panic' has been coined to describe some of these shifts of interest. The first published reference to a moral panic was by the British sociologist, Jock Young, when discussing public concern about statistics showing an apparently alarming increase in drug abuse. He observed that 'the moral panic over drug-taking results in the setting-up of drug squads' by police departments, which in turn produced an increase in drug-related arrests (Young 1971). His essential point is that the interaction of the media, public opinion, interest groups and social control agents, such as the police, produce an amplifying effect which gives rise to the phenomenon now identified as a moral panic. However, S. Cohen (1972/80) can certainly take the credit for publicizing the concept by exploring the reactions of the media, the public and the police to the youth disturbances and seaside fights between mods and rockers in 1960s Britain. K. Thompson (1998) has suggested that moral panics about sex are increasingly the most frequent and have the most serious repercussions in modern society. So children at risk from sexual abuse, from video nasties or from sex on the screen, can be 'captured' in this context.

In the 1990s there was a rapid succession of moral panics – indeed, journalists as much as academics increasingly use the term. The danger is to regard the issues which emerge as moral panics as unrelated episodes of collective behaviour; moral panics may be symptomatic of developments that are of wider significance. K. Thompson (1998) locates the study of moral panics within a sociology of morals, focusing on changes in forms of moral regulation and reactions to them.

This is just part of a more general point that patterns of deviance can change and shifts of focus can take place, but neither happens as drastically as we are sometimes led to believe. Pearson (1983) demonstrated the importance of historical research when he showed that the supposedly 'new' moral panic about football hooliganism in the 1970s was not really new. His work exploded the myth that street crime and hooliganism are

Plate 16.1 | 'A Briton in time of peace'
Source: Punch Publications 1856

the product of a permissive society or evidence of rapid moral decline from the stable traditions of the past. Pearson stresses the violent realities of street life in the past. He shows that successive generations have voiced identical fears of social breakdown and moral degeneration. In his lively study, we can begin to identify the parallels between the 'garotters' and original 'hooligan' gangs of late Victorian London and the 'muggers' of contemporary urban streets. Pearson discovered that the word 'hooligan' made an abrupt entrance into common English usage, as a term to describe gangs of rowdy youths, during the hot summer of 1898. The word was new but the problem was not – there had been considerable unease about what was happening in earlier periods, as plate 16.1 shows.

Drug-taking and crime

Different types of deviance come into focus at different times, but the question of drug-taking seems to be of continuous interest. In fact, there are many perceptions of drug use. Indeed, much drug-taking is condoned or even encouraged when directed by a medical doctor, while other drug-taking is harshly condemned. Since the late 1980s, however, increasing concern has developed regarding the possible connection between drug-taking and crime, in particular violent crime. The tragic killing in 1997 of a 5-year-old boy as he walked down the street hand in hand with his stepfather, a former heroin addict and drug dealer, in Bolton, Greater Manchester, indicated this. Dillon Hull was shot through the head during a bungled assassination attempt on his step-father. In passing sentence at the end of a five-week trial, Mr Justice Forbes said 'This is a crime which sent shockwaves through the country. On a summer's afternoon, a child was shot in broad daylight in a residential area of Bolton and ordinary citizens were brought into contact with horrifying violence and death' (*Guardian*, 18 November 1998). When the drug underworld clashes with the ordinary world in such tragic circumstances, it highlights the question of the possible link between drug-taking and crime.

In fact, this link has attracted interest for a long time. Bean and Wilkinson (1988) have noted how the links can be examined in terms of three main questions: to what extent does drug use lead to crime, to what extent does crime lead to drug use, and to what extent do crime and drug use emerge from a common set of circumstances? Bean and Wilkinson draw upon the results of a major study in Nottingham and note how the rather static and deterministic approach implied in the first two propositions offers little by way of explanation of a relationship between drug-taking and crime. They argue that, following the third approach, one can usefully consider to what extent crime is part of the drug user's world. They focus on the users' link to the illicit supply system, suggesting that the system is central to the users' world whether for crime or for drugs. Indeed, they conclude that:

> our evidence, in Nottingham at least, suggests that the presence and structure of an illicit drug supply system provide the best evidence for the link between drug-taking and crime. The crimes committed, and the nature and extent of those crimes, all point to contact with the illicit supply system which not only involves illegal drug transactions but crimes related to those transactions. These in turn are related to the users' position on the illicit supply network. (pp. 538–9)

The simple relationships so often posited between drug-taking and crime are not so straightforward; they can be misleading and are often wrong.

Summary

1 There are varieties of deviance. The major division is between criminal and non-criminal forms of deviance.
2 Crimes divide into consensus crimes (which outrage and scare the public) and conflict crimes (where public opinion is much more divided about the appropriate status). Non-criminal forms of deviance can be divided into social deviations and social diversions.
3 There are significant shifts in definitions of deviance over time. The most important shifts involve the movement between criminal and non-criminal status. Historical research often indicates that a supposedly new moral panic, such as football hooliganism, is not necessarily a startlingly new phenomenon.
4 Moral panics may be symptomatic of developments that are of wider significance.
5 Links between different types of deviance, such as drug-taking and crime, are often complex. However, varieties of deviance may sometimes emerge from a common set of circumstances.

16.3   Crime statistics

There is a whole set of problems in studying official rates of deviance. Crime figures may well tell you more about the organizations that produce the figures than the actual occurrence of crime and deviance. Sociologists have warned (and to some extent the message has got through) of the dangers of reading too much into the official crime figures. Even a cursory glance at the newspapers today suggests that the media will continue to make allegedly rising crime rates a major issue. Bad news attracts more attention than good news. In the early 1990s politicians were becoming less willing to highlight the crime figures, and ministers considered whether to have less frequent publication of the crime statistics. However, more recently, there has been some good news about crime figures and so the government has been less reluctant to talk about crime statistics. Certainly, though, most general elections have a 'law'n'order' emphasis, when the success or otherwise of the government in dealing with crime becomes a major issue. Criminal statistics, both real and spurious, are thrown into the debate. Understanding what criminal statistics actually mean is crucial. Can we rely on them? How is it that such opposite conclusions can be drawn from their use?

Sociologists have somewhat diverse views on the value of official statistics in resolving debates about the extent of deviance and the social origins of deviants. Some continue to stress that official crime statistics are seriously misleading, owing to the vast numbers of crimes that are not reported to the police (known as the 'dark figure'). Other criminologists think that some of the criticisms of the official statistics have been exaggerated, arguing that crime statistics do reflect a reality. So, for example, radical sociologists tend to believe that the law is essentially a 'class law' (that is, operating against the interests of the working class), and hence, they argue, what is so surprising about a disproportionate number of working-class people appearing in the crime statistics?

The intricacies of the construction of official crime statistics are dealt with quite adequately in several texts (e.g. Box 1981; Bottomley and Pease 1986). Official statistics on crime and criminals are both limited and biased. They overrepresent the contribution to 'conventional' crimes of the lower class, especially ethnically oppressed males. They also fail to reveal the extent of corporate and governmental crimes, including crimes committed by agents of social control, such as the police. So when we study the official statistics, we need to recognize that they tell only an incomplete story. Nevertheless, we still need to face basic questions such as the extent of crime, who is at risk and how we should handle the fear of crime. A major development in the 1980s which enables us to probe more accurately some of these issues was the rise in interest in victimization surveys. Surveys of victimization involve asking samples of the general population about crimes (whether or not reported to the police) that may have been committed against them in some preceding period (usually a year). Certainly they provide a measure of crime much closer to reality than the statistics of offences recorded by the police and court statistics, which are published annually under the title *Criminal Statistics*. In truth, the latter provide a useful index of the workload of the police and a record of the working of the court system, but are not a reliable indicator of crime levels.

The decision by the Conservative government in mid-1981 to carry out the first national survey of crime victimization not only heralded a series of these government studies but also spawned in the 1980s some fascinating local studies, for example in Merseyside (Kinsey 1985), in Islington (Jones, Maclean and Young 1986; A. Crawford et al. 1990) and in Edinburgh (S. Anderson et al. 1990), which both complemented and challenged some of the findings from the national studies. The importance of such local surveys cannot be overestimated. However, there is no doubt that surveys do have their limitations. For example, they have had considerable difficulty in probing the number of offences against women – domestic violence, indecent assault, attempted rape and actual rape. In the first British Crime Survey (BCS), the number of sexual offences was clearly an underestimate for at least two reasons. Respondents may be reluctant to relive a painful or embarrassing experience for the benefit of a survey interviewer. Furthermore, with domestic violence, a respondent's assailant may be in the same room at the time of the interview. The questions about sexual attack were changed for the subsequent BCSs, but it still seems unlikely that they probe this area very accurately. However, it is important to recognize that one can identify the kind of bias – the counts of sexual offences and domestic or non-stranger violence are always likely to be underestimates in these types of survey.

In contrast, studies conducted by the women's movement have consistently shown more disturbing figures. A pioneering survey directed by R. Hall (1985) indicated that more than one in six women questioned in the survey claimed to have been the victim of a rape. In fact, this survey claims that nearly one in three women had been sexually assaulted, one in five had survived an attempted rape, and nearly one in every 100 had been raped by a gang or by more than one man. Importantly, the reporting rates to the police were disturbingly low. Only 8 per cent of those surveyed had reported rape to the police and 18 per cent had reported sexual assault. While these figures were vigorously challenged at the time, increasingly the problems faced by women have been recognized, and the dangers of assault are not minimal. Nevertheless, different ways of doing surveys and asking questions may begin to explain some of the apparently very different results.

In fact, Hall's figures refer to sexual assaults on women *at any point in their lives*, while the BCS figures refer to *one particular year*, so, of course, one can expect what seem to be widespread discrepancies. Certainly, in comparing figures, there are considerable dangers which need to be considered. What is classed as 'rape'? Does it include 'marital rape', for example? What is the response rate? In Hall's survey 62 per cent of the women responded, and one needs to ask whether particular kinds of persons tend to respond to questionnaires. If women are interviewed, to whom would they tell such intimate details of their lives, which may have remained secret but are never forgotten? Certainly sexual assaults are measured by the BCS, but owing to the small number of incidents reported to the survey the results are not considered reliable.

Despite the dangers and the shortcomings, there is still considerable value in the information collected by the ongoing BCS. There have now been seven sweeps of the survey – carried out in 1982, 1984, 1988, 1992, 1994, 1996 and 1998. The first survey was carried out in England, Wales and Scotland, as was the third survey. The second survey and all sweeps since 1992 were carried out in England and Wales alone. Scotland now has its own survey and so the title 'British Crime Survey' is something of a misnomer. There has been an increasing sophistication in methodological terms, while the possibility of comparing the results of later surveys with earlier ones has been retained. It has been possible to analyse this national study at a local level. Indeed, there is now concern that insurance companies may use the results to fix differential insurance rates in areas shown to be at higher risk.

The British Crime Survey

The BCS asks adults in private households about their experience of victimization in the previous year. Most questions on victimization have remained the same in each sweep of the BCS, but other topics have varied. The 1998 BCS had a nationally representative sample of 14,947 people aged 16 and above out of 18,983 addresses – a creditable response rate of 79 per cent.

The value of the BCSs is that they yield estimates of the extent of various crimes that include incidents unreported to the police. They cover violence against the person, and theft of and damage to private property. The BCS estimated there were 16,437,000 crimes in 1997 against people living in private households.

Figure 16.2 shows BCS estimates of the number of criminal incidents in 1997 by crime type. What becomes quite evident from figure 16.2 is that the vast majority of crimes do not involve violence. The most common offences involve some type of theft (62 per cent of the total). Vandalism against vehicles and other household and personal property make up a further 18 per cent of offences covered by the BCS. A minority of crimes are categorized as violent offences (20 per cent), and the majority of these are common assaults that involve at most minimal injury (14 per cent); only 4 per cent involve significant injury (wounding) and 2 per cent are muggings (robbery and snatch

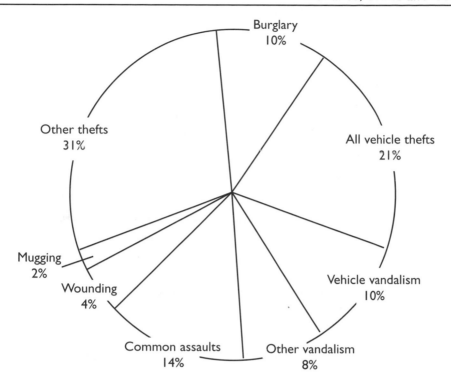

Figure 16.2 | BCS estimates of certain offences, England and Wales, 1997
Source: Mirrlees-Black et al. 1998. Crown copyright

thefts). Thus, while serious crimes of violence certainly occurred, in numerical terms they were overshadowed by the large number of comparatively trivial offences, particularly involving motor vehicles. All the BCSs show an inverse relationship between the seriousness and the frequency of incidents. This last finding, of course, gives some support for Hagan's use of the pyramid structure in considering varieties of deviance (figure 16.1).

In the BCS, violence is defined as the offences of wounding, common assault, robbery and snatch theft: robbery and snatch thefts are combined for the category of mugging. However, regrouping the offences to develop a typology of violence according to the relationship between offender(s) and victim shows how the most common type of violent crime is between people known to each other in some way: 43 per cent of all violence involves acquaintances (that is, where the victim knows the offender at least by sight), and a further 25 per cent involves people in a domestic relationship. In contrast, a fifth (20 per cent) of violence is committed by strangers and 12 per cent involves mugging. As figure 16.3 shows, six out of ten incidents of violence in 1997 were against men. Assaults by strangers were particularly likely to be aimed at men; over eight in ten were in 1997. However, women were the victims in seven out of ten domestic incidents. The danger from those known to the victim is clear enough, but the authors of BCS remind us that the survey probably underestimates these types of violence. Fights

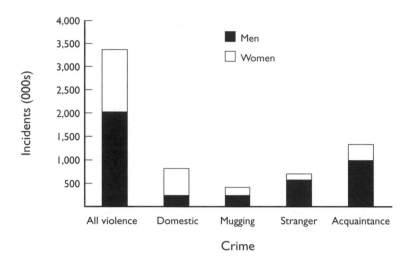

Figure 16.3 | BCS: number of violent crimes against men and women, 1997
Source: Mirrlees-Black et al. 1998. Crown copyright

between friends may be forgiven and even forgotten, while victims of domestic violence may be too fearful to report their experiences to interviewers.

In a fascinating manner, the material from the BCSs enables us to probe the dark figure of unreported and unrecorded crime. Of the crimes mentioned in the 1998 BCS, 44 per cent were said by their victims to have been reported to or become known to the police. Therefore, the majority of crimes are not reported to the police at all. However, reporting varies considerably by type of offence. As figure 16.4 shows, thefts of cars are reported most often: 97 per cent of such cases in 1997. Similarly, burglaries in which something was stolen were also usually reported (85 per cent). The necessity of reporting to the police in order to make an insurance claim will be an important factor. In contrast, theft from the person (35 per cent) and vandalism (26 per cent) were the least likely to be reported.

In fact, many of the offences reported to the police do not get recorded as crime. Just over half (54 per cent) of crime which was said to have been reported to the police was recorded by the police in 1997. Again, there are variations according to the type of offence, with thefts of vehicles most likely to be recorded. Apart from technical difficulties in matching the data which might explain some of the discrepancy between the number of *reported* crimes and the number *recorded*, police discretion is an important factor: perhaps the police do not accept the victims' accounts of incidents or there is simply insufficient evidence to say that a crime has been committed.

The gap between survey estimates of total crime committed and the figures of offences recorded by the police is an important one. Indeed, the value of the BCSs in covering both recorded and unrecorded crime is that one can have some idea of what an apparent rise in crime rates actually means. As the span of time increases since the first BCS, long-term trends can more easily be identified. In brief, do the police figures which the media tend to use in telling us about crime really reveal an accurate picture about

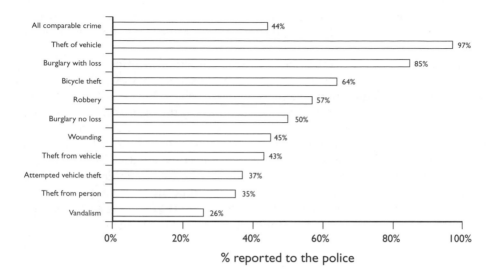

Figure 16.4 | BCS: proportion of offences reported to the police, 1997
Source: Mirrlees-Black et al. 1998. Crown copyright

criminal activity? To measure this one needs to consider the relationship between trends in reporting crime to the BCSs and police-recorded crime. Figure 16.5 helps to explain what has been happening since the early 1980s. The figures for 1981 are indexed at 100, so that rises and falls can be easily identified. Over the full period, the number of recorded crimes rose by 67 per cent; the number of reported crimes (as measured by BCS) rose by 92 per cent; and the total number of crimes identified by BCS, whether reported

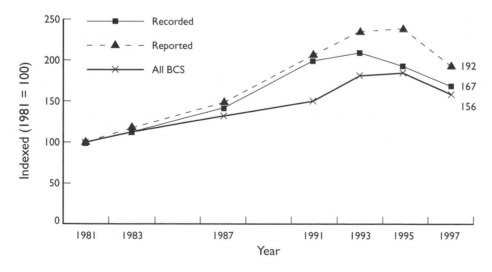

Figure 16.5 | Indexed trends in BCS and police-recorded crime, 1981–97
Source: Mirrlees-Black et al. 1998. Crown copyright

or not, by 56 per cent. So this illustrates that there are important differences between the three measures of crime. However, there were also some interesting shifts over the period.

During the 1980s, recorded crime rose more than the crime identified by the BCS; this seemed to be the result of people reporting more of the crimes they experienced, and the police perhaps recording more of the reports they received. Between 1991 and 1993, recorded crime stabilized, whereas the crime identified by the BCSs continued to rise, as did reported crime. This suggested that there had been a fall in the amount of reported crime which was actually recorded by the police. Between 1993 and 1995, recorded crime continued to fall, while reported crime and the crime identified by the BCS levelled off. However, between 1995 and 1997 there was a remarkable fall in all three measures. The police recorded a 12 per cent fall in crime and the comparable figures emerging from the BCS indicated a fall of 15 per cent. For the first time since the start of the BCSs in 1981, both measures are declining and so provide strong evidence that there really has been a recent fall in crime.

Risks and fears of crime

One aspect which has been of particular interest since the 1970s or so is the question of the fear of crime. Indeed, some commentators suggested in the 1980s that fear of crime in Britain was becoming as great a problem as crime itself. In an early statement of the issue, Hough and Mayhew (1983) tend to question the appropriateness of the fear of crime, suggesting that this in turn can lead to a downward spiral:

> Increasingly it is being said that fear of crime in Britain is becoming as great a problem as crime itself. Criminologists suggest that preoccupation with crime is out of all proportion to the risks; that fear is needlessly reducing the quality of people's lives; and that fear of crime can itself lead to crime – by turning cities at night into empty, forbidding, places. (p. 22)

Certainly it is an issue which provokes controversy, for fear of crime can reduce the quality of people's lives. The crucial question, of course, is whether fear of crime is needless or not. Is the fear of crime commensurate with the risks for people in their communities? This was a matter of some controversy in the 1980s but perhaps there has been more agreement about this in the 1990s.

The problem was that the risks of experiencing most crime seemed comparatively low when one considered the national figures. This led to the view being espoused that many people worried unnecessarily about crime and that fear about crime could be confronted simply by telling people that the actual risks of being attacked were really quite low. So, for instance, the first BCS suggested that 'the "average" citizen would suffer a robbery once every five centuries; burglary once every 40 years; and assault resulting in injury (even slight) once every century' (J. Young 1991, p. 103). Hence, for the 'average' citizen it certainly seemed irrational to get seriously worried about most crime. However, this was challenged on at least two grounds: first, that for some people the risks were much higher than the national figures were suggesting; second, if, say, old people stayed indoors believing that they might be mugged if they went out, the comparatively low figures of old people being mugged might simply reflect the fact that they tended to stay out of potential harm's way. Both of these points relate to the issue of 'unequal risks'.

Embracing a 'new realist' approach, Young and his colleagues at the Middlesex Centre for Criminology (Jones, Maclean and Young 1986; A. Crawford et al. 1990) argued that local surveys enable us to move beyond the abstraction of aggregate national statistics. They have identified that for people living in certain areas the fear of crime is not an empty one. As Young (1991) points out, 'crime is extremely geographically focused and policing varies widely between the suburbs and the inner city' (p.47). In combining these very different geographical areas to produce national figures, he suggests we distort what life is really like for those living in some parts of an inner city. In other words, Young's work began to challenge the notion of the irrational fear of crime. Young's point is that fears become highly rational for certain groups, particularly those living in certain city areas. So, for example, he suggests it may be unwise to ascribe irrationality to women regarding their fears of violence. Not only are crimes such as domestic violence often masked in official figures, but women also experience harassment on a level which is unknown to most men. Women simply do not know which of the minor incivilities, as Young terms the wide range of abuse, could escalate to more serious violence. Even burglary is feared, not only as a property crime, but as a possible precursor to sexual assault. As Young (1991) notes, 'if crime deteriorates the quality of life for men, it has a much more dramatic impact on the lives of women in the inner city' (p. 48). So Young argues powerfully that we should take seriously the public's fear of crime. In reality, for most adults, the biggest single area of risk of crime is with motor vehicles. However, fear is not simply about frequency. For example, being the victim of one vehicle crime a year is for many little more than a nuisance, while being raped once in a lifetime is a traumatic event that will never be forgotten. Young's point (1991) is that social surveys help us to differentiate the safety needs of different sectors of the community.

The BCS estimated that 34 per cent of adults in 1997 were victims of at least one of the crimes the BCS covers. This was a fall from 39 per cent in 1995. Those analysing the BCS now fully appreciate the issue of unequal risks and they focus on variations in risks for different groups, looking at three offence types: burglary, thefts involving vehicles, and violent crime. Certainly vulnerability to crime differs for different communities and individuals. Where people live, the financial resources they have, the structure of their households, and their own personal lifestyles are among the main factors shown to be associated with risk of victimization (Mirrlees-Black et al. 1998). The risk factors are interrelated. So, for example, high burglary risks are shown for younger households, single parents, the unemployed, and private renters; these may often be the same people. Curiously, those with few resources are at greater risk of burglary. Locality is also an important indicator of risk. While, on average, 5.6 per cent of households experienced at least one burglary (either attempted or successful) in 1997, figure 16.6 shows how the risk of burglary varies enormously for selected household types. If you are living in a young household (that is, where the head of household is aged 16–24) in an inner city, you are over eight times more likely to be burgled than if you are living in an older household (in which the head is aged 65 or older) in a rural area.

Nationally, 15.7 per cent of households owning vehicles in 1997 experienced at least one vehicle-related theft. As with burglary risks, vehicle-related theft varied considerably. However, although the risk patterns are similar to those for burglary, the differences are not quite so marked, as figure 16.7 shows.

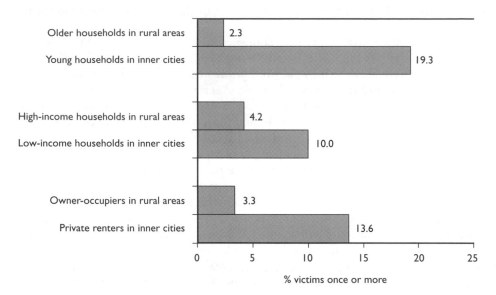

Young households are those in which the head of household is aged 16–24. Older households are those in which the head is aged 65 or older. Low-income households are those with an annual household income of less than £5,000. High-income households are those with a household income of £30,000 or more.

Figure 16.6 | Risks of burglary for selected household types, 1997
Source: Mirrlees-Black et al. 1998. Crown copyright

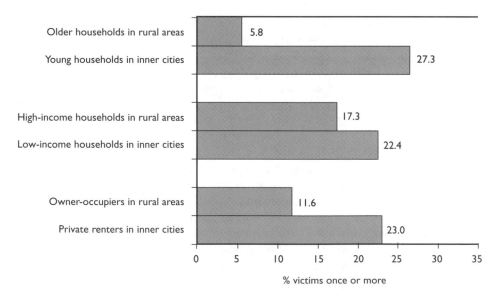

See notes to figure 16.6. Based on vehicle-owning households only

Figure 16.7 | Risks of vehicle-related thefts for selected household types, 1997
Source: Mirrlees-Black et al. 1998. Crown copyright

In terms of violent crime nationally, 4.7 per cent of adults in 1997 were victims once or more of some type of violence (wounding, common assault, robbery and snatch theft). There are reservations about the accuracy of the BCS in relation to all forms of violence. Nevertheless, the BCS provides some important clues about the risk of violence. This differs markedly among adults depending upon their personal characteristics, and those of the household to which they belong (see table 16.1). Those at higher risk were:

- young men and young women;
- single adults;
- one adult living alone with children (single parents);
- unemployed adults;
- adults in low-income households: under £5,000 a year;
- adults in accommodation rented privately or from a council or housing association;
- adults in flats or terraced property;
- adults who go out more often.

It is now recognized that the burden of crime falls on some sectors of the population more than others. Certainly the elderly do not actually experience as much crime as some other groups. In fact, taking violence as one example, young adult men experience the most. While young men aged 16–24 formed only 5 per cent of the BCS sample, they experienced 25 per cent of all incidents of violent crime. Similarly, young women also experience a larger proportion of all violence than would be expected given their number in the population.

While the 'facts' may now be much clearer, there is still much room for debate. The BCS, although now a technically impressive instrument, does not really help to explain *why* certain groups face a heightened risk or, indeed, why other groups have a much lower risk. Curiously, the increasing fear of crime, often encouraged by media 'scare stories', may have had an impact, which in turn may have changed some people's behaviour. In investigating the extent and sources of the fear of crime, earlier BCS findings indicated that women, the elderly and those in inner cities registered most anxiety about walking alone in their neighbourhood after dark. As mentioned earlier, many people may manage such fear by staying indoors after dark. Even being indoors may not provide much comfort for some. Burglary causes widespread anxiety, particularly among some women, but the concern may be more about the danger from burglary turning to rape. Having managed to cast those fears aside, perhaps a fear remains of domestic violence when a partner returns from his evening out.

While the main battles on the 'facts' of victimization may have been solved, unpacking the national averages for various types of crime simply means that some people may find out that they are at much less risk than they might have expected whilst others are at much greater risk than the 'average' figures suggest. Sadly, for some, whether indoors or out of doors, their chances of experiencing crime victimization are really quite high.

TABLE 16.1	Proportion of adult victims of violence, by personal characteristics, 1997 (percentages)

Category	Victims once or more	Category	Victims once or more
Men	6.1	Tenure	3.2
16–24	30.9	Owner-occupiers	3.2
25–44	7.0	Social renters	6.3
45–64	3.0	Private renters	9.4
65–74	0.2		
75+	1.0		
Women	3.6	Accommodation type	
16–24	8.8	Detached house	3.1
25–44	4.6	Semi-detached house	4.1
45–64	2.0	Mid-terrace	5.9
65–74	0.8	End terrace	6.3
75+	0.2	Flats/maisonettes	6.4
Living arrangements		Hours out average weekday	
Married	2.7	< 3 hours	2.0
Cohabiting	6.4	3–5 hours	3.6
Single	11.3	5 hours +	6.3
Separated	8.4		
Divorced	6.0		
Widowed	0.6		
Head of household under 60		Evenings out in last week	
Single adult and child(ren)	11.9	None	3.0
Adults and child(ren)	5.6	One	4.1
No children	6.0	Two/three	5.7
		Four/five	7.2
Employment status		Six/seven	12.8
In employment	5.6		
Unemployed	11.8	Evening pub/wine bar visits last month	
Economically inactive	5.9	None	2.9
		Less than three times a week	5.6
Household income		Three or more times	10.6
<£5k	6.6		
£5 to <£10k	2.9		
£10k to <£20k	4.1		
£20k to <£30k	4.7		
£30k		All adults	4.7

Source: Mirrlees-Black et al. 1998. Crown copyright

Hidden crime

It is crucial to remember that what criminologists and politicians pay attention to is not necessarily the most serious kinds of deviance. In the 1950s and 1960s, criminologists paid enormous attention to youth gangs, but this interest cannot be explained completely by the actual seriousness of gang delinquency and its extent relative to other kinds of criminal activity. In the 1970s, mugging and football hooliganism occupied a disproportionate amount of media attention. While it would be foolish to deny that these problems exist, they may not be so widespread or even so important as the media and the politicians tend to suggest. Indeed, there are other hazards for the community that do not figure in the criminal statistics but are potentially much more serious and widespread in their effects.

Indeed, environmental pollution, health and safety in factories and even unethical business practices may be much more crucial to the survival and well-being of the community than many of the issues highlighted by the media and the politicians. However, it is difficult to find such activities recorded in *Criminal Statistics*, and those who design victimization surveys usually fail to consider these kinds of problems. More importantly, though – and this illustrates the most serious drawback of victimization surveys – what happens if people are not even aware that they are victims? For example, environmental pollution may be affecting everyone, but if no one notices, then there can be no record. To do something about deviance, one must know that it exists.

There are increasing challenges to the commonly accepted notion that the job of the criminal law is to protect *all* the members of society. Questions about who makes the law and who really benefits from it have led to the view that, in fact, the criminal law does not serve the interests of the majority in society, but only appears to do so. It is suggested that the criminal law is virtually dictated by small and powerful groups in society and, as a result, serves the interests of these groups and works against the interests of larger but much less powerful ones. Certainly, much of the activity of large, powerful organizations, such as companies and corporations, is potentially very dangerous, but it is often not covered by the harsh rigours of the criminal law. We need to recognize the ability of transnational corporations to shape new legislation relating to their corporate activities. This clearly enables corporations to prevent some of the avoidable deaths, injuries and economic deprivation they sometimes cause from being included in the criminal law and, as a consequence, in crime statistics. In this sense, then, crime statistics and victimization surveys provide evidence of the extent of only a particular kind of deviance and not necessarily the most dangerous and destructive behaviour.

Summary

1   Official crime statistics may indicate more about the work of the organizations producing the figures than about the actual occurrence of crime and deviance.
2   Surveys of crime victimization show an inverse relationship between the severity and the frequency of incidents of crime. The vast majority of crimes do not involve violence against the person but are offences against property.

3   There is a varying ratio of reported and unreported crime (the 'dark figure'). The BCSs indicate that thefts of cars are reported most often, as well as most burglaries. Theft from the person and vandalism are the least likely to be reported.

4   The occurrence of offences against women – domestic violence, indecent assault and rape – is very difficult to estimate accurately.

5   Those who are most fearful of crime are the least victimized. Part of the explanation is that fear leads many people to avoid risky situations and, thereby, to minimize their chances of becoming victims. However, for those living in certain areas, fear of crime reflects its likely incidence.

6   Official statistics and victimization surveys provide evidence of only particular kinds of deviance. Other, particularly corporate, activity that is potentially dangerous may not be covered by the harsh rigours of the criminal law.

16.4   The criminal justice system

Since the 1970s, there has been a new interest in the societal response to acts and persons labelled deviant. There is a wide range of agencies involved in formal social control, from the police, judiciary and prison service to other agencies less obviously part of the control framework, namely social workers and the medical profession. The focus has largely been on the decision-making activities of agencies of social control. There has been increasing concern about structurally generated injustices, reflected in class prejudice, racism and sexism. Questions have been raised about the assumed prejudice of decision-makers, and there has been an increasing recognition – though not always by government – of the limited access of socially disadvantaged persons to resources for their protection.

It is important, first of all, to identify a typical sequence of agency responses to deviance, starting with initial detection and going through to the final outcome. An important contribution of sociologists has been to indicate the processes by which social control itself can play a considerable part in transforming a 'normal' person into a 'deviant'. The process has not significantly changed over the years, and Box (1981) usefully summarizes much of the work that identifies the bureaucratic and social processes through which an individual becomes officially registered as deviant.

Figure 16.8 identifies the major stages in becoming deviant as well as – and most importantly – routes out of deviance. Sociologists have become known for suggesting that social control may well lead to further deviance, although it would be foolish to think this was an inevitable process. Nevertheless, the crucial point remains that as each cycle of offence–detection–punishment–stigmatization is completed (follow the thick black line in figure 16.8) the chances of the next cycle are increased.

In fact, the process of becoming an official deviant is rarely completed. The bureaucratic and social process shown as figure 16.8 is more like a hurdle race than a flat race, with many potential offenders falling at each hurdle before the process is complete. As table 16.2 demonstrates, it is just a minority of crimes which result in a conviction or even a caution. Of all offences, under one half (46 per cent) are reported to the police, 23 per cent are actually recorded by the police, 5 per cent are cleared up, and only 3 per cent finally result in a caution or a conviction.

While few crimes have an outcome in terms of a caution or a conviction, the public

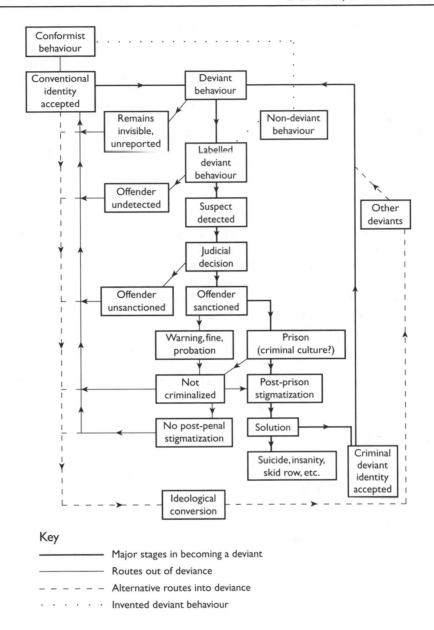

Figure 16.8 | The bureaucratic and social process of becoming an official deviant
Source: Box 1981, p. 21

expenditure on the criminal justice system is enormous. As table 16.3 shows, the major part is spent on the police.

In terms of criminal deviance the two most important gatekeepers are the police and the judiciary. In the Western world, there has been much work on the police as

TABLE 16.2 | **Crimes committed: by outcome, England and Wales, 1995 (percentages)**[a]

Crime	Reported	Recorded	Cleared up	Resulting in caution or conviction
Domestic burglary	66	37	9	2
Wounding	39	20	15	12
Vandalism	29	13	3	3
All offences	46	23	5	3

[a] As a percentage of offences committed
Source: *Social Trends* 1998, p. 156

guardians of 'public morality', particularly on what happens during the 'on-the-street' encounters with suspects or suspicious persons. In fact, it is when the police officer is in the community that his or her discretion is widest. Backing up the police as guardians of moral boundaries are judges and magistrates, who have similar scope for considerable discretion, although their actions are more public and open to review than those of the police officer 'on the beat'. In brief, the concern is that the personal, social or political sympathies of social control agents may influence the type of action taken or even whether any action is taken at all; is justice fair and equal for all? Box's particular concern was that *'when processing individuals who have behaved similarly,* the judicial system will discriminate against some, particularly the poor, the unemployed, and the ethnically oppressed' (1981, p. 180). Little has happened since he wrote that observation to suggest that much has changed, except that we should widen our concern to consider women as well.

The overall issue is whether the legal system behaves differently towards some groups compared with others. So, for example, Eaton (1986) focused on women and magistrates' courts, but her work has relevance for the criminal justice system as a whole. Her basic question concerned the equality of men and women before the court. She concludes 'by recognizing that *within its own terms* Hillbury Court treats men and women equally, i.e. they receive similar sentences when they appear in similar circumstances' (p. 97). However, her main point is that men and women rarely appear in similar circumstances, and so 'formal equality within the strictly defined area of the court does not affect the substantial inequality of women and men who appear before the court' (p. 97). She argues that men and women are socialized, educated and employed to act and react in different ways, stressing that these differences are most forcefully expressed within the family. Eaton makes a strong case that by upholding the dominant model of the family 'the court is contributing to the cultural reproduction of society and, thereby, to the continued subordination of women.' Hence, pointing to the familial ideology which underpins summary justice, she maintains that women are not equal to men in court, since the court is operating from a perspective which defines women as different and subordinate.

Eaton's argument about gender inequality remains important, for perhaps it is not simply about equality of sentencing. In fact, women going before the courts are less likely than men to receive a prison sentence for the same offence. The findings are based on other factors being equal, like the seriousness of the crime and any previous convic-

| TABLE 16.3 | Public expenditure on the criminal justice system, England and Wales, 1988–9 to 1996–7 (£ million at 1996–7 prices)[a] |

	1988–9	1990–1	1992–3	1993–4	1995–6	1996–7
Police	5,397	5,876	6,464	6,625	6,817	6,782
Prisons	1,454	1,777	1,776	1,615	1,704	1,695
Lord Chancellor's Department[b]	–	646	780	767	765	1,003
Probation	353	402	468	515	465	462
Magistrates' courts	389	367	393	439	428	321
Crown Prosecuiton Service	218	258	304	303	304	288

[a] Adjusted to 1996–7 prices using the GDP market prices deflator adjusted to remove the distortion caused by the abolition of domestic rates
[b] Criminal work only: in 1996–7 includes areas that have not been previously accounted for such as the Duty Solicitors' Scheme
Source: Social Trends 1998, p. 169

tions, but not the personal circumstances of the offender. This study was essentially examining whether policy had changed since the 1991 Criminal Justice Act, which laid down basic rules for the use of jail sentences, community service and fines. The research considered sentencing in 3,000 cases at magistrates' courts and 1,800 cases at crown courts in 1994–5.

Similarly, there is now much more information about the experience of ethnic minorities in the criminal justice system. Interestingly, the study just mentioned also found no evidence that black and Asian offenders were more likely to be sent to jail than their white counterparts, assuming other circumstances were the same. However, there is no doubt that there are concerns about the treatment of minority ethnic groups which go beyond sentencing.

The special focus on ethnic minority risks in some of the BCSs has been helpful. So, for example, Mayhew et al. (1989) consider whether Afro-Caribbeans and Asians are disproportionately victims of crime. This study also inquires whether there is a racial element in the offences they experience. Certainly the evidence is that both Afro-Caribbeans and Asians tend to be more at risk than whites for many types of crime. Most importantly, Mayhew et al. (1989) stress that this finding is largely explained by social and demographic factors, particularly the areas in which Afro-Caribbeans and Asians live. Nevertheless, even after taking account of these factors, ethnic minorities are probably more vulnerable to crime than whites. Asians in particular are at greater risk from vandalism and robbery or theft from the person. Furthermore, ethnic minorities, particularly Asians, see many offences against them as being racially motivated. In fact, Asians seem rather more vulnerable to victimization by groups of strangers, and to rather more serious offences. Certainly people from ethnic minority groups tend to worry much more about crime than white people, as table 16.4 indicates. A much higher percentage in each ethnic group were 'very worried' by each type of crime. The heightened concern is not unrealistic, as victimization studies indicate.

Moving on to the reaction of social control agents, some pioneering studies (e.g. D. J. Smith and Gray 1983) have shown for some time that young black men are much more likely to be apprehended by the police than their white counterparts. Recent evidence

TABLE 16.4 | **Fear of crime:[a] by type of crime and ethnic group, England and Wales, 1996 (percentages)**

Crime	White	Black	Indian	Pakistani/ Bangladeshi
Rape[b]	31	43	51	49
Theft from car[c]	24	42	40	40
Burglary	21	40	47	44
Theft of car[c]	20	35	35	33
Mugging	18	32	40	38
Racially motivated attacks	7	27	35	38

[a] Percentage of people aged 16 and over in each ethnic group who were very worried about each type of crime
[b] Females only
[c] Percentage of car owners
Source: Social Trends 1998, p. 161

suggests that in some areas black people are nearly eight times more likely to be stopped and searched by police than white people (*Guardian*, 27 July 1998). The overall recorded rate of stop and search in England and Wales is 17 per 1,000 of the population. However, the rate varies widely among police forces, with the ethnic variation of particular concern. Four forces stop more than 100 black people per 1,000 population: Merseyside (189), the Metropolitan police (141), Cleveland (135) and Dyfed Powys (158). In Surrey and Merseyside the rate for black people is at least seven times higher than for white people. At the other end of the scale, only two police forces, Cumbria and Northumberland (out of the 43 forces in England and Wales), stop and search more white people proportionately than people from ethnic minorities.

Other evidence also suggests somewhat different treatment, in so far as black male offenders reach the courts at an earlier stage in their criminal careers (McConville and Baldwin 1982; Crow 1987) and are likely to receive longer custodial sentences than their white counterparts (NACRO 1989; Crow 1987). While black people are overrepresented in the criminal statistics, they continue to be underrepresented in the criminal justice system: 'although they make up 5.2 per cent of the population they represent only 1 per cent of police officers and less than 1 per cent of prison officers' (*Guardian*, 16 November 1992). Holdaway's (1996) work has explored reasons for this. There can be both direct and indirect discrimination. Holdaway quotes an example of institutional discrimination where for many years the English police had a height requirement which excluded many Asian recruits. While it applied to all applicants, Asians, who tend to be smaller, were unfairly disadvantaged, as indeed were women.

While pointing to the contribution of 'black criminology', Rice (1990) powerfully reminds us of the neglect of black women in these studies. She stresses that 'concern about the high rates of arrest of black people on the streets does not extend to black women who are harassed by the police on suspicion of soliciting' (p. 58). She notes that black women make up over 20 per cent of the female prison population, but only 5 per cent of all women. (Overall the proportion of black prisoners rose from 12.6 per cent in 1985 to 16 per cent in 1992.) There is nothing new in this phenomenon of discrimination in the bureaucratic procedures in the processing of crime. In short, the poor, the unemployed and ethnic minorities always get a bad deal, whether one is focusing on the last decade of the twentieth century or indeed any other time or place.

Summary

1 Social control can play a considerable part in transforming a normal person into a deviant.
2 It is just a minority of crimes which result in a conviction or even a caution.
3 In terms of criminal deviance, the two most important gatekeepers are the police and the judiciary.
4 The crucial issue is whether the legal system behaves differently towards some groups compared with others. The evidence is mixed, but the powerless tend to get a bad deal.

16.5 The police

In the sense that deviance can only be understood as a political process, then, of course, any form of policing becomes political. The notion that the police may be serving a political function rather than occupying an independent role between conflicting groups has been the focus of considerable public debate since 1980 or so. Much of the interest in the police started when people considered the policing of areas, such as Brixton and Toxteth, which experienced the rioting on the streets in 1981 that led to the Scarman Report (1981). The controversial policing of industrial disputes and strikes, particularly the miners' strike of 1984–5, raised similar issues. It became evident that no longer could the government of the day expect us to accept without question the idea that the police are necessarily acting for the general welfare of the community. Certainly, the police have been, quite literally, in the middle of disputes between various sections of the community in ways not previously experienced in post-war Britain. Furthermore, because of the presence of television in virtually every home, these encounters between police and protesters have been witnessed by a much wider audience than ever before. In some situations, the police have been accused of simply being the agents of the government, helping to impose a particular industrial and economic strategy upon the nation. Such accusations have deeply concerned some members of the police force, who do not regard their task as helping to carry out the political will of the government in this way. There is quite widespread concern that the police have increasingly been drawn into the political arena.

Two major issues continue to underpin debates on changing police behaviour: the growth of professionalism within the police; and whether there has been a shift from consensus policing (that is, policing by consent) to something much more akin to para-military policing. Even more dramatically, some commentators have been asking whether Britain is turning into a police state. A contemporary development in the police, which raises the spectre of 'Big Brother', is the use of computerized information systems in processing crime and of surveillance technology, such as closed circuit television (CCTV), in trying to catch criminals. One study (Ackroyd et al. 1992) has shown how the introduction of technology involving computerized information systems has difficulties, limitations, dangers and, before cynicism entirely takes over, some important gains. There seems little doubt that policing is an increasingly difficult job both to define and to do.

In recent years there have been quite dramatic changes in the nature of policing. The police, like the prison service, is a disciplined force similar in structure to the military. Holdaway (1983) was among the first to note how the traditional militaristic style of command in the police has changed to one of 'management'. More specifically, he identified the emergence of 'managerial professionalism'. While discipline in the force has remained paramount, it is now maintained more by persuasion, consultation and encouragement than by enforcing blind obedience to authoritative commands. However, despite the changes, the continuing dominance of the occupational values of the lower ranks is evident. The 'cop culture' survived the various changes associated with the introduction of professional policing. In brief, the old views and practices of the rank-and-file police officers still persist, and these attitudes contribute to a concern about the harassment of the public, or at least sections of it (particularly the black community). The failure of the police to deal appropriately with the murder of the young black youth Stephen Lawrence led to a major inquiry, which revealed serious shortcomings in police procedures and practice.

The emergence of 'managerial professionalism' within the police has been accompanied by a concern about the growth of police powers. However, in considering this possible growth, there is an important distinction between an increase in police resources on the one hand, and a strengthening of their legal powers on the other. There has been a substantial increase in police personnel levels. Indeed, 'law and order' was one of the few areas in the public sector where expenditure increased quite significantly from the time of the Conservatives taking office in 1979. So while in 1961 there was only one police officer for every 602 people in Britain, by 1982 this had increased to one per 394. However, it is important to recognize that the ratio of the resident population to police officers varies quite considerably throughout England and Wales. The Suffolk police force area had the greatest number of people per police officer in 1997 with 557, while the Metropolitan Police force area had about half this number, with 281 (*Social Trends* 1998). Certainly, as table 16.3 showed, there has been a significant increase in resources for the police over the past decade, but by the 1990s government support for significant expansion seemed to be over, and financial stringencies have increasingly been the focus in recent years.

Whether the legal powers of the police have been extended is a much more contentious issue. One of the main planks of the Conservative government's law-and-order policy in the 1980s was the 1984 Police and Criminal Evidence Act. As a result of this Act, sweeping reforms of police powers and practices, coupled with a new code of rights for citizens, came into force. The changes provoked criticism from all sides. Civil libertarians saw the legislation essentially as a strengthening of police powers (such as those to stop and search, arrest, enter, search and seize), with only illusory safeguards for suspects. The police, for their part, feared that their investigations were being increasingly hampered by the need to adhere to detailed codes of practice (such as the first statutory scheme of rules for detention and questioning in police stations). So, in theory at least, the extension of police powers is hemmed in by wide-ranging safeguards.

A focus of the Conservative government's law-and-order policy in the 1990s was the

Plate 16.2 | CCTV cameras watch people in public space
Source: Nick Abercrombie

1994 Criminal Justice and Public Order Act. Certainly, in theory at least, such legislation has strengthened the legal position of the police when operating in certain contexts. However, a recent Home Office report has suggested that this Act has made little difference to police practice (*Guardian,* 8 December 1998). There are at least two reasons for this. First, one can perhaps overstate the growth of police powers by understating their previous powers. In other words, the police have always had quite strong powers if they had wished to use them. Second, and more importantly, changing legislation will not overnight change cultural attitudes. So the police may be reluctant to use their new-found powers while, if they do, the rest of the criminal justice system, such as the magistracy, may be unwilling to punish as punitively as the legislators might have expected or, indeed, wished. Hence, protesters, for instance, may be fined rather than imprisoned.

The 1990s were a difficult decade for the police. There have been widely publicized accounts of quashed convictions and triumphant appeals – the Darvell brothers, Judith Ward, Stefan Kiszko, the Guildford Four, the Birmingham Six and the McGuire Seven. The tactics of the now disbanded West Midlands Serious Crime Squad produced widespread concern.

In the 1990s there was a noticeable shift in the public presentation of the police and in the recognition of possible causes of crime. So, for example, Sir Peter Imbert, retiring commissioner of the Metropolitan Police, signalled a volte-face in the willingness to identify some link in crime growth to inner-city deprivation, saying 'society ignores at its peril the importance of the deprived and disadvantaged underclass in the growth of crime', and going on to say that 'in the years to come, the idea of better service delivery would have more impact on policing than rigid enforcement' *(The Times*, 30 July 1992). Further, the chief inspector of police for England and Wales, Sir John Woodcock, was reported as acknowledging that officers were 'economical with the truth' as a matter of course and that the service was 'shot through with corner cutting and expediency' but that 'the police showed a willingness to admit fault and to change' (*Guardian,* 14 October 1992). While it would be unwise to suggest that a few well-chosen public words by senior policemen represent a fundamental change of direction, they do perhaps indicate that the dangers of some of the excesses of the past couple of decades have been recognized and that the challenge to the credibility of the police service is a serious one.

This all results in a curious paradox. It seems indisputable that there has been a growth in police powers since 1980 or so, but there has been increasing concern that the police cannot afford to come under fundamental criticism from the public as to the way they approach their task of policing. At a time when there is more scope, in theory at least, for paramilitary policing, there is perhaps an increasing recognition that consensus policing is what most of the British public actually want.

Summary

1 Since the late 1980s, the police have shifted quite dramatically from having a low profile in society to being a high-profile occupation.
2 The two major issues concerning the police are the growth of professionalism

within the force and the shift from consensus policing (that is, policing by consent) to something more akin to military policing.

3   While there has been a growth in police powers which could encourage paramilitary policing, consensus policing is what most of the public want.

16.6   Prisons and punishment

There are many, varied relationships between forms of punishment and the society within which they are exercised. Methods of punishment are historically specific, different ones being employed under different economic, social and indeed religious conditions. Changes in these conditions make it possible, desirable and in some cases even necessary to abandon certain methods of punishment in favour of others. In trying to identify differences between the new Labour government of 1997 and the nearly two decades of Conservative rule preceding it, one can recognize a definite shift of emphasis, although some of the measures which the parliamentary Labour Party challenged in opposition, such as the privatization of prisons, seem to have been embraced in government. Nevertheless, while certainly not rejecting a penology based on retribution and deterrence, the new Labour government is much more willing also to focus on rehabilitation and reform.

The Labour government had some familiar problems to face, such as overcrowded and many outdated prisons, but also some new concerns which had been getting media attention in the 1990s, namely mentally disordered offenders being released back into the community, and sex offenders continuing to be potential threats to children. Both these concerns relate to the broader issue of 'care in the community' (see chapter 14 for further discussion of this issue). 'Care in the community' is not a new concept in the area of crime. Indeed, the idea of probation in the community began its development in the late nineteenth century, with the move to full-time officials dealing with offenders in the community being introduced in the 1907 Probation of Offenders Act. However, the increased focus on dealing with deviants of various kinds in the community rather than in institutions has brought both a new set of problems and a new slant on some old ones.

Since the 1970s, there has been much focus on the possibilities of decarceration and deinstitutionalization. Thorpe et al. (1980) note that the term 'decarceration' is really shorthand for a state-sponsored policy of closing down asylums, prisons and reformatories and replacing them with 'a range of facilities which will enable [delinquents] to be supported in the community'. Thorpe et al. focus on delinquents, but discussion about decarceration also encompasses areas of mental health (questioning the use of psychiatric hospitals), gerontology (old people's homes), and so on. In the 1980s there was largely a bipartisan approach in Parliament, with both major parties accepting the overall approach of either closing down psychiatric institutions or trying to reduce the prison population. The various community control schemes for criminals can easily be presented as enlightened reforms, for few would deny that schemes that enable criminals to be dealt with in the community rather than being sent into custody should be applauded. However, the situation is rather more complex than it at first appears. In fact, most of the discussion about decarceration programmes stems from the United States of America, which still has one of the highest rates of imprisonment in the world. Similarly, in Britain there has also been much talk of deinstitutionalization programmes, which are more enthusiastically embraced by governments as they recognize that they may be a cheaper as well as a more effective alternative. So, for example, the average cost of holding someone in custody for a month is £2,000, compared with £89 for a probation order and £76 for a community service order *(The Times,* 2 November 1992). Nevertheless, with 150 prisoners per 100,000 population, Great Britain has the third highest prisoner rate in the European Union (EU) after Portugal and Spain, as figure 16.9 shows.

Although the time-honoured tradition of 'slopping-out' (that is, emptying overnight human waste into recesses) had largely been phased out by the early 1990s, prison conditions in Britain were being increasingly criticized. A devastating indictment was made in the report of the Council of Europe Committee for the Prevention of Torture and Inhuman or Degrading Treatment, in what was probably the most embarrassing critique so far of the deficiencies of some of our largest Victorian jails. Its inspectors said that conditions at Leeds, Brixton and Wandsworth prisons violated basic human rights by subjecting inmates to a pernicious combination of overcrowding, bad hygiene and inactivity. While the early 1990s witnessed the biggest prison building programme since the start of the twentieth century, few of the old prisons were being closed down. The contradictions were evident, for the Criminal Justice Act which came into force in 1992 was based on the principle that prison was of highly dubious value, both to the particular offender and to the interests of wider society; but prison continued to be used widely, despite efforts by the then Conservative government to encourage a distinction between imposing long sentences for serious offenders and for the 'dangerous', and imposing

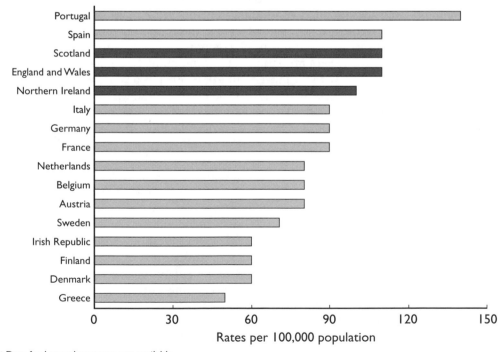

ᵃ Data for Luxembourg are not available

Figure 16.9 | Prison population: EU comparison,ᵃ 1996
Source: Social Trends 1998, p. 166

more community sentences and less prison for the less serious offenders, particularly those who commit several minor offences.

A dramatic change of governmental policy came with the appointment of Michael Howard as home secretary. Howard – at a time of rising national crime rates – espoused a supposedly populist philosophy that 'prison works'. Hence, after a decade of a decreasing proportion of convicted prisoners being sentenced to prison, figure 16.10 shows the sudden rise in sentenced prisoners.

In 1996 there were 83,000 receptions under sentence into Prison Service establishments in England and Wales. While this figure was 7 per cent lower than in the previous year, close examination of figure 16.10 shows that this was due to a sharp fall in the number of defaulters, as receptions of both adult and young offenders increased over this period. A rejection of the 'prison works' philosophy by the new Labour government of 1997 will almost certainly mean that the rise in the prison population will not continue to the same extent. Nevertheless, the plans to increase prison capacity by opening seven new prisons between July 1997 and June 2000 (the first of these, HMP *Parc* at Bridgend, opened in November 1997) can still be justified on the basis that some prisons need replacing. There is often a confusion about the numbers in prison. The above figures relate to those entering as sentenced prisoners during each year, but in addition there are also those who are on remand in prison awaiting trial. These latter are a source of concern when their time in custody as unconvicted prisoners becomes unreasonable. Another way of calculating the prisoner population is to consider the number in prison at any one time: in 1996 there were 61,000 people in Prison Service establishments, some 8 per cent more than in the previous year.

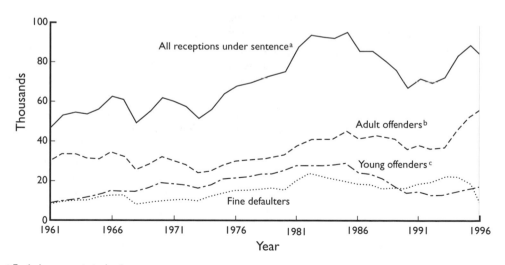

[a] Excludes non-criminal prisoners
[b] Includes approved places: excludes fine defaulters
[c] Excludes fine defaulters

Figure 16.10 | Receptions under sentence[a] into Prison Service establishments, England and Wales, 1961–96
Source: Social Trends 1998, p. 165

It would be tempting to equate the rise in the prison population with the recent fall in crime (see section 16.3). However, the relationship between imprisonment and crime levels is not a straightforward one, and probably more important was the deteriorating economic situation in the mid-1990s.

Mentally disordered offenders

Since the late 1980s, the risk that some mentally disturbed people represent to the wider community has come to be recognized as a major public policy issue. Certainly a series of cases, highlighted by the media, has cast doubt on the ability of the notion of care in the community to provide adequate protection to the public. The best-known is probably the case of Christopher Clunis, who murdered Jonathan Zito in an unprovoked attack at a London Underground station. The subsequent inquiry (Ritchie 1994) identified a catalogue of errors, with the failure to communicate or share information as a particular problem. Other tragic cases, followed by similar reports, highlighted a gap between the criminal justice and mental health systems which seems to leave the public at risk. It is of little comfort to point out that such cases, involving serious crimes of violence against members of the public, are comparatively rare, and the splash in the media when such cases occur provides counter-evidence which quite understandably worries the public.

A thoughtful report by the National Association for the Care and Resettlement of Offenders' (NACRO's) Mental Health Advisory Committee (NACRO 1998) both encapsulates the issues and provides some important guidance. In fact, assessing risk is not a precise science and the search for technical solutions – such as detailed assessment tools – is hazardous. We should not have unrealistic expectations of those who are asked to make such assessments. Furthermore, protecting the public is only one side of the coin, and the rights and interests – the civil liberties – of mentally disturbed people (the vast majority of whom will never be dangerous) is the other side which needs to be recognized. A balance has to be achieved between these two rather different kinds of demand. Nevertheless, in terms of the safety of the public, the NACRO report points to two key elements in the recent failures in the system. First, the problems presented by the minority of potentially violent or dangerous patients were not adequately recognized when present mental health policies were being developed in the 1970s, leaving local services ill-equipped to deal with them, and access to specialist forensic support severely limited. Second, these problem cases reflect the wider context of mental health services never having been allocated adequate resources to meet either the general needs of their patients, or the special problems presented by the high-risk group. Indeed, there is some evidence that the level of resources for mental health services has actually fallen.

There is a general problem relating to the needs of mentally disturbed patients, but there is specific concern about offenders with severe personality disorders (often termed psychopaths) who do not meet the criteria for detention under mental health legislation. The NACRO report (1998) proposes a new jurisdiction outside the existing criminal and mental health legislation to deal with such persons. It is suggested that such new arrangements should include a positive approach to the management of the offenders concerned, focusing on education and rehabilitation. However, a drawback to such proposals is that psychopaths do not seem to respond to treatment. There are no easy solutions. However, as the government has declared its commitment to carrying through a programme of reform to deliver safe and comprehensive mental health services (Department of Health Press Release 98/315, 29 July 1998), this is a topic which will be a focus of debate in the next few years.

Sex offenders

Each decade seems to have a moral panic or concern about sexual offending. In Britain, rising concern about the visibility of prostitution and several scandals brought organized prostitution to public attention in the 1950s; the move towards partial decriminalization of homosexuality was the focus of the 1960s; the new wave of the women's movement took rape as a major issue in the 1970s; and the main moral panic of the 1980s was about child sexual abuse within the family. In the early 1990s, the multiple murders of young women associated with Fred and Rosemary West in Gloucestershire seemed to proclaim the start of a new era of serial sex killing, but a focus on the issue of the monitoring of sexual offenders in the community had a spectacular rise in the market of public concerns, and a remarkably quick response in terms of legislation coming onto the statute book. A registration scheme for sexual offenders, embodied in the Sex Offenders Act 1997 as well as other legislation, demonstrated that action was taking place. Some of the provisions made are quite measured, but there is also the issue as to whether the focus has been used to feed a political agenda of the law-and-order lobby. What started as a concern about the safety of children quickly became a more generalized concern about sex offending. In fact, there is a considerable range of sex offending and there are dangers in considering sex offenders as a homogeneous group. Identifying the serious risks is difficult, but still needs to be done. However, believing in the containment of sex crime by increased control over convicted sex offenders may be illusory. A concentrated focus on known offenders – many of whom may genuinely want to break free from the criminal justice system – may distract our attention dangerously away from the fact that serious perils also come from persons who have never been apprehended for a sexual offence.

Community control

There is little doubt that there are currently confusions and tensions about punishment and the control of deviants. After a period of deinstitutionalization and decarceration, followed by a brief period in the 1990s when the notion that 'prison works' was embraced by the then Conservative government, there is now a period of consolidation taking place, when there are at least attempts to separate the best and worst parts of the various control systems. Certainly no one wants the risks which arise from having deviants in the community, while few would want a widespread return to the era when institutions – whether they be called prisons or hospitals – were the main focus of containment. However, balancing the various demands is no easy task.

In setting up community controls, some fear that there is no liberalization in the new methods but, rather, a deepening and increasing repression of dissent and difference. As imprisonment is no less used, perhaps it is simply that a wider framework of formal social control is being developed. Of course, one explanation of the massive increase in the number of people controlled by the criminal justice system is that this is simply a response to increased crime. Let us consider these developments in a more systematic way.

In some pioneering work S. Cohen (1985) has been influential in exposing some of the illusions of the community control movement. He notes that in some respects de-carceration has not been taking place particularly rapidly. However, he is not surprised that the establishment of various supposed alternatives to incarceration does not necessarily decrease imprisonment rates, or necessarily have beneficial effects on the rest of the system. He argues that there is so much investment in the 'delinquency business' that some see crime and delinquency as having a definite function: delinquents keep the courts busy and provide legal aid work for lawyers; the crime problem helps to justify the employment of more police; and delinquency management generates an expanding range of penal and social responses, drawing in more and more agencies and providing a range of services and intervention right across the delinquent and criminal career spectrum. In short, there is an enormous vested interest in the continuation of the crime and delinquency business. This concern is further heightened by the increasing intrusion of the private sector into the 'crime business' with an imperative to make profits from crime.

S. Cohen (1985) and others have argued that when new and extensive forms of intervention do result, they may actually be quite hard to distinguish from the old institutions and may produce in the community the very practices they were designed to replace. Cohen expands on the various problems of community control, and we will mention two aspects as examples here – what he calls blurring and widening.

- *Blurring*. This refers to the increasing invisibility of the boundaries of the social control apparatus. Prisons – segregated and insulated from the community – made the boundaries of control obvious enough. In today's world of community control, such boundaries are no longer as clear. As half-way houses, rehabilitation centres and cheap lodgings are usually only available in the more run-down areas of town, so certain inner-city areas, patrolled more visibly by the police and controlled less visibly by other agents of social control, will increasingly have the characteristics of an open prison. There is, we are sometimes told, a 'correctional continuum' or a 'correctional spectrum'. The danger from the civil liberties standpoint is that the same treatment is sometimes used for those who have actually committed an offence and those who are thought to be 'at risk' of committing one. Certain legal niceties about the difference between guilt and innocence are, therefore, sometimes blurred. As we focus more on risk, this danger is certainly heightened.
- *Widening*. On the surface, one of the ideological thrusts behind the new movements towards 'community' and 'alternatives' was that the state should do less, rather than more. In some respects – with the greater intervention of the private sector – it may seem that the state is doing less, but this is only a mask to what is actually happening. In fact, it is ironic that among the major results of the new network of social control has been an increase, rather than a decrease, both in the amount of intervention directed at many groups of offenders and in the total number of offenders who get into the system in the first place.

In other words the 'alternatives' are not alternatives at all, but new programmes that supplement the existing system or expand that system by attracting new populations. The net of social control is thus widened. Hence, there is concern that recent legislation (e.g. trade union laws and laws restricting the owners of dangerous dogs) increases the numbers and kinds of criminal deviant in our midst.

While S. Cohen (1985) points to some of the dangers in the new movement, he also stresses that to be aware of these dangers is not to defend the old system. Undoubtedly, some programmes of community treatment or diversion are genuine alternatives; they are more humane and less intrusive. However, this should not allow us to obscure what social control is all about. For Cohen, what is more striking is the continuities with the system that established state control of crime in Britain two centuries ago. Certainly, the move to community entails more subtle calibrations of care, control, welfare, punishment and treatment. New categories and subcategories of deviant are being created before our very eyes. Cohen concludes that 'community' only exists for middle-class, white, healthy, middle-aged, socially powerful males. The rest have all been classified by them as various kinds of deviant who are only fit to live in ghettos which are patrolled as open prisons in the community. Sadly, the lyrics from the Tom Robinson Band's song 'Power in the Darkness', which headed this chapter, begin to have an authentic ring about them.

Summary

1   Methods of punishment are historically specific, different ones being employed under different economic, social and indeed religious conditions.
2   In the 1990s there was a sudden rise in the number of sentenced prisoners following a change in government policy.
3   A balance needs to be achieved between freedom and control for mentally disordered offenders.
4   In the 1990s there was a particular focus on the dangers of sex offenders in the community.
5   With the increase in community controls and the continued high use of imprisonment, a wider framework of formal social control is being developed.
6   Two problems of community control are identified by S. Cohen (1985) as the blurring and the widening of boundaries.

Related topics

Further information on the relations between ethnic minorities and law enforcement agencies can be found in section 8.5, where there is also more material on differential exposure to risk of being a victim of crime. Other aspects of policing are referred to in section 13.4. Women's exposure to male violence is discussed in section 7.7.

Further reading

There are many books in this area but Maguire, Morgan and Reiner (1997) is the most authoritative text. Croall (1998) is a good, comprehensive introduction to the study of crime in Britain. The work of the late Steven Box remains impressive. Box (1981) provides an excellent overview of the theoretical issues on deviance and is particularly helpful in discussing the social construction of official statistics. His two later books (1983, 1987) focus on topics which remain important contemporary issues. Another good background book is Heidensohn (1989), while Bottomley and Pease (1986) provide a useful account of the criminal justice system.

Cross-references to *Readings in Contemporary British Society*

Virdee on racial harassment; **Hetherington** on travellers and Stonehenge; **Thompson** on moral panics, deviance and the mass media; **Worrall** on juvenile delinquency and crime, punishment and the criminal justice system.

Glossary

Cross-references to other terms in this glossary appear in **bold type**.

absolute poverty the state in which people do not have the minimum level of income deemed necessary for living in a civilized way. Different societies will have different conceptions of this necessary minimum. *Compare* **relative poverty**.

absolute social mobility the total amount of movement of persons between classes during a specified period of time (normally within one or between two generations). *Compare* **relative social mobility**.

agenda setting the process whereby the mass media, especially television, radio and the press, determine what are important, newsworthy stories and what are not.

assimilation the process by which immigrant groups are absorbed into the host society.

associations the looser forms of social organization, such as voluntary organizations, friendship networks or religious institutions, that lie between the formal organization of employment and the immediate family.

bimodal distribution when the distribution of values of a variable is formed into two clusters. For example, if deaths from a disease largely affected the young or the old but not the middle-aged, those deaths would be bimodally distributed.

blue-collar a term referring to typical work clothing which was used to characterize manual occupations and to contrast them with non-manual (*see* **white-collar**) occupations, and which was considered a feature of the cultural differences between **working** and **middle classes**.

bunde social groups which have very powerful loyalties and are tightly organized but unstable. Examples are travellers and some religious cults.

bureaucracy a form of social organization which manifests a high degree of division of labour and specialization, formal rules, hierarchical structure of authority, and impersonal relationships between organizational members and clients.

capitalism a system of economic production, with distinctive institutions and **social relations**, which emerged in the West in the sixteenth century and which has continued to develop and extend its range since. As a system capitalism is characterized by private ownership of productive property, profit-making as a driving force, commodified transactions (*see* **commodification**), the reward of workers through wages and the use of **markets** as the principal mode of co-ordinating economic activity.

capitalist accumulation the process whereby the owners of the **means of production** use profits to build up a stock of capital which is then reinvested, with the consequence that owners increase their wealth and firms increase in size.

civil society that area of **social relations** that lies between the immediate family on the one hand and the institutions of employment and the state on the other.

class alignment used in studies of voting behaviour to describe the tendency of people belonging to the same class to vote for the same political party. *See also* **dealignment**.

class conflict the (variable) tendency for overt expression of antagonism between different social classes.

class differentials the different and unequal distribution of economic and social resources between classes.

class formation the process whereby underlying similarities in economic and social resources cause aggregates of people to see themselves as members of a class, sometimes thereafter to form the basis of collective organization and political mobilization.

class relations the abstract and concrete relationships that connect one class to another.

class solidarity a condition (variable in its degree) wherein people belonging to a particular social class perceive themselves to have similar interests and therefore feel sympathy and/or act jointly with other members of the same class.

class structure the architecture or pattern of **class relations** in a society, describing how classes, which may be differentiated horizontally or hierarchically, stand in relation to one another.

class struggles a term of Marxist origin which describes processes of conscious and organized antagonism between classes.

closed shop the situation where a condition of being employed in a particular job in a firm is membership of a specified trade union.

cohort study an investigation of a group of people who share a particular experience at a certain moment of time. For example, in studying the attitudes of university students, one might investigate first-year students in sociology, who form a cohort.

commodification the process by which goods and services acquire a monetary value and are capable of being bought and sold.

commodities goods and services that are produced in order to be bought and sold.

communist an individual, party, state or ideology professing the desirability of an alternative to capitalist (*see* **capitalism**) economic arrangements, emphasizing the disadvantages of private property ownership and the virtues of a more egalitarian distribution of resources.

community most usually, a collection of people within a geographical area; more loosely, a group of people who have characteristics in common.

concentration of ownership a process whereby a higher and higher proportion of sales becomes concentrated in fewer and fewer companies, and small independent firms account for a declining activity.

consumer society a kind of society in which there is an abundance of goods and services, which are increasingly used as components for **lifestyles**.

consumption patterns in a **consumer society**, the way different social groups acquire different goods and services manifesting different tastes and incomes.

corporate economy one dominated by the activities of large corporations.

counter-urbanization a process of migration away from cities towards their peripheries or to the country.

credentialism the tendency within modern societies to allocate people to occupational positions by means of the educational qualifications that they acquire.

crude death rate the number of deaths per 1,000 living members of the population per year. *See* **mortality**.

cults relatively small groups tightly bound together and organized around some kind of religious belief, though outside the main religious organizations.

cultural imperialism the imposition of its culture by one nation on others. The term is most usually used of the United States, whose mass media industries, it is claimed, are effectively forcing American values on other countries.

cultural turn a move within sociology from the 1980s onwards emphasizing the importance of cultural forms in everyday life and thereby downplaying the role of economic or political factors.

culture of dependency the way in which people who receive state benefits become dependent on them and are therefore less inclined to look for work. It is not at all clear that such a culture exists.

dealignment a term used in voting studies to describe the declining probability of members of particular groups (especially classes) voting for a particular party. *See also* **class alignment**.

decarceration the process of taking people out of institutions such as prisons or mental hospitals.

deindustrialization the process identified by a decline in the proportion of workers involved in manufacturing industry (**secondary sector**) and an expansion of employment in service industries.

deinstitutionalization when people spend a great deal of time in institutions such as retirement homes or prisons it is claimed that they become institutionalized – passive and dependent. Deinstitutionalization refers to attempts to reverse this process. *See* **institutionalization**.

delayering reducing the number of levels in an organization, especially by eliminating intermediate positions in a hierarchy.

depersonalization of ownership the tendency whereby the proportion of shares held by individuals declines and large financial institutions, like pension and insurance companies, increase their holdings.

deskilling the reduction in the level of skill required of an individual worker, an occupation or the workforce as a whole, usually associated with changes in technology or the reorganization of working practices.

deviant behaviour behaviour that offends against social **norms** or values.

direct discrimination the open prevention of members of minority groups from gaining access to jobs, education or housing which are available to the rest of the population. *Compare* **indirect discrimination**.

discourse an ordered and structured use of language which organizes the way in which people see their world.

discrimination the process whereby members of social groups are disadvantaged by comparison with the rest of the population. Such discrimination can be **direct** and open or **indirect** and even unconscious.

disposable income that income left to people to spend after income taxes and national insurance payments have been deducted *Compare* **gross**, **original** and **post-tax incomes**.

division of labour the way in which work, of all types, is distributed between organizations and people.

domestic labour unpaid work performed within the household, for family or household members.

double shift the condition of women who both engage in paid work and have principal and extensive responsibility for **domestic labour** within the household.

downsizing a policy of reducing the number of workers in a given organization, especially by transferring some activities to subcontractors or other independent small organizations.

downward social mobility movement down the class hierarchy. *Compare* **upward social mobility**.

dual labour market a conceptualization of the **labour market** which identifies a sharp difference between a primary market of jobs which are comparatively well paid, secure and have career structures and a secondary market where jobs are impermanent, often part-time and lowly paid. It has the associated implication that certain categories of person, especially women and members of **ethnic minority** groups, tend to be concentrated in and restricted to the secondary market.

effort bargain an agreement, often tacit, regarding the level of wages paid by an employer in exchange for an accepted intensity of effort on the part of employees.

embourgeoisement thesis the argument prominent in the 1950s that greater affluence was leading to normative and cultural convergence between classes, with the **working class** adopting values and patterns of behaviour similar to those of the **middle class**.

entrepreneurial capitalist a type of capitalist (*see* **capitalism**) who has direct and immediate control over all aspects of business operations. *Compare* **executive**, **finance** and **rentier capitalists**.

environmentalist environmentalist approaches to health seek the causes of ill-health in the environment of the patient rather than in his or her biological constitution.

epidemiology the study of the incidence of disease in the population. For example, epidemiologists might seek to discover the differing incidence of cancer between men and women.

essentialism the view that there are invariant truths about the social world or that social phenomena are determined by an invariant core of properties. Essentialist theories are usually counterposed to those that stress the changeable quality of social phenomena. For example, essentialist theories of identity suggest that people have an invariant core of selfhood. Non-essentialist theories argue that identity changes in a way that depends on the social context.

ethnic groups   social groups distinguished by a common culture and a strong sense of a shared identity based on religion, language and history.

ethnic minority   an **ethnic group** which forms a minority of a population.

exchange-value   in Marxist social theory, the value of a **commodity** which is determined by the labour time needed to create it. The term is contrasted with **use-value**.

executive capitalist   a type of capitalist (*see* **capitalism**) who is involved exclusively in the strategic management of an enterprise but who does not have a controlling block of shares in it. *Compare* **entrepreneurial**, **finance** and **rentier capitalists**.

extended family   the wider network of relatives (e.g. grandparents, cousins, aunts) outside the immediate or **nuclear family**.

femininity   a set of distinctive culturally specific characteristics attributed to and prescribed for women. *Compare* **masculinity**.

finance capitalist   a company or individual working in the financial sector. More technically, in Marxist economic theory, finance **capitalism** is the most developed stage of capitalism, characterized by a high degree of concentration, centralization and **monopoly**.

flexibility   a concept trying to capture recent changes in the nature of economic production – applied variously to technology, products, **labour processes** and employment contracts – and claimed to be a key feature of the emerging post-Fordist (*see* **post-Fordism**) economy. It implies more adaptable machines, more varied products, more versatile workers and more performance-related contracts.

Fordism   a system of economic regulation, characterized by the production of mass manufactured foods, for mass consumption, so called because the Ford motor company furnished a prototype of the techniques of factory organization and marketing. The term is also used to describe modern industrial societies of the West in the period 1945–75.

fractions   usually used in the sense of class fractions to mean distinctive groupings within social classes, perhaps with particular occupational characteristics or positions in the **labour market**.

franchise   in the political context, persons enfranchised are those entitled to vote in elections, the categories of persons with such entitlement having changed over time; in the economic context, the arrangement whereby a company leases the right to sell particular branded products to other smaller, independent oganizations or individual tenants.

full employment   a goal of the **welfare state**, entailing the abolition of unemployment, such that the only persons wanting employment and without a job at any point in time would be those in the process of moving between positions, implying a level of unemployment around 2 per cent.

gatekeepers   people or organizations that regulate access, formally or informally, to information, resources or social position. News organizations, for example, are gatekeepers in that they control what news appears in public and what does not.

gender   the social distinction between males and females.

gender differentials   the different and unequal distribution of economic and social resources between men and women.

gendered subjects   individuals as produced by **discourse**.

gender roles   socially defined attributes and expectations associated with positions or situations which are different for men and women.

gender struggles   processes of conscious and organized conflict between men and women.

gentrification   the process by which houses in decaying and relatively poor areas of a city are bought by **middle-class** people, thus raising property values in the area.

glass ceiling   a barrier to prevent women rising to the highest positions in an organization as a result of informal exclusionary practices.

globalization   the process by which the world has been increasingly transformed into an integrated global system, with greater flows of money, goods, information and people between nation-states, which are becoming less independent of one another.

green belt an area of open countryside around a city in which building, except on a limited scale, is not permitted.

gross income the total amount of income from all sources before any deductions for income tax or national insurance. *Compare* **disposable**, **original** and **post-tax incomes**.

hidden curriculum social knowledge, behavioural traits and expectations inculcated in young people inexplicitly and indirectly by educational institutions, which serve to prepare students for their likely future roles in the **division of labour**, including their acceptance of the discipline of the workplace.

horizontal segregation the separation of women into different occupation groups from men. *Compare* **vertical segregation**.

household a single person, family or group in living accommodation.

human resource management a **managerial strategy** designed to obtain improved employee performance by altering employees' attitudes to work, increasing both their commitment to carrying out tasks effectively and their identification with firm and product.

ideal type a simplified and abstract model or conceptualization of a social phenomenon. For example, the ideal type of **bureaucracy** is a model which shows its internal workings but which does not occur in precisely that form in any real bureaucracy.

immiseration the progressive lowering of the standard of living of a social group over time. Karl Marx held that, as **capitalism** developed, the **working class** would get progressively poorer.

indirect discrimination the prevention of members of minority groups from gaining access to jobs, education or housing by means that are not direct or open but are concealed or the accidental product of some other behaviour. *Compare* **direct discrimination**.

industrial relations all aspects of relationships between employers and workers, including negotiation over contracts and conditions of employment, worker and employer organizations, and the forms and incidence of conflict; also, the specialized field of study of these matters.

institutionalization institutionalized people are those who have spent a great deal of time in institutions such as prisons, mental hospitals or retirement homes and have, as a result, become passive and dependent. *See* **deinstitutionalization**.

inter-generational social mobility movement from one class to another occurring between generations, measured by comparing the class positions of children with their parents'. *Compare* **intra-generational social mobility**; *see also* **social mobility**.

intermediate class a concept particularly associated with a version of J. H. Goldthorpe's model of the class structure, identifying persons who derive their livelihood from routine **white-collar** and technical occupations or from ownership of a small business. *Compare* **working** and **service classes**.

internal labour market a process occurring within some economic organizations where recruitment to more senior positions is from existing personnel at lower levels within the organization, thus offering promotion opportunities and a career structure for at least some of the labour force.

internationalization the way that social organizations originally confined to one country are spread to others. For example, many large media organizations are international in their ownership and operations.

intra-generational social mobility the movement of an individual between classes during his or her own lifetime. *Compare* **inter-generational social mobility**; *see also* **social mobility**.

labour market an abstract mechanism and institutional arrangement through which economic organizations requiring workers and persons seeking employment are linked together with a view to establishing mutually acceptable agreement to exchange wages for labour.

labour process the operational aspect of jobs, both the specific content of the work involved and the exercise of authority, which underlies relationships between employers, managers, supervisors and workers.

life course similar to **life-cycle** but without the connotation that its stages are fixed. Life course carries with it the implication that the stages through which a life passes are actually extremely varied from individual to individual.

life-cycle the passage of a person through critical life events such as birth, childhood, adolescence, mid-life, old age and death. The term does not refer to a purely biological notion of maturation but implies that the various stages are socially defined.

lifestyles patterns of **social relations**, the consumption of material goods, tastes and attitudes which form a whole way of life which can differentiate one social group from another.

managerial strategy a prescribed way of controlling or monitoring the performance of employees to ensure that work is completed in a sufficiently quick, reliable and effective manner to secure the economic objectives of the firm.

marital mobility the achievement of **social mobility** through marriage, most usually used to account for an aspect of the social mobility of women.

market a means by which buyers and sellers of goods and services are brought together so that exchanges can take place.

marketable wealth the value of the assets held by a person that can be sold. *Compare* **non-marketable wealth**.

market economy a form of economic organization in which there are well-developed means by which goods and services can be bought and sold, usually through the medium of money, and there are few, if any, controls exercised by the state on the free operation of those **markets**.

market relations the relationships that obtain between buyers and sellers in a **market**.

masculinity a set of distinctive, culturally specific characteristics attributed to and prescribed for men. *Compare* **femininity**.

means of production typically employed within Marxist social theory to mean the materials, tools and techniques employed in the production of goods.

meritocracy a society ruled by persons who merit their positions of power, usually interpreted as one where individuals with the most talent, best qualifications and greatest propensity for hard work, irrespective of family background, occupy the highest positions.

middle class a social class, whose precise composition and boundaries are disputed among sociologists, which is comprised of **non-manual** workers and/or whose members share some distinctive cultural and political traits. *Compare* **upper** and **working classes**.

monopoly the circumstance in which there is only one producer of a particular **commodity**, thus permitting premium pricing.

moral panic an anxious overreaction by politicians, the police, the judiciary, newspapers and television, and the general public to some perceived problem deemed to affect society as a whole. Recent examples are AIDS, BSE and the activities of travellers.

morbidity the incidence in the population of particular medical conditions.

mortality the death rate per 1,000 living members of the population. It can be expressed crudely for the population as a whole or for particular groups within the population, e.g. age or gender groups. *See* **crude death rate**.

multinational companies those which have establishments (offices, factories, branches) in more than one country.

nationalism a belief in the importance of the nation founded on the assumption that a population with common characteristics such as language, ethnicity and religion also constitutes a unified political entity.

news values the set of assumptions held by journalists about which events constitute news, and which do not, and about the manner in which those events should be treated.

non-manual occupational groups not required to undertake manual labour, including routine clerical, managerial and professional occupations.

non-marketable wealth the value of those assets held by a person that cannot be sold. The most common forms of non-marketable wealth are pension entitlements. *Compare* **marketable wealth**.

norms values or rules which act as guidelines for social action.

nuclear family the immediate family consisting of parents (or parent) and their dependent children. *Compare* **extended family**.

objective class position the location in the class structure to which an individual is allocated through one of the classificatory schemes devised by social scientists or the national statistical office. *Compare* **subjective class position**.

occupational closure a strategic manoeuvre by practitioners of an occupation to exercise control over recruitment to that occupation with a view to restricting the supply of labour and improving their own conditions of work, used especially in relation to the professions, in which a professional association controls entry qualifications.

occupational control the determination of the key features of an occupation, including levels of payment, recruitment and working practices, used mostly in the exploration of the capacity of professional practitioners to regulate their own conditions of employment.

occupational culture distinctive **norms** and practices, formal and informal, associated with particular occupational groups.

occupational group strategy procedures espoused by practitioners of an occupation to enhance their collective conditions of work and remuneration.

occupational structure the total number of types of occupation available at any given time, classified systematically in the light of the similarities and differences in their attributes.

original income the income accruing to an individual before any deductions for income tax or national insurance. *Compare* **disposable**, **gross** and **post-tax incomes**.

panel study a technique of sociological investigation that involves collecting data from the same group of people over a period of time and therefore several blocks of data collection.

partisan dealignment the process wherein **partisanship** becomes weaker, which involves the preferences and support by individuals for a particular political party becoming less constant.

partisanship sustained preference and support for a political party.

patriarchy the dominance of men over women.

petit bourgeois the characteristic traits and attitudes of a social class (the petite bourgeoisie) who own small businesses and have no (or very few) employees.

positional goods those associated with a particular status position or membership of a valued social group.

post-Fordism a description, contested, of the contemporary phase in the organization of the formal economy characterized by flexible technologies (*see* **flexibility**) and diverse and specialized products, requiring more autonomous and versatile workers whose remuneration is geared more to individual performance. *Compare* **Fordism**.

postmodern experience contemporary societies are said to embody a postmodern culture. There is a great deal of disagreement about its constituents, or even whether it exists, but the following are among those features claimed for it: a collapse of large-scale systems of belief, e.g. communism; a society that lives in images rather than reality; relativism – the absence of objective standards of truth; irony and self-awareness; a disrespect for traditional artistic boundaries, e.g. between high and popular culture; and an interest in the depthless or superficial.

post-tax income that income left to a person after deductions for income tax and national insurance. *Compare* **disposable**, **gross** and **original incomes**.

pressure groups organizations designed to bring pressure to bear on government to achieve specific objectives.

primary sector industries, like mining, agriculture and fishing, whose products are typically raw materials directly extracted from earth or sea. Compare **secondary** and **tertiary sectors**.

privatization the process whereby public assets, e.g. British Gas, are sold off to private investors; also, the way in which people are turning inwards to their immediate families, or even themselves, with a corresponding reduction in contacts with extended family members, friends or the community.

proletarian a person whose livelihood depends on wages paid in exchange for labour and who has no control over the labour process.

Protestant ethic a term introduced into sociology by Max Weber, referring to a collection of beliefs that emphasize hard work, thrift and independence. In the sixteenth century such beliefs were closely associated with an emerging Protestant religion in its opposition to Catholicism.

psephology the study of voting behaviour.

qualitative studies those sociological investigations that do not depend on precise measurement and quantification but rely instead on achieving in-depth and detailed understanding of particular social behaviour of a relatively few subjects. *Compare* **quantitative studies**.

quango an abbreviation of quasi-autonomous non-governmental organization, meaning an organization that is generally not for profit, is in receipt of public funds, but is partly independent of government control.

quantitative studies those sociological investigations that rely on precise measurement so the findings can be expressed in a numerical form. *Compare* **qualitative studies.**

racism actions or policies that are determined by beliefs about racial characteristics.

redistributive policies policies that are designed to alter or redistribute resources, usually from rich to poor.

regionalization a process whereby resources or political power are distributed to regions of a country rather than held centrally.

relative poverty a conception of poverty which argues that people are poor when they are very much worse off than other people in their society. The consequence of such an understanding is that, as living standards rise, the level at which people are said to be in poverty will also rise. *Compare* **absolute poverty.**

relative social mobility an estimation of the chance of **upward social mobility** of a member of one social class compared with someone from another class. The concept was devised to control for the steady growth of jobs at the top of the occupational structure, which inevitably increases the level of **absolute mobility** upwards for members of all subordinate classes. However, to the extent that individuals originating in the highest classes rarely experience **downward social mobility** they retain a capacity to protect their privileges, a fact which would be concealed if changes in the occupational structure were not considered. Hence, sociologists calculate *relative* chances of mobility.

rentier capitalist one who is not active in the control of business organizations but who has stakes in the ownership of several enterprises. *Compare* **entrepreneurial, executive** and **finance capitalists**.

restructuring adjustment and alteration to the structure of an institution, most usually referring to economic organizations and institutions.

risk society one in which political conflicts are defined by the perception of risks of various kinds which affect everyone in a society, e.g. global warming, environmental pollution and AIDS.

ruralist ideology a set of beliefs that emphasizes the virtues of living in the country and the importance of country values.

scapes the networks that connect together organizations, places and machines. Examples are the global transport system and the cables that carry computer information.

secondary sector manufacturing industries which transform raw materials into tangible goods. *Compare* **primary** and **tertiary sectors**.

self-actualization the process by which people are able to be active and take the initiative rather than wait for organizations to solve their problems.

self-perpetuating oligarchies small numbers of persons currently occupying positions of power in a particular sphere of social life, who also control access to those positions, and who recruit new members from among their own families, friends or associates.

service class a section of the **middle class** in professional and managerial occupations whose conditions of employment are comparatively advantageous in terms of high levels of autonomy at work and high salaries. Its members share some distinctive political and cultural traits, including typically being highly educated.

sink estates housing estates, managed by local authorities, to which the poorest groups among the population are allocated and where, consequently, a disproportionate amount of socially problematic behaviour is found.

social capital that network of personal relationships, contacts and personal support that people build up outside the immediate family. Elements of social capital therefore include participation in voluntary organizations or **community** projects, friendship networks, or membership of religious institutions or political parties.

social engineering the practice by governments or large organizations of trying to change social behaviour. For example, equal opportunities policies are sometimes described as social engineering.

social exclusion a term describing the way in which certain social groups are excluded from full participation in society. It has been most recently applied to the poor, who are not only materially deprived but also unable to play their part in the cultural, sporting, political and educational life of their society.

socialization the process whereby people learn skills, aptitudes, and conformity to the expectations, patterns of behaviour and culture of those around them.

social mobility the movement of persons from one class to another. *See also* **inter-generational** and **intra-generational social mobility**.

social movements various forms of collective action aimed at social reorganization. Social movements tend to be less tightly organized than, say, political parties.

social relations the patterned and structured relationships between individuals that persist over time.

social wage that contribution to household income which is provided by the state, whether in cash or in kind; a manifestation of policies for social welfare.

stratification the hierarchical ordering of individuals and groups with respect to their possession of valued resources (typically money, power or status).

subjective class position the location in the **class structure** which individuals consider, or report, themselves to occupy. *Compare* **objective class position.**

suburbanization the movement of population out of the inner city or the countryside into the suburbs.

symmetrical family an allegedly new family form in which partners are centred on the home, the **extended family** counts for less and the **nuclear family** for more, and there is greater sharing of domestic tasks between husband and wife.

Taylorism a doctrine, devised by F. W. Taylor, advocating an optimal way of organizing the **labour process** for maximum efficiency. It was one pillar of the Fordist (*see* **Fordism**) system of economic regulation.

tertiary sector tends to be a residual category grouping industries not clearly in either **primary** or **secondary sectors**; industries which deliver services rather than goods.

time-space compression in modern societies the world seems to be compressed, in that events appear to move at a greater pace while it takes ever less time to travel from one place to another. Time appears to speed up and space to shrink.

underclass a disputed concept implying that there is a class of the population with distinctive cultural traits who are dependent on state benefits and/or poorly paid and are therefore locked into disadvantaged circumstances.

unemployment the condition of lacking remunerated work, usually referring to adults of working age who would wish to be employed.

union density a measure of the membership of trade unions, calculated as the number currently enrolled as members as a proportion of all those employees potentially eligible to be members.

unskilled occupations requiring of potential employees no qualifications, training or experience.

upper class a superordinate social class whose power and privilege derive from ownership of property and control of key economic, social and political institutions. *Compare* **middle** and **working classes**.

upward social mobility movement between positions in the class structure which entails an improvement in condition. *Compare* **downward social mobility**.

use-value a term, central to Marxist economics, which designates the value of a good or service in terms of its practical usefulness, rather than by its price or **exchange-value**.

vertical segregation the concentration of men and women in different hierarchical levels within an occupation. Compare **horizontal segregation** *and see* **glass ceiling**.

wealth the total value of assets held by an individual.

welfare state a state that takes on responsibility for the welfare of its citizens, including providing for their health, education and basic income.

white-collar the aggregate of occupations not requiring manual labour (and its associated clothing conventions: *see* **blue-collar**), which, at least for most of the twentieth century, implied superior working conditions.

working class a social class, whose precise composition and boundaries are disputed among sociologists, which is comprised of manual (and sometimes routine **white-collar**) employees and/or whose members share distinctive cultural and political traits.

Bibliography

Abercrombie, N. (1996) *Television and Society*. Cambridge: Polity Press.

Abercrombie, N. and Longhurst, B. (1998) *Audiences: A Sociological Theory of Performance and Imagination*. London: Sage.

Abercrombie, N., Hill, S. R. and Turner, B. S. (2000) *Penguin Dictionary of Sociology*. Harmondsworth: Penguin.

Abercrombie, N., Baker, J., Brett, S. and Foster, J. (1970) Superstition and religion: the God of the gaps. *Sociological Yearbook of Religion in Britain*, 3: 93–129.

Acheson Report (1998), *Independent Inquiry into Inequalities in Health*. London: Stationery Office.

Acker, S. (1994), *Gendered Education*. Buckingham: Open University Press.

Ackroyd, S., Harper, R., Hughes, J. A., Shapiro, D. and Soothill, K. (1992) *New Technology and Practical Police Work*. Milton Keynes: Open University Press.

Adkins, L. (1995), *Gendered Work: Sexuality, Family and the Labour Market*. Buckingham: Open University Press.

Albrow, M. (1996) *The Global Age*. Cambridge: Polity Press.

Alcock, P. (1993) *Understanding Poverty*. Basingstoke: Macmillan.

Alcock, P. (1997) *Understanding Poverty*. 2nd edn. Basingstoke: Macmillan.

Allan, G. (1979) *A Sociology of Friendship and Kinship*. London: George Allen and Unwin.

Allan, G. (1989) *Friendship: Developing a Sociological Perspective*. Hemel Hempstead: Harvester Wheatsheaf.

Allan, G. and Crow, G. (1991) Privatization, home-centredness and leisure. *Leisure Studies*, 10: 19–32.

Allat, P. and Yeandle, S. (1992) *Youth Unemployment and the Family: Creating the Domestic Sphere*. London: Macmillan.

Al-Rasheed, M. (1996) The Other-Others: hidden Arabs? In Peach, C. (ed.), *Ethnicity in the 1991 Census. Vol. 2: The Ethnic Minority Populations of Great Britain*. London: OPCS.

Anderson, M. (1971) *Family Structure in Nineteenth Century Lancashire*. Cambridge: Cambridge University Press.

Anderson, S., Grove-Smith, C., Kinsey, R. and Wood, J. (1990) *The Edinburgh Crime Survey: First Report*. Edinburgh: Scottish Office.

Arber, S. and Ginn, J., eds (1995) *Connecting Gender and Ageing? A Sociological Approach*. Buckingham: Open University Press.

Arnot, M., David, M. and Weiher, G. (1996) *Educational Reforms and Gender Equality in Schools*. Manchester: Equal Opportunities Commission.

Atkinson, A., Gordon, J. and Harrison, J. (1986) *Trends in the Distribution of Wealth in Britain,*

1923–1981. STICERDTIDI discussion paper no. 7. London: London School of Economics.

Axtmann, R., ed. (1998) *Globalization and Europe*. London: Pinter.

Aye Maung, N. and Mirrlees-Black, C. (1994) *Racially Motivated Crime: A British Crime Survey Analysis*. Home Office Research and Planning Unit Paper 82. London: Home Office.

Backett, K. (1987) The negotiation of fatherhood. In Lewis, C. and O'Brien, M. (eds), *Reassessing Fatherhood*. London: Sage.

Baker, D., Gamble, A. and Ludlam, S. (1992) Response: the social background of British MPs. *Sociology*, 26(4): 695–8.

Ball, S. J. (1981) *Beachside Comprehensive: A Case Study of Secondary Schooling*. Cambridge: Cambridge University Press.

Ballard, R. (1996) The Pakistanis: stability and introspection. In Peach, C. (ed.), *Ethnicity in the 1991 Census. Vol. 2: The Ethnic Minority Populations of Great Britain*. London: OPCS.

Banks, J. and Banks, O. (1964) *Feminism and Family Planning in Victorian England*. Liverpool: Liverpool University Press.

Banks, M., Bates, I., Breakwell, G., Bynner, J., Ember, N., Jamieson, L. and Roberts, K. (1992) *Careers and Identities*. Buckingham: Open University Press.

Banks, O. (1955) *Parity and Prestige in English Secondary Education*. London: Routledge and Kegan Paul.

Barber, M. (1996) *The Learning Game*. London: Victor Gollancz.

Barker, E. (1989) *New Religious Movements*. London: HMSO.

Barrett, F. (1989) *The Independent Guide to Real Holidays Abroad*. London: *Independent*.

Barwise, P. and Ehrenberg, A. (1988) *Television and its Audience*. London: Sage.

Bauman, Z. (1990) *Thinking Sociologically*. Oxford: Blackwell.

Bean, P. T. and Wilkinson, C. K. (1988) Drug taking, crime and the illicit supply system. *British Journal of Addiction*, 83: 533–9.

Bechhofer, F. and Elliott, B. (1968) An approach to a study of small shopkeepers and the class structure. *European Journal of Sociology*, 9: 2.

Beck, U. (1992) *Risk Society: Towards a New Modernity*. London: Sage.

Beckford, J. (1985) *Cult Controversies*. London: Tavistock.

Bell, D. (1973) *The Coming of Post-Industrial Society*. New York: Basic Books.

Berger, P. (1968) *The Social Reality of Religion*. London: Faber and Faber.

Berle, A. A. and Means, G. C. (1932) *The Modern Corporation and Private Property*. New York: Macmillan.

Bernades, J. (1997) *Family Studies*. London: Routledge.

Berrington, A. (1996) Marriage patterns and inter-ethnic unions. In Coleman, D. and Salt, J. (eds), *Ethnicity in the 1991 Census. Vol. 1: Demographic Characteristics of the Ethnic Minority Populations*. London: OPCS.

Berthoud, R. (1997) Income and standards of living. In Modood, T., Berthoud, R., Lakey, J., Nazroo, J., Smith, P., Virdee, S. and Beishon, S. (eds), *Ethnic Minorities in Britain: Diversity and Disadvantage*. London: Policy Studies Institute.

Beveridge, W. (1942) *Social Insurance and Allied Services*. Cmd 6404. London: HMSO.

Beynon, H., Hudson, R. and Sadler, D. (1986) *The Growth and Internationalisation of Teesside's Chemical Industry*. Working Paper no. 3. Durham: Middlesbrough Locality Study.

Billam, A. (1995) Reading newspapers. Unpublished research, University of Lancaster.

Billig, M. (1995) *Banal Nationalism*. London: Sage.

Black Report (1980) *Inequalities in Health: Report of a Research Working Group*. London: DHSS.

Blackburn, R. and Mann, M. (1979) *The Working Class in the Labour Market*. London: Macmillan.

Blackman, S. (1995) *Youth: Positions and Oppositions*. Aldershot: Avebury.

Blau, P. and Duncan, O. (1967) *The American Occupational Structure*. New York: Wiley.

Blaxter, M. (1990) *Health and Lifestyles*. London: Routledge.

Bosanquet, N. (1994) Improving health. In Jowell, R., Curtice, J., Brook, L. and Ahrendt, D. (eds), *British Social Attitudes: 11th Report*. Aldershot: Dartmouth.

Bottomley, S. K. and Pease, K. (1986) *Crime and Punishment: Interpreting the Data*. Milton

Keynes: Open University Press.

Bowe, R., Ball, S. and Gold, A. (1992) *Reforming Education and Changing Schools*. London: Routledge.

Bowles, S. and Gintis, H. (1976) *Schooling in Capitalist America*. London: Routledge.

Box, S. (1981) *Deviance, Reality and Society*. 2nd edn. London: Holt, Rinehart and Winston.

Box, S. (1983) *Power, Crime and Mystification*. London: Tavistock.

Box, S. (1987) *Recession, Crime and Punishment*. London: Macmillan.

Boyd, D. (1973) *Elites and their Education*. Slough: NFER.

Bradshaw, J. and Holmes, H. (1989) *Living on the Edge: A Study of the Living Standards of Families on Benefit in Tyne and Wear*. Newcastle upon Tyne: Child Poverty Action Group.

Bradshaw, J. and Millar, J. (1991) *Lone Parent Families in the UK*. DSS Research Report 6. London: HMSO.

Braverman, H. (1974) *Labor and Monopoly Capital: The Degradation of Work in the Twentieth Century*. New York: Monthly Review Press.

Brierley, P. (1991) *'Christian' England*. London: MARC Europe.

Brierley, P. and Wraight, H. (1995) *UK Christian Handbook 1996/7*. London: Christian Research.

Brown, P. (1987) *Schooling Ordinary Kids*. London: Tavistock.

Brunner, E. (1945) *Holiday Making and the Holiday Trades*. Oxford: Oxford University Press.

Brymin, M. and Sanders, D. (1997) Party identification, political preferences and material conditions: evidence from the BHPS, 1991–2. *Party Politics*, 3: 53–77.

Buck, N., Gershuny, J., Rose, D. and Scott, J. (1994) *Changing Households: The British Household Panel Survey 1990–1992*. University of Essex: ESRC Research Centre on Micro-Social Change.

Buckingham, D. (1987) *Public Secrets: EastEnders and its Audience*. London: British Film Institute.

Buckingham, D. (1993) *Children Talking Television*. London: Falmer Press.

Bulmer, M. (1996) The ethnic group question in the 1991 Census of population. In Coleman, D. and Salt, J. (eds), *Ethnicity in the 1991 Census. Vol. 1: Demographic Characteristics of the Ethnic Minority Populations*. London: OPCS.

Burchall, B. (1994) The effects of labour market position, job insecurity, and unemployment on psychological health. In Gallie, D., Marsh, C. and Vogler, C. (eds), *Social Change and the Experience of Unemployment*. Oxford: Oxford University Press.

Burrows, R. (1991) A socio-economic anatomy of the British petty bourgeoisie: a multivariate analysis. In Burrows, R. (ed.), *Deciphering the Enterprise Culture: Entrepreneurship, Petty Capitalism and the Restructuring of Britain*. London: Routledge.

Butler, D. and Kavanagh, D. (1998) *The British General Election of 1997*. London: Macmillan.

Butler, T. (1995) Gentrification and the new urban middle classes in Butler, T. and Savage, M. (1995).

Butler, T. and Savage, M., eds (1995) *Social Change and the Middle Classes*. London: UCL Press.

Callender, C. (1992) Redundancy, unemployment and poverty. In Millar, J. and Glendinning, C. (eds), *Women and Poverty in Britain in the 1990s*. London: Harvester Wheatsheaf.

Carrier, J. and Kendall, I. (1998) *Health and the National Health Service*. London: Athlone Press.

Carroll, J. A. (1998) Reflexive accounts – the lives of retired professional women. Unpublished PhD thesis, Lancaster University.

Castells, M. (1997) *The Power of Identity*. Oxford: Blackwell.

Central Statistical Office (1998) *Social Focus on Women*. London: HMSO.

Chaney, D. (1996) *Lifestyles*. London: Routledge and Kegan Paul.

Charles, N. (1990) Women and class – a problematic relationship. *Sociological Review*, 38: 43–89.

Clarke, I. M. (1982) The changing international division of labour within ICI. In Taylor, M. and Thrift, N. (eds), *The Geography of Multinationals: Studies in the Spatial Development and Economic Consequences of Multinational Corporations*. London: Croom Helm.

Clarke, R. (1993) Trends in concentration in UK manufacturing. In Casson, M. and Creedy, J.

(eds), *Industrial Concentration and Economic Inequality*. Aldershot: Edward Elgar.

Cloke, P., Phillips, M. and Thrift, N. (1995) The new middle class and the social constructs of rural living. In Butcher, T. and Savage, M. (eds), *Social Change and the Middle Classes*, London: UCL Press.

Clough, R. C. (1996) Homes for heroines and heroes? Inaugural lecture, Lancaster University.

Clough, R. (1998) *Living in Someone Else's Home*. London: Counsel and Care.

Cockburn, C. (1983) *Brothers: Male Dominance and Technological Change*. London: Pluto Press.

Cohen, R., Coxell, J., Craig, G. and Sadiq-Sangster, A. (1992) *Hardship Britain*. London: Child Poverty Action Group.

Cohen, S. (1972/80) *Folk Devils and Moral Panics: The Creation of the Mods and Rockers*. London: MacGibbon and Kee. New edn with introduction (1980), Oxford: Martin Robertson.

Cohen, S. (1985) *Visions of Social Control*. Cambridge: Polity Press.

Cohen, S. (1991) *Rock Culture in Liverpool: Popular Music in the Making*. Oxford: Oxford University Press.

Coleman, D. and Salt, J. (1996a) The ethnic group question in the 1991 Census: a new landmark in British social statistics. In Coleman, D. and Salt, J. (eds), *Ethnicity in the 1991 Census. Vol. 1: Demographic Characteristics of the Ethnic Minority Populations*. London: OPCS.

Coleman, D. and Salt, J., eds (1996b) *Ethnicity in the 1991 Census. Vol. 1: Demographic Characteristics of the Ethnic Minority Populations*. London: OPCS.

Collett, P. and Lamb, R. (1985) Watching people watching television. Unpublished report to the IBA.

Compston, H. (1997) The European Union. In Compston, H. (ed.), *The New Politics of Unemployment*. London: Routledge.

Connolly, P. (1995) Boys will be boys? Racism, sexuality and the construction of masculine identities among infant boys. In Holland, J., Blair, M. and Sheldon, S. (eds), *Debates and Issues in Feminist Research and Pedagogy*. Clevedon: Multi-Lingual Matters.

Cooke, A. (1994) *The Economics of Leisure and Sport*. London: Routledge.

Crawford, A., Jones, T., Woodhouse, T. and Young, J. (1990) *The Second Islington Crime Survey*. London: University of Middlesex, Centre for Criminology.

Crawford, R. (1998) You are dangerous to your health: the ideology and politics of victim blaming. In Mackay, L., Soothill, K. and Melia, K. (eds), *Classic Texts in Health Care*. Oxford: Butterworth-Heinemann.

Crewe, I., Day, N. and Fox, A. (1991) *The British Electorate, 1963–1987: A Compendium of Data from the British Election Studies*. Cambridge: Cambridge University Press.

Critcher, C., Bramham, P. and Tomlinson, A., eds (1995) *Sociology of Leisure: A Reader*. London: E. and F. N. Spon.

Croall, H. (1998) *Crime and Society in Britain*. London: Longman.

Crompton, R. (1993) *Class and Stratification*. Cambridge: Polity Press.

Crompton, R. (1995) Women's employment and the 'middle class'. In Butler, T. and Savage, M. (eds), *Social Change and the Middle Classes*. London: UCL Press.

Crompton, R. (1996) *Women and Work in Modern Britain*. Oxford: Oxford University Press.

Crompton, R. and Jones, G. (1984) *White-Collar Proletariat: Deskilling and Gender in Clerical Work*. London: Macmillan/Philadelphia: Temple University Press.

Crompton, R. and Sanderson, K. (1990) *Gendered Jobs and Social Change*. London: Routledge.

Crow, I. (1987) Black people and criminal justice in the UK. *Howard Journal of Criminal Justice*, 26(4): 303–14.

Cully, M. and Woodland, S. (1998) Trade union membership and recognition 1996–97: an analysis of data from the Certification Officer and the Labour Force Survey. *Labour Market Trends*, July: 353–64.

Cultural Trends (1993) 18. London: Policy Studies Institute.

Cultural Trends (1995a) 25. London: Policy Studies Institute.

Cultural Trends (1995b) 26. London: Policy Studies Institute.

Cumberbatch, G., McGregor, R. and Brown, J. with Morrison, D. (1986) *Television and the*

Miners' Strike. London: Broadcasting Research Unit.

Currie, R., Gilbert, A. and Horsley, L. (1977) *Churches and Churchgoers: Patterns of Church Growth in the British Isles since 1700*. Oxford: Oxford University Press.

Curtice, J. and Steed, M. (1998) The results analysed: appendix II. In Butler, D. and Kavanagh, D. (eds), *The British General Election of 1997*. London: Macmillan.

Dale, R. (1997) The state and the governance of education. In Halsey, A. H., Lauder, H., Brown, P. and Stuart Wells, A. (eds), *Education: Culture, Economy and Society*. Oxford: Oxford University Press.

Daley, P. (1996) Black-African: students who stayed. In Peach, C. (ed.), *Ethnicity in the 1991 Census. Vol. 2: The Ethnic Minority Populations of Great Britain*. London: OPCS.

Daniel, W. (1990) *The Unemployed Flow*. London: Policy Studies Institute.

David, M., West, A. and Ribbens, J. (1994) *Mother's Intuition? Choosing Secondary Schools*. London: Falmer.

Davie, G. (1994) *Religion in Britain since 1945: Believing without Belonging*. Oxford: Blackwell.

Davies, J. (1998) Labour disputes in 1997. *Labour Market Trends*, June: 299–311.

Dawtrey, L., Holland, J. and Hamner, M. with Sheldon, S., eds (1995) *Equality and Inequality in Education Policy*. Buckingham: Open University Press.

Deacon, A. (1998) Employment. In Alcock, P., Erskine, A. and May, M. (eds), *The Student's Companion to Social Policy*. Oxford: Blackwell.

Dearlove, J. and Saunders, P. (1991) *Introduction to British Politics: Analysing a Capitalist Democracy*. 2nd edn. Cambridge: Polity Press.

Deem, R. (1986) *All Work and No Plan: The Sociology of Women and Leisure*. Milton Keynes: Open University Press.

Deem, R. (1994) School governing bodies – public concerns or private interests? In Scott, D. (ed.), *Accountability and Control in Educational Settings*. London: Cassell.

Deem, R. (1996) Women, the city and holidays. *Leisure Studies*, 15(2): 1–15.

Deem, R. and Gilroy, S. (1998) Physical activity, life-long learning and empowerment – situating sport in women's leisure. *Sport, Education and Society*, 3(1): 89–104.

Deem, R., Brehony, K. J. and Heath, S. (1995) *Active Citizenship and the Governing of Schools*. Buckingham: Open University Press.

Denver, D. (1994) *Elections and Voting Behaviour in Britain*. 2nd edn. Hemel Hempstead: Harvester Wheatsheaf.

Denver, D. (1998) The government that could do no right. In King, A., Denver, D., McLean, I., Norris, P., Norton, P., Sanders, D. and Seyd, P. *New Labour Triumphs: Britain at the Polls*. Chatham, NJ: Chatham House Publishers.

Devine, F. (1989) Privatized families and their homes. In Allan, G. and Crow, G. (eds), *Home and Family: Creating the Domestic Sphere*. London: Macmillan.

Devine, F. (1992) *Affluent Workers Revisited: Privatism and the Working Class*. Edinburgh: Edinburgh University Press.

Devine, F. (1997) *Social Class in America and Britain*. Edinburgh: Edinburgh University Press.

DFEE (Department for Education and Employment) (1995) *Education and Training Statistics for the UK 1995*. London: HMSO.

DFEE (Department for Education and Employment) (1997) *Education and Training Statistics for the UK 1997*. London: HMSO.

DFEE (Department for Education and Employment) (1998) *Education and Training Statistics for the UK 1998*. London: HMSO.

DHSS (Department of Health and Social Security)(1984) *The Health Service in England: Annual Report*. London: HMSO.

Dicken, P. (1998) *Global Shift*. 3rd edn. London: Paul Chapman.

DOH (Department of Health) (1992) *The Health of the Nation*. Cm 1523. London: HMSO.

DOH (Department of Health) (1998) *Our Healthier Nation: a Contract for Health*. London: Stationery Office.

Driver, S. and Martell, L. (1998) *New Labour. Politics after Thatcherism*. Cambridge: Polity Press.

DSS (Department of Social Security) (1998a) Facts and figures. http://www.dss.gov.uk/hq/facts/

mainframe.htm

DSS (Department of Social Security) (1998b) *Households Below Average Income Statistics*. Published press release. London: Department of Social Security.

Dunleavy, P. and O'Leary, B. (1987) *Theories of the State: The Politics of Liberal Democracy*. London: Macmillan.

Dunning, E., Murphy, P. and Williams, J. (1988) *The Roots of Football Hooliganism: An Historical and Sociological Study*. London: Routledge.

Eaton, M. (1986) *Justice for Women? Family, Court and Social Control*. Milton Keynes: Open University Press.

Edgell, S. (1993) *Class*. London: Routledge.

Edwards, A., Fitz, J. et al. (1989) *The State and Private Education: An Evaluation of the Assisted Places Scheme*. London: Falmer.

Employment Gazette (1987a) London: Department of Employment, HMSO.

Employment Gazette (1987b) London: Department of Employment, HMSO.

Employment Gazette (1994) London: Department of Employment.

Employment Gazette (1995) London: DFEE and CSO.

Erikson, R. and Goldthorpe, J. (1992) *The Constant Flux: A Study of Class Mobility in Industrial Society*. Oxford: Oxford University Press.

Esping-Andersen, G., ed. (1993) *Changing Classes: Stratification and Mobility in Post-Industrial Societies*. London: Sage.

European Commission (1997) The employment situation in the European Union. http://europa.eu.int/en/comm/dg05/elm/summit/en/backgr/situat.htm.

Eurostat (1991) *Labour Force Survey: Results 1991*.

Eurostat (1996) *Labour Force Survey: Results 1996*.

Eurostat (1998) Euro-zone unemployment. http://www.EUROPA.EU.INT/en/comm/eurostat/compres/en/11898/6311898a.htm.

Evetts, J. (1990) *Women in Primary Teaching*. London: Unwin Hyman.

Evetts, J. (1994) *Becoming a Secondary Headteacher*. London: Cassell.

Family Expenditure Survey (1962–89, various years) London: HMSO.

Fielding, T. (1995) Migration and middle-class formation in England and Wales, 1981–91. In Butler, T. and Savage, M. (eds), *Social Change and the Middle Classes*. London: UCL Press.

Finch, J. and Mason, J. (1993) *Negotiating Family Responsibilities*. London: Routledge.

Finke, R. and Starke, R. (1992) *The Churching of America*.

Finnegan, R. (1989) *The Hidden Musicians: Music Making in an English Town*. Cambridge: Cambridge University Press.

Fitz, J., Halpin, D. et al. (1993) *Grant Maintained Schools: Education in the Market Place*. London: Kogan Page.

Fox, A. (1974) *Beyond Contract: Work, Power and Trust Relations*. London: Faber and Faber.

Frankenberg, R. (1966) *Communities in Britain*. Harmondsworth: Penguin.

Frazer, E. (1988) Teenage girls talk about class. *Sociology*, 22(3): 343–58.

Frith, S. and Horne, H. (1987) *Art into Pop*. London: Routledge.

Fryer, P. (1984) *Staying Power: The History of Black People in Britain*. London: Pluto Press.

Fuller, M. (1980) Black girls in a London comprehensive. In Deem, R. (ed.), *Schooling for Women's Work*. London: Routledge.

Furlong, A. and Cartmel, F. (1997) *Young People and Social Change: Individualisation and Risk in Late Modernity*. Buckingham: Open University Press.

Further Education Development Agency (1997) *Flagship Survey: Women and Men in FE Management*. London: Further Education Development Agency.

Gabriel, Y. (1988) *Working Lives in Catering*. London: Routledge.

Gallie, D. and Marsh, C. (1994) The experience of unemployment. In Gallie, D., Marsh, C. and Vogler, C. (eds), *Social Change and the Experience of Unemployment*. Oxford: Oxford University Press.

Gallie, D. and Vogler, C. (1994) Labour market deprivation, welfare, and collectivism. In Gallie, D., Marsh, C. and Vogler, C. (eds), *Social Change and the Experience of Umemployment*.

Oxford: Oxford University Press.

Gallie, D., Gershuny, J. and Vogler, C. (1994) Unemployment, the household and social networks. In Gallie, D., Marsh, C. and Vogler, C. (eds), *Social Change and the Experience of Unemployment*. Oxford: Oxford University Press.

Gallie, D., White, M., Cheng, Y. and Tomlinson, M. (1998) *Restructuring the Employment Relationship*. Oxford: Oxford University Press.

Gallup Political Index Report (1991)

Gardner, C. and Sheppard, J. (1989) *Consuming Passion*. London: Unwin Hyman.

Gaskell, J. (1992) *Gender Matters from School to Work*. Milton Keynes: Open University Press.

General Household Survey (1988) London: HMSO.

General Household Survey (1996) London: HMSO.

Gershuny, J. (1978) *After Industrial Society*. London: Macmillan.

Gershuny, J. (1992) Change in the domestic division of labour in the UK, 1975–1987: dependent labour versus adaptive partnership. In Abercrombie, N. and Warde, A. (eds), *Social Change in Contemporary Britain*. Cambridge: Polity Press.

Gershuny, J. and Jones, S. (1987) The changing work/leisure balance in Britain, 1961–1984. In Home, J., Jary, D. and Tomlinson, A. (eds), *Sport, Leisure and Social Relations*. London: Routledge.

Gewirtz, S., Ball, S. and Bowe, R. (1995) *Markets, Choice and Equity in Education*. Buckingham: Open University Press.

Giddens, A. (1990) *The Consequences of Modernity*. Cambridge: Polity Press.

Giddens, A. (1992) *The Transformation of Intimacy: Sexuality, Love and Eroticism in Modern Societies*. Cambridge: Polity Press.

Giddens, A. (1997) *Sociology*. 3rd edn. Cambridge: Polity Press.

Giddens, A. (1998) *The Third Way: The Renewal of Social Democracy*. Cambridge: Polity Press.

Gillespie, M. (1993) Soap viewing, gossip and rumour amongst Punjabi youth in Southall. In Drummond, P., Paterson, R. and Willis, J. (eds), *National Identity and Europe*. London: British Film Institute.

Gilligan, C. (1982) *In a Different Voice*. Cambridge MA: Harvard University Press.

Gilroy, P. (1987) *There Ain't No Black in the Union Jack*. London: Hutchinson.

Gilroy, P. (1993) *The Black Atlantic: Modernity and Double Consciousness*. London: Verso.

Glasgow University Media Group (1976) *Bad News*. London: Routledge and Kegan Paul.

Glasgow University Media Group (1980) *More Bad News*. London: Routledge and Kegan Paul.

Glasgow University Media Group (1982) *Really Bad News*. London: Writers and Readers.

Glasgow University Media Group (1985) *War and Peace News*. Milton Keynes: Open University Press.

Glasgow University Media Group (1993) *Getting the Message*. London: Routledge.

Goldthorpe, J. (1996) Class analysis and the reorientation of class theory: the case of predicting differentials in educational attainment. *British Journal of Sociology*, 17(3): 481–505.

Goldthorpe, J. and Marshall, G. (1992) The promising future of class analysis: a response to recent critiques. *Sociology*, 26(3): 381–400.

Goldthorpe, J. (with Llewellyn, C. and Payne, C.) (1980) *Social Mobility and Class Structure in Modern Britain*. 1st edn. Oxford: Clarendon Press.

Goldthorpe, J. (with Llewellyn, C. and Payne, C.) (1987) *Social Mobility and Class Structure in Modern Britain*. 2nd edn. Oxford: Clarendon Press.

Goldthorpe, J. H., Lockwood, D., Bechhofer, F. and Platt, J. (1969) *The Affluent Worker in the Class Structure*. Cambridge: Cambridge University Press.

Good, F. (1990) Estimates of the distribution of personal wealth: I marketable wealth of individuals 1976 to 1988. *Economic Trends*, October: 137–57.

Goodhardt, G., Ehrenberg, A. and Collins, M. (1987) *The Television Audience: Patterns of Viewing*. London: Gower.

Gratton, C. and Tice, A. (1994) Trends in sports participation in Britain: 1977–1987. *Leisure Studies*, 13: 49–66.

Greeley, A. (1992) Religion in Britain, Ireland and the USA. In Jowell, R., Brook, L., Prior, G. and

Taylor, B. (eds), *British Social Attitudes 9*. Aldershot: Dartmouth.

Green, E., Hebron, S., and Woodward, D. (1990) *Women's Leisure, What Leisure*. London: Macmillan.

Green, K. (1993). Returning to the primary classroom. *Journal of Teacher Development*, 2(3): 134–40.

Gregson, N. and Lowe, M. (1993) Renegotiating domestic division of labour? A study of dual career households in north east and south east England. *Sociological Review*, 41(3): 475–505.

Gregson, N. and Lowe, M. (1994) *Servicing the Middle Classes*. London: Routledge.

Griffiths, V. A. (1995) *Adolescent Girls and their Friends: A Feminist Ethnography*. Aldershot: Avebury.

Grimsley, M. and Bhat, A. (1990) Health. In Bhat, A., Carr-Hill, R. and Ohri, S. (eds), *Britain's Black Population*. 2nd edn. Aldershot: Gower.

Grint, K. (1998) *The Sociology of Work: An Introduction*. 2nd edn. Cambridge: Polity Press.

Gunter, B., Sancho-Aldridge, J. and Winstone, P. (1994) *Television: The Public's View*. London: John Libbey.

Hagan, J. (1984) *The Disreputable Pleasures*. Toronto: McGraw-Hill.

Hakim, C. (1998) *Social Change and Innovation in the Labour Market*. Oxford: Oxford Universty Press.

Hales, C. P. (1986) What do managers do? A critical review of the evidence. *Journal of Management Studies*, 23(1): 88–115.

Halford, S. Savage, M. and Witz, A. (1997) *Gender, Careers and Organisations: Current Developments in Banking, Nursing and Local Government*. London: Macmillan.

Hall, P. A. (1998) Social capital in Britain. Paper to the American Political Science Association Meeting, Boston, September.

Hall, R. (1985) *Ask any Woman*. London: Falling Wall Press.

Hall, S. (1983) The great moving right show. In Hall, S. and Jacques, M. (eds), *The Politics of Thatcherism*. London: Lawrence and Wishart.

Halpin, D. and Troyna, B. (1995) The politics of educational policy borrowing. *Comparative Education*, 31(3): 303–10.

Halsey, A. H., Heath, A. F. and Ridge, J. M. (1980) *Origins and Destinations: Family, Class and Education in Modern Britain*. Oxford: Clarendon Press.

Halsey, A. H., Lauder, H., Brown, P. and Stuart Wells, A., eds (1997) *Education: Culture, Economy and Society*. Oxford: Oxford University Press.

Hannah, L. (1976) *The Rise of the Corporate Economy*. London: Methuen.

Hannah, L. (1983) *The Rise of the Corporate Economy*. 2nd edn. London: Methuen.

Harbury, C. D. and Hitchens, D. M. W. N. (1979) *Inheritance and Wealth Inequality in Britain*. London: George Allen and Unwin.

Hargreaves, I. and Christie, I., eds (1998) *Tomorrow's Politics: The Third Way and Beyond*. London: Demos.

Hargreaves, J. (1986) *Sport, Power and Culture*. Cambridge: Polity Press.

Harrison, A., ed. (1992) *Health Care UK 1991*. London: King's Fund Institute.

Harrison, P. (1985) *Inside the Inner City*. Harmondsworth: Penguin.

Hassell, K., Noyce, P. and Jesson, J. (1998) White and ethnic minority self-employment in retail pharmacy in Britain: an historical and comparative analysis. *Work, Employment and Society*, 12(2), 245–72.

Haw, K. (1998) *Educating Muslim Girls*. Buckingham: Open University Press.

Heaphy, B. Donovan, C. et al. (1997) Sex, money and the kitchen sink: power in same-sex couple relationships. British Sociological Association Conference, York. Unpublished conference paper.

Heath, A. (1981) *Social Mobility*. London: Collins.

Heath, A. and Savage, M. (1995) Political alignment with the middle classes, 1972–89. In Butler, T. and Savage, M. (eds), *Social Change and the Middle Classes*. London: UCL Press.

Heath, A., Jowell, R. and Curtice, J. (1985) *How Britain Votes*. Oxford: Pergamon.

Heath, A., Jowell, R. and Curtice, J. with Taylor, B., eds (1994) *Labour's Last Chance? The 1992 Election and Beyond*. Aldershot: Dartmouth.

Heath, A., Jowell, R., Curtice, J., Evans, G., Field, J. and Witherspoon, S. (1991) *Understanding Political Change: The British Voter 1964–1987.* Oxford: Pergamon.

Heath, S. J. (1997) *Preparation for Life? Vocationalism and the Equal Opportunities Challenge.* Aldershot: Ashgate.

Heelas, P. (1996) *The New Age Movement.* Oxford: Blackwell.

Heidensohn, F. (1989) *Crime and Society.* London: Macmillan.

Held, D., McGrew, A., Goldblatt, D. and Perraton, J. (1999) *Global Transformations.* Cambridge: Polity Press.

Hendrick, H. (1997) *Children, Childhood and English Society 1880–1990.* Cambridge: Cambridge University Press.

Hermes, J. (1995) *Reading Women's Magazines.* Cambridge: Polity Press.

Hesse, B., Rai, D. K., Bennett, C. and McGilchrist, P. (1992) *Beneath the Surface: Racial Harassment.* Aldershot: Avebury

Hetherington, K. (1992) Stonehenge and its festivals: spaces of consumption. In Shields, R. (ed.), *Lifestyle Shopping.* London: Routledge.

Hetherington, K. (1998) *Expressions of Identity: Space, Performance, Politics.* London: Sage.

Hewison, R. (1987) *The Heritage Industry.* London: Methuen.

Hewitt, P. (1993) *About Time: The Revolution in Work and Family Life.* London: IPPR/Rivers Oram Press.

Hey, V. (1997) *The Company She Keeps: An Ethnography of Girls' Friendship.* Buckingham: Open University Press.

Hills, J. (1995) *Joseph Rowntree Foundation Inquiry into Income and Wealth. Vol. 2.* York: Joseph Rowntree Foundation.

Hills, J. (1996) Introduction: after the turning point. In Hills, J. (ed.), *New Inequalities: The Changing Distribution of Income and Wealth in the United Kingdom.* Cambridge: Cambridge University Press.

Hirst, P. and Thompson, G. (1996) *Globalization in Question.* Cambridge: Polity Press.

Hobson, D. (1982) *Crossroads: The Drama of a Soap Opera.* London: Methuen.

Hochschild, A. (1997) *The Time Bind: When Work Becomes Home and Home Becomes Work.* New York: Henry Holt.

Hockey, J. (1990) *Experiences of Death: An Anthropological Account.* Edinburgh: Edinburgh University Press.

Hockey, J. and James, A. (1993) *Ageing and Dependency in the Life Course.* London: Sage.

Hoggett, P. and Bishop, J. (1986), *Organizing Around Enthusiasms: Mutual Aid in Leisure.* London: Comedia.

Holdaway, S. (1983) *Inside the British Police.* Oxford: Blackwell.

Holdaway, S. (1996) *The Racialization of British Policing.* London: Macmillan.

Holdaway, S. (1997) Responding to racialized divisions within the workforce – the experience of black and Asian police officers in England. *Ethnic and Racial Studies*, 20(1): 69–90.

Hough, M. and Mayhew, P. (1983) *The British Crime Survey: First Report.* London: HMSO.

Houlihan, B. (1991) *The Government and Politics of Sport.* London: Routledge.

Hughes, J., Martin, J. and Sharrock, W. W. (1995) *Understanding Classical Sociology.* London: Sage.

Husband, C., ed. (1987) *'Race' in Britain. Continuity and Change.* 2nd edn. London: Hutchinson.

Hymer, S. H. (1972) The multinational company and the law of uneven development. In Bhagwati, J. N. (ed.), *Economics and World Order.* London: Macmillan.

Inland Revenue (1994) *Inland Revenue Statistics, 1994.* London: HMSO.

Irwin, S. (1995) *Rights of Passage.* London: UCL Press.

Jacobson, J. (1997) Religion and ethnicity: dual and alternative sources of identity among young British Pakistanis. *Ethnic and Racial Studies*, 20(2): 238–56.

Jamieson, J. (1998) *Intimacy.* Cambridge: Polity Press.

Jerrome, D. (1981) The significance of friendship for women in later life. *Ageing and Society*, 1(2): 175–97.

Jessop, B. (1994) The transition to post-Fordism and the Schumpeterian workfare state. In Burrows, R. and Loader, B. (eds), *Towards a Post-Fordist Welfare State?* London: Routledge.

Johnson, T. (1972) *Professions and Power.* London: Macmillan.

Jones, T., Maclean, B. and Young, J. (1986) *The Islington Crime Survey.* London: Gower.

Judge, K., Mulligan, J.-A. and New, B. (1997) The NHS: new prescriptions needed? In Jowell, R., Curtice, J., Park, A., Brook, L., Thomson, K. and Bryson, C. (eds), *British Social Attitudes: 14th Report.* Aldershot: Dartmouth.

Keith, M. (1993) *Race and Policing.* London: UCL Press.

Kelly, M. P. (1980) *White Collar Proletariat.* London: Routledge and Kegan Paul.

Kelman, S. (1998) The social nature of the definition problem in health. In Mackay, L., Soothill, K. and Melia, K. (eds), *Classic Texts in Health Care.* Oxford: Butterworth-Heinemann.

Kennedy, H. (1997) *Learning Works: Widening Participation in Further Education.* London: Further Education Funding Council.

Kenway, J. (1997) Taking stock of gender reform policies for Australian schools: past, present and future. *British Educational Research Journal,* 23(3): 329–44.

Kerckhoff, A. C., Fogelman, K., Crook, D. and Reeder, D. (1996) *Going Comprehensive in England and Wales.* London: Woburn Press.

Kiernan, K. and Wicks, M. (1990) *Family Change and Future Policy.* London: Family Policy Studies Centre.

King, A., Denver, D., McLean, I., Norris, P., Norton, P., Saunders, D. and Seyd, P. (1998) *New Labour Triumphs: Britain at the Polls.* Chatham, NJ: Chatham House Publishers.

Kinsey, R. (1985) *Merseyside Crime and Police Surveys: Final Report.* Edinburgh: Centre for Criminology, University of Edinburgh.

Labour Market Trends (1996) April. London: HMSO.

Labour Market Trends (1998a) September. London: ONS.

Labour Market Trends (1998b) October. London: ONS.

Labour Market Trends (1998c) November. London: ONS.

Lakey, J. (1997) Neighbourhoods and housing. In Modood, T., Berthoud, R., Lakey, J., Nazroo, J., Smith, P., Virdee, S. and Beishon, S. (eds), *Ethnic Minorities in Britain: Diversity and Disadvantage.* London: Policy Studies Institute.

Laslett, P. (1965) *The World We Have Lost.* London: Methuen.

Lee, D. and Turner, B., eds (1996) *Conflicts about Class: Debating Inequality in Late Industrialism.* Harlow: Longman.

Lees, S. (1993) *Sugar and Spice: Sexuality and Adolescent Girls.* London: Penguin.

Leichter, H. (1980) *A Comparative Approach to Policy Analysis: Health Care Policy in Four Nations.* Cambridge: Cambridge University Press.

Leonard, D. (1980) *Sex and Generation.* London: Tavistock.

Leonard, M. (1998) *Rediscovering Europe.* London: Demos.

Living in Britain (1994). London: HMSO.

Living in Britain (1996). London: HMSO.

Lloyd, C. and Seifert, R. (1995) Restructuring in the NHS: the impact of the 1990 reforms on the management of labour. *Work, Employment and Society,* 9(2): 359–78.

Lockwood, D. (1958) *The Blackcoated Worker.* London: George Allen and Unwin.

London Research Centre (1996) *The Capital Divided: Mapping Poverty and Social Exclusion in London.* London: LRC.

Longhurst, B. (1995) *Popular Music and Society.* Cambridge: Polity Press.

Lowe, S. (1997) Homelessness and the law. In Pleace, N., Burrows, R. and Quilgars, D. (eds), *Homelessness and Social Policy.* London: Routledge.

Lunt, P. K. and Livingstone, S. M. (1992) *Mass Consumption and Personal Identity.* Buckingham: Open University Press.

Lury, C. (1996) *Consumer Culture.* Cambridge: Polity Press.

Luthra, M. (1997) *Britain's Black Population.* Oxford: Blackwell.

Mac an Ghaill, M. (1988) *Young, Gifted and Black: Student–Teacher Relations in the Schooling of Black Youth.* Milton Keynes: Open University Press.

Mac an Ghaill, M. (1994) *The Making of Men.* Buckingham: Open University Press.

Macdonald, S. (1997) A people's story: heritage, identity and authenticity. In Rojek, C. and Urry, J. (eds), *Touring Cultures*. London: Routledge.

Mackay, L., Soothill, K. and Melia, K., eds (1998) *Classic Texts in Health Care*. Oxford: Butterworth-Heinemann.

Macnaghten, P. and Urry, J. (1998) *Contested Natures*. London: Routledge.

Maffesoli, M. (1996) *The Time of the Tribes*. London: Sage.

Maguire, M., Morgan, R. and Reiner, R., eds (1997) *The Oxford Handbook of Criminology*. 2nd edn. Oxford: Clarendon Press.

Mann, M. (1993) *The Sources of Social Power: The Rise of Classes and Nation-States. Vol. 2*. Cambridge: Cambridge University Press.

Mann, M. (1998) Is there a society called Euro? In Axtmann, R. (ed.), *Globalization and Europe*. London: Pinter.

Marshall, G., Rose, D., Newby, H. and Vogler, C. (1988) *Social Class in Modern Britain*. London: Unwin Hyman.

Marshall, G., Swift, A. and Roberts, S. (1997), *Against the Odds? Social Class and Social Justice in Industrial Societies*. Oxford: Clarendon Press.

Martin, B. and Mason, S. (1994) Current trends in leisure: taking account of time. In *Leisure Studies*, 13(2): 133–9.

Marx, K. and Engels, F. (1872) *The Communist Manifesto*, reprinted in Marx, K. and Engels, F., *Selected Works*. London: Lawrence and Wishart, 1968.

Mason, D. (1995) *Race and Ethnicity in Modern Britain*. Oxford: Oxford University Press.

Mayhew, P., Elliott, D. and Dowds, L. (1989) *1988 British Crime Survey*. Home Office Research Study No. 111. London: HMSO.

McConville, M. and Baldwin, J. (1982) The influence of race on sentencing in England. *Criminal Law Review*, October: 652–8.

McCrone, D. (1992) *Understanding Scotland*. London: Routledge.

McCrone, D., Morris, A. and Kiely, R. (1995) *Scotland – The Brand: The Making of Scottish Heritage*. Edinburgh: Edinburgh University Press.

McGlone, F. and Cronin, N. (1994) A Crisis in Care? The Future of Family and State Care for Older People in the European Union. London: Family Policy Centre.

McGlone, F., Park, A. and Roberts, C. (1996) Relative values: kinship and friendship. In Jowell, R., Curtice, J., Park, A., Brook L. and Thomson, K. (eds), *British Social Attitudes 13*. Aldershot, Dartmouth.

McIlroy J. (1995) *Trade Unions in Britain Today*. 2nd edn. Manchester: Manchester University Press.

Mckay, G. (1996) *Senseless Acts of Beauty*. London: Verso.

McNair, B. (1996) *News and Journalism in the UK*. London: Routledge.

McNaught, A. (1984) *Race and Health Care in the United Kingdom*. London: Centre for Health Service Management Studies, Polytechnic of the South Bank.

Meegan, R. (1989) Paradise postponed: the growth and decline of Merseyside's outer estates. In Cooke, P. (ed.), *Localities*. London: Unwin Hyman.

Miles, A. (1988) *Home Informatics*. London: Pinter.

Millward, N., Stevens, M., Smart, D. and Hawes, W. (1992) *Workplace Industrial Relations in Transition*. Aldershot: Dartford.

Mirrlees-Black, C. (1995) Estimating the extent of domestic violence: findings from the 1992 BCS. *Home Office Research Bulletin*, 37: 1–9.

Mirrlees-Black, C., Budd, T., Partridge, S. and Mayhew, P. (1998) The 1998 British Crime Survey: England and Wales. *Home Office Statistical Bulletin*, 21/98.

Mirza, H. (1993) The social construction of black womanhood in British educational research: towards a new understanding. In Arnot, M. and Weiler, K. (eds), *Feminism and Social Justice in Education*. London, Falmer.

Mitchell, J. (1984) *What is to be Done about Illness and Health?* Harmondsworth: Penguin.

Modood, T. (1997a) Culture and identity. In Modood, T., Berthoud, R., Lakey, J., Nazroo, J., Smith, P., Virdee, S. and Beishon, S. (eds), *Ethnic Minorities in Britain: Diversity and Disadvan-*

tage. London: Policy Studies Institute.

Modood, T. (1997b) Employment. In Modood, T., Berthoud, R., Lakey, J., Nazroo, J., Smith, P., Virdee, S. and Beishon, S. (eds), *Ethnic Minorities in Britain: Diversity and Disadvantage*. London: Policy Studies Institute.

Modood, T. (1997c) Qualifications and English language. In Modood, T., Berthoud, R., Lakey, J., Nazroo, J., Smith, P., Virdee, S. and Beishon, S. (eds), *Ethnic Minorities in Britain: Diversity and Disadvantage*. London: Policy Studies Institute.

Modood, T. (1997d) Conclusion: ethnic diversity and disadvantage. In Modood, T., Berthoud, R., Lakey, J., Nazroo, J., Smith, P., Virdee, S. and Beishon, S. (eds), *Ethnic Minorities in Britain: Diversity and Disadvantage*. London: Policy Studies Institute.

Modood, T., Berthoud, R., Lakey, J., Nazroo, J., Smith, P., Virdee, S. and Beishon, S., eds (1997) *Ethnic Minorities in Britain: Diversity and Disadvantage*. London, Policy Studies Institute.

Moorhouse, H. F. (1976) Attitudes to class and class relations in Britain. *Sociology*, 10(3): 469–96.

Moorhouse, H. F. (1989) Models of work, models of leisure. In Rojek, C. (ed.), *Leisure for Leisure*. London: Macmillan.

Moorhouse, H. F. (1991) *Driving Ambitions: An Analysis of the American Hot-rod Enthusiasm*. Manchester: Manchester University Press.

Morgan, D. (1996) *Family Connections: An Introduction to Family Studies*. Cambridge: Polity Press.

Morgan, G. (1986) *Images of Organization*. London: Sage.

Morley, D. (1986) *Family Television*. London: Comedia.

Morris, L. (1990) *The Workings of the Household*. Cambridge: Polity Press.

Morris, L. (1995) *Social Divisions: Economic Decline and Social Structural Change*. London: UCL Press.

Murphy, M. (1996) Household and family structure among ethnic minority groups. In Coleman, D. and Salt, J. (eds), *Ethnicity in the 1991 Census. Vol 1: Demographic Characteristics of the Ethnic Minority Populations*. London: OPCS.

Murray, C. (1990) *The Emerging British Underclass*. London: Institute of Economic Affairs.

Myerscough, J. (1988) *The Economic Importance of the Arts*. London: Policy Studies Institute.

NACRO (1989) *Some Facts and Figures about Black People in the Criminal Justice System*. London: NACRO.

NACRO (1998) *Risks and Rights: Mentally Disturbed Offenders and Public Protection*. London: NACRO.

National Committee of Inquiry into Higher Education (1997) *Higher Education in the Learning Society*. London: HMSO.

Nava, M. (1992) *Changing Cultures: Feminism, Youth and Consumerism*. London: Sage.

Nettleton, S. (1995) *The Sociology of Health and Illness*. Cambridge: Polity Press.

New Earnings Survey (1974–98, various years) London: HMSO.

Newby, H. (1985) *Green and Pleasant Land? Social Change in Rural England*. London: Wildwood House.

Nicholson-Lord, D. (1992) In the consumer's cathedral. *Independent on Sunday*, 13 December: 3.

Nutt, D. (1998) Women without children – their family and friendship networks. Unpublished PhD thesis, Lancaster University.

O'Brien, M. and Penna, S. (1998) *Theorising Welfare: Enlightenment and Modern Society*. London: Sage.

O'Connor, P. (1992) *Friendships Between Women*. Hemel Hempstead: Harvester Wheatsheaf.

OECD (Organization for Economic Co-operation and Development) (1994) *Economic Surveys 1994: United Kingdom*. Paris.

OECD (Organization for Economic Co-operation and Development) (1998) *Economic Surveys 1998: United Kingdom*. Paris.

Offe, C. (1985) New social movements: challenging the boundaries of institutional politics. *Social Research*, 52(4): 817–68.

ONS (Office for National Statistics) (1997) *Family Spending: A Report on the 1996–97 Family*

Expenditure Survey. London: ONS.

ONS (Office for National Statistics) (1998a), *Travel Trends: A Report on the 1997 International Passenger Survey*. London: Stationery Office.

ONS (Office for National Statistics) (1998b) *Living in Britain: Results from the 1996 General Household Survey*. London: Stationery Office.

OPCS (Office of Populations, Censuses and Surveys) (1994) *1991 Census: Economic Activity, Great Britain*. London: HMSO.

Otley, C. B. (1973) The educational background of British army officers. *Sociology*, 7.

Owen, D. (1996a) Size, structure and growth of the ethnic minority populations. In Coleman, D. and Salt, J. (eds), *Ethnicity in the 1991 Census. Vol. 1: Demographic Characteristics of the Ethnic Minority Populations*. London: OPCS.

Owen, D. (1996b) The other-Asians: the salad bowl. In Peach, C. (ed.), *Ethnicity in the 1991 Census. Vol. 2: The Ethnic Minority Populations of Great Britain*. London: OPCS.

Pahl, R. E. (1984) *Divisions of Labour*. Oxford: Blackwell.

Pahl, R. (1988) Some remarks on informal work, social polarisation and the social structure. *International Journal of Urban and Regional Research*, 12(2): 247–67.

Pahl, R. (1993) Does class analysis without class theory have a promising future? *Sociology*, 27(2): 253–8.

Pahl, R. and Wallace, C. (1985) Household work strategies in the recession. In Redclift, N. and Mingione, E. (eds), *Beyond Employment*. Oxford: Blackwell.

Pakulski, J. and Waters, M. (1996) *The Death of Class*. London: Sage.

Parkin, F. (1971) *Class Inequality and Political Order*. London: MacGibbon and Keel.

Parry, N. and Parry, J. (1976) *The Rise of the Medical Profession*. London: Croom Helm.

Parsons, T. (1956) The American family: its relation to personality and to the social structure. In Parsons, T. and Bales, R. F. (eds), *Family, Socialization and Interaction Processes*. London: Routledge and Kegan Paul.

Peach, C., ed. (1996a) *Ethnicity in the 1991 Census. Vol. 2: The Ethnic Minority Populations of Great Britain*. London: OPCS.

Peach, C. (1996b) Black-Caribbeans: class, gender and geography. In Peach, C. (ed.), *Ethnicity in the 1991 Census. Vol. 2: The Ethnic Minority Populations of Great Britain*. London: OPCS.

Peach, C. (1996c) Introduction. In Peach, C. (ed.), *Ethnicity in the 1991 Census. Vol. 2: The Ethnic Minority Populations of Great Britain*. London: OPCS.

Pearson, G. (1983) *Hooligan: A History of Respectable Fears*. London: Macmillan.

Penn, R., Rose, M. and Rubery, J. (eds) (1994) *Skill and Occupational Change*. Oxford: OUP.

Peterson, R. A. and Berger, D. G. (1990), Cycles in symbol production: the case of popular music. In Frith, S. and Goodwin, A. (eds), *On Record: Rock, Pop and the Written Word*. London: Routledge.

Phizacklea, A. (1990) *Unpacking the Fashion Industry*. London: Routledge.

Pierson, C. (1996) *The Modern State*. London: Routledge.

Pierson, C. (1997) *Beyond the Welfare State: The New Political Economy of Welfare*. 2nd edn. Cambridge: Polity Press.

Pilcher, J. (1995) *Age and Generation in Modern Britain*. Oxford: Oxford University Press.

Pleace, N., Burrows, R. and Quilgars, D. (1997) Homelessness in contemporary Britain: conceptualisation and measurement. In Pleace, N., Burrows, R. and Quilgars, D. (eds), *Homelessness and Social Policy*. London: Routledge.

Power, S., Edwards, T. et al. (1998) Schools, families and academically able students: contrasting modes of involvement in secondary education. *British Journal of Sociology of Education*, 19(2): 157–76.

Price, R. and Bain, G. S. (1988) The labour force. In Halsey, A. H. (ed.), *British Social Trends since 1900*. London: Macmillan.

Prosser, N. (1995) Another aspect of rural deprivation – spatial aspects of young women's leisure in a rural area. In McFee, G., Murphy, W. and Whannel, G. (eds), *Leisure Cultures: Values, Gender, Lifestyles*. Brighton: Leisure Studies Association.

Randle, K. (1996) The white-coated worker: professional autonomy in a period of change. *Work,*

Employment and Society, 10(4): 737–53.

Reid, I. (1989) *Social Class Differences in Britain: Life-chances and Life-Styles*. 3rd edn. London: Fontana.

Rice, M. (1990) Challenging orthodoxies in feminist theory: a black feminist critique. In Gelsthorpe, L. and Morris, A. (eds), *Feminist Perspectives in Criminology*. Milton Keynes: Open University Press.

Richardson, J. and Lambert, J. (1985) *The Sociology of Race*. Ormskirk: Causeway Press.

Riddell, S. (1992) *Gender and the Politics of the Curriculum*. London: Routledge.

Rietveld, H. (1993) Living the dream. In Redhead, S. (ed.), *Rave Off*. Manchester: Manchester University Press.

Ritchie, J. (1994) *Inquiry into the Care and Treatment of Christopher Clunis*. London: HMSO.

Ritzer, G. (1998) *The McDonaldization Thesis*. London: Sage.

Robbins, T. (1988) *Cults, Converts and Charisma: The Sociology of New Religious Movements*. London: Sage.

Roberts, C., Davies, E. and Jupp, T. (1992) *Language and Discrimination: A Study of Communication in Multi-Ethnic Workplaces*. London: Longman.

Roberts, K. (1989), Great Britain: socio-economic polarization and the implications for leisure. In Olszewska, A. and Roberts, K. (eds), *Leisure and Life-Style*. London: Sage.

Roberts, K. (1997) Same activities, different meanings: British youth cultures in the 1990s. *Leisure Studies*, 16(1): 1–15.

Roberts, K. and Parsell, G. (1994) Youth cultures in Britain: the middle class take-over. *Leisure Studies*, 13(2): 33–48.

Robinson, D. C., Buck, E. B. and Cuthbert, M. (1991) *Music at the Margins*. London: Sage.

Rojek, C. (1985) *Capitalism and Leisure Theory*. London: Tavistock.

Rojek, C. (1989) *Leisure for Leisure*. London: Macmillan.

Ross, A. (1994) *The Chicago Gangster Theory of Life: Nature's Debt to Society*. London: Verso.

Routh, G. (1980) *Occupation and Pay in Great Britain, 1906–79*. 2nd edn. London: Macmillan.

Routh, G. (1987) *Occupations of the People of Great Britain, 1801–1981*. London: Macmillan.

Royal Commission on the Distribution of Income and Wealth (1979) *Report No. 7*. London: HMSO.

Royal Commission on the Poor Laws and the Relief of Distress (1909) Cmnd 4499. London: HMSO.

Runciman, W. G. (1983) *A Treatise on Social Theory. Vol. 1: The Methodology of Social Theory*. Cambridge: Cambridge University Press.

Salt, J. (1996) Immigration and ethnic group. In Coleman, D. and Salt, J. (eds), *Ethnicity in the 1991 Census. Vol. 1: Demographic Characteristics of the Ethnic Minority Populations*. London: OPCS.

Samuel, R. (1988) *Theatres of Memory. Vol. 1*. London: Verso.

Samuel, R. (1994) *Theatres of Memory*. London: Verso.

Sanders, D. (1998) The new electoral battleground. In King, A., Denver, D., McLean, I., Norris, P., Norton, P., Sanders, D. and Seyd, P., *New Labour Triumphs: Britain at the Polls*. Chatham, NJ: Chatham House Publishers.

Saunders, P. (1989) *Social Class and Stratification*. London: Longman.

Saunders, P. (1990) *A Nation of Home Owners*. London: Unwin Hyman.

Saunders, P. (1995) Might Britain be a meritocracy? *Sociology*, 29(1): 23–41.

Saunders, P. (1996) *Unequal but Fair?* London: IEA.

Saunders, P. and Harris, C. (1994) *Privatization and Popular Capitalism*. Milton Keynes: Open University Press.

Savage, M. (1994) British class division in European perspective. In Warde, A. and Abercrombie, N. (eds), *Stratification and Social Inequality: Studies in British Society*. Lancaster: Framework.

Savage, M. and Egerton, M. (1997) Social mobility, individual ability and the inheritance of class inequality. *Sociology*, 31(4): 645–72.

Savage, M. and Warde, A. (1993) *Urban Sociology, Capitalism and Modernity*. London: Macmillan.

Savage, M., Barlow, J., Dickens, P. and Fielding, T. (1992) *Property, Bureaucracy and Culture:*

Middle-Class Formation in Contemporary Britain. London: Routledge.

Scarman Report (1981) *The Brixton Disorders 10–12 April 1981*. London: HMSO.

Schieber, G., Poullier, J.-P. and Greenwald, L. (1992) US health expenditure performance: an international comparison and data update. *Health Care Financing Review*, 13(4): 1–87.

Schlesinger, P. (1978) *Putting Reality Together: BBC News*. London: Constable.

Schor, J. (1992) *The Overworked American: The Unexpected Decline of Leisure*. Cambridge MA: Harvard University Press.

Schumpeter, J. (1943) *Capitalism, Socialism and Democracy*. London: Allen and Unwin.

Scott, A. (1990) *Ideology and the New Social Movements*. London: Unwin Hyman.

Scott, A., ed. (1997) *The Limits of Globalization*. London. Routledge.

Scott, J. (1982) *The Upper Classes: Property and Privilege in Britain*. London: Macmillan.

Scott, J. (1985) The British upper class. In Coates, D., Johnston G. and Bush R. (eds), *A Socialist Anatomy of Britain*. Cambridge: Polity Press.

Scott, J. (1990) Corporate control and corporate rule: Britain in an international perspective. *British Journal of Sociology*, 41(3).

Scott, J. (1991) *Who Rules Britain?* Cambridge: Polity Press.

Scott, J. (1994) *Poverty and Wealth: Citizenship, Deprivation and Privilege*. London: Longman.

Scott, S., Jackson, S. and Backett, K. (1998) Swings and roundabouts: risk anxiety and the everyday worlds of children. *Sociology*, 23(4): 689–706.

SCPR (Social and Community Planning Research) (1988) *British Social Attitudes: The Fifth Report*. Aldershot: Gower.

Scraton, S. (1992) *Shaping Up to Womanhood: Gender and Girls' Physical Education*. Milton Keynes: Open University Press.

Seabrook, J. (1978) *What Went Wrong? Working People and the Ideals of the Labour Movement*. London: Gollancz.

Sennett, R. (1986) *The Fall of Public Man*. London: Faber and Faber.

Sewell, T. (1998) Loose cannons: exploding the myth of the 'black macho' lad. In Epstein, D., Elwood, J., Hey, V. and Maw, J. (eds), *Failing Boys? Issues in Gender and Achievement*. Buckingham: Open University Press.

Seyd, P. and Whiteley, P. (1992) *Labour's Grass Roots: The Politics of Party Membership*. Oxford: Clarendon Press.

Sharpley, R. (1994) *Tourism, Tourists and Society*. Huntingdon: ELM.

Sharpley, R. and Sharpley, J. (1997) *Rural Tourism: An Introduction*. London: International Thompson Business Press.

Sheldon, T. S. and Parker, H. (1992) Race and ethnicity in health research. *Journal of Public Health Medicine*, 14(2): 104–10.

Shilling, C. (1989) *Schooling for Work in Capitalist Britain*. Brighton: Falmer.

Simpson, S. (1996) Non-response to the 1991 Census: the effect on ethnic group enumeration. In Coleman, D. and Salt, J. (eds), *Ethnicity in the 1991 Census. Vol. 1: Demographic Characteristics of the Ethnic Minority Populations*. London: OPCS.

Sinfield, A. (1981) *What Unemployment Means*. Oxford: Martin Robertson.

Skeggs, B. (1997) *Formations of Class and Gender: Becoming Respectable*. London: Sage.

Skellington, R. with Morris, P. (1992) *'Race' in Britain Today*. London: Sage.

Skelton, A. (1993). On becoming a male physical education teacher: the informal culture of students and the construction of hegemonic masculinity. *Gender and Education*, 5(3): 289–304.

Skelton, C. (1994). Sex, male teachers and young children. *Gender and Education*, 6(1): 87–94.

Smart, C. (1999), The new parenthood: fathers and mothers after divorce. In Silva, E. B. and Smart, C. (eds), *The New Family?* London: Sage.

Smart, C. and Neale, B. (1999) *Family Fragments*. Cambridge: Polity Press.

Smith, A. (1986) State-making and nation-building. In Hall J. (ed.), *States in History*. Oxford: Blackwell.

Smith, D. J. (1977) *Racial Disadvantage in Britain*. Harmondsworth: Penguin.

Smith, D. J. and Gray, J. (1983) The police in action. In *Police and People in England. Vol. 4*.

London: Policy Studies Institute.

Snyder, P. (1992) *The European Women's Almanac*. London: Scarlet Press.

Social Focus on Women and Men (1983). London: HMSO.

Social Focus on Women and Men (1998). London: HMSO.

Social Trends (1992). London: HMSO.

Social Trends (1995). London: HMSO.

Social Trends (1996). London: HMSO.

Social Trends (1997). London: HMSO.

Social Trends (1998). London: HMSO.

Social Trends (1999). London: HMSO.

Solomon, M. (1992) Public opinion and the National Health Service. In Harrison, A. (ed.), *Health Care UK 1991*. London: King's Fund Institute.

Soothill, K., Mackay, L. and Melia, K. (1998) Introduction. In Mackay, L., Soothill, K. and Melia, K. (eds), *Classic Texts in Health Care*. Oxford: Butterworth-Heinemann.

Stark, E. (1977) The epidemic as a social event. *International Journal of Health Services*, 7(4): 691–705.

Stewart, A., Prandy, K. and Blackburn, R. M. (1980) *Social Stratification and Occupations*. London: Macmillan.

Stewart, J. (1997) Poverty and social security. Unpublished paper. Department of Applied Social Science, Lancaster University.

Thompson, K. (1998) *Moral Panics*. London: Routledge.

Thompson, P. (1989) *The Nature of Work: An Introduction to Debates on the Labour Process*. London: Macmillan.

Thompson, P. and Findlay, P. (1999) Changing the people. In Ray, L. J. and Sayer A. (eds), *Culture and Economy after the Cultural Turn*. London: Sage.

Thorne, B. (1993) *Gender Play: Girls and Boys in School*. Buckingham: Open University Press.

Thornton, S. (1995) *Club Cultures*. Cambridge: Polity Press.

Thorpe, D., Smith, D., Green., C. J. and Paley, J. H. (1980) *Out of Care*. London: George Allen and Unwin.

Tomlinson Report (1992) *Report of the Inquiry into London's Health Service, Medical Education, and Research*. London: HMSO.

Tonge, J. (1997) Britain. In Compston, H. (ed.), *The New Politics of Unemployment*. London: Routledge.

Townsend, P. (1979) *Poverty in the United Kingdom*. Harmondsworth: Penguin.

Townsend, P., Phillimore, P. and Beattie, A. (1988) *Health and Deprivation: Inequality and the North*. London: Croom Helm.

Trowler, P. (1998). *Education Policy: A Policy Sociology Approach*. Eastbourne: Gildredge Press.

Tunstall, J. (1993) *Television Producers*. London: Routledge.

Turner, E., Riddell, S. et al. (1995). *Gender Equality in Scottish Schools: The Impact of Recent Educational Reforms*. Glasgow: Equal Opportunities Commission.

Urry, J. (1990) *The Tourist Gaze*. London: Sage.

Urry, J. (1995) *Consuming Places*. London: Routledge.

Vincent, C. and Warren, S. (1998) Becoming a 'better' parent? Motherhood, education and transition. *British Journal of Sociology of Education*, 19(2): 177–93.

Virdee, S. (1997) Racial harassment. In Modood, T., Berthoud, R., Lakey, J., Nazroo, J., Smith, P., Virdee, S. and Beishon, S. (eds), *Ethnic Minorities in Britain: Diversity and Disadvantage*. London: Policy Studies Institute.

Walby, S. (1990) *Theorizing Patriarchy*. Cambridge: Polity Press.

Walby, S. (1997) *Gender Transformations*. London: Routledge.

Wallis, R. (1984) *The Elementary Forms of the New Religious Life*. London: Routledge and Kegan Paul.

Walvin, J. (1978) *Besides the Seaside*. London: Allen Lane.

Ward, C. and Hardy, D. (1986) *Goodnight Campers! The History of the British Holiday Camp*. London: Mansell.

Warde, A. (1989) The furure of work. *Social Studies Review*, 5(1): 11–15.

Warde, A. (1991) Gentrification as consumption: issues of class and gender. *Environment and Planning D: Society and Space*, 9(2): 223–32.

Warde, A. (1997) *Consumption, Food and Taste*. London: Sage.

Warness, T. (1996) The age structure and ageing of the ethnic groups. In Coleman, D. and Salt, J. (eds), *Ethnicity in the 1991 Census. Vol. 1: Demographic Characteristics of the Ethnic Minority Populations*. London: OPCS.

Waters, I. (1989), *Entertainment, Arts and Cultural Services*. London: Longman.

Waters, M. (1995) *Globalization*. London: Routledge.

Weber, M. (1968) *Economy and Society*. New York: Free Press.

Wenger, G. C. (1994a) *The Supportive Network: Coping with Old Age*. London: Allen and Unwin.

Wenger, G. C. (1994b) *Understanding Support Networks and Community Care*. Aldershot: Avebury.

Westergaard, J. (1995), *Who Gets What? The Hardening of Class Inequality in the Late Twentieth Century*. Cambridge: Polity Press.

Westergaard, J. (1996) Class in Britain since 1979: facts, theories and ideologies. In Lee, D. and Turner, B. (eds), *Conflicts about Class: Debating Inequality in Late Industrialism*. Harlow: Longman.

Westwood, S. (1984) *All Day, Every Day*. London: Pluto Press.

Wheelock, J. (1990) *Husbands at Home: The Domestic Economy in a Post Industrial Society*. London: Routledge.

White, M. (1991) *Against Unemployment*. London: Policy Studies Institute.

Whitehead, M. (1992) *The Health Divide*. Harmondsworth: Penguin.

Wicke, P. (1990) *Rock Music*. Cambridge: Cambridge University Press.

Widgery, D. (1988) *The National Health: A Radical Perspective*. London: Hogarth Press.

Wilkinson, H. (1996) Mothers marketing' work: the experiences of mothers making choices for children with special needs. *Discourse*, 17(3): 315–24.

Williams, G. (1994) *Britain's Media: How They Are Related*. London: Campaign for Press and Broadcasting Fredom.

Williams, R. (1990) Paper presented to Annual Conference of the Society of Social Medicine, Glasgow.

Willis, P. (1977) *Learning to Labour*. London: Saxon House.

Willis, P. (1990) *Common Culture*. Buckingham: Open University Press.

Witz, A. (1991) *Professions and Patriarchy*. London: Routledge.

Woods, P. (1995) *Creative Teachers in Primary Schools*. Buckingham: Open University Press.

Working for Patients (1989) Cmnd 555. London: HMSO.

Wright, C., Weekes, D. et al. (1998) Masculinised discourses within education and the construction of black male identities among African Caribbean youth. *British Journal of Sociology of Education*, 19(1): 75–87.

WTO (World Tourism Organization) (1997) *Yearbook of Tourism Statistics*. Madrid: WTO.

Wynne, D., ed. (1992), *The Culture Industry: The Arts in Urban Regeneration*. Aldershot: Avebury.

Wynne, D. (1998) *Leisure, Lifestyle and the New Middle Class: A Case Study*. London: Routledge.

Young, J. (1971) The role of the police as amplifiers of deviancy. In Cohen, S. and Taylor, L. (eds), *Images of Deviance*. Harmondsworth: Penguin.

Young, J. (1991) Ten principles of realism. Paper presented at the British Criminology Conference, York.

Young, M. and Willmott, P. (1957) *Family and Kinship in East London*. London: Routledge and Kegan Paul.

Young, M. and Wilmott, P. (1973) *The Symmetrical Family*. London: Routledge and Kegan Paul.

Index